Symbian OS Internals

TITLES PUBLISHED BY SYMBIAN PRESS

❑   Wireless Java for Symbian Devices
Jonathan Allin
0471 486841   512pp   2001   Paperback

❑   Symbian OS Communications Programming
Michael J Jipping
0470 844302   418pp   2002   Paperback

❑   Programming for the Series 60 Platform and Symbian OS
Digia
0470 849487   550pp   2002   Paperback

❑   Symbian OS C++ for Mobile Phones, Volume 1
Richard Harrison
0470 856114   826pp   2003   Paperback

❑   Programming Java 2 Micro Edition on Symbian OS
Martin de Jode
0470 092238   498pp   2004   Paperback

❑   Symbian OS C++ for Mobile Phones, Volume 2
Richard Harrison
0470 871083   448pp   2004   Paperback

❑   Symbian OS Explained
Jo Stichbury
0470 021306   448pp   2004   Paperback

❑   Programming PC Connectivity Applications for Symbian OS
Ian McDowall
0470 090537   480pp   2004   Paperback

❑   Rapid Mobile Enterprise Development for Symbian OS
Ewan Spence
0470 014857   324pp   2005   Paperback

❑   Symbian for Software Leaders
David Wood
0470 016833   326pp   2005   Hardback

Symbian OS Internals

Real-time Kernel Programming

Jane Sales

With

Andrew Rogers, Andrew Thoelke, Carlos Freitas, Corinne Dive-Reclus, Dennis May, Douglas Feather, Morgan Henry, Peter Scobie, Jasmine Strong, Jason Parker, Stefan Williams and Tony Lofthouse

And

Jon Coppeard and Martin Tasker

Reviewed by

Andrew Ford, Andrew Jordan, Andrew Thoelke, David Bachelor, Dennis May, Jason Parker, Jonathan Medhurst, Jo Stichbury, Mark Shackman, Nigel Henshaw, Peter Scobie, Richard Fitzgerald, Simon Trimmer, Tony Lofthouse, Trevor Blight and William Roberts

Symbian Press

Head of Symbian Press

Phil Northam

Managing Editor

Freddie Gjertsen

John Wiley & Sons, Ltd

Copyright © 2005   Symbian Ltd
Published by   John Wiley & Sons, Ltd
                    The Atrium, Southern Gate, Chichester,
                    West Sussex PO19 8SQ, England
                    Telephone (+44) 1243 779777

Email (for orders and customer service enquiries): cs-books@wiley.co.uk
Visit our Home Page on www.wiley.com

Reprinted with corrections February 2006

Other Wiley Editorial Offices

John Wiley & Sons Inc., 111 River Street, Hoboken, NJ 07030, USA

Jossey-Bass, 989 Market Street, San Francisco, CA 94103-1741, USA

Wiley-VCH Verlag GmbH, Boschstr. 12, D-69469 Weinheim, Germany

John Wiley & Sons Australia Ltd, 42 McDougall Street, Milton, Queensland 4064, Australia

John Wiley & Sons (Asia) Pte Ltd, 2 Clementi Loop #02-01, Jin Xing Distripark, Singapore 129809

John Wiley & Sons Canada Ltd, 22 Worcester Road, Etobicoke, Ontario,
Canada M9W 1L1

Wiley also publishes its books in a variety of electronic formats. Some content that
appears in print may not be available in electronic books.

Library of Congress Cataloging-in-Publication Data

Sales, Jane.
  Symbian OS internals : real-time kernel programming / Jane Sales
with Andrew Rogers [. . . et al.].
     p. cm.
  Includes bibliographical references and index.
  ISBN-13 978-0-470-02524-6 (pbk. : alk. paper)
  ISBN-10 0-470-02524-7 (pbk. : alk. paper)
  1. Real-time control.   I. Title.
TJ217.7.S25 2005
629.8—dc22
                                                        2005018263

British Library Cataloguing in Publication Data

A catalogue record for this book is available from the British Library

ISBN-13 978-0-470-02524-6
ISBN-10 0-470-02524-7

Typeset in 10/12pt Optima by Laserwords Private Limited, Chennai, India
Printed and bound in Great Britain by Bell & Bain, Glasgow
This book is printed on acid-free paper responsibly manufactured from sustainable
forestry in which at least two trees are planted for each one used for paper production.

Contents

Symbian Press Acknowledgements

Many people put many hours into the creation of this book, none more so than the authors and reviewers. Symbian Press would like to thank each of them without restraint for their perseverance and dedication, with a special mention for Dennis, who always seemed to be holding the short straw.

Thanks are also due to Stephen Evans and Akin Oyesola for their patience whilst some of their most vital engineers were distracted from "real work" for week after long week. And also to Robert Palmer, Igor Masrna, Andy Salter and Terrence Smith, for their close reading of the text.

About this Book

The latest versions of Symbian OS are based upon Symbian's new real-time kernel. This kernel is designed to make phone-related development easier: base-porting will be easier, device driver development will be easier, software development will be easier.

Symbian OS Internals is a detailed exposition on the new real-time kernel, providing the reader with the insights of the software engineers who designed and wrote it. In the main it is an explanatory text which seeks to describe the functioning of the kernel, and, where relevant, to indicate key differences from its predecessor.

This book is invaluable for:

Those who are involved in porting Symbian OS. This book is not a base-porting manual, since this is already provided by Symbian; but it benefits the base-porting engineer by giving him or her a more solid understanding of the OS being ported.

Those writing device drivers. This book provides an in-depth explanation of how Symbian OS drivers work. Device drivers have changed considerably with the introduction of a single code, so this helps fill the knowledge gap for those converting them to the new kernel.

Those who wish to know how the Symbian OS kernel works. This book provides a detailed commentary on the internals of Symbian OS, providing information for the varied needs of readers, helping: students studying real-time operating systems, middleware programmers to understand the behavior of underlying systems, systems engineers to understand how Symbian OS compares to other similar operating systems, and, for those designing for high performance, how to achieve it.

About the Authors

Jane Sales, lead author

Jane joined Symbian (then Psion) in 1995 to lead the team whose goal was to create a new 32-bit operating system, now known as EKA1. This goal was realized two years later, when the Psion Series 5 was released. Since then, Jane has taken on a variety of roles within Symbian, including product management, systems architecture and setting up a small product-focused research group in Japan.

Jane studied at Jesus College, Oxford, where she gained an MA in mathematics in 1982. After that, she became part of a small team building a microcomputer to which they ported CCP/M. It was the start of a long-lasting love of systems programming.

In 2003, Jane moved to the South of France and began work on this book. She would like to thank her husband, Roger, for his moral and financial support over the succeeding 18 months.

Corinne Dive-Reclus

Corinne joined Symbian in 2001 after several years at Baltimore Ltd., where she designed the embedded software of ACCE (Advanced Configurable Crypto Environment), a cryptographic hardware module certified FIPS 140-1 Level 4.

In 1987, her first job was as a presales engineer at Sun Microsystems, France where she was exposed to the concept of Network Computing & Internet and to its very first remote attacks – at a time when this was still confidential. Being more interested in development than presales, she subsequently worked as a software engineer for Concept and Implicit, developing an RAD (Rapid Application Development) programming language for the creation of distributed data-oriented applications.

Since joining Symbian, Corinne has been the Platform Security System Architect, and has worked on the platform security architecture from its initial design to its implementation in Symbian v9. To ensure that all layers of the operating system will contribute to its overall security, she worked extensively with Andrew Thoelke and Dennis May to validate the security features of EKA2, design new services such as Publish&Subscribe and Capability Model, as well as defining the new behavior of the file server, known as Data Caging. For this work, Corinne received the Symbian Technical Innovation award in 2003.

Fulfilling an early passion for Prehistoric Archaeology & Computing, Corinne graduated from the Ecole Nationale Superieure de Geologie, a unique French institution combining a five-year curriculum in Engineering and Earth Science.

Douglas Feather

Douglas joined Symbian (then Psion) in 1994. He started by leading the writing of the text formatting engine for the Psion S5. He has also worked in the Web Browser and Core Apps teams where he rewrote most of the versit parser to greatly improve its performance. For five out of the last seven years he has worked mainly on the Window Server, where he added full color support, fading support, a framework to allow digital ink to be drawn over the other applications, support for multiple screens and transparent windows.

Douglas has a BSc in Mathematics from Southampton University and a PhD in Number Theory from Nottingham University. He is a committed Christian and regularly engages in vigorous theological debate, to defend the biblical truths about Jesus Christ, at Speaker's Corner (Hyde Park, London) on Sunday afternoons.

Carlos Freitas

Carlos joined Symbian in 2000, working on device and media drivers and porting the Base. His involvement with EKA2 dates from 2002 when he ported the newly released Kernel and several device drivers to a new hardware reference platform. He has since assumed responsibility for documenting, improving and maintaining the power management framework.

Carlos is a licentiate in Electronics and Telecommunications Engineering from the University of Porto, Portugal, and had a CERN bursary to research advanced optical communications. Prior to Symbian Carlos worked on both hardware and embedded software development under a number of Operating Systems such as VxWorks, μItron and WinCE.

Morgan Henry

Morgan joined Symbian (then Psion) in 1995 working in the kernel team on EKA1, where he met some amazing people. Once he regained his composure he was responsible for the kernel port for the Nokia 9210 – "the world's first open Symbian OS phone". During his time in the kernel team he invented the EKA1 power management framework, a cross platform DMA framework, co-developed Symbian's ROM-building tools, and worked on the partner-OS solution for single-core dual-OS phones.

Morgan is responsible for the Symbian OS kernel debug architecture for both EKA1 and EKA2, and has worked with many tools vendors, taking the project from research to production.

Before joining Symbian, Morgan dabbled in graphic design, but he now finds himself as a System Architect. He's not sure how that happened. Most recently he has been working on requirements and designs across several technology areas to shape future versions of Symbian OS.

Morgan maintains an active interest in drawing, painting and animation. He holds a BSc in Mathematics and Computer Science from Queen Mary and Westfield College, London.

Tony Lofthouse

Tony joined Symbian in 2002, having previous worked for the Santa Cruz Operation (SCO) Inc. in the Base Drivers team on the UnixWare Operating System and Veritas Inc. in the VxFS file-system team.

At Symbian he has been a lead developer on various Symbian OS hardware reference platform base ports for the Development Boards group. Tony now works in the Base department and is the technical architect for the Development Boards technology stream.

He received a BSc in Computer Science from the University of Southampton in 1996. Prior to this he had a brief career in contaminated land environmental research, but along with sometimes being cold and wet, decided this was too risky.

Dennis May

Dennis May joined Symbian (then Psion) in 1996, having previously worked on RF hardware design and software development for mobile satellite communication systems and on layer 1 software development for a GSM mobile handset.

Dennis initially worked on the development of the Psion Series 5 PDA and subsequently rewrote the Symbian maths library, worked on improvements to the EKA1 kernel and ported Symbian OS to new platforms. He went on to become the original architect and creator of the EKA2 kernel, which he designed to improve on the original kernel in the areas of real-time performance, portability and robustness.

Dennis has made several other contributions to Symbian, including work in the areas of build tools and automated testing, and he is an inventor of patented ideas relating to platform security, file systems, memory management and kernel synchronization primitives. He also had a hand in the design of the ARM architecture 6 memory management unit.

Dennis is currently working as kernel technology architect at Symbian, leading the kernel team in the continued development of the EKA2 kernel.

Dennis received a BA in Mathematics from Trinity Hall, Cambridge, in 1990 and an MSc in Communications and Signal Processing from Imperial College, London, in 1991.

Jason Parker

Jason joined Symbian (then Psion) in 1998, where he became a founding member of the Base Porting Group (BPG). He currently leads BPG and the recently formed Multimedia Porting Group (MMPG) within Symbian's Technical Consulting division.

Jason engages with Symbian semiconductor partners to ensure their SoC designs are optimized for Symbian phones. He and his teams have been instrumental in building many of Symbian's leading-edge phones. They have contributed practical technologies into the EKA2 project, including ROLF (now renamed as ROFS) and the Flash Logger. They built the first working EKA2 prototype phone and are leading the development of commercial EKA2 handsets.

Before joining Symbian, Jason developed real-time software for bespoke embedded systems. Projects included a multi-channel digital video recording system and 3D military simulators.

Jason holds a BSc in Mathematics and Physics from the University of York, and an MSc in Remote Sensing and Image Processing from Edinburgh University. Outside of Symbian, he can be found climbing the world's mountains.

Andrew Rogers

Andrew Rogers joined Symbian in 2002. He then spent time working on Bluetooth, USB, Infrared and OBEX with teams in Cambridge before joining the base kernel team in London to work on EKA2. Whilst with the base kernel team Andrew migrated the whole OS to a new data type for TInt64 and oversaw the introduction of support for the Symbian User::Leave()/TRAP framework to be implemented in terms of C++ exceptions, including implementing the support for this on the Win32 emulator himself.

More recently, Andrew has spent the last 4 months working in Korea as a member of Symbian's technical consultancy department, but has now returned to Cambridge to work as a consultant on European phone projects.

Andrew has a BA in Computer Science from Sidney Sussex College, Cambridge. In his "spare" time he has been known to bring up support on EKA2 for other Win32 compilers and has also been responsible for implementing changes to the IPC mechanism to prevent problems caused by race conditions between connect and disconnect messages, whilst he is not chasing round after his two young children or writing.

Peter Scobie

Peter joined Symbian (then Psion) in 1992 after eight years working for various telecommunications and process control companies – including Dacom, Combustion Engineering and Plessey Telecommunications.

At Psion he initially led the production software team which developed software for the test systems used in the manufacture of the Psion Series 3a. Then he moved into the hand-held computer software department and was part of the original development team for the EKA1 kernel – working on EPOC Release 1 used in the Psion Series 5. During this time he designed and developed the local media sub-system and the PC Card Controller. He then worked on the development of the MultiMediaCard controller and the LFFS file system. He is still working in the base department and is now technical architect for the peripherals technology stream.

Peter has a BSc in Electrical and Electronic Engineering from Loughborough University of Technology. Outside of work Peter enjoys canoeing, sailing and coaching for his eldest son's football team.

Jasmine Strong

Jasmine Strong joined Symbian in 2003, having previously worked for Texas Instruments, designing the system-on-chip architecture of the new generation of OMAP processors. At Symbian, she has worked on performance profiling and improvements for the EKA2 kernel, using her long experience with ARM processors to exploit their special characteristics.

Jasmine has worked in embedded systems since 1998, when she started a project to produce the world's first internet-enabled walk-in freezer cabinet. Her eclectic career has touched upon many different areas, from hydrocarbon physics to digital television.

Jasmine has been programming ARM processors since the late 1980s and is a keen motorcyclist and photographer. When she's not at work or tearing around at high speeds, Jasmine keeps a weblog.

Andrew Thoelke

Andrew joined Symbian (then Psion) in 1994 and became one of the key developers of OVAL, a rapid application development language similar to Visual Basic, for the Psion Series3a computers. He has since worked on projects throughout the lifetime of Symbian OS, and spanning many of its technology areas such as kernel, data storage, messaging, Java and platform security. He has been deeply involved in the design, development and promotion of EKA2 for the last four years, taking this project from research to production.

Today he has one of the most senior technical roles within Symbian, influencing both the technical strategy of the organization and the ongoing architectural development of Symbian OS.

He graduated from Sidney Sussex College, Cambridge with an MA in Mathematics shortly before beginning his career at Symbian.

Stefan Williams

Stefan joined Symbian in 2002 where he now works in the position of File Server Technical Lead. During his time with Symbian, Stefan has been actively involved in many aspects the Peripherals and File Server sub-systems, with most recent contributions including the design and implementation of the SDIO framework, USB Mass Storage controller and various kernel porting activities.

A graduate of Imperial College, London, Stefan has an MEng in Electrical and Electronic Engineering and has previously worked on several major design commissions and commercial products, including PC-based data acquisition and signal analysis software, real-time TDR-based fault analysis systems and distributed embedded network solutions.

Stefan would like to thank his son, Derry, for not complaining too much while Dad spent his weekends writing – and promises to start being fun again!

1

Introducing EKA2

by Jane Sales with Martin Tasker

The ability to quote is a serviceable substitute for wit.
W. Somerset Maugham

1.1 The history of EKA2

Kernel design is one of the most exciting opportunities in software engineering. EKA2 is the second iteration of Symbian's 32-bit kernel architecture, and this in turn follows 8- and 16-bit kernels designed in the 1980s for Psion's personal organizers and PDAs.

Psion's Organiser, launched in 1984, was based on an 8-bit processor and supported only built-in applications. For such a device, the only kernel needed was a bootstrap loader and a small collection of system services. There was no clear requirement to differentiate the 8-bit kernel from middleware or application software.

In 1986, Psion launched the Organiser II, an 8-bit machine offering expansion based on the interpreted OPL language. The demands on the OS were slightly greater – sufficiently good memory management, for example, to support an interpreted language.

A major evolution came when, beginning in 1990, Psion launched a range of machines including a laptop, a clamshell organizer and an industrial organizer, all based on a single OS. The 16-bit EPOC kernel was tied to the Intel 8086 architecture and supported expansion, with applications written not only in OPL, but also in the native C APIs of the EPOC OS – thus opening up the OS itself to any number of aftermarket application writers.

This openness placed massive new demands on the kernel. For one thing, it had to be documented and made accessible to aftermarket programmers. Perhaps some applications would be poorly written: the kernel had to provide memory protection so a bug in one program would not crash another – or even crash the whole OS. Applications demanded sophisticated memory management for their own working memory. A potentially limitless number of event-driven services had to execute efficiently on a highly resource-constrained machine. And all this had to be delivered on the platform of the 8086's segmented memory model, with challenges that PC programmers of the day will readily recall.

The 16-bit EPOC kernel thus had to address many of the requirements which are met by EKA2 today, because of its positioning between the embedded real-time operating systems and classic desktop operating systems such as Windows. Although it was similar to embedded RTOSes (it ran from ROM), it was bigger because it supported richer functionality and was open to aftermarket applications. Although it was similar to desktop OSes (it was open and used the 8086 architecture), it was smaller because the memory and power resources available were considerably less.

Two further evolutionary steps were necessary to arrive at EKA2.

EPOC32, released in Psion's Series 5 PDA in 1997, began life in 1994. Its kernel, retrospectively dubbed EKA1, carried over the best features of the 16-bit EPOC kernel and fixed several significant issues. Firstly, EKA1 was thoroughly 32-bit – with no relics of the awkwardness in EPOC resulting from the 8086-segmented memory architecture. Secondly, the EKA1 kernel was designed from the beginning with hardware variety and evolution in mind – unlike 16-bit EPOC, which had been tied closely to a single 80186-based chipset. Many implementation details were changed as a result of these fundamentals, but EKA1 was otherwise surprisingly similar in spirit to 16-bit EPOC.

At that time, one of the proudest moments of my career took place – in my spare bedroom! The rest of the team were out of the office, so I worked at home for a week, frantically trying to achieve the first ever boot of the kernel before they got back. And late on the Friday afternoon, the null thread finally printed out its debug message – EKA1 was born.

But EKA1 was not destined to be the end of the story. The Symbian OS system for supporting event-driven programming was efficient overall, but provided no real-time guarantees. The kernel itself was designed with robustness – key for PDAs that hold a user's personal data – as the primary goal. As Symbian OS began to address the processing needs of mobile phones, it became apparent that an OS that *could* provide real-time guarantees was really needed.

There were other influences on EKA2 too. The experience gained from real hardware porting in the context of EKA1 was beginning to demonstrate that EKA1's module boundaries were not always drawn in the right place to make porting easy. Some ports, which should have required only a driver change, in practice required the kernel to be re-built.

So a new kernel architecture was conceived and, to distinguish it from the original 32-bit EPOC kernel, it was named EKA2 (EPOC Kernel Architecture 2), with the term EKA1 being invented for the original.

EKA2 was conceived in 1998 and, little by little, brought from drawing board to market. By 2003, Symbian's lead licensees and semiconductor partners were committed to adopting EKA2 for future products.

This book was written to provide a detailed exposition on the new real-time kernel, providing the reader with the insights of the software engineers who designed and wrote it.

This chapter is designed as the foundations for that book and should give you a good understanding of the overall architecture of the new real-time kernel, and of the reasoning behind our design choices. I will also say a little about the design of the emulator, and then return to this subject in more detail a couple of times later in the book.

1.2 Basic OS concepts

I'd like to start with a basic definition of an operating system (OS):

The operating system is the fundamental software that controls the overall operation of the computer it runs on. It is responsible for the management of hardware – controlling and integrating the various hardware components in the system. The OS is also responsible for the management of software – for example, the loading of applications such as email clients and spreadsheets.

The operating system is usually the first software that is loaded into a computer's memory when that computer boots. The OS then continues the start-up process by loading device drivers and applications. These, along with all the other software on the computer, depend on the operating system to provide them with services such as disk access, memory management, task scheduling, and interfacing with the user.

Symbian OS has a design that is more modular than many other operating systems. So, for example, disk services are in the main performed by the file server, and screen and user input services by the window server. However, there is one element that you can think of as the heart of the operating system – the element that is responsible for memory management, task management and task scheduling. That element is of course the kernel, EKA2.

There are many different flavors of operating system in the world, so let's apply some adjectives to Symbian OS, and EKA2 in particular:

Symbian OS and EKA2 are **modular**. As I've already said, operating system functionality is provided in separate building blocks, not one monolithic unit. Furthermore, EKA2 is modular too, as you can see in Figure 1.1.

EKA2 is **single user**. There is no concept of multiple logins to a Symbian OS smartphone, unlike Windows, Mac OS X, UNIX or traditional mainframe operating systems.

EKA2 is **multi-tasking**. It switches CPU time between multiple threads, giving the user of the mobile phone the impression that multiple applications are running at the same time.

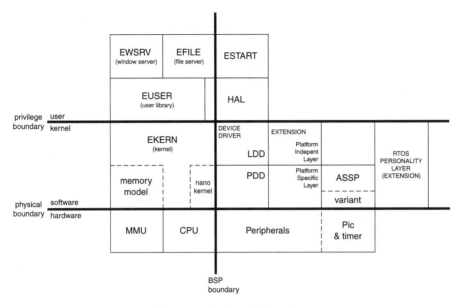

Figure 1.1 Symbian OS overview

EKA2 is a **preemptively** multi-tasking OS. EKA2 does not rely on one thread to relinquish CPU time to another, but reschedules threads perforce, from a timer tick.

EKA2 is a **priority-based** multi-tasking OS with **priority inheritance**. EKA2 allocates CPU time based on a thread's priority and minimizes the delays to a high-priority thread when a low-priority thread holds a mutex it needs.

EKA2 is **real-time**. Its services are (mostly) bounded, that is it completes them in a known amount of time.

EKA2 can be a **ROM-based** OS.

EKA2 is suitable for **open but resource-constrained** environments. We designed it for mobile phones, and so it needs less of key resources such as memory, power and hard disk than open desktop operating systems such as Windows or Linux.

1.3   Symbian OS design

1.3.1   Design goals

When creating EKA2 we set ourselves a number of design constraints. We started by deciding what we didn't want to lose from EKA1. This meant that we wanted to ensure that the new kernel was still:

1. In the embedded OS tradition

2. Suitable for resource-constrained environments

3. Modular: consisting of microkernel and user-side servers

4. Portable to a range of evolving chipsets

5. Robust against badly written user code

6. Of high integrity, ensuring the safety of user data.

Then we decided on our new goals. The key goal was that the new kernel would be real-time and have enhanced overall performance. We decided that we would meet this if we could run a GSM protocol stack on our new operating system. A side benefit, and a worthy one, would be the ability to better support high-bandwidth activities such as comms and multimedia. This goal broke down into several sub-goals and requirements:

1. Latency $\leq$ 1 ms from interrupt to user thread

2. Latency $\leq$ 500 μs from interrupt to kernel thread

3. Fast mutex operations

4. OS calls to be of determined length where possible

5. OS calls to be preemptible

6. Priority-order waiting on semaphores and mutexes

7. Timers with a finer resolution.

Then we considered how else we could improve the operating system, and we came up with the following list:

1. Ease porting – although EKA1 had been designed to be portable, we could go much further to make life easier for those porting the OS to new hardware

2. Be robust against malicious (rather than merely badly written) user code

3. Enable single-core solutions, in which embedded and user-application code run on the same processor core

4. Provide a better emulator for code development and debugging, that emulator being a closer match to real hardware

5. Simplify life for device driver writers.

And as we considered these design goals, we were aware that there was one over-riding constraint on our design. That constraint was to be backwards source compatibility with the EKA1's EUSER class library.

EUSER is the interface to the kernel for all Symbian OS applications, and there are a lot of them out there!

1.3.2   Symbian OS kernel architecture

With those design goals in mind, we designed an operating system whose architecture, at the highest level, looked like that in Figure 1.1. You can see the major building blocks of the kernel. I've also included two other key system components that are usually considered to be part of the operating system, and that I will cover in this book: the file server and the window server. I'll cover each of these building blocks and give you an idea of its basic functionality.

1.3.2.1   Nanokernel

The main function of the nanokernel is to provide simple, supervisor-mode threads, along with their scheduling and synchronization operations. We named the nanokernel as we did because the services it provides are even more primitive than those provided by most embedded real-time operating systems (RTOSes). However, we have carefully chosen those services to be sufficient to support a GSM signaling stack.

The nanokernel is the initial handler for all interrupts. It then passes the majority of them to the variant layer for dispatch. It also provides simple timing functions, such as the nanokernel timer (NTimer) API, which gives a callback after a specified number of ticks, and the sleep API (NKern::Sleep), which makes the current thread wait for a specified number of ticks.

The simple synchronization objects I mentioned earlier are the nanokernel mutex (NFastMutex) and the nanokernel semaphore (NFast-Semaphore). Both of these forbid more than one thread from waiting on them.

Finally, the nanokernel provides deferred function calls (DFCs) and the oddly named immediate deferred function calls (IDFCs). If you want to find out more about these, then please turn to Chapter 6, *Interrupts and Exceptions.*

An important difference in EKA2 from EKA1 that should be noted is that neither the nanokernel nor the Symbian OS kernel link to the user library, EUSER. Instead, the nanokernel uses its own library of utility functions, and makes these available to the rest of the kernel, and device drivers too.

Another key difference from EKA1, somewhat related to the one I have just discussed, is that EKA2 does not support a kernel-side leaving mechanism. This means that errors are reported by returning an error code – or panicking the thread.

The majority of the time, the nanokernel is preemptible. Usually it runs unlocked and with interrupts enabled, but we do have to prevent other threads from running in a few sections of code, such as thread state changes and access to the ready list. We designed these critical sections to be as short as possible and to have bounded execution times, the goal being to maintain deterministic real-time performance. We protect the critical sections in the nanokernel by disabling preemption – this is possible because these sections are very short. In general, we use a mutex known as the system lock to protect critical code in the Symbian OS kernel and memory model, but the only place where the nanokernel uses this lock is to protect the scheduler's address space switch hook on the moving memory model.

What are the limitations on the nanokernel? The main one to note is that it does not do any dynamic memory allocation; that is, it can't allocate or free memory. In all of the nanokernel's operations, it assumes that memory has been preallocated by other parts of the operating system.

1.3.2.2 Symbian OS kernel

The Symbian OS kernel provides the kernel functionality needed by Symbian OS, building on the simple threads and services provided by the nanokernel to provide more complex objects, such as user-mode threads, processes, reference-counted objects and handles, dynamically loaded libraries, inter-thread communication and more.

These objects also include a range of more sophisticated synchronization objects: Symbian OS semaphores and mutexes. Symbian OS semaphores are standard counting semaphores which support multiple waiting threads and which release waiting threads in priority order. Symbian OS mutexes are fully nestable (a thread can hold several mutexes at once, and can hold the same mutex multiple times). They also support priority inheritance: the holding thread inherits the priority of the highest priority waiting thread, if that is higher than its usual priority.

In contrast to the nanokernel, the Symbian OS kernel does allow dynamic memory allocation. It provides a kernel memory allocator – the kernel heap, which uses low-level memory services provided by an entity known as the memory model. The Symbian OS is completely MMU agnostic – we isolate all assumptions about memory to the memory model, which I describe in more detail in the next section.

The Symbian OS kernel is fully preemptible: an interrupt can cause it to reschedule at any point in its execution, even in the middle of a context switch. This means that the Symbian OS kernel can have no effect whatsoever on thread latency.

We use system lock mutex, provided by the nanokernel, to protect the most fundamental parts of the Symbian OS kernel, such as:

(i) The state of DThread objects. When Symbian OS threads interact with semaphores and mutexes, they undergo state transitions that are protected by the system lock

(ii)   The state of most Symbian OS synchronization objects: IPC (servers and sessions), semaphores, mutexes, message queues, publish and subscribe properties

(iii) Handle arrays are valid for reading (but not writing) when the system lock is held. All the executive functions that take a handle hold the system lock while translating it – see Chapter 5, *Kernel Services*, for more on this subject.

1.3.2.3   *Memory model*

In EKA2, we confine our assumptions about the memory architecture of the ASIC to one module, the memory model. Thus the memory model encapsulates significant MMU differences, such as whether a cache is virtually tagged or physically tagged, and indeed, whether there is an MMU at all. In EKA1, assumptions about memory and the MMU were spread throughout the operating system, making it difficult to produce a mobile phone based on an ASIC without an MMU, for example. This has become much easier with the advent of EKA2, since the memory model allows you to model memory in different ways, and to change that decision relatively easily.

Symbian currently provides four different memory models:

1.   Direct (no MMU)

2.   Moving (similar to EKA1)

3.   Multiple (used for ASICs with physically tagged caches such as Intel X86 and later ARM cores)

4.   Emulator (used by the Symbian OS emulator that runs on Windows).

The memory model provides low-level memory management services, such as a per-process address space and memory mapping. It performs the context switch when asked to do so by the scheduler and is involved in inter-process data transfer.

The memory model also helps in the creation of processes as an instantiation of an executable image loaded by the file server, and takes part in making inter-process data transfers.

If you are interested in finding out more about the memory model, turn to Chapter 7, *Memory Models*.

1.3.2.4   *Personality layer*

We designed the nanokernel to provide just enough functionality to run a GSM signaling stack. The idea behind this was to allow mobile phone manufacturers to run both their signaling stacks and their personal information management (PIM) software on a single processor, providing considerable cost savings over the usual two-processor solution.

Most mobile phone manufacturers have written their signaling stacks for existing RTOSes such as Nucleus or μITRON. These signaling stacks represent a considerable investment in time and money, and it would be very time-consuming for the mobile phone manufacturers to port them to the nanokernel – not to mention the increase in defects that would probably ensue from such an exercise.

Because of this, we designed the nanokernel to allow third parties to write personality layers. A personality layer is an emulation layer over the nanokernel that provides the RTOS API to client software. The personality layer would translate an RTOS call into a call (or calls) to the nanokernel to achieve the same ends. In this way, we allow source code written for that RTOS to run under Symbian OS with little or no modification.

For a more detailed description of personality layers, and the nanokernel design decisions that support them, turn to Chapter 17, *Real Time*.

1.3.2.5   *ASSP/variant extension*

Typically, the CPU and the majority of hardware peripherals on mobile devices are implemented on a semiconductor device integrated circuit commonly referred to as an ASSP (Application-Specific Standard Product). To reduce both the bill of materials and the size of a phone, it is becoming common to add an increasing number of components to the ASSP. This might include stacking RAM and flash components on the same silicon package, or incorporating components into the silicon layout; for example, a DSP (digital signal processor) for audio/video processing, dedicated graphics processors and telephony baseband processors running GSM or CDMA communication stacks.

We refer to any hardware components outside the ASSP as variant-specific components. These typically include components such as flash and RAM storage technology, display devices, baseband and Bluetooth units. They are typically interfaced to the processor over semiconductor-vendor-specific buses and interconnect, or more standard communications lines such as USB and serial UARTs. ASSPs also tend to provide configurable GPIO (general purpose I/O) lines for custom functions such as MMC card detect and touch-screen pen down interrupt lines.

So, in Symbian OS, the ASSP/variant extension provides the hardware-dependent services required by the kernel – for example, timer tick interrupts and real-time clock access. In the days of EKA1, we built the ASSP into the kernel, and the separate variant layer described in the next section was mandatory. This made for unnecessary re-compilation of the kernel when porting to a new ASSP, so in EKA2 we have completely separated the ASSP from the kernel. Of course, this means that if you are porting EKA2, you no longer need to recompile the kernel every time you tweak your hardware.

1.3.2.6 Variant

In EKA2, we don't insist that you make a division between the ASSP and the variant, as we do in EKA1. You may provide one single variant DLL if you wish. Nevertheless, if you were porting the OS to a family of similar ASICs, you would probably choose to split it, putting the generic code for the family of ASICs in the ASSP extension, and the code for a particular ASIC in the variant DLL. For example, within Symbian, the Intel SA1100 ASSP has two variants, Brutus and Assabet.

1.3.2.7 Device drivers

On Symbian OS, you use device drivers to control peripherals: drivers provide the interface between those peripherals and the rest of Symbian OS. If you want, you may split your device driver in a similar way to the ASSP and variant, providing a hardware-independent logical device driver, or LDD, and a hardware-dependent physical device driver, or PDD.

Device drivers may run in the client thread or in a kernel thread: our new multi-threaded kernel design makes porting device drivers to Symbian OS from other operating systems much easier.

Symbian provides standard LDDs for a wide range of peripheral types (such as media devices, the USB controller and serial communications devices) – nevertheless, phone manufacturers will often develop their own interfaces for custom hardware.

Device drivers have changed considerably from EKA1 to EKA2. See Chapter 12, *Drivers and Extensions*, for more details.

1.3.2.8 Extensions

Extensions are merely device drivers that the kernel automatically starts at boot-time, so you can think of them as a way to extend the kernel's functionality. For example, the crash debugger is a kernel extension, allowing you to include it or exclude it from a ROM as you wish, without having to recompile the kernel.

The variant and the ASSP that I discussed earlier are important extensions that the kernel loads quite early in the boot process. After this, the kernel continues to boot until it finally starts the scheduler and enters the supervisor thread, which initializes all remaining kernel extensions. Extensions loaded at this late stage are not critical to the operation of the kernel itself, but are typically used to perform early initialization of hardware components and to provide permanently available services for devices such as the LCD, DMA, I2C and peripheral bus controllers.

The final kernel extension to be initialized is the EXSTART extension, which is responsible for loading the file server. I discuss system boot in more detail in Chapter 16, *Boot Processes*.

1.3.2.9 EUSER

The user library, EUSER, provides three main types of function to its clients:

1. Class library methods that execute entirely user-side, such as most methods in the array and descriptor classes (descriptors are the Symbian OS version of strings)

2. Access to kernel functions requiring the kernel to make privileged accesses on behalf of the user thread, such as checking the time or locale settings

3. Access to kernel functions requiring the kernel to manipulate its own memory on behalf of a user thread, such as process creation or loading a library.

Every Symbian OS thread gains its access to kernel services through the EUSER library. It is this interface that we have largely maintained between EKA1 and EKA2, resulting in minimal disruption to application authors.

1.3.2.10 File server

The file server is a user-mode server that allows user-mode threads to manipulate drives, directories and files. Please turn to Chapter 9, *The File Server*, for more details.

1.3.2.11 Window server

The window server is a user-mode server that shares the screen, keyboard and pointer between all Symbian OS applications. See Chapter 11, *The Window Server*, for more details.

1.3.2.12 Software layering

We can also consider the architecture of Symbian OS from a software layering perspective, as shown in Figure 1.2.

If you are familiar with EKA1, you will notice that the layering of EKA2 is a little different. Nonetheless, there are strong similarities, as we move down from the most generic, independent layer, in which code is shared between all platforms, to the most specific variant layer, in which code is written for a particular ASIC on a particular development board or in a particular mobile phone.

We call the top four software layers "the kernel layer", and the bottom two, "the peripheral layer". These last form a key part of the *board support package* that a phone manufacturer implements when porting Symbian OS to new hardware. This also comprises the bootstrap and device drivers and extensions.

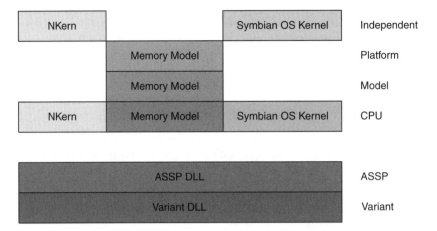

Figure 1.2 Kernel layering

The independent layer makes up about 60% of the kernel source code. It provides the basic building blocks of the nanokernel and the Symbian OS kernel – nanothreads, threads, processes, chunks, client-server and more. These base classes are derived in lower layers to provide implementations for the particular hardware on which Symbian OS is running.

The platform layer is concerned with executable images – whether Symbian OS is running on the emulator or real hardware – hence its alternative name of the image layer. Only the memory model has code at this level, and it provides two implementations, EPOC for device hardware and WIN32 for the emulator.

The model layer is all about the organization of per-process memory, and again only the memory model has code at this level. The memory model provides four different implementations – moving, multiple, direct and emulator. I will discuss these in more depth in Chapter 7, *Memory Models*.

The CPU layer is for code that differs according to the processor that Symbian OS is running on; this is where assembler code belongs. The nanokernel, memory model and Symbian OS kernel all have code in this layer. At the time of writing, Symbian provides three possible CPU layers – X86 (a port to PC hardware), ARM (mobile phones) and Win32 (for the emulator).

The CPU layer of the memory model has code that is CPU- and MMU-specific, as well as specific to the type of memory model. The nanokernel's CPU layer contains most of the knowledge of the core CPU architecture – how exceptions and interrupts are handled, which registers need to be saved on a context switch and so on. A good proportion of the code in the CPU layer of the Symbian OS kernel is independent layer functionality that has been assembler-coded for improved performance.

The variant layer provides the hardware-specific implementation of the control functions expected by the nanokernel and the Symbian OS kernel. As I mentioned earlier, the phone manufacturer can choose whether to split this layer into an ASSP and a variant when porting to new hardware.

This variant layer can also provide hardware-specific implementations of hardware abstraction layer (HAL) functions, although these may equally be implemented in the kernel itself or in extensions.

In Chapter 5, *Kernel Services*, I will explain what services each layer exposes to the other layers.

1.3.3   Design solutions

Now I'm going to talk about the design decisions that we took for EKA2, and how they helped us to achieve the goals that we had set ourselves.

1.3.3.1   Multi-threaded preemptible kernel

To decrease thread latency, we chose to make EKA2 multi-threaded, allowing the preemption of low-priority kernel operations by high-priority ones.

EKA2 has five threads, and they are:

1.   The null thread – idles the CPU, de-fragments RAM. This is also known as the idle thread

2.   The supervisor thread – cleans up killed threads and processes, provides asynchronous object deletion

3.   DFC thread 0 – runs DFCs for general device drivers, such as comms, keyboard and digitizer

4.   DFC thread 1 – runs the nanokernel's timer queue

5.   Timer thread – runs Symbian OS relative and absolute timers (`After()`, `At()`).

I'll describe the purpose of these five threads in more detail in Chapter 3, *Threads, Processes and Libraries*.

The multi-threaded nature of the kernel also helped us to achieve another of our goals – making life easier for device driver writers. You often want to port a device driver from another operating system, but the single-threaded device driver model of EKA1 meant that porting a multi-threaded device driver was not a simple task – you usually had to redesign the driver from scratch. In EKA2, device drivers can make use of DFC thread 0, or can even create threads of their own if they wish. Device driver designs from other operating systems can be re-used and porting is now much simpler.

1.3.3.2   Nanokernel

We chose to have a separate nanokernel, because it has several advantages:

1. Very low and predictable interrupt and thread latencies. This is because only the nanokernel disables either interrupts or rescheduling. (There are a handful of exceptions to this, but they are not important here.) The vast majority of the Symbian OS kernel, and the memory model, run with both interrupts and preemption enabled. Because the nanokernel provides only a small selection of primitives, it is easy to determine the longest period for which we disable interrupts or rescheduling

2. Simpler and better emulation. The Symbian OS emulator running under Windows has far more code in common with a real device, which means that the emulation is more faithful than that obtained with the EKA1 emulator

3. Support for single-core phones. The nanokernel allows you to run an RTOS and its GSM signaling stack alongside Symbian OS and its PIM software. For more detail see Section 1.3.2.4.

1.3.3.3   Modularity

The increased modularity of the new kernel makes porting the operating system to new ASSPs much easier. A large proportion of the processor-specific code is in the nanokernel, and differences in memory and MMU are confined to the memory model.

The memory model makes it easy for you to use the direct memory model in the early stages of a port to a new CPU architecture, changing to the moving or multiple models later on when you've done more debugging. It allows you to port the OS in smaller, simpler stages.

1.3.3.4   Design limitations

Designing for real-time performance led to a couple of design limitations on EKA2:

1. To ensure deterministic interrupt latencies, we could not allow an unlimited number of interrupt service routines to bind to one interrupt source as was possible in EKA1. Now only one ISR may bind to an interrupt

2. To ensure bounded context switch times, we had to restrict the number of chunks in a process to a maximum of 16 – from an unlimited number in EKA1. (A chunk is the Symbian OS object that is fundamental to memory allocation – for more details see Chapter 7, *Memory Models*.)

It's important to note that not all EKA2 services are bounded in time: for example, the allocation and freeing of memory are potentially unbounded. This is discussed in Chapter 17, *Real Time*.

1.3.4 The Symbian OS emulator

1.3.4.1 Design decisions

The emulator has two main uses – developing Symbian OS software and demonstrating that software.

The first of these use cases makes more demands on kernel services, so we concentrated on it when we drew up our requirements. At the highest level, it gave us just a couple of key requirements for the emulator:

1. It needs to support development and debugging using standard tools on the host platform

2. It should provide as faithful an emulation as possible of Symbian OS on target hardware.

These requirements seem to conflict, because the first requires the use of entities in the hosted platform (until now, always Windows) that do not exist in the same form in the "real" Symbian OS. For example:

1. Source-level debugging requires that the object code is stored in standard Windows executable files that the Windows debugger can recognize and that are loaded via the standard Windows loader

2. Debugging multi-threaded software requires that the Windows debugger recognize those threads. This means that we should implement emulated threads as Windows threads.

In the end, we decided to write the EKA2 emulator as a port of the EKA2 kernel, rather than trying to make the Symbian OS kernel API work over Win32 APIs. We used Windows as little as possible so as to share the maximum amount of Symbian OS code (and hence behavior) between the emulator and real mobile phones.

Indeed, if you look at Figure 1.3 and compare the code that runs on a real device to the code that runs on the Win32 emulator, you will find a great deal in common. Both systems contain the same core kernel code, from the Symbian OS kernel and the nanokernel. At the lower, architecture-specific, levels of the nanokernel, we have an emulated "Win32" CPU rather than an ARM CPU or an X86 CPU. This means that the emulator is effectively a port to a different processor. For example, the emulator has processes and scheduling that are almost identical to those on a real device.

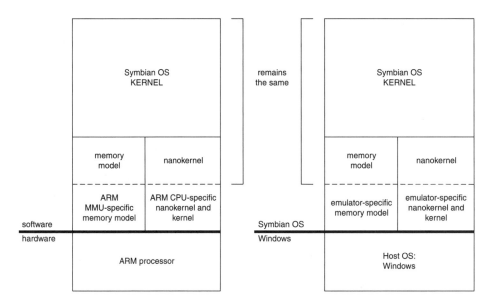

Figure 1.3   Emulator code re-use

The memory model, however, is completely different on the emulator and a real mobile phone. On the emulator, it is always the special emulator memory model, which has knowledge of the different image files that are loaded to create processes. These are standard Win32 PE EXE files, and so we satisfy our earlier requirement for source-level debugging. In theory, this approach could make it easier for us to implement an emulator on platforms other than Windows.

1.4   Summary

I hope that this chapter has given you a good overview of the history and design of the Symbian OS kernel. Next I shall look at Symbian OS as a platform for real device hardware.

2

Hardware for Symbian OS

by Jason Parker

If it draws blood, it's hardware.

Unknown

This chapter explores the hardware that Symbian OS is designed to run on: a mobile phone. This is often known as the device platform. I'll examine the core hardware that is needed to run Symbian OS, and try to help you to appreciate the design choices that underlie a world-class Symbian phone. With this knowledge, I hope that you will also gain a deeper insight into the operating environment of Symbian OS.

Information on running Symbian OS on the EKA2 emulator, the platform that you will use during development, is placed in context throughout the book. The aim of this material is to let you see where you can rely on the similarities of the emulator to your phone hardware, and where you need to be aware of the differences.

2.1 Inside a Symbian OS phone

Symbian OS phones are designed first and foremost to be good telephones, with quality voice calls and excellent battery life. On top of that, Symbian OS phones are usually open platforms that provide opportunities for interesting and novel software. Achieving these goals requires hardware designed specifically for the task, high enough performance in the key use cases and an obsession for low power usage.

Looking into Symbian OS phone design, there are two complementary computing domains, the mobile radio interface of the baseband processor (BP), also known as the modem, and the application processor (AP), which runs the user interface and high-level code, under Symbian OS. Surrounding these domains is a collection of peripherals that make up the product: battery, display, speakers, SIM card and more.

Figure 2.1 depicts a common two-chip solution, where the BP and the AP are self-contained systems, with a high speed inter-processor

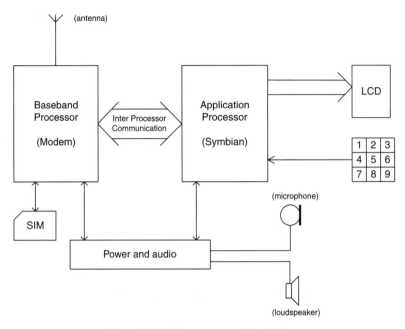

Figure 2.1   A common two-chip solution

communication (IPC) link between them. This is the preferred design for 3G phones, in which each domain can re-use existing software and hardware sub-systems.

The two-domain system of AP and BP isolates each processor from the other's requirements. The BP requires hard real-time software, periodic power management and provides security for the network. The AP expects to operate in two modes – full power when a user is interacting with the phone, and a deep sleep idle when nothing is happening. The AP code contains the frameworks and libraries for built-in applications and third-party code.

The overall quality of the product comes from the tight coupling between the two domains over the IPC, and their ability to co-ordinate the shared responsibilities of audio and power.

Designing hardware for Symbian OS phones requires a clear under-standing of the end-user use cases, the performance requirements that these put on the design, and a continual focus on power management.

2.1.1   Baseband processor (BP)

The baseband processor is the voice and data modem for the phone. It contains all the electronics required for the radios used in 2.5G and 3G telephony, a DSP to run the algorithms to decode the information, and a CPU to run the call control stack, which co-ordinates with the network base stations and communicates with the AP.

The software on the BP is called the telephony stack, and known as the stack for short. The stack is a complex system of code that has grown in step with the evolving telephony standards and their type certification regimes. A typical stack will contain between 2 and 8 MB of code, and require up to 2 MB of working RAM to execute. GSM calls are scheduled to a 4.6 ms time frame, in which all of the call activity needs to have completed before the start of the next frame. This requires a real-time operating system (RTOS) environment. It is tuned and tested to meet the stringent timing requirements under worst-case loads of voice and data calls.

BP power management is highly optimized for maximum call time and idle time, whilst still being connected to the network. When the phone is idle, the BP can put itself into a deep power-saving mode, only waking up every two seconds to listen to the paging channel for an incoming call or message.

The IPC interface to the AP has evolved from simple serial ports in early Symbian phones to 10 Mb/s multiplexed links. This link could use five bi-directional channels for telephony control, system control, packet data, streamed data and BP debug.

Audio data is routed to and from the BP through a dedicated digital audio bus, directly to the audio hardware. This bus provides minimal latency with guaranteed real-time performance and lower power consumption during a call by bypassing the AP. If voice call data was passed over the IPC to the AP, additional buffering would be incurred, a real-time load would be placed on the AP, and power consumption would go up.

The BP controls the SIM card, which contains the secret codes and algorithms required for network authentication.

The two-domain system of AP and BP provides many technical and engineering benefits, including design re-use, stability and security. These come at the cost of additional chips, physical size, and overall power consumption.

There are strong financial pressures towards the closer integration of the AP and BP domains for mid-tier phones. Example designs range from multiple cores on one ASIC, sharing memory but little else, up to the full integration of the telephony stack and Symbian OS. In this last case, the two co-exist on the same CPU, with all of the software integration issues that this incurs.

As you can see, baseband processors and their sophisticated telephony stacks are major topics that already fill several books on their own.

2.1.2 Application processor (AP)

The application processor is at the heart of a Symbian OS phone. Contained on a single piece of silicon, the AP is an example of a System-on-Chip. It has an ARM CPU, memory, display and audio interfaces, multimedia accelerators and many more peripherals. I will now focus on these components, their integration and how they interact with each other.

2.2   System-on-Chip (SoC)

SoCs are known by two other names: ASICs (Application-specific Integrated Circuits) for custom chips and ASSPs (Application-specific Semiconductor Parts) for commercial parts. All three terms are used imprecisely and interchangeably. SoCs are designed and manufactured by all of the major silicon companies: Texas Instruments have a product family called OMAP and Intel have their XScale range of processors. Figure 2.2 shows a typical System-on-Chip design.

Each sub-component within the SoC is an intellectual property (IP) block. The blocks are linked to interconnecting buses through industry standard interfaces. The IP blocks can be licensed from many sources. The most well known IP licensing company is ARM Ltd, who license ARM CPU cores.

The example SoC is driven by an ARM 926 CPU for Symbian OS, and a DSP for multimedia codecs. These two cores are both masters on the system bus, which is a high-speed, low-latency, 32-bit wide bus, connected to the DRAM controller. The system bus and memory controller funnel all data accesses into main memory, so they must be designed for high bandwidth and low latency transfers to avoid starving the CPU and reducing its effective performance.

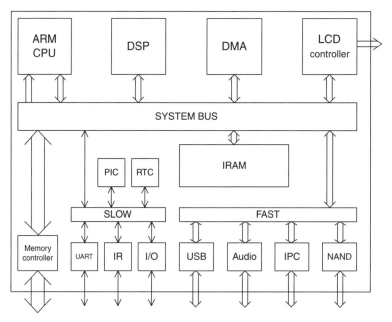

Figure 2.2   System-on-Chip

The DMA engine and LCD controller are additional bus masters, both accessing memory through the same bus. The remaining peripheral blocks are known as bus slaves – they cannot access memory directly, and require their masters to feed them with commands and data. The slave blocks are cascaded off the two peripheral buses, one of which is a relatively fast bus for DMA devices, and the other is a slow bus for simple low-bandwidth peripherals.

Peripheral buses are connected to the system bus through bus bridges. These translate between the bus formats and compensate for any speed differences, necessary since peripheral buses normally run slower than the system bus. A good SoC design will pay attention to these bridges to ensure that critical timed or high-bandwidth peripherals can be accessed quickly by the CPU.

Further information about ARM SoCs can be found in the book, *ARM System-on-Chip Architecture* by Steve Furber.[1]

2.2.1 Physical memory map

The buses and their connections determine the physical address map of the chip – with 32-bit addressing there is 4 GB of addressable space. Symbian OS uses the CPU's Memory Management Unit (MMU) to remap the reality of the chip's address space layout into a consistent virtual address space for the software.

As an example, the 4 GB address space of the SoC might be divided into large regions by the system bus controller. By only decoding the top three address bits, it produces eight regions, each 512 MB in size:

Address start	Address end	Content
0x00000000	0x1FFFFFFF	ROM Bank 0 (Boot Rom)
0x20000000	0x3FFFFFFF	ROM Bank 1
0x40000000	0x5FFFFFFF	DSP
0x60000000	0x7FFFFFFF	Fast Peripheral Bus
0x80000000	0x9FFFFFFF	Slow Peripheral Bus
0xA0000000	0xBFFFFFFF	IRAM
0xC0000000	0xDFFFFFFF	DRAM Bank 0
0xE0000000	0xFFFFFFFF	DRAM Bank 1

---

[1] *ARM System-on-Chip Architecture*, 2nd edn by Steve Furber. Addison-Wesley Professional.

These large regions are then further sub-divided.

With 32 MB of RAM installed in DRAM Bank 0, the remaining 480 MB of address space will contain aliases of the RAM contents if address bits 25 to 28 are not decoded by the hardware, as is typical:

0xC0000000	0xC1FFFFFF	32 MB RAM
0xC2000000	0xC3FFFFFF	32 MB Alias 1
0xC4000000	0xC5FFFFFF	32 MB Alias 2
. . .	. . .	. . .
0xDE000000	0xDFFFFFFF	32 MB Alias F

The peripheral bus's regions are sub-divided by their peripherals. The fast peripherals in the example SoC each have 64 KB of address for their register sets:

0x60000000	0x6000FFFF	NAND Interface
0x60010000	0x6001FFFF	IPC
0x60020000	0x6002FFFF	Audio
0x60030000	0x6003FFFF	USB
. . .	. . .	. . .
0x600x0000	0x7FFFFFFF	Empty Space

In practice, every ASSP will have a different physical address space and most of it will be unused or aliased. Reads and writes to unused space will produce a bus error.

A good design will have a consistent memory map for all of the bus masters, removing the need for any physical address translation, and reducing the likelihood of errors.

Normally the CPU will have access to every peripheral in the system, whereas the other masters will only have visibility of appropriate slaves. The LCD controller needs to pull frame data from memory, and the DMA engine will work between the fast peripherals and memory.

The physical address map is used by the bootstrap code when configuring the MMU. The DMA engine and the other bus masters will not contain their own MMUs. They only understand physical addresses and software that programs these devices must translate virtual addresses back to their physical values before using them.

2.2.2 Central Processing Unit (CPU)

Symbian OS requires a 32-bit microprocessor that combines high performance with low power consumption. It must be little endian, with a full MMU, user and supervisor modes, interrupts and exceptions. ARM designs fit this bill exactly and when this book was written all Symbian OS phones had an ARM-based CPU, as did 80% of the world's mobile phones.

To take these requirements in turn:

High performance is a relative term for a battery-powered device. Symbian phones today have CPUs clocked between 100 and 200 MHz, which is more than an order of magnitude slower than an average 3 GHz PC – yet the power they consume is three orders of magnitude less. Future application demands will push the CPU speeds into the 300 to 400 MHz range for peak performance.

Low power consumption is a design requirement for all components in a Symbian OS phone. During the CPU design, engineering trade-offs are evaluated and features are added to produce the most power-efficient core. Power saving comes from lean hardware design, the selective clocking of circuits and the addition of multiple low-power modes: Idle, Doze, Sleep, Deep Sleep and Off. I will discuss the mapping from hardware into the software frameworks that Symbian OS provides for power management in Chapter 15, *Power Management*.

The MMU, with the user and supervisor modes the CPU provides, allow for the virtualization of the user memory. EKA2 constructs a robust execution environment for applications, each isolated from the others with its own protected memory space. Application code executes in user mode with limitations and kernel code uses supervisor mode with fewer limitations, but even kernel code is still constrained by its virtual memory map. I describe the memory models that Symbian OS provides in Chapter 7, *Memory Models*.

Exceptions are CPU events that change the instruction flow in the core. Interrupt exceptions are generated by peripherals that are seeking attention. Software interrupts are used as a controlled switch from user to supervisor mode. The MMU will generate a data abort if code tries to access memory that is not mapped, and a prefetch abort if the CPU jumps to a code address that is not mapped. See Chapter 6, *Interrupts and Exceptions*, for more on interrupts and exceptions.

2.2.3 ARM

ARM have been designing RISC-based CPUs for over 20 years, and successfully licensing them to all of the world's semiconductor manufacturers for inclusion into their own SoCs. Intel has licensed version 5 of the ARM architecture to build the software-compatible XScale microprocessor.

As ARM developed successive generations of CPUs, they have added new instructions and features, and deprecated some rarely used old features. The ARM architectural version number, with some additional letters, defines the feature set. It specifies the instruction set, the operation of the MMU, the caches and debugging.

Symbian OS requires a CPU that supports ARM v5TE or greater. ARM v5TE is the baseline instruction set for all Symbian software. To ensure compatibility across multiple phones, application code should only use v5TE instructions. (The previous generation of EKA1 phones used the ARM v4T architecture.)

What does ARM v5TE actually mean? It is **v**ersion **5** of the ARM architecture, with the **T**HUMB instruction set and the **E**nhanced DSP instructions. The definition of the ARM v5TE instruction set can be found in the *ARM Architecture Reference Manual*.[2]

ARM cores and SoCs that are currently compatible with Symbian OS phone projects include:

Core	Architecture	SoC
ARM926	v5TE	Philips Nexperia PNX4008
ARM926	v5TE	Texas Instruments OMAP 1623
Xscale	v5TE	Intel XScale PXA260
ARM1136	v6	Texas Instruments OMAP 2420

THUMB was introduced in architecture v4T. It is a 16-bit sub-set of the ARM instruction set, designed to resolve the common RISC issue of poor code density with instructions that are all 32 bits. By using a 16-bit encoding scheme, THUMB compiled code is approximately 70% of the size of the ARM equivalent, but it needs 25% more instructions to do the same task. THUMB and ARM code can inter-work on the same system, using the BLX instruction to switch mode.

Most code in Symbian OS is compiled as THUMB, since the size of the ROM is intimately linked to the cost of a Symbian OS phone. The kernel is built for ARM for increased performance and it requires instructions which are missing from THUMB, such as coprocessor instructions needed to access the MMU and CPU state control registers. Application code can be built for ARM by adding ALWAYS_BUILD_AS_ARM into the application's

---

[2] *ARM Architecture Reference Manual*, 2nd edn by David Seal. Addison-Wesley Professional.

MMP file. Symbian does this for algorithmic code, since, for example, the JPEG decoder runs 30% faster when compiled for ARM.

The enhanced DSP instructions enable the more efficient implementation of 16-bit signal processing algorithms using an ARM CPU. These instructions are not used in normal procedural code and have little impact on the execution of Symbian OS.

2.2.4   Memory Management Unit (MMU)

Symbian OS requires a full Memory Management Unit to co-ordinate and enforce the use of virtual memory within an open OS. I discuss the use of the MMU in Chapter 7, *Memory Models*.

The MMU sits between the CPU and the system bus, translating virtual addresses used by software into physical addresses understood by the hardware. This lookup has to happen on every memory access.

The MMU breaks up the flat contiguous physical memory into pages. Mostly they are small, 4 KB pages, although larger 64 KB pages and 1 MB sections exist.

The Symbian OS virtual memory map re-orders scattered physical pages into an apparently ordered virtual memory space. The re-ordering information is expressed to the MMU through the use of page tables. Page tables are a hierarchical data structure that encode the entire 4 GB virtual address space in a sparse manner. On ARM systems the table has two levels, the Page Directory and Page Tables.

In much the same way as a physical address is decoded by the bus controllers, the bit fields within a virtual address are decoded by the MMU into the Page Directory, the Page Table and index into the memory page. This is explained in detail in Section 7.2.1.

Bits	**31 → 20**	**19 → 12**	**11 → 0**
Address decode	Top 12 bits map to Page Directory	Middle 8 bits map to Page Table	Bottom 12 bits are offset in page

Virtual address decoding for a small page

On every memory access the MMU performs a virtual to physical lookup to get the correct bus address and to validate page permissions. The process of looking up a physical address from a virtual one is known as "walking" the page tables. This takes the time required for two memory accesses, the read of the Page Directory followed by the Page Table read.

To speed up the address translation the MMU caches recently looked-up results within a Translation Look-aside Buffer (TLB). If a virtual to physical lookup cannot be found in a TLB, the MMU has table walking hardware to perform a new virtual lookup and it will save the result into a TLB entry.

The TLBs must be flushed if the page tables are changed. This can happen on a context switch, during debug or the unloading of code.

At startup the CPU will run using physical addresses and the bootstrap code will build the initial set of page tables. When the MMU is turned on the CPU will switch into virtual memory operation, ready for the kernel boot sequence.

2.2.5   Caches

The CPUs used in every Symbian phone require caches to achieve optimum performance. The job of a cache is to insulate the fast CPU from its slower memory system by holding local copies of recently accessed data or instructions.

ARM CPUs have Harvard architectures, with separate instruction and data ports, resulting in separate instruction and data caches (ICache, DCache).

Caches work by taking advantage of the repetitive local characteristics of executing code. Code that is in a loop will execute the same instructions and access the same or similar data structures. As long as the CPU's view into memory is consistent, it does not care where the data is located at any instant in time – whether it is found in RAM or in the cache. However, the kernel does not cache memory mapped peripherals because the controlling software requires strict ordering of reads and writes into the peripheral registers.

Caches are organized in cache lines, which typically contain 32 bytes of data from a 32-byte aligned address, and a tag to store this source address. A 16 KB cache would contain 512 lines.

When the CPU requests data, the cache tests to see if it has a line that matches the requested address. If it does, the data is returned immediately – this is called a cache hit. If the cache does not contain the data, then a cache miss has occurred. After a miss, there will be a cache line fill of the required data from the memory system, and then the CPU will continue execution. To make space for this new cache line, an older cache line will be evicted from the cache.

The efficiency of a cache is measured by its *hit ratio* – the ratio of cache hits to total accesses. On Symbian OS, the approximate numbers are 95% for the ICache and 90% for the DCache.

With a high hit rate, the CPU can run close to its maximum speed without being stalled by the memory system. This is good for performance and even better for battery life, since a cache hit requires substantially less power than an external memory access.

Line fill operations are optimized for the memory system, to take advantage of sequential burst modes from the memory chips.

Once the MMU has been set up and the cache enabled, all of its operation is automatic and the system runs faster. EKA2 only needs to issue cache control commands if the caches need to be flushed. This can be due to any of the following:

- A memory map change on a context switch

- New code being loaded or existing code discarded

- Self-modifying code generation

- Using DMA from cached memory.

2.2.5.1   *Virtual and physical caches*

The CPU is isolated from the system bus by the MMU and caches, so their order of operation has an impact on Symbian OS (see Figure 2.3).

When the CPU is connected directly to the cache, the cache uses virtual addresses, and it in turn talks through the MMU to generate physical addresses on the system bus (left-hand side of Figure 2.3).

A physically addressed cache will be connected directly to the system bus and will be indexed with real physical addresses. The virtual to physical lookup will occur in the MMU, which is located between the CPU and the cache (right-hand side of Figure 2.3).

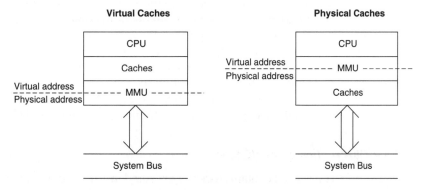

Figure 2.3   Virtual and physical caches

2.2.5.2   *ARM v5 virtual cache*

In ARM v5 and earlier systems, the MMU was placed outside the CPU and caches, resulting in caches that worked within the virtual memory domain of the MMU.

In this design, all data stored in the cache is indexed by its virtual address, so when the CPU requests data with a virtual address, no MMU translation is required for a cache hit. If there is a miss, the MMU is invoked to generate a physical bus address for the cache miss. This design reduces the workload on the MMU and saves power.

The downside to virtual caches is that the kernel has to empty them every time it modifies the page tables. The kernel can invalidate the ICache (discard it) but it has to flush all of the dirty data in the DCache to the memory system.

Unfortunately, the Symbian OS moving memory model modifies the virtual address map when it performs inter-process context switch. This means that a cache flush is needed that can take many milliseconds, resulting in a significant loss of system performance. In Section 7.2.1, you will see that Symbian OS uses a technique called fixed processes to minimize these cache flushes.

2.2.5.3   ARM v6 physical cache

ARM architecture v6 delivered a whole new MMU, with new page table layout, physical caches, process ASIDs, support for level 2 caches and IO memory space.

An ARM v6 CPU, such as the 1136, uses physical addresses at all times in the cache. This requires the MMU to work harder by performing a virtual to physical lookup on every request from the CPU core. This will normally be through a TLB lookup.

The advantage to this scheme is that the caches are always in sync with the physical memory map, no matter how the virtual map changes. This removes the cache flush penalty from context switches.

To further improve performance, the v6 MMU model introduced Application Space Identifiers, known as ASIDs. Each ASID has its own 4 or 8 KB PDE, for the bottom 1 or 2 GB of address space. Changing the ASID will instantly swap out this address space.

As I will explain in Section 7.4.2, EKA2 assigns an ASID to every process it creates, resulting in extremely fast context switches.

2.2.5.4   Instruction cache (ICache)

The ICache contains recently executed instructions, ready for their re-use. Instructions cannot be modified in the ICache, so it can be treated as a read-only device.

When a line needs to be evicted on a cache miss, it is immediately overwritten by the new instructions. This is permitted, since it is read-only and cannot have changed. Cache flushing operations are only needed when code is unloaded from the system and to ensure the coherency of generated or self-modifying code.

Code compiled for the THUMB instruction set gains an advantage over ARM by being able to fit twice as many instructions into the ICache. This helps to offset its slower performance.

2.2.5.5 Data cache (DCache)

When the CPU is reading data, the DCache works in the same way as the ICache. Data hits within the cache are returned immediately and missed data will be sourced from main memory, replacing a recently evicted line.

The complexity comes with data writes into the DCache and the combinations of strategies to return it to memory.

With write-through caching, every time the CPU writes data, it will be immediately written out to memory, through the write buffer, and the data will update the cached copy if it hits.

Write-through caching ensures that memory always stays coherent with the cache. Cache line evictions and cache cleaning operations do not need to write anything back to memory, enabling them to discard lines at will.

The downside is that the system bus has to support the full write speed of the CPU and the cache is only being effective for reads.

Symbian OS uses write-through caching for the LCD frame buffer, to ensure consistent pixels on the display. Writes of new pixel data will gain a small speed-up because of the write buffer, and read–modify–write operations will be aided by the cache. But running all of Symbian OS in a write-through cached system reduces performance by over 30%.

To make full use of the DCache for writes as well as reads, Symbian OS uses a scheme called copy-back. Write hits into the cache remain in the cache, where they may be overwritten again. Copy-back results in a massive reduction of write traffic to memory by only writing data when it is evicted.

Cache lines that have been modified are tagged by dirty bits – normally two of them for a pair of half lines. When it is time to evict the cache line, the dirty bits are evaluated, and dirty half lines are written back out to memory through the write buffer. Half lines are used to reduce the write bandwidth overhead of unmodified data, since clean data can be discarded.

Flushing the entire contents of a copy-back cache will take some milliseconds, as it may be populated entirely with dirty data.

2.3 Random Access Memory (RAM)

Random Access Memory (RAM) is the home of all the live data within the system, and often the executing code. The quantity of RAM determines the type and number of applications you can run simultaneously, the access speed of the RAM contributes to their performance.

A Symbian OS phone will have between 8 and 64 MB of RAM. The OS itself has modest needs and the total requirement is determined by the expected use cases. Multimedia uses lots of RAM for mega-pixel cameras images and video recording. If NAND Flash memory is used, megabytes of code have to be copied into RAM, unlike NOR flashes that execute in place.

The RAM chip is a significant part of the total cost of a phone, both in dollar terms, and in the cost of the additional power drain required to maintain its state.

It is not only the CPU that places heavy demands on the memory subsystem; all of the bus master peripherals read and write into RAM too. Their demands and contention have to be considered during the system design. Working out real-world use cases, with bandwidth and latency calculations, is essential for understanding the requirements placed on the memory system.

2.3.1 Mobile SDRAM

In the last few years, memory manufacturers have started to produce RAM specifically for the mobile phone market, known as Low Power or Mobile SDRAM.

This memory has been optimized for lower power consumption and slower interface speeds of about 100 MHz, compared to normal PC memory that is four times faster.

Mobile memories have additional features to help maintain battery life. Power down mode enables the memory controller to disable the RAM part without the need for external control circuitry.

Data within a DRAM has to be periodically updated to maintain its state. When idle, DRAMs do this using self-refresh circuitry. Temperature Compensated Self Refresh (TCSR) and Partial Array Self Refresh (PASR) are used to reduce the power consumption when idle. The combination of TCSR and PASR can reduce the standby current from 150 to 115 μA.

2.3.2 Internal RAM (IRAM)

Memory that is embedded within the SoC is known as internal RAM (IRAM). There is much less of this than main memory.

When booting a system from NAND Flash, core-loader code is copied from the first block of NAND into RAM. IRAM is an ideal target for this code due to its simple setup. Once the core-loader is running from IRAM, it will initialize main RAM so that the core OS image can be decompressed and copied there.

IRAM can be used as an internal frame buffer. An LCD controller driving a dumb display needs to re-read the entire frame buffer 60 times a second. Thus a 16-bit QVGA display will require 8.78 MB of data in one second. By moving the frame buffer into IRAM, the system can make a large saving in power and main memory bandwidth. A dedicated IRAM frame buffer can be further optimized for LCD access and to reduce its power needs.

IRAM can also be useful as a scratch pad or message box between multiple processors on the SoC.

Note that putting small quantities of code into IRAM does not speed up the execution of that code, since the ICache is already doing a better and faster job.

2.4 Flash memory

Symbian phones use Flash memory as their principal store of system code and user data. Flash memory is a silicon-based non-volatile storage medium that can be programmed and erased electronically.

The use of Flash memory is bound by its physical operation. Individual bits can only be transformed from the one state into the zero state. To restore a bit back to a one requires the erasure of a whole block or segment of Flash, typically 64 KB. Writing a one into a bit position containing a zero will leave it unchanged.

Flash memory comes in two major types: NOR and NAND. The names refer to their fundamental silicon gate design. Symbian OS phones make best use of both types of Flash through the selection of file systems – I will explain this in detail in Chapter 9, *The File Server*.

The built-in system code and applications appear to Symbian software as one large read-only drive, known as the Z: drive. This composite file system is made up of execute in place (XIP) code and code that is loaded on demand from the Read Only File System (ROFS). The Z: drive is sometimes known as the ROM image.

User data and installed applications reside on the internal, writable C: drive. The C: drive is implemented using one of two different file systems: LFFS (Log Flash File System) for NOR or a standard FAT file system above a Flash Translation Layer (FTL) on top of NAND.

A typical Symbian phone today will use between 32 and 64 MB of Flash for the code and user data – this is the total ROM budget.

Symbian uses many techniques to minimize the code and data sizes within a phone, such as THUMB instruction set, prelinked XIP images, compressed executables, compressed data formats and coding standards that emphasize minimal code size.

2.4.1 NOR Flash

NOR Flash is used to store XIP code that is run directly by the CPU. It is connected to a static memory bus on the SoC and can be accessed in random order just like RAM. The ARM CPU can boot directly out of NOR Flash if the Flash is located at physical address zero (0x00000000).

For user data, Symbian uses the Log Flash File System (LFFS) on top of NOR Flash. This file system is optimized to take advantage of NOR Flash characteristics. I describe LFFS in detail in Chapter 9, *The File Server*.

NOR flashes allow for unlimited writes to the same data block, to turn the ones into zeros. Flashes usually have a write buffer of around 32 to 64 bytes that allows a number of bytes to be written in parallel to increase speed. A buffered write will take between 50 and 600 μs depending on the bit patterns of the data already in the Flash and the data being written. All zeros or all ones can be fast, and patterns such as 0xA5A5 will be slow.

Erasing a NOR segment is slow, taking about half a second to one second. But erases can be suspended and later restarted – LFFS uses this feature to perform background cleanup of deleted data while remaining responsive to foreground requests.

Completed writes and erases will update the status register within the Flash, and may generate an external interrupt. Without an interrupt, the CPU will need to use a high-speed timer to poll the Flash for completion.

By using NOR flashes with Read–While–Write capabilities, it is possible to build a Symbian OS phone with one NOR part containing XIP code and LFFS data.

2.4.2 NAND Flash

NAND Flash is treated as a block-based disk, rather than randomly addressable memory. Unlike NOR, it does not have any address lines, so cannot appear in the memory map. This means that code cannot execute directly from NAND and it has to be copied into RAM first. This results in the need for extra RAM in a NAND phone compared to a similar NOR device. NAND Flash writes are about 10 times faster than those on NOR Flash.

A phone cannot boot directly from NAND. The process is more complex, requiring a set of boot loaders that build upon each other, finally resulting in a few megabytes of core Symbian OS image, the ROM, being loaded into RAM, where it will execute.

NAND is also inherently less reliable than NOR. New parts will come with defective blocks and are susceptible to bit errors during operation. To alleviate the second problem, an Error Correction Code (ECC) is calculated for every page of data, typically 512 bytes. On every read, the ECC is re-calculated and the difference between it and the stored ECC value is used to correct single-bit errors, at runtime. Multi-bit errors cannot be recovered and the page is considered corrupt.

The lower price of NAND compared to NOR makes it attractive for mass-market phone projects, even after taking into account the extra RAM required.

NAND Flash parts are attached to the SoC using a dedicated interface that is connected directly to the NAND chip pins through an 8-bit or 16-bit bus. The interface block will use the DMA interface for data transfers, and contains circuits to calculate the ECC on writes and reads.

The NAND interface reads and writes into the NAND Flash using pages of data. A small block NAND device uses 512-byte pages, and a large block device uses 2048-byte pages. Data is erased by block, where a block will contain 32 or 64 pages.

2.5 Interrupts

Peripherals in the system demand attention from the CPU by generating interrupts. Every peripheral will have one or more interrupt lines attached to the Programmable Interrupt Controller (PIC), which in turn will funnel the outstanding interrupts into the CPU. ARM cores only have two interrupt inputs, the normal Interrupt ReQuest (IRQ) and the Fast Interrupt reQuest (FIQ). The FIQ has higher priority than IRQ and an additional set of banked registers.

The EKA2 interrupt dispatch code determines the source of an interrupt by reading the PIC registers, and then calls the correct service function. This is all explained in Chapter 6, *Interrupts and Exceptions.*

In Figure 2.4, you can see a 62 interrupt system, incorporating a two-layer design that re-uses the same PIC block to cascade from level 2 into level 1.

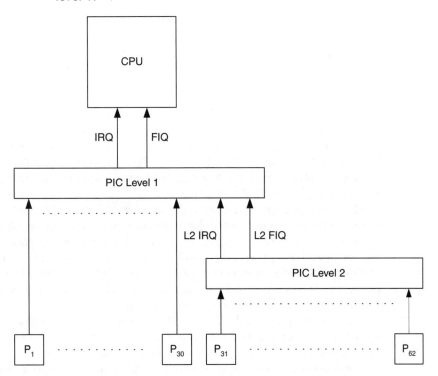

Figure 2.4 Two-layer interrupt controller

Each interrupt within a layer will be represented by one of the 32 bits inside the controlling register set. The registers allow the interrupt dispatch software to configure, enable and detect the correct interrupt:

Interrupt Type	IRQ	FIQ
Output Status	True	False
Enabled	True	False
Latched Interrupt Input	True	False
Detect Type	Edge	Level
Polarity	Rising Edge/High Level	Falling Edge/Low Level

Examples of interrupt types in use include:

A serial port output FIFO will have a half-empty setting, generating a high level whenever there is space within the FIFO. Once enough data has been written into the FIFO by an interrupt service routine, the interrupt output will drop back.

A rising edge interrupt would be used to detect the short VSync pulse generated by the LCD controller on the start of a new output frame.

To determine the current pending interrupt, the software dispatcher must read the status and enable registers from the PIC, AND them together, and look for a set bit to determine which interrupt to dispatch. The bit number is then used to index a table of function pointers to the correct interrupt service routine (ISR). By putting the highest priority interrupt in the upper bits of level 1, the first valid bit can be found quickly using the count leading zeros (CLZ) instruction.

The interrupt dispatch latency is the time between the IRQ input being raised and the execution of the first instruction in the ISR, and is the time taken up by the software dispatcher described in the previous paragraph and the thread preamble code. It will run for tens of instructions, resulting in about a 50-cycle interrupt cost, or 250 ns on a 200 MHz core. The total overhead of an interrupt, once the post-amble code and kernel dispatcher is taken into account, will be approaching 1 μs.

You can use more sophisticated PICs to reduce the interrupt latency. Bit patterns are replaced by a status register containing the highest priority interrupt number for the dispatch software to use immediately.

The ARM vectored interrupt controller (VIC) is an even more complex system, in which the CPU has a dedicated VIC port. It allows for the

ISR address to be injected directly into the CPU, removing the overhead of software interrupt dispatch, and saving a few tens of cycles per interrupt. Symbian OS phones do not require a VIC and its associated silicon complexity, as they do not have hard real-time interrupts with nanosecond latencies.

When designing a phone you should aim to minimize the number of active interrupts within the system, as this will increase the overall system interrupt response robustness and reduce power consumption. This can be done by using DMA interfaced peripherals, and by not polling peripherals from fast timers.

2.6   Timers

In Chapter 5, *Kernel Services*, I will explain EKA2's use of the millisecond timer. EKA2 uses a 1 ms tick timer to drive time slicing and the timer queues, and to keep track of wall clock time.

The minimum hardware requirement is for a high-speed timer capable of generating regular 1 ms interrupts without drifting. The timer counter needs to be readable, writable, and the maximum cycle period should be many seconds.

The speed of the timer clock source is not essential to Symbian OS, but somewhere between 32 kHz and 1 MHz is common. Slower clock sources have lower power consumption, and faster clock rates allow more flexible use of the timers, beyond the kernel millisecond tick (see Figure 2.5).

The preferred hardware implementation is a free-running 32-bit counter coupled with a set of 32-bit match registers to generate the timer interrupts. They enable simple software schemes for anti-jitter, idle tick suppression and profiling. Self-reloading countdown timers are an alternative hardware option, but they are less flexible.

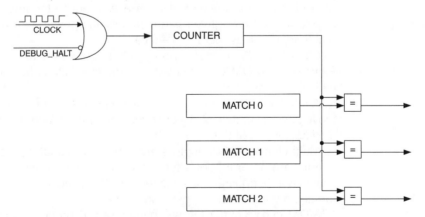

Figure 2.5   High-speed timer with three match registers

The normal operation of the millisecond timer with match registers is straightforward. The external clock source drives the counter, and on every increment the match registers are tested. If they match, their interrupt line is raised, the millisecond timer ISR will execute, kernel millisecond tick processing will occur and then the ISR will re-queue the interrupt by adding 1 ms worth of clock ticks to the match register.

The counter is always allowed to be free-running and the match register is always incremented from the previous match value. This produces a drift-free millisecond interrupt. If the input clock frequency is not an exact multiple of 1 Hz, anti-jitter software will generate an average 1 ms timer, by adding or removing a few extra clock cycles per millisecond interrupt.

For the kernel to keep accurate track of time when the CPU is asleep, the timer input clock and the counter circuits must be powered from an independent source to the core.

To debug software running in a system with high-speed timers, it is essential that the JTAG debugger hardware suspends the timers while it halts the CPU. It does this by the input of a DEBUG_HALT signal into the timer block. Stopping the timers ensures that the OS is not flooded by timer interrupts during debug single steps, and that the kernel timer queues are not broken by too much unexpected time elapsing.

Multiple timers are required within a real system even though EKA2 itself only needs one. Peripherals with sub-millisecond timing requirements, for example those polling a NOR Flash for write completion, will use an extra timer. Spare timers can also be used for accurate performance profiling.

2.7 Direct Memory Access (DMA)

Direct Memory Access (DMA) is used by Symbian OS to offload the burden of high bandwidth memory to peripheral data transfers and allow the CPU to perform other tasks. DMA can reduce the interrupt load by a factor of 100 for a given peripheral, saving power and increasing the real-time robustness of that interface.

Chapter 13, *Peripheral Support,* will describe how the EKA2 software framework for DMA is used with the different DMA hardware options and device drivers.

A DMA engine is a bus master peripheral. It can be programmed to move large quantities of data between peripherals and memory without the intervention of the CPU.

Multi-channel DMA engines are capable of handling more than one transfer at one time. SoCs for Symbian phones should have as many channels as peripheral ports that require DMA, and an additional channel for memory-to-memory copies can be useful.

A DMA channel transfer will be initiated by programming the control registers with burst configuration commands, transfer size, the physical addresses of the target RAM and the peripheral FIFO. This is followed by a DMA start command. The transfers of data will be hardware flow controlled by the peripheral interface, since the peripherals will always be slower than the system RAM.

In a memory to peripheral transfer, the DMA engine will wait until the peripheral signals that it is ready for more data. The engine will read a burst of data, typically 8, 16 or 32 bytes, into a DMA internal buffer, and it will then write out the data into the peripheral FIFO. The channel will increment the read address ready for the next burst until the total transfer has completed, when it will raise a completion interrupt.

A DMA engine that raises an interrupt at the end of every transfer is single-buffered. The CPU will have to service an interrupt and re-queue the next DMA transfer before any more data will flow. An audio interface will have a real-time response window determined by its FIFO depth and drain rate. The DMA ISR must complete within this time to avoid data underflow. For example, this time would be about 160 μs for 16-bit stereo audio.

Double-buffered DMA engines allow the framework to queue up the next transfer while the current one is taking place, by having a duplicate set of channel registers that the engine switches between. Double-buffering increases the real-time response window up to the duration of a whole transfer, for example about 20 ms for a 4 KB audio transfer buffer.

Scatter-gather DMA engines add another layer of sophistication and programmability. A list of DMA commands is assembled in RAM, and then the channel is told to process it by loading the first command into the engine. At the end of each transfer, the DMA engine will load the next command – until it runs out of commands. New commands can be added or updated in the lists while DMA is in progress, so in theory my audio example need never stop.

Scatter-gather engines are good for transferring data into virtual memory systems where the RAM consists of fragmented pages. They are also good for complex peripheral interactions where data reads need to be interspersed with register reads. NAND controllers require 512 bytes of data, followed by 16 bytes of metadata and the reading of the ECC registers for each incoming block.

Power savings come from using DMA, since the CPU can be idle during a transfer, DMA bursts don't require interrupts or instructions to move a few bytes of data, and the DMA engine can be tuned to match the performance characteristics of the peripheral and memory systems.

2.8 Liquid Crystal Display (LCD)

The primary display on Symbian OS phones is a color liquid crystal display. The job of the display is to turn pixels in the frame buffer into images we can see.

Displays in Symbian phones come in common sizes dictated by the user interface software layers, since the latter are graphically optimized to the screen size. The most common resolutions are 176×208 pixels as used in Series 60 phones and 240×320 pixels for UiQ.

The frame buffer is an area of contiguous physical memory, large enough to contain an array of pixels with the same dimension as the display.

The base port reserves memory for the frame buffer during initialization, and ensures the MMU maps it with write-through caching. A frame buffer for 16-bpp QVGA display will require 150 KB ($320 \times 240 \times 2$) of RAM.

Pixels have common formats depending on their storage containers. Most current mobile phones use 16 bits per pixel (bpp) in 565 format, where the top 5 bits are red, the middle 6 bits are green, and the bottom 5 bits are blue – giving 65,535 (2^{16}) unique colors:

15 → 11	10 → 5	4 → 0
RED	GREEN	BLUE

Phones with genuine 18-bpp displays are starting to be common, they display 262,144 colors. Symbian OS does not support 18-bit words – instead a 24-bpp representation is used inside a 32-bit word. This has an aRGB, 8888 format, where the "a" is empty space or an alpha value. The LCD controller will discard the bottom two bits of each color component byte:

31 → 24	23 → 16	15 → 8	7 → 0
alpha	RED	GREEN	BLUE

Mobile phone LCDs come in two distinct types, dumb and smart. A dumb display does not contain any control electronics; instead its pixels are driven directly by the LCD controller in the SoC. On the other hand, a smart display contains its own LCD controller, memory for the frame buffer, and a medium-bandwidth interface back to the SoC.

The dumb display controller within an SoC has to output a new copy of the display image around 60 times per second to persist the image on the LCD.

This 60 Hz update requires the controller to continually transfer data from memory using DMA as long as the display is switched on. Using IRAM as a frame buffer can help reduce the power cost and bandwidth overhead of the display. As I said earlier, a 16-bit QVGA with a 60 Hz refresh rate will require 8.78 MB of data every second, and looking to the future, a full 32-bit VGA display will require eight times as much data.

The interface to a smart display is optimized for two uses: incremental updates to the display when small elements change, and full bandwidth operation when multimedia video or games require it. For the small updates, the updated screen region is transferred into the display interface using a smart 2D DMA engine.

Smart displays save power by removing the need for full-bandwidth updates most of the time. Their internal circuitry is optimized to match the display characteristics exactly. They have additional low-power modes for idle phones that only want to display the clock. These have partial display refreshing and limited colors.

2.9   Audio

The audio sub-system of a Symbian OS phone contains two, mostly independent, streams of audio data. One is the telephony voice data and the other is multimedia data.

Two vital phone use cases are to have good quality voice calls and long talk times. Digital audio buses are dedicated to voice data to ensure this is the case.

The de facto raw hardware audio format used in a Symbian OS phone is 16-bit pulse code modulated (PCM) data. The quality ranges from 8 kHz mono for telephony audio up to 48 kHz stereo for music playback.

PCM audio hardware can be quite simple, requiring little setup to ensure the volume and correct output path are selected. Then all that is needed is to feed data to the hardware at the rate it demands – DMA hardware is very good for this. If data transfer stalls, the audio hardware will immediately produce audible pops, clicks and stutters.

2.9.1   Telephony audio

The telephony voice data is the essence of a phone call. It has stringent latency restrictions placed upon it to ensure that the user has a high-quality call without the effects of transatlantic satellite lag. To ensure this is the case, the system designers have optimized the controlling software and hardware paths for low latency response and low power consumption during a voice call.

The BP contains a DSP that performs the processing for voice band audio without passing through Symbian OS. During a call, Symbian OS will be in a low-power mode, only needing to wake up when the display needs updating.

A normal call will end up in the analogue audio circuits. They contain the analogue to digital and digital to analogue converters, which in turn are connected to the microphone and speakers. When using a BlueTooth (BT) headset the PCM data is transported directly into the BT module via its own dedicated interface.

Symbian OS needs an additional audio path to allow it to inject system sounds into the ongoing call. These are for such things as message alerts, low battery and a second incoming call. This injection of sounds can be done by passing the raw audio data over the IPC link to the BP, where the DSP will mix it into the audio stream.

2.9.2 Multimedia audio

Multimedia audio is a general term for every generated sound in the system that is not voice data.

The main multimedia sounds are:

- Ring tones, in many formats

- Alerts, for incoming messages

- Alarms, from clock and calendar

- Video telephony

- MP3 playback

- Games

- Recorded voice, dictaphone

- Video capture and playback.

The higher levels are all controlled by the Symbian multimedia framework (MMF) for media players, file formats and plug-ins.

The Multimedia Device Framework (MDF) will contain the codecs, and it will transfer PCM data to and from the device driver layer, DevSound.

Video telephony (VT) is a special case, in which live audio data does pass through Symbian OS. The audio elements of the call are multiplexed into the 64-kb/s data stream along with the video. The VT call system has to de-multiplex the incoming data stream, decode the audio and video elements, and then play them in sync. This is normally done in dedicated hardware or a DSP, since it would require all of a 200 MHz ARM CPU just to run the codecs.

The main complexity in the audio systems is the ever-growing number of audio sources and sinks, and the possible ways in which they can be connected. For example, current phones have multiple headsets, speakers, Bluetooth and FM radios. This is likely to remain an issue until hardware is capable of mixing and routing every audio source in all possible combinations. Today some audio use cases will be incompatible with others, requiring them to interrupt each other.

2.10 Power management

All Symbian OS phones are battery powered, and as I have stressed throughout this chapter, effective power management (PM) is crucial in designing a successful Symbian OS phone.

The overall design goals of the SoC team must be focused on adequate performance at low power. At every decision point the system's designers must ask themselves, "How will this affect the power consumption?" "Can I design this in another way that will have the same performance with lower power?" Only by constant attention to power use will a single battery charge give hours of talk and play time, and still leave hundreds of hours for standby.

The ARM CPUs used in Symbian OS phones are designed as answers to these questions, as they are the best low-power peripheral blocks in use. Schemes to reduce power consumption within the SoC include self-clocking circuits, serial ports that power down when idle and memory controllers that put RAM into low-power modes whenever possible.

Most importantly, the SoC should only include hardware capabilities that will be used. Use case analysis and feature justification are a good way of removing unnecessary power loads at the start of the design. An example of a bad design is an over-specified internal bus with more bandwidth than all of its slave peripherals.

I explain the EKA2 power model in Chapter 15, *Power Management*. This power management architecture is based on the runtime use of shared power resources by the peripherals. To closely match this model, the SoC power architecture needs to be partitioned for clean and orthogonal PM, enabling peripherals to have well-defined power and clock sources that can be turned on and off as needed.

The designers of CPUs like to invent all sorts of named power modes, for example Turbo, Run, Idle, Doze, Sleep, Deep Sleep and Off. The more power-saving the mode is, the more work is required to get into or out of the state. For example, a Deep Sleep state is likely to require flushing all the state out of the caches, and turning off the core, and waking from Deep Sleep will initially look like a boot to the CPU.

Almost all of these modes will map onto the Symbian OS idle mode, where the system is powered but doing nothing. Symbian OS tends to spend most of its time in idle mode, even going into it between presses on a phone keypad. As I've already hinted, the most important difference between the CPU power modes to Symbian OS is the time it takes to transition from Run to a mode and the time taken to get back to Run mode again. The decision about which CPU mode to use is determined heuristically within the idle software, based on recent use and pending timer events.

Dedicated hardware accelerators allow for excellent performance with low power consumption, whereas general purpose ARM software is infinitely reprogrammable, but execution is more expensive in power and time. The trick is to get the right balance between fixed hardware and flexible software, and ensure that the real phone requirements can be met two years after the silicon is finalized.

Power management is a pervasive topic. It requires careful hardware design and focused software to achieve the system design goals.

2.11   Summary

In this chapter I have described the core hardware that is needed to run Symbian OS, with some emphasis on the power management implications of those hardware choices. There are a great many more peripherals and topics that I do not have space to cover here, including:

- Real-time clock
- Touch screen
- IPC interface to BP
- Debug interfaces
- Flash programming
- Multiple displays
- IRDA
- Booting
- Removable media, SD, MMC
- 2D Graphics
- 3D Graphics
- DSP
- Multimedia accelerators
- USB interfaces
- Advance power management
- Bluetooth modules
- Watchdogs and resets
- Security hardware.

Within Symbian, we refer to the software layers that control the hardware, including the bootstrap, kernel port and device drivers as the baseport, and more generically as the Board Support Package (BSP).

To enable all of the hardware on a phone is the job of the people in the base porting team, who use their skills and experience to populate the lowest layers of hardware abstraction within Symbian OS. You can find further information in the Base Porting Kit (BPK) and Device Driver Kit (DDK) documentation, both of which are available to Symbian Partners, see ***www.symbian.com/partners*** for more information.

Designing hardware for a Symbian OS phone requires a system view of the final product. The designers need to consider real-world performance use cases, select hardware with enough (but not too much) capacity, and with every decision, they need to analyze power consumption.

I hope that this chapter will have given you an insight into the design choices you will need to make if you are building a Symbian OS phone.

In the next chapter, I will start to look at the fundamental entities that underlie the running of code on Symbian OS – threads, processes and libraries.

3

Threads, Processes and Libraries

by Jane Sales

One of the main causes of the fall of the Roman Empire was that, lacking zero, they had no way to indicate successful termination of their C programs.

Robert Firth

In this chapter, I will look at the entities – that is, threads, processes and libraries – that are concerned with executing code under Symbian OS. I'll begin by examining threads, which are the fundamental unit of execution of Symbian OS.

Because processes and threads touch so many components in Symbian OS, this chapter will refer to many areas that I will explain in more detail in other chapters.

3.1   What is a thread?

Under Symbian OS, our definition of a thread is that it is the unit of execution; it is the entity that the kernel schedules, the entity to which the kernel allocates CPU resources. You can think of a thread as a collection of kernel data structures that describe the point a program has reached in its execution. In fact, more accurately, these data structures describe *one of the points* a program has reached in its execution, because a program can contain more than one thread.

The Symbian OS definition of a process is that it is a collection of threads that share a particular address mapping. In other words, the particular mapping of virtual to physical memory at a particular time depends on the process that is running. Each thread within a process can read and write from any other thread's memory, since they share an address space. But more on this later – for now, let's concentrate on threads.

3.2   Nanokernel threads

The nanokernel provides the most basic thread support for Symbian OS in the form of nanokernel threads (which from now on I'll call nanothreads). The nanokernel provides support for the scheduling of nanothreads, and for their synchronization and timing services. The thread services the nanokernel provides are very simple – simpler even than those provided by a typical RTOS. We chose them to be the minimal set needed to support a GSM signaling stack.

Nanothreads only ever run in supervisor mode; they never run in user mode. Because of this, each nanothread needs only a single, supervisor mode stack. The nanokernel keeps the address of the nanothread's stack in the NThread class's iStackBase, and the stack's size in iStackSize. The kernel uses these two variables for initialization and, when an exception occurs, for stack checking to protect against stack overflows.

Each nanothread's member data also contains its last saved stack pointer value, iSavedSP. Whenever the nanothread blocks or is pre-empted, the scheduler saves the ARM processor's context on the nano-thread's stack. Next, the scheduler saves the value of the processor's supervisor-stack-pointer register in iSavedSP. Then the scheduler over-writes the processor's supervisor-stack-pointer register, by loading it from the iSavedSP of the new nanothread. Finally, the scheduler restores the processor's context from the new stack, thus bringing about a thread switch. I will cover scheduling in more detail later.

3.2.1   NThread class

The NThread class is derived from a base class, NThreadBase, which is defined in nk_priv.h. Here is a cut-down version of NThreadBase, showing the main points of interest:

```
class NThreadBase : public TPriListLink
  {
public:

  enum NThreadState
    {
    EReady,
    ESuspended,
    EWaitFastSemaphore,
    ESleep,
    EBlocked,
    EDead,
    EWaitDfc,
    ENumNStates
    };

  enum NThreadOperation
    {
    ESuspend=0,
```

```
        EResume=1,
        EForceResume=2,
        ERelease=3,
        EChangePriority=4,
        ELeaveCS=5,
        ETimeout=6,
        };

public:
    NThreadBase();
    TInt Create(SNThreadCreateInfo& anInfo,TBool aInitial);
    IMPORT_C void CheckSuspendThenReady();
    IMPORT_C void Ready();
    void DoCsFunction();
    IMPORT_C TBool Suspend(TInt aCount);
    IMPORT_C TBool Resume();
    IMPORT_C TBool ForceResume();
    IMPORT_C void Release(TInt aReturnCode);
    IMPORT_C void RequestSignal();
    IMPORT_C void SetPriority(TInt aPriority);
    void SetEntry(NThreadFunction aFunction);
    IMPORT_C void Kill();
    void Exit();
    void ForceExit();

public:
    NFastMutex* iHeldFastMutex;// fast mutex held
    NFastMutex* iWaitFastMutex;// fast mutex on which blocked
    TAny* iAddressSpace;
    TInt iTime;  // time remaining
    TInt iTimeslice;
    NFastSemaphore iRequestSemaphore;
    TAny* iWaitObj;// object on which this thread is waiting
    TInt iSuspendCount; // how many times we have been suspended
    TInt iCsCount; // critical section count
    TInt iCsFunction; // what to do on leaving CS:
                      // +n=suspend n times, 0=nothing, -1=exit
    NTimer iTimer;
    TInt iReturnValue;
    TLinAddr iStackBase;
    TInt iStackSize;
    const SNThreadHandlers* iHandlers; // + thread event handlers
    const SFastExecTable* iFastExecTable;
    const SSlowExecEntry* iSlowExecTable; //first entry iEntries[0]
    TLinAddr iSavedSP;
    TAny* iExtraContext; // coprocessor context
    TInt iExtraContextSize; // +ve=dynamically allocated
                            //  0=none, -ve=statically allocated
    };
```

You can see that the thread base class itself is derived from TPriList
Link – this means that the thread is part of a priority-ordered doubly
linked list, which is used in scheduling.

The NThread class itself is CPU-dependent – at the moment three
versions of it exist, one for ARM, one for X86 and the other for the
emulator. To give you a flavor for the kind of functionality that you find
in NThread, here is a cut-down ARM version:

```
class NThread : public NThreadBase
   {
public:
   TInt Create(SNThreadCreateInfo& aInfo, TBool aInitial);
   inline void Stillborn() {}

// Value indicating what event caused thread to
// enter privileged mode.
   enum TUserContextType
      {
      EContextNone=0,          /* Thread has no user context */
      EContextException=1, /* HW exception while in user mode */
      EContextUndefined,
      EContextUserInterrupt, /* Preempted by int in user mode */
      // Killed while preempted by interrupt taken in user mode
      EContextUserInterruptDied,
      // Preempted by interrupt taken in executive call handler
      EContextSvsrInterrupt1,
      // Killed while preempted by interrupt taken in
      // executive call handler
      EContextSvsrInterrupt1Died,
      // Preempted by interrupt taken in executive call handler
      EContextSvsrInterrupt2,
      // Killed while preempted by interrupt taken in
      // executive call handler */
      EContextSvsrInterrupt2Died,
      EContextWFAR, // Blocked on User::WaitForAnyRequest()
      // Killed while blocked on User::WaitForAnyRequest()
      EContextWFARDied,
      EContextExec, // Slow executive call
      EContextKernel, // Kernel-side context (for kernel threads)
      };

   IMPORT_C static const TArmContextElement*
                   const* UserContextTables();
   IMPORT_C TUserContextType UserContextType();
   inline TInt SetUserContextType()
       { return iSpare3=UserContextType(); }
   inline void ResetUserContextType()
      {if(iSpare3>EContextUndefined) iSpare3=EContextUndefined; }
   void GetUserContext(TArmRegSet& aContext,
                   TUint32& aAvailRegistersMask);
   void SetUserContext(const TArmRegSet& aContext);

   void ModifyUsp(TLinAddr aUsp);

#ifdef __CPU_ARM_USE_DOMAINS
   TUint32 Dacr();
   void SetDacr(TUint32 aDacr);
   TUint32 ModifyDacr(TUint32 aClearMask, TUint32 aSetMask);
#endif

#ifdef __CPU_HAS_COPROCESSOR_ACCESS_REG
   void SetCar(TUint32 aDacr);
#endif
   IMPORT_C TUint32 Car();
   IMPORT_C TUint32 ModifyCar(TUint32 aClearMask, TUint32 aSetMask);
```

```
#ifdef __CPU_HAS_VFP
  void SetFpExc(TUint32 aDacr);
#endif
  IMPORT_C TUint32 FpExc();
  IMPORT_C TUint32 ModifyFpExc(TUint32 aClearMask, TUint32 aSetMask);
  };
```

Key member data of NThread and NThreadBase

iPriority
The thread's absolute scheduling priority, between 0 and 63 inclusive.

iNState
The state of the thread, that is, ready or blocked. Essentially this determines which queue if any the thread is linked into.

iAttributes
Bit mask that determines scheduling policy with respect to the system lock and whether the thread requires an address space switch in general.

iAddressSpace
Address space identifier for the thread, used to determine whether the correct address space is already active. The actual value has no significance to the nanokernel, only to the Symbian OS memory model.

iTime
Counter used to count timer ticks before thread should yield to next equal priority thread.

iTimeslice
Number of low-level timer ticks before thread yields to equal priority threads. If negative, it will not yield unless it blocks.

iRequestSemaphore
An NFastSemaphore that we use for general "wait for any event". For Symbian OS threads, it serves as the Symbian OS request semaphore.

iSuspendCount
Integer, ≤ 0, which equals minus the number of times a thread has been explicitly suspended.

iCsCount
Integer, ≥ 0, which indicates whether the thread may currently be killed or suspended. These actions can only happen if this count is zero, otherwise they are deferred.

iCsFunction
Integer that indicates what if any action was deferred due to iCsCount being non-zero. If zero, no action is required; if positive, it equals the number of explicit suspensions that have been deferred; if negative, it indicates that a thread exit has been deferred.

`iTimer`
Nanokernel timer object used to sleep the thread for a specified time and to implement wait-for-event-with-timeout functions.

`iExitHandler`
Pointer to function. If it is not NULL the kernel will call the function when this thread exits, in the context of the exiting thread.

`iStateHandler`
Pointer to function that is called if the thread is suspended, resumed, released from waiting or has its priority changed and the `iNState` is not a standard nanokernel thread state. Used to implement RTOS emulation layers.

`iExceptionHandler`
Pointer to function called if the thread takes an exception. On ARM, the function is called if a prefetch abort, data abort or undefined instruction trap occurs. The function is always executed in `mode_svc`[1] in the context of the current thread, regardless of the exception type.

`iFastExecTable`
Pointer to table of fast executive calls for this thread.

`iSlowExecTable`
Pointer to table of slow executive calls for this thread – see Section 5.2.1.7 for details.

3.2.2   Nanothread creation

The nanokernel provides the static API below to allow kernel modules outside of the nanokernel to create a nanothread:

```
NKern::ThreadCreate(NThread* aThread, SNThreadCreateInfo& aInfo)
```

This function takes an `SNThreadCreateInfo` structure as a parameter. The caller also passes a pointer to a new `NThread` object, which it has instantiated beforehand. This must be done because the nanokernel cannot allocate or free memory.

3.2.2.1   *SNThreadCreateInfo*

The `SNThreadCreateInfo` structure looks like this:

```
struct SNThreadCreateInfo
    {
```

---

[1] An ARM CPU mode that is associated with a different register set. See Chapter 6, *Interrupts and Exceptions,* for more on this.

```
NThreadFunction iFunction;
TAny* iStackBase;
TInt iStackSize;
TInt iPriority;
TInt iTimeslice;
TUint8 iAttributes;
const SNThreadHandlers* iHandlers;
const SFastExecTable* iFastExecTable;
const SSlowExecTable* iSlowExecTable;
const TUint32* iParameterBlock;
TInt iParameterBlockSize;
// if 0,iParameterBlock is initial data
// otherwise it points to n bytes of initial data
};
```

Key member data of SNThreadCreateInfo

`iFunction`
Address of code to execute.

`iStackBase`
Base of stack for new `NThread`. This must be preallocated by the caller – the nanokernel does not allocate it.

`iHandlers`
Points to the handlers for different situations, namely:

- `iExitHandler`: called when a thread terminates execution

- `iStateHandler`: called to handle state changes when the `iNState` is not recognized by the nanokernel (used so OS personality layers can implement new `NThread` states)

- `iExceptionHandler`: called to handle an exception

- `iTimeoutHandler`: called when the `NThread::iTimer` timer expires.

3.2.2.2 SNThreadHandlers

The SNThreadHandlers structure looks like this:

```
struct SNThreadHandlers
  {
  NThreadExitHandler iExitHandler;
  NThreadStateHandler iStateHandler;
  NThreadExceptionHandler iExceptionHandler;
  NThreadTimeoutHandler iTimeoutHandler;
  };
```

Key member data of SNThreadCreateInfo

`iParameterBlock`
Either a pointer to a block of parameters for the thread, or a single 32-bit parameter.

`iParameterBlockSize`
If zero, `iParameterBlock` is a single 32-bit parameter. If non-zero, it is a pointer.

`iFastExecTable`
Allows personality layer to pass in a pointer to a table of exec calls to be used for this thread.

`iSlowExecTable`
Allows personality layer to pass in a pointer to a table of exec calls to be used for this thread.

3.2.2.3 *Creating a nanothread*

Returning to `NKern::ThreadCreate()`, you can see that the caller passes in the address of the stack that the nanothread will use. This is because the nanokernel cannot allocate memory – so anyone creating a nanothread must first allocate a stack for it.

`NThread::Create()`

```
TInt NThread::Create(SNThreadCreateInfo& aInfo, TBool aInitial)
  {

  TInt r=NThreadBase::Create(aInfo,aInitial);
  if (r!=KErrNone)
    return r;
  if (!aInitial)
    {
    TUint32* sp=(TUint32*)(iStackBase+iStackSize-
                    aInfo.iParameterBlockSize);
    TUint32 r6=(TUint32)aInfo.iParameterBlock;
    if (aInfo.iParameterBlockSize)
      {
      wordmove (sp,aInfo.iParameterBlock,
            aInfo.iParameterBlockSize);
      r6=(TUint32)sp;
      }
    *--sp=(TUint32)__StartThread;          // PC
    *--sp=0;                               // R11
    *--sp=0;                               // R10
    *--sp=0;                               // R9
    *--sp=0;                               // R8
    *--sp=0;                               // R7
    *--sp=r6;                              // R6
    *--sp=(TUint32)aInfo.iFunction;        // R5
    *--sp=(TUint32)this;                   // R4
    *--sp=0x13;                            // SPSR_SVC
    *--sp=0;                               // R14_USR
    *--sp=0;                               // R13_USR
    iSavedSP=(TLinAddr)sp;
    }
```

`NThreadBase::Create()`

```
TInt NThreadBase::Create(SNThreadCreateInfo& aInfo, TBool aInitial)
    {
    if (aInfo.iPriority<0 || aInfo.iPriority>63)
                        return KErrArgument;
    new (this) NThreadBase;
    iStackBase=(TLinAddr)aInfo.iStackBase;
    iStackSize=aInfo.iStackSize;
    iTimeslice=(aInfo.iTimeslice>0)?aInfo.iTimeslice:-1;
    iTime=iTimeslice;
    iPriority=TUint8(aInfo.iPriority);
    iHandlers = aInfo.iHandlers ? aInfo.iHandlers :
                        &NThread_Default_Handlers;
    iFastExecTable=aInfo.iFastExecTable?aInfo.iFastExecTable:
                                    &DefaultFastExecTable;
    iSlowExecTable=(aInfo.iSlowExecTable?aInfo.iSlowExecTable:
                        &DefaultSlowExecTable)->iEntries;
    iSpare2=(TUint8)aInfo.iAttributes;
    // iSpare2 is NThread attributes
    if (aInitial)
        {
        iNState=EReady;
        iSuspendCount=0;
        TheScheduler.Add(this);
        TheScheduler.iCurrentThread=this;
        TheScheduler.iKernCSLocked=0;
        // now that current thread is defined
        }
    else
        {
        iNState=ESuspended;
        iSuspendCount=-1;
        }
    return KErrNone;
    }
```

The static function `NKern::ThreadCreate()` merely calls `NThread::Create()` (the first code sample), which then calls `NThreadBase::Create()`(the second sample). This function sets up various properties of the new thread, including:

- its stack

- its priority

- its timeslice

- its slow and fast exec tables.

`NThreadBase::Create()` then puts the new nanothread into the suspended state and returns.

`NThread::Create()` sets up a stack frame for the new nanothread, first copying over the parameter block (if any) and then creating register values, ready for the thread to pop them. The kernel gives the thread's program counter register (on the stack) the value of `__StartThread` (see the following code sample). To find out more about where in memory we create the thread's stack, see Chapter 7, *Memory Models*.

__StartThread

```
__NAKED__ void __StartThread()
{
// On entry r4->current thread, r5->entry point, r6->parameter block
asm("mov r0, r6 ");
asm("mov lr, pc ");
asm("movs pc, r5 ");
asm("b  " CSM_ZN5NKern4ExitEv);
}
```

`__StartThread` merely assigns some registers, so that `iFunction` is called with the `iParameterBlock` function as its argument. If `iFunction` returns, `__StartThread` branches to `Kern::Exit` to terminate the thread.

3.2.3   Nanothread lifecycle

3.2.3.1   *Nanothread states*

A nanokernel thread can be in one of several states, enumerated by `NThreadState` and determined by the `NThread`'s `iNState` member data. I will describe these states below:

`iNState==EReady`
Threads in this state are eligible for execution. They are linked into the ready list. The highest priority `EReady` thread is the one that will actually execute at any given time, unless it is blocked on a fast mutex.

`iNState==ESuspended`
A thread in this state has been explicitly suspended by another thread rather than blocking on a wait object.

`iNState==EWaitFastSemaphore`
A thread in this state is blocked waiting for a fast semaphore to be signaled.

`iNState==EWaitDfc`
The thread is a DFC-handling thread and it is blocked waiting for a DFC to be added to the DFC queue that it is servicing. (For more on DFCs, see Section 6.3.2.3.)

`iNState==ESleep`
A thread in this state is blocked waiting for a specific time period to elapse.

`iNState==EBlocked`
The thread is blocked on a wait object implemented in a layer above the nanokernel. This generally means it is blocked on a Symbian OS semaphore or mutex.

`iNState=EDead`
A thread in this state has terminated and will not execute again.

`iNState=other`
If you are writing a personality layer (see Chapter 17, *Real Time*) then you may choose to allow your nanothreads to have extra states; that is your `iNState` will be able to take a value other than those above. You must then provide an `iStateHandler` in your `NThread`, and then the kernel will call this function if there is a transition in state for this nanothread – if it is resumed, blocked and so on.

3.2.4 Mutual exclusion of nanothreads

3.2.4.1 Critical sections

A critical section is any sequence of code for which a thread, once it has entered the section, must be allowed to complete it. In other words, the nanokernel must not suspend or kill a thread that is in a critical section.

The nanokernel has sections of code that update kernel global data, and where preemption is enabled. This could lead to problems: imagine that thread MARLOW is in the middle of updating a global data structure, when thread BACON preempts it. Then the global data structure is left in a half-modified state, and if BACON tries to access that data a system crash may well result. We can guard against this scenario by protecting each such global data structure by a mutex, but we need to do more than this.

Imagine this time that, while MARLOW is in the middle of updating the global data structure, BACON preempts MARLOW and suspends or kills it. Let's consider the two situations – suspended or killed – separately.

Assume BACON suspended MARLOW, and that BACON is the only thread that might release MARLOW. MARLOW still holds the mutex protecting the global data structure. So now, if BACON tries to access the same global data structure, a deadlock results, because no other thread will release MARLOW.

Assume BACON killed MARLOW. Now we have a situation similar to our first one – we have left the global data structure in a half-modified state, rendering it unusable by any other thread and having the potential to crash the entire system.

To prevent either of these situations from occurring, we give each thread a critical section count, `iCsCount`. We increment this every time the thread enters a critical section of kernel code, and decrement it when the thread leaves the critical section.

Then, when thread BACON preempts thread MARLOW, and tries to suspend or kill it, the nanokernel first checks MARLOW's critical section count. If the count is zero, the nanokernel can immediately suspend or kill the thread on behalf of thread BACON.

If MARLOW's critical section count is non-zero, then the nanokernel must delay its actions until MARLOW leaves the critical section. The nanokernel sets a flag in MARLOW's iCsFunction member, to indicate

a)   That further action is required

b)   Whether the thread should suspend or exit.

The nanokernel decrements the thread's iCsCount when the thread leaves the critical section. If the thread's iCsCount becomes zero, then the kernel checks the thread's iCsFunction to see if further action is required. If iCsFunction is set, then the nanokernel suspends or kills the thread, according to the value placed in iCsFunction. Note that thread BACON, which called Suspend() or Kill(), is not blocked at any stage – it simply carries on executing.

3.2.4.2   Fast mutexes

But what of the actual mutex used to protect global data structures? Keeping the design goals for the nanokernel as a whole in mind, we derived the following requirements for a fast mutex that would efficiently protect short, critical sections of code:

1.   The mutex must be very fast in the case where there is no contention for the mutex

2.   The mutex must have a low RAM footprint

3.   A thread may not wait on a fast mutex if it already holds a fast mutex (fast mutexes are non-nestable)

4.   A thread may not block or exit while holding a fast mutex.

The nanokernel then ensures that a thread is not suspended or terminated while holding a fast mutex. It does this by treating a nanothread that holds a fast mutex as if it were in a critical section – that is, the nanokernel delays suspending or terminating the nanothread until it releases the fast mutex.

This leaves us with the case in which the thread attempts to exit while holding a fast mutex, for example as a result of taking an exception. In this case, as in the one where a thread attempts to exit while in a critical section, the kernel will fault.

If a nanothread holds a fast mutex, then, on a timeslice, the nanokernel will not schedule another nanothread of the same priority in its place.

This is done to reduce the time spent unnecessarily switching between threads in short critical sections.

How fast mutexes work

Each nanothread has a pointer to the fast mutex currently **held** by the thread (iHeldFastMutex). We only need one fast-mutex pointer, because, as I said earlier, we chose to design EKA2 with non-nestable fast mutexes. Naturally, the fast mutex pointer is NULL if the nanothread does not hold a fast mutex.

Each nanokernel thread also has a pointer to the fast mutex on which it is currently **blocked** (iWaitFastMutex). Again, this pointer is NULL if the nanothread is not blocked on a fast mutex.

There are two key elements in the fast mutex class. The first is a pointer to the holding thread (iHoldingThread), which is NULL if the mutex is free. The second is a flag (iWaiting), which indicates either that there was contention for the mutex or that the nanokernel deferred an action (such as suspension, termination or round-robinning) because the mutex was held.

The algorithm for waiting on a fast mutex is:

```
1.   Lock the kernel
2.   IF (iHoldingThread!=NULL)
3.     iWaiting = TRUE
4.     Current thread->iWaitFastMutex = this
5.     Yield to iHoldingThread //return with ints disabled, kernel unlocked
6.     Lock the kernel
7.     Reenable interrupts
8.     Current thread -> iWaitFastMutex = NULL
9.   ENDIF
10.  Current thread -> iHeldFastMutex = this
11.  iHoldingThread = Current thread
12.  Unlock the kernel
```

If the mutex is free, this simply reduces to two variable assignments, and so is very fast. On single-processor systems (all of them to date!), we further optimize this by disabling interrupts rather than locking the kernel when we check iHoldingThread.

It is worth looking carefully at the section of pseudo code between the IF and the ENDIF, lines 2 to 9. You can see that as the kernel blocks the thread, it does not remove it from the ready list. Instead, it performs the Yield to iHoldingThread operation, which immediately switches the context to the thread that holds the mutex. We have to be careful in the case where we are using the moving memory model (see Chapter 7, *Memory Models*, for more on what this means). The context switch that we have just done does not call the memory model hook provided to allow slow process changes, so the memory model does not get chance to perform any page table manipulations. We cannot allow it to do so, because we want a fast mutex operation, and page table manipulations are usually slow. This means that **the kernel doesn't guarantee a user address space to be consistent while the current thread holds a fast mutex**. (If we are using the multiple memory model, then all is well, since we can perform the address space change, as in this case it is very fast.)

This scheme also gives us priority inheritance on fast mutexes. This comes about because the blocked thread remains on the ready list, so a reschedule can only be triggered if another thread becomes ready whose priority is at least as great as the highest priority blocked thread (see Section 3.6). So the holding thread can only be scheduled out by a thread whose priority is greater than any thread already on the list – in effect its priority is raised to that of the highest priority blocked thread.

The algorithm for releasing a fast mutex is:

```
1.  Lock the kernel
2.  iHoldingThread = NULL
3.  Current thread -> iHeldFastMutex = NULL
4.  IF iWaiting
5.  iWaiting = FALSE
6.  Set TheScheduler.iRescheduleNeededFlag to cause reschedule
7.  IF CurrentThread->iCsFunction & & CurrentThread->iCsCount==0
8.  Do critical section exit processing for current thread
9.  ENDIF
10. ENDIF
11. Unlock the kernel
```

If iWaiting is NULL, then again this becomes just two variable assignments. And again, on single-processor systems we have optimized this by disabling interrupts rather than locking the kernel while checking iWaiting.

Remember that the nanokernel would have set the iWaiting flag if another nanothread had attempted to acquire the mutex while the first nanothread held it.

The nanokernel would also have set the iWaiting flag if another nanothread had attempted to suspend or kill the first one – in this case it would delay the function to be performed, and keep a record of which function is to be performed later by storing it in iCsFunction.

Finally, the nanokernel would also have set the iWaiting flag if the first nanothread's timeslice had expired, because it will delay the round-robin with other equal priority threads until the fast mutex is released.

Have another look at lines 7 and 8 of the pseudo code. They say that the critical section exit processing will be called whenever we are not in a critical section **and** there is a delayed function to be performed (iCsFunction != NULL). We can reach this point for two reasons. The first is that the thread was executing in a critical section when it was killed or suspended, and now it has exited that critical section. The second is the thread held a fast mutex when it was killed or suspended, and now it has released the fast mutex. The exit processing is the same in both cases.

3.2.5   Nanothread death

You can kill a nanothread by calling `NThread::Kill()`, but beware – this method is only intended for use by personality layers and the EPOC layer, and should not be called directly on a Symbian OS thread. This is because a Symbian OS thread is an extension of a nanothread, and needs to also perform its own actions on thread death, such as setting the thread exit category and the reason code.

So, we believe that killing threads is not a good thing to do and it is much better to ask them nicely to stop! We have implemented this philosophy in the kernel process's Symbian OS threads. The practical consequence of this is that these threads don't need to enter critical sections – so if you were to kill them at the wrong point, you would have the problems outlined in Section 3.2.4.1.

If the subject thread **is** in a critical section, then the kernel will not kill it immediately, but will mark it "exit pending" and kill it once it has exited its critical section.

In either case, the exiting thread first invokes its exit handler, which I'll discuss next.

3.2.5.1   Exit handler

An exiting thread will invoke its exit handler (`iExitHandler`) if one exists. The exit handler runs with the kernel unlocked and the exiting thread in a critical section, so it is impossible to suspend the thread while running its exit handler.

The exit handler can return a pointer to a DFC (deferred function call) that will be queued just before the thread actually terminates, that is just before the kernel sets the thread's `iNState` to `EDead`. The Symbian OS kernel also uses the DFC to perform final cleanup after the thread has terminated – for example to delete the thread control block.

3.2.6   Threads in the emulator

The Win32 `NThread` class has the following members to add to those of the generic `NThreadBase`:

Field	Description
`iWinThread`	Win32 handle that refers to the host thread that underlies this thread.
`iScheduleLock`	Win32 event object used to block the host thread when not scheduled by the nanokernel. Every nanokernel thread except the current thread will either be suspended in the host OS, in which case `iWakeup` is `EResume` or `EResumeLocked`, otherwise it will be waiting on this event object in its control block.

`iDivert`	A function pointer used to divert a thread from normal return from the scheduler. Diverting threads using a forced change of context in the host OS is unsafe and is only used for forced termination of a thread that is suspended.
`iInKernel`	A counter used to determine if the thread is in "kernel" mode. A zero value indicates "user" mode. This state is analogous to being in supervisor mode on ARM – it is used primarily to determine the course of action following an exception.
`iWakeup`	Records the method required to resume the thread when it becomes the current thread.

3.2.6.1   Thread creation

Instantiating a thread in the emulator is a little more complex than on a target phone, as we must create and initialize a host thread, acquire the resources to control its scheduling, and hand the initial data over to the thread. On the target, we hand the initial data over by directly manipulating the new thread stack before it runs; on the emulator this is best avoided as it involves directly manipulating the context of a live host thread. The nanokernel API allows an arbitrary block of data to be passed to the new thread. Because the new thread does not run synchronously with the create call, but rather when the new thread is next scheduled to run, we must hand over this data before the creating thread returns from `NThread::Create()`.

When creating a new nanokernel thread in the emulator, we create an event object for the reschedule lock, then create a host OS thread to run the `NThread::StartThread()` method, passing an `SCreateThread` parameter block. The parameter block contains a reference to the thread creation information and a fast mutex used to synchronize the data block handover. The handover requires that the new thread runs to copy the data, but it must be stopped again straight afterwards, because when `NThread::Create()` returns the new thread must be left in a `NThread::ESuspended` state. Now I'll describe in detail how we achieve this.

We create the new Windows thread, leaving it suspended within Windows. `NThread::Create()` then marks the new thread as preempted (within the nanokernel) so that it will be resumed when the nanokernel schedules it to run. The creating thread then locks the kernel, sets up the handover mutex so that it is held by the new thread, and sets a deferred suspension on the new thread. (The deferred suspension is not immediately effective as the new thread holds a fast mutex.) When the creating thread waits on the same fast mutex, the scheduler runs the new thread from its entry point.

The new thread now initializes. It sets an exception handler for the Windows thread so that the emulator can manage access violations, and then copies the data out of the parameter block. Initialization is then complete so the new thread signals the handover mutex. This action activates the deferred suspension, leaving the new thread suspended as required. Signaling the mutex also wakes up the creating thread, which was blocked on the mutex. The creating thread can now release the mutex again and return, as the new thread is ready to run.

When the new thread is resumed, it invokes the supplied thread entry point function and then exits if that returns.

3.2.6.2 *Thread exit*

On target, a nanothread is considered dead when its state is `NThread::EDead` and after it enters `TScheduler::Reschedule` for the last time and schedules another thread to run. Because of its state, it will never be scheduled to run again, and its control block can be destroyed.

If the emulator followed this model directly, the Windows thread would be left blocked on its `iRescheduleLock`. Although the host thread and event object could then be discarded when the thread's control block is destroyed by calling the `TerminateThread()` function (as in EKA1), Windows does not recommend such use of this function.

Instead, we want the Windows thread to exit cleanly by calling the `ExitThread()` function. To do this, we ensure that we handle the final thread switch (detected by checking a thread state of `EDead`) slightly differently. We wake up the next Windows thread to run but do not block the dying thread. Instead, the dying thread releases the thread and event handles before calling `ExitThread()`.

3.2.6.3 *Forced exit – diverting threads*

When one thread kills another, the victim has to be diverted from its current activity into the thread exit processing. As we saw before, doing such a diversion by making a forced change of context in Windows can destabilize Windows itself.

The vast majority of situations in which this occurs involve a thread that has voluntarily rescheduled, by calling `TScheduler::Reschedule()`, rather than being preempted, due to an interrupt. In these situations we can divert safely by making the return path from `TScheduler::Reschedule()` check to see if a diversion is needed. We use the `NThread::iDivert` member to record the existence of a diversion on the thread.

This only leaves the rare case where the thread has been preempted, in which case diversion has to involve changing the Windows thread context – there is no other alternative.

This doesn't crash Windows for two reasons:

1. We don't run the emulator on versions of Windows that suffer like this (such as Windows 98)

2. We ensure that we don't kill the thread when it is executing code inside a Windows "kernel" function.

Also we recommend that any threads interacting with Windows should use `Emulator::Lock()` and `Unlock()` to prevent preemption whilst "inside" Windows.

3.3   Symbian OS threads

The Symbian OS kernel builds on nanothreads to provide support for user-mode threads that are used by standard Symbian OS user applications. We represent these threads using the `DThread` class.

Earlier in this chapter, I said that nanothreads always execute in supervisor mode and have a single supervisor-mode stack. Each Symbian OS thread object contains a nanothread object; this nanothread is what the kernel actually schedules. The nanokernel cannot allocate memory, so when it is creating a Symbian OS thread, the Symbian OS kernel must allocate the memory for the nanothread's supervisor stack before it makes the `ThreadCreate()` call to the nanokernel.

Each user-mode Symbian OS thread naturally has a user-mode stack, so, to spell it out, user-mode Symbian OS threads each have two stacks (Figure 3.1). The supervisor-mode stack associated with the nanothread is used by kernel-side code run in the thread's context – that is, the system calls made by the thread.

The use of per-thread supervisor stacks is a fundamental difference from EKA1, in which each thread had only one stack. By adding the supervisor stack to each thread, we allow kernel-side code to be preempted and thus achieve low thread latencies. You can read more about this in Section 5.2.1.3.

EKA2 also provides each Symbian OS thread with:

*   Access to a set of executive functions to enable user-mode threads to gain access to kernel functionality

*   An exception handler, which enables the kernel to handle exceptions in user-mode threads (typically caused by programming errors)

*   An exit handler, which allows resources to be freed and other threads to be notified when a thread terminates.

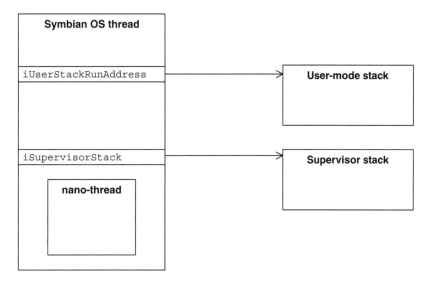

Figure 3.1   Stacks for a user-mode Symbian OS thread

3.3.1   Symbian OS thread creation

3.3.1.1   *Creating a thread: 1*

User-mode code creates a Symbian OS thread by calling `RThread::Create()`. By default, this method creates a thread belonging to the current process, and returns an open handle to the newly created thread back to the caller.

The `RThread::Create()` method goes via an exec call (see Chapter 5, *Kernel Services*) to the kernel, where it ends up inside the method `DThread::Create(SThreadCreateInfo&aInfo)`.

SThreadCreateInfo
The basic `SThreadCreateInfo` structure looks like this:

```
struct SThreadCreateInfo
    {
    TAny* iHandle;
    TInt iType;
    TThreadFunction iFunction;
    TAny* iPtr;
    TAny* iSupervisorStack;
    TInt iSupervisorStackSize;
    TAny* iUserStack;
    TInt iUserStackSize;
    TInt iInitialThreadPriority;
    TPtrC iName;
    TInt iTotalSize;        // Size including any extras
    };
```

Key member data of SThreadCreateInfo

iHandle
Handle on thread, returned to caller.

iType
Type of thread (EThreadInitial, EThreadSupervisor, EThread-MinimalSupervisor or EThreadUser). Indicates whether thread can execute in user mode and whether creation should be fast or normal.

iFunction
Where to begin execution of this thread.

iPtr
The pointer passed as an argument to iFunction.

iSupervisorStack
Pointer to supervisor stack. If 0, a stack will be created for it.

iSupervisorStackSize
Size of supervisor stack. Zero means to use the default value of 4 KB.

iUserStack
Pointer to user stack. This is returned to caller, not passed in.

iUserStackSize
Size of user stack. Zero means to use the default value of 8 KB.

iInitialThreadPriority
Initial priority for this thread.

iName
Name of the thread. If this is non-zero then the thread is a global object.

iTotalSize
Size including any extras. This must be a multiple of 8 bytes.

SStdEpocThreadCreateInfo

The basic SThreadCreateInfo structure is then derived by SStdE-pocThreadCreateInfo to provide three more fields, like so:

```
struct SStdEpocThreadCreateInfo : public SThreadCreateInfo
  {
  RAllocator* iAllocator;
  TInt iHeapInitialSize;
  TInt iHeapMaxSize;
  TInt iPadding; // Make size a multiple of 8 bytes
  };
```

This structure adds a pointer to the RAM allocator and an initial and a maximum size for the heap. It forms the control block that is pushed onto a thread's stack before that thread starts. The extra fields are used by the standard entry point function to set up the thread's heap – the kernel does not use them itself.

We chose to derive from SThreadCreateInfo so that we could support other kinds of threads in personality layers. Those new types of thread would probably need to pass different parameters to the thread's entry point instead. The authors of the personality layer can do this easily, by deriving a new class from SThreadCreateInfo.

3.3.1.2 Creating a thread: 2

The DThread constructor sets the state of the new thread to ECreated. The thread stays in this state throughout the construction process, then, once the thread is completely constructed, the kernel changes its status to EReady. This ensures that there are no anomalies arising from the death of a partly created thread.

Then the DThread::Create() method creates a user stack for the thread. To find out more about where in memory we create the thread's stack, see Chapter 7, *Memory Models*.

Next DThread::Create() calls DThread::DoCreate(). This method continues the work of setting up the thread, calling NKern::ThreadCreate() to create the nanokernel portion of the Symbian OS thread.

On return from DoCreate(), DThread::Create() adds the thread to the object container for threads (assuming it is neither the initial thread, nor a minimal supervisor thread). For more on object containers, see Chapter 5, *Kernel Services*.

When the Symbian OS thread first starts to run, it executes __StartThread. This calls DThread::EpocThreadFunction(), which checks to see if the thread is a kernel or user thread.

If it is a kernel thread, then DThread::EpocThreadFunction() calls the thread function – this is the function that the caller specified in Kern::ThreadCreate().

If it is a user thread, then the thread creation information is copied to the user stack. Then the CPU is switched to user mode and the process's entry point is called, with a parameter that is either KModuleEntryReasonProcessInit for the first thread in the process, or KModuleEntryReasonThreadInit for subsequent threads.

The process's entry point is __E32Startup in e32\euser\epoc\arm\uc_exe.cia. This code compiles into eexe.lib – Symbian's equivalent of crt0.obj on Windows.

The process entry point then calls RunThread(), which calls User Heap::SetupThreadHeap(). This is the function that will create the thread's heap if required.

Then, if this is the first thread in the process, the constructors for static data are called before calling E32Main(). Otherwise, the thread function is called straight away.

3.3.1.3   *Over-riding the Symbian OS allocators*

You may have noticed that EKA2 does not create the thread's heap. Instead, threads create their own heaps (or share an existing heap) when they first run. This makes it possible for the process itself to hook in and over-ride the normal heap creation function. In this way, you can choose to make a particular process use a memory allocator other than the standard one that Symbian provides in EUSER. You can also insert additional heap tracking or diagnostic functions. However, you should note that the function `UserHeap::SetupThreadHeap()` must be in a static library if you want to automatically over-ride heap creation in a process; the code for the `RAllocator`-derived class can be in a DLL. You do need to be careful when over-riding `UserHeap::SetupThreadHeap()`, because it is called before static data is initialized.

3.3.2   The DThread class

As we've already seen, the `DThread` class represents a Symbian OS thread. Now let's find out a little more about it. `DThread` derives from `DObject`, which makes it a dynamically allocated reference counted object inside the kernel (see Chapter 5, *Kernel Services*, for more on this). The `DThread` has an embedded nanothread (`iNThread`), which enables the nanokernel to schedule it.

We then derive the `DThread` class further to give a concrete CPU/MMU specific class – on ARM CPUs this is called `DArmPlatThread`. `DArmPlatThread` contains some CPU specifics but in general, it does not add much functionality to `DThread`.

Here is a cut-down version of the `DThread` class to give you a flavor for the kind of thing it includes:

```
class DThread : public DObject
  {
public:
  enum {EDefaultUserTimeSliceMs = 20};

  enum TThreadState
    {
    ECreated,
    EDead,
    EReady,
    EWaitSemaphore,
    EWaitSemaphoreSuspended,
    EWaitMutex,
    EWaitMutexSuspended,
    EHoldMutexPending,
    EWaitCondVar,
    EWaitCondVarSuspended,
    };
```

```
  enum TOperation
    {
    ESuspend=0,
    EResume=1,
    EForceResume=2,
    EReleaseWait=3,
    EChangePriority=4,
    };

public:
  DThread();
  void Destruct();
  TInt Create(SThreadCreateInfo& aInfo);
  TInt SetPriority(TThreadPriority aPriority);
  IMPORT_C void RequestComplete(TRequestStatus*& aStatus,
                                               TInt aReason);
  IMPORT_C TInt DesRead(const TAny* aPtr, TUint8* aDes,
                    TInt aMax, TInt aOffset, TInt aMode);
  IMPORT_C TInt DesWrite(const TAny* aPtr, const TUint8* aDes,
                      TInt aLength, TInt aOffset, TInt aMode,
                                 DThread* aOriginatingThread);

// not memory model dependent
  TInt DoCreate(SThreadCreateInfo& aInfo);
  IMPORT_C void SetThreadPriority(TInt aThreadPriority);
  void SetDefaultPriority(TInt aDefaultPriority);
  void AbortTimer(TBool aAbortAbsolute);
  void Suspend(TInt aCount);
  void Resume();
  void ForceResume();
  void Exit();
  void Die(TExitType aType, TInt aReason,
                 const TDesC& aCategory);
  TInt Logon(TRequestStatus* aStatus, TBool aRendezvous);
  void Rendezvous(TInt aReason);

// memory model dependent
  TInt AllocateSupervisorStack();
  void FreeSupervisorStack();
  void FreeUserStack();
  TInt AllocateUserStack(TInt aSize);
  TInt RawRead(const TAny* aSrc, TAny* aDest, TInt aLength,
                                               TInt aFlags);
  TInt RawWrite(const TAny* aDest, const TAny* aSrc,
      TInt aLength, TInt aFlags, DThread* aOriginatingThread);
  DChunk* OpenSharedChunk(const TAny* aAddress, TBool aWrite,
                                               TInt& aOffset)

  static void DefaultUnknownStateHandler(DThread* aThread,
                        TInt& aOperation, TInt aParameter);
  static void EpocThreadFunction(TAny* aPtr);
  static TDfc* EpocThreadExitHandler(NThread* aThread);
  static void EpocThreadTimeoutHandler(NThread* aThread,
                                               TInt aOp);
public:
  TUint32 iIpcCount;
  TLinAddr iUserStackRunAddress;
```

```
TInt iUserStackSize;
TUint32 iFlags;
DProcess* iOwningProcess;
SDblQueLink iProcessLink;
TInt iThreadPriority;
DObjectIx* iHandles;
TUint iId;
RAllocator* iAllocator;
RAllocator* iCreatedAllocator;
TTrap* iFrame;
TTrapHandler* iTrapHandler;
RArray<STls> iTls;
CActiveScheduler* iScheduler;
TExceptionHandler iExceptionHandler;
TUint iExceptionMask;
TExcTrap* iExcTrap;
TInt iDebugMask;
TThreadMessage iKernMsg;
DObject* iTempObj;
DObject* iExtTempObj;
TAny* iTempAlloc;
SDblQue iOwnedLogons;
SDblQue iTargetLogons;
RMessageK iSyncMsg;
TDfc iKillDfc;
SDblQue iClosingLibs;
TPriListLink iWaitLink;
TInt iDefaultPriority; // default scheduling priority
TAny* iWaitObj; // object on which this thread is waiting
// handler for extra thread states - used by RTOS
// personality layers
TUnknownStateHandler iUnknownStateHandler;
// pointer to extra data used by RTOS personality layers
TAny* iExtras;
TAny* iSupervisorStack;// thread's supervisor mode stack
TInt iSupervisorStackSize;
TUint8 iSupervisorStackAllocated;
TUint8 iThreadType;
TUint8 iExitType;
TUint8 iPad1;
TInt iExitReason;
TBufC<KMaxExitCategoryName> iExitCategory;
// list of held mutexes, used only for acquisition
// order checking
SDblQue iMutexList;
// things to clean up when we die
TPriList<TThreadCleanup,KNumPriorities> iCleanupQ;
TTimer iTimer;
NThread iNThread;
};
```

Key member data of DThread

`iFlags`
Thread flags (system critical, last chance, process permanent, original).

`iExitType`
Top level thread exit reason (kill, terminate or panic) or `EExitPending` if thread still running.

iExitReason

Exit code (return value from thread main function or reason supplied to kill, terminate or panic call).

iExitCategory

String providing additional exit information in case of panic.

iThreadType

Type of thread: `EThreadInitial`, `EThreadSupervisor`, `EThread-MinimalSupervisor` or `EThreadUser`.

iOwningProcess

Pointer to `DProcess` object that represents the process to which this thread belongs.

iThreadPriority

Priority of this thread in either absolute or process-relative form. Values between 0 and 63 represent absolute priorities; values between −8 and −2 represent priorities relative to that of the owning process.

iHandles

Pointer to array (`DObjectIx`) of thread-local handles for this thread.

iId

Symbian OS thread ID of this thread (unsigned 32-bit integer).

iAllocator

Pointer to the user-side heap being used by this thread. This is stored by the kernel on behalf of the user code and is not used by the kernel itself.

iExceptionHandler

Pointer to this thread's user-side exception handler. This will be invoked in user mode in the context of this thread if a handled exception occurs.

iExceptionMask

Bit mask indicating which types of exception the user-side exception handler handles. These are defined by the enum `TExcType`.

iExcTrap

Pointer to the thread's exception trap handler. The handler will be invoked if an exception occurs in the context of this thread. The trap part of the handler provides the ability to return to the beginning of a protected code section with an error code. `NULL` if no such handler is currently active.

iDebugMask

Per-thread debug mask. This is ANDed with the global debug mask to generate the debug mask used for all kernel tracing in the context of this thread.

iKernMsg

Kernel-side message sent synchronously to kernel-side threads. Used for communication with device driver threads.

iOwnedLogons
Doubly linked list of thread logons owned by this thread (that is, this thread is the one which requests notification of another thread terminating).

iTargetLogons
Doubly linked list of thread logons whose target is this thread (that is, another thread requests notification if this thread terminates).

iSyncMsg
Symbian OS IPC message (RMessageK) reserved for sending synchronous IPC messages.

iKillDfc
The Symbian OS exit handler returns a pointer to this DFC when the thread terminates. The nanokernel queues the DFC immediately before terminating the thread. The DFC runs in the context of the supervisor thread and is used to clean up any resources used by the thread, including the DThread object itself.

iClosingLibs
This is a doubly linked list holding a list of DLibrary objects which require user-side destructors to be called in the context of this thread.

iMState
This is actually the iSpare1 field of iWaitLink. It indicates the state of this thread with respect to Symbian OS wait objects.

iWaitLink
This is a priority queue link field used to link the thread on to the wait queue of a Symbian OS wait object. Note that the priority of this link should always be equal to the thread's nanokernel priority.

iWaitObj
This is a pointer to the Symbian OS wait object to which this thread is currently attached, NULL if the thread is not attached to any wait object.

iSupervisorStack
Base address of thread's supervisor mode stack.

iCleanupQ
Priority-ordered list (64 priorities, same structure as scheduler) used to hold callbacks to be invoked if the thread terminates. Also used to implement priority inheritance – adding a high-priority cleanup queue entry will raise a thread's priority. Thread scheduling priority is calculated as the maximum of iDefaultPriority and the highest priority of any entry in the cleanup queue.

iNThread
The nanokernel thread control block corresponding to this thread.

3.3.3 Types of Symbian OS thread

There are four types of Symbian OS thread, which are determined by the `iThreadType` field in `DThread`. This takes on one of the values in the enumeration `TThreadType`.

`iType==EThreadInitial`

There is only ever one initial thread in the system, and this is the first thread to run on a device at boot time. This thread's execution begins at the reset vector and eventually becomes the null thread, which is the thread with the lowest possible priority in the system. For more on Symbian OS bootup, see Chapter 16, *Boot Processes.*

`iType==EThreadSupervisor`

Supervisor threads run only in supervisor mode, never in user mode. The memory model allocates a supervisor stack for these threads; you may vary its size by passing in a parameter during thread creation. Usually it is best to pass in a value of 0, which tells the kernel to use the default size of 4 KB (one page).

Supervisor threads have time slicing enabled by default, with a timeslice of 20 ms.

`iType==EThreadMinimalSupervisor`

These threads are intended for use by RTOS personality layers and are similar to supervisor threads. The key requirement for an RTOS threads is a fast creation time, so the kernel does not give these threads.

The memory model can allocate the supervisor stack just as it does for supervisor threads, but if you wish, you can preallocate an area of memory and pass a pointer to it when you create the thread.

Finally, RTOS threads generally don't need time slicing, so we disable it by default.

`iType==EThreadUser`

These are the threads used to run standard user applications. They run in user mode for most of the time, although they do run in supervisor mode during executive calls.

As we have seen, these threads have two stacks, a user-mode one and a supervisor-mode one; the memory model allocates both of these dynamically. The memory model allocates the supervisor stack in the same way as for supervisor threads, with a default stack size of 4 KB. It allocates the user stack during thread create time; it creates the user stack in the address space of the process to which the thread belongs. (I will discuss this in more detail in Chapter 7, *Memory Models.*) The creator of a user thread can specify the size of the user stack at creation time.

User threads have time slicing enabled by default, with a timeslice of 20 ms.

3.3.3.1 Identifying Symbian OS and personality layer threads

The easiest way to determine if a given NThread is a Symbian OS thread or belongs to an executing personality layer is to examine the nanothread's handlers:

```
// additional thread event handlers for this NThread
SNThreadHandlers* NThreadBase::iHandlers()
```

The function I use looks like this:

```
SNThreadHandlers *gEpocThreadHandlers;

// Grab the thread handlers from a thread that we
// know is a Symbian OS thread.
// The extension and DLL loader is guaranteed to be
// a Symbian OS thread, so we can use an extension
// entry point to capture its thread handlers.

// Extension entry point
DECLARE_STANDARD_EXTENSION()
  {
  gEpocThreadHandlers=(SNThreadHandlers*)
          CurrentThread()->iHandlers;
  ...
  }

// Get Symbian OS thread from a NThread
// if there isn't one, it's a personality
// layer thread, return NULL.
DThread *GetEpocThread(NThread *aNThread)
  {
  if (aNThread->iHandlers != gEpocThreadHandlers)
          return NULL; // personality layer thread
  DThread* pT = _LOFF(aNThread, DThread, iNThread);
  return pT;
  }
```

The method I use is quite simple. First, in a global variable I save a pointer to the handlers of the extension and DLL loader (a thread that is known to be a Symbian OS thread). Then, later, I compare my thread's nanothread's iHandlers pointer, and if it is the same as the global variable, then my thread is a Symbian OS thread too.

3.3.4 Symbian OS thread lifecycle

3.3.4.1 Symbian OS thread states

Each Symbian OS thread has a state, known as the M-state. (This is in addition to the N-state of each Symbian OS thread's embedded nanothread.) When the Symbian OS thread waits on or is released from a Symbian OS semaphore or mutex, its M-state changes.

The M-state may take on any of the values in the enumeration `TThreadState` – a complete list follows. An RTOS may add more M-states; I'll discuss this further in the next section, 3.3.4.2.

`iMState==ECreated`
This is the initial state of all Symbian OS threads. It is a transient state – the kernel puts the thread into this state when it creates the `DThread` control block and keeps the thread in this state until the kernel is ready to resume it, at which point it changes the state to `EReady`.

`iMState==EDead`
This is the final state of all Symbian OS threads. A thread enters this state when it reaches the end of its exit handler, just before the nanokernel terminates it.

`iMState==EReady`
A thread is in this state when it is not waiting on, or attached to, any Symbian OS kernel wait object (semaphore or mutex). This state does not necessarily imply that the thread is actually ready to run – this is indicated by the N-state. For example, a thread that is explicitly suspended or waiting on a nanokernel wait object (generally a fast semaphore) has `iMState==EReady`, if it is not attached to any Symbian OS wait object.

`iMState==EWaitSemaphore`
This state indicates that the thread is currently blocked waiting for a Symbian OS semaphore and is enqueued on the semaphore's wait queue. The thread's `iWaitObj` field points to the semaphore.

`iMState==EWaitSemaphoreSuspended`
This state indicates that another thread has explicitly suspended this thread after it blocked on a Symbian OS semaphore and was enqueued on the semaphore's suspended queue. The thread's `iWaitObj` field points to the semaphore.

`iMState==EWaitMutex`
This state indicates that the thread is currently blocked waiting for a Symbian OS mutex and is enqueued on the mutex wait queue. The thread's `iWaitObj` field points to the mutex.

`iMState==EWaitMutexSuspended`
This state indicates that another thread has explicitly suspended this thread after it blocked on a Symbian OS mutex and was enqueued on the mutex suspended queue. The thread's `iWaitObj` field points to the mutex.

`iMState==EHoldMutexPending`
This state indicates that the thread has been woken up from the `EWait-Mutex` state but has not yet claimed the mutex. The thread is enqueued on the mutex pending queue and the thread's `iWaitObj` field points to the mutex.

`iMState==EWaitCondVar`
This state indicates that the thread is waiting on a condition variable. The thread is enqueued on the condition variable's wait queue, `iWaitQ`, and its `iWaitObj` field points to the condition variable.

`iMState==EWaitCondVarSuspended`
This state indicates that the thread has been suspended while waiting on a condition variable. The thread is removed from the condition variable's `iWaitQ`, and enqueued on `iSuspendQ`. The thread's `iWaitObj` field points to the condition variable.

M-state changes
A thread's M-state can change because of any of the following operations:

1. The thread blocks on a wait object

2. The thread is released from a wait object

3. The thread is suspended

4. The thread is resumed

5. The thread's priority is changed. This can cause a transition from `EWaitMutex` to `EHoldMutexPending` if the mutex is free and the thread's priority is increased

6. The thread is killed. Multiple state changes can occur in this case as the thread proceeds through the exit handler. The first state change will occur as a result of a `ReleaseWait()` call at the beginning of the exit handler. This call cancels the thread's wait on any Symbian OS wait object and detaches the thread from the wait object, that is it removes it from any queues related to the wait object. The final state change will be to the `EDead` state at the end of the exit handler.

The first five of these operations are protected by the system lock mutex. In the case of thread exit, the initial call to make the thread exit is protected by the system lock, as is the `ReleaseWait()` call, but the exit handler runs without the system lock for some of the time.

3.3.4.2   Other M-states

RTOS personality layers can add new M-states to indicate that threads are waiting on non-Symbian OS wait objects. To make this easier to implement, each Symbian OS thread has an unknown state handler, `iUnknownStateHandler`. Let's see how it works.

Assume that a thread is in an M-state unknown to the kernel (that is, not one of those I have discussed above). Then the kernel will call the unknown state handler after the kernel suspends, resumes, kills or changes the priority of that thread. The unknown state handler can then adjust the RTOS wait object's queues and transition the M-state if necessary.

The unknown state handler is not involved in all state transitions: the RTOS personality layer code will block and release threads from an RTOS wait object directly.

It is worth noting that the Symbian OS thread unknown state handler, `iUnknownStateHandler`, is completely different to the nanokernel thread unknown state handler, `iNThread->iHandlers->iState Handler`. Which you use depends on exactly how you implement your RTOS personality layer. Clearly there are two choices:

Over the nanokernel
This is the usual method, described in Chapter 17, *Real Time*. Personality layer threads are bare `NThreads` and you use `NThread::iHandlers->iStateHandler` to add extra wait states for new wait objects.

Over the Symbian OS kernel
In this case, personality layer threads are Symbian OS kernel threads, and `DThread::iUnknownStateHandler` would be used to add extra wait states for new wait objects. The advantage of using this method is that you can make use of Symbian OS kernel services in your personality layer threads (for example semaphores, mutexes and memory allocation). The disadvantage is that Symbian OS threads use a lot more memory – over 800 bytes per `DThread`, plus 4 KB of stack.

3.3.5   Cleanup queues

Each Symbian OS thread has a cleanup queue, `iCleanup`. This queue holds thread cleanup items, which are `TThreadCleanup`-derived objects.

TThreadCleanup

```
class TThreadCleanup : public TPriListLink
  {
public:
  IMPORT_C TThreadCleanup();
  void ChangePriority(TInt aNewPriority);
  IMPORT_C void Remove();
  virtual void Cleanup()=0;
public:
  DThread* iThread;
public:
  friend class Monitor;
  };
```

The cleanup queue is a priority queue, with each of the cleanup items on it having a priority between 0 and 63. Each cleanup item also has a callback function. When the Symbian OS thread terminates, its thread exit handler calls the callback functions in descending order of priority – it always holds the system lock while it does this. It is, however, permissible for a cleanup item's callback to release the system lock, for example to delete the cleanup item itself or to perform some other long-running operation. (The kernel also locks the system when it modifies the cleanup queue.)

The kernel sets the priority of cleanup items that are used purely to provide notification of thread exit to zero.

Currently the Symbian OS kernel uses thread cleanup items for two purposes:

1. It associates a TThreadMutexCleanup object with every Symbian OS mutex. The kernel adds this item to the cleanup queue of the mutex-holding thread so that it can release the mutex if the thread terminates

2. The kernel uses cleanup items with non-zero priority to implement priority inheritance for Symbian OS mutexes; it does this by adjusting the priority of the TThreadMutexCleanupItem.

3.3.5.1 *Priority inheritence*

How does this priority inheritance work? We define the priority of a Symbian OS thread to be the maximum of its own priority, and that of any cleanup item on its queue. Now suppose that a low-priority thread owns a mutex when a higher-priority thread comes along and blocks on that mutex. The kernel will then adjust the priority of the cleanup item associated with the mutex to be equal to the priority of the high-priority thread. Thus the low-priority thread's priority, which is the maximum of its own priority and any cleanup item it owns, is also boosted, since it owns the cleanup item associated with the mutex. If there are no higher-priority ready threads in the system, it will continue to run until it releases the mutex, at which point its priority drops to its normal level.

3.3.5.2 *Notification of device driver client termination*

There is a third use for thread cleanup items: device drivers can use them to get notification of their clients terminating unexpectedly. For example, the local media sub-system uses this mechanism to ensure that the resources held by the driver on behalf of the client thread are cleaned up if the client thread terminates. It has to use this method, since multiple threads in the same process may use a single logical channel to communicate with the driver, meaning that the channel Close() method will not necessarily be called when a client thread terminates.

3.3.6   Thread logon and rendezvous

Thread logon is a mechanism that allows a thread to request notification that another thread has reached a given point in its execution or has terminated. The first form of notification is known as a rendezvous.

Each thread has two doubly linked lists: one of target logons (iTargetLogons – representing threads which are requesting notification of a rendezvous with or the termination of this thread) and one of owned logons (iOwnedLogons – representing requests by this thread to be notified of a rendezvous with other threads or when other threads terminate). Rendezvous requests are stored at the head of iOwnedLogons and logon (termination) requests are stored at the tail of this list.

The kernel handles process rendezvous and logon using an identical mechanism.

The TLogon::LogonLock fast mutex protects all these lists (over all the threads and processes in the system). When a rendezvous is signaled by a thread, the target logon list is iterated from the head and all rendezvous requests completed. When a thread terminates, the thread exit handler completes all the logons on its target logon list (both rendezvous and termination) with the exit reason and discards any remaining logons on its owned logon list.

We use the iExiting field to prevent a new logon from being added to a thread after it has completed all its target logons, which would result in the new logon never being completed. The iExiting flag is set to ETrue at the beginning of the thread exit handler. Any attempt to add a new logon to (or rendezvous with) a thread whose iExiting flag is set will fail and will complete immediately with KErrDied.

Since thread logons need notification of thread exit just as cleanup items do, why do we need a separate mechanism for them rather than just adding them to the thread cleanup list? This is because the kernel protects thread cleanup queues with the system lock held and so they must be fast, with a bounded execution time. But, of course a thread may have any number of logons outstanding, and canceling a logon requires the kernel to walk the list of outstanding logons. This means that the time for which the system lock could be held is unbounded.

You might be wondering why this is so. After all, the kernel releases the system lock after it processes each cleanup item. However, the situations are subtly different. The kernel processes cleanup items when a thread exits, walking the queue and processing each cleanup item. However, rather than searching for and removing a particular item, it simply wants to remove all items, so it can use an algorithm like this one:

```
FOREVER
  {
  LOCK();
  // remove the first item (if any) from the list
```

```
// and return a pointer to it.
// p is null when there are no more items left
p = GetFirstItem();
UNLOCK();
if (p)
  Cleanup(p);
else
  break;
}
```

But when attempting to cancel a logon, the kernel needs to search the list for a particular item and remove just that one item. If it releases the lock at any point during this scan it can "lose its place" – the last item it checked may be removed from the list and placed on another list, or even destroyed, before this portion of code runs again. So the kernel must hold the lock throughout the scan, and this means that it cannot use the system lock.

We also considered the fact that processes don't have cleanup queues. Once we had taken this into account, it made sense to create an entirely new mechanism for thread logons, knowing we could re-use it for process logons. So, we use a separate queue for logons, and we protect this queue with a different mutex.

3.3.7 Symbian OS thread-synchronization objects

The Symbian OS kernel provides support for more complex thread-synchronization objects than the nanokernel does. These objects are Symbian OS semaphores and mutexes.

Symbian OS semaphores are standard counting semaphores which support multiple waiting threads (unlike nanokernel fast semaphores) and which release waiting threads in priority order.

Symbian OS mutexes are fully nestable – a thread can hold several mutexes at once and can also hold the same mutex several times. They support priority inheritance – the holding thread inherits the priority of the highest-priority waiting thread if that is higher than the holding thread's usual priority. The kernel and memory model use Symbian OS mutexes extensively to protect long-running critical code sections.

3.3.7.1 Semaphores – DSemaphore

Symbian OS semaphores are standard counting semaphores. The semaphore maintains a count: if the count is positive or zero, no threads are waiting; if it is negative, the count is equal to minus the number of waiting threads.

There are two basic operations on semaphores:

- WAIT. This decrements the count atomically. If the count remains non-negative the calling thread continues to run; if the count becomes negative the calling thread is blocked

- SIGNAL. This increments the count atomically. If the count was originally negative, the kernel releases the next waiting thread.

The kernel protects Symbian OS semaphore operations by the system lock.

It is important to note that DSemaphore operations rely on fields that are present in DThread but not in NThread. This means that only Symbian OS threads may invoke Symbian OS semaphore operations – **it is not permitted for an IDFC or a non-Symbian OS thread to signal a Symbian OS semaphore**.

We use the DSemaphore class to represent a Symbian OS semaphore. This class is derived from DObject, which makes it a dynamically allocated reference counted object. DSemaphore is the kernel object referred to by a user-side RSemaphore handle:

```
class DSemaphore : public DObject
  {
public:
  TInt Create(DObject* aOwner, const TDesC* aName,
       TInt aInitialCount, TBool aVisible=ETrue);
public:
  ~DSemaphore();
  void WaitCancel(DThread* aThread);
  void WaitCancelSuspended(DThread* aThread);
  void SuspendWaitingThread(DThread* aThread);
  void ResumeWaitingThread(DThread* aThread);
  void ChangeWaitingThreadPriority(DThread* aThread, TInt aNewPriority);
public:
  TInt Wait(TInt aNTicks);
  void Signal();
  void SignalN(TInt aCount);
  void Reset();
public:
  TInt iCount;
  TUint8 iResetting;
  TUint8 iPad1;
  TUint8 iPad2;
  TUint8 iPad3;
  SDblQue iSuspendedQ;
  TThreadWaitList iWaitQ;
public:
  friend class Monitor;
  };
```

Key member data of DSemaphore

iCount
The semaphore count.

`iResetting`

A flag set while the semaphore is being reset; this occurs just prior to the semaphore being deleted and involves releasing any waiting or suspended threads. The flag is used to prevent any more threads from waiting on the semaphore.

`iSuspendedQ`

This is a doubly linked list of threads which are both waiting on the semaphore and explicitly suspended. These threads will have `iWaitObj` pointing to this semaphore and will have M-state `EWaitSemaphore-Suspended`.

`iWaitQ`

A list, in decreasing priority order, of threads that are waiting on the semaphore and not explicitly suspended. Note that this is a difference from EKA1 – under the old version of Symbian OS, the kernel released threads in the order that they had waited on the semaphore.

Threads in this list will have their `iWaitObj` pointing to this semaphore and their M-state will be `EWaitSemaphore`.

Note that the `iWaitObj` field under discussion here is the `DThread` member, not the `NThread` member of the same name.

Threads that are explicitly suspended as well as waiting on a semaphore are not kept on the semaphore wait queue; instead, the kernel keeps them on a separate suspended queue, `iSuspendedQ`, which is just a standard doubly linked list. We do not regard such threads as waiting for the semaphore – if the semaphore is signaled, they will not acquire it and the semaphore count will simply increase and may become positive. To acquire the semaphore, they must be explicitly released, at which point the kernel removes them from `iSuspendedQ` and adds them to `iWaitQ`.

3.3.7.2   Mutexes – DMutex

Symbian OS mutexes provide mutual exclusion between threads, but without the restrictions imposed by the nanokernel mutex. So,

- It is possible to wait on a Symbian OS mutex multiple times, provided it is signaled the same number of times

- It is possible to hold several Symbian OS mutexes simultaneously, although care is required to avoid deadlocks (I'll discuss this later)

- It is possible to block while holding a Symbian OS mutex. Symbian OS mutexes provide priority inheritance.

The freedom from the restrictions of the nanokernel mutex comes at a price in terms of performance; operations on Symbian OS mutexes are more complicated and hence slower than those on NFastMutex.

Our motivation in designing DMutex was the requirement that the mutex should be held, whenever possible, by the highest priority thread that requires the mutex. Of course, this is not possible if the mutex is already held when a higher-priority thread requests the mutex – in this case, the delay before the higher-priority thread acquires the mutex should be kept to a minimum. The design meets these criteria in these ways:

1. The kernel defers a thread's acquisition of a mutex to the last possible moment. A thread cannot acquire a mutex on behalf of another thread; it can only acquire a mutex for itself. When a thread signals a mutex, the kernel does not directly hand the mutex over to the highest-priority waiting thread; it merely frees the mutex and **releases** the highest-priority waiting thread. The waiting thread must actually run to claim the mutex. We chose this design to take care of the case in which a high-priority thread acquires and releases a mutex several times in succession. Imagine we have a high-priority thread HAIKU that owns a mutex and a lower-priority thread EPIC that is the highest-priority thread waiting on that mutex. If HAIKU released the mutex and the kernel then handed it over to EPIC immediately, then HAIKU would not be able to reclaim the mutex so would be delayed by the lower-priority thread

2. The kernel queues threads waiting for a mutex and releases them in priority order. So when the kernel releases a mutex the highest-priority waiting thread will run and acquire the mutex, if its priority is higher than the current thread's priority

3. Mutexes implement priority inheritance. If a low priority thread, EPIC, is holding a mutex when a higher-priority thread, HAIKU, waits on the same mutex, then the kernel elevates the priority of EPIC to that of HAIKU. This ensures that another thread SONNET, of medium priority, which might prevent EPIC from running and releasing the mutex, does not delay HAIKU

4. If the kernel suspends a thread that is waiting on a mutex, it removes it from the wait queue and places it on a separate suspended queue. The kernel no longer regards the thread as waiting for the mutex: the kernel will never hand over the mutex to a thread that is suspended. This is because this would result in the mutex being held for an indeterminate period.

We need three thread M-states to describe the interaction of a thread with a mutex. The most obvious of these is the EWaitMutex state, which indicates that the thread is blocked waiting for the mutex. The kernel adds a thread in `EWaitMutex` state to the priority-ordered mutex wait queue.

Point 4 requires the existence of a second state, `EWaitMutexSuspended`; this is because threads that are both waiting for a mutex and explicitly suspended are not enqueued on the wait queue but on the suspended queue. The kernel needs to perform different actions in the event, for example, of the thread being killed, and so different states are required.

Point 1 requires the existence of a third state, `EHoldMutexPending`. When the kernel releases a mutex, it marks the mutex as free and releases the highest-priority waiting thread. Typically, that thread will then run and acquire the mutex. Note that although there may be other threads on the wait queue, we release only one thread, the highest priority one. We do this for efficiency – there is no point releasing all those other threads since this is time-consuming and only the highest-priority thread among them will be able to acquire the mutex anyway. But this presents us with a problem: if we release the highest-priority thread and it is killed before it has had chance to acquire the mutex, then the mutex remains free but none of the waiting threads can claim it – because they are all blocked.

The solution is simply that the kernel moves the next highest-priority thread from the `EWaitMutex` state to `EHoldMutexPending`.

The thread that holds the mutex is in the `EReady` state. It is linked to the mutex by way of its cleanup queue and each mutex has a `TThreadCleanup` object embedded in it. When a thread acquires the mutex, the kernel adds the `TThreadCleanup` object to the thread's cleanup queue. (While the mutex remains free, the cleanup item is not linked to any queue and its cleanup item's thread pointer is `NULL`.) The priority of the cleanup item is equal to that of the highest-priority thread on the mutex wait queue. The kernel first sets this priority when a thread acquires the mutex, just before adding the cleanup item to the thread's cleanup queue. If another thread subsequently waits for the mutex then the kernel adjusts the priority of the cleanup item (if the new waiting thread has a higher priority than any other). Raising the cleanup item's priority may then cause the holding thread's priority to increase (if the new cleanup priority is higher than the holding thread's default priority). In this way, the holding thread's priority will never be less than that of any waiting thread, and so we get priority inheritance.

What happens if the holding thread is itself blocked on another mutex? In this case the kernel may elevate the priority of the holding thread of the second mutex if necessary. In principle, a sequence like this may be arbitrarily long, which would result in an arbitrarily long execution time for the mutex wait operation. To avoid this, we terminate the chain once we have traversed 10 mutexes. **Priority inheritance will no longer operate if a chain of mutexes exceeds this length.**

To ensure that the highest-priority thread always acquires the mutex first, the kernel must take action whenever a thread performs any of the following operations on a thread associated with the mutex:

- Suspends

- Resumes

- Kills

- Changes priority.

The following table summarizes the required actions. (The row indicates the relationship of the thread to the mutex, the column indicates the operation performed on the thread.)

	Suspend	Resume	Kill	Priority change
Holding thread	No action.	No action.	Signal mutex.	Priority of thread will not drop below that of highest-priority waiting thread.
Waiting	Change thread state to wait/suspend. Adjust cleanup priority.	Not applicable.	Remove from wait queue and adjust cleanup priority.	If priority raised and mutex free, make thread pending. If mutex not free adjust cleanup priority.
Waiting/suspended	No action.	If mutex free make thread pending else make thread waiting and adjust cleanup priority.	Remove from suspended queue and adjust cleanup priority.	No action.
Pending	If mutex free and wait queue non-empty, make highest-priority waiting thread pending.	No action.	Remove thread from pending queue. If mutex free and wait queue non-empty, make highest priority waiting thread pending.	If mutex free and thread priority reduced below that of highest-priority waiting thread, make the latter pending.

The kernel and memory model use DMutex extensively to protect global data structures that are accessed by multiple threads. The kernel protects DMutex operations using the system lock fast mutex.

Note that DMutex operations rely on fields that are present in DThread but not in NThread. Hence only Symbian OS threads may invoke mutex operations; **it is not permitted for an IDFC or a non-Symbian OS thread to use a Symbian OS mutex.**

We represent a Symbian OS mutex by the DMutex class. Like many others, this class is derived from DObject, which makes it a dynamically allocated reference counted object. DMutex is the kernel object referred to by a user-side RMutex handle:

```
class DMutex : public DObject
  {
public:
  TInt Create(DObject* aOwner, const TDesC* aName,
                  TBool aVisible, TUint aOrder);
public:
  DMutex();
  ~DMutex();
  TInt HighestWaitingPriority();
  void WaitCancel(DThread* aThread);
  void WaitCancelSuspended(DThread* aThread);
  void SuspendWaitingThread(DThread* aThread);
  void ResumeWaitingThread(DThread* aThread);
  void ChangeWaitingThreadPriority(DThread* aThread,
                                TInt aNewPriority);
  void SuspendPendingThread(DThread* aThread);
  void RemovePendingThread(DThread* aThread);
  void ChangePendingThreadPriority(DThread* aThread,
                                TInt aNewPriority);
  void WakeUpNextThread();
public:
  TInt Wait();
  void Signal();
  void Reset();
public:
  TInt iHoldCount;
  TInt iWaitCount;
  TUint8 iResetting;
  TUint8 iOrder;
  TUint8 iPad1;
  TUint8 iPad2;
  TThreadMutexCleanup iCleanup;
  SDblQue iSuspendedQ;
  SDblQue iPendingQ;
  TThreadWaitList iWaitQ;
#ifdef _DEBUG
  SDblQueLink iORderLink;
#endif
public:
  friend class Monitor;
  };
```

Key member data of DMutex
iHoldCount
Count of the number of times the holding thread has waited on this mutex in a nested fashion. We increment this field if the holding thread waits

again and decrement it if it signals the mutex; in the latter case we release the mutex if iHoldCount becomes zero.

iWaitCount

Count of the number of waiting threads plus the number of waiting and suspended threads. This is used only to implement the RMutex::Count() method.

iResetting

This flag is set while the mutex is being reset; this occurs just prior to the mutex being deleted and involves releasing and unlinking any waiting, suspended or pending threads. The flag is used to prevent further threads waiting on the mutex.

iCleanup

A TThreadCleanup entry used both to enable the mutex to be released if the holding thread exits and also to enable the holding thread to inherit the priority of the highest-priority waiting thread. The iThread member of iCleanup is a pointer to the holding thread; a NULL value for iCleanup.iThread indicates that the mutex is free.

iSuspendedQ

A doubly linked list of threads that are both waiting on the mutex and explicitly suspended. These threads have iWaitObj pointing to this mutex and have M-state EWaitMutexSuspended.

iPendingQ

A doubly linked list of threads, released by the kernel after waiting on a mutex, but which have not yet claimed that mutex. These threads have iWaitObj pointing to this mutex and have M-state EHoldMutex Pending.

iWaitQ

A 64-priority list of threads that are waiting on the mutex and that are not explicitly suspended. These threads have iWaitObj pointing to the mutex and have M-state EWaitMutex.

3.3.7.3 Condition variables – DCondVar

Often, a thread will need to block until some data that it shares with other threads reaches a particular value. In Symbian OS, it can do this by using a POSIX-style condition variable.

Condition variables provide a different type of synchronization to locking mechanisms like mutexes. Mutexes are used to make other threads wait while the thread holding the mutex executes code in a critical section. In contrast, a thread uses a condition variable to make itself wait until an expression involving shared data attains a particular state.

The kernel-side object is `DCondVar`, and its class definition is shown in the first of the two code samples which follow. Access to `DCondVar` from user-side is via `RCondVar`, which is shown in the second sample.

Condition variables are always used in association with a mutex to protect the shared data. In Symbian OS, this is, of course, an `RMutex` object.

DCondVar

```
class DCondVar : public DObject
  {
public:
  TInt Create(DObject* aOwner, const TDesC* aName, TBool aVisible);
public:
  DCondVar();
  ~DCondVar();
  void WaitCancel(DThread* aThread);
  void WaitCancelSuspended(DThread* aThread);
  void SuspendWaitingThread(DThread* aThread);
  void ResumeWaitingThread(DThread* aThread);
  void ChangeWaitingThreadPriority(DThread* aThread, TInt
                                              aNewPriority);
public:
  TInt Wait(DMutex* aMutex, TInt aTimeout);
  void Signal();
  void Broadcast(DMutex* aMutex);
  void Reset();
  void UnBlockThread(DThread* aThread, TBool aUnlock);
public:
  TUint8 iResetting;
  TUint8 iPad1;
  TUint8 iPad2;
  TUint8 iPad3;
  DMutex* iMutex;
  TInt iWaitCount;
  SDblQue iSuspendedQ;
  TThreadWaitList iWaitQ;
public:
  friend class Monitor;
  };
```

RCondVar

```
class RCondVar : public RHandleBase
  {
public:
  IMPORT_C TInt CreateLocal(TOwnerType aType=EOwnerProcess);
  IMPORT_C TInt CreateGlobal(const TDesC& aName,
               TOwnerType aType=EOwnerProcess);
  IMPORT_C TInt OpenGlobal(const TDesC& aName,
               TOwnerType aType=EOwnerProcess);
  IMPORT_C TInt Open(RMessagePtr2 aMessage, TInt aParam,
                        TOwnerType aType=EOwnerProcess);
  IMPORT_C TInt Open(TInt aArgumentIndex,
          TOwnerType aType=EOwnerProcess);
```

```
IMPORT_C TInt Wait(RMutex& aMutex);
IMPORT_C TInt TimedWait(RMutex& aMutex, TInt aTimeout);
IMPORT_C void Signal();
IMPORT_C void Broadcast();
};
```

You can see that the condition to be tested lives outside of the condition variable. This is because the condition is application-defined, and allows it to be as complex as you wish. The only real requirement is that the volatile data being tested by the condition is protected by the mutex that is being used with the condition variable.

Let's look at how condition variables are used in practice.

One common use case for condition variables is the implemention of thread-safe message queues, providing a producer/consumer communication mechanism for passing messages between multiple threads. Here we want to block producer threads when the message queue is full and we want to block consumer threads when the queue is empty. Assume that the queue is a doubly linked list of messages. Clearly we will need to protect this list with a mutex (let's call it myMutex), so that producers and consumers do not interfere with each other as they add and remove messages from the queue.

Now let's look at this from the point of view of the consumer thread, and let's suppose that there are no messages for it to process. How does it deal with this situation? The consumer thread could repeatedly lock and unlock myMutex, each time checking the linked list for more messages. But this busy polling is extremely inefficient. It is far better for the consumer thread to first wait on myMutex, and then on the condition variable, by calling RCondVar::Wait(RMutex&aMutex). This method will only return when there is a new message on the list. What goes on behind the scenes when this happens?

The consumer thread ends up in DCondVar::Wait(). This is kernel code, but it is running in the consumer thread's context. Almost the first thing DCondVar::Wait() does is to release the mutex. The function then blocks – this means the consumer thread does not run again until the condition variable is signaled. Now that myMutex is unlocked, other threads that were blocked on the mutex may become runnable, and can access and modify the message-status variable.

Suppose a producer thread signals the condition variable. What then happens to our sleeping consumer thread? Immediately after it wakes, still in DCondVar::Wait(), it re-aquires the mutex, preventing access by other threads and making it safe for it to examine the shared data itself.

So we have seen that usage pattern for condition variables is as follows:

```
mutex.Wait();
while(!CONDITION)
```

```
        // possible race condition here if signalling thread
        // does not hold mutex
    condvar.Wait(mutex);
    STATEMENTS;
    mutex.Signal();
```

Here CONDITION is an arbitrary condition involving any number of user-side variables whose integrity is protected by the mutex. You have to loop while testing the condition since there is no guarantee that the condition has been satisfied when the condition variable is signaled. Different threads may be waiting on different conditions or the condition may have already been absorbed by another thread. All that can be said is that the thread will awaken whenever something happens which might affect the condition.

And what about the producer thread? How does it signal the condition variable? There are two methods in RCondVar that allow it to do this: Signal() and Broadcast().

Signal() unblocks a single, waiting thread. If there are several of these, then the kernel unblocks the highest-priority thread that is not explicitly suspended. If there are no threads currently waiting this call does nothing.

The calling thread does not **have** to hold the mutex when it calls Signal() but we recommend that it does so. Otherwise a race condition can result if it signals the condition variable just between the waiting thread testing the condition and calling Wait().

Broadcast() unblocks all the threads that are waiting on the condition variable. As for Signal(), it is best if the thread that calls Broadcast() holds the mutex first.

I hope that I have also shown that, although RCondVar is used for explicit communications between threads, the communications are anonymous. The producer thread does not necessarily know that the consumer thread is waiting on the condition variable that it signaled. And the consumer thread does not know that it was the producer thread that woke it up from its wait on the condition variable.

3.3.8 Symbian OS thread death

All Symbian OS threads have an exit handler installed, which performs first stage cleanup of the thread in the context of the exiting thread. This first stage includes:

- Restoring the thread to a consistent state – for example removing the thread from any mutexes or semaphores on which it was waiting

- Running thread-exit cleanup handlers

- Completing logons.

The kernel can't perform its entire cleanup in the exiting thread's context – for example it can't free the thread's supervisor stack or control block. So the kernel performs a second phase of exit processing in the supervisor thread context. Each DThread has a DFC, given by iKillDfc, which is queued on the supervisor thread just before the exiting thread actually terminates. The DFC completes the cleanup process – closing thread handles, freeing stacks and freeing the thread control block. If this is the last thread in a process, then it also closes process handles and frees the process control block.

3.3.8.1   Types of Symbian OS thread

When we start to think about thread death, there are four different types of Symbian OS thread we need to consider. These are specified by the iFlags member data, and defined in u32std.h:

```
KThreadFlagProcessCritical = 1
KThreadFlagProcessPermanent = 2
KthreadFlagSystemCritical = 4
KthreadFlagSystemPermanent = 8
```

The corresponding user-side enumerations are in e32std.h:

```
enum TCritical
    {
    ENotCritical,
    EProcessCritical,
    EProcessPermanent,
    EAllThreadsCritical,
    ESystemCritical,
    ESystemPermanent
    };
```

The meanings of the values in this enumeration are:

ENotCritical
The thread or process is not critical. No special action is taken on thread or process exit or panic.

EProcessCritical
Indicates that a thread panic causes the process to panic.

EProcessPermanent
Indicates that a thread exit of any kind causes the process to exit.

EAllThreadsCritical
Indicates that if any thread in a process panics, then the process panics.

`ESystemCritical`

Indicates that a thread or process is system-critical. If that thread or process panics, then the entire system is rebooted. Clearly this is a drastic step to take, so we ensure that only a process with the "Protected Server" capability can set a thread to system-critical.

`ESystemPermanent`

Indicates that a thread or process is system-permanent. If that thread or process exits, then the entire system is rebooted. Clearly this too is a drastic step to take, so again we ensure that only a process with the "Protected Server" capability can set a thread to system-permanent.

3.3.9   Kernel threads

The Symbian OS kernel itself creates five kernel threads at boot time, and these threads continue to run until the mobile phone is rebooted. (In fact, there may even be more than five threads on a phone, since kernel extensions can create them too.) Next I will briefly describe each kernel thread and its purpose in the system.

3.3.9.1   The null thread

Earlier I described how the null thread (also known as the idle thread) is the first thread to run on a device at boot time. This thread's execution begins at the reset vector. Just after the reset is applied, there are no `NThread` or `DThread` objects in existence, of course – but the thread of execution that begins here eventually becomes the null thread, which is the thread with the lowest possible priority in the system. Since there is no point in time slicing the null thread, the kernel sets a variable in the thread to disable time slicing. This thread has `iType==EThreadInitial`, and is the only thread in the system with this type.

Because of the unusual way this thread comes into being, the bootstrap must allocate and map its stack before kernel execution begins. This means that the stack is in a special place – at the start of the chunk containing the kernel heap. For more on Symbian OS bootup, see Chapter 16, *Boot Processes*.

As we said, the null thread has the lowest possible priority in the system. This means that the null thread will gain control only when no other thread is ready to run. Generally the null thread simply loops forever executing a "wait for interrupt" instruction, which places the CPU in a low-power mode where instruction execution stops until a hardware interrupt is asserted.

The main task that the null thread performs in its infinite loop is to delay the nanokernel timer tick for as long as possible. The null thread inspects the nanokernel timer queue and determines how many ticks will elapse before the first timer is due to expire. It then updates the hardware timer to skip that number of ticks, so that the next timer interrupt coincides with the expiry of the first timer on the queue. In this way, we save power by not reactivating the CPU several times just to discover that there is nothing to be done. For more details of Symbian OS power management, see Chapter 15, *Power Management.*

3.3.9.2   *The supervisor thread*

This is the second thread to run after a system reset. It is responsible for the final phase of kernel initialization and for phase 3 of the variant initialization, which initializes the interrupt dispatcher and enables the nanokernel tick timer interrupt. For more details of the supervisor thread's role in start-up, see Chapter 16, *Boot Processes.*

Once the OS is running, the primary functions of the supervisor thread are cleanup activities and providing notification of non-time-critical events to user-side code. The supervisor thread's priority is set so that it is higher than applications and most user-mode code but lower than anything that is time-critical.

The supervisor thread performs many of its functions via deferred function calls, or DFCs, which I will discuss in Chapter 5, *Interrupts and Exceptions.* DFCs that run in the supervisor thread can't expect any real-time guarantees – and would typically be unbounded operations anyway, often involving the freeing of memory. To sum up, DFCs in the supervisor thread perform these tasks:

1.   Thread and process cleanup on exit

2.   Asynchronous deletion. For more on this, see Chapter 7, *Memory Models*

3.   Asynchronous change notifier completion. (User code uses the `RChangeNotifier` class to get notification from the kernel of important changes, such of change of locale.) Sometimes the kernel needs to signal change notifiers either from time-critical code (for example the midnight crossover detection in `TSecondQ`) or from places where low-level kernel mutexes are held (for example the memory threshold detection code may run with the kernel heap mutex held). The signaling of change notifiers is unbounded (since there may be arbitrarily many of them) and involves waiting on the change notifier container's mutex. To avoid timing and deadlock problems, the kernel provides the function `Kern::AsyncNotify Changes()`. This function accumulates the set of changes that it needs to signal in a bit mask, `K::AsyncChanges`, and queues a DFC on the supervisor thread to signal the change notifiers

4. Asynchronous freeing of physical RAM. For more on this, see Chapter 7, *Memory Models*

5. The completion of publish and subscribe property subscriptions.

3.3.9.3 DFC thread 0

This thread has priority 27 (usually the second highest in the system), and it simply runs a DFC queue. The kernel does not use this queue itself, but provides it for those device drivers that do not have stringent real-time requirements, to give them a context that they can use for their non-ISR processing. You can think of this queue as approximately equivalent to the single DFC queue that EKA1 provided. The presence of this single "general purpose" DFC thread in the kernel saves memory, because each device driver does not have to create its own thread. The function `Kern::DfcQue0()` returns a pointer to the DFC queue serviced by this thread.

Symbian device drivers that use this thread include serial comms, sound, ethernet, keyboard and digitizer.

3.3.9.4 DFC thread 1

This thread has priority 48; it is generally the highest-priority thread in the system. The nanokernel timer DFC runs on this thread.

DFC thread 1 is available for use by other device drivers if necessary; the function `Kern::DfcQue1()` returns a pointer to the DFC queue serviced by this thread.

You should beware of using DFC thread 1 for anything other than running the nanokernel timer queue. You should also beware of creating a higher-priority thread than this one. If you delay the nanokernel timer DFC by more than 16 nanokernel timer ticks, you run the risk of adversely affecting the accuracy of the nanokernel timers.

3.3.9.5 The timer thread

This thread has priority 27. It manages the Symbian OS timer queues.

The timer thread is also available for device drivers to use if they need it – the function `Kern::TimerDfcQ()` returns a pointer to the DFC queue serviced by this thread.

3.3.10 Threads – conclusion

In this section I've discussed both nanothreads and Symbian OS threads. I'll now go on to describe a Symbian OS object that has no nanokernel equivalent – the process.

3.4   What is a process?

Under Symbian OS, a process is both a single instantiation of an executable image file and a collection of one or more threads that share a particular address space (or memory mapping). This address space may, or may not, be different to that of other processes in the system – this depends on whether the processor in the mobile phone has an MMU, and on which particular memory model the phone manufacturer has chosen to use.

In most cases, designers will want to ensure that they protect processes from each other by choosing the memory model appropriately. In this case, a thread in one process will not be able to directly access the memory belonging to a thread in another process – although, it will of course be able to directly access the memory of any thread in the same process. So you can see that, with the appropriate choice of memory model, the process is the fundamental unit of memory protection under Symbian OS.

The loader creates a process by first asking the kernel to create a `DProcess` object, then loading the image and informing the kernel that it has done so. The kernel creates a single thread, marks it as the main thread, and starts execution at the process's entry point. The main thread is marked as `KThreadFlagProcessPermanent` (see Section 3.3.8), but the application can change this later.

As well as sharing an address space, the threads in a process are connected in other ways:

- You can specify their priorities relative to the process priority; changing the process priority will change the priorities of all such threads. (You may also specify absolute thread priorities – these do not change when the process priority is changed)

- If the process exits or is terminated, then the kernel terminates all the threads in the process with the same exit information

- Threads in the same process can share object handles; this is not possible for threads in different processes

- A user thread can create a new thread only in its own process.

This section is quite a lot shorter than the one on threads, since the two things that are mainly of interest for processes are how they are loaded, which I will cover in Chapter 10, *The Loader*, and the role they play in address spaces, which I will cover in Chapter 7, *Memory Models*. All that remains is to discuss the Symbian OS representation of the process, `DProcess`.

3.5   DProcess class

Like many other classes in the kernel, this class is derived from DObject, which makes it a dynamically allocated reference counted object. DProcess is the kernel object referred to by a user-side RProcess handle. Here a cut-down version of the class:

```cpp
class DProcess : public DObject
    {
public:
  DProcess();
  ~DProcess();
  TInt Create(TBool aKernelProcess, TProcessCreateInfo& aInfo,
                                      HBuf* aCommandLine);
  TInt SetPriority(TProcessPriority aPriority);
  TInt Logon(TRequestStatus* aStatus, TBool aRendezvous);
  void Rendezvous(TInt aReason);
  TInt AddCodeSeg(DCodeSeg* aSeg, DLibrary* aLib, SDblQue& aQ);
  TInt RemoveCodeSeg(DCodeSeg* aCodeSeg, SDblQue* aQ);
  TBool HasCapabilityNoDiagnostic(TCapability aCapability);
private:
  virtual TInt NewChunk(DChunk*& aChunk, SChunkCreateInfo& aInfo,
                                      TLinAddr& aRunAddr)=0;
  virtual TInt AddChunk(DChunk* aChunk,TBool isReadOnly)=0;
  virtual TInt DoCreate(TBool aKernelProcess,
                  TProcessCreateInfo& aInfo)=0;
  virtual TInt Loaded(TProcessCreateInfo& aInfo);
public:
  TInt NewThread(DThread*& aThread, SThreadCreateInfo& aInfo,
                            TInt* aHandle, TOwnerType aType);
  virtual void Resume();
  void Die(TExitType aType,TInt aReason,const TDesC &aCategory);
public:
  TInt iPriority;
  SDblQue iThreadQ;
  TUint8 iExitType;
  TUint8 iPad1;
  TUint8 iPad2;
  TUint8 iPad3;
  TInt iExitReason;
  TBufC<KMaxExitCategoryName> iExitCategory;
  DObjectIx* iHandles;
  TUidType iUids;
  TInt iGeneration;
  TUint iId;
  TUint32 iFlags;
  HBuf* iCommandLine;
  DProcess* iOwningProcess;
  SDblQue iTargetLogons;
  RArray<SCodeSegEntry> iDynamicCode;
  SSecurityInfo iS;
  SSecurityInfo iCreatorInfo;
  TUint iCreatorId;
  TUint iSecurityZone;
  TInt iEnvironmentData[KArgIndex];
public:
  enum TProcessAttributes {
```

```
  EPrivate=2,
  ESupervisor=0x80000000,
  EBeingLoaded=0x08000000,
  EResumed=0x00010000 };
TInt iAttributes;
TLinAddr iDataBssRunAddress;
DChunk* iDataBssStackChunk;
DCodeSeg* iCodeSeg;
DCodeSeg* iTempCodeSeg;
DMutex* iProcessLock;
DMutex* iDllLock; // can be held while in user mode
// user address to jump to for new threads, exceptions
TLinAddr iReentryPoint;
};
```

Key member data of DProcess

iThreadQ

Doubly linked list of all threads belonging to this process. Accesses to this list are protected by the process lock mutex.

iHandles

Pointer to array (DObjectIx) of process-global handles for this process.

iDataBssStackChunk

Pointer to chunk-holding process global data (.data and .bss sections) and, in most cases, user stacks of threads belonging to this process. The memory model determines whether or not user stacks are placed in this chunk.

iDataBssRunAddress

Run address of base of initialized data.

iDynamicCode

RArray listing all explicitly dynamically loaded code segments which are attached to this process – that is, only ones corresponding to DLLs which have been explicitly loaded, not the process EXE code segment (iCodeSeg) or code segments which are attached to the process only due to implicit linkages from other code segments. For each such code segment this array contains two pointers – a pointer to the DCodeSeg object and a pointer to the DLibrary or (for the kernel process only) the DLogicalDevice DPhysicalDevice object that represents the process's use of the code segment.

iCodeSeg

Pointer to DCodeSeg object that represents the executable image used to create this process. This value is set when the process is fully loaded and ready to be resumed.

iTempCodeSeg

Temporary pointer to DCodeSeg object that represents the executable image used to create this process. This value is only used during process creation; it is set to NULL when the process is fully loaded and ready to be resumed.

`iAttributes`
Process attributes. Some of these are generic (private, supervisor, being loaded, resumed); the memory model defines some more.

`iFlags`
Process flags (just-in-time debug).

`iProcessLock`
Pointer to DMutex object used to protect the process thread list and in some memory models, the process address space list.

`iDllLock`
Pointer to DMutex object used to protect DLL static data constructors and destructors that run user-side in this process. Note that this mutex is held while running user-mode code and hence the thread need not enter a critical section before acquiring it; these are the only mutexes used by the kernel with this property.

3.5.1   Processes in the emulator

The increased code-sharing in the EKA2 emulator means that the EKA2 emulator provides much better emulation of Symbian OS processes than the EKA1 emulator did. The emulator can instantiate a process from a .EXE file and has the same object and thread ownership model as on target hardware. The EKA1 emulator failed to emulate processes at all.

That said, debugging multiple processes on a host OS is difficult and so the EKA2 emulator still executes as a single process in the host OS. Indeed, the emulator does not provide a complete emulation of processes as found on target platforms. In particular, the following aspects of processes are not completely emulated:

1. Memory protection between processes, or between user and kernel mode

2. Full support for multiple instances of a DLL with writable static data.

The EKA1 emulator shares both these failings.

3.5.1.1   When a .EXE is not an EXE

Under Windows, a process is instantiated from a *Portable Executable* (PE) format file of type EXE. However, a process instantiated in this way may not load and link further EXE files. This means that the emulator must use a PE file of type DLL to create a new emulated Symbian OS process.

The Symbian tool chain could build all EXE targets for the emulator as host DLLs. These would then be easily loaded into the emulator as an emulated process. Unfortunately this prevents the EXE from being invoked from the Windows command line, something which has proved useful with EKA1. It also makes it impossible to load multiple instances of a process that has static data, because static data support is provided by the host OS, and the emulator is a single process in the host OS.

We solved this dilemma by making certain assumptions about the PE file format and the Windows platform:

1. The difference between a DLL and an EXE is a single bit in the PE file header

2. Identical copies of a DLL with different file names load as independent modules in the host OS.

This is currently true for all the Win32 platforms we have tested.

When creating a process within the emulator, we go through the following steps:

1. We copy the EXE file to a new filename

2. We set the "DLL" type bit and clear the Win32 entry point

3. We load the copy as a DLL

4. We find the Symbian OS entry point by looking for the `_E32Startup` export.

As a result, if you set the target type to EXE, then the tool chain creates a file that can bootstrap the emulator and that can also be loaded as a process within the emulator multiple times.

3.5.1.2 *Entry points*

The DLL and EXE entry point scheme used in the emulator has been changed, allowing the emulator to fully control how and when these functions are called. It also enables the Symbian OS "EXE" scheme I have just described.

The entry point in a Win32 DLL is not used at all, and the entry point for a Win32 EXE merely bootstraps the emulator by calling `BootEpoc()`.

The Symbian OS entry points are implemented by exporting a named symbol from the DLL or EXE. The DLL entry point is "`_E32Dll`" and the EXE entry point is "`_E32Startup`". The export management tools recognize these symbols and ensure that they are not included in frozen exports files and are always exported by name as the last symbol from the file.

3.6 Scheduling

EKA2 implements a priority-driven, preemptive scheduling scheme. The highest-priority ready thread, or one of several ready threads of equal highest priority, will usually run. (The exception, which I discussed earlier, is when a high-priority thread is waiting on a nanokernel fast mutex held by a lower-priority thread – in this case, the lower-priority thread runs.)

Within Symbian OS, scheduling is the responsibility of the nanokernel. Threads that are eligible for execution (that is, threads that are not waiting for an event) are called "ready" and are kept on a priority-ordered list, the ready list.

Each nanothread has an integer priority between 0 and 63 inclusive. As we have said, the highest-priority thread that is ready to run will run. If there are several threads at the same priority, then one of two things may happen. Firstly, the threads may be executed in a round-robin fashion, with the timeslice selectable on a thread-by-thread basis. Secondly, they may be executed in FIFO order – that is the first thread to become ready at that priority will run until it blocks and other threads at the same priority will not run until the first thread blocks. Which of these two methods is chosen is a property of the thread itself, not the scheduler.

Each thread has its own timeslice (iTimeslice) and time count (iTime). Whenever the thread blocks or the kernel rotates the thread to the end of the queue of threads at the same priority, the kernel sets the iTime field equal to iTimeslice. The low-level tick interrupt then decrements the current thread's iTime if it is positive and triggers a reschedule if it becomes zero. So you can see that if iTimeslice is positive, the thread will run for iTimeslice low level timer ticks before yielding to the next thread at the same priority. If iTimeslice is negative, the thread will only yield to other threads at the same priority if it blocks.

The ready list, shown graphically in Figure 3.2, holds all the threads that are currently eligible for execution. It is always accessed with the kernel locked so, to maintain low thread latency, operations on the ready list need to be bounded and as fast as possible. We achieve this by using 64 separate queues, one for each possible thread priority – the kernel places each ready thread in the queue corresponding to its priority. The kernel also maintains a 64-bit mask to indicate which queues have entries; bit n in the mask is set if and only if the queue for priority n has entries.

So, to insert an entry, the kernel simply adds it to the tail of the queue corresponding to its priority (no searching is required) and sets the corresponding bit in the bit mask. To remove an entry, the kernel first unlinks it from its queue, then, if that queue is now empty, resets the bit in

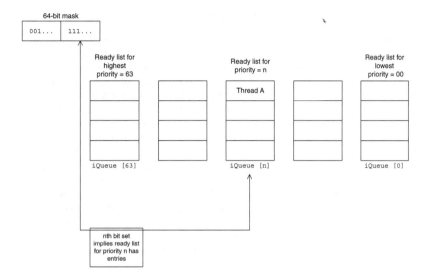

Figure 3.2 The ready list

the bit mask. To find the highest-priority entry, the kernel finds the most significant 1 in the bit mask (which can be done with a binary search or with a single instruction on some CPUs), and then finds the first entry on the corresponding queue. You can see that this implementation gives us bounded (and small) execution times for insertion and removal of entries and for finding the highest-priority entry.

To save on memory, we use a single pointer for each queue. This is NULL if the queue is empty, otherwise it points to the first entry on the queue. We arrange the entries in the queue in a doubly linked ring. We use the same priority ordered list implementation for DFC queues, and semaphore and mutex wait queues.

The kernel also maintains a flag (TheScheduler.iReschedule-NeededFlag) that indicates whether a thread switch may be required. It sets this flag whenever it adds a thread to the ready list, and that thread's priority is greater than the highest priority of any other thread already on the list. The nanokernel timer tick interrupt also sets this flag when the current thread's timeslice has expired.

When the kernel subsequently becomes unlocked, it checks this flag to determine whether a reschedule is needed, and clears the flag when it performs the reschedule.

The scheduler is responsible both for running IDFCs (immediate deferred function calls) and for selecting the next thread to run and switching to it. It does not do any page table manipulations to switch processes – instead it provides a hook that the Symbian OS memory model uses to arrange for such code to be called.

Here is a summary of the scheduler control block:

Field	Description
iPresent[2]	64-bit mask with a 1 in bit position n if and only if iQueue[n] is non-empty, that is, if and only if there is a thread of priority n on the ready list.
iQueue[64]	64 pointers, one for each possible thread priority. If there is no ready thread at priority n, iQueue[n]=NULL, else iQueue[n] points to the first ready thread at priority n.
iRescheduleNeededFlag	Boolean flag that is set if a reschedule is needed when the kernel is locked, and cleared by the scheduler when it runs.
iDfcPendingFlag	Boolean flag, set when an IDFC is queued and cleared when all pending IDFCs have been processed.
iKernCSLocked	The kernel lock (otherwise known as the preemption lock).
iDfcs	Doubly linked list of pending IDFCs.
iMonitorExceptionHandler	Pointer to exception handler installed by the crash debugger.
iProcessHandler	Pointer to the process address space switch handler in the Symbian OS memory model.
iLock	The system lock fast mutex.
iCurrentThread	Pointer to the currently executing NThread.
iAddressSpace	The identifier of the currently active process address space.
iExtras[16]	Space reserved for extra data used by the Symbian OS process switch handler.

Now let's look at the full scheduler algorithm. Before we start, we'll define some terms.

Non-volatile registers: those CPU registers that are preserved across a function call (r4–r11 and r13 on ARM).

CPU-specific registers: those registers, outside the normal supervisor-mode register set, that are required to exist on a per-thread basis. Examples on ARM include the DACR (domain access control register, CP15 CR3) and user mode R13 and R14.

System lock: a fast mutex, iLock, which the kernel uses to protect address space changes, among other things.

Kernel lock: a counter, iKernCSLocked, which is always ≥ 0. Zero is the normal state and indicates that IDFCs and a reschedule may run immediately following an interrupt. Non-zero values indicate that IDFCs and reschedules must be deferred until the count is decremented to zero. Also known as the preemption lock.

The kernel calls the scheduler in two different situations. The first is at the end of an interrupt service routine, if the following conditions are met:

1. IDFCs are pending or a reschedule is pending

2. The kernel is not locked (iKernCSLocked==0)

3. On ARM the interrupted mode must be usr or svc. (Other modes are non-preemptible since they don't have per-thread stacks.)

The kernel also calls the scheduler when it becomes unlocked (iKernCS-Locked decrements to zero), if the following condition is met:

4. Either IDFCs are pending or a reschedule is pending. (This will be the case if the current thread has just completed a nanokernel function that has blocked it or made a higher-priority thread ready.)

Here is the full scheduler algorithm for the moving memory model:

```
// Enter with kernel locked
// Active stack is supervisor stack of current thread

1    Disable interrupts
2    start_resched:
3    IF IDFCs pending (iDfcPendingFlag TRUE)
4    Run IDFCs (with interrupts enabled but kernel locked)
5    iDfcPendingFlag = FALSE
6    ENDIF
7    IF reschedule not needed (iRescheduleNeededFlag FALSE)
8    iKernCSLocked=0 (unlock the kernel)
9    Return
10   ENDIF
11   Reenable interrupts
12   Save nonvolatile registers and CPU specific registers on stack
13   iCurrentThread->iSavedSP = current stack pointer
14   iRescheduleNeededFlag = FALSE
15   next_thread = first thread in highest priority non-empty ready queue
16   IF next_thread->iTime==0 (ie timeslice expired)
17   IF another thread is ready at same priority as next_thread
18   IF next_thread holds a fast mutex
19   next_thread->iHeldFastMutex->iWaiting=TRUE
20   goto resched_end
21   ENDIF
22   next_thread->iTime=next_thread->iTimeslice (new timeslice)
23   next_thread=thread after next_thread in round-robin order
24   ENDIF
25   ENDIF
```

```
26  IF next_thread holds a fast mutex
27  IF next_thread holds system lock
28  goto resched_end
29  ENDIF
30  IF next_thread requires implicit system lock
31  IF system lock is held OR next_thread requires address space
                                                      switch
32  next_thread->iHeldFastMutex->iWaiting=TRUE
33  ENDIF
34  ENDIF
35  goto resched_end
36  ENDIF
37  IF next_thread is blocked on a fast mutex
38  IF next_thread->iWaitFastMutex->iHoldingThread (mutex is still
                                                       locked)
39  next_thread=next_thread->iWaitFastMutex->iHoldingThread
40  goto resched_end
41  ENDIF
42  ENDIF
43  IF next_thread does not require implicit system lock
44  goto resched_end
45  ENDIF
46  IF system lock held by another thread
47  next_thread=system lock holding thread
48  system lock iWaiting = TRUE
49  goto resched_end
50  ENDIF
51  IF thread does not require address space switch
52  goto resched_end
53  ENDIF
54  iCurrentThread=next_thread
55  current stack pointer = next_thread->iSavedSP
56  Restore CPU specific registers from stack
57  system lock iHoldingThread = next_thread
58  next_thread->iHeldFastMutex = system lock
59  Unlock kernel (scheduler may go recursive here, but only once)
60  Invoke address space switch handler
61  Lock the kernel
62  system lock iHoldingThread = NULL
63  next_thread->iHeldFastMutex = NULL
64  IF system lock iWaiting (there was contention for the system lock)
65  system lock iWaiting = FALSE
66  iRescheduleNeededFlag = TRUE (so we reschedule again)
67  IF next_thread has critical section operation pending
68  Do pending operation
69  ENDIF
70  ENDIF
71  goto switch_threads

72  resched_end:   // switch threads without doing process switch
73  iCurrentThread=next_thread
74  current stack pointer = next_thread->iSavedSP
75  Restore CPU specific registers from stack

76  switch_threads:
77  Restore nonvolatile registers from stack
78  Disable interrupts
79  IF IDFCs pending or another reschedule needed
```

```
80   goto start_resched
81   ENDIF
82   iKernCSLocked=0 (unlock the kernel)
83   Return with interrupts disabled
```

Lines 1–10 are concerned with running IDFCs. We check for the presence of IDFCs with interrupts disabled, since an interrupt could add an IDFC. If IDFCs are present, we call them at this point; we do this with interrupts enabled and with the kernel locked. IDFCs run in the order in which they were added to the queue. An IDFC could add a thread to the ready list; if that thread has a sufficiently high priority, the kernel sets iRescheduleNeededFlag. We remove each IDFC from the pending queue just before we execute it. We then disable interrupts again and make another check to see if more IDFCs are pending. If there are no more IDFCs, the kernel clears the iDfcPendingFlag. Interrupts are still disabled here. Next we check iRescheduleNeededFlag. This could have been set in several different ways:

1. By the current thread just before calling the scheduler (for example if that thread needs to block waiting for an event)

2. By an IDFC

3. By the timer tick interrupt, if the current thread's timeslice has expired.

If the flag is clear, no further action is needed and the scheduler returns. If it is set, we proceed to switch threads.

Lines 11–14 are straightforward: we can re-enable interrupts at this point since the most they could do is queue another IDFC that would eventually cause the scheduler to loop. We save the current thread's register context on the stack, which is the thread's own supervisor mode stack. Then we store the stack pointer in the current thread's iSavedSP field and clear iRescheduleNeededFlag since we are about to do a reschedule.

Line 15 implements the basic scheduling policy. The most significant bit in the 64-bit mask indicates the highest priority of any ready thread. We select the first thread on the queue corresponding to that priority as a candidate to run.

Lines 16–25 deal with round-robin scheduling of threads at the same priority. The system tick interrupt decrements the current thread's iTime field; when this reaches zero the thread's timeslice has expired, so the iRescheduleNeededFlag is set, which causes a reschedule at the next possible point – either at the end of the tick ISR or when the kernel is next unlocked. Line 16 checks to see if the selected thread's timeslice has expired. If it has, and there is another thread at the same priority, and the originally selected thread does not hold a fast mutex, then we select the next thread in round-robin order and we reset the original thread's timeslice.

If the original thread does hold a fast mutex, we defer the round-robin and set the fast mutex iWaiting flag so that the round-robin will be triggered when the thread releases the mutex. We defer the round-robin to reduce the time that might be wasted by context switching to another thread that then immediately waits on the same mutex and causes another context switch. This would be a particular problem with threads waiting on the system lock. We expect that a fast mutex will only be held for short periods at a time and so the overall pattern of round-robin scheduling will not be disturbed to any great extent.

Lines 26–36 deal with the case where the selected thread holds a fast mutex. If the thread holds the system lock, we can simply switch straight to the thread with no further checking, since the address space cannot have been changed since the thread last ran. Also, the thread cannot be blocked on another fast mutex (because it holds one and they do not nest).

If the selected thread holds a fast mutex other than the system lock, we still switch to it, and we don't have to call out to do address space changes, since we don't guarantee that the user-mode address space is valid during a critical section protected by a fast mutex (unless it's the system lock). However, if an address space change would normally be required, we set the mutex iWaiting flag to ensure that the address space change does actually occur when the fast mutex is released. In addition, if the thread has the KThreadAttImplicitSystemLock attribute and the system lock is currently held, we set the mutex iWaiting flag. This is to ensure that the thread doesn't exit the mutex-protected critical section while the system lock is held.

Lines 37–42 deal with the case where the selected thread is actually blocked on a fast mutex. Such threads stay on the ready list, so the kernel may select them during a reschedule. We do not want to waste time by switching to the thread and letting it run, only to immediately switch to the holding thread. So we check for this case in the scheduler and go straight to the mutex holding thread, thus saving a context switch. This check also guarantees that the YieldTo function used in NFastMutex wait operations cannot return until the mutex has been released. Notice that we need to check both iWaitFastMutex and iWaitFastMutex->iHoldingThread, since when the holding thread releases the mutex, iHoldingThread will be set to NULL but iWaitFastMutex will still point to the mutex. As before, there is no need to do any address space changing if we switch to the mutex holding thread. There is also no need to set the fast mutex iWaiting flag here since it must already have been set when the selected thread blocked on it.

Lines 43–50 deal with threads requiring an implicit system lock. We mainly use this mechanism for threads requiring long-running address space switches: to perform such a switch the scheduler must claim the system lock. Threads that do not need implicit system lock will also not need the scheduler to call the address-space-switch hook; the scheduler can simply switch to them at this point (lines 43–45). If the selected thread does require an implicit system lock, the scheduler then checks if the lock is free. If it is not, the scheduler switches to the system lock holding thread. It also sets the system lock's iWaiting flag since there is now a thread implicitly waiting on the system lock.

If we reach line 51, the selected thread needs an implicit system lock and the lock is free. If the thread does not need an address space change, we can now switch it in – the system lock is not claimed (lines 51–53). If the thread does require an address space change – that is, it has the KThreadAttAddressSpace attribute and its iAddressSpace value differs from the currently active one – then the scheduler calls out to do this address space change (line 60).

In lines 54–56 we do the actual thread switch. We change stacks and restore the CPU-specific registers from the new thread's stack. At this point, the new thread is effectively running with the kernel locked. Lines 57–58 claim the system lock for the new thread – we know that it's free here. Then we unlock the kernel (line 59). From this point on, further preemption can occur. It's also worth noting that the scheduler will go recursive here if an IDFC was queued by an interrupt serviced during the first part of the reschedule. There can only be one recursion, however, since the second reschedule would find the system lock held and so could not reach the same point in the code.

Line 60 calls the address space switch handler in the Symbian OS memory model to perform any MMU page table manipulations required to change to the required address space. The switch hander is also responsible for changing the iAddressSpace field in the scheduler to reflect the new situation. Since the switch handler runs with the kernel unlocked, it does not directly affect thread latency. But it does affect latency indirectly, since most Symbian OS user mode threads need an address space switch to run and many kernel functions wait on the system lock. The switch handler also affects the predictability of execution time for Symbian OS kernel functions. This means that we want the system lock to only be held for a very short time. To accommodate this, the address space switch handler does the operation in stages and checks the system lock's iWaiting flag after each stage. If the flag is set, the switch handler simply returns and we trigger a further reschedule (line 64) to allow the higher-priority thread to run. We set the iAddressSpace field in the scheduler to NULL just before we make the first change to the address space and we set it to the value corresponding to the new thread just after the last change is made. This ensures that we take the correct action if the address space switch handler is preempted and another reschedule occurs in the middle of it.

After we've done the address space switch, we lock the kernel again and release the system lock (lines 61–70). If contention occurred for the lock, we do not call the scheduler again directly as would normally be the case in a fast mutex signal; instead we set the `iRescheduleNeededFlag`, which will cause the scheduler to loop. Attempting recursion at this point would be incorrect, because the system lock is now free and there would be nothing to limit the recursion depth. [The processing of a deferred critical section operation (line 68) could cause the scheduler to go recursive, but only in the case where the thread was exiting; clearly, this cannot occur more than once. A deferred suspension would simply remove the thread from the ready list and set the `iRescheduleNeededFlag`, which would then cause the scheduler to loop.]

Lines 73–75 cover the case in which an address space switch was not required. They do the actual thread switch by switching to the new thread's stack and restoring the CPU-specific registers.

In lines 76 and onwards we finish the reschedule. First we restore the non-volatile registers, then we disable interrupts and make a final check of `iDfcPendingFlag` and `iRescheduleNeededFlag`. We need to do this because interrupts have been enabled for most of the reschedule and these could either have queued an IDFC or expired the current thread's timeslice. Furthermore, the `iRescheduleNeededFlag` may have been set because of system lock contention during the processing of an address space change. In any case, if either of these flags is set, we loop right back to the beginning to run IDFCs and/or select a new thread. If neither of the flags is set, then we unlock the kernel and exit from the scheduler in the context of the new thread.

The scheduler always returns with interrupts disabled. We need to make sure of this to prevent unbounded stack usage because of repeated interrupts in the same thread. When an interrupt occurs, the kernel pushes the volatile registers (that is, those modified by a normal function call) onto the thread's supervisor stack before calling the scheduler. If interrupts were re-enabled between unlocking the kernel and popping these registers, another interrupt could occur and push the volatile registers again before causing another reschedule. And so it might continue, if interrupts were not disabled.

The algorithm and the explanation above apply to the moving memory model. The emulator and direct memory models do not do any address space switching, simplifying scheduling. The multiple memory model uses a simplified address space switching scheme, since switching is very fast. The multiple memory model scheduling algorithm becomes:

```
// Enter with kernel locked
// Active stack is supervisor stack of current thread
1   Disable interrupts
2   start_reschedule:
3   IF IDFCs pending (iDfcPendingFlag TRUE)
```

```
4   Run IDFCs (with interrupts enabled but kernel locked)
5   iDfcPendingFlag = FALSE
6   ENDIF
7   IF reschedule not needed (iRescheduleNeededFlag FALSE)
8   iKernCSLocked=0 (unlock the kernel)
9   Return
10  ENDIF
11  Reenable interrupts
12  Save non-volatile registers and CPU specific registers on stack
13  iCurrentThread->iSavedSP = current stack pointer
14  iRescheduleNeededFlag = FALSE
15  next_thread = first thread in highest priority non-empty ready
                                                               queue
16  IF next_thread->iTime==0 (ie timeslice expired)
17  IF another thread is ready at same priority as next_thread
18  IF next_thread holds a fast mutex
19  next_thread->iHeldFastMutex->iWaiting=TRUE
20  goto resched_end
21  ENDIF
22  next_thread->iTime=next_thread->iTimeslice (new timeslice)
23  next_thread=thread after next_thread in round-robin order
24  ENDIF
25  ENDIF
26  IF next_thread holds a fast mutex
27  IF next_thread holds system lock
28  goto resched_end
29  ELSE IF next_thread requires implicit system lock and system
                                                        lock held
30  next_thread->iHeldFastMutex->iWaiting=TRUE
31  goto resched_end
32  ENDIF
33  ENDIF
34  IF next_thread is blocked on a fast mutex
35  IF next_thread->iWaitFastMutex->iHoldingThread (mutex is still
                                                             locked)
36  next_thread=next_thread->iWaitFastMutex->iHoldingThread
37  goto resched_end
38  ENDIF
39  ENDIF
40  IF next_thread does not require implicit system lock
41  goto resched_end
42  ELSE IF system lock held by another thread
43  next_thread=system lock holding thread
44  system lock iWaiting = TRUE
45  ENDIF
46  resched_end:
47  iCurrentThread=next_thread
48  current stack pointer = next_thread->iSavedSP
49  switch_threads:
50  Restore CPU specific registers from stack
51  IF next_thread requires address space switch
52  Invoke address space switch handler (kernel still locked)
53  ENDIF
54  Restore nonvolatile registers from stack
55  Disable interrupts
56  IF IDFCs pending or another reschedule needed
57  goto start_resched
58  ENDIF
```

```
59  iKernCSLocked=0 (unlock the kernel)
60  Return with interrupts disabled
```

The main difference here is that we can invoke the address space switch handler with preemption disabled. This is because we can change address spaces in just a few assembly language instructions.

3.6.1   Scheduling of Symbian OS thread

As I said in the previous section, scheduling is the responsibility of the nanokernel, and the scheduler deals in nanothreads, not Symbian OS threads. Symbian OS only contributes to scheduling in the setting of thread priorities.

The Symbian OS thread class, DThread, has a member iThread-Priority. This specifies the priority in either absolute or process-relative form. Values between 0 and 63 inclusive represent absolute priorities (corresponding directly to nanokernel priorities) and negative values between −8 and −2 represent process-relative values (−1 is not used).

A call to the user-side API RThread::SetPriority() sets the iThreadPriority field using a value derived from the TThread-Priority argument that is passed to it. The kernel combines the iThreadPriority field with the process priority of the thread's owning process using a mapping table to produce the iDefaultPriority field. The following code shows how this is done.

Calculating Thread Priority

```
// Mapping table for thread+process priority to
// thread absolute priority

LOCAL_D const TUint8 ThreadPriorityTable[64] =
  {
//Idle MuchLess Less Normal More MuchMore RealTime
/*Low*/           1,  1,  2,  3,  4,  5, 22, 0,
/*Background*/    3,  5,  6,  7,  8,  9, 22, 0,
/*Foreground*/    3, 10, 11, 12, 13, 14, 22, 0,
/*High*/          3, 17, 18, 19, 20, 22, 23, 0,
/*SystemServer1*/ 9, 15, 16, 21, 24, 25, 28, 0,
/*SystemServer2*/ 9, 15, 16, 21, 24, 25, 28, 0,
/*SystemServer3*/ 9, 15, 16, 21, 24, 25, 28, 0,
/*RealTimeServer*/ 18, 26, 27, 28, 29, 30, 31, 0
  };

TInt DThread::CalcDefaultThreadPriority()
  {
  TInt r;
  TInt tp=iThreadPriority;
  if (tp>=0) // absolute thread priorities
    r=(tp<KNumPriorities)?tp:KNumPriorities-1;
  else
```

```
{
tp+=8;
if (tp<0)
    tp=0;
    TInt pp=iOwningProcess->iPriority; // proc priority 0-7
    TInt i=(pp<<3)+tp;
    // map thread+process priority to actual priority
    r=ThreadPriorityTable[i];
    return r;
    }
}
```

This `iDefaultPriority`, returned from `CalcDefaultThreadPriority()` is the actual scheduling priority used by the thread when it doesn't hold a Symbian OS mutex, and so it is not subject to priority inheritance.

What about when the thread does hold a mutex? As we saw in Section 3.3.5.1, the nanokernel priority of a Symbian OS thread is given by the maximum of its `iDefaultPriority` value and the maximum priority of any entry on the thread's cleanup queue. Some of the cleanup queue entries result from mutexes held by the thread and, as we saw, the kernel adjusts their priorities to provide priority inheritance.

3.6.2 Scheduling in the emulator

As we saw in Chapter 1, *Introducing EKA2*, the emulator uses the host OS (Win32) threads. This means that the nanokernel needs to provide its own scheduling mechanism as Windows does not provide the 64 priority levels we have in Symbian OS. (Win32 only really provides five usable distinct priorities within a process.)

To make this work, we cannot allow Windows to arbitrarily schedule Symbian OS threads to run. The nanokernel achieves this by only making one Symbian OS thread ready to run as a Win32 thread; all the others will either be waiting on a Win32 event object or suspended. A side effect of this policy is that all Symbian OS threads can have the same standard Win32 priority.

3.6.2.1 Disabling preemption

EKA2 provides two mechanisms to disable preemption and rescheduling:

1. Masking interrupts – disables interrupt dispatch and thus preemption

2. Locking the kernel – disables preemption and rescheduling.

The emulator only has to emulate the first of these, since the second uses the same implementation as the target mobile phone.

We provide the interrupt mask in the emulator using something similar to a Win32 critical section object. Unlike the `RCriticalSection` of Symbian OS, this is re-entrant, allowing a single thread to wait on a critical section multiple times. The key difference to the standard Win32 critical section is the ability to operate correctly on a multi-processor PC in conjunction with the emulator's "interrupt" mechanism.

We disable interrupts by entering this critical section. This is effective as "interrupts" must do the same, and so they are blocked until the thread that owns the critical section releases it (by restoring interrupts). Thus this also prevents a thread being preempted whilst it has masked interrupts, as desired.

3.6.2.2   TScheduler::Reschedule

The kernel lock is just a simple counter, rather than the Win32 critical section used in EKA1; this allows the emulator to hand over the lock between threads when rescheduling exactly as the target scheduler does. The result is that the scheduler code follows the same algorithm as the nanokernel with regards to:

- Disabling interrupts

- Running IDFCs

- Selecting a new thread

- Exiting the scheduler.

The major difference in scheduling is in the handover code between threads. Any Symbian OS thread which is not the current thread will either be waiting on a Win32 event object, the "reschedule lock", or suspended. Suspension is rare, and only occurs if the thread was preempted rather than voluntarily rescheduling. I discuss preemption in more detail in the next section; this section will concentrate on the normal case.

The handover from the old (executing) thread is usually done by signaling the new thread's reschedule lock and then waiting on the old one's lock. The new thread starts running from the same point in the code (because there is only one place where the waiting is done), the kernel is still locked and the algorithm continues as normal.

This is slightly different to the behavior on a real target phone. On the latter, there is no "waiting", as the thread state is saved to its stack before the new thread state is restored. The scheduler knows that there is only one true thread of execution in the CPU and just changes the register context to effect the switch. But in the emulator we have two "real" execution contexts (ours, and the new thread) and we need to give the impression that execution is being directly handed off from one to the other.

Note that blocked threads nearly always have the same functions at the top of the call stack, `SwitchThreads()` and `TScheduler::Reschedule()`.

Also note that this handover in the emulator works equally well when the new thread is the same as the old thread.

3.6.2.3 "Interrupts" and preemption

Interaction with the hardware in the emulator is always via the host OS. As a result, there are no real interrupts to handle in the emulator. Interaction with the host is always done using native threads, which make use of the host OS APIs for timer services, file I/O, UI and so on.

The emulator creates a number of Win32 threads to act as "event" or "interrupt" sources. These are not Symbian OS threads, therefore they are effectively unknown to the nanokernel scheduler. They run at a host priority above that of the Symbian OS threads to ensure that they respond to events immediately and cause preemption within the emulator.

The emulator provides two routines which act as the interrupt preamble and post-amble, `StartOfInterrupt()` and `EndOfInterrupt()`. The preamble routine, `StartOfInterrupt()`, disables interrupts and then suspends the host thread that is the current nanokernel thread. This ensures that the "interrupt" behaves like a real interrupt, executing while the current thread does nothing, even on multi-processor PCs. The post-amble routine, `EndOfInterrupt()`, does something similar to the ARM interrupt post-amble on a real phone – checking the kernel lock state and the need for a reschedule. If a reschedule is needed, the routine leaves the current thread suspended and causes a reschedule, otherwise it resumes the thread and enables interrupts again.

Unlike on a real phone, the end of interrupt function cannot cause the current thread to branch off to the scheduler because it is not safe to divert a Win32 thread from an arbitrary location – this can cause the entire host OS to hang. Instead we mark the current thread as preempted, leave it suspended, and signal another dedicated interrupt-rescheduler thread to do the reschedule on behalf of the preempted thread. This interrupt-rescheduler thread is a nanokernel thread that spends its entire life inside `TScheduler::Reschedule()` – it is not on the ready list and so the nanokernel never selects it to be run, but `EndOfInterrupt()` can wake it up when necessary to schedule the next thread.

When the nanokernel selects a preempted thread to run rather than signaling the reschedule lock, the emulator must resume the host thread. However, life is not that simple – there's more to do. On a phone, when the nanokernel schedules a thread, the kernel is locked. The kernel then makes a final check of the `iDfcPending` and `iRescheduleNeeded` flags before unlocking and resuming where it left off. In the emulator, if we merely resume the preempted thread, then we will just do the final item in that list, and miss out the checks. This means that the current thread must do the checks (restarting the reschedule if required) and unlock the kernel on behalf of the preempted thread. This makes the handover to a preempted thread rather more complex than it is on the mobile phone. The beauty of this method is that no side effects are apparent to users of the emulator. The Win32 version of the nanokernel has some pretty tricky code in it, but this ensures that the rest of the kernel just works – because it presents the same model as on real hardware.

3.6.2.4 Idling

In the emulator, there is no way to "idle the CPU" from the Symbian OS null (idle) thread and the obvious alternative – going round in an infinite loop – is not very nice to the PC!

The null thread calls `NThread::Idle()` to go into idle mode on both the emulator and a phone. On the emulator, this sets a flag to indicate that the emulator is idle, and then waits on the thread's reschedule lock. The `EndOfInterrupt()` function detects this state as a special case and instead of using the interrupt-rescheduler thread, it just wakes up the null thread. The null thread then reschedules. Next time the null thread is scheduled, it returns from `NThread::Idle()` and so behaves in a similar fashion to its counterpart on real phones.

3.7 Dynamically loaded libraries

I have talked about threads and processes; I will finish this chapter with a short discussion on dynamically loaded libraries, or DLLs. You can find more on this subject in Chapter 8, *Platform Security* and Chapter 10, *The Loader*.

3.7.1 The DLibrary class

The kernel creates a kernel-side library object (`DLibrary`) for every DLL that is explicitly loaded into a user process; that is, one that is the target of an `RLibrary::Load()` rather than one that is implicitly linked to by another executable. Library objects are specific to, and owned by, the process for which they were created; if two processes both load the same DLL, the kernel creates two separate `DLibrary` objects. A library has two main uses:

1. It represents a link from a process to the global code graph. Each process always has at least one such connection – the `DProcess::iCodeSeg` pointer. This pointer, set up by the kernel at

process load time, links each process to its own EXE code segment. DLibrary objects represent additional links to the code graph, created at run time.

2.   It provides a state machine to ensure that constructors and destructors for objects resident in .data and .bss sections are called correctly.

Libraries have two reference counts. One is the standard DObject reference count (since DLibrary derives from DObject); a non-zero value for this reference count simply stops the DLibrary itself being deleted – it does not stop the underlying code segment being deleted or removed from any process.

The second reference count (iMapCount) is the number of user references on the library, which is equal to the number of handles on the library opened by the process or by any of its threads. The kernel always updates this count with the CodeSegLock mutex held. When the last user handle is closed, iMapCount will reach zero and this triggers the calling of static destructors and the removal of the library code segment from the process address space.

The loader creates DLibrary objects on behalf of a client loading a DLL. A process may not have more than one DLibrary referring to the same code segment. If a process loads the same library twice, the kernel will open a second handle for it on the already existing DLibrary and its map count will be incremented.

A DLibrary object transitions through the following states during its life:

- ECreated – transient state in which object is created. Switches to ELoaded or EAttached when library and corresponding code segment are added to the target process

- ELoaded – code segment is loaded and attached to the target process but the kernel has not called static constructors

- EAttaching – the target process is currently running the code segment static constructors. Transitions to EAttached when constructors have completed

- EAttached – static constructors have completed and the code segment is fully available for use by the target process

- EDetachPending – the last user handle has been closed on the DLibrary but static destructors have not yet been called. Transitions to EDetaching just before running static destructors

- EDetaching – the target process is currently running the code segment static destructors. Transitions to ELoaded when destructors have completed.

Let's have a look at the `Dlibrary` class:

```
class DLibrary : public DObject
    {
public:
  enum TState
      {
      ECreated=0,          // initial state
      ELoaded=1,           // code segment loaded
      EAttaching=2,        // calling constructors
      EAttached=3,         // all constructors done
      EDetachPending=4,    // about to call destructors
      EDetaching=5,        // calling destructors
      };
public:
  static TInt New(DLibrary*& aLib, DProcess* aProcess,
                                   DCodeSeg* aSeg);
  DLibrary();
  void RemoveFromProcess();
  virtual ~DLibrary();
  virtual TInt Close(TAny* aPtr);
  virtual TInt AddToProcess(DProcess* aProcess);
  virtual void DoAppendName(TDes& aName);
public:
  TInt iMapCount;
  TUint8 iState;
  SDblQueLink iThreadLink; // attaches to opening/closing thread
  DCodeSeg* iCodeSeg;
  };
```

Key member data of DLibrary

`iMapCount`

Count of the number of times this library is mapped into the process; equal to the number of user handles the process and its threads have on this library.

`iState`

Records progress in calling user-side constructors or destructors during library loading and unloading.

`iThreadLink`

Doubly linked list field, which is used to attach the library to the thread that is running user-side constructors or destructors. This is needed to enable cleanup if the thread terminates while running one of these functions.

`iCodeSeg`

Pointer to the code segment to which this library refers.

3.7.2   Code segments

I mentioned that a library represents a link from a process to the global code graph, and that this link is held in the `iCodeSeg` pointer. This pointer denotes a kernel object known as a `DCodeSeg`.

A DCodeSeg is an object that represents the contents of an executable, relocated for particular code and data addresses. Executable programs (EXEs) or dynamically loaded libraries (DLLs), execute in place (XIP) or RAM-loaded – whatever the combination, the code is represented by a DCodeSeg.

On EKA1, EXEs and DLLs were handled separately and differently, which gave us problems when we came to load a DLL that linked back to an EXE.

Under EKA2, the unification of the support for loading code under the DCodeSeg has made matters much simpler. Multiple instances of the same process will use the same DCodeSeg unless a RAM-loaded fixed process needs different data addresses. Similarly, if a DLL is loaded into several processes, the same DCodeSeg is attached to all the processes (the code is shared), unless different data addresses are required. This happens when a RAM-loaded DLL with writable static data is then loaded into more than one fixed process, or into a combination of fixed and non-fixed processes.

I will discuss this in greater depth in Chapter 10, *The Loader*.

3.8 Summary

In this chapter I have talked about threads in the nanokernel, and Symbian OS threads, processes and libraries. Of course, these are fundamental operating system concepts, and you will find that they form an important basis for other parts of this book.

In the next chapter, I shall talk about some of the ways in which threads and processes can communicate with each other.

4

Inter-thread Communication

by Andrew Rogers and Jane Sales

Be not deceived: evil communications corrupt good manners.
1 Corinthians 15:33

In the last chapter, I introduced Symbian OS threads. Now I will go on to discuss some of the mechanisms that those threads can use to communicate with one another.

Symbian OS provides several such mechanisms, including shared I/O buffers, publish and subscribe, message queues and client-server. Each of the methods has its particular merits and restrictions. I will examine each of them in turn, discussing their implementation and the general class of problem each is intended to solve. Since the most widely used of these is the client-server mechanism used to communicate with system servers, I will start there.

4.1 Client-server ITC

Client-server is the original Symbian OS inter-thread communication (ITC) mechanism, having been present from the earliest implementations of EPOC32 in the Psion Series 5 right up to the latest mobile phones deployed on the secure platform of Symbian OS v9.

This mechanism allows a client to connect to a server using a unique, global name, establishing a "session" that provides the context for all further requests. Multiple sessions can be established to a server, both from within a single thread and from within multiple threads and processes. Clients queue messages in the kernel; the server then retrieves these messages and processes each in turn. When the processing of a request is finished, the server signals the client that its request is complete. The implementation of the client-server mechanism guarantees request completion, even under out-of-memory and server death conditions. The combination of a robust service request mechanism and a service provider guaranteed to be unique within the system was designed to make the client-server mechanism suitable for providing centralized and controlled access to system resources.

The managing of central resources using the client-server paradigm can be seen throughout Symbian OS, with all the major services provided by Symbian OS being implemented using this method. The file server (F32), the window server (WSERV), the telephony server (ETEL), the comms server (C32) and the socket server (ESOCK) are all examples of central resources managed by a server and accessed by a client interface to them.

However, my intention in this chapter is to give you the inner workings of client-server. It is not to teach you how to write your own server based on this framework, or to show you how to use any of the existing servers within Symbian OS. For that, please refer to a Symbian OS SDK or *Symbian OS Explained*.[1] Since this book focuses on EKA2, I will only discuss the newest version of client-server (IPCv2). I will summarize the differences from the legacy client-server framework (IPCv1) in a separate section at the end.

4.1.1   History

The design and architecture of the client-server system have evolved with the platform. In the original, pre-Symbian OS v6.0 implementation of client-server, a session was explicitly tied to the thread that had created it. In Symbian OS v6.0, we generalized the concept of a session from this very "client-centric" implementation by adding the concept of a "shared session" that could be used by all the threads within the process.

Though they appeared less client-centric in the user API, we implemented shared sessions within the kernel by creating objects tied to the session to represent each "share". The share managed per-thread resources for the session, including a handle to the client thread for the server. The handle from the share that corresponded to the thread that sent a given message was then passed in the message delivered to the server, so that when the server performed an operation to access a client's address space using a message handle, it was actually performed in the kernel using a handle associated with the client (in the share) rather than the message itself.

With the advent of a secure platform on EKA2, Symbian OS client-server has undergone a second evolution to an entirely "message-centric" architecture known as IPCv2. IPCv2 performs all accesses to memory in a client's address space using a handle that is explicitly associated with a message, rather than the client that sent it. This allows us to deprecate and then remove APIs that allow direct access to an arbitrary thread's address space with nothing more than a handle to that thread.

---

[1] *Symbian OS Explained: Effective C++ Programming for Smartphones*, by Jo Stichbury. Symbian Press.

Earlier versions of EKA2 supported the legacy client-server APIs (IPCv1), using a special category of handle values, which directly referred to kernel-side message objects. The kernel passed these back as the client thread handle in legacy messages. When the kernel detected the use of such a handle by legacy code during translation of a user-side handle to a kernel-side object, it located the corresponding kernel-side message object, extracted the client thread associated with that message, then used it to perform the requested operation. This legacy support was removed with the move to the secure Symbian OS v9.

Also, as part of the changes we made to implement a secure Symbian OS, we chose several categories of kernel-side objects to be able to be shared securely and anonymously between two separate processes. Handles to such "protected" objects may be passed between processes both by an extended "command line" API and via the client-server mechanism. We have extended the "command line" API to allow a parent to pass handles to its children, and we have extended the client-server mechanism to enable a message to be completed with a handle rather than a standard error code.

These "protected" objects can provide a mechanism for secure data transfer between processes. In particular, this new class of objects includes server sessions, so that a session to a server can be shared between two separate processes. This means that in EKA2 a new method of sharing a session has now become possible: global (inter-process) session sharing. An interesting range of features can be designed using this new paradigm. For example, secure sharing of protected files between processes can be accomplished using a shared file server session.

4.1.2   Design challenges

The design of the kernel-side client-server architecture that I will describe in more detail below is inherently a difficult matter. Even in the most basic of configurations, with only a single client thread communicating with a single-threaded server, there are several things that can happen concurrently:

- A client may send a message (asynchronously)

- A client may close a session

- Either the client or the server thread may die, resulting in kernel-side object cleanup being invoked

- A server thread may complete a message (in a multi-threaded server, possibly a different thread than the one owning the handle to the kernel-side server object)

- The server may close the handle to the kernel-side server object.

All of these actions require the state of kernel-side objects to be updated and, since these actions may execute concurrently and preempt one another, they need to be carefully synchronized to avoid corruption of the kernel data structures. To make this task as simple and efficient as possible, it was important that our design minimized the complexity of these objects, their states and the transitions needed to perform client-server communication.

Design simplicity was a key priority on EKA2. This was because, if the required synchronization (using the system lock) is not performed in a constant-order manner, unbounded delays can occur and there is no possibility of Symbian OS offering hard real-time guarantees. Also, care needs to be taken to allow the server itself to respond to messages it has received within bounded time limits, so that servers which offer real-time guarantees themselves can be created. To this end, we added support in IPCv2 for asynchronous session creation and destruction, allowing the server's RunL() duration to be small and bounded. In this way we have provided a platform on which, for example, guaranteed multimedia services can be offered.

However, the design of client-server on EKA2 is further complicated due to the need to provide a secure IPC architecture. This has meant adding checks that operations performed on a client's address space are valid and providing a mechanism whereby the identity of a server may be securely verified. It has also meant adding the ability for sessions to be shared so that requirements for a secure platform such as secure file sharing can be implemented using client-server.

I'll now describe both the new user-side architecture of IPCv2 and the kernel architecture that supports it.

4.1.3   User-side architecture – server

The key component in the user-side architecture is the server object itself. This is simply a standard active object,[2] queuing requests on an asynchronous service API provided by the kernel to retrieve messages sent to the server by its clients. On the completion of such a request (receiving a message), the server active object's RunL() usually dispatches the message to a session object which has been created to manage the connection between the server and its client.

Session objects manage the server-side resources associated with a session and are created by the server when a connect message is received from the client. In this case, the server's RunL() calls the virtual NewSessionL() which returns an instance of a CSession2derived class. You would implement the server active object by deriving from CServer2 and the session object by deriving from CSession2. The server-side architecture is shown in Figure 4.1 and CServer2 is implemented as follows:

---

[2] For a comprehensive explanation of the use of active objects in Symbian OS C++, consult *Symbian OS Explained* by Jo Stichbury, Symbian Press.

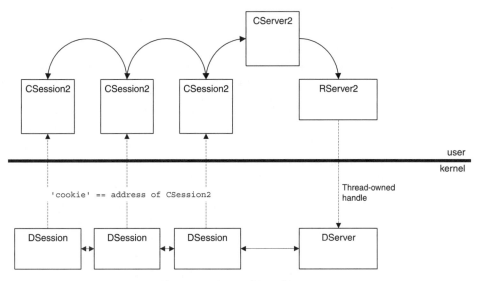

Figure 4.1   Server-side architecture

```
class CServer2 : public CActive
  {
public:
  enum TServerType
    {
    EUnsharableSessions = EIpcSession_Unsharable,
    ESharableSessions = EIpcSession_Sharable,
    EGlobalSharableSessions = EIpcSession_GlobalSharable,
    };
public:
  IMPORT_C virtual ~CServer2() =0;
  IMPORT_C TInt Start(const TDesC& aName);
  IMPORT_C void StartL(const TDesC& aName);
  IMPORT_C void ReStart();
  inline RServer2 Server() const { return iServer; }
protected:
  inline const RMessage2& Message() const;
  IMPORT_C CServer2(TInt aPriority,
                        TServerType aType=EUnsharableSessions);
  IMPORT_C void DoCancel();
  IMPORT_C void RunL();
  IMPORT_C TInt RunError(TInt aError);
  IMPORT_C virtual void DoConnect(const RMessage2& aMessage);
private:
  IMPORT_C virtual CSession2* NewSessionL(const TVersion& aVersion,
                              const RMessage2& aMessage) const =0;
private:
  TInt iSessionType;
  RServer2 iServer;
  RMessage2 iMessage;
  TDblQue<CSession2> iSessionQ;
protected:
  TDblQueIter<CSession2> iSessionIter;
  };
```

The server keeps track of the current message it is processing (`iMessage`) and manages a queue of the session objects so they can be cleaned up during the destruction of the server (`iSessionQ`).

Upon reception of a (session) connect message, the server calls `NewSessionL()` to create a new `CSession2`-derived session object and then appends the new session object to the end of the server queue. Finally, the server uses the connect message to pass a "cookie" (in the form of the address of the newly-created session object) to the kernel, which the kernel can then use to identify the particular session a given message is associated with.

The server implementation can over-ride `DoConnect()` in order to provide asynchronous session creation. It works in a similar way to the method I described in the previous paragraph, except that the memory allocation for the new session is performed in a separate thread and the connect message is completed asynchronously, rather than after a (potentially long) synchronous wait in `DoConnect()`. The separate thread will simply consist of a base call to `DoConnect()` as there is no public API to perform the actions of `DoConnect()` separately, such as setting the session's "cookie".

Your `CServer2`-derived server active object uses an instance of the private class `RServer2` – which holds a handle to the equivalent kernel-side server object, `DServer` – to receive messages from the kernel. The handle to the kernel-side kernel object, contained in the `iServer` member, remains open throughout the lifetime of the server object and is `Close()`d in its destructor.

The server active object receives messages from the kernel by queuing a request on the `RServer2`. This is done automatically for you in `Start()` after the kernel-side server object has been successfully created. A request is also automatically requeued after processing a message in the server's `RunL()`. The request to receive another message from the kernel is canceled in the server object's `DoCancel()` and the server active object `Cancel()`s itself in its destructor, as with any other active object.

The kernel-side (`DServer`) object is created via a call to `Start()` on your `CServer2`-derived object and the level of session sharability the server will support, as enumerated in `CServer2::TServerType`, is determined at this time. You specify the level of sharability a given session actually has when a client calls `RSessionBase::CreateSession()`. The sharability of a new session is opaque to the server itself, which will only know that a new session has been created. Therefore it is the kernel's responsibility to police sharability – both when creating new sessions and also when opening handles to existing ones.

`CSession2`, from which you derive session objects used to manage per-session resources in your server, is shown below:

```
class CSession2 : public CBase
    {
    friend class CServer2;
public:
    IMPORT_C virtual ~CSession2() =0;
private:
    IMPORT_C virtual void CreateL(); // Default method, does nothing
public:
    inline const CServer2* Server() const;
    IMPORT_C void ResourceCountMarkStart();
    IMPORT_C void ResourceCountMarkEnd(const RMessage2& aMessage);
    IMPORT_C virtual TInt CountResources();
    virtual void ServiceL(const RMessage2& aMessage) =0;
    IMPORT_C virtual void ServiceError(const RMessage2& aMessage,
                                                   TInt aError);
protected:
    IMPORT_C CSession2();
    IMPORT_C virtual void Disconnect(const RMessage2& aMessage);
private:
    TInt iResourceCountMark;
    TDblQueLink iLink;
    const CServer2* iServer;
    };
```

The heart of the session object is the ServiceL() method. On reception of a message, the server uses the cookie the kernel returns to it as a pointer to a session object and then passes the message to that session by calling ServiceL(). The session class will then perform appropriate actions to fulfill the request contained in the message and at some future point the message will be completed to signal the completion of the request to the client.

The virtual method Disconnect() is used to allow the session to implement asynchronous session deletion in a similar manner to that described for asynchronous session creation using CServer2::DoConnect().

The server can access the kernel-side message objects using RMessagePtr2, which encapsulates both the handle to the message object and descriptor APIs for accessing the client's memory space using the message. A small number of APIs to allow manipulation of the client thread are available to allow the server to enforce certain behavior of its client, for example, enforcing that the client passes certain parameters by panicking it if it presents a message containing invalid values. Finally, RMessagePtr2 also presents APIs that allow the security attributes of the client to be examined and checked against predetermined security policies. The security of these APIs is ensured as the kernel verifies that the thread using them has a valid handle to a kernel message object.

The client constructs a message for a particular session by specifying a "function number" to identify the operation that is being requested and optionally up to four message parameters. These parameters may be either plain integers, pointers or may be descriptors that the server will then be able to use to access the client's address space. Using templated argument types and an overloaded function that maps argument types to a bitfield, the class `TIpcArgs` (which is used to marshall message arguments in IPCv2) generates a bit mask at compile time which describes the types of its arguments.

This bit mask is stored in the kernel-side message object. This allows the kernel to check whether operations requested by the server using the message are correct – for example, checking the source and target descriptors are either both 8-bit or both 16-bit descriptors. It also allows the kernel to check that the requested operation is permitted by the client, for example by checking that when the server requests to write to a client descriptor, the client descriptor is `TDes`-derived (modifiable) rather than `TDesC`-derived (constant).

You should beware that though you can still pass pointers in IPCv2, there are no longer any APIs to directly access memory in another thread's address space using an arbitrary pointer and a handle to the thread as this is inherently insecure. The ability to pass a pointer between a client and server is therefore only of any value when the client and server are within the same process. In this case, the use of a pointer is obviously not limited to pointing to a descriptor, but may also be used to point to an arbitrary data structure containing information to be shared between the client and server:

```
class RMessagePtr2
    {
public:
  inline RMessagePtr2();
  inline TBool IsNull();
  inline TInt Handle();
#ifndef __KERNEL_MODE__
  inline TBool ClientDataCaging();
  IMPORT_C void Complete(TInt aReason);
  IMPORT_C void Complete(RHandleBase aHandle);
  IMPORT_C TInt GetDesLength(TInt aParam);
  IMPORT_C TInt GetDesLengthL(TInt aParam);
  IMPORT_C TInt GetDesMaxLength(TInt aParam);
  IMPORT_C TInt GetDesMaxLengthL(TInt aParam);
  IMPORT_C void ReadL(TInt aParam,TDes8& aDes,TInt aOffset=0);
  IMPORT_C void ReadL(TInt aParam,TDes16 &aDes,TInt aOffset=0);
  IMPORT_C void WriteL(TInt aParam,const TDesC8& aDes,TInt aOffset=0);
  IMPORT_C void WriteL(TInt aParam,const TDesC16& aDes,TInt aOffset=0);
  IMPORT_C TInt Read(TInt aParam,TDes8& aDes,TInt aOffset=0);
  IMPORT_C TInt Read(TInt aParam,TDes16 &aDes,TInt aOffset=0);
  IMPORT_C TInt Write(TInt aParam,const TDesC8& aDes,TInt aOffset=0);
  IMPORT_C TInt Write(TInt aParam,const TDesC16& aDes,TInt aOffset=0);
  IMPORT_C void Panic(const TDesC& aCategory,TInt aReason);
  IMPORT_C void Kill(TInt aReason);
  IMPORT_C void Terminate(TInt aReason);
  IMPORT_C TInt SetProcessPriority(TProcessPriority aPriority);
```

```
  inline    void SetProcessPriorityL(TProcessPriority aPriority);
  IMPORT_C TInt Client(RThread& aClient,
                         TOwnerType aOwnerType=EOwnerProcess);
  inline    void ClientL(RThread& aClient,
                         TOwnerType aOwnerType=EOwnerProcess);
  IMPORT_C TUint ClientProcessFlags();
  IMPORT_C TSecureId SecureId();
  IMPORT_C TVendorId VendorId();
  inline TBool HasCapability(TCapability aCapability,
                             const char* aDiagnostic=0);
  inline void HasCapabilityL(TCapability aCapability,
                             const char* aDiagnosticMessage=0);
  inline TBool HasCapability(TCapability aCapability1,
              TCapability aCapability2, const char* aDiagnostic=0);
  inline void HasCapabilityL(TCapability aCapability1,
         TCapability aCapability2, const char* aDiagnosticMessage=0);
  inline TUid Identity() const { return SecureId(); }
#endif
protected:
  TInt iHandle;
  };

inline TBool operator==(RMessagePtr2 aLeft,RMessagePtr2 aRight);
inline TBool operator!=(RMessagePtr2 aLeft,RMessagePtr2 aRight);
```

RMessage2 expands the API provided by RMessagePtr2 by bringing a copy of the message arguments and the cookie (CSession2 pointer) stored in the kernel over into user space, allowing access to both. RMessage2 also contains a number of spare words that do not correspond to data stored in the kernel. One of these, iFlags, is used to provide the "Authorised()" APIs which are used by a utility server base class, CPolicyServer, which allows simple implementation of a server that validates given security policies upon session creation and reception of each message. For full details of CPolicyServer and its use, refer to a recent Symbian OS SDK.

```
class RMessage2 : public RMessagePtr2
  {
  friend class CServer2;
public:
  enum TsessionMessages
    {
    EConnect=-1,
    EDisConnect=-2
    };
public:
  inline RMessage2();
#ifndef __KERNEL_MODE__
  IMPORT_C explicit RMessage2(const RMessagePtr2& aPtr);
  void SetAuthorised() const;
  void ClearAuthorised() const;
  TBool Authorised() const;
#endif
```

```
  inline TInt Function() const;
  inline TInt Int0() const;
  inline TInt Int1() const;
  inline TInt Int2() const;
  inline TInt Int3() const;
  inline const TAny* Ptr0() const;
  inline const TAny* Ptr1() const;
  inline const TAny* Ptr2() const;
  inline const TAny* Ptr3() const;
  inline CSession2* Session() const;
protected:
  TInt iFunction;
  TInt iArgs[KMaxMessageArguments];
private:
  TInt iSpare1;
protected:
  const TAny* iSessionPtr;
private:
  mutable TInt iFlags; // Currently only used for *Authorised above
  TInt iSpare3;        // Reserved for future use
  friend class RMessage;
  };
```

4.1.4   User-side architecture – client

The client-side architecture is shown in Figure 4.2.

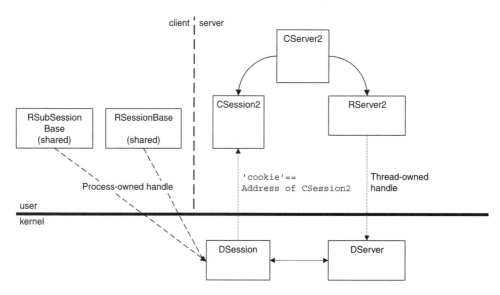

Figure 4.2   Client-side architecture

The remainder of the user-side support for client-server consists of two client base classes, one for sessions and another for sub-sessions. The session class is RSessionBase, as follows:

```
class RSessionBase : public RHandleBase
    {
    friend class RSubSessionBase;
public:
    enum TAttachMode
        {
        EExplicitAttach,
        EAutoAttach
        };
public:
    inline TInt ShareAuto()        { return DoShare(EAutoAttach); }
    inline TInt ShareProtected()
        { return DoShare(EAutoAttach|KCreateProtectedObject); }
    IMPORT_C TInt Open(RMessagePtr2 aMessage,TInt aParam,
                                        TOwnerType aType=EOwnerProcess);
    IMPORT_C TInt Open(RMessagePtr2 aMessage,TInt aParam,
        const TSecurityPolicy& aServerPolicy, TOwnerType aType=EOwnerProcess);
    IMPORT_C TInt Open(TInt aArgumentIndex, TOwnerType aType=EOwnerProcess);
protected:
    IMPORT_C TInt Open(TInt aArgumentIndex,
        const TSecurityPolicy& aServerPolicy, TOwnerType aType=EOwnerProcess);
    inline TInt CreateSession(const TDesC& aServer,
                        const TVersion& aVersion);
    IMPORT_C TInt CreateSession(const TDesC& aServer,
        const TVersion& aVersion,TInt aAsyncMessageSlots);
    IMPORT_C TInt CreateSession(const TDesC& aServer,
            const TVersion& aVersion,TInt aAsyncMessageSlots,
            TIpcSessionType aType,const TSecurityPolicy* aPolicy=0,
            TRequestStatus* aStatus=0);
    inline TInt CreateSession(RServer2 aServer,const TVersion& aVersion);
    IMPORT_C TInt CreateSession(RServer2 aServer,const TVersion& aVersion,
                                TInt aAsyncMessageSlots);
    IMPORT_C TInt CreateSession(RServer2 aServer,const TVersion& aVersion,
            TInt aAsyncMessageSlots,TIpcSessionType aType,
            const TSecurityPolicy* aPolicy=0, TRequestStatus* aStatus=0);
    inline TInt Send(TInt aFunction,const TIpcArgs& aArgs) const;
    inline void SendReceive(TInt aFunction,const TIpcArgs& aArgs,
                                        TRequestStatus& aStatus) const;
    inline TInt SendReceive(TInt aFunction,const TIpcArgs& aArgs) const;
    inline TInt Send(TInt aFunction) const;
    inline void SendReceive(TInt aFunction,TRequestStatus& aStatus) const;
    inline TInt SendReceive(TInt aFunction) const;
private:
    TInt SendAsync(TInt aFunction,const TIpcArgs* aArgs,
                                        TRequestStatus* aStatus) const;
    TInt SendSync(TInt aFunction,const TIpcArgs* aArgs) const;
    IMPORT_C TInt DoShare(TInt aAttachMode);
    TInt DoConnect(const TVersion &aVersion,TRequestStatus* aStatus);
    };
```

Sub-sessions are simply a lightweight wrapper over the functionality of session objects, as already described above. They are useful because it is often the case that clients wish to use multiple instances of an API that would otherwise be associated with the session, for example a client might wish to have multiple instances of the file API from the file server. Sessions are relatively heavyweight in terms of the kernel overhead associated with them, so rather than insist that a new session be created to support such paradigms, we provide a simple mechanism for multiplexing multiple "sub-sessions" over a single session in the RSubSessionBase class.

You enable sub-session creation by specifying a specific function that the server will use to create resources required to manage the sub-session. As well as this, the sub-session creation function generates a "sub-session cookie" that RSubSessionBase then stores, which is automatically passed as the fourth argument of any future messages to that session. (This leaves only three parameters for use by the sub-session requests.) When a session object receives a request that it recognizes as being for a sub-session, it uses the cookie in the fourth argument to identify the sub-session and then processes the message accordingly. You should note that the sub-session cookie is only shared by the client and server and is opaque to the kernel, which sees it as any other message parameter. For example, requests to the RFile API appear to the kernel as identical to requests to the file server session API, RFs, of which it is a sub-session.

From the following declaration of RSubSessionBase, it can be seen that it is simply a wrapper around the RSessionBase API implemented using a private RSessionBase member and a copy of the sub-session cookie used to identify the sub-session to the server:

```
class RSubSessionBase
   {
public:
  inline TInt SubSessionHandle() const;
protected:
  inline RSubSessionBase();
  IMPORT_C const RSessionBase Session() const;
  inline TInt CreateSubSession(const RSessionBase& aSession,
                      TInt aFunction,const TIpcArgs& aArgs);
  inline TInt CreateSubSession(const RSessionBase& aSession,
                                     TInt aFunction);
  IMPORT_C TInt CreateAutoCloseSubSession(RSessionBase& aSession,
                       TInt aFunction,const TIpcArgs& aArgs);
  IMPORT_C void CloseSubSession(TInt aFunction);
  inline TInt Send(TInt aFunction,const TIpcArgs& aArgs) const;
  inline void SendReceive(TInt aFunction,const TIpcArgs& aArgs,
                             TRequestStatus& aStatus) const;
  inline TInt SendReceive(TInt aFunction,const TIpcArgs& aArgs) const;
  inline TInt Send(TInt aFunction) const;
  inline void SendReceive(TInt aFunction,TRequestStatus& aStatus) const;
  inline TInt SendReceive(TInt aFunction) const;
private:
  RSessionBase iSession;
  TInt iSubSessionHandle;
  };
```

Note that because a thread blocks on the synchronous API, only one synchronous server message may be sent by a thread at a time. This allows a significant optimization in the allocation of kernel-side memory used to hold messages.

The session and sub-session creation functions have new overloads in IPCv2 that allow the session to be created asynchronously, so the server cannot maliciously block the client whilst connecting to it.

The other methods of note in `RSessionBase` are the `ShareXxx()` methods. Previously, in EKA1, a session could only be created in a non-shared state. If sharing was required, then the client had to explicitly call `Share()` (not present in IPCv2) or `ShareAuto()` to create a process-relative session handle. A similar method has been added in EKA2 to explicitly create a process-relative handle that is also "protected" and may be passed to another process – `ShareProtected()`.

However, creating a duplicate handle is an expensive operation, so we have now provided a new overload of `RSessionBase::Create-Session()` which allows the sharability of the session to be determined from the creation of the session, thereby avoiding the need to perform the expensive handle duplication operation. This then is the preferred and recommended way of creating a shared session on EKA2. Before a client in a separate thread or process can use a given session, the session must either be created with the required level of sharability or a call to a `ShareXxx()` method must be made before the separate thread or process sends any messages to the session, or a panic will occur in the client.

If the return value from a client call to `RSessionBase::Create-Session()` indicates that the server is not running, then the client DLL may wish to launch the server process itself and then make another attempt to create a session with the server. When doing this, the client code needs to be able to detect whether and when the server has started up successfully. To do this in the past, the client had to pass a structure containing its thread ID and a pointer to a request status object in its address space to the server via the server's command line. The server would then use this structure to signal successful startup to the client using `RThread::RequestComplete()`. The introduction of thread and process rendezvous, as described in Section 3.3.6, removes the need for this mechanism and simplifies server startup code considerably.

4.1.5   Kernel-side architecture

4.1.5.1   Server – queue management

The kernel-side architecture reflects the structure of the user-side client-server architecture it is designed to support. The first kernel-side object I'll discuss is the server object, corresponding to the `RServer2` handle held by the server process. The kernel-side server object has two purposes:

- To ensure the uniqueness of the user-mode server within the system
- To provide a FIFO queue of messages to be delivered to the server thread. A client may deliver messages to the server at any time, but the server thread only receives the messages one at a time as it sequentially requests them from the kernel.

The first requirement is easy to achieve: during server creation the kernel adds the server object being added to a global object container for servers. As I will show in the next chapter, object containers mandate the uniqueness of names within them. Also, another check is performed at server creation: the server may only specify a name beginning with "!" if the server has the ProtServ capability. This allows the client to be certain that servers with names beginning with "!" have not been spoofed by some other malicious code.

To fulfill the second requirement, server objects use the state machine shown in Figure 4.3 to manage their FIFO queue of messages.

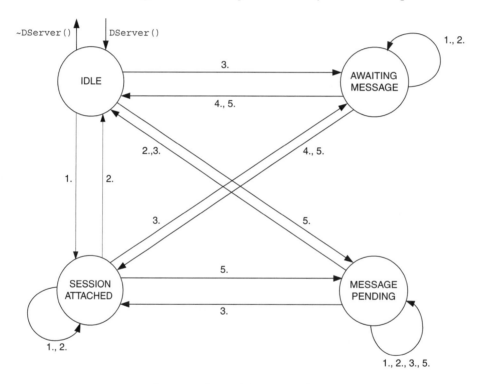

Figure 4.3　Server object state machine

The labeled state transitions listed below are executed under the protection of the system lock, to maintain state integrity. Each of these transitions is designed to hold the system lock for constant execution time. This maintains the real-time characteristics of the kernel as there will always be a maximum, constant time for which the system lock will be held before being released:

1.　`DSession::Add()`

2.　`DSession::Detach()`

3. `DServer::Receive()`

4. `DServer::Cancel()`,
   `DServer::Close()` [when closing last reference]

5. `DServer::Deliver()`

The states in the above transition diagram are defined as follows:

	Session queue	Message queue	[User] Server request status
IDLE	Empty	Empty	NULL
SESSION ATTACHED	Non-empty	Empty	NULL
AWAITING MESSAGE	Don't care	Empty	Non-NULL
MESSAGE PENDING	Don't care	Non-empty	NULL

The implementation of this state machine can be seen in the methods and members of the `DServer` class:

```
class DServer : public DObject
  {
public:
  DServer();
  virtual ~DServer();
  virtual TInt Close(TAny*);
  virtual TInt RequestUserHandle(DThread* aThread, TOwnerType aType);

  // aMessage bit 0 = 0 -> RMessage, bit 0 = 1 -> RMessage2
  void Receive(TRequestStatus& aStatus, TAny* aMessage);
  void Cancel();
  void Accept(RMessageK* aMsg);
  void Deliver(RMessageK* aMsg);
public:
  inline TBool IsClosing();
public:
  DThread* iOwningThread; // thread which receives messages
  TAny* iMsgDest; // where to deliver messages
  TRequestStatus* iStatus; // completed to signal message arrival
  SDblQue iSessionQ; // list of sessions
  SDblQue iDeliveredQ; // messages delivered but not yet accepted
  TUint8  iSessionType; // TIpcSessionType
  };
```

The server object itself is created by `ExecHandler::ServerCreate()`, called (indirectly via `RServer2`) from `CServer2::Start()`. Once `ExecHandler::ServerCreate()` has created the kernel-side server object, it opens a handle on the current (server) thread, so the pointer to the server thread (`iOwningThread`) is always valid.

This is required because a process-relative handle may be created to the server object by any thread in the server's process, using `Dupli-cate()` and hence the server objects may be held open after the server thread terminates. The first handle to the server object that is created and subsequently vested within the `RServer2` will be a process-relative handle if the server is anonymous (that is, has a zero-length name) and thread-relative otherwise. To exercise control over the use of `Dupli-cate()`, `DServer` over-rides `DObject`'s `RequestUserHandle()` method, which is called whenever a user-mode thread wishes to create a handle to an object. `DServer` enforces the policy that handles to it may only be created within the server's process. The server object then closes the reference to the server thread in its destructor, so the thread object will only ever be safely destroyed after the server object has finished using it.

`DServer::Receive()` and `DServer::Cancel()` provide the kernel-side implementation of the private `RServer2` API used to retrieve messages for the server. These receive and cancel functions provide an API for an asynchronous request to de-queue the message at the head of the FIFO queue. After de-queuing a message, the request is completed on the server thread. If a message is present in the server's queue when the request is made, this operation is performed immediately. Otherwise no action is taken and the next message delivered to the `DServer` object is used to immediately complete this request, rather than being placed on the server's queue.

The server thread may choose to block until a message is available (for example, using `User::WaitForRequest()`) or may use another method to wait for the request completion. In the case of a standard Symbian OS server, the `CServer2`-derived class is an active object and uses the active scheduler as a mechanism to wait for the request for the next message to be completed.

The procedure of writing a message to the server process's address space and signaling it to notify it of the completion of its request for a message is known as "accepting" a message. `DServer::Deliver()` is the client thread's API to deliver a message to the server's message queue. Both `DServer::Receive()` and `DServer::Deliver()` will accept a message immediately, where appropriate. These methods both call a common subroutine `DServer::Accept()`, which contains the code to accept a message. It updates the message's state to reflect the fact the server has accepted its delivery before writing the message to the server's address space and finally signaling the server's request status to indicate completion of its request.

The kernel-side message object (`RMessageK`) is converted into the correct format for user-side message object by using a utility classes whose structure mirrors `RMessage2`:

```
class RMessageU2
    {
public:
    inline RMessageU2(const RMessageK& a);
public:
    TInt iHandle;
    TInt iFunction;
    TInt iArgs[KMaxMessageArguments];
    TUint32 iSpare1;
    const TAny* iSessionPtr;
    };
```

Note that the iSpare1 member of RMessageU2 is simply zeroed by the kernel when writing the message to the user (that is, the server thread), but the other "unused" members of RMessage2 will not be overwritten by the kernel when it writes a message to user-space. A separate structure is used here as the format of RMessageK is private to the kernel itself and this class therefore provides translation between the internal message format used by the kernel and the public message format of RMessage2 used by user-side code.

Most of the methods mentioned above can be written to hold the system lock for a constant time with relative ease as they encompass tasks such as adding to or removing from a doubly linked list, updating state and performing a fast write of a small amount of data. However, when the DServer object is closed for the last time in DServer::Close(), the session list has to be iterated to detach all the sessions still attached to the server. This must be done under the protection of the system lock so that the server's state is updated in a consistent manner. As there are an arbitrary number of sessions to detach, this operation has an execution time linearly proportional to the number of sessions, as opposed to a constant execution time.

This operation is therefore carefully split up into *n* separate operations, each of which only hold the system lock for a constant time and each of which leave the data structures in a consistent state. DServer::Close() acquires the system lock before detaching each session by calling DSession::Detach(), which will release the lock before returning. DSession::Detach() is an operation made up of freeing an arbitrary number of uncompleted messages that have been sent by that session to the server. Again, this operation is split up by acquiring the system lock before freeing each message and then releasing it again afterwards, so the system lock is never held for more than a constant, bounded time whilst one message is freed or one session is removed from the server's queue.

To achieve the consistency required whilst splitting up these operations, the fact that a server or session is closing (iAccessCount is 0) is used to restrict what actions may occur. For example, new sessions cannot be attached to a server whilst it is closing and messages cannot be completed whilst a session is closing.

4.1.5.2   Sessions – delivery and message pool management

In the previous section, I described how sessions provide the context for communication between the client and server. Specifically, the kernel session objects manage the delivery of messages to the server and ensure message completion, even under out-of-memory conditions. They also manage user-mode access to a session, as specified by the session's "sharability".

To ensure message completion, the session object maintains a queue of message objects distinct from that of the server. This queue also includes messages sent by the session that have not yet been completed by the server. The interaction of this queue with both the lifetime of the client and the server is controlled via the state machine shown in Figure 4.4.

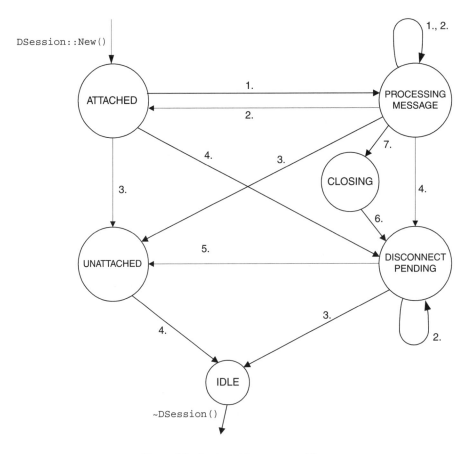

Figure 4.4   Session object state machine

Again, the labeled state transitions listed below are executed under the protection of the system lock to maintain state integrity. These transitions are also designed to hold the system lock for a constant execution time, in order to maintain the real-time characteristics of the kernel:

1. `DSession::Send()`

2. `ExecHandler::MessageComplete()`

3. `DSession::Detach()`

4. `DSession::Close()` [when closing last reference]
   [no connect message pending or not accepted by server]

5. `DSession::CloseFromDisconnect()`

6. `ExecHandler::SetSessionPtr()`

7. `DSession::Close()` [when closing last reference]
   [connect message pending and accepted by server]

The states in Figure 4.4 are defined like this:

	Server queue (of sessions)	Client references	Message queue
ATTACHED	Queued	Open	Empty
PROCESSING MESSAGE	Queued	Open	Non-empty
CLOSING	Queued	Closed	Non-empty, contains connect msg.
DISCONNECT PENDING	Queued	Closed	Non-empty
UNATTACHED	De-queued	Open	Empty
IDLE	De-queued	Closed	Empty

The implementation of `DSession` to support this is as follows:

```
class DSession : public DObject
   {
public:
  DSession();
  virtual ~DSession();
  virtual TInt Close(TAny*);
  virtual TInt RequestUserHandle(DThread* aThread, TOwnerType aType);
```

```
  void Detach(TInt aReason);
  RMessageK* GetNextFreeMessage();
  RMessageK* ExpandGlobalPool();
  void CloseFromDisconnect();
  static TInt New(DSession*& aS, TInt aMsgSlots, TInt aMode);
  TInt Add(DServer* aSvr, const TSecurityPolicy* aSecurityPolicy);
  TInt MakeHandle();
  TInt Send(TInt aFunction, const TInt* aPtr, TRequestStatus* aStatus);
  TInt SendSync(TInt aFunction, const TInt* aPtr,
                                        TRequestStatus* aStatus);
  TInt Send(RMessageK* aMsg, TInt aFunction, const TInt* aPtr,
                                        TRequestStatus* aStatus);
public:
  inline TBool IsClosing();
public:
  DServer* iServer;    // pointer to kernel-side server object
  SDblQueLink iServerLink; // link to attach session to server
  const TAny* iSessionPtr;
  // pointer to server-side CSession2 (user cookie)
  TUint16 iTotalAccessCount;
  TUint8 iSessionType; // TIpcSessionType
  TUint8 iSvrSessionType;// TIpcSessionType
  TInt iMsgCount;
  // total number of outstanding messages on this session
  TInt iMsgLimit;
  // max number of outstanding messages on this session
  SDblQue iMsgQ;
  // q of outstanding msgs on this session (by iSessionLink)
  RMessageK* iNextFreeMessage; // pointer to next free message in
                               // per-session message pool, if any
  RMessageK* iPool; // pointer to per-session message pool, if any
  RMessageK* iConnectMsg; // pointer to connect msg, if any
  RMessageKBase iDisconnectMsg; // vestigial disconnect message
  };
```

The session is a standard kernel reference-counted object that user-mode clients hold references to via handles (I'll discuss this mechanism in the next chapter, *Kernel Services*). However, the lifetime of the session must extend beyond that given by client handles, because it needs to stay in existence whilst the server processes the disconnect message that is sent to the server when a session is closed. To do this, we use iTotalAccessCount, modified under the protection of the system lock, to keep track of both whether there are any client references and when the session is attached to a server, giving it a count of 1 for either, or 2 for both. The **IDLE** state is equivalent to iTotalAccessCount reaching 0.

The creation of a session is performed as two distinct operations in two separate executive calls by the client – firstly the creation of the kernel-side session object itself and secondly the sending of the connect message to the server. The second part of this operation is identical to sending any other message to a server. However, since both a client can connect asynchronously and the server can create a session asynchronously it is now possible for a client to close its handle to the session before the session object has been created in the server.

Normally, closing the last handle to the session would result in a disconnect message being immediately delivered to the server, but if this were done in this case the disconnect message could be accepted by the server, and would contain a null cookie as the session object had not yet been created. There would then be a race between the server setting the cookie after creating the session object and it completing the disconnect request. If the disconnect message is completed first, the kernel-side session object is no longer valid when the server tries to set the cookie using the connect message and it will be panicked. Otherwise, if the session cookie is set first, then the disconnect message will complete as a no-op, since the cookie within it is null, and a session object is leaked in the server.

To avoid either of these situations, we have introduced the **CLOSING** state. If a connect message has been delivered but not yet completed when the last user handle to the session is closed, the delivery of the disconnect message to the server is delayed until the session cookie is updated to indicate successful creation of a user-side session object. If the connect message completes without the cookie having been updated, there is no user-side session object to clean up but a disconnect message is still sent to ensure the lifetime of the session object extends until the completion of other messages which may have been sent to the unconnected session. If there is an undelivered connect message, this is immediately removed from the queue to avoid the possibility of an orphan session object being created.

Note that the ability to create process-relative session handles and the asynchronous nature of sending a connect message mean that you can send other messages to a server both before and after a connect message has been sent, and before the connect message has been completed, so care must be taken over this possibility. However, when a disconnect message is sent no more messages may be sent to the session by virtue of the fact that it is sent once all user-side handles to the session have been closed. Therefore the disconnect message is always the last message to a session that is completed by the server and the session object may be safely destroyed after completing it, without causing lifetime issues for the server.

There are two methods to send synchronous and asynchronous messages – SendSync() and Send() (first overload above), respectively. These validate certain preconditions, select an appropriate message object to store the new message, and then pass the selected message object to this method:

```
Send(RMessageK* aMsg, TInt aFunction, const TInt* aPtr,
                    TRequestStatus* aStatus);
```

This method populates the message object, increments the current thread's IPC count (DThread::iIpcCount), adds the message to the session's queue and delivers it to the server. If the server has terminated, or is in the process of doing so, sending the message fails immediately.

Neither Send() method permits the sending of a disconnect message, since this is sent automatically by DSession::Close() when the last client session handle is closed.

At the other end of a normal message's life, it is completed in ExecHandler::MessageComplete() (called from RMessage-Ptr2::Complete()). If the message is a disconnect message, then execution is simply transferred to DSession::CloseFromDisconnect(). If not, then what happens next is pretty much the reverse of the send procedure: the message is removed from the session queue, the sending thread's IPC count is decremented and the client thread's request is completed. The only exception to this is if the session is closing; this happens if the client has closed all handles to the session but the disconnect message has not yet been completed by the server. In this case the client thread's request is not completed.

Messages can also be completed from DSession::Detach(), which is called either when the server terminates (that is, when the last reference to the server is closed in DServer::Close()) or when completing a disconnect message. In this case, the message is again removed from the session queue, the sending thread's IPC count decremented and the client request is completed (if the session is not closing).

We have just seen that it is possible for a message not to be completed – this happens when the session is closing, as we saw above. And yet previously I said that guaranteed message completion is one of the properties of the client-server system. The explanation here is that the client having an outstanding message when calling Close() on a session is considered to be a client-side programming error. There is clearly a race between the server completing such outstanding asynchronous requests and the disconnect request being processed. Those requests processed after the session has been closed cannot be completed whereas those before can, so the behavior of client-server has always been undefined by Symbian in this situation.

The actual behavior of EKA2 differs from EKA1 here. In EKA1, disconnect messages overtake all undelivered messages to the server and these undelivered messages are discarded. Now, in EKA2, the server processes all delivered messages before processing the disconnect message – although, as we've seen, such messages can still not be completed to the client. All this said, we don't advise you to rely on this new behavior of EKA2, because we explicitly state this to be a programming error and may change the behavior of this area in future.

One of the other main functions of the session object is to control the session's "sharability". With the advent of a fully message-centric design, there is no requirement for the session to hold a handle to the client thread, and providing different levels of accessibility to a session – restricted to one thread, restricted to one process or sharable with any thread – is now a simple matter of recording the stated intentions of the user-mode server in `iSvrSessionType` and then creating a handle to the session for any client that is allowed access to it, when requested. That is, whether a given thread can access a session is now determined purely by whether it has a handle to the session or not as the access check is performed at handle-creation time.

This accounts for the introduction of the new method `DObject::RequestUserHandle()`. Suppose a server only supports non-sharable sessions. Then a user-mode thread with a handle to a session could just duplicate that handle, making a process-relative handle, and over-ride the settings of the server. But `DSession`'s over-ridden `RequestUserHandle()` checks the value in `iSvrSessionType` to see whether the requested sharing level is allowed by the server, and thereby enforces the user-mode server's requested policy on session sharing.

To maintain backwards compatibility, the user-side APIs for creating sessions default to creating a session that is "unshareable", even if shared sessions are supported by the server. This "current sharability level" – specified when creating the initial handle to the session, is stored in `iSessionType` and is validated against the "sharability" level the server supports. To share this session with other threads, the session has either to explicitly create a session that supports the level of sharability required (the preferred method) or subsequently call `ShareAuto()` (to share within process) or `ShareProtected()` (to share between processes), as required. If the `ShareXxx()` method succeeds, it creates a new process-relative handle and closes the old one. The new session creation overloads that allow the "sharability" of a session to be specified from session creation are the preferred method, as they avoid the expensive operation of creating a new handle where it is not needed.

These new session creation overloads also support an optional security policy that the client can use to verify the security credentials of the server it is connecting to. Similarly, there are overloads of the new APIs to open a handle to a session shared over client-server IPC or from a creator process which allow the session to be validated against a security policy. This allows you to prevent a handle to a spoof server being passed by these mechanisms, as you may verify the identity of the server whose session you are accepting a handle to. The initial session type and security policy parameters are then marshalled into the call to `DSession::Add()`, where they are used to fail session creation if the server does not meet the required policy.

The final responsibility of the session is to find – and allocate if necessary – kernel memory for messages to be stored in. I will discuss these message pools in the next section. At session creation time, you can specify whether the session uses a pool specific to the session or a global kernel pool. The session stores the type of pool it is using in `iPool`. If it is using a per-session pool, then it maintains a pointer to the next available free message in `iNextFreeMessage`.

During a send, the session will then use one of the session's disconnect message, the thread's synchronous message or the next free message from the selected pool. If the session is using the global pool and there are no more free messages the system lock is relinquished (to avoid holding it for an unbounded period of time whilst allocating), the message pool is expanded, then the lock is reclaimed and sending proceeds as before.

4.1.5.3 Messages – minimal states and message pool design

Next, I'll consider the design of message pools, that is, the memory used to store messages within the kernel. There is one important constraint on the design of the message pools, namely that there must always be a free message available for a session to send a disconnect message to the server, so that resources may be correctly freed in OOM situations. This disconnect message is naturally associated with the session whose disconnection it is notifying and will always be available if the message is embedded within the session object itself. To minimize the memory used by this disconnect message object, we have designed the message object to have a base class, RMessageKBase, which contains only the data required for the disconnect message, and then derive from it the (larger) message class, RMessageK, which is used for normal messages:

```
class RMessageKBase : public SDblQueLink
    {
public:
  TBool IsFree() const { return !iNext; }
  TBool IsDelivered() const
    { return iNext!=0 && (TLinAddr(iNext) & 3)==0; }
  TBool IsAccepted() const
    { return ((TLinAddr)iNext & 3)==3; }
public:
  TInt iFunction;
    };
```

```
class RMessageK : public RMessageKBase
    {
public:
  enum TMsgType {EDisc=0, ESync=1, ESession=2, EGlobal=3};
  inline TInt ArgType(TInt aParam) const;
  inline TInt Arg(TInt aParam) const;
  void Free();
  static RMessageK* NewMsgBlock(TInt aCount, TInt aType);
  IMPORT_C DThread* Thread() const;
  static RMessageK* MessageK(TInt aHandle, DThread* aThread);
  IMPORT_C static RMessageK* MessageK(TInt aHandle);
public:
  TInt iArgs[4];
  TUint16 iArgFlags; // describes which arguments are descriptors/handles
  TUint8 iPool; // 0=disconnect msg, 1=thread sync message,
                // 2=from session pool, 3=from global pool
```

```
TUint8 iPad;
DSession* iSession; // pointer to session
SDblQueLink iSessionLink; // attaches message to session
DThread* iClient; // pointer to client thread (not reference counted)
TRequestStatus* iStatus; // pointer to user side TRequestStatus
};
```

After we have ensured that session cleanup works properly, the next most important concern in designing the message allocation strategy is to minimize the memory that the kernel uses for sending messages. In the original client-server implementation of Symbian OS v5, a fixed number of message objects were allocated for each session, resulting in poor message object utilization, considering that most IPC calls were synchronous and hence only one of the message objects was in use at any one time!

Analysis of the client-server system, by instrumenting EUSER and EKERN, has shown that as many as 99% of the calls to RSession-Base::SendReceive() are to the synchronous overload. Obviously, a thread cannot send a synchronous message to more than one server at a time, because it waits for the synchronous message's completion inside EUSER immediately after dispatching it. This means that we can use a per-thread message object to avoid having to allocate message objects for all the synchronous messages that are sent. This message object (RMessageK) is embedded within the DThread object, and therefore avoids allocation issues by being allocated as part of the thread object itself.

Thus all that remains to be determined is the allocation strategy for message objects used by asynchronous IPC (such messages are typically used for remote I/O such as sockets or for event notification). These message objects are allocated on a per-session basis, or dynamically from a global pool. As we only need a small number of them, the overhead for non-utilization of these message objects is not large.

You may wonder why we do not insist on a global pool, and cut memory requirements further. This is because for real-time code a guaranteed response time is important, and a global, dynamic pool does not provide those guarantees (as it may require memory allocation in the kernel). This means that we must provide the option of creating a per-session pool, which allows the real-time code to manage the time it takes to process an asynchronous request precisely. That said, it is more common for servers to use asynchronous message completion for event notification, in which case using the dynamic global pool becomes more attractive due to its smaller memory footprint. This is therefore the recommended option where real-time guarantees are not required for any asynchronous IPC calls to the server.

This allocation scheme allows any number of threads to invoke synchronous IPC on a server using the same session without having to increase the session's message pool and it also provides guaranteed message sending for synchronous IPC.

We have achieved further memory savings by minimizing the state that is required within the message objects themselves. There are only three states that a message can have, as shown in Figure 4.5.

FREE   The message is not currently in use
DELIVERED   The message has been sent but the server hasn't seen it yet
ACCEPTED   The server has received the message but not yet completed it.

To assure a message's cleanup when a session closes, we attach it to a session queue whilst it is not free. We also have to ensure no message can persist beyond the lifetime of the thread that sent it, as such a message can no longer be completed. By assuming a strategy that messages should never be discarded prematurely (for example, when the thread Exit () s), but only at the last possible moment (just before the thread object is destroyed), we can avoid the complication of maintaining an open reference on the thread and the associated state required for this. When a thread exits, therefore, we need not iterate through a queue to discard **DELIVERED** messages – they are simply allowed to propagate through the server as usual. Instead of an open reference on the thread in each message, we need only maintain a count of the outstanding messages for each thread (in DThread::iIpcCount).

When a thread exits it checks this count and if it is non-zero it increments its own reference count so it is not destroyed and sets a flag (the top bit of the message count) to indicate this has been done. Completing a message decrements the outstanding message count for the client thread and if its value reaches 0x80000000, this means the

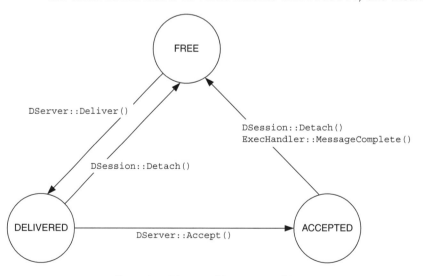

Figure 4.5   Message object state machine

message count for the thread has reached zero and the flag has been set. The extra reference on the thread is then closed, allowing it to be safely destroyed.

Closing a session does not unilaterally discard **DELIVERED** messages either – again they are simply allowed to propagate through the server. This means that session close needs only to send the disconnect message to the server and has no need to iterate its queue of messages.

So, we only need to perform message queue iteration either when the server itself terminates or when the server completes a disconnect message. In the latter case, the iteration is needed to free any remaining **ACCEPTED** messages (no **DELIVERED** messages can remain since the disconnect message is guaranteed to be the last message received from that session). The messages concerned are not on any other queue so there is no contention when we iterate over the session queue. When the server itself terminates, the complete system of server and sessions is frozen, because clients are not allowed to send a message to the server whilst it is terminating, so again there is no contention on the session queue when a message is being completed and hence no need for an intermediate **COMPLETED** state to deal with delayed removal of messages from the session queue.

The three states are then encoded in a minimal way into the doubly linked list fields:

	iLink.iNext	**iLink.iPrev**
FREE	NULL	N/A
DELIVERED	Valid address (multiple of 4) [bottom bits == 00b]	N/A
ACCEPTED	~(this) [bottom bits == 11b]	~&(server DProcess)

4.1.5.4 Message handles

Another key design decision we took for message objects was not to derive them from DObject. This means that they do not have standard object containers and user handles. Rather, the user-side handle for an RMessageK is in fact its address on the kernel heap. To verify the handles that user-mode operations give, the kernel uses the fact that a user-side component only ever has a valid handle to a message when it is in the **ACCEPTED** state and does the following:

- Checks the address and size of the object are within the kernel heap

- If so, reads the memory under an exception trap (the machine coded versions of these functions use the magic exception immunity mechanism, see Section 5.4.3.1)

- Check that `msg.iNext == ~(& msg)`

- Check that `msg.iPrev == ~(requestingThread->`
  `iOwning Process).`

If these tests pass, then the message object is taken to be valid and the requested operation can proceed.

4.1.6   Changes for IPCv2

The main change from the IPCv1 implementation of client-server has been the removal of the insecure APIs. These were:

```
class CSharableSession
class CSession
class CServer
class RMessagePtr
class RMessage
class RServer

RSessionBase::Share(TAttachMode aAttachMode=EExplicitAttach)
RSessionBase::Attach()
RSessionBase::Send(TInt aFunction,TAny* aPtr)
RSessionBase::SendReceive(TInt aFunction,TAny* aPtr,
                          TRequestStatus& aStatus)
RSessionBase::SendReceive(TInt aFunction,TAny* aPtr)
RSubSessionBase::CreateSubSession(RSessionBase&,TInt aFunction,
                                  const TAny* aPtr)
RSubSessionBase::Send(TInt aFunction,const TAny* aPtr)
RSubSessionBase::SendReceive(TInt aFunction,const TAny* aPtr,
                             TRequestStatus&)
RSubSessionBase::SendReceive(TInt aFunction,const TAny* aPtr)
RThread::GetDesLength(const TAny* aPtr)
RThread::GetDesMaxLength(const TAny* aPtr)
RThread::ReadL(const TAny* aPtr,TDes8& aDes,TInt anOffset)
RThread::ReadL(const TAny* aPtr,TDes16 &aDes,TInt anOffset)
RThread::WriteL(const TAny* aPtr,const TDesC8& aDes,TInt anOffset)
RThread::WriteL(const TAny* aPtr,const TDesC16& aDes,TInt anOffset)
RThread::RequestComplete(TRequestStatus*& aStatus,TInt aReason)
RThread::Kill(TInt aReason)
RThread::Terminate(TInt aReason)
RThread::Panic(const TDesC& aCategory,TInt aReason)
```

We have replaced these APIs with the framework I have described above. To aid migration to the new APIs, all EKA1-based Symbian OS releases from 7.0 s onwards contain both the new `Rendezvous()` thread/process APIs discussed in Section 3.3.6, and a functioning (but not secure) implementation of the IPCv2 APIs.

4.1.6.1 *IPCv2 summary*

To summarize, IPCv2 has brought the following benefits and features:

- Secure access to the client's address space based on the permissions and data types it specifies in messages to the server

- The ability to prevent spoofing of server names and to validate a security policy against the server when connecting to a session or opening a handle to a shared session

- Real-time server performance is possible through the use of asynchronous session connect and disconnect operations

- The ability to share server sessions between processes

- Asynchronous creation of a connection with a server to prevent a malicious server blocking a client indefinitely.

4.2 Asynchronous message queues

A message queue is a mechanism for passing data between threads, which may be in the same process, or in different processes. The message itself is usually an instance of a class, and its size must be a multiple of 4 bytes.

The asynchronous message queue mechanism provides a way to send a message without needing to know the identity of a recipient, or indeed, if anyone is actually listening.

You define and fix the size of the queue when you create it, choosing the maximum number of messages it can contain and the size of those messages. So, you would normally create a new queue to deal with messages of a particular type. There is no fixed maximum to either the message size or the queue size – these are only limited by system resources.

Many readers and writers may share a single queue. Sending and receiving messages are real-time operations and operate with real-time guarantees.

We represent a message queue by a DMsgQueue kernel-side object, to which the reader and the writer can open a handle. This is a reference-counted object derived from DObject, which means that it is not persistent; the kernel deletes it when the last handle to it is closed. The queue itself is simply a block of memory divided into slots. Here is the DMsgQueue class that manages it:

```
class DMsgQueue : public DObject
  {
public:
  enum TQueueState {EEmpty, EPartial, EFull};
  enum {KMaxLength = 256};
public:
```

```
  ~DMsgQueue();
  TInt Create(DObject* aOwner, const TDesC* aName,
       TInt aMsgLength, TInt aSlotCount, TBool aVisible = ETrue);
  TInt Send(const TAny* aPtr, TInt aLength);
  TInt Receive(TAny* aPtr, TInt aLength);
  void NotifySpaceAvailable(TRequestStatus* aStatus);
  void NotifyDataAvailable(TRequestStatus* aStatus);
  void CancelSpaceAvailable();
  void CancelDataAvailable();
  TInt MessageSize() const;
private:
  void CancelRequest(DThread* aThread, TRequestStatus*& aStatus);
  void CompleteRequestIfPending(DThread* aThread,
               TRequestStatus*& aStatus, TInt aCompletionVal);
private:
  TUint8* iMsgPool;
  TUint8* iFirstFreeSlot;
  TUint8* iFirstFullSlot;
  TUint8* iEndOfPool;
  DThread* iThreadWaitingOnSpaceAvail;
  DThread* iThreadWaitingOnDataAvail;
  TRequestStatus* iDataAvailStat;
  TRequestStatus* iSpaceAvailStat;
  TUint16 iMaxMsgLength;
  TUint8 iState;
  TUint8 iSpare;
public:
  friend class Monitor;
  };
```

Key member data of DMsgQueue

iMsgPool

A pointer to the block of memory used for the message slots.

iFirstFreeSlot

A pointer to the first free slot in the message pool, unless the pool is full,
iState==EFull.

iFirstFullSlot

A pointer to the first full slot in the message pool, unless the pool is
empty, iState==EEmpty.

iEndOfPool

A pointer to the byte of memory that is just past the end of the poll of
message slots.

iState

Whether the pool is empty, full or somewhere in between.

You perform actions (such as creation, opening, writing and reading) to a
message queue through a message queue handle, which is an RMsgQueue
object. This is a templated class, where the template parameter defines
the message type.

RMsgQueue is derived from RMsgQueueBase, which together form
a thin template class/base class pair. RMsgQueueBase provides the

implementation, while `RMsgQueue` provides type safety. An `RMsgQueueBase` object is a valid message queue handle, but does not offer the type safety that `RMsgQueue` does.

4.2.1 Visibility

A message queue can be:

1. Named and be visible to all processes – a global queue

2. Nameless, but accessible from other processes. A handle may be passed to another process by a process currently owning a handle to the queue, using a handle-sharing mechanism – a protected queue

3. Nameless and local to the current process, hence not visible to any other process – a local queue.

The choice clearly depends on the use you have in mind for the queue.

4.3 Kernel-side messages

Kernel-side messages are a means of communication that are used to communicate with a Symbian OS thread that is executing kernel-side code. Typically, you would use this communication method if you were writing a device driver – to communicate between your client thread, usually a user-mode thread, and a supervisor-mode thread running the actual device driver code.

The mechanism consists of a message containing data, and a queue that is associated with a DFC. The DFC runs to process each message.

We represent a kernel-side message by a `TMessageBase` object; this allows a single 32-bit argument to be passed, and returns a single 32-bit value. If you want to pass more arguments, then you must derive a new message class from `TMessageBase`.

Every Symbian OS thread has a `TThreadMessage` object embedded within it. `TThreadMessage` is derived from `TMessageBase`, and contains space for 10 extra 32-bit arguments. You can use these objects for communication with device driver threads.

Both `TMessageBase` and `TThreadMessage` are defined in `kernel.h`. The following example shows the `TMessageBase` class:

```
class TMessageBase : public SDblQueLink
    {
public:
  enum TState {EFree,EDelivered,EAccepted};
public:
  TMessageBase() : iState(EFree), iQueue(NULL) {}
  IMPORT_C void Send(TMessageQue* aQ);
  IMPORT_C TInt SendReceive(TMessageQue* aQ);
  IMPORT_C void Forward(TMessageQue* aQ, TBool aReceiveNext);
```

```
  IMPORT_C void Complete(TInt aResult, TBool aReceiveNext);
  IMPORT_C void Cancel();
  IMPORT_C void PanicClient(const TDesC& aCategory, TInt aReason);
public:
  IMPORT_C DThread* Client();
public:
  TUint8 iState;
  TMessageQue* iQueue;
  NFastSemaphore iSem;
  TInt iValue;
  };
```

Key member data of TMessageBase

iState
Indicates whether message is free, delivered or accepted.

iQueue
A pointer to the message queue to which the message was delivered.

iSem
A fast semaphore used to block the sending thread if the message was sent synchronously. The iOwningThread field of this semaphore is used as a pointer to the thread that sent the message.

iValue
Used to hold a single integer argument when the message is sent; holds completion code when message is completed.

TMessageQue
The kernel sends kernel-side messages to a message queue, which is represented by a TMessageQue object. This consists of a DFC and a doubly linked list of received messages. The class is shown below:

```
class TMessageQue : private TDfc
  {
public:
  IMPORT_C TMessageQue(TDfcFn aFunction, TAny* aPtr,
                   TDfcQue* aDfcQ, TInt aPriority);
  IMPORT_C void Receive();
  IMPORT_C TMessageBase* Poll();
  IMPORT_C TMessageBase* Last();
  IMPORT_C void CompleteAll(TInt aResult);
  using TDfc::SetDfcQ;
public:
  inline static void Lock() {NKern::FMWait(&MsgLock);}
  inline static void Unlock() {NKern::FMSignal(&MsgLock);}
  inline void UnlockAndKick() {Enque(&MsgLock);}
public:
  SDblQue iQ;
  TBool iReady;
  TMessageBase* iMessage;
  static NFastMutex MsgLock;
  friend class TMessageBase;
  };
```

Key member data of TMessageQue
TDfc (the base class)
This DFC is attached to the thread receiving the messages. It runs whenever the message queue is ready to receive and a message is available.

iQ
A doubly linked list of messages that have been delivered to this queue.

iReady
A Boolean flag indicating whether the message queue is ready to receive. If TRUE, the DFC will run as soon as a message is delivered; if FALSE the message will simply remain on the delivered queue and the DFC will not run.

iMessage
Pointer to the last message accepted by the receiving thread.

Kernel-side messaging in operation
When a message is sent to the queue, either:

- The kernel accepts the message immediately, and the receiving thread's DFC runs. This happens if the message queue is ready to receive, which is the case if the message queue is empty and the receiving thread has requested the next message.

Or

- The kernel places the message on the delivered message queue, and the DFC does not run. This happens if there are other messages queued ahead of this one or if the receiving thread has not (yet) requested another message.

A kernel-side message may be in one of three states at any time:

1. FREE – represented by the TMessageBase::EFree enum value. This indicates that the message is not currently in use

2. DELIVERED – represented by the TMessageBase::EDelivered enum value. This indicates that the message is attached to a message queue but is not currently in use by the receiving thread. It may be removed from the queue and discarded with no ill effects on the receiving thread

3. ACCEPTED – represented by the TMessageBase::EAccepted enum value. This indicates that the message is not attached to a message queue but is currently in use by the receiving thread. The message may not be discarded.

Transitions between these states, including adding the message to and removing it from a message queue, occur under the protection of the global `TMessageQue::MsgLock` fast mutex. We need to use a mutex to avoid queue corruption in the case of, for example, multiple threads sending to the same message queue at the same time. By using a fast mutex, we ensure that message-passing operations may only be invoked from a thread context.

You can send kernel-side messages either synchronously or asynchronously. Each `TMessageBase` object contains an `NFastSemaphore` on which the sending thread will wait after sending a synchronous message. The receiving thread signals the semaphore after the kernel has processed the message and written the completion code. The kernel then releases the sending thread, and when it runs, it picks up the return code.

The `NFastSemaphore` also contains a pointer to the sending `NThread`; this serves to identify the sending thread and is therefore set up for both synchronous and asynchronous message send. We reference count this pointer – incrementing the access count of the originating `DThread` when the message is sent. This prevents the sending `DThread` object disappearing if the thread terminates unexpectedly. When the kernel completes the message it removes the extra access asynchronously – the thread completing the message will not need to close the `DThread` itself. We do this to avoid unpredictable execution times for message completion. Also note that even messages that are sent asynchronously must be completed; this is so that the kernel can set the message state back to FREE and remove the access count from the sending thread.

The kernel always sends the `TThreadMessage` objects embedded in Symbian OS thread control blocks synchronously – this ensures that one message per thread will always suffice. The kernel cancels these messages if the corresponding thread terminates. Canceling an ACCEPTED message has no effect, but canceling a DELIVERED message means that the kernel will remove the message from the queue and also remove the access count held by the message on the sending thread. Because of this, the receiving thread should only use any of the member data of `TMessageBase` if the message is in the ACCEPTED state.

4.4 Publish and subscribe

Publish and subscribe, also known as ''properties'', provides:

1. System-wide global variables

2. A new IPC mechanism, for asynchronous peer-to-peer communication between threads.

An overview is given in Figure 4.6.

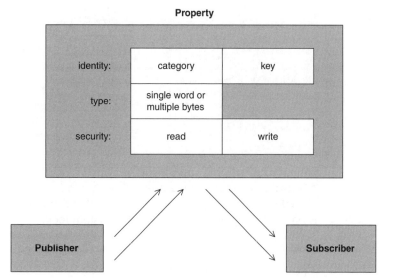

Figure 4.6 Publish and subscribe overview

Publish and subscribe can be used by both user and kernel code, through similar APIs, and so this method also allows communication between user and kernel code.

From the user side, you would use the `RProperty` handle, defined in `e32property.h`:

```
class RProperty : public RHandleBase
  {
public:
  enum { KMaxPropertySize = 512 };
  enum { KMaxLargePropertySize = 65535 };
  enum TType
    {
    EInt,
    EByteArray,
    EText = EByteArray,
    ELargeByteArray,
    ELargeText = ELargeByteArray,
    ETypeLimit,
    ETypeMask = 0xff
    };
public:
  IMPORT_C static TInt Define(TUid aCategory, TUint aKey,
                       TInt aAttr, TInt aPreallocate=0);
  IMPORT_C static TInt Define(TUid aCategory, TUint aKey,
          TInt aAttr, const TSecurityPolicy& aReadPolicy,
                   const TSecurityPolicy& aWritePolicy,
                                     TInt aPreallocated=0);
  IMPORT_C static TInt Delete(TUid aCategory, TUint aKey);
  IMPORT_C static TInt Get(TUid aCategory, TUint aKey, TInt& aValue);
  IMPORT_C static TInt Get(TUid aCategory, TUint aKey, TDes8& aValue);
  IMPORT_C static TInt Set(TUid aCategory, TUint aKey, TInt aValue);
```

```
IMPORT_C static TInt Set(TUid aCategory, TUint aKey,
                             const TDesC8& aValue);
IMPORT_C TInt Attach(TUid aCategory, TUint aKey,
            TOwnerType aType = EOwnerProcess);
IMPORT_C void Subscribe(TRequestStatus& aRequest);
IMPORT_C void Cancel();
IMPORT_C TInt Get(TInt& aValue);
IMPORT_C TInt Get(TDes8& aValue);
IMPORT_C TInt Set(TInt aValue);
IMPORT_C TInt Set(const TDesC8& aValue);
};
```

From the kernel side, you use the `RPropertyRef` and `TPropertySub-sRequest` classes defined in `sproperty.h`, and the `TPropertyInfo` class defined in `u32property.h`. Note that `TPropertySubsRequest` is on a single queue protected by the system lock.

```
class RPropertyRef
  {
public:
  RPropertyRef() {iProp = NULL;}
  IMPORT_C TInt Attach(TUid aCategory, TInt aKey);
  IMPORT_C TInt Open(TUid aCategory, TInt aKey);
  IMPORT_C void Close();
  IMPORT_C TInt Define(TInt aAttr, const TSecurityPolicy& aReadPolicy,
                           const TSecurityPolicy& aWritePolicy,
                  TInt aPreallocate=0, DProcess* aProcess = NULL);
  IMPORT_C TInt Delete(DProcess* aProcess = NULL);
  IMPORT_C TInt Subscribe(TPropertySubsRequest& aRequest,
                          DProcess* aProcess = NULL);
  IMPORT_C void Cancel(TPropertySubsRequest& aRequest);
  IMPORT_C TInt Get(TInt& aValue, DProcess* aProcess = NULL);
  IMPORT_C TInt Set(TInt aValue, DProcess* aProcess = NULL);
  IMPORT_C TInt Get(TDes8& aDes, DProcess* aProcess = NULL);
  IMPORT_C TInt Set(const TDesC8& aDes, DProcess* aProcess = NULL);
  IMPORT_C TBool GetStatus(TPropertyStatus& aStatus);
private:
  TProperty* iProp;
  };

class TPropertySubsRequest : public SDblQueLink
  {
public:
  TPropertySubsRequest(TPropertyCompleteFn aCompleteFn, TAny* aPtr)
    {
    iNext = NULL;
    iCompleteFn = aCompleteFn;
    iPtr = aPtr;
    }
  TPropertyCompleteFn iCompleteFn;
  TAny* iPtr;
private:
  friend class TProperty;
  DProcess* iProcess;
  };
```

```
class TPropertyInfo
    {
public:
    TUintiAttr;
    TUint16 iSize;
    RProperty::TType iType;
    TSecurityPolicy iReadPolicy;
    TSecurityPolicy iWritePolicy;
    };
```

4.4.1 Key entities

There are three key entities in the publish and subscribe system. I will describe them below; you may also want to refer back to the overview in Figure 4.6.

Properties
This is data: either a single 32-bit data value or a variable-length set of bytes, identified by a 64-bit integer.

Publishers
Publishers are threads that define and update a property.

Subscribers
Subscribers are threads that listen for changes to a property and can get the current value of a property.

Now let's have a look at properties in a little more detail.

4.4.2 Properties

Internally, the kernel stores a property as an instance of the TProperty class, defined in sproperty.cpp. I will give a very cut-down version here, as this is a surprisingly large class:

```
class TProperty
    {
public:
    static TInt Init();
    static TInt Attach(TUid aCategory, TUint aKey, TProperty** aProp);
    static TInt Open(TUid aCategory, TUint aKey, TProperty** aProp);
    void Close();
    TInt Define(const TPropertyInfo*, DProcess*);
    TInt Delete(DProcess*);
    TInt Subscribe(TPropertySubsRequest* aSubs, DProcess*);
    void Cancel(TPropertySubsRequest* aSubs);
    TInt GetI(TInt* aValue, DProcess*);
    TInt GetB(TUint8* aBuf, TInt* aSize, DProcess*, TBool aUser);
    TInt SetI(TInt aValue, DProcess*);
    TInt SetB(const TUint8*, TInt aSize, DProcess*, TBool aUser);
    const TUid iCategory;
    const TUint iKey;
private:
    enum { KCompletionDfcPriority = 2 };
    static TDfc CompletionDfc;
```

```
  static SDblQue CompletionQue;
  static DMutex* FeatureLock;

  static TProperty* Table[KHashTableLimit];
  TUint8 iType;
  TUint8 iAttr;
  TCompiledSecurityPolicy iReadPolicy;
  TCompiledSecurityPolicy iWritePolicy;
  TUint32 iOwner;
  TUint iRefCount;

// The property value
// Meaningful for defined properties only
//      (ie. iType != RProperty::ETypeLimit)
  union // the value is protected by the system lock
    {
    TBuf* iBuf;
    TInt iValue;
    };
  };
```

A property has three key attributes: identity, type and security.

The identity and type of a property is the only information that must be shared between a publisher and a subscriber – there is no need to provide interface classes or functions, though that may often be desirable.

Identity

A property is identified by a 64-bit integer made up of two 32-bit parts: the category and the key.

A property is said to belong to a category, which is a standard Symbian OS UID.

The key is a 32-bit value that identifies a specific property within a category. The meaning applied to the key depends on the kind of enumeration scheme set up for the category. At its simplest, a key can be an index value. It can also be another UID, if you are designing the category to be generally extensible.

Type

A property can be:

1.   A single 32-bit value

2.   A contiguous set of bytes, referred to as a byte-array. The length of this can go as high as `KMaxLargePropertySize`, 65,535 bytes, but real-time guarantees are made only if the length is below `RProperty::KMaxPropertySize`, 512 bytes. Memory for the smaller byte arrays may be allocated at definition time: if this is done publishing cannot fail with `KErrNoMemory`, and we can satisfy those real-time guarantees

3.   Unicode text. This is for properties and accessor functions that accept Unicode descriptors, and is just a convenience for programmers wishing

to store Unicode text properties. The implementation treats Unicode text as a byte-array; the API hides the detail.

Security

A property has two `TCompiledSecurityPolicy` members. One of these is for read operations – that is, `Get()` and `Subscribe()` calls on `RProperty` – and the other is for write operations – that is `Set()` calls on `RProperty`.

These members are set up when the property is defined, passing in two `TSecurityPolicy` parameters to the `RProperty::Define()` function:

```
IMPORT_C static TInt Define(TUid aCategory, TUint aKey, TInt aAttr,
                            const TSecurityPolicy& aReadPolicy,
                            const TSecurityPolicy& aWritePolicy,
                            TInt aPreallocated=0);
```

You can turn to Chapter 8, *Platform Security*, for more information.

4.4.3 Using publish and subscribe

There are six basic operations that you can perform on a property: define, delete, publish, retrieve, subscribe and unsubscribe.

I give an overview of these operations in the table below, and in subsequent sections I will describe some of these functions in more detail.

Define	Create a property variable and define its type and access controls.
Delete	Remove a property from the system.
Publish	Change the value of a property.
Retrieve	Get the current value of a property.
Subscribe	Register for notification of changes to a property.
Unsubscribe	Say that you no longer want to be notified of changes.

4.4.4 Defining a property

As we saw above, you define a property by using the `RProperty::Define()` function to specify the attributes of the property.

You don't have to define a property before it is accessed. This means that either the publisher, or one of the subscribers, may define a property.

On a secure implementation of Symbian OS, outstanding subscriptions at the point of definition may be completed with `KErrPermissionDenied` if they fail the security policy check.

Once defined, the property persists in the kernel until the operating system reboots or the property is deleted. The property's lifetime is not tied to that of the thread or process that defined it. This means that it is a good idea to check the return code from `RProperty::Define()` in case that the property was previously defined and not deleted.

You can delete a property using the `RProperty::Delete()` function. The kernel will complete any outstanding subscriptions for this property with `KErrNotFound`.

Note that only an instance of a process from the same EXE as the process which defined the property is allowed to delete it, as the SID of the process (as defined in the EXE image) is checked against the SID of the defining process. Also note that in a secure implementation of Symbian OS, you may only define a property with a category equal to the SID of the process within which you are executing if the category being defined is greater than `KUidSecurityThresholdCategoryValue`. Any process may define a property with a category less than `KUidSecurityThresholdCategoryValue` if it has the `WriteDeviceData` capability, to ease migration of legacy code whilst still enforcing security on defining properties.

```
const TUid KMyPropertyCat={0x10012345};
enum TMyPropertyKeys= {EMyPropertyCounter,EMyPropertyName};

// define first property to be integer type
Tint r=RProperty::Define(KMyPropertyCat,EMyPropertyCounter,
                                        RProperty::EInt);
if (r!=KErrAlreadyExists)
  User::LeaveIfError(r);

// define second property to be a byte array,
// allocating 100 bytes
r=RProperty::Define(KMyPropertyCat,EMyPropertyName,
                    RProperty::EByteArray,100);
if (r!=KErrAlreadyExists)
  User::LeaveIfError(r);

// much later on...

// delete the 'name' property
TInt r=RProperty::Delete(KMyPropertyCat,EMyPropertyName);
if (r!=KErrNotFound)
  User::LeaveIfError(r);
```

4.4.5   Creating and closing a handle to a property

You carry out some property operations (such as defining and deleting properties) by specifying a category and key, but other operations (such as subscribing) require a reference to the property to be established beforehand. Some operations, such as publishing, can be done in either way.

To create a reference to a property, you use the `RProperty::Attach()` member function. After this has completed successfully, the `RProperty` object will act like a normal handle to a kernel resource.

When the handle is no longer required, it can be released in the standard way by calling the inherited `RHandleBase::Close()` member function. You should note that releasing the handle does not cause the property to disappear – this only happens if the property is deleted.

As I said before, it is quite legitimate to attach to a property that has not been defined, and in this case no error will be returned. This enables the lazy definition of properties.

```
// attach to the 'counter' property
RProperty counter;
Tint r=counter.Attach(KMyPropertyCat,EMyPropertyName,EOwnerThread);
User::LeaveIfError(r);

// use the counter object...

// when finished, release the handle
counter.Close();
```

4.4.6 Publishing and retrieving property values

You can publish properties using the `RProperty::Set()` family of functions, and read them using the `RProperty::Get()` family. You can either use a previously attached `RProperty` handle, or you can specify the property category and key with the new value. The former method is guaranteed to have a bounded execution time in most circumstances and is suitable for high-priority, real-time tasks. If you specify a category and key, then the kernel makes no real-time guarantees. See Section 4.4.8 for more on the real-time behavior of publish and subscribe.

The kernel reads and writes property values atomically, so it is not possible for threads reading the property to get a garbled value, or for more than one published value to be confused.

The kernel completes all outstanding subscriptions for the property when a value is published, even if it is exactly the same as the existing value. This means that a property can be used as a simple broadcast notification service.

If you publish a property that is not defined, the `Get()` and `Set()` functions just return an error, rather than panicking your thread. This happens because you may not have made a programming error, see Section 4.4.4.

```
// publish a new name value
TFileName n;
RProcess().Filename(n);
TInt r=RProperty::Set(KMyPropertyCat,EMyPropertyName,n);
User::LeaveIfError(r);

// retrieve the first 10 characters of the name value
TBuf<10> name;
r=RProperty::Get(KMyPropertyCat,EMyPropertyName,name);
if (r!=KErrOverflow)
  User::LeaveIfError(r);

// retrieve and publish a new value using the attached 'counter'
// property
TInt count;
r=counter.Get(count);
if (r==KErrNone)
  r=counter.Set(++count);
User::LeaveIfError(r);
```

If another thread is executing the same sequence to increment `count`, then this last example contains a race condition!

4.4.7   Subscribing to properties

A thread requests notification of property update using the `RProperty::Subscribe()` member function on an already attached property object. You can only make a single subscription from a single `RProperty` instance at any one time, and you can cancel this subscription request later with the `RProperty::Cancel()` member function.

If you subscribe to a property, you are requesting a single notification of when the property is next updated. The kernel does not generate an ongoing sequence of notifications for every update of the property value. Neither does the kernel tell you what the changed value is. Essentially, the notification should be interpreted as "Property X has changed" rather than "Property X has changed to Y". You must explicitly retrieve the new value if you need it. This means that multiple updates may be collapsed into one notification, and that you, as the subscriber, may not have visibility of all the intermediate values.

This might appear to introduce a window of opportunity for a subscriber to be out of sync with the property value without receiving notification of the update – in particular, if the property is updated again before the subscriber thread has the chance to process the original notification. However, a simple programming pattern (outlined in the example below) ensures this does not happen.

```
// Active object that tracks changes to the 'name' property
class CPropertyWatch : public CActive
  {
  enum {EPriority=0};
public:
```

```
  static CPropertyWatch* NewL();
private:
  CPropertyWatch();
  void ConstructL();
  ~CPropertyWatch();
  void RunL();
  void DoCancel();
private:
  RProperty iProperty;
  };

CPropertyWatch* CPropertyWatch::NewL()
  {
  CPropertyWatch* me=new(ELeave) CPropertyWatch;
  CleanupStack::PushL(me);
  me->ConstructL();
  CleanupStack::Pop(me);
  return me;
  }

CPropertyWatch::CPropertyWatch() :CActive(EPriority){}
void CPropertyWatch::ConstructL()
  {
  User::LeaveIfError(iProperty.Attach(KMyPropertyCat,
                                      KMyPropertyName));
  CActiveScheduler::Add(this);
  // initial subscription and process current property value
  RunL();
  }

CPropertyWatch::~CPropertyWatch()
  {
  Cancel();
  iProperty.Close();
  }

void CPropertyWatch::DoCancel()
  {
  iProperty.Cancel();
  }

void CPropertyWatch::RunL()
  {
  // resubscribe before processing new value to prevent
  // missing updates
  iProperty.Subscribe(iStatus);
  SetActive();

  // property updated, get new value
  TFileName n;
  if (iProperty.Get(n)==KErrNotFound)
    {
    // property deleted, do necessary actions here...
    NameDeleted();
    }
  else
    {
    // use new value ...
```

```
    NameChanged(n);
    }
}
```

4.4.8   Real-time issues

When designing this functionality, we wanted to ensure that publishing a new value to a property was a real-time service, since time-critical threads will surely need to invoke it. For example a communication protocol could use publish and subscribe to indicate that a connection has been established.

However, there can be an arbitrarily large number of subscriptions on any given property, which makes publishing to that property unbounded. We solved this problem by using a DFC queued on the supervisor thread to do the actual completion of subscriptions. The publisher updates the value of the property and the kernel then places the property on a queue of properties for which notifications are outstanding. The DFC, in the supervisor context, then drains the queue and notifies subscribers.

As I showed earlier, you should publish or retrieve properties by using a previously attached `RProperty` handle, rather than by specifying the property category and key with the new value. This is guaranteed to have a bounded execution time, unless you are publishing a byte-array property that has grown in size. In this case the kernel will have to allocate memory for the byte-array, and memory allocation is an unbounded operation.

4.5   Shared chunks and shared I/O buffers

Shared I/O buffers and shared chunks are mechanisms which allow you to share memory between a user-side process and a kernel-side process, with a minimum of overhead. Such sharing avoids the expensive and time-consuming act of copying (potentially) large amounts of data around the system. Note that shared I/O buffers are a legacy mechanism primarily aimed at providing compatibility with EKA1 and that shared chunks, which are much more efficient and flexible, are the preferred mechanism for sharing memory between device drivers and user threads in EKA2. To understand how these mechanisms work, you need to know a little more about how Symbian OS manages its memory, so I will cover them in Chapter 7, *Memory Models*.

4.6   Summary

In this chapter, I have covered several of the mechanisms that EKA2 provides to allow communication between threads: client-server, message queues, publish and subscribe, shared I/O buffers and shared chunks. In the next chapter, I will describe how EKA2 provides services to user-mode threads.

5

Kernel Services

by Jane Sales

*On two occasions I have been asked (by members of Parliament!):
"Pray, Mr. Babbage, if you put into the machine wrong figures, will the
right answers come out?" I am not able rightly to apprehend the kind of
confusion of ideas that could provoke such a question.*

Charles Babbage

EKA2 provides a variety of services to user-mode threads. In this chapter I
will explain the mechanism it uses to do so, which we call an "executive
call", and then I will describe a few example services to give you a feel
for them.

Of course, the kernel does not just provide services for user-mode
threads – each part of the kernel provides services to the other parts of
the kernel too. I will consider interfaces between modules such as the
nanokernel and the memory model, and interfaces between the different
abstraction levels of the kernel, such as the independent layer and the
CPU layer.

But first of all I will look inside the basic object and handle mechanism
used by Symbian OS. This is at the heart of the communication between
the user side and the kernel.

5.1 Objects and handles

5.1.1 Handles – the RHandleBase class

User-side code always references a kernel-side object through an object
known as a handle. Handles are objects derived from the base class
`RHandleBase`:

```
class RHandleBase
    {
public:
    enum
```

```
    {
  EReadAccess=0x1,
  EWriteAccess=0x2,
  EDirectReadAccess=0x4,
  EDirectWriteAccess=0x8,
  };
public:
  inline RHandleBase();
  inline TInt Handle() const;
  inline void SetHandle(TInt aHandle);
  inline TInt SetReturnedHandle(TInt aHandleOrError);
  static void DoExtendedClose();
  IMPORT_C void Close();
  IMPORT_C TName Name() const;
  IMPORT_C TFullName FullName() const;
  IMPORT_C void SetHandleNC(TInt aHandle);
  IMPORT_C TInt Duplicate(const RThread& aSrc,
            TOwnerType aType=EOwnerProcess);
  IMPORT_C void HandleInfo(THandleInfo* anInfo);
  IMPORT_C TUint Attributes() const;
protected:
  inline RHandleBase(TInt aHandle);
  IMPORT_C TInt Open(const TFindHandleBase& aHandle,TOwnerType aType);
      static TInt SetReturnedHandle(TInt aHandleOrError,
                                    RHandleBase& aHandle);
  TInt OpenByName(const TDesC &aName,TOwnerType aOwnerType,
                                         TInt aObjectType);
private:
  static void DoExtendedCloseL();
protected:
  TInt iHandle;
  };
```

Here you can see some of the fundamental methods that we can
perform on handles: we can open and close them, retrieve their short
name and their full name, and we can duplicate them. You can also
see that RHandleBase's only member data is a single 32-bit integer,
iHandle. To show you how the kernel forms this integer, I will first
need to explain a container class, DObjectIx, which is known as the
object index. This class is a container for kernel-side objects derived from
DObject, which I will discuss first.

5.1.2   Reference-counted kernel objects

A large part of the kernel interface presented to user-side code is concerned with creation and manipulation of kernel objects represented
by user-side RHandleBase-derived classes. These kernel objects have
some basic properties in common.

5.1.2.1   Reference counted

Kernel objects are reference counted: multiple references can exist to
each object and the kernel only destroys the object when all references
have been removed.

5.1.2.2   Accessed using handles

User-side code accesses kernel objects indirectly using handles, rather than directly using pointers. The kernel translates a handle into a pointer by looking it up in a thread or process handle array. The use of handles allows the kernel to check the validity of kernel object references made by user code.

5.1.2.3   Named

Kernel objects may have names that you can use to find the object. Moreover, the name can be scoped relative to another kernel object (the owner). I will expand more on this later.

5.1.2.4   The DObject class

As I mentioned earlier, kernel objects are represented using classes derived from the DObject class. This base class provides the necessary reference counts, object names and name scoping relative to the owner object. DObject is in turn derived from DBase – this class provides kernel-side behavior equivalent to that provided by the user-side class CBase; that is, it zero-fills memory before object construction and provides a virtual destructor. It also offers the ability to trigger asynchronous deletion of the object, which is important in time-critical code.

Here is a slightly cut-down version of the DObject class:

```
class DObject : public DBase
   {
public:
   enum TCloseReturn
      {
      EObjectDeleted=1,
      EObjectUnmapped=2,
      };
   enum TObjectProtection
      {
      ELocal=0,
      EProtected,
      EGlobal,
      };
public:
   inline TInt Inc() {return NKern::SafeInc(iAccessCount);}
   inline TInt Dec() {return NKern::SafeDec(iAccessCount);}
   IMPORT_C DObject();
   IMPORT_C ~DObject();
   inline TInt Open() { return(Inc()?KErrNone:KErrGeneral); }
   IMPORT_C void CheckedOpen();
   IMPORT_C virtual TInt Close(TAny* aPtr);
   IMPORT_C virtual TInt RequestUserHandle(DThread* aThread,
                                           TOwnerType aType);
   IMPORT_C virtual TInt AddToProcess(DProcess* aProcess);
   IMPORT_C TInt AsyncClose();
```

```
    IMPORT_C virtual void DoAppendName(TDes& aName);
    IMPORT_C void DoAppendFullName(TDes& aFullName);
    IMPORT_C void Name(TDes& aName);
    IMPORT_C void AppendName(TDes& aName);
    IMPORT_C void FullName(TDes& aFullName);
    IMPORT_C void AppendFullName(TDes& aFullName);
    IMPORT_C TInt SetName(const TDesC* aName);
    IMPORT_C TInt SetOwner(DObject* aOwner);
    IMPORT_C void TraceAppendName(TDes8& aName, TBool aLock);
    IMPORT_C void TraceAppendFullName(TDes8& aFullName, TBool aLock);
    inline DObject* Owner();
    inline TInt AccessCount();
    inline TInt UniqueID();
    inline HBuf* NameBuf();
    inline void SetProtection(TObjectProtection aProtection);
    inline TUint Protection();
public:
    TInt iAccessCount;
    DObject* iOwner;
    TUint8 iContainerID;
    TUint8 iProtection;
    TUint8 iSpare[2];
    HBuf* iName;
public:
    static NFastMutex Lock;
    };
```

Key member data of DObject

iAccessCount
This counts how many references exist to the object – it is always non-negative.

iOwner
This is a reference-counted pointer to the DObject (thread or process) that is the owner of this object.

iContainerID
This is the ID of the DObjectCon that contains this object. I will discuss this later in this chapter.

iName
This is a pointer to a kernel-heap-allocated descriptor that holds this object's name. It is NULL if the object is unnamed.

iProtection
This is a TObjectProtection value, which notes if the object is private to the owning thread or process.

5.1.2.5 DObjects explained

The DObject class is new to EKA2. In EKA1 we derived our kernel classes from the user library's object class, CObject. In EKA2, we chose to create a new, kernel-only, DObject class to break the dependency between the kernel and the user library. In the same way, we created DObjectIx for the kernel to use instead of CObjectIx.

When a user thread requests the creation of an object represented by a handle, the kernel creates a DObject with an access count of 1, representing the pointer returned to the creating thread. If another thread then wishes to open this object, the kernel calls DObject::Open() on its behalf, incrementing the DObject's access count. We wanted it to be possible to call this method from anywhere, even in an ISR or DFC, so we prevented it from being over-ridden in a derived class. The result is that DObject::Open() always atomically executes the following operation:

```
if (iAccessCount==0)
  return KErrGeneral;
else
  {
  ++iAccessCount;
  return KErrNone;
  }
```

The access count is incremented, unless it was zero – this is an error, because, as we've seen, every DObject is created with an access count of 1.

The DObject::Dec() method does the opposite – it atomically executes the following operation:

```
if (iAccessCount==0)
  return 0;
else
  return iAccessCount--;
```

The Open() and Dec() methods are not protected by fast mutexes; they simply use atomic instructions or disable interrupts for a short time.

When a user thread closes a handle, the kernel invokes the DObject::Close(TAny*) method to remove a reference from the object. It calls Dec(), then proceeds to delete the object if the returned value is 1, indicating that the last reference has been closed:

```
EXPORT_C TInt DObject::Close(TAny* aPtr)
  {
  if (Dec()==1)
    {
    NKern::LockSystem(); // in case it is still in use
    NKern::UnlockSystem();
    DBase::Delete(this);
    return EObjectDeleted;
    }
  return 0;
  }
```

Since `Close()` may cause the freeing of memory on the kernel heap, the rules about when kernel heap operations may be performed apply; this means that we can't call it from an ISR or a DFC, for example. This contrasts with `Open()`, which as we've seen can be called from anywhere. We therefore allow the `Close()` method to be over-ridden by making it virtual.

The kernel deletes a `DObject` only when its access count becomes zero – in fact, this always happens via the `Close()` method. It is possible that a `DObject` with a zero access count is in the process of being destroyed. This is why `Open()` must fail if the object's access count is zero.

The parameter `aPtr` passed to `Close()` is either `NULL` or a pointer to the process that is closing a handle on the object. The kernel uses the pointer when the object being closed is a chunk, to remove the chunk from the process address space.

`DObject` also provides an `AsyncClose()` method. This is the same as `Close()` except that the parameter is always `NULL` and the kernel does the delete (if one is needed) asynchronously in the supervisor thread. Of course, `AsyncClose()` will only work if the derived class does not over-ride `Close()`.

There are two names associated with a `DObject` – the name (also known as the short name) and the full name.

The short name is either:

1. The string pointed to by `iName`

2. If `iName=NULL`, it is "`Local-XXXXXXXX`" where `XXXXXXXX` is the hexadecimal address of the `DObject`.

Object short names can be up to 80 characters in length. This makes them shorter than in EKA1, where the maximum was 128 characters. There's another difference too: EKA1 supported Unicode names, whereas in EKA2, names must be in ASCII. We made this decision for several reasons:

- If the kernel were to support Unicode internally, then we would have to duplicate many Unicode functions and large folding tables inside the kernel

- An ASCII compare is much simpler than a Unicode folded compare, so searching for objects by name is faster

- The naming of objects is a programmer convenience, and programmers generally write code in ASCII source files.

The object's full name is longer; it can be anything up to 256 characters in length. We define it recursively as the full name of the `DObject`'s owner appended with "`::<short name of this object>`". The limit of 80 characters on the length of the short name guarantees that the full name cannot exceed 256 characters, because there can be a maximum of three objects in the owner chain: the DObject might be owned by a thread that is owned by a process. For example, a semaphore named ALAZON, owned by the thread EPOS, in turn part of the LEXIS process, would be called LEXIS::EPOS::ALAZON. If you're worrying about thread-relative threads, don't – we no longer allow them in EKA2.

We use a global fast mutex, DObject::Lock, to protect the operations of getting an object's name, setting its name and setting its owner. We do this to avoid inconsistent results when one thread renames an object while another is reading its name or full name. (Obviously, we protect the setting of the owner because this changes the full name of the object.)

The method that reads an object's short name, DObject::DoAppendName(), can be over-ridden in a derived class. In fact, the
DLibrary and DProcess classes do over-ride it, because they both include the UID in the object name, and DProcess adds a generation number too.

5.1.2.6 Object indexes and handles

Now that I've described the DObject class, I can return to the object index class that is used to record the handles held by user threads or processes on kernel objects.

A handle is a 32-bit integer, split into bit fields like this:

Bits	Function
0-14	15-bit index into the DObjectIx holding the handle.
15	No close flag. If set to 1 the handle cannot be closed using RHandleBase::Close().
16-29	14-bit instance count (taken from DObjectIx::iNextInstance). This field is never zero for a valid handle.
30	Local handle flag. If set to 1 the handle is thread-local, otherwise it is process-global.
31	0 for normal handles, 1 for special handles. Supported special handles are: FFFF8000 – always refers to the current process FFFF8001 – always refers to the current thread.

Let's have a look at the `DObjectIx` class, along with the `SDObjectIxRec` structure that it makes use of:

```
struct SDObjectIxRec
  {
  TInt16 instance;
  TInt16 uniqueID;
  DObject* obj;
  };

class DObjectIx : public DBase
  {
public:
  enum
  {ENoClose=KHandleNoClose, ELocalHandle=0x40000000};
public:
  IMPORT_C static DObjectIx* New(TAny* aPtr);
  IMPORT_C ~DObjectIx();
  IMPORT_C TInt Add(DObject* aObj, TInt& aHandle);
  IMPORT_C TInt Remove(TInt aHandle, DObject*& aObject, TAny*& aPtr);
  IMPORT_C DObject* At(TInt aHandle,TInt aUniqueID);
  IMPORT_C DObject* At(TInt aHandle);
  IMPORT_C TInt At(DObject* aObject);
  IMPORT_C TInt Count(DObject* aObject);
  IMPORT_C DObject* operator[](TInt aIndex);
  TInt LastHandle();
  static void Wait();
  static void Signal();
  inline TInt Count();
  inline TInt ActiveCount();
protected:
  IMPORT_C DObjectIx(TAny* aPtr);
private:
  void UpdateState();
  TInt iNextInstance;
  TInt iAllocated;     // Max entries before realloc needed
  TInt iCount; // At least 1 above the highest active index
  TInt iActiveCount; // No of actual entries in the index
  SDObjectIxRec* iObjects;
  TAny* iPtr;
  TInt iFree;      // The index of the first free slot or -1.
  TInt iUpdateDisabled;
public:
  static DMutex* HandleMutex;
  };
```

Key member data of *DObjectIx*

iNextInstance
This is a counter that starts at 1, and is incremented every time an object is added to the index. It is incremented again if it would become zero modulo 16384, so that the lower 14 bits range from 1 to 16383.

iAllocated
This is the number of slots currently allocated in the `iObjects` array.

`iCount`
This field is 1 + the highest index of any occupied slot in the `iObjects` array.

`iActiveCount`
This is the number of occupied slots in the `iObjects` array.

`iObjects`
This is a pointer to the array of object index records. Each record contains a pointer to a `DObject`, the instance counter modulo 16384 when the entry was added and the unique ID of the `DObjectCon` in which the `DObject` is held.

`iPtr`
This is a pointer to the process that is the ultimate owner of all handles in this index (that is, the thread's owning process for a thread-local handle array). This is passed as a parameter to `DObject::Close()` when a handle is closed.

Finding objects from handles
To translate a handle into a `DObject` pointer, the kernel follows the following steps, which are shown graphically in Figure 5.1:

1. Uses bit 30 of the handle to choose a `DObjectIx` (either the current thread's or the current process's handle array)

2. Takes the bottom 15 bits to use as an index, and checks this index against the `DObjectIx::iCount` value to ensure it is within the array

3. Uses the index to access an entry in the `iObjects` array of the `DObjectIx`

4. Compares the handle's instance value (bits 16–29) against the instance value stored in the `iObjects` array entry.[1] (We set the latter from the `DObjectIx::iNextInstance` value when the `DObjectIx` entry was made[2])

5. If the two instance values are the same, then the handle is valid

6. Checks the unique ID value in the `iObjects` array entry to ensure that the object pointed to is of the expected type

7. Finally, extracts the `DObject` pointer from the `iObjects` array entry.

---

[1] Note that the instance value provides protection against a stale handle being re-used after it has been closed and after the kernel has reallocated its index slot to a new handle. Handle lookup always occurs with the system locked to protect against changes in the handle array while it is being examined.

[2] Which is when the handle was created.

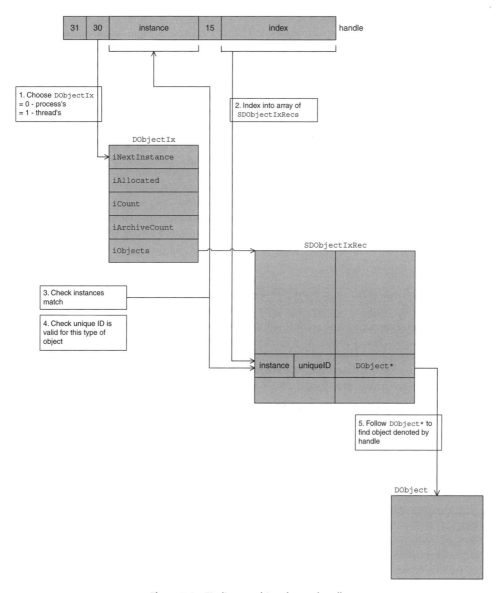

Figure 5.1   Finding an object from a handle

Protection of handle mechanisms

The adding and removing of handles requires some care. The kernel protects additions and removals from `DObjectIx` arrays with a global mutex, `DObjectIx::HandleMutex`. The mutex allows the `Exec::HandleInfo()` function to prevent any handle creation and deletion while it inspects the handle array of every thread and process.

The kernel doesn't protect the lookup of handles, though – this would slow it down too much. Instead it looks up handles while holding only the system lock.

If the `iObjects` array needs to grow as a result of adding a handle, the kernel uses the `Kern::SafeReAlloc()` function. This allocates a new larger block first, copies the old contents into it, fills the extra space in the new block with zeros, and then acquires the system lock before replacing the pointer with the address of the new block and deleting the old block. This ensures that any code running with the system locked always sees a valid handle array.

Since a handle contains an index into the `iObjects` array, the removal of an entry from the `iObjects` array cannot result in all the later entries being moved as that would make all the existing handles to those objects invalid. Instead, the kernel sets the entry's object pointer to `NULL` and adds the entry to the front of the linked list of free slots – that is, it sets `iFree` to point to the entry. When it next adds an object to the index, it will use up the slot denoted by `iFree`.

5.1.2.7   *Object containers*

Object containers exist for two reasons:

1.   So that the kernel can find objects by name

2.   So that the kernel can enumerate all the objects of a certain type.

With some exceptions, such as internal kernel mutexes, whenever the kernel creates a `DObject`-derived object it adds that object to the `DObjectCon` that corresponds to the object's type.

The kernel removes the object from the container when it deletes it – which, as we saw earlier, happens when the object's access count drops to zero. In fact, the removal of the object from the container is the last action that the kernel does before it frees the memory – because it is the `DObject` destructor that removes the dying `DObject` from the container.

When the kernel adds an object to a container, it checks that the object's full name is unique among the objects in that container. This ensures that the kernel can find the object unambiguously using its full name.

Each `DObjectCon` has its own `DMutex` that protects all accesses to the container, including those that simply index into the container. The kernel indexes into a `DObjectCon` much more rarely than it indexes into a `DObjectIx`, so the overhead of waiting on the mutex is not significant in this case.

Array management for `DObjectCon` is simpler than for `DObjectIx`. The first `iCount` slots are occupied with no gaps – removing an entry

will move all the following entries down one. When the kernel adds a
new entry, it always goes at the end of the array.

Here is the DObjectCon class:

```
class DObjectCon : public DBase
  {
protected:
  enum {ENotOwnerID};
public:
  ~DObjectCon();
  static DObjectCon* New(TInt aUniqueID);
  IMPORT_C void Remove(DObject* aObj);
  IMPORT_C TInt Add(DObject* aObj);
  IMPORT_C DObject* operator[](TInt aIndex);
  IMPORT_C DObject* At(TInt aFindHandle);
  IMPORT_C TInt CheckUniqueFullName(DObject* aOwner, const TDesC& aName);
  IMPORT_C TInt CheckUniqueFullName(DObject* aObject);
  IMPORT_C TInt FindByName(TInt& aFindHandle, const TDesC& aMatch,
                                              TKName& aName);
  IMPORT_C TInt FindByFullName(TInt& aFindHandle, const TDesC& aMatch,
                                                  TFullName& aFullName);
  IMPORT_C TInt OpenByFullName(DObject*& aObject, const TDesC& aMatch);
  inline TInt UniqueID() {return iUniqueID;}
  inline TInt Count() {return iCount;}
  inline void Wait() {Kern::MutexWait(*iMutex);}
  inline void Signal() {Kern::MutexSignal(*iMutex);}
  inline DMutex* Lock() {return iMutex;}
protected:
  DObjectCon(TInt aUniqueID);
  TBool NamesMatch(DObject* aObject, DObject* aCurrentObject);
  TBool NamesMatch(DObject* aObject, const TDesC& aObjectName,
                                     DObject* aCurrentObject);
public:
  TInt iUniqueID;
private:
  TInt iAllocated;
  TInt iCount;
  DObject** iObjects;
  DMutex* iMutex;
  };
```

Key member data of DObjectCon

iUniqueID
This is an identity number indicating the type of kernel object held
in this container. The value used is 1 + the corresponding value in
the TObjectType enumeration – for example the identity number for
threads is 1.

iAllocated
This is the number of slots currently allocated in the iObjects array.

`iCount`
This is the number of slots currently occupied in the `iObjects` array.

`iObjects`
This is the pointer to the array of pointers to `DObjects` that are currently held in this container.

`iMutex`
This is the pointer to the `DMutex` mutex object that the kernel uses to protect accesses to this container.

5.2 Services provided to user threads

5.2.1 Executive call mechanism

The kernel provides services to user-mode code using a mechanism that we call *executive calls*, or *exec calls* for short.

Exec calls begin as a standard user-side function, and then use a software exception as a gateway to allow them to enter kernel code. The software exception instruction switches the CPU into supervisor mode and starts the execution of kernel code at a defined entry point – see Chapter 6, *Interrupts and Exceptions*, for more on this.

The CPU's instruction set generally limits the number of possible entry points from software interrupts or traps – for example, on an ARM CPU there is only one SWI instruction to enter supervisor mode. Because of this, we use a dispatcher in the nanokernel to decode a parameter passed from user side, determine the function required and then call it. On ARM CPUs, the parameter is the opcode used with the SWI instruction, and this determines the function that the dispatcher calls.

This calling mechanism results in a very loose coupling between the kernel and user processes, and this means that we can make design changes within the kernel more easily.

5.2.1.1 Flow of execution in an executive call

Now I'll show the flow of execution from a user-mode application to supervisor-mode kernel code and back again. Let's choose an example to trace:

```
TUint8* Exec::ChunkBase(ChunkHandle)
```

This executive call returns a pointer to the start of a chunk belonging to the calling thread. The parameter passed is the handle of the chunk within the thread.

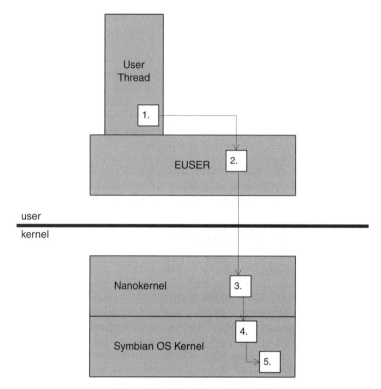

Figure 5.2   Kernel executive call

You can follow my explanation in Figure 5.2.

1. **User thread:** Let's assume that a user-side thread is executing the following section of code:

```
RChunk newChunk=0;
newChunk=OpenGlobal(_L(''SharedChunk''),ETrue);
TUint* base=0;
base=newChunk.Base();
```

This code segment opens a shared chunk and stores the handle returned in newChunk. Next it wants to find out the base address of this chunk, which it does by calling RChunk::Base(). I will trace this operation from the user side into the kernel, via an executive call.

The code for the RChunk::Base() method is found in the file \e32\euser\us_exec.cpp and looks like this:

```
EXPORT_C TUint8 *RChunk::Base() const
  {
  return(Exec::ChunkBase(iHandle));
  }
```

So RChunk::Base() calls Exec::ChunkBase(), which is in the user library, EUSER.DLL.

2. **User library:** Exec::ChunkBase() is in the file \epoc32\include\exec_user.h, and is generated by entering "ABLD MAKE-FILE GENEXEC" in the E32 directory. The ABLD tool takes the file execs.txt, and uses it to generate the source code for the user-side executive calls. The portion of execs.txt we are interested in is this:

```
slow
  {
  name = ChunkBase
  return = TUint8*
  handle = chunk
  }
```

You can see that it tells the tools to generate a function named ChunkBase which returns a pointer to TUint, and which is passed a handle to a chunk.

The generated Exec::ChunkBase() function looks like this:

```
__EXECDECL__ TUint8* Exec::ChunkBase(TInt)
  {
  SLOW_EXEC1(EExecChunkBase);
  }
```

In \e32\include\u32exec.h we have:

```
#elif defined(__CPU_ARM)

// Executive call macros for AR
#define EXECUTIVE_FAST 0x00800000
#define EXECUTIVE_SLOW 0x00000000
#define __DISPATCH(n)                            \
  asm("mov ip, lr ");                            \
  asm("swi %a0" : : "i" (n));

#define FAST_EXEC0(n) __DISPATCH((n)|EXECUTIVE_FAST)
#define FAST_EXEC1(n) __DISPATCH((n)|EXECUTIVE_FAST)
#define SLOW_EXEC0(n) __DISPATCH((n)|EXECUTIVE_SLOW)
#define SLOW_EXEC1(n) __DISPATCH((n)|EXECUTIVE_SLOW)
#define SLOW_EXEC2(n) __DISPATCH((n)|EXECUTIVE_SLOW)
#define SLOW_EXEC3(n) __DISPATCH((n)|EXECUTIVE_SLOW)
#define SLOW_EXEC4(n) __DISPATCH((n)|EXECUTIVE_SLOW)
```

When you disentangle the macros, you can see that Exec::ChunkBase() makes this SWI call to enter supervisor mode:

```
SWI EExecChunkBase
```

EExecChunkBase is an enumeration that gives the opcode for the SWI call.

3. **Nanokernel dispatcher:**   We enter the nanokernel at the function
    __ArmVectorSwi, in vectors.cia. This function makes much
    use of the executive tables, which are defined like this:

    ```
    GLREF_D const TUint32 EpocFastExecTable[];
    GLREF_D const TUint32 EpocSlowExecTable[];
    ```

Essentially, the fast executive table consists of a number of 32-bit entries,
the nth of which is the address of the handler for the nth fast exec call.
The slow executive table consists of pairs of 32-bit entries, the first of
which is a set of attribute flags, and the second of which is the address
of the slow exec call handler. I will cover this subject in more detail in
Section 5.2.1.6.

The function __ArmVectorSwi first checks bit 23 of the ARM opcode
to find out whether this is a slow exec call or a fast one. If bit 23 is 1, then
this is a fast exec call, and the dispatcher will switch interrupts off before
indexing into the fast exec table, and calling the relevant kernel function.

In our case, bit 23 is 0, so ours is a slow exec call. Next the
dispatcher checks bit 31 in the attribute word of the slow exec table.
EExecChunkBase has this bit set, so the dispatcher locks the system by
taking the system lock fast mutex.

The dispatcher goes on to check another bit in the attribute word to
see if it should call the Symbian OS preprocessing handler, PreprocessHandler, the address of which it discovers from the second word
of the slow exec table. The dispatcher always claims the system lock
before calling PreprocessHandler.

Again, in our case this bit is set, so the dispatcher calls PreprocessHandler. I'll discuss this in the next section.

On returning from PreprocessHandler, the dispatcher finally calls
the relevant OS function: in our case this is ExecHandler::ChunkBase().

Finally the dispatcher checks a bit to see whether it should release the
system lock fast mutex, and after doing so if required, it returns to the
user library.

4. **Preprocessing handler (optional):**   The preprocessing handler is part
    of the Symbian OS kernel (rather than the nanokernel) and is found
    in cexec.cia. It looks up handles to kernel objects.
    The preprocessing handler has access to the following information:

    • The arguments passed to the executive function, which include
      the handle to look up. The preprocessing handler may modify
      these arguments as part of its execution

    • The attribute flags of the executive call, the bottom five bits of
      which specify the type of kernel object that the handle refers to.

On return, the preprocessing handler will have replaced the handle with a pointer to the kernel object to which it refers.

There are various special handles that the preprocessing handler must pay attention to. Firstly, there are the two handles defined in `e32const.h`:

```
//A flag used by the kernel to indicate the current process.
const TInt KCurrentProcessHandle=0xffff0000|KHandleNoClose;

//A flag used by the kernel to indicate the current thread.
const TInt KCurrentThreadHandle=0xffff0001|KHandleNoClose;
```

Then there are three special handle types:

```
// lookup IPC message handle, allow disconnect
EIpcMessageD=0x20,

// lookup IPC message handle, don't allow disconnect
EIpcMessage=0x21,

// lookup IPC message client, don't allow disconnect
EIpcClient=0x22,
```

Handles like of this type are "magic" values that refer to a client/server IPC message. In the case of `EIpcClient` type, this means "the thread that sent the message". The magic value is in fact the address of the `RMessageK` object stored within the kernel! Don't worry – the kernel performs strict validation checks on this object to prevent security breaches.

Returning to our simpler example, the preprocessing handler merely looks up the handle in the owning thread or process, and returns with a pointer to the corresponding `DChunk`.

5. **OS function:** The exec handling function that the dispatcher calls may be almost anywhere in kernel – in the nanokernel, the Symbian OS kernel, the memory model or even the variant.

   In our example, `ExecHandler::ChunkBase()` is in the file `sexec.cpp`, which is part of the Symbian OS kernel. This function simply retrieves the base of the chunk from the `DChunk`, like this:

```
TUint8 *ExecHandler::ChunkBase(DChunk* aChunk)
// Return the address of the base of the Chunk.
  {
  return (TUint8 *)aChunk->Base();
  }
```

5.2.1.2 *Context of executive call*

An exec call executes in the context of the calling user-mode thread, not that of any kernel thread. The only changes that happen on entry to the kernel are:

- The processor switches into supervisor mode

- The active stack changes from the current thread's user stack to the current thread's supervisor stack.

Because of this, you can't make an exec call from an interrupt service routine or an IDFC, because in these situations there is no thread context.

5.2.1.3   Changes from EKA1

The exec call mechanism has changed considerably from EKA1 to EKA2. On EKA1, exec calls borrow the kernel server or the null thread stack, rather than running on the calling thread's own supervisor stack as they do on EKA2. For this, and other reasons, EKA1 exec calls have the following restrictions:

1.   They are not preemptible

2.   They can't block in the kernel

3.   They can't allocate and free kernel memory.

On EKA1, if a user-mode thread needed to call a service that allocated or freed kernel memory (for example, a service that created or destroyed objects derived from CObject), then that user-mode thread had to make a special kind of kernel call, known as a kernel server call. This is no longer the case in EKA2.

As we've seen, on EKA2 exec calls run on the supervisor stack of the calling thread. This means that exec calls can be preempted and they can block in the kernel. Furthermore, because EKA2 does not link to EUSER, exec calls may allocate and free kernel memory.

5.2.1.4   Accessing user-mode memory

Earlier in this chapter, I said that an exec call runs in the context of the calling thread. This means that on systems with an MMU and multiple processes running in separate address spaces, the active address space is still that of the process to which the calling thread belongs. It is therefore theoretically possible for the kernel-side exec call to directly access the memory of the user process that called it, by dereferencing a pointer or using memcpy(). However, in practice we do not allow this. This is because the exec call is executing kernel code with supervisor privileges, and can therefore read and write anywhere in the processor's address space, which of course includes kernel memory. If the exec call dereferences a pointer given to it by a user thread without checking that pointer, then we are effectively giving the user thread the freedom to access all of the address space too. This defeats platform security and makes it more likely that an invalid pointer from the user application will overwrite a key part of the kernel, crashing the mobile phone.

5.2.1.5   The kumem functions

Does this mean that exec calls can't access the memory of the user process that called them? No, because we provide the special kernel functions kumemget(), kumemput() and kumemset() to dereference the pointers that are passed from user code. You should use these functions yourself if you are writing a device driver or an extension that is passed pointers to user data from user-side code.

The kumem functions access memory with special CPU instructions that perform the access at user privilege level – for example LDRT/STRT on ARM. Here is the relevant portion of the kumemget() function, this time on X86 for a change:

```
_asm mov ax, gs
_asm mov ds, ax
_asm call CopyInterSeg
```

On entry to the function, GS contains the data segment of the caller – this is obviously a user-mode data segment in the case of an exec call. We move GS to DS before we call CopyInterSeg(), which copies ECX bytes from DS:ESI to ES:EDI. This means that the user's data segment is used as the source of the copy, and the memory move therefore respects the privileges of the caller.

5.2.1.6   Slow and fast executive calls compared

I mentioned earlier that the dispatcher checks a bit in the SWI opcode to determine whether the exec call is a slow or a fast one. In this section I'll discuss these two forms of exec call in more detail and point out the differences between them.

Slow executive calls

Slow exec calls run with interrupts enabled and the kernel unlocked. This means that they can be preempted at any point in their execution.

As we saw in the walk-through, slow exec calls have a mechanism for automatically performing certain actions when in the dispatcher. This mechanism relies on particular bits being set in the attribute word of the slow executive table.

Using this mechanism, a slow exec call may:

- Acquire the system lock fast mutex before calling the kernel handler
- Release the system lock after calling the kernel handler
- Call a Symbian OS preprocessing handler to look up a Symbian OS handle. In this case, the call always acquires the system lock too.

A key difference between slow and fast execs is that the user side can pass many more parameters to a slow exec call. In their standard form, slow execs can have up to four direct 32-bit arguments and can return one 32-bit value. If this isn't enough, then the slow exec call can also copy as many as eight additional 32-bit values from user space to the current thread's supervisor stack. If this is done, then we have to use one of the four direct arguments to point to the additional arguments, so we can pass a maximum of eleven arguments in total.

These extra exec call arguments are a new feature of EKA2 that is not available on EKA1. On EKA1, you could pass extra arguments, but only by passing a pointer to an arbitrary amount of additional user-mode data as one of the four standard parameters. The EKA1 kernel would then access this data directly, which, as I discussed in Section 5.2.1.4, is not safe. EKA2 allows the extra arguments to be passed in a way that does not compromise robustness or security, because the new kernel uses the kumem functions to access the additional data.

The mechanism by which the extra parameters are passed is dependent on the CPU architecture. If the processor has sufficient registers, then we use those that are not already in use. For example, on ARM, we pass the extra arguments in R4-R11; this means that the user-side Exec:: functions must save these registers and load the additional arguments into them before executing the SWI instruction to enter the kernel. The Exec:: functions must then restore those registers on return from the kernel. The dispatcher pushes R4–R11 onto the supervisor stack and then sets R2 (the third normal argument) to the address of the saved R4.

On X86, we use the third argument to pass a pointer to the additional arguments in user memory. The dispatcher copies the specified number of arguments from user memory space to the current thread's supervisor stack and modifies the third argument to refer to the copied arguments. If the SWI opcode has its system lock bit set, then the dispatcher copies the arguments before it acquires the system lock. We do it this way in case an exception occurs during the copying of the additional arguments because the supplied address is invalid. Then, if this does happen, the kernel can terminate the current thread without a problem.

Regardless of the CPU architecture, the executive handler always accesses the additional arguments by using the third normal argument as a pointer to them. By the time the executive handler runs, the dispatcher will have copied the additional arguments to the current thread's supervisor stack, and changed the third argument to refer to that copy. This means that the executive handler does not need to check that the referenced address is a valid user mode address.

Fast exec calls

As we saw earlier, slow exec calls run with interrupts enabled. Fast exec calls, on the contrary, run with all interrupts disabled. This is another difference from EKA1, where they ran with IRQ interrupts disabled and FIQ interrupts enabled. Because of this, EKA2 fast exec calls must be very short. There aren't many of them, and typically they get or set a single, easily accessible, item of kernel data. For example, there is a fast exec call to get the current thread's heap pointer.

We saw that slow exec calls can pass up to eleven parameters. Fast exec calls, on the other hand, can only pass one 32-bit parameter. They may also return a single 32-bit value.

5.2.1.7   Executive tables

I have already mentioned that we specify the range of valid fast and slow executive calls and their associated handlers using two tables – the fast executive table and the slow executive table. Every nanokernel thread in the system has two pointers, one to each of these tables. The kernel sets up these pointers when the thread is created, which means that the available executive calls can be changed on a thread-by-thread basis. All Symbian OS threads do in fact use the same tables, but this feature makes it possible for threads in an RTOS personality layer to use different tables, if desired. It is worth noting that you would only need to use this feature if you had user-mode personality layer threads. If your threads only ever run in supervisor mode, then you can call your required personality layer services directly.

The fast executive table
The fast executive table is composed of a number of 32-bit entries, like so:

Word index	Description
0	Number of fast executive calls supported.
n ≥ 1	Address of handler for fast executive call number n.

You can see that fast executive call 0 has no entry in the table. This is because it is always assigned to wait on the current thread's request semaphore.

If a thread makes a fast executive call with a number that is greater than or equal to the number of calls specified in the table, then the kernel calls the invalid executive handler, which is specified in the slow executive table.

The slow executive table
The slow executive table is composed of three single-word entries followed by an arbitrary number of two-word entries, like so:

Word index	Description
0	Number of slow executive calls supported.
1	Address of handler for invalid call number.
2	Address of handler for argument preprocessing.
3+2n	Attribute flags for slow executive call number n.
4+2n	Address of handler for slow executive call number n.

If a thread makes a slow executive call with a number that is greater than or equal to the number of calls specified in the table, then the kernel calls the invalid executive handler, which is specified in word 1 of the table. Invalid fast exec calls are routed here too, but even in this case the kernel treats the invalid handler as a slow executive call with its attribute flags all zero.

I've mentioned the attribute flags already in the walk-through and in my discussions about the differences between slow and fast exec calls. These flags determine any additional actions that the dispatcher performs before calling the handler and after returning from it. Here are the details of the functions associated with each bit:

Bit	Description
31	If this bit is set to 1, the system lock fast mutex will be acquired prior to calling the executive handler.
30	If this bit is set to 1, the system lock fast mutex will be released after returning from the executive handler.
29	If this bit is set to 1, the preprocessing handler will be called prior to calling the executive handler. Note that if bit 31 is also set to 1, the system lock is acquired before calling the preprocessing handler.
26, 27, 28	These bits make a three-bit wide field indicating the number of additional arguments required by the executive call. A value of 0 indicates that there are no additional arguments; a value of n, where $1 \le n \le 7$ indicates that there are $n + 1$ additional arguments. Thus up to eight additional arguments may be specified.

5.2.1.8   Kernel server calls

If you know EKA1, you may be wondering why I haven't mentioned kernel server calls. Let me explain a little bit about them, and then I hope the reason will become clear.

As I've said, EKA1 makes use of the EUSER library. The heap functions in EUSER allocate and free memory on the heap of the current thread. This made it difficult for any EKA1 exec calls that resulted in the creation (or destruction) of kernel objects – those objects must be created on the kernel heap, but during the executive call the thread context is that of the thread making the executive call.

So, to ensure that the memory was allocated on the kernel heap, we had to engineer a switch to a kernel thread context. To do this, an EKA1 thread executes a special exec call that makes a request from the kernel server thread and then blocks awaiting the reply. At the next reschedule, the kernel server thread will run (as it is the highest priority thread in the system) and obviously it can then create or destroy objects on its own heap on behalf of the user thread.

EKA2 has its own memory allocation routines, and does not link to EUSER. This means that EKA2 exec calls can allocate and free kernel memory and we do not need kernel server calls.

5.2.2   Executive calls in the emulator

The emulator can't use a software interrupt to implement executive calls, so instead it uses a function call but with a special calling convention.

The executive dispatcher lives in the nanokernel, but the calls themselves are in the user library (EUSER.DLL). To prevent EUSER.DLL depending on EKERN.EXE, this call is not done using the standard import machinery. Instead, there is a function pointer to the dispatcher in EUSER, which is initialized lazily to point to the first ordinal in EKERN.EXE – this is the only export from EKERN that must be maintained in EKA2's emulator. The executive functions in EUSER first set up two parameters (the executive number and the pointer to the parameters, which are all on the thread stack), then they jump to the nanokernel dispatcher function.

The dispatcher then handles the executive in a way which is similar to that on a phone: the executive function runs with the thread in "kernel mode", fast executive calls run with interrupts disabled and slow executive calls can manipulate the system lock and have preprocessing done on their parameters.

5.3   Example user-accessible services

In this section, I'm just aiming to give you a feel for the kind of services that the kernel provides via EUSER, and how we decide to categorize each exec call.

5.3.1   Fast exec calls

As we saw, fast executive calls run with all interrupts off, so they must do their tasks very quickly and then return to the user. Generally these calls just get or set a single word of kernel memory. Here are some examples:

```
RAllocator* Exec::Heap()
```
Returns the current thread's heap.

```
TUint32 Exec::FastCounter()
```
Returns the value of the fast counter, which can be used in profiling.

```
Exec::SetDebugMask(TUint32)
```
Sets the kernel's debug bit mask to determine the level of `printf()` debugging displayed on the serial port. Often used in debug code to restrict debug printing to key areas of interest.

5.3.2   Slow exec calls

5.3.2.1   Services that don't claim the system lock

These services are ones which do not need to lock the system to protect them from their own side effects – that is, two concurrent calls to the same exec call will not interfere with each other. These services often read, rather than modify, kernel data. Examples are:

```
void Exec::IMB_Range(TAny* aBase, TUint aLength)
```
Performs all necessary cache management for the address range `aBase` to `aBase+aLength` in order that whatever has been written there can be executed. This is known as an instruction memory barrier (IMB).

```
TUint Exec::TickCount()
```
Returns the number of system ticks since boot.

```
void Exec::DebugPrint(TAny* aDebugText, TInt aMode)
```
Passes in a descriptor with text to print out as a debug string, and a mode to print in.

5.3.2.2   Services that claim the system lock

As we've seen, certain slow exec calls have a bit set in their attribute word to say that the dispatcher should lock the system before calling the executive handler in the kernel. The main reason for this is to protect certain kernel resources against multiple accesses.

Examples of this type of service are:

```
TUint32 Exec::MathRandom()
```
Returns a random number. Since this code is not re-entrant, the system is locked.

`void Exec::CaptureEventHook()`

The window server calls this function to capture the event hook. Only one thread may own this event hook, so the system is locked to prevent a second thread gaining access to the function before the first thread has flagged that it has taken the hook by setting the kernel variable `K::EventThread` to point to itself. On the secure kernel, this function panics if the thread taking the event hook is not the window server thread.

Services passing handles

Certain slow exec calls have a bit set in their attribute word to say that the dispatcher should call a preprocessing handler in the Symbian OS kernel before calling the executive handler in the kernel. The preprocessing handler takes the first argument of the slow exec call, which is always a handle, and translates it into a `DObject` derived object pointer.

Any slow exec call that calls the preprocessing handler also claims the system lock.

Examples of this type of service are:

`TUint8* Exec::ChunkBase(ChunkHandle aHandle)`

Returns a pointer to the start of a chunk.

`TInt Exec::ThreadId(ThreadHandle aHandle)`

Returns the ID of the given thread.

`TlibraryFunction LibraryLookup(LibraryHandle aHandle, TInt aFunction)`

Returns the address of the required function number in the given library.

Services where the dispatcher doesn't release the lock

These exec calls claim the system lock on entry, but don't unlock it on exit. This is because the exec handler functions release the system lock themselves.

Examples of this type of service are:

`void Exec::MutexWait(MutexHandle aHandle)`

Waits on the given mutex.

`void Exec::ProcessSetPriority(ProcessHandle aProcess, TProcessPriority aPriority)`

Sets the priority of the given process.

`void Exec::SemaphoreSignalN(SemHandle aHandle, TInt aNum)`

Signals the given semaphore a number of times.

5.3.3 HAL functions

As we've seen, the EKA2 kernel is not linked to, and never calls, the user library, EUSER.DLL. This is a major difference from EKA1, which often used the user library as a way to call its own services, going via an executive call and a supervisor mode SWI to the required service, even though it was already executing in supervisor mode.

Not only does EKA2 not call EUSER, it rarely makes a SWI call either – clearly a good thing for its performance. In fact, there is only one place where EKA2 does make a SWI call – `Kern::HalFunction()`. This function is used to request a service from a kernel extension, and user threads call it via the function `UserSvr::HalFunction()`.

The hardware abstraction layer, or HAL, consists of a set of hardware or system attributes that can be set or read by software. These are broken down into groups of like functionality, as enumerated by `THalFunctionGroup`:

```
enum THalFunctionGroup
  {
  EHalGroupKernel=0,
  EHalGroupVariant=1,
  EHalGroupMedia=2,
  EHalGroupPower=3,
  EHalGroupDisplay=4,
  EHalGroupDigitiser=5,
  EHalGroupSound=6,
  EHalGroupMouse=7,
  EHalGroupEmulator=8,
  EHalGroupKeyboard=9,
  };
```

Each of these groups then has a set of attributes. For example, the first group, `EHalGroupKernel`, has these attributes:

```
enum TKernelHalFunction
  {
  EKernelHalMemoryInfo,
  EKernelHalRomInfo,
  EKernelHalStartupReason,
  EKernelHalFaultReason,
  EKernelHalExceptionId,
  EKernelHalExceptionInfo,
  EKernelHalCpuInfo,
  EKernelHalPageSizeInBytes,
  EKernelHalTickPeriod,
  EKernelHalMemModelInfo,
  };
```

Each HAL group has a handler function that manages the group's attributes. This handler can be dynamically installed by using the function

`Kern::AddHalEntry()`. For example, some HAL groups correspond to a particular hardware device, like the screen display or keyboards, and the kernel extension or device drivers for these devices will install a handler.

As I said earlier, the kernel accesses HAL functions via `Kern::HalFunction()`:

```
EXPORT_C __NAKED__ TInt Kern::HalFunction(TInt /*aGroup*/,
                    TInt /*aFunction*/, TAny* /*a1*/,
                    TAny* /*a2*/, TInt /*aDeviceNumber*/)
    {
    asm("ldr ip, [sp, #0] ");
    asm("orr r0, r0, ip, lsl #16 ");
    asm("mov ip, lr ");
    asm("swi %a0" : : "i"(EExecHalFunction|EXECUTIVE_SLOW));
    }
```

You can see that the first and second parameters are the group and the number of the function. The remaining parameters, if present, are passed to the HAL function itself.

5.4   Services provided by the kernel to the kernel

In the introduction to this book, I mentioned that we could consider the architecture of EKA2 from a software layering perspective, as shown in Figure 5.3, and went on to discuss the kind of software that appeared at each layer.

In this chapter, I am more concerned with the services each layer provides to the other layers.

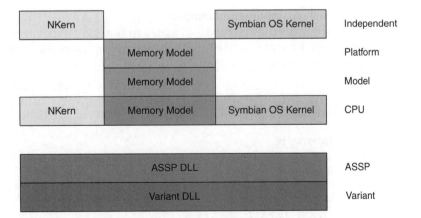

Figure 5.3   Software layering

5.4.1   Independent layer

5.4.1.1   Nanokernel

The static interface to the independent nanokernel is provided through the class `NKern`, which is defined in `nkern.h`. The APIs in this class cover a few key areas of interest, which I'll discuss now.

Threads

`NKern` provides a static interface to nanothread manipulation, using an `NThread*` parameter. This allows callers to create a nanothread, to kill it, to suspend it, to release it and more. Here are a couple of examples:

```
static void ThreadKill(NThread* aThread)
static void ThreadSetPriority(NThread* aThread, TInt aPriority);
```

Timers

As we saw in Chapter 2, *Hardware for Symbian OS*, the kernel needs hardware to provide a periodic tick interrupt; this timer must be started from the ASSP's or variant's `Init3()` function. The period of this tick determines the timer resolution and is usually set to 1 ms – hence it is frequently known as the millisecond timer. The tick interrupt's interrupt handler calls the `Tick()` method in the nanokernel's timer queue class, `NTimerQ`.

Nanokernel timers provide the most fundamental system timing functions in the operating system. Symbian OS tick-based timers and time-of-day functions are both derived from nanokernel timers. In addition, the nanokernel timer service supports timed wait services, if implemented. The tick interrupt is also used to drive the round-robin scheduling for equal-priority thread.

I will discuss timers in more detail in Section 5.5.

Fast semaphores and mutexes

The `NKern` semaphore and mutex APIs allow their callers to wait on and signal nanokernel fast mutexes and semaphores. Here are the two fast mutex APIs:

```
static void FMWait(NFastMutex* aMutex);
static void FMSignal(NFastMutex* aMutex);
```

Interrupts

The `NKern` interrupt APIs allow their callers to enable and disable interrupts: globally, or to a certain level. For example:

```
static TInt DisableAllInterrupts();
void EnableAllInterrupts();
```

Read-modify-write

The `NKern` read-modify-write APIs allow their callers to atomically increment or decrement a counter, preventing side-effects from two threads attempting to access the same counter. For example:

```
static TInt LockedInc(TInt& aCount);
static TInt LockedDec(TInt& aCount);
```

Key concrete classes

The independent nanokernel also provides key classes that are used by the rest of the kernel. I have covered or will cover these in other chapters, so here it will suffice to enumerate them:

- `NFastSemaphore`
- `NFastMutex`
- `TDfc`.

5.4.1.2 Symbian OS kernel

The static interface to the independent Symbian OS is provided through the class `Kern`, which is defined in `kernel.h`. The APIs in this class cover a wide miscellany of topics, of which I'll pick out a few.

Thread read and write

The `Kern` class provides APIs to allow other parts of the kernel to safely read and write from threads' address spaces.

```
static TInt ThreadDesRead(DThread* aThread, const TAny* aSrc,
                    TDes8& aDest, TInt aOffset, TInt aMode);
static TInt ThreadRawRead(DThread* aThread, const TAny* aSrc,
                                 TAny* aDest, TInt aSize);
static TInt ThreadDesWrite(DThread* aThread, TAny* aDest,
            const TDesC8& aSrc, TInt aOffset, TInt aMode,
                               Thread* aOrigThread);
static TInt ThreadRawWrite(DThread* aThread, TAny* aDest,
                     const TAny* aSrc, TInt aSize,
                        DThread* aOrigThread=NULL);
```

Access to kernel variables

In this case, a variety of examples is worth a thousand words:

```
static TTimeK SystemTime();
static DPowerModel* PowerModel();
static DObjectCon* const *Containers();
static TSuperPage& SuperPage();
static TMachineConfig& MachineConfig();
static DThread& CurrentThread();
static DProcess& CurrentProcess();
```

Key concrete classes

At this level, the Symbian OS kernel provides the abstractions of key kernel objects such as DThread, DProcess, and DChunk. I discuss these in detail in Chapter 3, *Threads, Processes and Libraries* and Chapter 7, *Memory Models*.

5.4.2   Platform (or image) layer

5.4.2.1   *Memory model*

The memory model is the only module in the platform layer, because this layer is essentially concerned with executable images on disk, and processes in memory. This means that there are only two possibilities at the platform layer: EPOC for a real mobile phone platform or WIN32 for the emulator.

The platform layer provides static APIs to the independent layer in the class P, which is defined in kern_priv.h. This is very short, so I'll show you all of it:

```
class P
  {
public:
  static TInt InitSystemTime();
  static void CreateVariant();
  static void StartExtensions();
  static void KernelInfo(TProcessCreateInfo& aInfo,
                         TAny*& aStack, TAny*& aHeap);
  static void NormalizeExecutableFileName(TDes& aFileName);
  static void SetSuperPageSignature();
  static TBool CheckSuperPageSignature();
  static DProcess* NewProcess();
  };
```

You can see that the platform layer takes part, as expected, in certain key initializations. It starts the system clock (reading the system time on Win32, the RTC on a mobile phone), starts the extensions (including the variant) and then creates the actual variant object by calling A::CreateVariant(). I will talk about this more in Chapter 16, *Boot Processes*.

Key concrete classes

The most important class with a platform specific implementation is the Symbian OS process, DProcess. The implementation is provided by the derived DEpocProcess class on the EPOC platform and DWin32Process on the emulator.

5.4.3   Model layer

5.4.3.1   *Memory model*

The model layer is the place in which we have isolated all the kernel's assumptions about memory hardware and layout. The main functions that this layer provides are low-level memory management – how the MMU is used and how the address space is configured.

Symbian OS currently supports four memory models – one for the WIN32 platform (the emulator model) and three for the EPOC platform (moving, multiple and direct). If you want to find out more, turn to Chapter 7, *Memory Models*.

There are two static interfaces to the memory model. The first is defined in the class Epoc, in platform.h. This is a common interface to all EPOC memory models, which is provided for use by extensions and device drivers. It looks like this:

```
class Epoc
    {
public:
  IMPORT_C static void SetMonitorEntryPoint(TDfcFn aFunction);
  IMPORT_C static void SetMonitorExceptionHandler(TLinAddr aHandler);
  IMPORT_C static TAny* ExceptionInfo();
  IMPORT_C static const TRomHeader& RomHeader();
  IMPORT_C static TInt AllocShadowPage(TLinAddr aRomAddr);
  IMPORT_C static TInt FreeShadowPage(TLinAddr aRomAddr);
  IMPORT_C static TInt FreezeShadowPage(TLinAddr aRomAddr);
  IMPORT_C static TInt AllocPhysicalRam(TInt aSize, TPhysAddr& aPhysAddr,
                                                     TInt aAlign=0);
  IMPORT_C static TInt FreePhysicalRam(TPhysAddr aPhysAddr, TInt aSize);
  IMPORT_C static TInt ClaimPhysicalRam(TPhysAddr aPhysAddr, TInt aSize);
  IMPORT_C static TPhysAddr LinearToPhysical(TLinAddr aLinAddr);
  IMPORT_C static void RomProcessInfo(TProcessCreateInfo& aInfo,
                        const TRomImageHeader& aRomImageHeader);
    };
```

You can see that this interface provides functions for allocating physical RAM, for finding information in ROM, and for converting linear addresses to physical ones.

The second interface to the memory model is in class M, in kern_priv.h. This consists of functions provided by the memory model to the independent layer. Here it is:

```
class M
    {
public:
  static void Init1();
  static void Init2();
  static TInt InitSvHeapChunk(DChunk* aChunk, TInt aSize);
  static TInt InitSvStackChunk();
  static TBool IsRomAddress(const TAny* aPtr);
  static TInt PageSizeInBytes();
  static void SetupCacheFlushPtr(TInt aCache, SCacheInfo& c);
  static void FsRegisterThread();
```

```
static DCodeSeg* NewCodeSeg(TCodeSegCreateInfo& aInfo);
};
```

You can see that this class mainly provides initialization functions that the independent layer calls during startup.

Key concrete classes

At this level you can find model specific implementations of many key Symbian OS classes. For example, DMemModelChunk derives from DChunk and DMemModelThread derives from DThread. On the EPOC platform the DMemModelProcess class derives from DEpocProcess, which in turn derives from DProcess. On the emulator the concrete class representing a process is DWin32Process, which derives directly from DProcess.

5.4.4　CPU layer

5.4.4.1　Nanokernel and Symbian OS kernel

The CPU layer is where we make assumptions about the particular processor we're running on – is it X86 or ARM? This is the layer in which you might expect to see some assembler making an appearance. In fact, a sizable proportion of the code in the ARM CPU layer of the Symbian OS kernel is actually independent layer functionality that has been assembler coded for improved performance.

There are two static interfaces to the CPU layer nanokernel and Symbian OS kernel. The first is provided in the class Arm, which is defined in arm.h, and is an interface to the ARM CPU layer for the use of the variant. (There is a similar class X86 for the X86 CPU layer.) The Arm class looks like this:

```
class Arm
    {
public:
  enum {EDebugPortJTAG=42};
  static void Init1Interrupts();
  static TInt AdjustRegistersAfterAbort(TAny* aContext);
  static void GetUserSpAndLr(TAny* /*aReg[2]*/);
  static void SetUserSpAndLr(TAny* /*aReg[2]*/);
  IMPORT_C static void SetIrqHandler(TLinAddr aHandler);
  IMPORT_C static void SetFiqHandler(TLinAddr aHandler);
  IMPORT_C static TInt DebugOutJTAG(TUint aChar);
  IMPORT_C static TInt DebugInJTAG(TUint32& aRxData);
  IMPORT_C static void SetCpInfo(TInt aCpNum,
                          const SCpInfo* aInfo);
  IMPORT_C static void SetStaticCpContextSize(TInt aSize);
  IMPORT_C static void AllocExtraContext(TInt aRequiredSize);
  static void CpInit0();
  static void CpInit1();
```

```
static Uint64 IrqStack[KIrqStackSize/8];
static Uint64 FiqStack[KFiqStackSize/8];
static Uint64 ExceptionStack[KExceptionStackSize/8];
}
```

You can see that a key use case is to allow the variant to install primary interrupt dispatchers.

The second interface class, class A, provided in kern_priv.h, contains CPU layer APIs that are called by both the memory model and independent layer – but mainly the latter.

```
class A
  {
public:
  static void Init1();
  static void Init2();
  static void Init3();
  static void DebugPrint(const TDesC8& aDes);
  static void UserDebugPrint(const TText* aPtr, TInt aLen,
                                            TBool aNewLine);
  static TInt CreateVariant(const TAny* aFile);
  static TInt NullThread(TAny*);
  static DPlatChunkHw* NewHwChunk();
  static TPtr8 MachineConfiguration();
  static void StartCrashDebugger(const TDesC8& aDes, TInt aFault);
  static TInt MsTickPeriod();
  static TInt CallSupervisorFunction(TSupervisorFunction aFunction,
                                            TAny* aParameter);
  static TInt VariantHal(TInt aFunction, TAny* a1, TAny* a2);
  static TInt SystemTimeInSecondsFrom2000(TInt& aTime);
  static TInt SetSystemTimeInSecondsFrom2000(TInt aTime);
  };
```

Again you can see that a large part of this interface's purpose is to assist at initialization time.

5.4.4.2 Memory model

The memory model also appears in the CPU layer. In fact, the bottom layer of the memory model is both CPU- and MMU-specific, as well as specific to the type of memory model.

The key class that the memory model provides is ArmMmu (or X86Mmu on X86 processors). This class is derived from Mmu, which in its turn is derived from MmuBase. The methods provided by this class allow the standard MMU operations, such as the mapping and unmapping of pages, the changing of page permissions and so on. Here are a few examples:

```
virtual void Map(TLinAddr aLinAddr, TPhysAddr aPhysAddr, TInt aSize,
                 TPde aPdePerm, TPte aPtePerm, TInt aMapShift);
```

```
virtual void Unmap(TLinAddr aLinAddr, TInt aSize);
virtual void ApplyTopLevelPermissions(TLinAddr anAddr, TUint aChunkSize,
                                                      TPde aPermissions);
```

Key concrete classes

At this level, you can see MMU-specific portions of key Symbian OS classes, namely DArmPlatThread, DArmPlatChunk and DArmPlat-Process.

5.4.5 Variant layer

The variant provides the hardware-specific implementation of the control functions expected by the nanokernel and Symbian OS kernel.

The class Asic, provided in assp.h, contains pure virtual APIs, which are to be provided by the variant and called by the CPU layer. So, if you are creating a variant, you would derive it from the Asic class:

```
class Asic
  {
public:
      // initialisation
  virtual TMachineStartupType StartupReason()=0;
  virtual void Init1()=0;
  virtual void Init3()=0;

      // debug
  virtual void DebugOutput(TUint aChar)=0;

      // power management
  virtual void Idle()=0;

      // timing
  virtual TInt MsTickPeriod()=0;
  virtual TInt SystemTimeInSecondsFrom2000(TInt& aTime)=0;
  virtual TInt SetSystemTimeInSecondsFrom2000(Tint aTime)=0;
  virtual TUint32 NanoWaitCalibration()=0;

      // HAL
  virtual TInt VariantHal(TInt aFunction, TAny* a1, TAny* a2)=0;

      // Machine configuration
  virtual TPtr8 MachineConfiguration()=0;
  };
```

The variant provides other interfaces that are available for use by device drivers and extensions. A key example is the Interrupt class provided in assp.h:

```
class Interrupt
  {
```

```
public:
  IMPORT_C static TInt Bind(TInt aId, TIsr aIsr, TAny* aPtr);
  IMPORT_C static TInt Unbind(TInt aId);
  IMPORT_C static TInt Enable(TInt aId);
  IMPORT_C static TInt Disable(TInt aId);
  IMPORT_C static TInt Clear(TInt aId);
  IMPORT_C static TInt SetPriority(TInt aId, TInt aPriority);
  };
```

The variant performs interrupt dispatch for the system; the methods in the `Interrupt` class allow device drivers and extensions to install their own interrupt handlers.

The CPU layer can also provide hardware-specific implementations of HAL functions, although these may equally be implemented in the kernel itself or in an extension.

5.5 Timers

Timers are both a fundamental need for the functioning of EKA2, and a service that EKA2 provides to its users. In this section, I will discuss the detailed operation of nanokernel and Symbian OS timers.

5.5.1 Nanokernel timers

Earlier in this chapter, I said that nanokernel timers, `NTimer`, provide the most fundamental system timing functions in the operating system. Let's look now at how they are implemented.

The main requirements for `NTimer` are:

- Timers can be started and stopped from any kernel code – ISRs, IDFCs or threads, so the timer start and stop functions should have small deterministic execution times

- It should be possible to generate periodic timers with no drift due to delays in servicing the timer

- It should be possible to disable the timer tick if the CPU is expected to be idle for several ticks without affecting the accuracy of the timed intervals, to minimize system power consumption.

The timer queue uses 67 separate doubly linked lists. Of these, the 32 pairs of final queues hold timers that are due to expire within the next 32 ticks. Of the other three, one is used to support timers whose handlers are called back in a DFC (the completed queue) and the other two (the holding queue and the ordered queue) hold timers which are due to expire more than 32 ticks in the future.

The timer queue contains a tick count, which is incremented on every tick interrupt. The tick count modulo 32 determines which of the 32 pairs of linked lists is checked on that tick. One list of the pair holds timers that require the handler to be called at the end of the tick ISR itself, and the other holds timers that require the handler to be called from a DFC following the tick interrupt. This second list, if non-empty, is appended to the end of the completed queue and the timer DFC is queued to process the callbacks. A 32-bit mask is also maintained – this corresponds to the 32 pairs of final queues, with one bit representing each pair. A bit is set if either of the corresponding pair of final queues has an entry.

If a timer is queued for a time less than 33 ticks in the future, the kernel just places that timer on the respective final queue. Timers that are queued for more than 32 ticks in the future are placed on the holding queue in FIFO order. Every 16 ticks, the tick interrupt service routine checks the holding queue, and if it is not empty, queues the timer DFC. This transfers any timers on the holding queue that are now due to expire in less than 33 ticks to their respective final queue. It transfers timers that still expire in more than 32 ticks to the ordered queue. As its name implies, entries on this queue always appear in increasing order of expiry time.

The timer DFC also drains the ordered queue. Every 16 ticks the interrupt service routine checks the ordered queue; if this is non-empty and the first entry expires in less than 33 ticks, then the ISR queues a DFC. The DFC will then walk the ordered queue, transferring entries to the final queues, until it reaches the end of the ordered queue or reaches an entry that expires in more than 32 ticks.

The kernel uses the ordered queue, in combination with the bit mask for the final queues and the holding queue, to determine the number of ticks until the next timer queue operation. In fact, this would generally be done in the null (idle) thread, just before it puts the CPU into idle mode. The null thread can then disable the timer tick for that number of ticks, allowing the CPU to sleep undisturbed for longer, and possibly allowing a lower-power sleep mode to be used. The bit mask for final queues is used to determine the number of ticks before the next final queue expiry. If the holding queue is non-empty, the number of ticks before the sort operation is calculated from the tick number – the sort operation is triggered if the tick count is zero modulo 16. If the ordered queue is non-empty, the time at which transfer of the first entry (that is, the one that expires first) to the relevant final queue would occur is calculated. The minimum of these three time values gives the number of ticks that can be skipped. It can be seen that this calculation has a small, predictable execution time, which is just as well since it will be done with interrupts disabled.

To be able to cancel timers, we need to keep track of which queue a timer is on. Each timer has a state that gives this information, and the following states are defined:

- **Idle.** The timer is not linked into any queue and is not currently set to expire. However the expiry handler may actually be running. No action is required to cancel a timer in this state

- **Holding.** The timer is linked into the holding queue. To cancel a timer in this state, simply remove it from the holding queue

- **Transferring.** The timer is in transit from the holding queue to the ordered queue. It is not actually linked into either. To cancel a timer in this state, no dequeuing is needed, but a flag must be set to notify the timer DFC that the timer currently being transferred has been canceled. The timer DFC will then abort the transfer

- **Ordered.** The timer is linked into the ordered queue. To cancel a timer in this state, simply remove it from the ordered queue

- **Critical.** The timer is linked into the ordered queue and is currently being inspected by the timer DFC while transferring another timer from the holding queue to its correct position on the ordered queue. To cancel a timer in this state it is removed from the ordered queue and a flag is also set to notify the timer DFC that the current critical timer has been canceled. The timer DFC will then restart the sort operation

- **Final.** The timer is linked into the final queue corresponding to its expiry time. To cancel a timer in this state, first remove it from the queue, then check the two final queues corresponding to the expiry time of the timer being canceled; if both are now empty, clear the corresponding bit in the `iPresent` bit mask.

Timers for less than 32 ticks in the future will simply transition from `Idle` to `Final`, whereas timers for longer periods will generally transition through all these states.

When a timer expires, we set its state back to `Idle` just before calling the timer handler. This means that care needs to be taken when canceling a timer whose expiry handler runs in the timer DFC. If the thread calling `Cancel()` has a priority above the timer DFC thread or `Cancel()` is called from an ISR or IDFC then `Cancel()` may occur during the execution of the timer handler. Since the state has been set back to `Idle`, the cancel will not do anything. If the memory containing the timer control block is now freed and reassigned to something else, contention may occur with the expiry handler. This is not usually a problem since threads of such high priority will not usually delete objects. It would, however, be a problem on an SMP system since the canceling thread could overlap the handler even if it had a lower priority.

We provide two functions to start a nanokernel timer:

`OneShot(aTime, aDfc)`
This sets a timer for `aTime` ticks from now. If `aDfc` is TRUE, the callback occurs in the context of the timer DFC, otherwise it occurs in the timer ISR.

`Again(aTime)`
This sets a timer for `aTime` ticks from its last expiry time. This is used to implement periodic timers that are immune to delays in processing the timer callbacks. The callback occurs in the same context as the previous one.

Summary of nanokernel timer control block:

Field	Description
iNext, iPrev	Link pointers for linking the timer into timer queues.
iPtr	Argument passed to callback function when timer completes.
iFunction	Pointer to timer expiry handler function.
iTriggerTime	Number of the tick at which timer is due to expire.
iCompleteInDfc	Boolean flag – TRUE means run timer expiry handler in DFC, FALSE means run it in ISR.
iState	Indicates which queue the timer is currently linked into, if any, and whether the timer is currently being moved.

Summary of nanokernel timer queue control block:

Field	Description
iTickQ[32]	32 pairs of linked lists, one pair corresponding to each of the next 32 ticks. One of the pair holds timers to be completed in the tick ISR and the other holds timers to be completed in the timer DFC.
iPresent	Bit mask corresponding to iTickQ[32]. Bit n is set if and only if iTickQ[n] is non-empty – that is at least one of the two linked lists is non-empty.

Field	Description
iMsCount	The number of the next tick.
iHoldingQ	Queue of timers that expire more than 32 ticks in the future, ordered by time at which timers were queued.
iOrderedQ	Queue of timers that expire more than 32 ticks in the future, ordered by expiry time.
iCompletedQ	Queue of timers that have expired and are waiting to have their handlers called back in the timer DFC.
iDfc	DFC used to transfer timers between queues and to call back handlers for timers requiring DFC callback.
iTransferringCancelled	Boolean flag set if the timer that is currently being transferred from iHoldingQ to iOrderedQ is canceled. Cleared when a new timer is removed from iHoldingQ for transfer to iOrderedQ.
iCriticalCancelled	Boolean flag set if the timer on the ordered queue that is currently being inspected during a sort is canceled. Cleared when the sort steps on to a new timer.
iDebugFn	Only used for testing/debugging.
iDebugPtr	Only used for testing/debugging.
iTickPeriod	The period of the nanokernel timer tick in microseconds.
iRounding	Spare entry for use by the ASSP/variant code involved in generating the tick interrupt.

Figure 5.4 gives an approximate overview of the nanokernel timer and shows how it fits with the Symbian OS tick timer, which I will cover in the next section. To the left of the figure, you can see the control block of the nanokernel timer, which has pointers to the final timer queues (timers due to expire in less than 32 ticks) and pointers to the holding queue and

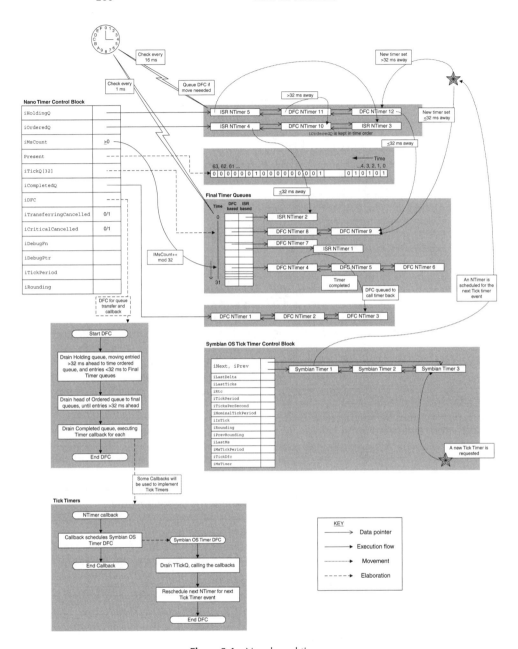

Figure 5.4 Nanokernel timers

ordered queue, for timers that are further in the future. You can also see
how Symbian OS tick timers interact with nanokernel timers – the head of
a doubly linked list of "SymbianTimers" (actually `TTickLink` objects)
is used to schedule a nanokernel timer for the next tick timer event.

The figure also shows how DFCs drain the nanokernel timer queues, with some of the callbacks being used to schedule Symbian OS tick timers – which I'll discuss next.

5.5.2 Symbian OS tick timers

Tick timers are general-purpose interval timers that are used where there is no need for high resolution or great accuracy. They correspond to the timing functions available to user-side code on EKA1. We represent a tick timer using a `TTickLink` object, which I will describe in detail later in this section. We keep active `TTickLink` objects on a doubly linked queue in order of expiry time. This queue is contained in a single `TTickQ` object instance, along with other global state related to Symbian OS timers. Adding `TTickLinks` to this queue is an O(N) operation so we use a mutex, `TTickQ::Mutex`, to protect the queue.

The tick queue operates according to a notional "Symbian OS nominal tick" which has a period of 15.625 ms (64 Hz frequency) – that is, the behavior is the same as that which would be obtained by using a 64 Hz periodic tick interrupt. In fact there is no such periodic tick – instead a single `NTimer` is used to trigger expiry of `TTickLink` timers. It is always set to expire either when the first `TTickLink` should expire or in 65536 Symbian OS ticks (1024 seconds), whichever is the sooner. The limit is imposed to ensure that differences calculated in microseconds never overflow a 32-bit signed quantity. When the `NTimer` expires, it activates a DFC that runs in the Symbian OS timer thread (TimerThread). This DFC dequeues and calls handlers for any `TTickLink` timers that have expired, and then requeues the `NTimer` for the next `TTickLink` timer expiry. The timer mutex is acquired at the beginning of the DFC and released at the end, so the mutex is held while the expiry handlers are called.

Under this system, adding a new `TTickLink` to the queue will in general mean that we need to requeue the `NTimer` if the new timer expires earlier than the previous earliest timer. The exception to this rule is if the `TTickLink` is added from another `TTickLink` expiry handler; in this case the main DFC routine will requeue the `NTimer` after all `TTickLink` expiry handlers for this tick have been called. We use the `TTickQ::iInTick` flag to indicate that the DFC is in progress; it is set by the DFC after acquiring the timer mutex, so the code to add a `TTickLink` (which also runs with the timer mutex held) will see it set if and only if called from the tick DFC itself.

We've seen that the usual `NTimer` resolution is 1 ms, which means that a period of 15.625 ms cannot be generated exactly. And, of course, the `NTimer` resolution may not be 1 ms for manufacturer/device-specific reasons. Hence the `TTickLink` timer queue uses a "pulse swallowing" type algorithm – it sets up the NTimer to generate intervals that are a multiple of 1 ms, such that the average period of the Symbian OS tick is 15.625 ms. For example, if a periodic TTickLink were active with a period of 1 nominal Symbian OS tick, the NTimer would actually trigger at either 15 ms or 16 ms intervals with five out of every eight intervals being 16 ms and the other three out of eight being 15 ms. This works by calculating the required NTimer interval in microseconds and accumulating the error incurred in rounding to the period of NTimer. The error is taken into account on the next calculation. In addition, we use the zero-drift mode of NTimer, where the interval is timed relative to the last timer expiry. In fact the Symbian OS timers are all calculated relative to the last such expiry. A count of nominal ticks is maintained to support the User::TickCount() function and a similar count is maintained to serve as universal time. These counts are updated at the beginning of the DFC that services the TTickQ. The nanokernel tick count at which the NTimer triggered is saved and the tick count and RTC count are incremented by the number of nominal ticks elapsed between this and the previous NTimer expiry. To obtain the current universal time in microseconds since 00:00:00 01-01-0AD (standard Symbian OS time storage format), we use the following formula:

```
iRtc*iNominalTickPeriod + (NTickCount()-iLastMs-1)*NTimer period
```

where NTickCount() is the current NTimer tick count and the other fields are defined in the tables below. The extra −1 in the second term is due to the fact that NTickCount() is incremented immediately after determining which timers to complete. This scheme allows the system time to be obtained to a 1 ms resolution (or whatever the resolution of NTimer is on a particular platform).

Summary of fields in TTickLink:

Field	Description
iNext, iPrev	Link pointers used to attach this object to the system tick timer queue (TTickQ).
iDelta	Number of OS ticks between the expiry of this timer and the expiry of the following one (pointed to by iNext). Never negative, but could be zero for timers expiring at the same time.
iPeriod	Period of this timer in OS ticks or zero for a one-shot timer.

Field	Description
`iPtr`	Argument passed to callback function when this timer expires.
`iCallBack`	Pointer to function to be called when this timer expires.
`iLastLock`	If this timer is being used to implement a Symbian OS "locked" timer, this holds the value of `TTickQ::iRtc` at the last expiry of this timer. If this timer is not being used for a locked timer or has not yet expired, this value is −1.

Summary of fields in `TTickQ`:

Field	Description
`iNext, iPrev`	Link pointers used to point to first and last entries on a time-ordered queue of `TTickLink` objects.
`iLastDelta`	Number of OS ticks which elapse between the last tick timer expiry and the time when `iMsTimer` next triggers – used to increment `iLastTicks` and `iRtc`.
`iLastTicks`	OS tick count at point when `iMsTimer` last triggered.
`iRtc`	The absolute time at the point when `iMsTimer` last triggered, measured in nominal OS ticks from 00:00:00 1st January 0AD.
`iTickPeriod`	The current actual length of an OS tick in microseconds. This may differ from the nominal tick period if a tracking system is being used to make the `iRtc` value follow a hardware RTC. This value may change as a result of the operation of any such tracking system.
`iTicksPerSecond`	Number of nominal OS ticks in one second of elapsed time.
`iNominalTickPeriod`	The nominal length of an OS tick in microseconds. This value is never changed, unlike `iTickPeriod`.
`iInTick`	Boolean flag set to indicate that processing of the tick queue initiated by `iMsTimer` expiry is underway.
`iRounding`	The number of microseconds added to the last delta value when `iMsTimer` was last set up in order to make the period an integral number of nanokernel timer ticks.

Field	Description
iPrevRounding	The value of iRounding at the point where iMsTimer last triggered. Each time the timer is queued, iPrevRounding is used in the calculation of when the timer should trigger and the rounding applied to that time to obtain an integral number of nanokernel ticks is stored in iRounding.
iLastMs	The nanokernel tick count at which iMsTimer last triggered.
iMsTickPeriod	The period of the nanokernel tick in microseconds.
iTickDfc	DFC queued by the expiry of iMsTimer. Runs in context of TimerThread and processes any Symbian OS timers which have just expired.
iMsTimer	Nanokernel timer used to initiate Symbian OS timer processing. It is always queued to trigger at the time when the next TtickLink timer should expire.

5.5.2.1 Second timers

Second timers are used when an event needs to occur at a specific date and time of day rather than after a specified interval, and are typically used for system alarms. They have a resolution of 1 second. They will also power up the system at the expiry time if they need to.

We represent a second timer by a TSecondLink object and attach active timers to a TSecondQ absolute timer queue object, of which a single instance exists. Each TSecondLink stores the absolute time at which it should trigger (measured in nominal OS ticks from 00:00:00 1st January 0AD UTC) and they are linked into the queue in chronological order of expiry time, earliest first. The second timer queue is driven from the tick timer queue. It contains a TTickLink timer which is set to expire at either the trigger time of the first TSecondLink on the queue or at the next midnight local time, whichever is the earlier. When this TTickLink timer triggers, it calls back the handlers for TSecondLink timers that have expired, and then requeues the TTickLink timer. The same mutex (timer mutex) is used to protect the TTickQ and TSecondQ objects, and the handlers are called with the timer mutex held. We use the expiry at midnight to signal change notifiers that midnight crossover has occurred. In a similar way to TTickQ, when a new TSecondLink is queued, the TTickLink timer may need to be canceled and requeued, unless it is queued from inside the TSecondQ expiry handler. Again we use an iInTick field to indicate the latter condition.

Summary of fields in `TSecondLink`:

Field	Description
iNext, iPrev	Link pointers used to attach this object to the system absolute timer queue (TSecondQ).
iTime	The absolute time when this timer should trigger, measured in nominal OS ticks from 00:00:00 1st January 0AD.
iPtr	Argument passed to callback function when this timer expires.
iCallBack	Pointer to function to be called when this timer expires.

Summary of fields in `TSecondQ`:

Field	Description
iNext, iPrev	Link pointers used to point to first and last entries in a time-ordered queue of TSecondLink objects.
iExpired	Boolean flag set when any TSecondLink timer expires and cleared by the power model just before initiating the machine power down sequence. Used by the power model to abort power down if an absolute timer expires during the power-down sequence.
iInTick	Boolean flag set to indicate that processing of the second timer queue initiated by iTimer expiry is underway.
iNextTrigger	The absolute time when iTimer will next trigger, measured in nominal OS ticks from 00:00:00 1st January 0AD.
iMidnight	The absolute time of the next midnight, measured in nominal OS ticks from 00:00:00 1st January 0AD.
iTicksPerDay	Number of nominal OS ticks in 1 day.
iTimer	TTickLink timer object used to initiate second queue timer processing. It is always queued to trigger either at the time when the next TSecondLink timer should expire or at the next midnight, whichever is earlier.
iWakeUpDfc	DFC used to restart the TTickQ and TSecondQ following machine power down and power up and changes to the system time.

5.6 Summary

In this chapter, I have described the wide variety of services that EKA2 provides, both to user-mode threads and within the kernel too. I have also described the basic objects used by the kernel, and the handle mechanism used to identify them.

A key part of the executive call was the SWI instruction, or software interrupt, used to switch the processor from user mode to supervisor mode. In the next chapter, I will look at software interrupts – and hardware interrupts, exceptions, faults and traps – in more detail.

6

Interrupts and Exceptions

by Dennis May

*Einstein argued that there must be simplified explanations of nature,
because God is not capricious or arbitrary. No such faith comforts the
software engineer.*

Fred Brooks

When talking about microprocessors, we use the term exception to
refer to any event, other than the execution of explicit branch or jump
instructions, which causes the normal sequential execution of instructions
to be modified. On processor architectures with multiple privilege levels,
these events typically cause a transition from a less privileged execution
level to a more privileged one.

On the types of processor that run Symbian OS, there are many events
that cause exceptions. These events form six categories, which I will
describe in the next six sections of this chapter. Although the words
used to describe the categories are the same throughout the computer
industry, their exact meanings tend to differ – so, even if you are familiar
with this subject, please do skim these next few sections. In Symbian, we
categorize the events from the perspective of the software event handlers,
so our terms will probably not match the categories given by people who
define them from a processor architecture perspective.

Whenever an exception occurs, the processor stops what it was doing,
and begins execution in a defined state from a (new) defined location.
But before doing so, it may save some information, such as the program
counter, to allow the original program flow to be resumed. Whether this
occurs, and how much information is saved, depends on the nature of
the exception. I will say more on this later.

6.1 Exception types

6.1.1 Interrupts

An interrupt is an exception that is not caused directly by program
execution. In most cases, hardware external to the processor core signals

an interrupt – for example, peripheral devices indicate that they have data available or require data to be supplied. What differentiates an interrupt from other exceptions is that it occurs asynchronously to program execution; in other words, it is not caused by the sequential execution of an instruction. Usually an interrupt is serviced as soon as the currently executing instruction is complete, although on some processors interrupts may occur in the middle of an instruction, and on others not every instruction can be followed by an interrupt.

Whenever an interrupt occurs the processor must save enough state to allow the interrupted program to be resumed and to continue execution precisely as if the interrupt had never occurred. This state always includes the program counter, which specifies the address of the instruction that would have been executed next, had the interrupt not occurred. The saved state also includes the processor status and the condition code register, which contains the interrupt mask level in effect at the time the interrupt occurred. The processor will then disable interrupts whose priority is lower than or equal to that of the one accepted.

Interrupts may be maskable or non-maskable. Maskable interrupts can be disabled by software; they are then held pending until software enables them again. There is no way to turn off non-maskable interrupts – they are always recognized by the processor.

Although the way in which the processor handles interrupts and other exceptions may be similar, the asynchronous nature of interrupts means that their software handlers are very different. In this book, I will always use the term exception to mean any exception **other than** an interrupt, and I will always refer to interrupts explicitly by name.

6.1.2   Resets

A reset causes the processor to reinitialize its whole state, and to start execution from a known location in memory. For example the ARM processor will disable all interrupts, enter supervisor mode and fetch the first instruction to be executed from physical address 0.

Most processors do not save any information about the program that was executing when the reset happened – all of the processor's state is wiped clean. However, on some processors, this is not the case – the processor only initializes enough state to allow it to deterministically execute a boot sequence.

Resets may be caused by hardware, for example when power is first applied to the system, or by software, for example when an unrecoverable error is detected.

6.1.3   Aborts

An abort is an exception that occurs because of an unrecoverable error. The processor may save some information relating to previous program execution, but this can only be used for diagnostic purposes and does not allow the kernel to recover the situation and continue execution of the program.

Aborts occur if the programmer accesses nonexistent or unmapped memory. They also occur when there is inconsistent processor state due to a system programming error. An example of this happens on an IA-32 processor if the programmer loads the ring 0 stack pointer with an invalid address. Any attempt to use the stack would then cause a stack fault exception. However, the processing of this exception requires that information be pushed onto the ring 0 stack, which is invalid. This is a system programming error.[1]

Depending on the nature of the error, an abort may be handled by the processor as a reset or it may be handled in software. Aborts due to incorrect physical addresses will be handled in software, since it is possible that the fault could be localized to a single program. However aborts due to inconsistent processor state, such as the example given, cannot be recovered by software and so are handled as a reset. In fact IA-32 processors will halt in the case of the stack fault example given and external logic will then reset the system. If the abort is handled in software, then the operating system may deal with it either by terminating the currently running program or by triggering a software reset of the system. Symbian OS deals with aborts by terminating the current thread of execution if it is a user thread or by rebooting the system if the abort occurs in kernel-side code.

6.1.4 Faults

A fault is an exception that occurs during instruction execution, signifying an error that may be recoverable – unlike an abort. The operating system can attempt to rectify the cause of the fault and then retry the instruction.

An example of this is a page fault. Suppose an instruction references a virtual memory address that is not currently mapped to any physical memory page. An operating system that supports demand paging (any of the common desktop operating systems) will first check that the virtual address accessed is valid; if it is, it will load the page containing the address referenced from backing store, and then retry the instruction.

6.1.5 Traps

A trap is an exception that replaces execution of a particular instruction. The usual recovery action ends with program execution resuming at the instruction after the one that caused the trap.

---

[1] Another example can occur on processors such as the Motorola MCore M340 and the Renesas SuperH, on which there are dedicated registers for handling exceptions. Whenever an exception occurs, the processor flags these registers as in use and disables interrupts. The system software must mark the registers as free after saving them and can only re-enable interrupts after this. If another exception occurs while the registers are still marked as in use, the processor treats this as an abort, because of the inconsistent processor state.

An example of this is an undefined instruction. This can be used to aid the emulation of coprocessors or other hardware blocks that are not physically present in the device. The instructions that normally access the coprocessor or hardware will be treated as undefined instructions and cause an exception; the exception handler emulates the missing hardware and then program execution resumes after the trapped instruction.

6.1.6 Programmed exceptions

Programmed exceptions result from the execution of specific instructions whose sole purpose is to cause an exception. These are of great importance to the functioning of an operating system. On a processor with multiple privilege levels, application code usually runs at the lowest privilege level, and the kernel of the operating system runs at the highest privilege level. How then can an application call the operating system to perform some task for it? The application cannot execute kernel code using a standard call mechanism – instead it must cause an exception, which executes at the highest privilege level. Programmed exceptions are the means by which application code gains access to operating system functionality, and for this reason they are also known as system calls.

When a system call is made, a call number is supplied – either as part of the instruction opcode that causes the exception (for example the ARM SWI instruction has 24 bits available for this), or in a register. The exception handler uses this to index into the kernel's system call table to locate the address of the required kernel function. Enough processor registers will be saved to make the system call appear as a standard C function call, although this register saving may be split between the kernel-side exception handler and a user-side shim[2] which contains the programmed exception instruction. For more details, please turn back to Chapter 5, *Kernel Services*.

6.2 Exceptions on real hardware

In the following sections, I describe in detail the types of exception that can occur on real hardware, and how they are handled on the ARM and Intel IA-32 (also known as X86) processor architectures.

6.2.1 ARM

The ARM architecture uses banked registers and a fixed-size, fixed-address vector table to deal with exceptions. In ARM terminology, there are seven execution modes:

---

[2] A *shim* is a small section of code which simply passes control to another piece of code without doing any work itself other than possibly some rearrangement of parameters.

1. User (usr). This is the only non-privileged mode – that is, certain instructions cannot be executed in user mode, and the MMU will block access to memory regions which are set up for privileged access only. User mode is entered explicitly by executing any of the instructions that write to the mode bits of the CPSR. Once the CPU is executing in user mode, only an exception can cause a transition to another mode. Under Symbian OS the majority of code (everything other than the kernel, device drivers and board support package code) executes in user mode.

2. System (sys). This is the only privileged mode that is not entered by an exception. It can only be entered by executing an instruction that explicitly writes to the mode bits of the CPSR. It is exited either by writing to the mode bits of the CPSR or by an exception. Symbian OS does not use system mode.

3. Supervisor (svc). This is a privileged mode entered whenever the CPU is reset or when a SWI instruction is executed. It is exited either by writing to the mode bits of the CPSR or by an exception other than reset or SWI. With the exception of interrupt service routines and most of the exception preambles, all Symbian OS kernel-side code executes in supervisor mode.

4. Abort (abt). This is a privileged mode that is entered whenever a prefetch abort or data abort exception occurs. Symbian OS makes only minimal use of this mode – the exception preamble switches to supervisor mode after saving a small number of registers.

5. Undefined (und). This is a privileged mode that is entered whenever an undefined instruction exception occurs. Symbian OS makes only minimal use of this mode – the exception preamble switches to supervisor mode after saving a small number of registers.

6. Interrupt (irq). This is a privileged mode that is entered whenever the processor accepts an IRQ interrupt. Under Symbian OS, service routines for IRQ interrupts execute in this mode, unless nested IRQs are supported. IRQ mode is exited either by writing to the CPSR, for example when returning from the interrupt, or if another exception occurs, for example an FIQ interrupt preempting the IRQ service routine.

7. Fast Interrupt (fiq). This is a privileged mode that is entered whenever the processor accepts an FIQ interrupt. Under Symbian OS, service routines for FIQ interrupts execute in this mode. FIQ mode is exited either by writing to the CPSR, for example when returning from the interrupt, or if another exception occurs. Under Symbian OS, this last case should never happen, because prefetch aborts, undefined instructions and SWIs are prohibited in interrupt service routines, and all interrupts are masked during an FIQ service routine.

The low 5 bits of the status register (CPSR) determine which mode is currently active. ARM supports two privilege levels – privileged and non-privileged. All execution modes except user mode are privileged. The ARM architecture supports 16 general purpose registers, labeled R0–R15. However, an instruction referring to one of these registers does not always access the same physical register. Accesses to registers R8–R14 refer to different physical registers depending upon the current execution mode.

Figure 6.1 illustrates which physical registers are accessed in each execution mode. You can see that R0–R7 are the same across all modes – the user mode registers are always used. We say that R0–R7 are never banked.

R13 and R14 are banked across all modes apart from system mode – each mode that can be entered because of an exception has its own R13

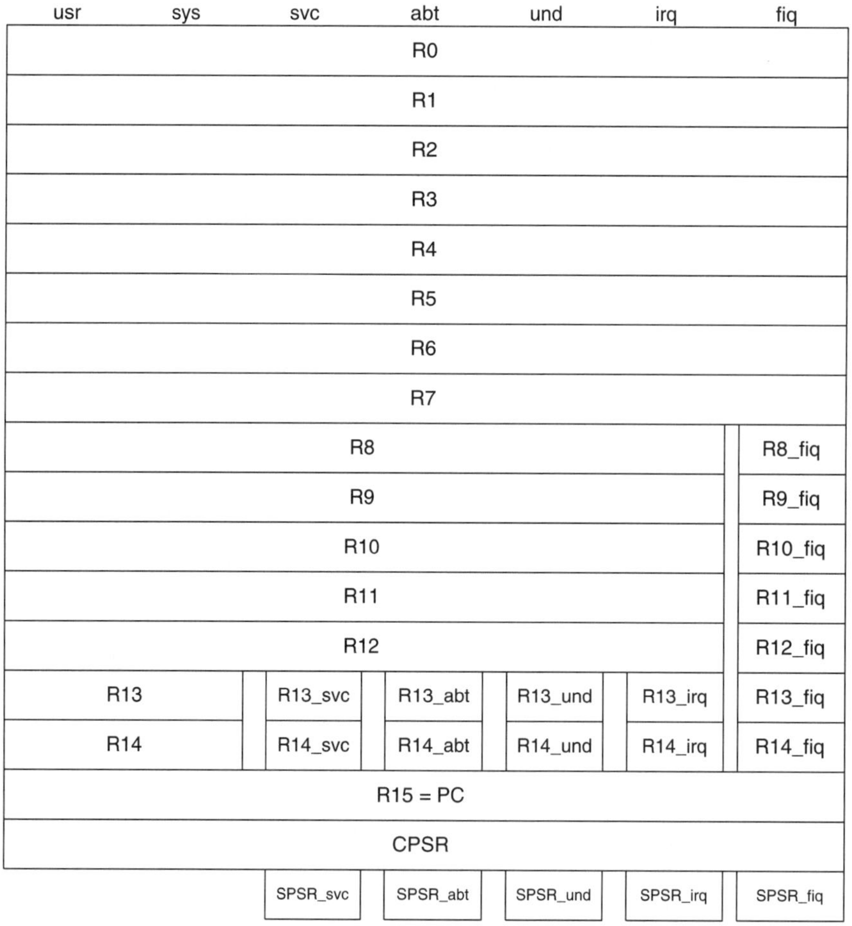

usr	sys	svc	abt	und	irq	fiq
R0						
R1						
R2						
R3						
R4						
R5						
R6						
R7						
R8						R8_fiq
R9						R9_fiq
R10						R10_fiq
R11						R11_fiq
R12						R12_fiq
R13		R13_svc	R13_abt	R13_und	R13_irq	R13_fiq
R14		R14_svc	R14_abt	R14_und	R14_irq	R14_fiq
R15 = PC						
CPSR						
		SPSR_svc	SPSR_abt	SPSR_und	SPSR_irq	SPSR_fiq

Figure 6.1   ARM registers

and R14. These registers generally hold the stack pointer and the return address from function calls respectively.

Also, each mode that can be entered by an exception has a SPSR (saved processor status register).

The actions taken by ARM CPUs on recognizing an exception are:

1. For exceptions other than resets, the CPU saves the return address from the exception in the banked R14 for the respective exception mode

2. For exceptions other than resets, the CPU copies the current value of the CPSR to the SPSR for the respective exception mode

3. The CPU changes the execution mode to that appropriate for the type of exception

4. The CPU disables normal (IRQ) interrupts. If it is processing an FIQ (fast interrupt) it disables FIQs, otherwise it leaves them enabled

5. The CPU continues execution at the vector address for the exception concerned. It always starts execution in ARM (not Thumb) mode. This means that the first part of the exception handler must be written in 32-bit ARM instructions rather than 16-bit Thumb instructions. Of course the handler can change to Thumb mode if it wishes.

Figure 6.2 illustrates these actions.

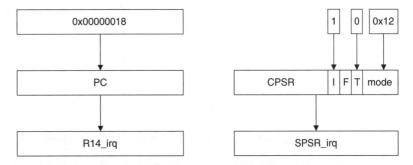

Figure 6.2   ARM CPU response to IRQ interrupt

When an exception is recognized, the processor only saves the return address and CPSR. Of course an exception handler will need to make use of some working registers too. The software handler must save these on the stack, and then restore them from the stack before returning from the exception. The banked R13 ensures that the exception handler has access to a valid stack area to which it can save its working registers.

The following table lists all the exceptions supported by the ARM architecture, along with the execution mode into which the exception puts the processor and the vector address for the exception:

Exception	Mode	Vector	Category
Reset	svc	0×00	Reset
Undefined Instruction	und	0×04	Fault, Trap or Abort
SWI	svc	0×08	Programmed Exception
Prefetch Abort	abt	$0 \times 0C$	Fault or Abort
Data Abort	abt	0×10	Fault or Abort
IRQ	irq	0×18	Interrupt
FIQ	fiq	$0 \times 1C$	Interrupt

As you can see in the previous table, the ARM core directly supports only two interrupt sources. External logic drives two signals, IRQ and FIQ, to signal these interrupts. FIQ has a higher priority than IRQ; if both are asserted simultaneously the FIQ is recognized first. What is more, IRQ interrupts are masked when an FIQ is recognized but FIQ interrupts are not masked when an IRQ is recognized. This means that FIQ interrupts can usually interrupt the service routine for an IRQ interrupt. Registers R8–R12 are banked for FIQ mode, which allows some FIQ interrupts to be serviced without the need to save working registers on the stack. This reduces the time taken to service the interrupt.

For most systems, and certainly for systems running Symbian OS, more than two interrupt sources are required. Because of this, we use an external interrupt controller. This accepts a number (typically 32 to 128) of interrupt signals from various peripherals.

The interrupt controller may provide the following services:

- Allow individual interrupt sources to be masked
- Allow the processor to look in one central place to discover which sources are currently pending
- Allow each source to be routed to either the IRQ or FIQ input to the processor
- Allow edge-triggered inputs to be latched before being fed to the processor.

The interrupt controller asserts the IRQ input to the processor if any interrupt source is:

1. Pending

2. Not masked

3. Routed to IRQ.

A similar rule applies to FIQ. On accepting an interrupt, the processor must check the interrupt controller to discover which sources are both pending and enabled. It then applies a software prioritization scheme to select one of these to be serviced. When the service routine completes, the procedure is repeated and another interrupt may be serviced. This continues until there are no more pending interrupts.

6.2.2 Intel IA-32

Most RISC processors use exception handling schemes similar to the one I described for ARM, in which special registers are used to hold return information from exceptions. The IA-32 architecture, coming from a CISC heritage, handles exceptions differently. The IA-32 architecture has an explicitly designated stack pointer register, ESP, along with special instructions that reference the stack (PUSH and POP). When it recognizes an exception, an IA-32 processor will push the return address and return status register onto the stack.

Before I go on to talk about IA-32 exception handling, it might be useful if I describe IA-32 memory addressing. Since Symbian OS runs in IA-32 protected mode, I will only cover that mode here. IA-32 protected mode uses a two-component memory address consisting of a segment selector and a 16- or 32-bit offset. The segment selector is specified by one of six 16-bit segment selector registers, as shown in the following table:

Register	Name	Description
CS	Code Segment	Specifies the segment for all instruction fetches. EIP specifies the offset component for instruction fetches.
SS	Stack Segment	Specifies the segment for all explicit stack instructions, including subroutine calls and returns and exception handling. ESP specifies the offset for explicit stack operations.
DS	Data Segment	Specifies the segment for data memory references other than those to the stack.
ES	Extra Segment	Specifies the segment for data memory references which explicitly indicate that ES is to be used.
FS	Second Extra Segment	Similar to ES.
GS	Third Extra Segment	Similar to ES.

The segment selectors are interpreted as follows:

- Bits 0 and 1 are known as the requestor privilege level (RPL) of the selector

- Bit 2 specifies whether the selector is local (1) or global (0). Symbian OS uses only global selectors

- Bits 3–15 form a 13-bit index into a descriptor table.

Bits 3–15 of the selector point to an 8-byte entry in the global descriptor table (GDT), which gives the base address of the segment, its size, privilege level and type (code, data, system information).

We find the effective memory address by adding the segment base address from the GDT entry to the 16- or 32-bit offset. This effective address is known as a linear address in IA-32 terminology. If paging is disabled, it is used directly as a physical address, but if it is not, then it is translated to a physical address using the page tables.

The IA-32 architecture supports four privilege levels (also known as *rings*). Level 0 is the most privileged; all instructions and resources are available at this level. Level 3 is the least privileged; application code usually runs at this level.

The RPL of the selector currently in CS is known as the current privilege level (CPL) and specifies the privilege level of the code that is currently executing. For segment registers other than CS, the RPL indicates the privilege level of the code that originated the selector – hence the name, requestor privilege level. So the RPL may not be the same as the CPL of the code currently executing – for example the selector may have been passed in as an argument from less privileged code. The kumem functions use this method to ensure that user code is not allowed to write with kernel privileges; see Section 5.2.1.5 for more on this.

Symbian OS uses five segments and only privilege levels 0 and 3. We have one level 0 code segment and one level 0 data segment, both covering the entire 4GB linear address space. We also have one level 3 code segment and one level 3 data segment, each covering the lower 3GB of linear address space. Finally, we have a single task state segment, which I will describe later in this chapter.

Returning to IA-32 exception handling, each exception other than reset has an 8-bit vector number associated with it. Numbers 0 to 31 are reserved for standard exceptions such as interrupts, page faults and division-by-zero, as described in the following table of all supported exceptions on IA-32 architectures.

Vector	Description	Category	Error code
–	Reset	Reset	–
0	Division by zero	Abort	No
1	RESERVED		
2	Non-maskable Interrupt (NMI)	Interrupt	No
3	Breakpoint	Programmed Exception	No
4	Overflow	Abort	No
5	Out of bounds (BOUND instruction)	Abort	No
6	Invalid opcode	Trap or Abort	No
7	Device not available	Fault or Abort	No
8	Double Fault	Abort	Yes
9	RESERVED		
10	Invalid Task State Segment (TSS)	Abort	Yes
11	Segment not present	Fault or Abort	Yes
12	Stack segment error	Abort	Yes
13	General protection error	Abort	Yes
14	Page Fault	Fault or Abort	Yes
15	RESERVED		
16	Floating point error	Trap or Abort	No
17	Alignment check error	Abort	Yes
18	Machine check error (Pentium and later)	Abort	No
19	SIMD Floating point exception (Pentium III and later)	Trap or Abort	No
20–31	RESERVED		
32–255	User defined exception; either hardware interrupt signaled via the INTR line or execution of INT instruction	Programmed Exception or Interrupt	No

When an exception is recognized, the processor uses the vector number to index the interrupt descriptor table (IDT). This is a table of 8-byte entries whose linear base is stored in the IDTR register. Each entry contains one of the following:

- A task gate; these are not used by Symbian OS

- A trap gate; this specifies a new CS and EIP indicating an address to which instruction execution should be transferred

- An interrupt gate; this is the same as a trap gate apart from the interrupt mask behavior.

Since a new CS selector is specified, a change of privilege level can occur when an exception is handled. The processor will not permit an exception to transfer control to a less privileged level. On Symbian OS, all exception handlers execute at level 0.

In the interests of security and robustness, it is a general principle that more privileged code must not rely on the validity of any data or addresses passed by less privileged code. So if an exception results in a change of CPL, the processor changes the stack from the current SS:ESP, which is accessible to less privileged code.

The processor uses the task state segment (TSS) in stack switching. The task register (TR) contains a segment selector that refers to a TSS descriptor in the GDT. The TSS descriptor specifies where in the linear address space the TSS resides. The TSS contains various fields related to the IA-32 hardware task switching mechanism but the only one relevant to Symbian OS is the privilege level 0 initial stack pointer, SS0:ESP0. When an exception occurs and control is transferred to privilege level 0 from a less privileged level, SS:ESP is loaded with the SS0:ESP0 value from the TSS. In Symbian OS this is always set to point to the top of the current thread's supervisor stack.

With this background information given, I can now describe in detail the response of an IA-32 processor to an exception:

1. The processor uses the exception vector number to index the IDT and obtain the CS:EIP of the exception handler

2. If the new CS specified in the IDT necessitates a transfer to a more privileged level, the processor loads SS and ESP from the currently active TSS and then pushes the original SS and ESP onto the new stack. All subsequent stack operations use the new stack

3. The processor pushes the EFLAGS register and then the current CS and EIP values

4. If the IDT entry contains an interrupt gate, the processor clears the IF flag so that maskable interrupts are disabled. A trap gate does not affect the IF flag

5. Depending on the type of exception, the processor may push an error code

6. The processor transfers control to the handler indicated by the CS and EIP values read from the IDT.

Like the ARM, the IA-32 architecture supports only two physical interrupt inputs to the processor. However, these inputs behave very differently to those on the ARM.

The NMI line always causes a vector 2 interrupt and may not be masked by software. It is of limited use in most IA-32 systems. Most hardware interrupts are directed to the INTR line. Interrupts signaled on this line are maskable by clearing the IF flags in the EFLAGS register.

IA-32 processors are used with external interrupt controller hardware, typically located in the motherboard chipset. The interrupt controller, which accepts inputs from a number of interrupt sources, allows the interrupt sources to be individually masked and prioritized. It also associates a vector number with each interrupt source.

When an enabled interrupt source becomes active, the interrupt controller signals an interrupt to the processor and passes the associated vector number. If interrupts are enabled (IF = 1) the processor calls the appropriate vector handler, as listed in the IDT. While the interrupt is in service the interrupt controller prevents lower priority interrupt sources from being signaled to the processor.

At the end of the software handler, the processor signals EOI (end of interrupt) to the interrupt controller. At this point lower priority interrupts can once more be signaled to the processor.

6.3 Interrupts

In this section, I will return to EKA2, and describe how it handles interrupts.

6.3.1 EKA2 interrupt handling

There are four phases in the handling of any interrupt. Figure 6.3 illustrates these four phases, and shows where in the kernel the code for each phase is located.

Interrupts occur very frequently during normal system operation – the system tick interrupts every millisecond and during some I/O operations, such as bulk data transfer over USB, an interrupt may occur every 50 μs. Because of this, the interrupt handling code is optimized for speed. The fewest possible registers are saved at each stage and the entire interrupt code path within the kernel and the dispatcher is written in hand-optimized assembler.

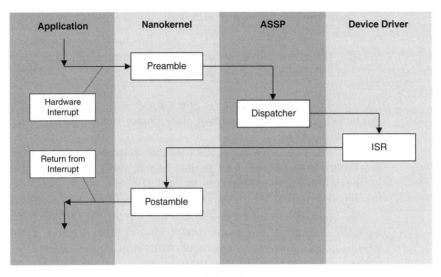

Figure 6.3   Code flow during interrupt

6.3.1.1   Preamble

The first code to execute following the processor response to an interrupt is the preamble, which is part of the nanokernel.

On ARM processors the preamble is entered directly from both the IRQ and the FIQ vectors.

On IA-32 processors, each IDT entry points to a preamble entry stub that saves the vector number, and then jumps to a common interrupt preamble. The preamble's job is to establish the correct processor state, by taking care of any nonautomatic stack switching and register saving before the dispatcher and interrupt service routine run. Because interrupts are asynchronous to program execution, the preamble can make no assumptions about the processor state on entry.

EKA2 uses a separate stack for interrupts. This means that we don't need to reserve stack space for interrupts on each thread's supervisor stack, which reduces RAM usage. Depending on processor architecture, the switching of stacks may be performed automatically or by the software preamble:

- On ARM-based hardware, the stack is switched automatically, since an interrupt causes the processor to switch to mode_irq or mode_fiq and thus R13_irq or R13_fiq becomes the active stack pointer

- On IA-32 hardware, the processor interrupt response includes a switch to the current thread's supervisor stack if the interrupt occurs in user mode (CPL = 3). If the interrupt occurs in supervisor mode (CPL = 0), no stack switch occurs and so the active stack may be a thread supervisor stack or the interrupt stack, if another ISR was interrupted.

On the first of a nest of interrupts, the preamble switches to a separate interrupt stack and saves the original stack pointer on the new stack. This can be seen in lines 10–15 of the IA-32 preamble. The IrqNestCount variable is initialized to −1, so if incrementing it gives zero, this is the first of a nest of interrupts.

Symbian OS interrupt service routines are generally written in C++. Each processor has a calling convention that specifies which registers are preserved across function calls and which are not. On ARM, R0–R3, R12 and CPSR are destroyed by function calls; on IA-32, EAX, ECX, EDX and EFLAGS are destroyed by function calls. Lines 1 and 2 of the ARM interrupt preamble, and lines 1, 2, 3, 6 and 7 of the IA-32 interrupt preamble, save these registers.

ARM interrupt preamble

```
1        SUB      LR, LR, #4
2        STMFD    SP!, {R0-R3, R12, LR}
3        LDR      R12, IrqHandler
4        LDR      LR, ArmVectorIrq
5        LDR      PC, [R12]
```

IA-32 interrupt preamble

```
1        PUSH     DS
2        PUSH     ES
3        PUSH     EAX
4        MOV      AX, SS
5        CLD
6        PUSH     ECX
7        PUSH     EDX
8        MOV      DS, AX
9        MOV      ES, AX
10       MOV      EAX, ESP
11       INC      DWORD PTR IrqNestCount
12       JNZ      Nested
13       LEA      ESP, IrqStackTop
14       PUSH     EAX
15 Nested:
16       CALL     [IrqHandler]
```

The preamble may need to set up more state, depending on the processor architecture. On IA-32, the hardware interrupt response sets up the SS and CS segment selectors, but not DS and ES. The preamble saves these selectors, then sets them both equal to SS, which is the privilege level 0 data segment covering the entire 4 GB linear address range. In addition, it clears the D flag, so that the IA-32 repeated string operations work in the forward direction, from low to high addresses.

On ARM, no further state setup is needed unless we want to support nested interrupts. In this case, ISRs cannot execute in mode_irq. This is because a nested interrupt would corrupt R14_irq, which may hold the return address from a subroutine called during execution of the first ISR. So, if support for nested interrupts is required, a switch to mode_sys will occur during the preamble. If the interrupt occurred in mode_sys (as indicated by SPSR_irq), it must be a nested interrupt, so R13_usr points to the interrupt stack. If the interrupt occurred in any other mode, the preamble saves R13_usr, then sets R13_usr to point to the top of the interrupt stack. It must also save R14_usr, since it will be corrupted by any subroutine calls made by the ISR.

6.3.1.2   *Interrupt dispatcher*

The role of the dispatcher is to determine the source of the interrupt and to call the registered service routine for that source. It is written as part of the base port for a given hardware platform. On platforms with an ASSP, the dispatcher is usually part of the ASSP extension; otherwise it is part of the variant.

On hardware without vectored interrupt support – which includes most current ARM-based hardware – the dispatcher interrogates the interrupt controller to establish which interrupts are both pending and enabled. It then selects one of these according to a fixed priority scheme, and invokes the corresponding service routine. Once the service routine is completed, the dispatcher will loop and interrogate the interrupt controller again; this continues until there are no more pending interrupts. In the code sample Example ARM IRQ dispatcher, lines 5–8 discover which interrupts are pending and select the one corresponding to the highest numbered bit in the hardware IRQ pending register. If no interrupts are pending, line 7 returns from the dispatcher.

Example ARM IRQ dispatcher

```
1         STMFD   SP!, {R4-R6, LR}
2         LDR     R4, InterruptControllerBase
3         LDR     R5, Handlers
4 dispatch:
5         LDR     R12, [R4, #IRQPendingRegOffset]
6         CMP     R12, #0
7         LDMEQFD SP!, {R4-R6, PC}
8         CLZ     R3, R12
9         ADD     R0, R5, R3, LSL #3
10        ADR     LR, dispatch
11        LDMIA   R0, {R0, PC}
```

On hardware with vectored interrupt support, which includes IA-32 architectures, the dispatcher knows immediately from the vector number which interrupt source is involved. It immediately invokes the service routine and then returns.

EKA2 typically allows only one service routine for each interrupt – although since the dispatcher is outside the Symbian-supplied kernel, this decision is actually up to the base porter, who could easily change this code to allow several service routines to be associated with a single interrupt. It is fairly common among hardware designs to find several interrupts attached to the same line on the interrupt controller. This situation is normally handled by using a sub-dispatcher rather than by registering several handlers with the main dispatcher. A sub-dispatcher is a routine that is bound to a given interrupt source at system boot time, and which performs a similar function to the main dispatcher, but only for interrupts that are routed to a particular line. A common pattern is that the main interrupt dispatcher is in the ASSP and this deals with the different interrupt sources recognized by the on-chip interrupt controller. Sub-dispatchers are in the variant, and these deal with interrupts from "companion" chips – peripheral devices external to the ASSP. These chips generally produce a single combined interrupt output, which is recognized as a single source by the main interrupt controller.

6.3.1.3 Interrupt service routines

The role of the interrupt service routine (ISR) is to perform whatever action is necessary to service the peripheral that generated the interrupt and to remove the condition that caused it to interrupt. This usually involves transferring data to or from the peripheral.

ISRs may be located in the ASSP, variant, an extension or a device driver. ISRs are typically written in C++, although some frequently used ones such as the system tick ISR are written in assembler.

In Chapter 12, *Drivers and Extensions*, I will discuss ISRs in more detail, but this is for the most part irrelevant in understanding how Symbian OS handles interrupts. All we need to know now is that the ISR runs, and that it may make use of a small number of OS services, as follows:

- It may queue an IDFC or DFC (which I will describe in Sections 6.3.2.2 and 6.3.2.3) or, in the case of the millisecond tick ISR, trigger a reschedule directly if the current thread's timeslice has expired

- It may queue or cancel a nanokernel timer

- It may disable or enable interrupts using APIs provided by the ASSP or variant. I will talk about this more later.

Of these, the first is fundamental to the entire operation of the system. This is the way in which external events cause the appropriate kernel-side and user-side tasks to run.

6.3.1.4 Postamble

The postamble runs after the dispatcher returns, which it does when it has serviced all pending interrupts. The goal of the postamble is to restore the processor's state and permit the interrupted program to resume. However before this, it may need to schedule another thread to run.

The postamble performs the following actions:

1. It checks what code was running when the interrupt was triggered.
    If that code was not running as part of a thread, then the postamble
    returns from the interrupt immediately. This covers the case in which
    one interrupt occurs during servicing of another. It also covers any
    cases in which the processor is in a transitional state (a thread stack is
    not active). Such a state can occur in ARM processors just after an abort
    or undefined instruction exception. The processor enters mode_abt or
    mode_und and the active stack is a shared exception stack rather than
    a thread stack. This stack is only used briefly to save registers before
    switching to mode_svc. However because a non-thread related stack
    is in use, rescheduling cannot occur. Lines 1, 4, 6 and 7 in the code
    sample ARM IRQ postamble check for this – if the interrupted mode
    is neither usr nor svc, we return from the interrupt immediately.

ARM IRQ postamble

```
1       MRS     R0, SPSR
2       LDR     R1, TheScheduler
3       ADD     R12, SP, #24
4       AND     R2, R0, #0x1F
5       LDR     R3, [R1, #iKernCSLocked]
6       CMP     R2, #0x10
7       CMPNE   R2, #0x13
8       CMPEQ   R3, #0
9       BNE     IrqExit0
10      MOV     R2, #0xD2
11      MSR     CPSR, R2
12      LDR     R2, [R1, #iRescheduleNeededFlag]
13      ADD     R3, R3, #1
14      MOV     LR, #0x13
15      CMP     R2, #0
16      BEQ     IrqExit0
17      STR     R3, [R1, #iKernCSLocked]
18      MSR     CPSR, LR
19      LDMDB   R12!, {R1-R3}
20      STMFD   SP!, {R1-R3}
21      LDMDB   R12!, {R1-R3}
22      STMFD   SP!, {R1-R3}
23      STMFD   SP!, {R0, LR}
24      MOV     R2, #0x13
25      MOV     LR, #0x92
26      MSR     CPSR, LR
27      ADD     SP, R12, #24
28      MSR     CPSR, R2
29      BL      Reschedule
30      LDMFD   SP!, {R1, LR}
31      ADD     SP, SP, #24
32      MOV     R12, SP
33      MOV     R2, #0xD2
34      MSR     CPSR, R2
35      MSR     SPSR, R1
36      LDMDB   R12, {R0-R3, R12, PC}
```

```
37 IrqExit0:
38     LDMFD   SP!, {R0-R3, R12, PC}
```

2. It checks if preemption is disabled – if this is the case, it returns from the interrupt immediately (lines 5 and 8).

3. It checks if an IDFC (see Section 6.3.2.2) or a reschedule is pending; if not, it returns from the interrupt immediately. Lines 10, 11, 12, 15, 16 are responsible for this. Note that the postamble must perform this check with all interrupts disabled, not just those at the same hardware priority as the one just serviced. If this were not the case, a higher priority interrupt, such as an FIQ, could run and queue an IDFC just after the current interrupt (IRQ) performed the check. The FIQ postamble would not run the IDFC since it interrupted mode_irq, and the IRQ postamble would not run the IDFC since it already decided there was no IDFC pending. The IDFC would then be subject to an unpredictable delay, until either another interrupt occurred or the current thread performed some action that resulted in rescheduling.

4. It disables preemption and re-enables interrupts (lines 13, 14, 17, 18). It transfers all saved state from the interrupt stack to the supervisor stack of the interrupted thread (lines 3 and 19–28). It calls the scheduler. This runs any pending IDFCs and then performs a context switch if one is needed. The call to the scheduler returns when the interrupted thread is next scheduled. Internally, the scheduler performs context switches by switching stacks. Any thread that is not currently executing has a call to the scheduler at the top of its call stack.

5. It restores the interrupted thread state from the supervisor stack and returns from the interrupt (lines 30–36).

6.3.2 Interaction with scheduling

The processing required for an external event generally splits into a number of stages with different response time requirements. For example, consider a PPP connection over a serial port. The UART receives data and stores it in its internal FIFO. When the FIFO is half-full, the UART raises an interrupt, which must be serviced before the FIFO becomes completely full to avoid data loss.

So, the first stage of processing is to move the data from the UART's receive FIFO to an internal memory buffer – and the deadline for this is the time taken to receive half a FIFO of data. Let's say that this is 8 characters at 115,200 bps, which gives us a time of 694 μs.

The second stage of processing is to perform PPP framing, verify the frame check sequence, transition the PPP state machine and transmit any acknowledgment required. The deadline for this is determined by the time that the peer PPP entity will wait before timing out the acknowledgment. This will be much longer than the first stage deadline, so second-stage processing can occur at lower priority than the receive interrupt, in a thread. In this way, further receive interrupts will preempt the second stage processing of earlier frames.

In a similar way, the PPP thread must preempt other activities with longer deadlines and long-running activities. The receive interrupt signals the PPP thread that data is available, which triggers the preemption. In general terms, processing for events with short deadlines should preempt processing for events with longer deadlines. This is done by using threads with differing priorities for the different types of event, with the most time critical events being handled directly by ISRs.

6.3.2.1   The kernel lock

In previous sections, it has become clear that there must be a method by which interrupts can cause the appropriate threads to run so that an event can be processed. In this way, the response can occur in stages, with the most urgent part being handled by the ISR itself and less urgent parts being handled by threads of decreasing priority.

To ensure that response deadlines are met, the time between a hardware interrupt being signaled and the ISR running must be bounded (that is, it must have a maximum latency) and we want this latency to be as short as possible. This translates into a requirement that interrupts be enabled all the time apart from in sections of code whose execution time is bounded and as short as possible. To satisfy this requirement, most code, whether kernel- or user-side, executes with interrupts enabled. This includes code that manipulates global structures such as the thread ready list. To prevent such code from being re-entered and corrupting the global structure, a preemption lock (`iKernCSLocked`, usually known as the kernel lock) is employed.

The kernel lock is a simple counter that is normally zero. Sections of code that need to protect themselves against rescheduling increment the kernel lock at the beginning of the critical section and decrement it at the end. Then, when an interrupt occurs, the kernel will only attempt a reschedule if the kernel lock was zero at the time of the interrupt. This can be seen in step 2 of the interrupt postamble described in Section 6.3.1.4, and in lines 3 and 8 of the code sample ARM IRQ postamble.

Of course this method can only work if the ISR itself does not invoke any of these critical sections of code. We disable rescheduling in certain code sequences because they need to atomically manipulate structures such as the thread ready list. Disabling rescheduling prevents a second thread from running and modifying these structures while the first thread is still halfway through its modification. However disabling rescheduling does not disable interrupts, so an ISR that modified the thread ready list directly would still conflict with threads modifying it. Therefore ISRs may not add a thread to the ready list. In fact, they may not use any OS services other than those listed in Section 6.3.1.3.

6.3.2.2 IDFCs

Interrupts cause the scheduling of a thread by means of an Immediate Deferred Function Call (IDFC). IDFCs are objects that specify a function that will be called after the ISR, as soon as the system is in a suitable state. We call them "immediate" because they normally run before returning from the interrupt, not later on, in a kernel thread. The exception to this is if the kernel was locked when the interrupt occurred, in which case IDFCs are run immediately after the kernel is unlocked.

It works like this. First the ISR adds an IDFC to the IDFC pending queue, which is always accessed with interrupts disabled. When the scheduler next runs, it calls the function associated with the IDFC directly. (The function is not called by a thread.) This is how the state of the kernel lock governs when IDFCs are called. If an interrupt occurs when the kernel lock count is nonzero, the ISR runs but nothing else happens. If an interrupt occurs when the kernel lock count is zero, the ISR runs and afterwards, if IDFCs have been queued, the scheduler is called and it runs the IDFCs. The IDFCs may add one or more threads to the ready list, after which the scheduler may select a new thread to run.

IDFCs are called in the same order in which they were originally queued. They are called with interrupts enabled and with the kernel lock count equal to 1; this guarantees that they will not be re-entered or preempted, either by another IDFC or by a thread.

Most interrupts do not need further processing after the ISR has run. For example, the system tick ISR runs every millisecond but, unless a timer expires on this particular tick, no IDFCs need to run and no reschedule is required. In this common case, to save the time taken to run the scheduler (lines 17–36 in the code sample ARM IRQ postamble, as opposed to line 38) we use a flag, known as the *DFC pending flag*, to indicate that one or more IDFCs have been added to the pending queue. The interrupt postamble only needs to call the scheduler if this flag is set. The flag is reset when all pending IDFCs have been processed.

We use a similar flag, the *reschedule needed flag*, to indicate that changes to the ready list have occurred that may require a new thread to be scheduled. After IDFCs have been run, we will only select a new thread to run if this flag is set; the flag is cleared as part of the reschedule.

There are two places where the scheduler, and hence IDFCs, may run. The first is during the interrupt postamble (line 29 in the code sample ARM IRQ postamble) and the second is at the point where a thread releases the kernel lock.

In the first place, IDFCs will run if they were added by any of the ISRs that ran during interrupt processing. A new thread will then be selected to run if any of these IDFCs causes a thread with a priority greater than or equal to that of the interrupted thread to become ready.

In the second place, IDFCs will run if they have been added by the thread that held the kernel lock or by ISRs that ran while the kernel lock was held. A new thread may then be selected for three different reasons:

1. If any thread with a priority greater than or equal to that of the interrupted thread is made ready (either by the IDFCs or by the thread that held the kernel lock)

2. If the thread that held the kernel lock removes itself from the ready list

3. If thread priorities are changed by the thread that held the kernel lock.

Figure 6.4 illustrates the processing of an IDFC in the case where the kernel was originally locked and where no thread switch is required following the IDFC.

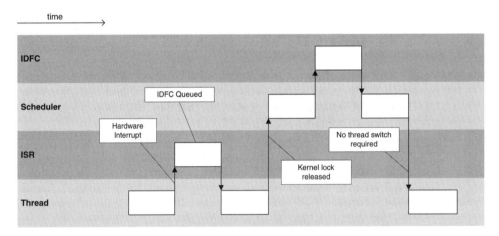

Figure 6.4   IDFC processing

6.3.2.3   *DFCs*

As I will explain in Section 6.3.2.4, IDFCs must be short and there are restrictions on which kernel services they may use. For these reasons IDFCs are rarely used directly except by RTOS personality layers. Instead, ISRs generally use Deferred Function Calls (known as DFCs) when they want to schedule a thread or perform other tasks not possible from within the ISR itself. DFCs make use of IDFCs in their implementation, so ISRs indirectly use IDFCs whenever they use DFCs.

A DFC is an object that specifies a function to be called in a particular kernel thread. DFCs are added to DFC queues. Exactly one kernel thread is associated with each DFC queue, but not all kernel threads are associated with a DFC queue.

DFCs have priorities that are between 0 and 7 inclusive. Within any given DFC queue, the associated kernel thread schedules DFCs co-operatively. It removes the highest priority DFC from the queue and calls its function. When the function returns, the kernel thread processes the next highest priority DFC; it processes DFCs with the same priority in the order that they were added to the queue. Once there are no DFCs remaining on the queue, the kernel thread blocks until another DFC is added to the queue. Each DFC must run to completion before any others on the same queue can run. However, since a different kernel thread services each DFC queue, a DFC running in a higher priority thread may preempt a DFC running in a lower priority thread.

A DFC may be queued from any context – from an ISR, IDFC or thread. However, the kernel handles these contexts a little differently. If an ISR queues a DFC, then the kernel adds it to the **IDFC** pending queue. (This is possible because IDFCs and DFCs are objects of the same type.) Then, when the scheduler runs, the nanokernel transfers the DFC to its final (DFC) queue and, if necessary, makes the corresponding kernel thread ready. Essentially, the DFC makes use of an IDFC with a callback function supplied by the kernel, which transfers the DFC to its final queue. This two-stage process is necessary because a DFC runs in a kernel thread and ISRs are not allowed to signal threads; however IDFCs are. Of course, if an IDFC or a thread queues a DFC, this two-stage procedure is not necessary; instead the kernel adds the DFC is directly to its final (DFC) queue.

Figure 6.5 illustrates the processing of a DFC queued by an ISR in the case where the kernel is unlocked when the interrupt occurs and where the DFC thread has higher priority than the interrupted thread.

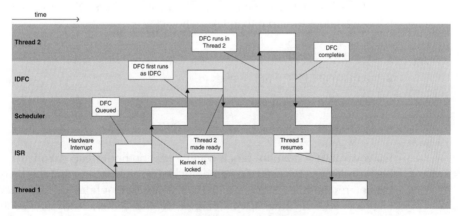

Figure 6.5 DFC processing

6.3.2.4 Kernel services in ISRs, IDFCs and DFCs

As I said earlier, to minimize interrupt latency we keep interrupts enabled most of the time – the only exceptions being a small number of short sections of code. Because of this, most operating system data structures might be in an inconsistent state during an ISR. This means that, during ISR processing, we can make no assumptions about the state of any of the following:

- The thread ready list

- Nanokernel threads

- Fast mutexes and fast semaphores

- DFC queues

- Virtual memory mappings for most memory areas accessible from user mode.

ISRs cannot manipulate any Symbian OS thread or wait object, since the system lock fast mutex must be held while doing that. Nor can an ISR access user memory, such as the stacks and heaps of a user-mode thread. In fact, the only services available to ISRs are:

- Queuing IDFCs and DFCs

- Queuing and canceling nanokernel timers

- Enabling and disabling interrupts.

Earlier, I said that IDFCs would only run after an ISR if the kernel were unlocked at the time the interrupt is serviced. This means that all nanokernel objects will be in a consistent state when IDFCs run, and so IDFCs can do a lot more than ISRs. They can:

- Make nanokernel threads ready

- Manipulate DFC final queues

- Signal fast semaphores

- Perform all operations available to ISRs.

However IDFCs may not block waiting for another thread to run. This is because IDFCs run with the kernel locked, which means that the kernel cannot reschedule. Since waiting on a fast semaphore or fast mutex is effectively blocking, IDFCs cannot do this either. And to take this argument to its conclusion, the prohibition on the use of fast mutexes in IDFCs also means that they may not perform any operations on Symbian OS threads or wait objects, since these are protected by the system lock fast mutex.

Similarly, the address space of a non-running user process is only guaranteed to be consistent when the system lock is held. Since it is not known which process is currently running when an IDFC runs, it may not access any user memory. Another reason for this prohibition is that exceptions are not tolerated during IDFCs.

Note that IDFCs run with preemption disabled, so they should be kept as short as possible.

DFCs run in the context of a kernel thread. In principle, this could be a bare nanokernel thread (`NThread`) but in practice, with the possible exception of code running in an RTOS personality layer, DFCs run in a Symbian OS kernel thread (`DThread`). This means that the full range of kernel services is available to DFCs, including but not limited to the following:

- Waiting on or signaling either nanokernel or Symbian OS wait objects

- Allocating or freeing memory on the kernel heap

- Accessing user memory

- Completing Symbian OS asynchronous requests (`TRequestStatus`).

6.3.2.5 Round-robin scheduling

The kernel schedules threads with equal priorities in a round-robin fashion. That is, each thread executes for a certain amount of time (its timeslice) and then the kernel schedules the next thread in cyclic order with the same priority. We implement this using the `iTime` field in the nanothread control block – this counts the number of nanokernel timer ticks remaining in the thread's time slice. The kernel decrements `iTime` on each nanokernel tick provided this field was initially positive. If `iTime` becomes zero, the kernel sets the reschedule needed flag, which causes the scheduler to run at the next opportunity. This is the only occasion where an interrupt triggers a reschedule directly rather than via an IDFC.

6.3.3 Using interrupts

6.3.3.1 The interrupt APIs

Device drivers and extensions gain access to interrupts via a generic interrupt management API, which I will describe later. The base porter implements this API in the ASSP module, if there is one, or in the variant, if there is not. In systems with an ASSP, parts of the implementation may remain in the variant – typically those parts dealing with interrupt sources outside the ASSP and that make use of a second-level dispatcher. However, the public functions themselves will be implemented in the ASSP.

The interrupt management API is encapsulated in a static class, `Interrupt`, defined as follows:

```
typedef void (*TIsr)(TAny*);

class Interrupt
    {
public:
    static TInt Bind(TInt aId, TIsr aIsr, TAny* aPtr);
    static TInt Unbind(TInt aId);
    static TInt Enable(TInt aId);
    static TInt Disable(TInt aId);
    static TInt Clear(TInt aId);
    static TInt SetPriority(TInt aId, TInt aPriority);
    };
```

The interrupt management API uses a 32-bit integer identifier to specify
the interrupt source that is referred to. The mapping between interrupt
sources and numeric identifiers is usually defined in a public header file
exported from the ASSP module. A second public header file, exported
from the variant, defines identifiers for interrupt sources external to
the ASSP.

Next I shall describe each interrupt management method in turn.

```
TInt Interrupt::Bind(TInt aId, TIsr aIsr, TAny* aPtr);
```

This method associates an ISR with the interrupt source whose numeric
identifier is specified by parameter aId. Parameter aIsr specifies the
interrupt service routine. Following a successful return from Interrupt::Bind(), interrupts from the specified source cause function
aIsr() to be called. The aPtr parameter is passed to aIsr as an
argument. This will typically be a pointer to some data required by the
ISR – for example the "physical channel" object for an interrupt in a
physical device driver.

   Interrupt::Bind() returns an error code if the specified interrupt
identifier is invalid or if the requested interrupt source has already
been bound.

```
TInt Interrupt::Unbind(TInt aId);
```

This method disables interrupts from the specified interrupt source and
then removes any ISR that is currently bound to it. An error code is
returned if the interrupt identifier is invalid or if there is no ISR associated
with the interrupt source.

```
TInt Interrupt::Enable(TInt aId);
```

This method enables interrupts from the specified interrupt source. Note
that this only enables the interrupt source in the main interrupt controller;
further setup in the peripheral itself may be necessary before interrupts

can actually occur. An error code is returned if the interrupt identifier is invalid or if there is no ISR associated with the interrupt source. An interrupt may not be enabled if it does not have an ISR associated with it.

```
TInt Interrupt::Disable(TInt aId);
```

This method disables interrupts from the specified interrupt source. Note that it only disables the interrupt source in the main interrupt controller; the peripheral itself is unaffected. An error code is returned if the interrupt identifier is invalid.

```
TInt Interrupt::Clear(TInt aId);
```

This method clears any pending interrupt from the specified source. It returns an error code if the interrupt identifier is invalid. This method is rarely used – most interrupts are cleared either implicitly during servicing or explicitly by writing to a hardware register. For example, a UART receive interrupt is usually cleared by reading all available data from the UART receive FIFO; a timer interrupt is cleared by writing to an acknowledgment register. The `Interrupt::Clear()` method is generally only used where the `aId` value is determined at runtime instead of being hard coded.

```
TInt Interrupt::SetPriority(TInt aId, TInt aPriority);
```

On hardware that supports multiple interrupt priority levels and that allows interrupt sources to have their priorities set dynamically, this call changes the hardware priority level of the specified interrupt source. The method returns an error code if this functionality is not supported or if the identifier is invalid. A typical use of this would be on ARM-based systems where the interrupt controller allows each interrupt source to be routed to either IRQ or FIQ. The board support package and device drivers for such a platform would call the `Interrupt::SetPriority()` API during initialization to configure the hardware to route each interrupt to either IRQ or FIQ as appropriate.

6.3.3.2 APIs for IDFCs and DFCs

IDFCs and DFCs are both represented by objects of the `TDfc` class. The public parts of this class are as follows:

```
typedef void (*TDfcFn)(TAny*);

class TDfc
    {
public:
    TDfc(TDfcFn aFn, TAny* aPtr);
    TDfc(TDfcFn aFn, TAny* aPtr, TInt aPri);
```

```
TDfc(TDfcFn aFn, TAny* aPtr, TDfcQue* aQ, TInt aPri);
void Add();
void Cancel();
void Enque();
void Enque(NFastMutex* aMutex);
void DoEnque();
inline TBool Queued();
inline TBool IsIDFC();
inline void SetDfcQ(TDfcQue* aQ);
inline void SetFunction(TDfcFn aFn);
};
```

Now let's look at these public functions in more detail:

```
TDfc(TDfcFn aFn, TAny* aPtr);
```

Whether the TDfc represents an IDFC or a DFC depends on how it is constructed. This constructor initializes the TDfc object as an IDFC. Function aFn will be called when the IDFC runs, and aPtr will be supplied as the argument to aFn.

```
TDfc(TDfcFn aFn, TAny* aPtr, TInt aPri);
TDfc(TDfcFn aFn, TAny* aPtr, TDfcQue* aQ, TInt aPri);
```

These constructors initialize the TDfc object as a DFC. Function aFn will be called when the DFC runs and aPtr will be supplied as the argument to it. Parameter aPri specifies the priority of the DFC within its DFC queue and must be between zero and seven inclusive. Parameter aQ specifies which DFC queue the DFC will run on. The version of the constructor without the parameter aQ will initialize the queue pointer to NULL, and the DFC queue to be used must be set with SetDfcQ before the DFC can be queued.

```
void Add();
```

This method places an IDFC or a DFC on the IDFC pending queue. The method is idempotent – if the object is already queued, no action is taken. This method is almost always called from an ISR. It may also be called from an IDFC or a thread context with preemption disabled, but it must not be called from a thread context with preemption enabled.

```
void Cancel();
```

This method removes an IDFC or DFC from any queue it is currently on. If the object is not currently queued, no action is taken. You must only call this method from IDFCs or threads, not from ISRs.

```
void Enque();
void DoEnque();
```

These methods place a DFC directly on its final queue without going via the IDFC pending queue. They must not be called on a `TDfc` object representing an IDFC. Both methods take no action if the DFC is already queued. You can only call the `DoEnque()` from an IDFC or a thread context with preemption disabled; it is the recommended way to queue a DFC from inside an IDFC. You may also call `Enque()` from a thread context with preemption enabled; it is the recommended way to queue a DFC from a thread.

```
void Enque(NFastMutex* aMutex);
```

This method is equivalent to `Enque()` followed immediately and atomically by signaling the specified fast mutex. If `aMutex` is NULL, the system lock is signaled. The call is atomic in that no reschedule may occur between the DFC being queued and the fast mutex being released. This method may only be called from a thread context.

The method is useful when both the thread queuing a DFC and the DFC thread itself need to access a data structure protected by a fast mutex. Let's consider what would happen if it did not exist. The first thread would acquire the mutex, update the structure, queue the DFC and then release the mutex. If, as is commonly the case, the DFC thread had the higher priority, a reschedule would occur immediately after the DFC was queued, with the fast mutex still held. The DFC would immediately try to acquire the mutex and find it locked, causing another reschedule back to the first thread. Finally, the first thread would release the fast mutex and there would be yet another reschedule back to the DFC thread, which could then claim the mutex and proceed. The use of an atomic "queue DFC and release mutex" operation eliminates the last two of these reschedules, since the DFC thread does not run until the mutex has been released.

```
TBool IsQueued();
```

This method returns `ETrue` if the `TDfc` object is currently on the IDFC pending queue or a DFC final queue.

```
TBool IsIDFC();
```

This method returns `ETrue` if the `TDfc` object represents an IDFC, `EFalse` if it represents a DFC.

```
void SetDfcQ(TDfcQue* aQ);
```

This sets the DFC queue on which a DFC will run. It is intended for use in conjunction with the `TDfc` constructor that does not specify a DFC queue, which is used when the queue is not known at the time the DFC is constructed. For example, this can happen in logical device drivers where the `DLogicalChannelBase`-derived object contains embedded DFCs, which are therefore constructed when the logical channel object is instantiated. This occurs before the logical channel has been bound to any physical device driver, so if the DFC queue is determined by the physical device driver, the `TDfc::SetDfcQ` method must be used to complete initialization of the DFCs once the queue is known.

The `TDfc::SetDfcQ` method must only be used on unqueued DFCs; it will not move a queued DFC from one queue to another.

```
void SetFunction(TDfcFn aFn);
```

This sets the callback function to be used by an IDFC or DFC.

6.4 Aborts, traps and faults

In this section, I will describe how Symbian OS handles aborts, traps and faults, and the uses it makes of them. I will use the generic term "exceptions" from here onwards to cover "aborts, traps and faults".

6.4.1 Response to exceptions

As with interrupts and system calls, the initial and final phases of exception handling occur in the nanokernel. The higher level processing occurs in a per-thread exception handler, which, for Symbian OS threads, is a standard handler in the Symbian OS kernel. Next I shall discuss each of these phases in more detail.

6.4.1.1 Preamble

The task of the exception preamble is similar to that of the interrupt preamble – to establish the correct context for the exception handlers to run, and to save the state of the system at the point where the exception occurred. However there are two main differences. The first is that the exception preamble saves the entire integer register set of the processor rather than just the minimum set required to restore the system state. The reasons for this are:

1. Exceptions are often indicative of programming errors, especially under Symbian OS, which doesn't support demand-paged virtual memory. Saving the entire register set allows us to generate more useful diagnostics

2. If an exception is intentional rather than the result of a programming error, we often need to modify the processor execution state before resuming the original program. For example, to run a user-side exception handler, we must modify the stack pointer and program counter of the running thread before resuming

3. Exceptions are quite rare events, so the performance penalty in saving and restoring all registers is acceptable.

The second difference from the interrupt preamble is that checks are made on the state of the system at the point where the exception occurred. Depending on the result of these checks, a kernel fault may be raised. This is because exceptions, unlike interrupts, are synchronized with program execution. Certain critical parts of kernel-side code are not expected to cause exceptions – if they do, a kernel fault is raised. This will immediately terminate normal system operation and either drop into the kernel's post-mortem debugger (if present) or (on a production device) cause the system to reboot.

Handling exceptions on ARM processors

On ARM processors, exceptions cause a transition to mode_abt or mode_und, and they disable IRQs but not FIQs. The exception modes have a single, small, shared stack between them – they do not have a per-thread stack. The preamble must switch the processor into mode_svc, so that the exception handler can run in the context of the thread causing the exception, and the kernel can reschedule correctly. The ARM exception preamble proceeds as follows:

1. Saves a small number of registers on the mode_abt or mode_und stack, including the address of the instruction that caused the exception

2. Checks the saved PSR to ensure that the exception occurred in either mode_usr or mode_svc. If not, the exception must have occurred either in an ISR or during the exception preamble itself. In either case, this is a fatal error, and a kernel fault will be raised

3. Enables IRQ interrupts. IDFCs queued by IRQs or FIQs will not run now, because the processor mode is abt or und, which is equivalent to the kernel lock being held (see Section 6.3.1.4)

4.   Checks if the kernel lock is currently held. If so, this is a fatal error, as code holding the kernel lock is not allowed to fault. If not, locks the kernel and switches to mode_svc. The current thread's supervisor mode stack is now active

5.   Checks that there is enough space remaining on the supervisor stack to store the full processor state. If not, the supervisor stack has overflowed, which is a fatal error

6.   Transfers the registers saved on the mode_abt or mode_und stack to the mode_svc stack. Saves the rest of the processor registers on the mode_svc stack. Also saves the fault address register and the fault status register, which give additional information about the cause of an MMU-detected exception such as a page fault

7.   Unlocks the kernel. Any deferred IDFCs and/or reschedules will run now

8.   Calls the exception handler registered for the current nanothread, passing a pointer to the saved processor state on the stack.

Handling exceptions on IA-32 processors

On IA-32 processors, exceptions automatically switch to privilege level 0 and the current thread's supervisor stack becomes active, as I described in Section 6.2.2. The return address from the exception is either the address of the aborted instruction for an abort or the address of the following instruction for a trap, and the processor automatically saves this on the supervisor stack along with the flag's register. If the exception occurred in user mode, the processor also automatically saves the user-side stack pointer. The processor does not disable interrupts (because Symbian OS uses trap gates for exceptions) and the preamble can be preempted at any time. This is not a problem because the current thread's supervisor stack is active throughout the preamble. The IA-32 exception preamble proceeds as follows:

1.   If the exception does not push an error code onto the stack (see Section 6.2.2), the preamble pushes a zero error code

2.   Saves all processor integer registers and segment selectors on the supervisor stack. Also pushes the fault address register; this is only valid for page faults but is nevertheless stored for all exceptions

3.   Checks the interrupt nest count. If it is greater than -1, then the exception occurred during an ISR, which we treat as a fatal error

4.   Checks if the kernel lock is currently held. If so, this is a fatal error

5.   Calls the exception handler registered for the current nanothread, passing a pointer to the saved processor state on the stack.

6.4.1.2 Postamble

If the exception was not fatal, then the postamble runs after the nano-thread's exception handler has returned. The postamble restores all of the processor state from the stack, with the exception of the supervisor stack pointer. The processor will restore this automatically by popping the saved state when it returns from the exception. The last instruction of the exception postamble will be a "return from exception" instruction, which restores both the program counter and the status register. Execution then returns to the saved program counter value, which means that either the processor retries the aborted instruction or it executes the instruction after the faulting one. It is worth pointing out that the exception handler may previously have modified the saved state by changing values in the stack, but these modifications only take effect at this point.

6.4.1.3 Symbian OS exception handler

All Symbian OS threads are provided with a standard exception handler. This implements several strategies for dealing with the exception. These strategies are tried one after another until either one of them successfully handles the exception or they all fail, in which case the thread causing the exception is terminated.

Magic handler

The first strategy is the so-called "magic" handler. This works slightly differently on the ARM and IA-32 versions of the kernel.

On ARM, the exception handler checks for a data abort occurring in mode_svc where the address of the aborted instruction is one of a short list known to the exception handler. If these conditions are all satisfied, the magic handler is used; this simply resumes execution at the instruction after the aborted instruction with the Z (zero) flag set, and R12 set to the data address that caused the data abort.

On IA-32, the exception handler checks for an exception occurring at CPL = 0, that is, in supervisor mode, and checks the iMagicEx-cHandler field of the current thread. If the latter is non-null and the exception occurred at CPL = 0, the Symbian OS exception handler calls the function pointed to by iMagicExcHandler, passing a pointer to the processor state saved by the exception preamble. If this function returns zero, it means that the magic handler has handled the exception and modified the saved processor state appropriately (typically the saved EIP will be modified), so the Symbian OS exception handler simply returns and execution resumes according to the modified saved state. If the return value is nonzero, the Symbian OS exception handler proceeds to the TExcTrap strategy.

The magic handler is used to safely handle[3] exceptions that are
caused by dereferencing user-supplied pointers in frequently used kernel
functions, such as `DThread::RequestComplete()`, which is used
to complete Symbian OS asynchronous requests. The advantage of the
magic handler is that it is very fast to set up – in fact on ARM it requires
no setup at all and on IA-32 we only need to write a single pointer to
the current thread control block. Fast set up is important, since the setup
overhead is incurred in the normal case where no exception occurs. The
disadvantage is that it can only be used in functions written in assembler
because the magic handler must inspect and manipulate saved processor
register values directly. In C++, we don't know what register the compiler
is going to use for what.

TExcTrap handlers

The second strategy is the use of the `TExcTrap` class. This supports the
catching of exceptions in C++ code and allows the handler to be written
in C++. The price of this additional flexibility is that it takes longer
to set up the `TExcTrap` before executing the code that might cause
an exception.

A thread wishing to catch exceptions occurring in a section of code
allocates a `TExcTrap` structure on its supervisor stack and initializes it
with a pointer to the function that is to be called if an exception occurs.
The initialization function saves the processor registers in the `TExcTrap`
structure and attaches this structure to the thread. If an exception occurs,
the Symbian OS exception handler sees that the thread has installed a
`TExcTrap` handler and calls the nominated handler function, passing
pointers to the `TExcTrap`, the current thread and to the processor
context saved by the nanokernel exception preamble. The handler can
then inspect the saved context and any additional information passed in
the `TExcTrap`, and decide to either retry the aborted instruction or to
return an error code. In the latter case the processor registers saved in the
`TExcTrap` are restored to allow C++ execution to continue correctly.

Coprocessor fault handler

The two strategies for handling exceptions that I have just described allow
the catching of exceptions that occur with a fast mutex held. If neither of
these methods successfully handles the exception, and the current thread
holds a fast mutex, then the kernel will treat this as a fatal error. It does
this because all of the exception-handling schemes that I am about to
describe make use of fast mutexes.

The next check the kernel makes is for coprocessor faults. On ARM,
the check is for "undefined instruction" exceptions on coprocessor
instructions; on IA-32 the check is for "device not available" exceptions.

---

[3] If it's good enough for Star Trek, it's good enough for me.

If the exception is of this type, and there is a context switch handler registered for the coprocessor involved, the registered handler is called. (We don't need to make the check on IA-32 as there is always a handler for the IA-32 FPU.) The return value indicates whether the exception has been handled successfully.

If the exception was handled successfully, the kernel restores the processor state and then either retries the coprocessor instruction or continues execution with the next instruction, depending on the reason for the exception. Coprocessor handlers can be used for two different purposes. One is to save and restore the coprocessor state as necessary to enable multiple threads to use the coprocessor. When a new thread attempts to use the coprocessor, an exception results; the exception handler saves the coprocessor state for the previous thread and restores the state for the current thread, and the instruction is then retried so it can execute correctly in the context of the current thread. This scheme is used for the IA-32 FPU and ARM VFP and I will describe it in more detail in Section 6.4.2.2. The other purpose for a coprocessor handler is to emulate a coprocessor that is not actually present. In this case execution will resume after the coprocessor instruction.

Kernel event handlers
The exception is then offered to all the kernel event handlers. The kernel calls each handler, passing a pointer to the processor context saved by the nanokernel exception preamble. The handler has the option to handle the exception, possibly modifying the saved processor context, and then resume the aborted program. Alternatively, it may ignore the exception, in which case it is offered to the next handler.

User-side exception handlers
If no kernel event handlers can deal with the exception, the last possibility for handling it is a user-side exception handler. If the exception occurred in user mode and a user-side exception handler is registered, then we modify the user-mode stack pointer and the return address from the exception to cause the current thread to run the user-side exception handler as soon as it returns to user mode.

If none of the previous methods are able to handle the exception, the current thread is terminated with the "KERN–EXEC 3" panic code.

6.4.2   Uses of exceptions

6.4.2.1   Trapping invalid pointers

Since Symbian OS does not support demand-paged virtual memory, any occurrence of a page fault must come from the use of an invalid memory pointer. In most cases this will result in the kernel terminating the thread that caused the page fault. Exceptions to this rule are:

- If the invalid pointer was passed in by other code, such as a server receiving a pointer from its client and using that pointer in an `RMessagePtr2::Read()` or `Write()` call. In this case the exception is caught within the kernel and an error code is returned to the server

- If the thread has set up a user-side exception handler to catch page faults.

6.4.2.2   Coprocessor lazy context switch

IA-32 and some ARM CPUs have floating point coprocessors that contain a substantial amount of extra register state. For example, the ARM vector floating point (VFP) processor contains 32 words of additional registers. Naturally, these additional registers need to be part of the state of each thread so that more than one thread may use the coprocessor and each thread will behave as if it had exclusive access.

In practice, most threads do not use the coprocessor and so we want to avoid paying the penalty of saving the coprocessor registers on every context switch. We do this by using "lazy" context switching. This relies on there being a simple method of disabling the coprocessor; any operation on a disabled coprocessor results in an exception. Both the IA-32 and ARM processor have such mechanisms:

- IA-32 has a flag (TS) in the CR0 control register which, when set, causes any FPU operations to raise a "Device Not Available" exception. The CR0 register is saved and restored as part of the normal thread context

- The ARM VFP has an enable bit in its FPEXC control register. When the enable bit is clear, any VFP operation causes an undefined instruction exception. The FPEXC register is saved and restored as part of the normal thread context

- Architecture 6 and some architecture 5 ARM devices also have a coprocessor access register (CAR). This register selectively enables and disables each of the 15 possible ARM coprocessors (other than CP15 which is always accessible). This allows the lazy context switch scheme to be used for all ARM coprocessors. If it exists, the CAR is saved and restored as part of the normal thread context.

The lazy context-switching scheme works as follows. Each thread starts off with no access to the coprocessor; that is, the coprocessor is disabled whenever the thread runs.

When a thread, HAIKU, attempts to use the coprocessor, an exception is raised. The exception handler checks if another thread, SONNET, currently has access to ("owns") the coprocessor. If so, the handler saves the current coprocessor state in SONNET's control block and then modifies SONNET's saved state so that the coprocessor will be disabled when SONNET next runs. If there wasn't a thread using the coprocessor, then the handler doesn't need to save the state of the coprocessor.

Then coprocessor access is enabled for the current thread, HAIKU, and the handler restores the coprocessor state from HAIKU's control block – this is the state at the point when HAIKU last used the coprocessor. If this is the first time HAIKU has used the coprocessor, a standard initial coprocessor state will have been stored in HAIKU's control block when HAIKU was created, and this standard state will be loaded into the coprocessor. HAIKU now owns the coprocessor.

The exception handler then returns, and the processor retries the original coprocessor instruction. This now succeeds because the coprocessor is enabled.

If a thread terminates while owning the coprocessor, the kernel marks the coprocessor as no longer being owned by any thread.

This scheme ensures that the kernel only saves and restores the coprocessor state when necessary. If, as is quite likely, the coprocessor is only used by one thread, then its state is never saved. (Of course, if the coprocessor were to be placed into a low power mode that caused it to lose state, the state would have to be saved before doing so and restored when the coprocessor was placed back into normal operating mode. However at the time of writing no coprocessors have such a low-power mode.)

6.4.2.3 Debugging

Exceptions are used in debugging to set software breakpoints. The debugger replaces the instruction at which the user wants to place a breakpoint with an undefined instruction. When control flow reaches that point, an exception occurs and the debugger gains control. Registers may be inspected and/or modified and then execution resumes after the undefined instruction. The debugger must somehow arrange for the replaced instruction to be executed, possibly by software emulation, before resuming execution. There is more on this subject in Chapter 14, *Kernel-Side Debug*.

6.4.3 APIs for exceptions

In the following sections, I will describe the kernel exception APIs that are available to device drivers and extensions.

6.4.3.1 The XTRAP macro

This is a macro wrapper over the TExcTrap handlers that I described in Section 6.4.1.3. The macro is used as follows:

```
XTRAP(result, handler, statements);
XTRAPD(result, handler, statements);
```

The specified `statements` are executed under a `TExcTrap` harness. The parameter `result` is an integer variable that will contain the value `KErrNone` after execution if no exception occurred. The macro `XTRAPD` declares the variable `result` whereas `XTRAP` uses a preexisting variable. The parameter `handler` is a pointer to a function with signature:

```
void (*TExcTrapHandler)(TExcTrap* aX, DThread* aThread, TAny* aContext);
```

This function is called if an exception occurs during the execution of `statements`.

If `XT_DEFAULT` is specified as the `handler` parameter, a default handler is used that returns an error code `KErrBadDescriptor` on any exception.

Parameter `aX` points to the `TExcTrap` harness which caught the exception, `aThread` points to the control block of the executing thread and `aContext` points to a processor dependent structure which contains the values of all the processor registers at the point where the exception occurred. In fact this is simply the processor state information saved in the exception preamble by the nanokernel. The ARM version of this is:

```
struct TArmExcInfo
  {
  TArmReg iCpsr;
  TInt    iExcCode;
  TArmReg iR13Svc;      // supervisor stack pointer
  TArmReg iR4;
  TArmReg iR5;
  TArmReg iR6;
  TArmReg iR7;
  TArmReg iR8;
  TArmReg iR9;
  TArmReg iR10;
  TArmReg iR11;
  TArmReg iR14Svc;      // supervisor mode LR
  TArmReg iFaultAddress;  // value of MMU FAR
  TArmReg iFaultStatus;       // value of MMU FSR
  TArmReg iSpsrSvc;     // supervisor mode SPSR
  TArmReg iR13; // user stack pointer
  TArmReg iR14; // user mode LR
  TArmReg iR0;
  TArmReg iR1;
  TArmReg iR2;
  TArmReg iR3;
  TArmReg iR12;
  TArmReg iR15; // address of aborted instruction
  };
```

If the exception can be handled, the function should call:

```
aX->Exception(errorcode);
```

This will cause the execution of the XTRAP macro to terminate imme-diately without completing execution of statements; the results variable is set to the errorcode passed in to the call.

If the exception cannot be handled, the function should just return. The other exception handling strategies described in Section 6.4.1.3 will then be attempted.

The XTRAP macro is used to catch exceptions occurring in supervisor mode, typically in conjunction with the kumemget() and kumemput() functions (described in Section 5.2.1.5) to access user-side memory from places where it would not be acceptable to terminate the current thread on an exception. Examples of these are code that runs with a fast mutex held or inside a thread critical section. The XTRAP macro is the only way to catch exceptions that occur with a fast mutex held.

6.4.3.2 *Kernel event handlers*

XTRAP handlers can only catch supervisor-mode exceptions in one thread, and are normally used to catch exceptions within a single function call. We use kernel event handlers when we want to catch exceptions occurring in multiple threads or in user-mode over extended periods of time. We implement kernel event handlers using the class DKernelEventHandler, the public interface of which follows:

```
class DKernelEventHandler : public DBase
    {
public:
// Values used to select where to insert the handler in the queue
enum TAddPolicy
    {
    EAppend,
    };


enum TReturnCode
    {
// Run next handler if set,
// ignore remaining handlers if cleared
    ERunNext = 1,
// Available for EEventUserTrace only.
// Ignore trace statement if set.
    ETraceHandled = 0x40000000,

// Available for hardware exceptions only.
// Do not panic thread if set.
    EExcHandled = 0x80000000,
    };

/** Pointer to C callback function called when an event occurs.
aEvent designates what event is dispatched.
a1 and a2 are event-specific.
aPrivateData is specified when the handler is created, typically a
pointer to the event handler.
The function is always called in thread critical section. */
```

```
typedef TUint (*TCallback)(TKernelEvent aEvent, TAny* a1, TAny* a2,
                                                 TAny* aP);

public:
  // external interface
  IMPORT_C static TBool DebugSupportEnabled();
  IMPORT_C DKernelEventHandler(TCallback aCb, TAny* aP);
  IMPORT_C TInt Add(TAddPolicy aPolicy = EAppend);
  IMPORT_C TInt Close();
  inline TBool IsQueued() const;
  };
```

If you are writing an extension or a device driver and you want to use a kernel event handler, follow these steps. First instantiate the `DKernelEventHandler` class on the kernel heap. This requires two parameters – `aCb` is a pointer to a function to be called back when any notifiable event occurs, and `aP` is an arbitrary cookie which is supplied as an argument to `aCb` when notifying an event.

After instantiating the class, call `Add()` on it to start receiving event callbacks. From this point on, whenever a notifiable event occurs, the kernel will call the specified function, `aCb`. It calls the function in the context of the thread that caused the event, with the thread itself in a critical section. The `aEvent` parameter to the callback indicates the event the callback relates to; the value `EEventHwExc` indicates a processor exception. For processor exception callbacks, parameter `a1` points to the saved processor state (for example, `TArmExcInfo` which I mentioned previously) and parameter `a2` is not used. The return value from the handler function will take one of the following values:

- `DKernelEventHandler::EExcHandled` if the exception has been handled and normal program execution should be resumed

- `DKernelEventHandler::ERunNext` if the exception has not been handled and the next kernel event handler (if any) should be run.

6.4.3.3 ARM coprocessor handlers

On ARM-based hardware, Symbian OS provides additional APIs to support lazy context switching and software support for coprocessors. ARM systems may have several coprocessors; examples of these are the Vector Floating Point (VFP), DSP and motion estimation units.

Here is the coprocessor API:

```
const TInt KMaxCoprocessors=16;

enum TCpOperation
  {
  EArmCp_Exc, /* UNDEF exc executing a coproc instr */
  EArmCp_ThreadExit, /* Coproc current owning thread exited */
```

```
    EArmCp_ContextInit /* Initialise coprocessor */
    };

struct SCpInfo;
typedef TInt (*TCpHandler)(SCpInfo*, TInt, TAny*);

struct SCpInfo
    {
    TCpHandler iHandler; /*Hdler:contextswitch,init&threadexit*/
    NThread* iThread; /*Current owning thread, NULL if none */
    TUint16 iContextSize; /* context size for this coprocr */
    TInt8 iCpRemap; /* Coproc no to remap this one to if >=0 */
    TUint8 iSpare;
    TInt iContextOffset; /* Offset in thread extra context */
    };

class Arm
    {
    ...
public:
    static void SetCpInfo(TInt aCpNum, const SCpInfo* aInfo);
    static void SetStaticCpContextSize(TInt aSize);
    static void AllocExtraContext(TInt aRequiredSize);
    static TUint32 Car();
    static TUint32 ModifyCar(TUint32 aClearMask, TUint32 aSetMask);
    static TUint32 FpExc();
    static TUint32 ModifyFpExc(TUint32 aClearMask, TUint32 aSetMask);
    ...
    };
```

The code responsible for handling the coprocessor (which may be in the kernel or in the ASSP, the variant or an extension) should call the following function during the Init1 initialization phase (see Chapter 16, *Boot Processes*, for a detailed description of the system initialization phases):

```
Arm::SetCpInfo(TInt aCpNum, const SCpInfo* aInfo);
```

Parameter aCpNum specifies the number of the coprocessor whose handler is being defined. Parameter aInfo specifies information about the coprocessor, as follows:

- SCpInfo::iHandler specifies the function that should be called at system boot if a thread exits or if an undefined instruction exception occurs trying to access the coprocessor. The second parameter passed to the function specifies which of these events has occurred, specified by the TCpOperation enumeration

- SCpInfo::iThread specifies which thread owns the coprocessor. On initialization this should be NULL

- SCpInfo::iContextSize specifies the size in bytes of the per-thread context for this coprocessor

- `SCpInfo::iCpRemap` specifies whether this coprocessor is really part of another coprocessor. If set to zero or a positive value, this specifies the number of the primary coprocessor. All events for this coprocessor will be redirected to the primary coprocessor. A value of −1 indicates that no redirection is required

- `SCpInfo::iContextOffset` is calculated by the kernel and need not be set. When the kernel calls back the handler function specified in `SCpInfo::iHandler` it passes the following parameters:

```
TInt h(SCpInfo* aInfo, TInt aOp, TAny* aContext);
```

If `aOp == EArmCp_ContextInit`, the system is in the `Init2` phase of boot. The handler should initialize the coprocessor and then save its state to the memory area pointed to by `aContext`. It should then disable access to the coprocessor.

If `aOp == EArmCp_ThreadExit`, a thread is exiting. The handler is called in the context of the exiting thread. If the exiting thread currently owns the coprocessor, the handler should mark the coprocessor as unowned, so that subsequent accesses do not try to save the state to a thread control block that no longer exists.

If `aOp == EArmCp_Exc`, an undefined instruction exception has occurred on an instruction targeted at this coprocessor. `aContext` points to the register state saved by the nanokernel exception preamble. The kernel calls the handler in the context of the thread attempting the instruction. If this is not the coprocessor's current owning thread, the handler should save the coprocessor state for the current owning thread and then disable the coprocessor for that thread. It should then enable the coprocessor for the current thread and restore the current thread's coprocessor state. If the exception is successfully handled the handler should return `KErrNone`, otherwise `KErrGeneral`.

The following functions are used to modify the access permissions for a coprocessor:

```
Arm::ModifyCar(TUint32 aClear, TUint32 aSet);
Arm::ModifyFpExc(TUint32 aClear, TUint32 aSet);
```

The functions return the original value of the register that they modify. Access to the VFP is controlled by the FPEXC register; access to other coprocessors is controlled by the CAR. Since these functions modify the hardware registers directly, they affect the current thread. To modify coprocessor access for another thread, the corresponding functions are used:

```
NThread::ModifyCar(TUint32 aClear, TUint32 aSet);
NThread::ModifyFpExc(TUint32 aClear, TUint32 aSet);
```

These do not modify the hardware registers – instead they modify the copy of those registers saved in the thread's control block.

6.4.4   Exceptions in the emulator

The emulator installs an exception handler on its Windows threads so that it can detect and handle exceptions occurring in Windows on that thread. This is similar to the data abort exception vector in the ARM code on a phone.

If the kernel is locked when an exception occurs the system halts, as this is a fatal error.

If the kernel is unlocked, the first action on taking an exception is to lock it. Next, we have to deal with the effect of a race condition between exception handling and forced exit – otherwise it is possible that a thread that has been killed will not actually die!

The exception handler then records the exception information and causes the thread to "return" to a second exception handler once the Windows exception mechanism has unwound. Running the second stage outside of the Windows exception handler allows the nanokernel to be in better control of the thread context; in particular it allows for the thread to be panicked and so on. The kernel remains locked through this process, so the saved exception data cannot be overwritten.

The second stage saves the full thread context including the original instruction pointer (this allows debuggers to display a complete call stack), then unlocks the kernel and invokes the nanokernel thread's exception handler. This handler can supply a final "user-mode" exception handler and parameters which is invoked before returning to the original exception location.

6.5   Summary

In this chapter, I've described interrupts and exceptions, and looked at their causes and the way in which processors react to them. I've shown how an operating system, in particular Symbian OS, makes use of exceptions, and I've gone on to examine how EKA2 handles them in detail. Finally, I have discussed the APIs that are available to allow you to make use of exceptions in base ports and device drivers.

The management of CPU resources is one of the key tasks of an operating system. The other is the management of memory, and it is this that I shall discuss in the next chapter, *Memory Models*.

7

Memory Models

by Andrew Thoelke

A memory is what is left when something happens and does not completely unhappen.

Edward de Bono

The kernel is responsible for two key resources on a device: the CPU and the memory. In Chapter 6, *Interrupts and Exceptions,* I described how the kernel shares the CPU between execution threads and interrupts.

In this chapter I will examine the high-level memory services provided by EKA2, and the way that the kernel interacts with the physical memory in the device to provide them. To isolate the kernel from different memory hardware designs, this interaction is encapsulated in a distinct architectural unit that we call the "memory model". As I describe the different memory models provided with EKA2 you will find out how they use the memory address space (the memory map) and their contribution to overall system behavior.

7.1 The memory model

At the application level – and to a large extent when writing kernel-side software – the main use of memory is for allocation from the free store using `operator new` or `malloc`. However, there are some more fundamental memory services that are used to provide the foundation from which such memory allocators can be built.

The kernel has the following responsibilities related to memory management:

1. Management of the physical memory resources: RAM, MMU and caches

2. Allocation of virtual and physical memory

3.   Per-process address space management

4.   Process isolation and kernel memory protection

5.   The memory aspects of the software loader.

As well as providing these essential services, we wanted to ensure that the design of the memory model does not impose hard or low limits on the operating system. In particular:

- The number of processes should be limited by physical resources rather than the memory model, and should certainly exceed 64

- Each process should have a large dedicated address space of 1–2 GB

- The amount of executable code that can be loaded by a process should be limited only by available ROM/RAM.

We found that the provision of efficient services to carry out these responsibilities is dependent on the memory architecture in the hardware. In particular, a design that is fast and small for some hardware may prove to be too slow or require too much memory if used on another. As one of the aims of EKA2 was to be readily portable to new hardware, including new MMU and memory architectures, we took all of the code that implements the different memory designs out of the generic kernel and provided a common interface. The resulting block of code we call the "memory model". This is itself layered, as I have already briefly described in Chapter 1, *Introducing EKA2*. I will repeat the key parts of the illustration I gave there as Figure 7.1.

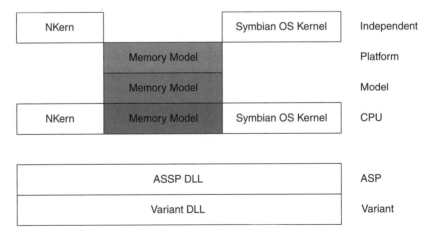

Figure 7.1   Memory model layering

At the highest level, we have to distinguish between a native implementation of EKA2 and an emulated one. In the former case, EKA2 is the OS that owns the CPU, the memory and all the peripherals, and the system boots from a ROM image. In the latter case another "host" OS provides basic services to EKA2, including memory allocation and software loading. This layer is referred to as the "platform".

As I mentioned in Chapter 1, *Introducing EKA2*, there are several ways to design an MMU and cache. We want to provide the best use of memory and performance for Symbian OS and so the different hardware architectures result in different memory model designs. The basic choices are as follows:

No MMU	Direct memory model
Virtually tagged cache	Moving memory model
Physically tagged cache	Multiple memory model
Emulator	Emulator memory model

I describe these different memory models in detail later in the chapter.

Even for identical memory architectures, different CPUs have different ways of controlling the MMU and cache and the final layer in the memory model, the "CPU" layer, supplies the specific code to control the memory in individual CPUs.

7.2 MMUs and caches

7.2.1 MMU

Before describing how EKA2 uses the RAM in the device to provide the memory services to the operating system and applications, it is worth explaining how the hardware presents the memory to the software.

EKA2 is a 32-bit operating system, which means that it assumes that all memory addresses can be represented in a 32-bit register. This limits the amount of simultaneously addressable memory to 4 GB. In practice there is far less physical memory than this, typically between 16 MB and 32 MB in the mobile phones available at the time of writing.

One of the important aspects of nearly all Symbian devices is that they are "open" – they allow the user to install third-party native applications and services. This is very different from a mobile handset based on an embedded OS, and is very significant for the way the OS must manage memory. It has several consequences:

1. In an embedded OS, one can determine the maximum memory requirement of each component. Then, at compilation time, one can

allocate exactly the memory that is needed to each component. This means that the exact amount of RAM needed is known when building the product. "Static allocation" of this kind is not viable with an open platform

2. There are certain types of application that ideally would use all available memory to provide maximum benefit to the user – for example, web browsers encountering complex web sites. Providing each such application with dedicated RAM would prove very expensive, particularly considering that most of this memory would be unused most of the time

3. The built-in software can be tested as thoroughly as required by the device manufacturer. However, third-party software added later can threaten the stability and integrity of the device. A poorly written or malicious program can be harmful if this software is allowed to directly interfere with the memory of the OS.

These issues make it important to make use of a piece of hardware found in higher-end devices: a memory management unit (MMU). This is responsible for the memory interface between the CPU and the memory hardware, which is typically a memory controller and one or more memory chips.

The rest of this section explores the various key features of a MMU and how EKA2 makes use of them.

7.2.1.1 *Virtual addresses and address translation*

One of the key services of an MMU is an abstraction between what the software considers to be a memory address and the real physical address of the RAM. The former is called the *virtual address* in this context and the latter the *physical address.*

This disconnection between the address in the software and the hardware address provides the mechanism to resolve the first two issues associated with an "open" OS. In particular, the OS can allocate a large range of virtual addresses for an application but only allocate the physical memory as and when the application requires it. Allocation of virtual addresses is often referred to as *reserving,* allocation of physical memory as *committing.*

The MMU and OS must maintain a mapping from virtual addresses to physical addresses in a form that allows the MMU to efficiently translate from the virtual to physical address whenever a memory access occurs. The most common structure used to hold this map is called a multi-level page directory, and the hardware supported by Symbian OS specifically supports two-level page directories. Some high-end CPUs now use three or more levels in the MMU, particularly 64-bit processors that support virtual address ranges with more than 32 bits. Figure 7.2 shows what a multi-level page directory might look like.

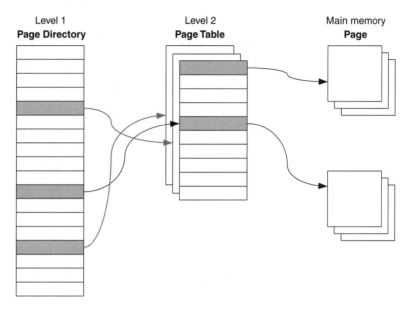

Figure 7.2   A multi-level page directory

The first level in a two-level directory is commonly referred to as the *page directory*. Conceptually there is just one of these directories used to do the mapping, although this is not always literally true – and we'll examine that in the next section. The directory is just a table of references to the items in the second level of the directory.

In the second level there are *page tables*. Typically there will be tens to hundreds of these objects in the mapping. Each page table itself contains a table of references to individual pieces of memory.

The memory itself has to be divided up into a collection of memory *pages* or *frames*. MMUs often support a small range of different page sizes: EKA2 prefers to use page sizes of 4 KB and 1 MB, but may also make use of others if available.

Perhaps the best way to understand how a virtual address is translated into a physical address through this structure would be to work through an example. To illustrate how address translation works, I shall concentrate on how an ARM MMU translates an address that refers to memory in a 4 KB page – this translation process is also called *page table walking*.

Let's suppose that a program has a string, "Hello world", at address 0x87654321 and issues an instruction to read the first character of this string. Figure 7.3 illustrates the work done by the MMU to find the memory page containing the string.

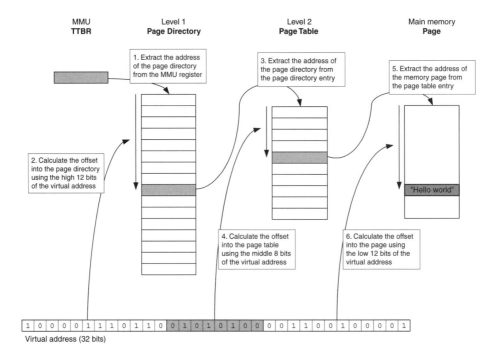

Figure 7.3 Algorithm for translating virtual addresses

Currently, ARM MMUs have a page directory which contains 2^{12} entries, each of which is 4 bytes – making the page directory 16 KB in size. Each entry is therefore responsible for 2^{20} bytes of address space, that is, 1 MB. When this entry refers to a page table containing 4 KB pages the page table will therefore have 2^8 entries. Again, each entry is 4 bytes, making the page table 1 KB in size.

First, the address provided by the program is broken up into three pieces. These provide three separate indexes into the different levels of the mapping.

Next the MMU locates the address of the page directory by reading its Translation Table Base Register (TTBR). The topmost 12 bits of the virtual address, in this case 0x876, is used as an index into the page directory. The MMU reads the entry from the page directory and determines that it refers to a page table for 4 KB pages.

Then, using the next 8 bits of the address, 0x54, as an offset into the page table, the MMU can read the page table entry. This now provides the physical address of the memory page.

The final 12 bits of the address are now combined with the page address to create the physical address of the string and this is used to fulfill the read request.

It is worth noting that the addresses in the TTBR, page directory entries and page table entries are all physical addresses. Otherwise, the MMU would have to use page table walking to do page table walking and the algorithm would never terminate!

Translation look-aside buffers

The algorithm described for translating addresses is quite simple, but if you consider that it requires two additional external memory accesses for each load or store operation it is easy to see that it is slow and inefficient.

To overcome this problem, MMUs provide a cache of the most recent successful address translations, and this is called the Translation Look-aside Buffer (TLB). This often stores the most recent 32 or 64 pages that were accessed, and allows the MMU to very quickly translate virtual addresses that correspond to one of those pages.

As with all caches, the kernel must manage the TLB to ensure that when the kernel makes changes to the underlying page tables it also modifies or discards any affected entries in the TLB.

TLBs are so effective that some MMUs do not provide the page-table walking algorithm in hardware at all. Instead they raise a CPU exception and expect that a software routine provided by the OS will look up the translation and set a TLB entry (if successful) before resuming the memory access that caused the exception. Although EKA2 could support this type of MMU, a reasonable implementation would require that the MMU provides special support for the software walking routine. For example, if the MMU reserved a region of the virtual address space to be directly mapped to physical memory without using the TLB, this would allow the table walking algorithm to read the page directory and page tables without incurring additional "TLB miss" exceptions.

7.2.1.2   Virtual address spaces

Earlier, I said that there is only one page directory in the mapping. This is true at any given time as the MMU has only one TTBR register which points to the base of the page directory. However, we can write to the TTBR and tell the MMU to use a different page directory when translating virtual addresses. This is one of the techniques that allows the same virtual address to map onto different physical addresses at different times.

Why would we want to do this?

The format of the executable code in Symbian OS is the basis for one of the reasons – in particular the way in which code refers to data. Symbian uses a *relocated* code format, in which the code has the actual (virtual) address of the data object. This is in contrast to *relocatable* code in which data references are all made relative to some external reference, usually a reserved register. It is almost amusing to note that only *relocated* code requires a set of *relocation data* in the executable file format so that the OS loader can correctly adjust all of the direct references within the code.

Consider an application, `TERCET.EXE` for instance, that has a global variable, `lasterror`, used to record the last error encountered in the program. Once this program has been loaded, linked and relocated there will be several memory blocks used for the program, and within them a direct reference from the program code to the address that the OS has decided to use for the `lasterror` variable (see Figure 7.4).

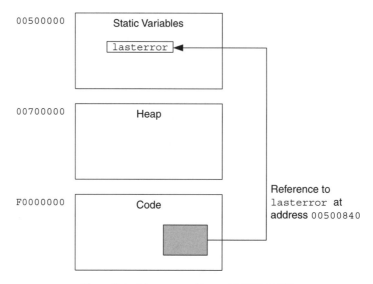

Figure 7.4   Memory used to run `TERCET.EXE`

This seems fine, we have a memory block allocated at virtual address `0xF0000000` for the program code, and another allocated at virtual address `0x00500000` for the program data, and in particular for the `lasterror` variable. There will be others for the program execution stack and the dynamic memory pool, or *heap*; however, unlike `lasterror` these do not have direct references from the program code.

Now suppose that the OS needs to run a second instance of TER-CET.EXE at the same time as the first. One of the definitions of a process in the OS is an independent memory address space. So as a separate process, the second copy of `TERCET.EXE` must have its own thread and execution stack, its own heap and its own copy of the global variables.

One way to achieve this would be to make a second copy of the program code and relocate this for different code and data addresses to the first instance (see Figure 7.5). Notice that this requires the code to be duplicated so that the second instance refers to a different location for the `lasterror` variable. Symbian OS doesn't do this for two reasons. Firstly, duplicating the code uses more RAM – which is already in short supply. Secondly, and more crucially, built-in software is usually executed in place (XIP) from Flash memory and so it has already been relocated for just one code and data address. And worse – we have discarded the relocation data to save space in the Flash memory, so we cannot make a copy of the code and relocate it for a new address.

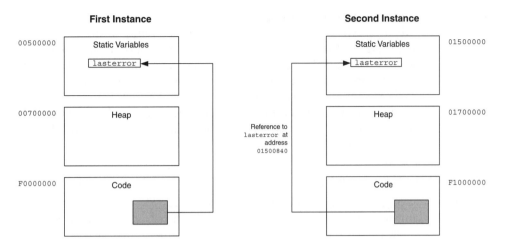

Figure 7.5 Memory used to run TERCET.EXE

So, in Symbian OS both instances of TERCET.EXE will share the same code memory – but this also implies that the address for lasterror is the same in both processes, 0x00500840 (see Figure 7.6).

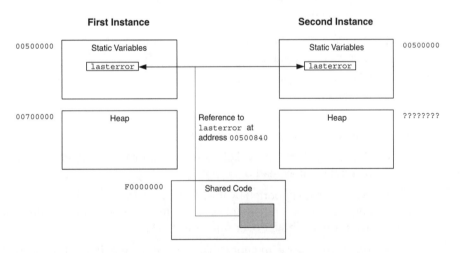

Figure 7.6 Running TERCET.EXE twice, sharing the code

We still need the two instances of TERCET.EXE to have separate memory blocks for their variables, so that when an instance of the process is running it finds its own variable mapped to address 0x00500840. So we need a way for the same virtual address to translate to two different physical addresses, depending on which process is currently running.

The solution is for each process in the OS to have its own mapping from virtual to physical addresses, and this mapping is called the process memory context. As I described in Chapter 3, *Threads, Processes and Libraries*, when we schedule a new thread to run, part of the work that has to be done is to determine if the new thread runs in the same process as the old one. When this is not the case, the memory context has to be changed to ensure that the correct mapping is used for virtual addresses in the new thread and process.

How this is achieved in Symbian OS depends on the type of MMU, and I describe this later in the chapter when I look at the different memory models.

7.2.1.3 *Memory protection*

One of the issues that an open OS must address is how to protect the operating system from software which is flawed or even malicious. If all software has direct access to the device memory, then it is not possible to limit the adverse effects that new software might have on a device.

We have already seen that the MMU provides an indirect mapping from the virtual address used by the software and the physical address of the memory provided by the OS. For each of the pages mapped by the MMU, we can supply attributes that describe an access policy for that memory. When used correctly and consistently by an OS this is a very powerful feature:

- We can protect the kernel data from direct and indirect attacks from user-mode programs

- We can protect the hardware that uses memory mapped I/O from being accessed directly by user-mode programs

- We can allow a process to read and write its own memory, but deny it access to that of any other process

- We can ensure that loaded software cannot be modified after loading by marking it as read-only

- When this is supported by the MMU, we can ensure that general heap and stack memory cannot be executed as program code, defending against many buffer over-run type attacks

- We can provide memory that can be shared by just some of the running processes.

Figure 7.7 illustrates these concepts by showing which memory should be made accessible to a thread when running in user or supervisor modes. The memory used by the kernel and two user programs, A and B, is shown where A and B share some code and some data. The left-hand images show memory accessible to a thread in program A in both user and kernel mode – note that the kernel memory is inaccessible to user-mode software. The top right image shows that program B cannot access

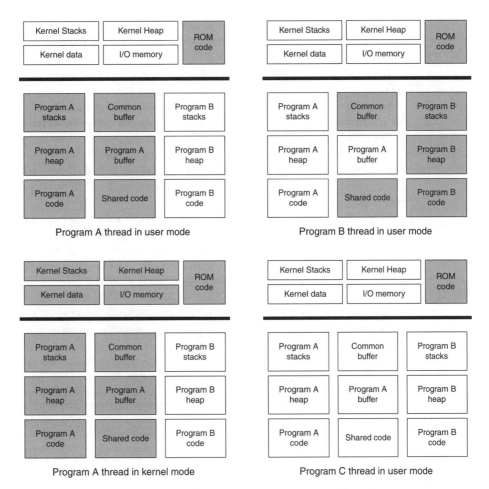

Figure 7.7 Memory accessible to a thread in user and kernel modes

memory used by program A except for memory that has been shared between these programs. The final image with program C, whose own memory is not shown, shows that this program has no access to any of the memory used by programs A and B. This demonstrates the ideal situation, and, as I will describe later, the different memory models sometimes provide less restricted access than is shown here for certain situations. Of course, any such relaxation is made very carefully to preserve the value of providing the memory protection in the first place.

7.2.1.4 Page faults

The MMU allows us to map all of a device's RAM, 16 MB say, into a much larger 4 GB virtual address space. Clearly many of the virtual addresses cannot map onto physical memory. What happens if we try to access one of these?

When walking through the page tables to translate an address, the MMU may find an entry that is marked as empty, or *not present* (in the page directory or a page table). When this occurs, the MMU raises a CPU prefetch or data abort exception, depending on whether the memory access was trying to read code or data.

Something very similar will occur if the MMU detects that the CPU is not permitted to access the page because it does not currently satisfy the access policy for the page.

In EKA2, this will usually result in a user-side thread terminating with KERN-EXEC 3 (unhandled exception) or the OS rebooting in the case of a kernel thread. I covered this in more detail in Chapter 6, *Interrupts and Exceptions*.

Operating systems designed for personal computers all use page faults and the MMU mapping to achieve another goal: demand paging. This is a scheme in which the operating system can effectively pretend that it has more physical memory than is really available. It does this by saving to disk memory pages that have not been used recently, and allowing another program to use the physical memory (for now). The memory mapping is adjusted to record that the old page is now saved to disk and is not present in memory. When this page is accessed once more a page fault occurs, and a special fault handler determines that the contents of the page are on disk, and arranges for it to be loaded back into spare physical memory before restarting the program that faulted.

EKA2 does not support demand paging.

7.2.2   Cache

The second key element of the hardware memory sub-system is the cache. This is very fast (1- or 2-cycle) memory that sits right next to the CPU. The data in the most recently accessed memory is contained here, substantially reducing the number of external memory accesses and therefore improving performance and efficiency.

In Chapter 2, *Hardware for Symbian OS*, I have discussed caches in some detail.

7.3   The memory model interface

The memory model is a distinct architectural block in the EKA2 kernel. As a result the rest of the kernel can be almost entirely independent of the chosen memory architecture and hardware support. To provide that encapsulation, the memory model defines a standard API to which all memory model implementations must conform.

The basic API is in the two classes P and M defined in kern_priv.h. P denotes the API exposed by the *platform* layer in the EKA2 software layer diagram, and M denotes the API exposed by the *model* layer in the same diagram:

```
class P
  {
  public:
  static TInt InitSystemTime();
  static void CreateVariant();
  static void StartExtensions();
  static void KernelInfo(TProcessCreateInfo& aInfo, TAny*& aStack,
                                                     TAny*& aHeap);
  static void NormalizeExecutableFileName(TDes& aFileName);
  static void SetSuperPageSignature();
  static TBool CheckSuperPageSignature();
  static DProcess* NewProcess();
  };

class M
  {
public:
  static void Init1();
  static void Init2();
  static TInt InitSvHeapChunk(DChunk* aChunk, TInt aSize);
  static TInt InitSvStackChunk();
  static TBool IsRomAddress(const TAny* aPtr);
  static TInt PageSizeInBytes();
  static void SetupCacheFlushPtr(TInt aCache, SCacheInfo& c);
  static void FsRegisterThread();
  static DCodeSeg* NewCodeSeg(TCodeSegCreateInfo& aInfo);
  };
```

This appears to be a very small API indeed, but it does hide a few secrets.

All but four of the functions are related to startup. The result of invoking the startup functions is both to initialize the memory model within the kernel, but also to configure the kernel for the memory model. In particular:

M::Init1()	During this initialization phase the process context switch callback is registered with the scheduler. This callback will be used for all address space changes triggered by a context switch.
M::SetupCacheFlushPtr()	Provides the memory address to be used by the cache manager when flushing the caches.

The two most interesting functions here are P::NewProcess() and M::NewCodeSeg(). These are not expected to return exact DProcess and `DCodeSeg` objects, but rather classes derived from them. We had a brief look at `DProcess` in Chapter 3, *Threads, Processes and Libraries*, but what you should note is that it has a number of virtual members – and among them are further factory functions `DProcess::NewChunk()` and `DProcess::NewThread()` designed to return memory model-specific classes derived from `DChunk` and `DThread`.

It is these four classes – `DProcess`, `DThread`, `DChunk` and `DCode-Seg` – that provide the main API between the generic layers of the kernel and the memory model.

7.3.1 DChunk

In Symbian OS, the *chunk* is the fundamental means by which the operating system allocates memory and makes it available to code outside of the memory model.

A chunk is a contiguous range of addressable (reserved) memory of which a sub-set will contain accessible (committed) memory. On systems without an MMU, the addresses are physical addresses, and the entire chunk is accessible.

On systems with an MMU, Symbian OS provides three fundamental types of chunk, depending on which sub-sets of the address range contain committed memory.

1. NORMAL. These chunks have a committed region consisting of a single contiguous range beginning at the chunk base address with a size that is a multiple of the MMU page size

2. DOUBLE ENDED. These chunks have a committed region consisting of a single contiguous range with arbitrary lower and upper endpoints within the reserved region, subject to the condition that both the lower and upper endpoints must be a multiple of the MMU page size

3. DISCONNECTED. These have a committed region consisting of an arbitrary set of MMU pages within the reserved region – that is, each page-sized address range within the reserved region that begins on a page boundary may be committed independently.

Although it is obvious that a normal chunk is just a special case of a double-ended chunk, and both of these are special cases of a disconnected chunk, we decided to separate the types because the specialized forms occur frequently and we can implement them more efficiently than the general purpose disconnected chunk. Figure 7.8 shows the different types of chunks and the common terminology used to describe their attributes.

As with other types of kernel resource, you can create chunks that are *local*, or private, to the creating process or chunks that are *global*. Local chunks cannot be mapped into any other process and thus the

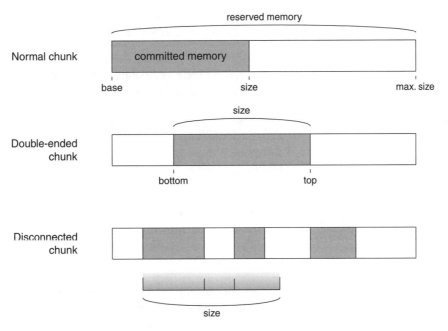

Figure 7.8 Fundamental chunk types

operating system uses them for any memory that does not need to be shared. Conversely, you can map a global chunk into one or more other processes. A process can discover and map global chunks that are named, whereas the only way for a process to access an unnamed global chunk is for it to receive a handle to the chunk from a process that already has one.

The operating system uses chunks for different purposes, and this information is also specified when creating a chunk. The memory model uses this information to determine where in the virtual address space to allocate a chunk, which access permissions must be applied and how to map the chunk into the kernel or user process memory context. The kernel uses the TChunkType enumeration to describe the purpose of the chunk to the memory model, and the following table explains the different types:

Value	Description
EKernelData	There is a single chunk of this type used to manage the global data for all XIP kernel-mode software, the initial (null) thread stack and the dynamic kernel heap. The virtual address for this chunk depends on the memory model, but is set during ROM

Value	Description
	construction and extracted from the ROM header at runtime. It is used to calculate the runtime data addresses for relocating the XIP code in ROM.
EKernelStack	There is single chunk of this type used to allocate all kernel-mode thread stacks. The difference with EKernelData is that the address range for this chunk is reserved dynamically during boot.
EKernelCode	There is at most a single chunk of this type, used to allocate memory for all non-XIP kernel-mode code, such as device drivers loaded from disk. It differs from the previous type by requiring execute permissions and I-cache management.
Edll EUserCode	The kernel uses these chunks to allocate memory or page mappings for non-XIP user-mode code. The memory model determines how these chunks are used and how code is allocated in them.
ERamDrive	This chunk contains the RAM drive, if present. The virtual address of the RAM drive is defined by the memory model – this allows the contents to be recovered after a software reboot.
EUserData	General purpose chunks for user-mode processes. The kernel uses these chunks for program variables, stacks and heaps. May be private to a process or shared with one or more other processes.
EDllData	This chunk allocates memory for writable static variables in user DLLs. The virtual address for this chunk must be fixed by the memory model, as it is used to calculate the runtime data address for XIP code in the ROM. Non-XIP DLLs have their data addresses allocated at load time. Each user process that links to or loads a DLL that has writable static data will have one of these chunks.
EuserSelfModCode	This is a special type of user-mode chunk that is allowed to contain executable code. For example, a JIT compiler in a Java runtime would use one for the

Value	Description
	compiled code sequences. This type of chunk differs from EUserData in the access permissions and also the cache management behavior.
ESharedKernelSingle ESharedKernelMultiple ESharedIo	The kernel provides these shared chunk types for memory that needs to be shared between device drivers and user-mode programs. Unlike other user-mode accessible chunks, these can only have the mapping adjusted by kernel software, which makes them suitable for direct access by hardware devices.
ESharedKernelMirror	Some memory models map shared chunks into the kernel memory context using an independent mapping – in this case, this chunk owns the additional mapping.

Here is the DChunk class:

```
class DChunk : public DObject
    {
public:
    enum TChunkAttributes
        {
        ENormal           =0x00,
        EDoubleEnded      =0x01,
        EDisconnected     =0x02,
        EConstructed      =0x04,
        EMemoryNotOwned   =0x08
        };

    enum TCommitType
        {
        ECommitDiscontiguous                = 0,
        ECommitContiguous                   = 1,
        ECommitPhysicalMask                 = 2,
        ECommitDiscontiguousPhysical        =
                ECommitDiscontiguous|ECommitPhysicalMask,
        ECommitContiguousPhysical           =
                ECommitContiguous|ECommitPhysicalMask,
        };

    DChunk();
    ~DChunk();
    TInt Create(SChunkCreateInfo& aInfo);
    inline TInt Size() const {return iSize;}
    inline TInt MaxSize() const {return iMaxSize;}
    inline TUint8 *Base() const {return iBase;}
```

```
inline TInt Bottom() const {return iStartPos;}
inline TInt Top() const {return iStartPos+iSize;}
inline DProcess* OwningProcess() const
                {return iOwningProcess;}
public:
virtual TInt AddToProcess(DProcess* aProcess);
virtual TInt DoCreate(SChunkCreateInfo& aInfo)=0;
virtual TInt Adjust(TInt aNewSize)=0;
virtual TInt AdjustDoubleEnded(TInt aBottom, TInt aTop)=0;
virtual TInt CheckAccess()=0;
virtual TInt Commit(TInt aOffset, TInt aSize, TCommitType aCommitType=
        DChunk::ECommitDiscontiguous, TUint32* aExtraArg=0)=0;
virtual TInt Allocate(TInt aSize, TInt aGuard=0, TInt aAlign=0)=0;
virtual TInt Decommit(TInt aOffset, TInt aSize)=0;
virtual TInt Address(TInt aOffset, TInt aSize,
                    TLinAddr& aKernelAddress)=0;
virtual TInt PhysicalAddress(TInt aOffset, TInt aSize,
                        TLinAddr& aKernelAddress,
                        TUint32& aPhysicalAddress,
                    TUint32* aPhysicalPageList=NULL)=0;
public:
DProcess* iOwningProcess;
TInt iSize;
TInt iMaxSize;
TUint8* iBase;
TInt iAttributes;
TInt iStartPos;
TUint iControllingOwner;
TUint iRestrictions;
TUint iMapAttr;
TDfc* iDestroyedDfc;
TChunkType iChunkType;
};
```

In the following table, I describe the meanings of some of DChunk's key member data:

Summary of fields in DChunk:

Field	Description
iOwningProcess	If the chunk is only ever mapped into a single process, this is the process control block for the process that created and owns this chunk. Otherwise this is NULL.
iSize	Size of committed memory in the chunk. Note that this does not include the gaps in a disconnected chunk.

Field	Description
iMaxSize	The reserved size of the chunk address region. This is usually the actual size reserved which may be larger than the requested size, depending on the MMU.
iBase	The virtual address of the first reserved byte in the chunk. This may change over time depending on which user-mode process is currently running, and may also be specific to a memory context that is not the current one – so dereferencing this value directly may not yield the expected results!
iAttributes	A set of flags indicating certain properties of the chunk. Some are generic – for example, double ended, disconnected, memory not owned. Some are memory model specific – for example, fixed access (protected by domain), fixed address, code (on moving model) and address allocation and mapping type flags on the multiple model.
iStartPos	The offset of the first committed byte in a double-ended chunk. Not used for other chunk types.
iControllingOwner	The process ID of the process that set restrictions on chunk.
iRestrictions	Set of flags that control which operations may be carried out on the chunk. For example, this is used to prevent *shared* chunks from being adjusted by user-mode software. Shared chunks are described in Section 7.5.3.2.
iMapAttr	Flags to control how the chunk is mapped into memory. Only used for shared chunks.
iDestroyedDfc	A DFC that is invoked once the chunk is fully destroyed. Chunk destruction is asynchronous and depends on all references to the chunk being released – this enables the device that owns the memory mapped by the chunk to know when the mapping has been removed.
iChunkType	The type of use that the chunk is put to. This is one of the TChunkType values already described.

We specify the chunk API entirely in terms of offsets from the base address. This is because the base address of a chunk is a virtual address, and thus may change depending on the memory context – in particular, different processes may have a different base address for the same chunk, or the kernel may find a chunk at a different base address than user code does. The precise circumstances under which the base address changes depend on the memory model.

We create a chunk with a specified maximum size, which determines the maximum size of the address range it covers; a chunk may never grow beyond this size. The memory model reserves a suitable region of virtual address space for the chunk which is at least as large as the maximum size, though it may be larger, depending on the particular MMU of the device.

The memory model provides chunk *adjust* functions which allow the committed region within the chunk to be changed in accordance with the chunk type:

`Adjust()`	Set the end of the committed region of a normal chunk. This will commit or release pages of memory as required to achieve the new size.
`AdjustDoubleEnded()`	Move one or both of the ends of the committed region of a double-ended chunk.
`Commit()`	Commit the pages containing the region specified. If any of the pages are already committed this will fail – so it is advisable to always specify page-aligned offsets.
`Decommit()`	Release the pages containing the region specified. This will ignore pages that are not committed without reporting an error.
`Allocate()`	Allocate and commit a region of the size requested. Optionally allocate a preceding *guard* region (which is not committed) and request larger than page-size alignment.

7.3.2   DCodeSeg

A code segment is responsible for the loaded contents of an executable image file, either an EXE or a DLL. This will be the relocated code and read-only data, as well as the relocated initial state of writable data, if it is present in the executable. We store this initial writable data in memory to avoid the need to re-read and relocate this from the executable file when initializing additional copies of the writable data section for the executable. As Symbian OS does not encourage the use of writable static data, this does not result in any significant waste of memory.

The code segment may own the memory for the code in different ways, depending on the memory model. In some cases, a single disconnected chunk manages all the memory for code segments, and in others the code segment manages the pages of memory directly.

As an optimization, code that is part of an XIP ROM does not usually have a code segment object to represent it in the kernel, unless it is directly referenced by a DProcess or DLibrary object.

Here are the other main responsibilities of code segments:

- Recording important information for the code segment, such as the code and data location, size and run address; the table of exception handlers; the code entry point; the directory of exports and more

- Maintaining the record of dependencies it has on other code segments. These are the dependencies that result from importing functions from other DLLs. Note that these dependencies can be circular, because mutual dependency between DLLs is legal. These dependencies are used to determine which code segments should be mapped in or out of a process as a result of a DLL being loaded or unloaded, or to determine when a code segment is unused and can be destroyed entirely

- Mapping the code segment into and out of a process address context when DLLs are loaded and unloaded. How, or if, this happens depends on how the memory model chooses to allocate and map code segments.

Chapter 10, *The Loader*, provides a thorough description of how code segments are used to manage executable code.

It is worth noting that EKA1 does not have a DCodeSeg object. In EKA1, the responsibilities of DCodeSeg were partly in DLibrary class and partly in DChunk. This arrangement suited the processor architectures and ROM available at the time it was designed. The complete redesign of this area for EKA2 was driven by the desire to exploit the very different memory model for ARMv6, and a need for a far more scalable design to manage hundreds of executables loaded from non-XIP Flash. EKA2 still has a DLibrary object, but it purely provides the kernel side of the user-mode RLibrary interface to dynamic code.

7.3.3 DProcess

Within the OS, a process is a container of one or more threads (see Chapter 3, *Threads, Processes and Libraries*) and an instantiation of an executable image file (see Chapter 10, *The Loader*). However, we have already seen that it is also the owner of a distinct, protected memory context. This means that it is concerned with both owning the memory belonging to the process (or being shared by the process), and also with owning the mapping of that memory into its virtual address space.

The memory model must maintain enough information with its process objects to be able to manage the process address context. This context is used by the memory model in the following situations:

- Process context switch. The previous context and protection must be removed from the MMU and the new one established. Changing the virtual to physical address map usually requires modifying one or more MMU registers, and may require invalidation of now-incorrect TLB entries and cache data due to changing the virtual to physical mapping

- Process termination. The memory model must be able to release all memory resources that the process owned or shared and return them to the system. Failure to do this would obviously result in slow exhaustion of the system memory and eventual reboot

- Inter-process communication – data transfers between processes. When a thread needs to read or write memory belonging to another process – this included when a kernel thread wishes to read or write user-mode memory – the memory model must be able to locate and map that memory to transfer the data.

7.3.4   DThread

Although the memory model is concerned with managing the process address space, a number of the operations that depend on the implementation of the memory model are logically carried out on threads, and so these operations are presented as members of the DThread class:

`AllocateSupervisorStack()`
`FreeSupervisorStack()`
`AllocateUserStack()`
`FreeUserStack()`
	The management of supervisor and user-mode thread stacks is memory model dependent. MMU enabled memory models typically allocate all thread stacks for a process in a single *disconnected* user-mode chunk, with uncommitted *guard pages* between each stack to catch stack overflow. Similarly, the kernel allocates all kernel-mode thread stacks in a single kernel chunk with guard pages between them.

`ReadDesHeader()`
`RawRead()`
`RawWrite()`
	These support the kernel reading from and writing to another thread's user memory. These methods will carry out any necessary checks to ensure that the specified "remote" memory is part of the thread's user memory address space. They can also check that the "local" memory buffer is within the executing thread's user memory context.
	This functionality is exposed to drivers via the `Kern::ThreadDesRead()` and `Kern::ThreadRawRead()` set of APIs, which in addition will trap any exceptions caused by unmapped addresses.
	The user-mode client/server `RMessagePtr2` APIs in turn use these for transferring data buffers between a client and server.

`ExcIpcHandler()`	This provides the exception handler used in conjunction with the exception trap (see my discussion of `XTRAP` in Chapter 6, *Interrupts and Exceptions*) as part of the inter-process copying I mentioned earlier. This enables an exception caused by providing a faulty remote address to be treated as an error response, but one caused by a faulty local address to be treated as a programming error, that is, a panic.
`RequestComplete()`	This is the kernel side of the Symbian OS programming patterns that use `TRequestStatus`, `User::WaitForRequest()` and active objects. Requests are always completed through this function, which writes the 32-bit status word into the target (requesting) thread's memory. As this is the basis for all inter-thread communication, performance is paramount, and so the memory model usually implements this operation as a special case of writing to another thread's memory space.

7.4   The memory models

Up to this point we have looked at a number of the problems faced when reconciling the need for Symbian OS to be open to third-party software, and yet robust against badly written or malicious programs. However, I have so far avoided providing the precise details of how these issues are resolved in EKA2. The reason for this is that the best solution depends on the design of the memory management hardware – and there are two very different designs of the level 1 memory sub-system employed in ARM processors. This has led to two different memory model implementations for devices running Symbian OS on ARM processors.

We developed the first implementation on EKA1, in the early days of Symbian OS, for version 3 of the ARM Architecture (ARMv3). The reason this is known as the *moving memory model* will become apparent as I explain its motivation and design. We developed and optimized this first implementation gradually, all the way through to version 5 of the ARM Architecture (ARMv5) and use it on both EKA1 and EKA2.

For version 6 of their architecture (ARMv6), ARM made a radical departure from their previous MMU and cache designs. At this point it made sense for Symbian OS to replace the moving model with a new design, the *multiple memory model*, which would make the most of the ARMv6 features and provide enhanced performance, reliability and robustness for Symbian OS.

For both of these memory models, we will look at the hardware architecture, describe how this is utilized to provide the memory model services and present the memory map, which depicts the way that the virtual address space is allocated to the OS.

For completeness, I will also briefly describe the two other memory models provided with EKA2: the *direct memory model*, enabling EKA2 to run without the use of an MMU, and the *emulator memory model*, which we use to provide a memory environment on the emulator that matches hardware as close as possible.

7.4.1   The moving model

We developed this memory model specifically for ARM processors up to and including those supporting ARMv5 architecture.

7.4.1.1   *Hardware*

The ARM Architecture Reference Manual[1] provides a detailed description of the memory sub-system in ARMv5. Here I will describe those features that have a significant impact on the memory model design.

---

[1] *ARM Architecture Reference Manual*, by Dave Seal. Addison-Wesley Professional.

Virtual address mapping

In ARMv5, the top-level page directory has 4096 entries, each of which is 4 bytes, making the directory 16 KB in size. Many operating systems that provide individual process address spaces use the simple technique of allocating a different page directory for each process – and then the context switch between processes is a straightforward change to the MMU's base register (the TTBR). However, on devices with limited RAM, we considered allocating 16 KB per process excessive and so we needed an alternative scheme for managing multiple address spaces.

Protection

ARMv5 provides two systems for protecting memory from unwanted accesses.

The first of these systems is the page table permissions: each page of memory that is mapped has bits to specify what kind of access is allowed from both user and supervisor modes. For example, a page can be marked as read-only to all modes, or no-access in user modes but read/write for supervisor modes. Obviously, memory that is not referenced in the current address map cannot be accessed either.

The second protection system is called *domains*. ARMv5 supports up to 16 domains. Each entry in the page directory contains a field to specify in which domain this address range lies. Thus, every mapped page lives in exactly one domain. The MMU has a register that controls the current access to each domain, with three settings: access to the domain is not allowed and always generates a fault, access to the domain is always allowed and page table permissions are ignored, or access to the domain is policed by the page table permissions.

Using domains allows large changes to the memory map and effective access permissions to be made by small changes to the page directory entries and to the *domain access control register* (DACR).

Caches

The ARMv5 cache design uses a virtually indexed and virtually tagged cache – this means that the virtual address is used to look up the set of cache lines that may contain the data being requested, and also to identify the exact cache cell that contains the data. The benefits are that no address translation is required if the data is in the cache, theoretically reducing power requirements. In practice, the MMU must still check the TLB to determine the access permissions for the memory.

However, as I discussed earlier, in a system that is managing multiple address spaces we expect the same virtual address to sometimes refer to two different physical addresses (depending on which process is current). This form of multiple mapping is sometimes referred to as a *homonym* – the same virtual address may "mean" more than one thing. There are also situations where we might wish to use two different virtual addresses to refer to the same physical memory, for example when sharing memory between processes or with a peripheral. This other form of multiple mapping is called a *synonym* – different virtual addresses have the same "meaning".

Figure 7.9 illustrates the problem of homonyms in ARMv5. Only one of the data items can be cached for the virtual address at any point in time because the MMU uses the virtual address to identify that item in the cache. We can only support the use of multiple overlapping address spaces by removing the virtual address and data from the cache during

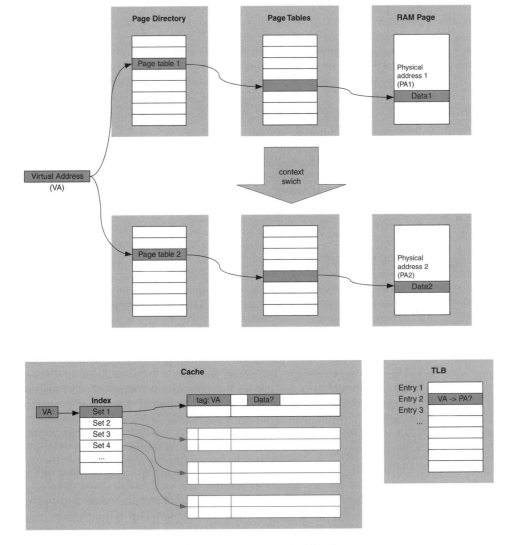

Figure 7.9   Homonyms in ARMv5

a context switch between the processes, ensuring that any updates are copied back to main memory. Otherwise the second process will only ever see (and access) the first process's memory.

In addition, the TLB cannot contain both of the mappings, and so the memory model also invalidates the TLB during a process context switch. As a result, a context switch that changes the virtual memory map impacts both performance and power consumption.

The problem of synonyms on such hardware is illustrated in Figure 7.10. This is slightly more complex, as the different virtual addresses will both appear in the cache in different places. This can result in confusing effects, because writing through one address may not be visible if read back through the other. This can only be solved by ensuring that the memory model does not map the same physical memory with two virtual addresses at the same time, and that if the virtual address needs to be changed then the cache data must be flushed.

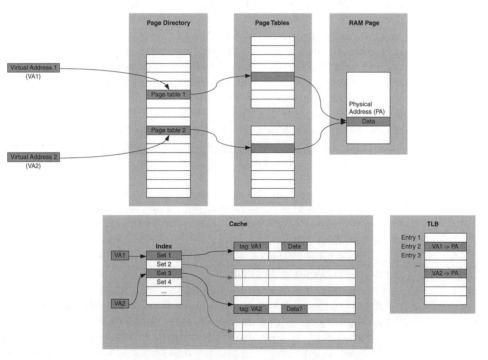

Figure 7.10   Synonyms in ARMv5

As with almost all new high-specification CPUs, the code and data caches are separated – this is sometimes referred to as a Harvard cache. (In Chapter 17, *Real Time*, I discuss the performance implications of different cache types.) Aside from general benefits that the Harvard cache is known to provide, the moving memory model specifically uses it to ensure that the instruction cache does not need to be managed on a context switch.

7.4.1.2 *Memory model concept*

The moving memory model uses a single page directory for the whole OS, and provides multiple overlapped process address spaces by moving blocks of memory (changing their virtual address) during a context switch. This is how the memory model derives its name.

Simple arithmetic shows that each page directory entry maps 1 MB of address space. Changing the domain specified in the entry provides easy control of the access policy for this memory range. The memory model can move this address range, whilst simultaneously changing the access permissions by writing a new entry in the page directory and resetting the old entry (two 32-bit writes).

For example, suppose we have a page table that maps a set of pages, each with "user no-access, supervisor read/write" permissions. Now we create a page directory entry in the second position in a page directory, allocate it to domain 0 and set the DACR to ignore-permissions for this domain. We can now access the pages using the address range 0x00100000-0x001fffff with full access from both user and supervisor modes as the permission bits are being ignored. On a context switch we remove this page directory entry and create a new one in the seventh position, this time setting the domain to 1 (with the DACR set to check-permissions for domain 1). After clearing the TLB entry for the old address range we can no longer use address 0x00100000 to access the memory. However, we can now use 0x00600000, but only from supervisor mode as the permission bits are now being checked. Figure 7.11 shows the effect of making these simple changes to the page directory.

This is the essential idea that we use to provide each process with identical virtual address spaces, but distinct and protected memory pages. During a context switch, we first move the old process's memory out of the common execution address, making it inaccessible to user mode at the same time, and then we move the new process's memory to the common execution address and make it accessible.

This is also one of the motivations behind the concept and implementation of the chunk, described in Section 7.3.1, which is the unit of "moving memory" within the higher layers of this memory model.

Unfortunately, as with many good ideas, this one is not without its drawbacks. If you remember, I earlier described the problem that can be caused by mapping memory at different virtual memory addresses, even when spread out in time – and that the solution is to flush the cache. This means that all modified data is copied back to main memory and all cached data is discarded and must be reloaded from main memory when required. As a result, a process context switch with this memory model is dominated by the time spent flushing the cache, and is typically 100 times slower than a thread context switch (within the same process). There is little hope that in future cache flushing will be made faster by

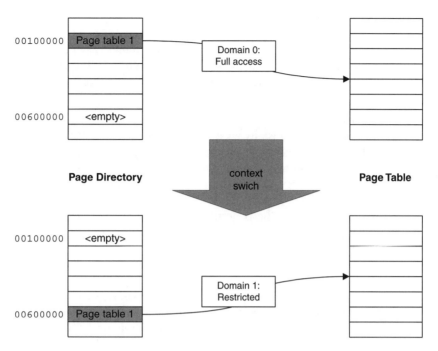

Figure 7.11 Remapping memory by modifying the page directory

new processors and memory, as performance gained there is lost flushing ever larger caches.

The moving memory model employs some of the other ARMv5 features, such as domains and split caches, to reduce the requirement for cache flushing. However, it cannot be entirely removed and still constitutes a measurable proportion of the execution time for Symbian OS.

It is interesting to note that ARMv5 provides an alternative to multiple page directories or moving page tables – the Fast Context Switch Extensions. In this mode, the MMU translates the virtual address before doing regular address translation using the page tables, and can eliminate the expensive cache flush on a context switch. In this mode, the MMU will replace the highest 7 bits of the virtual address with the value in the FCSE PID register, if these bits were all zero. This means that virtual addresses in the range 0x00000000 to 0x02000000 will be mapped to some other 32 MB range before the page tables are walked. On a process context switch all that is needed is to change the FCSE PID. Although popular with other open operating systems using ARMv5, this limits the system to 127 processes (the number of distinct, non-zero FCSE PID values) and each process to a virtual address space of 32 MB including code. The need for the kernel to use some of the memory map for other purposes can reduce these limits significantly. These limitations were not acceptable for Symbian OS.

7.4.1.3   Design

As I have already described, the moving memory model maintains a single page directory for the whole OS. The rest of this section provides a high-level view of the moving memory model design.

Address spaces

Allocated memory is always owned by a single-page table, and the page table will be owned by a single chunk. Thus a chunk is always responsible for a whole number of megabytes of virtual address space, and the base address is always aligned on a megabyte boundary.

Each chunk is always present in exactly one place in the memory map, and so all of the page tables that it owns will be referenced from consecutive page directory entries. One consequence of this is that there can never be more than 4096 distinct page tables at any one time.

The previous rule is not directly obvious from the requirements. Memory that is not accessible to the currently executing process does not always need to be in the memory map. However, much of Symbian OS execution involves inter-process activity and the implementations of the client/server system and thread I/O requests rely on having access to the memory of a non-current process. If we ensure that this memory is directly accessible to the kernel, we can simplify these algorithms considerably.

By default, the data chunks for a process are *moving* chunks and these have two address ranges allocated for them. The first is the *data section address* (or *run* address) which is the virtual address used by the process that creates the chunk and the range is as large as the maximum size for the chunk. The latter is necessary because the virtual address of the chunk is specified to never change as the chunk grows or shrinks. When a moving chunk is mapped into a second process, the memory model does not guarantee that the virtual address in the second process matches that in the first one. Thus the data section address is specific to each process that has access to the chunk.

The second address is the *kernel section address* (or *home address*) which is the virtual address occupied by the chunk when it is both inaccessible to the currently running process and the current process is not *fixed* – see the following optimizations section for an explanation of *fixed* processes. Page directory entries are only reserved in the kernel section for the currently committed memory in the chunk. If additional page tables are added to the chunk later, a new kernel section address will be allocated – this is not a problem as the kernel section address is only ever used transiently for inter-process memory accesses.

The memory model manages the chunks that are accessible to each process by maintaining for each process an address ordered list of all data chunks that are mapped by the process. Each entry on this list also contains the data section address for that chunk in the process. The chunk itself knows about its kernel section address, and whether it is currently mapped in the kernel section, or if it is mapped in the data section.

Protection

Using the memory moving technique shown in Figure 7.11, two domains are used to provide protection between the currently running process and the memory that should be inaccessible to the process, such as kernel memory or that belonging to other processes. Although it might be more obvious for the memory model to just use page permissions to achieve this, modifying the page permissions during a context switch would require changing every entry of the affected page tables – the scheme using domains only requires that the memory model modifies a handful of page directory entries.

Most chunks use page permissions that deny access from user mode, but allow read/write access from supervisor modes. Chunks that are not accessible to the current user process are allocated to domain 1, while those that are accessible to the current user process are allocated to domain 0. The domain access control register is set to allow all access to domain 0 (ignoring the permission bits), but makes the MMU check permissions for access to domain 1. This has the desired effect of allowing a process to access its own memory from user mode (chunks in the data section), but other memory is inaccessible except from supervisor modes.

Some chunks have slightly different permissions to improve the robustness of Symbian OS:

- Once loaded, all chunks containing code are marked as read-only, to prevent inadvertent or malicious modification of software

- The mappings for the RAM drive are allocated to domain 3. This domain is set to no-access by default, preventing even faulty kernel code from damaging the disk contents. The RAM disk media driver is granted access to this domain temporarily when modifying the disk contents.

Figure 7.12 illustrates the effective access control provided by the moving memory model, compared with the ideal presented earlier in the chapter. Note that the only compromise for user-mode software is the visibility of program code that has not been explicitly loaded by the program. However, this memory model does make all memory directly accessible from kernel mode. Kernel-mode software must already take care to ensure that user processes cannot read or corrupt kernel memory through the executive interface, so extending that care to guard against incorrect access to another process does not add any significant complexity to the OS.

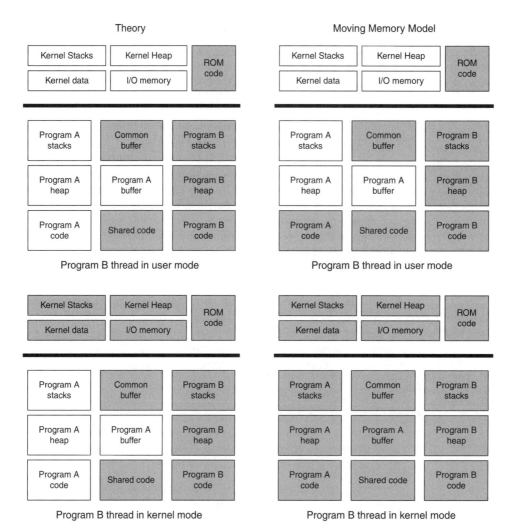

Figure 7.12   Memory accessible to a thread in the moving memory model

Optimizations

Every time an operation requires the moving of at least one chunk, the memory model must flush the relevant cache and TLB – therefore the memory model design attempts to reduce the number of chunks that need to be moved.

- A global chunk is used to allocate code segments. Thus code executes from the same address in all processes. Additionally, code loaded by one process is visible to the entire OS – although this is a compromise for system robustness, it avoids a very expensive operation to adjust the access permissions for all RAM-loaded code, and flush TLBs. Together this ensures that the memory model never needs to flush the I-cache on a context switch, significantly improving system performance

- Some chunks are fixed in memory, and their virtual address never changes. In these cases, we use domains to control access to the chunk by changing the DACR for the processes that are allowed access. This can reduce the number of chunks that need to be moved on a context switch

- Important and heavily used server processes can be marked as *fixed* processes. Instead of allocating the data chunks for these processes in the normal data section the memory model allocates them in the kernel section and they are never moved. The memory model allocates an MMU domain, if possible, to provide protection for the process memory. The result is that a context switch to or from a fixed process does not require a D-cache flush and may even preserve the data TLB. One consequence of using this feature is that we can only ever run a single instance of a fixed process, but this is quite a reasonable constraint for most of the server processes in the OS. Typical processes that we mark as fixed are the file server, comms server, window server, font/bitmap server and database server. When this attribute is used effectively in a device, it makes a notable improvement to overall performance.

Memory map
Figures 7.13 and 7.14 show how the virtual address space is divided in the moving memory model. These diagrams are not to scale and very large regions have been shortened, otherwise there would only be three or four visible regions on it!

7.4.1.4 Algorithms

In trying to understand how this memory model works it is useful to walk through a couple of typical operations to see how they are implemented.

Process context switch
The memory model provides the thread scheduler with a callback that should be used whenever an address space switch is required. I will describe what happens when the scheduler invokes that callback.

Switching the user-mode address space in the moving memory model is a complex operation, and can require a significant period of time – often more than 100 microseconds. To reduce the impact on the real time behavior of EKA2 of this slow operation, the address space switch is carried out with preemption enabled.

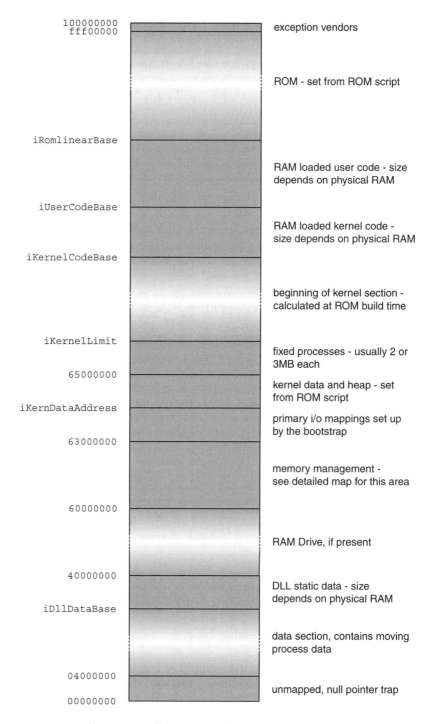

Figure 7.13 Full memory map for moving memory model

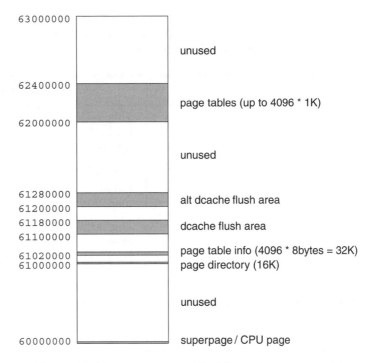

Figure 7.14   Memory management detail for moving memory model

The user-mode address space is a shared data object in the kernel, as more than one thread may wish to access the user-mode memory of a different process, for example during IPC or device driver data transfers. Therefore, changing and using the user-mode address space must be protected by a mutex of some form – the moving memory model uses the system lock for this. This decision has a significant impact on kernel-side software, and the memory model in particular – the system lock must be held whenever another process's user-mode memory is being accessed to ensure a consistent view of user-mode memory.

The context switch is such a long operation that holding the system lock for the entire duration would have an impact on the real time behavior of the OS, as kernel threads also need to acquire this lock to transfer data to and from user-mode memory. We tackle this problem by regularly checking during the context switch to see if another thread is waiting on the system lock. If this is the case, the context switch is abandoned and the waiting thread is allowed to run. This leaves the user-mode address space in a semi-consistent state: kernel software can locate and manipulate any user-mode chunk as required, but when the user-mode thread is scheduled again, more work will have to be done to complete the address space switch.

The *fixed process* optimization described in the previous section relies on the memory model keeping track of several processes. It keeps a record of the following processes:

Variable	Description
TheCurrentProcess	This is a kernel value that is really the owning process for the currently scheduled thread.
TheCurrentVMProcess	This is the user-mode process that last ran. It "owns" the user-mode memory map, and its memory is accessible.
TheCurrentDataSectionProcess	This is the user-mode process that has at least one moving chunk in the common address range – the *data section*.
TheCompleteDataSectionProcess	This is the user-mode process that has all of its moving chunks in the data section.

Some of these values may be NULL as a result of an abandoned context switch, or termination of the process.

The algorithm used by the process context switch is as follows:

1. If the new process is *fixed,* then skip to step 6

2. If the new process is not TheCompleteDataSectionProcess then flush the data cache as at least one chunk will have to be moved

3. If a process other than the new one occupies the *data section* then move all of its chunks to the *home section* and protect them

4. If a process other than the new one was the last user process then protect all of its chunks

5. Move the new process's chunks to the *data section* (if not already present) and unprotect them. Go to step 8

6. [Fixed process] Protect the chunks of TheCurrentVMProcess

7. Unprotect the chunks of the new process

8. Flush the TLB if any chunks were moved or permissions changed.

Thread request complete
This is the signaling mechanism at the heart of all inter-thread communications between user-mode programs and device drivers or servers.

The part related to the memory model is the completion of the request status, which is a 32-bit value in the requesting thread's user memory. The signaling thread provides the address and the value to write there to the `DThread::RequestComplete()` method, which is always called with the system lock held.

In the moving memory model, this is a fairly simple operation because all of the user-mode memory is visible in the memory map, either in the *data section* or in the *home section*. This function looks up the provided address in the chunks belonging to the process, and writes the data to the address where the memory is mapped now.

7.4.2 The multiple model

This memory model was developed primarily to support – and exploit – the new MMU developed for ARMv6. However, it is more generally applicable than the moving memory model and can also be used with MMUs found on other popular processors such as Intel x86 and Renesas SuperH.

7.4.2.1 Hardware

As with the ARMv5 memory architecture, I refer you to the ARM Architecture Reference Manual for the full details of the level 1 memory sub-system on ARMv6.

Virtual address mapping

As with ARMv5, the top-level page directory still contains 4096 entries. However, in contrast with ARMv5 the page directory on ARMv6 can be split into two pieces. Writing to an MMU control register, TTBCR, sets the size of the first piece of the directory to contain the first 32, 64, . . ., 2048 or 4096 page directory entries, with the remainder being located in the second page directory. To support this, the MMU now has two TTBR registers, TTBR0 and TTBR1.

The MMU also has an 8-bit application space identifier register (ASID). If this is updated to contain a unique value for each process, and the memory is marked as being process-specific, then TLB entries created from this mapping will include the ASID. As a result, we do not need to remove these TLB entries on a context switch – because the new process has a different ASID and will not match the old process's TLB entries.

Protection

Although ARMv6 still supports the concept of domains, this feature is now deprecated on the assumption that operating systems will opt to use the more powerful features of the new MMU.

However, ARM have enhanced the page table permissions by the addition of a never-execute bit. When set, this prevents the page being accessed as part of the instruction fetching. When used appropriately, this can prevent stack and heap memory being used to execute code, which in turn makes it significantly harder to create effective security exploits such as buffer over-run attacks.

Caches

The cache in ARMv6 has also been through a complete overhaul, and a virtually indexed, physically tagged cache replaces the virtually indexed, *virtually* tagged cache in ARMv5.

The cache is indexed using the virtual address, which enables the evaluation of the set of cache lines that could contain the data to run in parallel with the address translation process (hopefully in the TLB). Once the physical address is available, this is used to identify the exact location of the data in cache, if present.

The result of using a physically tagged cache is very significant – the problems associated with multiple mappings are effectively removed. When the same virtual address maps to different physical addresses (a homonym) the cache can still store both of these simultaneously because the tags for the cache entries contain distinct physical addresses (see Figure 7.15).

Also, two virtual addresses that map to the same physical address (a synonym) will both resolve to the same entry in the cache due to the physical tag and so the coherency problem is also eliminated. This rather nice result is not quite the whole picture – the use of the virtual address as the index to the cache adds another twist for synonyms which I will describe more fully later.

7.4.2.2 Memory model concept

The features of the ARMv6 MMU enable a number of the drawbacks of the moving memory model to be eliminated without compromising on the device constraints or OS requirements.

The split page directory of ARMv6 allows us to revisit the common idea of having one page directory for each process. This time, instead of requiring 16 KB for each process, we can choose to have just a part of the overall page directory specific to each process and the rest can be used for global and kernel memory. EKA2 always uses the top half (2 GB) for the kernel and global mappings, and the bottom half for per-process mapping. This reduces the per-process overhead to a more acceptable 8 KB, but retains up to 2 GB of virtual address space for each process. For devices with smaller amounts of RAM (<32 MB) we go further and only map the bottom 1 GB for each process reducing the overhead to just 4 KB for each process. The name of the model comes from it using multiple page directories.

The multiple memory model makes use of ASIDs to resolve the problem of mapping the same virtual address to different physical addresses, while the physically tagged cache ensures that multiple mappings of virtual or physical addresses can be correctly resolved without needing to flush data out of the cache. Figure 7.15 shows how these features allow the TLB and cache to contain multiple process memory contexts simultaneously, even when the processes map the same virtual address.

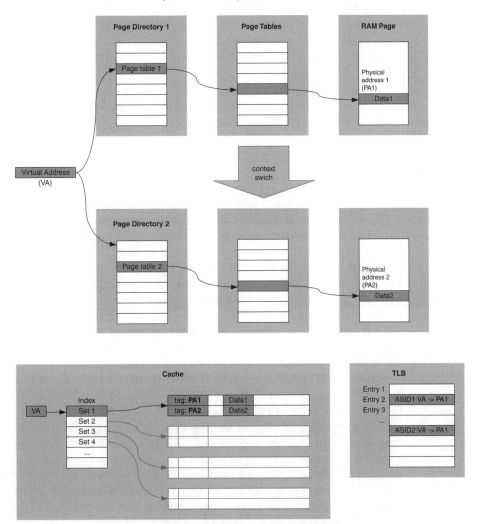

Figure 7.15   Homonyms in ARMv6

When compared with the moving memory model, this design:

- Still provides up to 2 GB of per-process virtual address space
- Requires moderate additional memory overhead for each process (4 or 8 KB)

- Has **no** requirement to flush the caches or TLBs on a context switch

- Does not make loaded program code globally visible

- Marks memory that holds data so that it cannot be executed as code.

The performance improvement that comes as a result of eliminating the cache flush on context switch is the most significant benefit of this memory model. It also ensures that this is a better memory model for the future, as we will see continuing increases in cache size and CPU to memory performance ratio.

The last two points in the previous list improve the robustness of the OS as a whole, but also increase the protection provided for platform security, which you can read more about in Chapter 8, *Platform Security*.

Revisiting the synonym problem

Although the multiple memory model is an improvement on the moving memory model, it is not without its own complexities. The most awkward issue is related to the solution for the synonym problem – providing a second or *alias* virtual address for the same physical address. The problem stems from the use of the virtual address as the initial index into the cache to select the small set of lines from which to determine an exact match using the physical address. Figure 7.16 primarily illustrates the ideal situation with a synonym mapping – where the cache resolves both virtual addresses to the same cache line and data.

However, the cache indexing is done using the lower bits of the virtual address. For obvious reasons, the bottom 12 bits of the virtual address and physical address are always identical (when using 4 KB pages). What could happen if the cache uses 13 bits for the index?

Suppose that the page at physical address 0x00010000 was mapped by two virtual addresses: 0x10000000 and 0x20001000. Then we write to the memory at 0x10000230, which results in an entry in the cache in the index set for 0x230 (low 13 bits) with the physical tag 0x00010230. If we now try to read the address 0x20001230 (which according to our mapping is the same memory), this will look up entries in the cache index set for 0x1230 and not find the previous entry. As a result the cache will end up containing two entries which refer to the original physical address. The dotted entry in the cache in Figure 7.16 illustrates this effect. This is the very problem we thought we had eliminated.

If the cache is small enough or the index sets within the cache large enough (commonly known as the cache associativity), then no more than 12 bits are used for the virtual index. In this case, the problem does not arise as there is a unique set within the cache for every physical address. If 13 or more bits of the virtual address are used for the cache index, then there can be multiple index sets in which a physical address may be found – which one depends on the virtual address used to map it. The

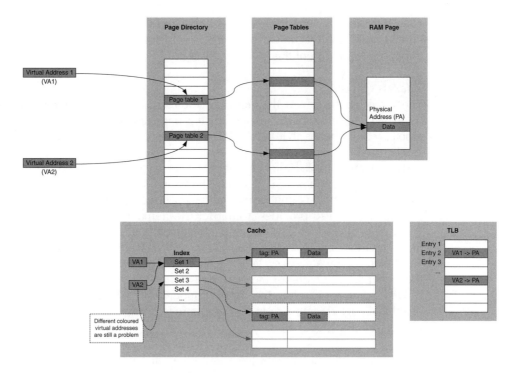

Figure 7.16 Synonyms in ARMv6

one or more bits of virtual address that select which of these sets are said to determine the *color* of the page.

The solution adopted by EKA2 for this problem is to ensure that all virtual to physical mappings share the same color – that is, all of the virtual addresses used to map a given physical page must have the same values for the bits that determine the color of the page. Thus every cache lookup using any of these virtual addresses will resolve to the same entry in the cache.

7.4.2.3 Design

In some respects the design of the multiple memory model is more straightforward, as there is never the need to work out where some memory happens to be at a given moment in time. If you know which process has the memory and you have the virtual address, it is just a matter of inspecting the process's page directory to locate the memory – remembering, of course, that the addresses in the page directory are physical addresses and translation to a virtual address is required to inspect the page table.

In this model, the concept of a chunk is less fundamental to the overall design. The design does not require such an object to exist – but as the

main interface between the memory model and the kernel is in terms of
chunks due to their significance for the moving memory model, they still
form an integral part of this memory model.

Address spaces

The kernel process owns the global page directory, which is referenced
by TTBR1. All of the pages mapped by this page directory are marked as
global, which means that the MMU will create global TLB entries that
can be used by any process.

The memory model allocates an ASID for each user-mode process.
ARMv6 only supports 256 distinct ASIDs and thus limits the OS to
running at most 256 concurrent processes. This is considered to be
sufficient! This also provides a limit for the number of per-process, or
local, page directories – so these are conveniently allocated in a simple
array. Memory is only committed for a local page directory when the
ASID is in use by a process. When a process is running, TTBR0 is set to
the local page directory for the process.

Depending on its type, the memory model will allocate a chunk in
the global page directory or in the local one. Examples of memory that is
allocated in the global directory:

- The global directory maps the XIP ROM as all processes must see this
  code

- All processes share the locale data so this is allocated in the global
  directory

- Any thread that is running in supervisor mode should have access to
  kernel data and this is allocated in the global chunk.

Examples of memory that is allocated in the local directory:

- Stack and heap chunks that are private to the process

- Shared chunks that may also be opened by other processes

- Program code that is loaded into RAM.

The last two of these examples are memory that the operating system
can map into more than one process. Unlike the moving memory model,
however, chunks that can be shared between user processes always have
the same base address in all processes. The multiple memory model
achieves this by using a single address allocator for all memory that can
be shared. This also ensures that shared memory does not suffer from the
coloring problem as the virtual address is common to all processes.

In the moving memory model, the DProcess objects maintain a
collection of the chunks that they currently have access to. This is also

necessary to ensure that on a context switch the chunk is made accessible to the program, as well as to allow address lookup when the process is not in context. In the multiple model, this collection still exists but only provides a means to track the number of times a given chunk has been opened within the process so that it can be removed from the memory map only after the last reference is closed. The process's local page directory maps the chunk to provide access when the program is running, and to provide lookup for the memory model with the process is not in context.

The model also keeps an inverse mapping from a shared chunk to the processes that have opened it, so that the memory model can reflect adjustments to the chunk size in all affected page directories.

Protection

Providing process memory protection with the multiple model is simpler than with the moving model, which required domains to make it efficient.

Multiple page directories provide most of the protection: memory that is private to a process is not present in the memory map when another process is running. The use of ASIDs and the physically tagged cache ensure that all cache data and mappings are only applied to the owning process. Thus, unlike the moving memory model, the multiple model applies full access permissions to memory mapped by the local page directory.

The model applies supervisor-only permissions to kernel data mapped by the global page directory, so that only supervisor modes can access this.

The model sets the never-execute permission on all data memory, such as stacks and heaps. This prevents buffer-over-run attacks being used to launch malicious code in the device.

Non-XIP user-mode program code is now mapped in the local page directory rather than globally. This allows the memory model to restrict the visibility of such code to just the processes that have explicitly loaded it.

The result is that the memory access matches the ideal situation described in Section 7.2.1.3.

Memory map

Figures 7.17 and 7.18 show how the multiple memory model divides virtual address space. I have depicted the case in which the local page directory is 8 KB in size. Again, these diagrams are not to scale.

A final word on chunks

Some might suggest that the chunk is a very high-level interface to provide the primary means of describing and controlling the memory allocated and mapped by a process, and that a simpler, lower-level interface would provide flexibility with less complexity.

The development of the disconnected chunk illustrates the need for increasing flexibility and support for alternative allocation strategies.

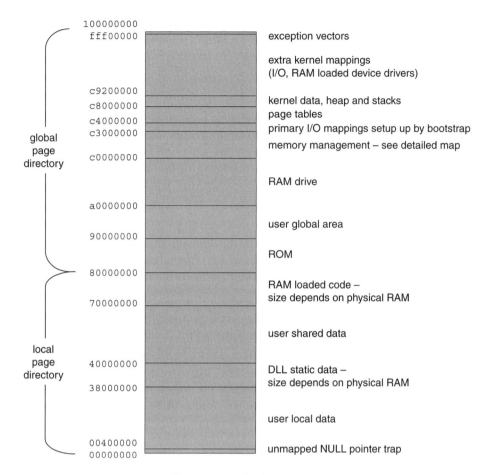

Figure 7.17 Full memory map for the multiple memory model

Within the multiple memory model there is an attempt to escape from the notion that all memory belongs to a chunk in the handling of program code that is loaded into memory.

However, because the moving memory model depends on the use of chunks to describe all of its memory, while Symbian OS supports ARMv5, chunks will continue to be the primary means of describing the memory that is mapped by a process, and as the abstract interface between generic kernel software and the memory model. Of course, even when no longer demanded by the underlying memory hardware, the chunk will always form part of the user-mode interface for memory management.

7.4.2.4 Algorithms

I will describe the same operations for the multiple memory model as I did for the moving model to illustrate the design.

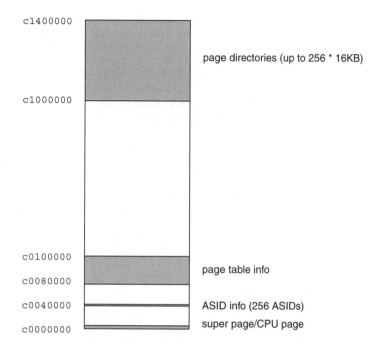

Figure 7.18 Memory management detail for the multiple memory model

Process context switch

The design of ARMv6 ensures that the address space switch is now a simple operation. It is fast enough that it can be executed with preemption disabled, making a process switch only marginally slower than a simple thread switch.

The process context switch involves modifying two MMU registers:

- `TTBR0` is set to the page directory for the new process

- `CONTEXTID` is set to the `ASID` for the new process.

The only extra work occurs if the new process contains user-mode "self-modifying" code chunks, and was not the last such process to run, in which case this function invalidates the dynamic branch prediction table before returning.

Thread request complete

In contrast, this is now a more complex operation than the equivalent in the moving memory model. This is because the memory to which we need to write is not visible in the current address space,

This function can afford to use a different, faster, technique for writing into another address space when compared with a general IPC data copy, because it doesn't need to simultaneously map both the signaling and requesting process memory. Instead, the current nanokernel thread changes its address space, effectively executing briefly within the memory context of the target thread.

The memory model manages this sleight of hand by changing the `TTBR0` and `CONTEXTID` registers to the values for the target thread with interrupts disabled. At the same time, it updates the current thread's `iAddressSpace` member to ensure that the right memory context is restored if the next operation is preempted. Now that the current thread has "jumped" into the target process address space, it can just write the result code before restoring the MMU state to return to the original address context.

Some care must be taken when writing to the request status to catch the use of an invalid memory address. The system lock is held and so `RequestComplete()` traps any exception and then processes the failure once the address space has been restored.

7.4.3   The direct model

This memory model disables the MMU and the OS assumes a direct mapping from virtual address to physical address. Although this enables Symbian OS to run on hardware that has no MMU, Symbian OS does not support this option in products as the lack of an MMU presents too many limitations for the OS as a whole:

- The manufacturer must divide the physical memory at build time between all the running processes in the OS, as memory chunks cannot be grown and shrunk without an MMU. This makes it difficult to support a variety of different memory-hungry use cases in a single device without supplying an excessive amount of RAM

- There is no memory protection between different user-mode processes or between user and kernel software – making the system significantly less robust. It would certainly be unwise to consider allowing such a device to support installation of additional software after production.

However, there are times when it is useful to be able to run part of Symbian OS – in particular the kernel and file server – with the MMU disabled, such as when porting EKA2 to a new CPU or a new CPU family. Such porting tasks are easier if the MMU is initially disabled to stabilize the essential parts of the board support package without debugging new memory hardware at the same time. Once EKA2 is running on the hardware, the porting team can enable the MMU and tackle any memory related problems independently.

7.4.4   The emulator model

As one might expect, we developed this memory model specifically to support the emulator hosted by the Windows operating system. To achieve the objectives set for the emulator regarding development and demonstration, we made some compromises regarding true emulation of the behavior of the hardware memory models.

It is here in the memory model that we find the most significant differences between target and emulator kernels.

The emulator does not run on the "bare metal" of the PC hardware, but is hosted as a process within the Windows operating system. As a result, the low-level memory support in the emulator memory model uses standard Windows APIs for basic memory allocation.

7.4.4.1   Virtual address mapping

The emulator runs as a single Win32 process, with the consequence that it only has a 2 GB virtual address range for all memory allocation. Compare this with a real device, where each application within the OS typically has approximately 1 GB of virtual address space for its own use.

To provide the programming model of the chunk, the emulator uses the low-level `VirtualAlloc()` Windows API, which can reserve, commit and release pages of the process address space. This also enables an emulation of the page-wise allocation of RAM to a chunk, and allows some approximation to be made of the amount of RAM being used by the OS at any time. However, the emulator does not allocate all memory in this way.

The emulator utilizes the Windows DLL format and the Windows loader – `LoadLibrary()` and friends – to enable standard Windows IDEs to be used for debugging of Symbian OS code in the emulator. As a result, Windows allocates and manages the memory used for code segments and the static data associated with DLLs and EXEs.

The emulator uses native Windows threads to provide Symbian OS threads, again enabling standard development tools to debug multi-threaded Symbian code. This results in Windows allocating and managing the software execution stack for the thread. As is typical for Windows threads, these stacks grow dynamically and can become very large – unlike the fixed size, fully committed stacks on target hardware.

7.4.4.2   Protection

The emulator runs within a single Windows process and thus within a single Windows address space. All memory committed to the emulator is accessible by any Symbian OS process within the emulator. As a result, the emulator provides no memory protection between Symbian OS processes, or between Symbian "user" and "kernel" memory.

Technically, it would be possible to make use of another Windows API, `VirtualProtect()`, which allows a program to change the access permissions for a region of committed memory, to, for example, temporarily make some memory inaccessible. The emulator could use this function to allow the current emulated Symbian OS process to only access its own memory chunks, and so provide some level of memory isolation between Symbian OS processes within the emulator. However, this would result in a poor multi-threaded debug experience as the memory for much of the OS would be unreadable by the debugger.

7.5   Programmer APIs

In Sections 7.2, *MMUs and caches*, and 7.3, *The memory model interface*, we looked at the very fundamental blocks of memory: the page and the objects used in the interface between the generic kernel and the memory model. Symbian OS provides a number of higher-level memory concepts and objects to provide user-mode and kernel-mode programmers with the right level of abstraction and control when allocating and using memory:

- The chunk forms the basic API for almost all memory allocation and ownership both inside the kernel and within user-mode processes

- One of the main consumers of chunks is the RHeap allocator class, which provides a free store allocator on top of a chunk. There are versions for both user- and kernel-side software. The standard C++ and C allocation functions use this allocator by default

- Kernel-mode software also has lower-level APIs designed for allocating memory, which are suitable for direct device or DMA access. These include physically contiguous RAM, shared I/O buffers and shared chunks.

7.5.1   Chunks

In Section 7.3.1, we looked at the principles of chunks, and how the memory model provides support for them. In this section we look at the programming interface for chunks.

Outside of the kernel executable, EKERN.EXE, kernel-mode software only uses chunks directly for allocation when creating shared chunks, and I will discuss these later in this section. The user-mode API for chunks is the RChunk class:

```
class RChunk : public RHandleBase
   {
public:
   enum TRestrictions
      {
      EPreventAdjust = 0x01
      };
public:
   inline TInt Open(...);
   IMPORT_C TInt CreateLocal(...);
   IMPORT_C TInt CreateLocalCode(...);
   IMPORT_C TInt CreateGlobal(...);
   IMPORT_C TInt CreateDoubleEndedLocal(...);
   IMPORT_C TInt CreateDoubleEndedGlobal(...);
   IMPORT_C TInt CreateDisconnectedLocal(...);
   IMPORT_C TInt CreateDisconnectedGlobal(...);
   IMPORT_C TInt Create(...);
   IMPORT_C TInt SetRestrictions(TUint aFlags);
   IMPORT_C TInt OpenGlobal(...);
   IMPORT_C TInt Open(RMessagePtr2,...);
   IMPORT_C TInt Open(TInt);
   IMPORT_C TInt Adjust(TInt aNewSize) const;
   IMPORT_C TInt AdjustDoubleEnded(TInt aBottom, TInt aTop) const;
   IMPORT_C TInt Commit(TInt anOffset, TInt aSize) const;
   IMPORT_C TInt Allocate(TInt aSize) const;
   IMPORT_C TInt Decommit(TInt anOffset, TInt aSize) const;
   IMPORT_C TUint8* Base() const;
   IMPORT_C TInt Size() const;
   IMPORT_C TInt Bottom() const;
   IMPORT_C TInt Top() const;
   IMPORT_C TInt MaxSize() const;
   inline TBool IsReadable() const;
   inline TBool IsWritable() const;
   };
```

This follows the standard handle pattern found with all kernel resources. It is a fairly simple API with approximately half of the members being ways to initialize the handle, either as a result of creating a new chunk or by gaining access to an already existing one. The different versions are used to create the different types of chunk and specify the visibility of the chunk. The other half of the class members either provide access to chunk attributes such as the base address (within the calling process address space), or provide the user-mode API to the various chunk adjust methods as already described in Section 7.3.1.

Aside from the use of global chunks to share memory between processes, programmers only rarely use a chunk directly to allocate memory. More often they utilize them as the underlying memory management for some form of allocator.

7.5.2   Free store allocators and heaps

An allocator is an object that services requests to acquire and release memory for a program. Behind every call to the new and delete operators in C++, or to the `malloc()` and `free()` functions in C, is an allocator. This object is concerned with taking the memory provided by the OS, usually in multi-page sized blocks, and dividing it up so that an application can use smaller pieces of it in an efficient manner.

7.5.2.1 Allocator APIs

The essential allocation support required for C++ and C is very similar, and in particular an allocator that supports standard C programs is good enough to implement support for C++. The key services of an allocator are just these three functions:

`malloc()` `operator new()`	Allocate and return a block of memory of at least the requested size in bytes, otherwise return NULL if the request cannot be satisfied. The allocator must ensure that it meets the alignment requirements of all object types. For example, the ABI for the ARM Architecture requires 8-byte alignment.
`free()` `operator delete()`	Release a block of memory previously allocated using `malloc()` or `realloc()`. Following this call the memory block should not be used by the program again.
`realloc()`	Grow or shrink a memory block previously allocated using `malloc()` or `realloc()`, preserving the contents and return the newly reallocated block. Note that this could trivially be implemented using `malloc()`, `memcpy()` and `free()`, but some allocation schemes may be able to satisfy this request "in place", thus avoiding the potentially expensive memory copy.

The last of these functions is clearly optional, and has no parallel in the C++ allocation operators. Of course, C++ also allows the programmer to provide specialized allocation services for a class by over-riding the default implementation of `operator new` – perhaps to improve performance, meet a strict alignment constraint, or to use a specific type or part of the physical memory.

This simple API does not describe the behavior of a free store allocator with multiple threads. The language standards do not define the behavior in this situation because there would be a performance penalty to using a thread-safe allocator in a single-threaded program. Thus the question of thread-safety is left to the implementation to determine. I will come back to how Symbian OS tackles this problem a little later.

7.5.2.2 Allocator strategies

If we examine the basic problem of dividing up pages of RAM into different sized pieces, we find that there are several different techniques for structuring and dividing the memory for allocation, and different algorithms for selecting exactly which portion of memory will be used to satisfy a particular allocation request.

Different allocation techniques have different ways of organizing their memory and acquiring and releasing it from the operating system. In Symbian OS an allocator is most likely going to use a chunk to provide the lower-level allocation, and will pick the type of chunk that best fits the allocation strategy and usage pattern. Here are some examples:

- Many *free store* allocators – that is, those supporting `operator new()` in C++ or `malloc()` and `free()` in C – assume that the storage is a single contiguous address range, and that requests for additional pages of memory extend the current committed memory at the "top". We can implement these using a standard chunk. The standard "heap" allocator in Symbian OS is one such allocator

- Some memory managers for non-native programming systems, such as Java, implement a handle/body system for objects – and effectively require two dynamically re-sizable contiguous memory regions. We can manage these two memory regions in a double-ended chunk, with one region growing upwards and the other downwards

- More advanced allocators may not require fully contiguous memory regions, and may also be able to release pages of memory back to the OS when no longer used by the program. This may result in better overall memory use in the OS. We use a disconnected chunk to support these.

Why should we bother with so many possible choices of data structure and algorithm for allocators? The simple answer is that there is no "ideal allocator". All allocator designs will favor some attributes over others. For example, some provide fast, real-time allocation but have a high memory overhead; others have a minimal memory overhead, but have poor worst-case performance. Different applications may need different allocators to meet their requirements.

7.5.2.3 Allocators in Symbian OS

We realized that Symbian OS has to achieve two aims with the allocator that it provides:

1. A good, general purpose allocator provided by default for all programs

2. The ability to customize or replace the default allocator for applica-
    tions that have special requirements.

EKA1 met the first of these needs with the `RHeap` allocator class. EKA2
provides the same choice of default allocator, but now also meets the
second need by providing an abstract allocator class. This is the definition
of `MAllocator` in `e32cmn.h`:

```
class MAllocator
    {
public:
  virtual TAny* Alloc(TInt)=0;
  virtual void Free(TAny*)=0;
  virtual TAny* ReAlloc(TAny*, TInt, TInt =0)=0;
  virtual TInt AllocLen(const TAny*) const =0;
  virtual TInt Compress()=0;
  virtual void Reset()=0;
  virtual TInt AllocSize(TInt&) const =0;
  virtual TInt Available(TInt&) const =0;
  virtual TInt DebugFunction(TInt, TAny*, TAny*)=0;
    };
```

The first three members are the basic allocator API that I described
earlier. The OS expects several other services from the allocator, as I
describe in the following table:

Alloc()	Basic allocation function, foundation for `malloc()` and similar allocator functions.
Free()	Basic de-allocation function, basis for `free()`, etc.
ReAlloc()	Reallocation function, basis for `realloc()`. There is an optional third parameter, to control allocator behavior in certain situations. This enables an allocator to provide compatibility with programs that may incorrectly assume that all allocators behave like the original `RHeap::ReAlloc()` function.
AllocLen()	Return the allocated length for the memory block. This is always at least as much as the memory requested, but is sometimes significantly larger.
Compress()	Release any unused pages of memory back to the OS, if possible. This function is deprecated, but retained for EKA1 compatibility. Allocators for EKA2 are expected to do this automatically as a side effect of `Free()` rather than wait for an explicit request.

Reset()	Release all allocated memory – effectively equivalent to Free() on all allocated blocks.
AllocSize()	Returns the number of blocks and the number of bytes currently allocated in this allocator.
Available()	Returns the number of bytes in this allocator that are unused and the largest allocation that would succeed without requesting more pages of memory from the OS.
DebugFunction()	Provide support for additional diagnostics, instrumentation and forced failure of the allocator, typically implemented only in a debug build of Symbian OS.

In practice, however, a concrete allocator will derive from the RAllo-cator class. This is the class that defines the full behavior expected by the free store API in Symbian OS. It provides commonly used additional functionality to the allocator, such as support for calling User::Leave() on allocation failure, rather than returning NULL. It also defines the forced failure support expected by Symbian OS.

Here is the RAllocator class as defined in e32cmn.h:

```
class RAllocator : public MAllocator
    {
public:
    enum TAllocFail
        {
        ERandom,
        ETrueRandom,
        ENone,
        EFailNext,
        EReset
        };
    enum TDbgHeapType { EUser, EKernel };
    enum TAllocDebugOp {ECount, EMarkStart, EMarkEnd,
                        ECheck, ESetFail, ECopyDebugInfo};
    enum TReAllocMode
        {
        ENeverMove=1,
        EAllowMoveOnShrink=2
        };
    enum TFlags {ESingleThreaded=1, EFixedSize=2};
    enum {EMaxHandles=32};
public:
    inline RAllocator();
    TInt Open();
    void Close();
    TAny* AllocZ(TInt);
    TAny* AllocZL(TInt);
    TAny* AllocL(TInt);
    TAny* AllocLC(TInt);
```

```
 void FreeZ(TAny*&);
 TAny* ReAllocL(TAny*, TInt, TInt=0);
 TInt Count() const;
 TInt Count(TInt&) const;
 void Check() const;
 void __DbgMarkStart();
 TUint32 __DbgMarkEnd(TInt);
 TInt __DbgMarkCheck(TBool, TInt, const TDesC8&, TInt);
 void __DbgMarkCheck(TBool, TInt, const TUint8*, TInt);
 void __DbgSetAllocFail(TAllocFail, TInt);
protected:
 virtual void DoClose();
protected:
 TInt iAccessCount;
 TInt iHandleCount;
 TInt* iHandles;
 TUint32 iFlags;
 TInt iCellCount;
 TInt iTotalAllocSize;
 };
```

We are still a step or two away from the APIs that programmers typically use to allocate memory. Symbian OS implements the standard C and C++ allocation functions using static members of the User class:

malloc() operator new()	User::Alloc()
free() operator delete()	User::Free()
realloc()	User::ReAlloc()

These User functions need to identify an allocator object to pass on the requests. The User::Allocator() function provides this service, returning a reference to the RAllocator object that is designated as the calling thread's current allocator.

The User class provides more functions related to manipulating and accessing the current allocator. Here is the relevant part of this class API:

```
class User : public UserHeap
 {
public:
 static TInt AllocLen(const TAny*);
 static TAny* Alloc(TInt);
 static TAny* AllocL(TInt);
 static TAny* AllocLC(TInt);
 static TAny* AllocZ(TInt);
 static TAny* AllocZL(TInt);
 static TInt AllocSize(TInt&);
 static TInt Available(TInt&);
```

```
static TInt CountAllocCells();
static TInt CountAllocCells(TInt&);
static void Free(TAny*);
static void FreeZ(TAny*&);
static TAny* ReAlloc(TAny*, TInt, TInt);
static TAny* ReAllocL(TAny*, TInt, TInt);
static RAllocator& Allocator();
static RAllocator* SwitchAllocator(RAllocator*);
};
```

We can see the almost one-to-one correspondence of this API with the
API provided by RAllocator. The User class implements all of these
functions in the same way: get the current allocator object and invoke
the corresponding member function.

It is possible to replace the current allocator with an alternative one
using the User::SwitchAllocator() function, which returns the
previous thread allocator object. There are several reasons that this may
be desirable, for example:

- Replacing the default allocator provided by the OS with one that uses
  a different allocation strategy better suited to the application

- Adding an adaptor to the allocator to provide additional instrumen-
  tation or debugging facilities. In this case, the new allocator will
  continue to use the previous allocator for the actual memory allocation but can intercept the actual allocation and de-allocation requests
  to do additional processing.

7.5.2.4   RHeap – the default allocator

Symbian OS provides a single allocator implementation, RHeap, providing a low memory overhead and generally good performance. The
same approach is used for both the user-mode free store, and the kernel
free store. One can describe this allocator as a "first fit, address ordered,
free list allocator". It is a simple data structure, and the allocation and
de-allocation algorithms are fairly straightforward.

RHeap supports different usage models:

- Using preallocated memory to provide a fixed size heap, or using a
  chunk to provide a dynamically sized heap

- Single-threaded or multi-threaded with light-weight locks

- Selectable cell alignment.

A dynamic RHeap uses a normal chunk, and so has a single region of
committed memory. Within that region, there will be both allocated and
free blocks. Each block is preceded by a 32-bit word which describes the
length of the block. The allocator does not need to track the allocated

blocks, as it is the program's responsibility to do this and later free them. The allocator does need to keep track of all the free blocks: it does this by linking them into a list – the "free list". The allocator uses the space within the free block (the first word) to maintain this list.

Free blocks that are neighbors in memory are coalesced into a single free block, so at any time the heap consists of a repeated pattern of one or more allocated blocks followed by a single free block. The free list is a singly linked queue maintained in address order – this enables the de-allocation algorithm to easily identify if the block being released is a direct neighbor of a block that is already free.

The allocation algorithm searches the free list from the start until a block is found that is large enough to satisfy the request. If the allocator finds such a block, the allocator splits the free block into the requested allocated block and any remaining free space, which is kept on the free list. Sometimes the block is only just large enough for the request (or the remaining space is too small to keep on the free list) in which case the whole block is returned by the request. If there is no free block large enough, the allocator tries to extend the chunk to create a larger free block at the end of the heap to satisfy the request.

The de-allocation algorithm searches the free list to find the last free block before the block being released and first one after it. If the block being released is a neighbor of either or both of these free blocks they are combined, otherwise the released block is just added into the list between these two free ones.

These algorithms are simple and so in general performance is fast. However, because both algorithms require the searching of an arbitrary length list, the performance is cannot be described as "real-time". However, this is no worse than the memory model allocation for adjusting chunks, which also does not have real-time behavior.

One drawback with this data structure is that large free blocks that lie inside the heap memory are not released back to the OS – the allocator can only release free memory that lies at the very end of the heap. However, the data structure has a very low memory overhead in general – approximately 4 bytes per allocated cell – though alignment requirements for modern compilers increase this to approximately 8 bytes.

So RHeap, despite its limitations, provides an excellent general purpose allocator for almost all applications within the OS. When better execution or memory performance is required, you can create custom allocators for individual applications.

7.5.3 Shared memory

In many cases, when an application must pass data across some memory context boundary, such as between two processes or between user and kernel contexts, it is most convenient to copy the data. This can be done in a controlled manner that ensures the data being transferred belongs to the sending memory context – and errors are reported correctly rather than causing the wrong program to terminate. However, when the amount of data to be transferred is large, or lower delays in transfer are required, it is more useful to be able to transfer the memory itself rather than copy the data. Some examples of such use cases would be streaming multiple channels of high bit-rate audio data to a software "mixer" or downloading large files over USB.

For any situation in which we need to share memory between two user-mode processes, we could use one or more global chunks to achieve this. Chunks can also be accessed by kernel-mode software or even directly by DMA. There is a problem with this approach, however.

The chunks that I have described so far have the property that memory is dynamically committed and released from the chunk at the request of user-mode software. For example, the kernel grows the heap chunk to satisfy a large allocation request, or releases some stack pages in response to thread termination. So you can see that it is possible that a page currently being accessed by a kernel thread or DMA might be unmapped by another thread – probably resulting in a system crash. The case of unmapping memory during DMA is particularly difficult to diagnose because DMA works with the physical address and will continue accessing the physical memory: the defect may only be discovered after the memory model reassigns the memory to another process and then suffers from "random" memory corruption.

To support the sharing of memory between hardware, kernel threads and user programs, we need different types of memory object.

7.5.3.1 *Shared I/O buffers*

The simplest of these objects is the *shared I/O buffer*. Kernel software, such as a device driver, can allocate a shared IO buffer to a fixed size, and may subsequently map and unmap the buffer from user process address space.

The major limitation with these buffers is that they cannot be mapped into more than one user-mode process at the same time. These are supported in EKA1, but have been superseded in EKA2 by the more powerful *shared chunk*. As a result of this, we deprecate use of shared I/O buffers with EKA2.

7.5.3.2 *Shared chunks*

A *shared chunk* is a more complex, though more capable, shared memory object and can be used in almost all memory sharing scenarios. It is very much like the global, disconnected chunk that I described in Section 7.3.1, but with one distinct difference: memory can only be committed and released by kernel code and not by user code.

A shared chunk is likely to be the answer if you are solving a problem with some of the following demands:

- The memory must be created and controlled by kernel-mode software

- The memory must be safe for use by ISRs and DMA

- The memory can be mapped into multiple user processes at the same time

- The memory can be mapped into multiple user processes in sequence

- The memory object can be transferred by user-side code between processes or to another device driver.

A device driver can map a shared chunk into multiple user processes, either in sequence or simultaneously. In addition, the driver can provide a user program with an RChunk handle to the chunk. This allows the user program to transfer the chunk to other processes and even hand it to other device drivers without the support of the device driver that created it originally.

See Chapter 13, *Peripheral Support,* for a fuller description of how shared chunks can be used by device drivers.

7.5.3.3 *Global and anonymous chunks*

As I have already mentioned, global chunks provide the most flexible way of sharing memory between user-mode processes. An anonymous chunk is a global chunk with no name; this restricts the discovery and access of the chunk from other processes. However, the limited value of anonymous chunks for sharing between kernel and user software has also been highlighted.

A global chunk is likely to be the solution if you are solving a problem with some of the following demands:

- The memory must be created and controlled by user-mode software

- The memory is not accessed directly from DMA/ISR

- The memory can be mapped into one or more user processes at the same time.

I will again point out that opening a shared chunk in two processes at the same time does not always guarantee that they will share the same address for the data. In fact, closing a chunk and re-opening it at a later point within a single program may result in a different base address being returned!

7.5.3.4 *Publish and subscribe*

There are, of course, other reasons for wanting to share memory, such as having some data that is global to the whole OS. In this case it is the universal access to the data and not the reduction in copying overhead that drives the desire for sharing.

Once again, a global chunk might serve this purpose on some occasions. But if the quantity of data is small, it is not possible to retain the chunk handle or data address between accesses, or some control is required for access to the data then another approach is needed.

Publish and subscribe may be the answer, as one way to look at this service is as a set of "global variables" that both user- and kernel-mode software can access by ID. The service also provides access control for each value, based around the platform security architecture, and some real-time guarantees. See Chapter 4, *Inter-thread Communication*, for a detailed description of this service.

7.6 Memory allocation

The following tables provide a comparison across the various memory models of how the memory models reserve and allocate the memory used for different purposes within the OS.

7.6.1 Kernel memory

	Moving memory model	Multiple memory model	Emulator model
Supervisor mode stack	Allocated as pages from the kernel's "SvStack" disconnected chunk, with 4 K uncommitted guard pages in between.		There is no supervisor "mode".
Non-XIP device driver code	Allocated as pages in the global "KERN$CODE" disconnected chunk.	Allocated as pages in the kernel's "$CODE" disconnected chunk.	Allocated by the Windows loader.
Non-XIP device driver static data	Allocated in the kernel heap.		Allocated by the Windows loader.
Free store/heap cells	Allocated in the kernel heap, which uses the kernel's dynamic "SvHeap" chunk.		

	Moving memory model	Multiple memory model	Emulator model
I/O address space	Some mapped by the bootstrap into reserved region. Otherwise created as mappings in the kernel section.		n/a
I/O and shared buffers	Created as chunks within the kernel section.		Created using a chunk.

7.6.2 User memory

	Moving model	Multiple model	Emulator model
User-mode stack	Allocated as pages from the process's ''$DAT'' disconnected chunk, with 8 K uncommitted guard pages in between.		Allocated by Windows when the thread is created.
Non-XIP code	Allocated and mapped as pages in the global ''USER$CODE'' disconnected chunk.	Allocated as pages in the User Code section. Mapped into the process in the process's ''$CODE'' disconnected chunk.	Allocated by the Windows loader.
EXE static data	Allocated as pages at the beginning of the process's ''$DAT'' chunk.		Allocated by the Windows loader.
DLL static data	Allocated as pages from the process's ''DLL$DATA'' disconnected chunk.		Allocated by the Windows loader.
Free store/heap cells	Allocated in the current allocator. By default this is a heap in an unnamed, private, dynamic chunk.		
Chunks	Further chunks can be created and are allocated in the user section of the address space.		
Thread Local Storage (TLS)	Each word of TLS is allocated in a map on the kernel heap. Access to the TLS data requires use of a kernel executive call.		
Publish & subscribe properties	Property data is allocated on the kernel heap, allowing it to be shared and protected.		

7.7   Low memory

On modern desktop computers, we certainly notice when the system runs
out of memory: everything begins to slow down, the hard disk starts to get
very busy and we get warning messages about running low on memory.
But we aren't generally informed that there is not enough memory to
carry out a request, as we would have been on a desktop system 10 years
ago – instead the system will struggle on, even if it becomes unusable.

This change in behavior is mainly because of demand paging and
virtual memory systems – the OS has the ability to save to disk a copy
of memory that has not been accessed recently and then copy it back in
to main memory again the next time a program tries to use the memory.
This way, the system can appear to have far more physical memory than
it really has. One side effect is that the "hard" limit of memory capacity
has become a softer restriction – very rarely will an application find that
a memory allocation request fails.

7.7.1   Handling allocation failure

As I said earlier, Symbian OS does not support demand paging and
has small amounts of physical memory when compared with desktop
devices. This combination means that all kernel, system and application
software must expect that all memory allocation requests will fail from
time to time. The result is that all software for Symbian OS must be
written carefully to ensure that *Out of Memory* (OOM) errors are handled
correctly and as gracefully as possible.

As well as correctly handling a failure to allocate memory, a server or
application must also manage all of its allocated memory. Long running
services (such as the kernel) must be able to free memory that was acquired
for a resource when a program releases that resource – the alternative is
the slow "leakage" of memory over time, eventually resulting in memory
exhaustion and system failure.

For user-side code, the TRAP and Leave mechanism, and the cleanup
stack provide much of the support required to manage memory allocation
and recovery on failure. These services are covered extensively in books
such as *Symbian OS C++ for Mobile Phones.*[2]

Within the EKA2 kernel, there are no mechanisms such as TRAP,
Leave and the cleanup stack. This contrasts with EKA1, in which we
used the TRAP mechanism inside the kernel. Our experience shows
that the use of TRAP, Leave and the cleanup stack make user-side
code simpler, more readable and often more compact. However, this
experience does not carry over to the implementation of EKA2 – the
presence of fine-grained synchronization and possibility of preemption at

---

[2] *Symbian OS C++ for Mobile Phones: Professional Development on Constrained
Devices*, by Richard Harrison. Symbian Press.

almost all points in the code often requires more complex error detection and recovery code. Additionally, optimizations to accelerate important operations or to reduce context switch "thrashing" remove the symmetry that is desirable for using a cleanup stack push/pop protocol.

So instead of providing an equivalent to TRAP, the kernel provides a number of supporting services that help ensure that threads executing in kernel mode do not leak memory, even during long running kernel services when it is quite possible that the thread may be terminated.

Thread critical sections

These bear little relation to the user-side synchronization primitive of the same name, RCriticalSection. Rather, these are code regions during which the thread cannot be unilaterally suspended or terminated – the thread will only act on suspend or exit requests once it leaves the critical section. The kernel uses these extensively to ensure that when a thread is modifying a shared data structure in the kernel, the modifications will run to completion rather than the thread stopping part way through.

Holding a fast mutex places a thread in an implicit critical section, as the scheduler depends on the fact that such a thread cannot block or otherwise be removed from the ready list.

Exception trapping

When inside a critical section, it is illegal for a thread to do any action that would result in the kernel terminating it – such as panicking it (due to invalid user arguments) or terminating it because it took an exception. The latter scenario can occur if a kernel service must copy data from memory supplied by the user-mode program, but the memory pointer provided is invalid.

This makes the copying of user-mode data difficult, particularly when the thread needs to hold the system lock at the same time (which is an implicit thread critical section). EKA2 provides an exception handling and trapping system, XTRAP, which behaves in a similar way to the user-side TRAP/Leave, but instead it can catch hardware exceptions such as those generated by faulty memory access. The kernel most frequently uses XTRAP to safely copy user-mode memory while inside a thread critical section. Any errors reported can then result in the thread safely exiting the critical section before reporting the failure.

Transient objects

Occasionally a thread needs to allocate a temporary object during part of a kernel executive call. As the owning reference to this object is the thread's registers and call stack, the thread would have to enter a critical section to prevent a memory leak happening if the thread were terminated. However, thread critical sections make error handling more complex as they require the use of exception trapping and deferring of error reporting until the critical section is released.

We provide some help here: each DThread in the kernel has two members to hold a DObject on which the thread has a temporary reference, and a temporary heap cell. If non-null, iTempObj and iExt-TempObj are closed and iTempAlloc is deleted during thread exit processing. Kernel code can use these members to "own" such temporary objects during an executive call, enabling the thread to release the critical section earlier.

7.7.2 System memory management

It is quite possible to write a single application that manages its own memory carefully, handles OOM scenarios and can adjust its behavior when less memory is available. However, a single application cannot easily determine whether it should release some non-critical memory (for example, a cache) so that another application can run.

However, the kernel provides some support to the system as a whole, to enable the implementation of system-wide memory management policies, typically within a component in the UI.

The memory model keeps track of the number of unused pages of memory. When this goes below a certain threshold, the kernel completes any RChangeNotifier subscriptions with EChangesFreeMemory. When the amount of free memory increases the kernel signals the notifiers again. In addition, should any RAM allocation request fail due to insufficient memory, the kernel signals the notifiers with EChangesOutOfMemory.

The EUSER function UserSvr::SetMemoryThresholds() sets two values that control when the memory model should signal the notifiers.

Typically, the UI component responsible for managing the system memory policy will set the thresholds and then monitor the notifier for indications that free memory is getting low or has been exhausted. When this occurs, the system might employ various strategies for freeing some currently used memory:

- The manager can request that applications reduce their memory consumption. For example, a browser could reduce a RAM cache it is using, or a Java Virtual Machine could garbage collect, and compact its memory space

- The manager can request (or demand) that applications and OS services that have not been used recently to save any data and then exit. This is quite acceptable on a phone, as the user-concept of running many applications at once is still very much one that is tied to computers and not to phones.

The mechanism by which such requests arrive at an application are presently specific to the UI, if they are used at all.

In some respects, you can envisage this system level memory manager as implementing an application level *garbage collector*. In future, it may well be that the algorithms used for selecting which applications should be asked to release memory or exit will borrow ideas from the already established problem domain of garbage collecting memory allocators.

7.8   Summary

In this chapter I have talked about the way in which the memory model makes use of the physical memory, the cache and the MMU to provide the memory services required by both the Symbian OS kernel- and user-mode programs.

I also showed how the MMU is used to provide memory protection between processes. In the next chapter, I will talk about how we build on this basis to provide a secure operating system.

8

Platform Security

by Corinne Dive-Reclus

Computers are like Old Testament gods; lots of rules and no mercy.
Joseph Campbell

In this chapter I will introduce a new concept – that of platform security. I will not explore this subject in too great a depth here, as it will shortly be the subject of a book of its own.[1] Instead, I will discuss how the core operating system components contribute to the implementation of platform security on Symbian OS.

8.1   Introduction

EKA2 was designed specifically for mobile phones, and so we had to meet the security requirements of both the mobile phone industry and the users of those mobile phones. This meant that we had to understand those requirements in detail, and in particular to understand the impact they would have on the essential components of the operating system, such as the kernel, the file server and the loader.

To decide how we could implement security in a mobile phone, it was important that we were aware of the user's perception of her phone, and the main differences between the well-known desktop environment and the mobile phone environment:

- For our typical end-users, mobile phones are **not** like computers: people expect them to be simple to use, reliable and predictable

- Mobile phones are personal: people do not share their mobile phones with others as they share their landline phone or family PC.

---

[1] *Platform Security for Symbian OS,* by Craig Heath. Symbian Press.

When we asked users what security they expect from a mobile phone, they responded:

1. I don't want nasty surprises when I receive my telephone bill

2. I want my private data to stay private!

So why not just re-use all the security measures from a desktop computer? The answer, of course, is that phones have specific characteristics, linked to the physical device itself and the way that it is used, that make them fundamentally different from the desktop environment:

1. There are the limitations imposed by the device itself – compared to a desktop, the screen is small and the keyboard is limited. This restricts the amount of information that can be displayed to the user (typically just one or two short sentences) and also the number and complexity of passwords the user is willing to enter

2. There is no IT support department to rely on: the user must not be asked questions that she cannot comprehend

3. The operating system is hidden: files and even processes are invisible. Let's take the case of the Sony Ericsson P900: when the user clicks on an application, she does not know (and should not need to know) whether this is starting a new process or re-using an existing one. Therefore the user should not be asked to make a security decision based on the name of a process or a file.

So the main goals of Symbian's platform security architecture were:

1. To protect the phone's integrity, because users want reliable phones

2. To protect the user's privacy

3. To control access to networks, because users care about their bills.

Our constraints on platform security were:

4. It must be easy for developers to use

5. It must be fast and lightweight

6. It must only expose security policy to users when they can understand it.

The platform security architecture of Symbian OS is based on three key concepts:

1. The OS process is the unit of trust

2. Capabilities are used to control access to sensitive resources

3. Data caging protects files against unauthorized access.

I shall now talk about these concepts in more detail.

8.2 Unit of trust

We define a unit of trust as the smallest entity to which we grant a set of permissions.

8.2.1 Concept

A phone only has a single user, so the security policy is not about protecting different users from each other, as in a desktop environment. Instead, it is about controlling exactly what applications are allowed to do when they run. It was clear that we should choose the unit of trust to be the process, because this is already the fundamental unit of memory protection on Symbian OS. (As I've shown in previous chapters, the kernel cannot protect individual threads from each other if they are running in the same process, because they all have unpoliced access to the same memory.) We identified three main levels of trust, and these are shown in Figure 8.1.

8.2.1.1 The Trusted Computing Base (TCB)

The *Trusted Computing Base* (TCB) is responsible for maintaining the *integrity* of the device and for applying the fundamental rules of platform security. Very few components – the kernel, the file server and, on open

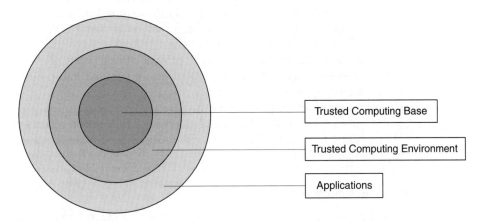

Figure 8.1 Processes and trust

devices, the software installer and its registry – are part of the TCB and have unrestricted access to the device's resources. The rest of the operating system implicitly trusts these to behave correctly; because of this, all TCB code is reviewed very strictly.

8.2.1.2   The Trusted Computing Environment (TCE)

Beyond the core of the TCB, other system components require access to some, but not all, sensitive system resources. For example, the window server requires direct access to keyboard events, but not to the ETEL server. The *Trusted Computing Environment* is composed of these key Symbian OS components that protect the device resources from *misuse*. In Symbian OS, server programs are used to control access to shared resources, so we define the TCE as the set of all system servers.

8.2.1.3   Applications

The final level of trust is ordinary applications. In most cases, these will not have any capabilities that can endanger the integrity of the phone, because they will access sensitive resources through components in the TCE and the TCB. In certain circumstances they may require capabilities – to access information private to the user, network services or local connectivity.

8.2.2   The kernel's role

As I mentioned before, the components in the TCB need to be entirely trustworthy – and because of this they are reviewed very carefully. The key component of the TCB is the main subject of this book, the kernel.

In a secure environment, the first duty of the kernel is to ensure the availability of hardware resources that critical processes require, and to provide access to those resources in a short, bounded period of time. I will discuss the real-time aspects of the kernel in Chapter 17, *Real Time*, and so will not dwell on them further here.

The second duty of the kernel is to provide strong protection of the process memory space (including its own) to guarantee that processes are protected against each other and therefore that the behavior of a trusted process cannot be compromised by another process. This aspect of the kernel is covered in Chapter 7, *Memory Models*, and again I will not discuss it further here. Instead I will proceed to enumerate the new security features of EKA2.

8.2.2.1   Access to user-mode memory

Any access to user-mode memory from within privileged code (that is, the kernel and device drivers) uses special accessor and copy methods to apply user-mode memory permissions to the access. This ensures that invalid data pointers passed to kernel functions by user processes do not cause the kernel to fail. See Section 5.2.1.5 for more details.

8.2.2.2 Thread stacks and heaps

Thread stacks and heaps are "private" chunks: they cannot be mapped and made accessible to processes other than their owner.

8.2.2.3 Process memory overwritten

When the kernel allocates memory to a process, it overwrites it with zeroes, to prevent any private data from the previous owner being accessible to the new process.

8.2.2.4 New IPC framework

We have replaced the existing Symbian OS inter-process communication (IPC) framework API (V1) with one designed for trusted IPC (V2). Please refer to Chapter 4, *Inter-thread Communication*, for more details. Here is an overview of the new features of the framework that provide increased security:

- The new server-side IPC classes have a "2" added to the EKA1 name to indicate that this is the version 2 of the IPC mechanism: for example, `CSession2`, `CServer2`, `RServer2`, `RMessage2`, `RMessagePtr2`

- We have removed old, insecure methods that allowed reading and writing arbitrary process data (for example, `RThread::ReadL()`) and we have replaced them with methods that only allow access to data areas specifically passed by the client in a message (for example, `RMessagePtr2::ReadL()`). Now the server can only access data that is associated with a valid message and it must now use the `RMessagePtr2` class to do this. This also means that the data is not available to the server after it has processed the message

- Parameters passed in an IPC request are now typed for increased robustness. For extra security, their lengths are also specified, even in the case of a pointer, to ensure that the server will not read or write more than the client expected to disclose: any attempt to read before the pointer's address or beyond its length will fail.

8.2.2.5 ARM v6 never-execute bit

If the hardware supports it, then EKA2 will take advantage of the ARMv6 never-execute bit in the page permissions (see Chapter 7, *Memory Models*, for more on this). This is used to deny the execution of code from stacks, heaps and static data, with the aim of preventing buffer-overflow attacks. (These inject malicious code into stacks or heaps over the limit of an array passed as a function parameter to trick a process into executing that code.) EKA2 only allows execution from execute-in-place ROM images, software loaded by the Symbian OS loader and explicitly created "local code" chunks (for compiled Java code such as JIT or DAC).

8.3 Capability model

8.3.1 Concept

A capability is an authorization token that indicates that its owner has been trusted to not abuse resources protected by the token. This authorization token can grant access to sensitive APIs such as device driver APIs or to data such as system settings.

8.3.2 Capability rules

The following capability rules are fundamental to the understanding of platform security. They strongly reenforce the first concept that the process is the unit of trust. They are worth reading carefully; they are somewhat less obvious than they may first appear.

Rule 1. Every process has a set of capabilities and its capabilities never change during its lifetime.

To build a Symbian OS executable, you have to create a project file (MMP). The Symbian OS build tools now require an additional line that defines what capabilities should be given to the executable in question. The build tools will read the MMP file and write the desired capabilities into the resulting binary, just as they do with UIDs.

MMP files are used to associate capabilities with every sort of executable code. Programs (.EXE), shared libraries (.DLL) all have their capabilities defined in this way. When it creates a process, the kernel reads the capabilities from the header of the program file on disk and associates those capabilities with the process for the remainder of its lifetime. The kernel stores the capabilities in memory, which is inaccessible to user-mode processes, to prevent tampering. It provides user-side APIs to allow user-side code to check that a process requesting a service has a specific set of capabilities.

In the following example, `litotes.exe` has been assigned two capabilities, `ReadUserData` and `WriteUserData`. These grant the application access to APIs that access and modify the user's private data, such as contacts.

```
// litotes.mmp
TARGET          litotes.exe
TARGETTYPE      exe
UID             0x00000000 0x00000123
SOURCEPATH      ..\litsource
SOURCE          litotes.cpp
USERINCLUDE     ..\include
SYSTEMINCLUDE   \epoc32\include
...
CAPABILITY      ReadUserData WriteUserData
```

Symbian OS provides three main methods for programs to use services provided by other executables:

1. Loading a DLL and calling its API

2. Making requests of server programs

3. Loading and calling a device driver.

In each case, the caller's capabilities must be checked. I will explain how this is done, taking each of these cases in turn.

8.3.2.1 Loading a DLL

As mentioned earlier, a DLL is executable code and its binary will contain a set of capabilities. But a DLL must always execute within the context of a process – the process that loads the DLL – and rule 1 stated that the capabilities of a process can never change. Together, these statements imply that the DLL code must run at the same capability level as the loading process. This leads to the principle of DLL loading, rule 2:

> **Rule 2. A process cannot load a DLL that has a smaller set of capabilities than it has itself.**

The need for this constraint follows from the fact that all DLL code runs at the capability level of the loading process. This means that DLL capabilities are different to process capabilities, in that they don't actually authorize anything; they only reflect the confidence placed in them to not abuse or compromise a host process with those capabilities.

DLL capabilities are policed by the loader, and so are checked only at load time. After that, all the code contained in the DLL will run with the same capabilities as the code directly owned by the process. This means that it will be subject to the same capability checking when it accesses services provided by other processes.

> **Rule 2b. A DLL cannot statically link to a DLL that has a smaller set of capabilities than it has itself.**

Rule 2b is a corollary of rule 2, as you can see if you replace the word "process" in rule 2 with the words "loading executable" – but it is clearer to restate it as I have just done.

The Symbian OS loader directly resolves static linkage between the loading executable (program or library) and the shared library. So, when a library is linked to another library, the loader does not take into account the top-level program. To see why, let's look at an example. Assume that a DLL, METAPHOR, with capability ReadUserData, wants to statically link to a DLL without this capability, SIMILE. When the linker resolves this static direct linkage, it does not know whether METAPHOR will be statically linked to a program with or without ReadUserData. If the final program EPITHET does have ReadUserData, and if METAPHOR were statically linked to SIMILE, then this would be unsafe as SIMILE might compromise EPITHET's use of ReadUserData capability.

Hence the secure route is to always reject the linkage when the linked DLL has a smaller set of capabilities than the linking one. This is illustrated in Figure 8.2.

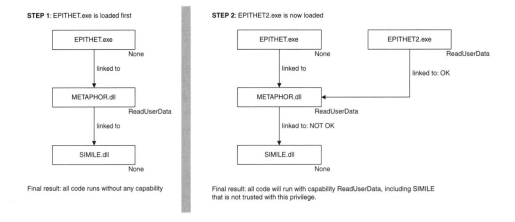

Figure 8.2   Capability rules and DLL linking

Rule 2 and its corollary prevent malicious or un-trusted code being loaded into sensitive processes, for example a plug-in into a system server. The rules also encourage the encapsulation of sensitive code inside well-known processes. The loader provides this security mechanism for all processes; relieving them of the burden of identifying which DLLs they can safely load or link to.

The following examples show how these rules are applied in the cases of statically and dynamically loaded DLLs respectively.

8.3.2.2 *Examples for statically linked DLLs*

Assume that the program PLOT.EXE is statically linked to the library RHYME.DLL and the library RHYME.DLL is statically linked to the library REASON.DLL.

Example 1
Also assume that:

1. PLOT.EXE holds Cap1 and Cap2

2. RHYME.DLL holds Cap1, Cap2 and Cap3

3. REASON.DLL holds Cap1 and Cap2.

Then the load fails because RHYME.DLL cannot load REASON.DLL according to rule 2b.

Example 2
Also assume that:

1. PLOT.EXE holds Cap1 and Cap2

2. RHYME.DLL holds Cap1, Cap2 and Cap3

3. REASON.DLL holds Cap1, Cap2 & Cap3 and Cap4.

Then the load succeeds; however RHYME.DLL cannot acquire the Cap4 capability held by REASON.DLL, and PLOT.EXE cannot acquire the Cap3 capability held by RHYME.DLL due to rule 1.

8.3.2.3 *Examples for dynamically loaded DLLs*

Assume that the program PLOT.EXE dynamically loads the library RHYME.DLL and the library RHYME.DLL then dynamically loads the library REASON.DLL.

Example 1
Also assume that:

1. PLOT.EXE holds Cap1 and Cap2

2. RHYME.DLL holds Cap1, Cap2 and Cap3

3. REASON.DLL holds Cap1 and Cap2.

The load succeeds because PLOT.EXE can load RHYME.DLL and REASON.DLL. You should note that the loading executable is the process PLOT.EXE and **not** the library RHYME.DLL, because the RLibrary::Load() request that the loader processes is sent by the process

PLOT.EXE. The fact that the call is within RHYME.DLL is irrelevant: once loaded the code from RHYME.DLL is run with the same capability set as PLOT.EXE (rule 1).

Example 2
Also assume that:

1. PLOT.EXE holds Cap1 and Cap2
2. RHYME.DLL holds Cap1, Cap2 and Cap3
3. REASON.DLL holds Cap1, Cap2 and Cap4.

Then the load succeeds because PLOT.EXE can load RHYME.DLL and REASON.DLL. Because of rule 1, the code loaded from RHYME.DLL and REASON.DLL will be run with the same capability set as PLOT.EXE – that is Cap1 and Cap2.

8.3.3 Client-server

The servers that make up the TCE police incoming requests from their clients to ensure that those clients hold the required capabilities. For example, if a client asks the ETEL server to make a phone call, ETEL checks that the client has the "network services" capability.

An alternative approach to restricting access that is sometimes used in security architectures is a check based on the caller's identity, using, for example, an access control list. The approach used by Symbian OS platform security is preferable, because adding a new requester (for example a new client of ETEL) does not impact the security policy of the enforcer, ETEL.

A server typically offers many functions to its clients, and each of these functions can require a different set of different capabilities, or none at all. The capabilities required may also differ according to the data the client passes to the server – for example, the file server's function to open a file does not require any capabilities if the client wants to open its own files, but requires a system capability if the client wants to open a file that it does not own.

This security check does not affect the way in which IPC messages are formatted. It would be pointless to require a client to pass its capabilities to the server directly, since a badly behaved client could lie about them. Instead, the kernel adds client capabilities to the IPC message as it transfers the call from the client to the server side.

Figure 8.3 shows an application ODE.EXE that wants to dial a phone number by invoking RCall::Dial(). This method is just a front-end to a client-server IPC communication.

The kernel receives the IPC message and adds ODE's capabilities to it before dispatching it to the ETEL server. ETEL can trust it to do this, since the kernel is part of the TCB.

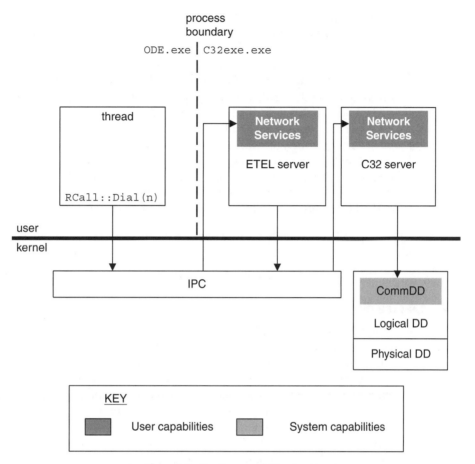

Figure 8.3 Runtime capability checking

ETEL can access ODE's capabilities via the RMessage2 class. It verifies that ODE has the network services capability before accepting the request. Several classes exist to help servers check access to their services:

- The server should derive from CPolicyServer

- Mapping of IPC messages and security policies are defined by using CPolicyServer::TPolicy

- Security policies are defined by using TPolicyElement which provides verification services such as:

```
IMPORT_C TBool CheckPolicy (RMessagePtr2 a MsgPtr, const char*
                                         aDiagnostic=0) const
```

These classes hide the format used to store capabilities. They are a useful abstraction guaranteeing binary compatibility to developers by isolating them from changes in the underlying internal format.

Now suppose that ODE.EXE does not have the network services capability. What happens if ODE decides to bypass ETEL by talking to C32 directly? This will not work – C32, knowing that some requests can come from external processes, does its own policing.

What will happen if ODE decided to talk to the base band device drivers directly? This still will not work: these device drivers cannot be used without the system capability CommDD.

Or perhaps you might think that you could write your own device driver to access the hardware. That will not work either – device drivers run within the same process space as the kernel, and the rules described in Section 8.3.1 would require this device driver implementation to have at least the same set of capabilities as the kernel itself.

The key points that you should bear in mind from this discussion are:

- Capabilities are **only worth checking** when a process boundary could be **crossed**

- The kernel is the **trusted intermediary** between a client and a server.

8.3.4 Device drivers

Device drivers run inside the kernel and so have access to all the resources of the mobile phone, without restriction. They are implicitly part of the TCB. Because of this, it is very important that drivers check the capabilities of user-side processes and that they protect themselves against bad parameters passed in by a client. For example, if a malicious client passes a pointer into another process or even the kernel, and the device driver does not check that the client has the correct permissions to access that memory, then the client is able to bypass platform security and fool the driver into returning secret data.

The general rules for device driver writers are:

1. Check that the client has sufficient capabilities to access the functionality provided by the driver

2. Do not trust any parameters passed in by the client; check that all parameters are valid

3. Do not use pointers passed by the client directly – always use the kernel functions that access the memory using the client's permissions (kumemget(), kumemput(), Kern::ThreadDesRead() and so on)

4. Device driver channels cannot be passed between processes.

For device drivers that are split into LDD and PDD parts, the recommended practice is to perform all client capability checking at the LDD level. This ensures the policy is provided consistently and securely across all physical driver implementations.

8.4 Data caging

8.4.1 Concept

The capability model is the most fundamental concept of platform security. Data caging, another key concept, is much more specific: it is about file access control. As I said at the beginning of this chapter, phones are single-user devices, so the emphasis is not on controlling the user's access to files, but on controlling the file access of the various *processes* running on her phone.

One point to bear in mind is that, compared to a typical desktop environment, phones are resource-constrained – they may have limited storage space, slow processors and limited battery life. It is vital that platform security does not reduce the speed of file access, or increase power consumption or the size of file system itself.

The solution that we came up with was to move away from traditional access control lists, and to implement a fixed access control policy that can be fully described by the following sentence:

Rule 3. The access rules of a file are entirely determined by its directory path, regardless of the drive.

We identified four different sets of access rules, which we represent by four separate directory hierarchies under the root "\".

8.4.1.1 \sys

Only TCB processes can read and write files under this directory. This directory tree contains data vital to the integrity of the platform, such as executables.

8.4.1.2 \resource

All processes can read files in this directory, but only TCB processes can write to them. This directory mostly contains bitmaps, fonts and help files that are not expected to change once installed.

8.4.1.3 \private

The file server provides all programs with a private sub-directory under \private, regardless of their level of trust. Only the appropriate process, TCB processes and the backup server can read and write files in a process's private directory. Other processes may neither read nor write.

8.4.1.4 *All other root files and directories*

There is no restriction on what a process can do to a file stored in any other directory, including the root directory itself. These are all completely public spaces.

8.4.2   Implementation

8.4.2.1   *Program SID*

Each program must be assigned a unique identifier, called the *secure identifier* or SID, so that the kernel can provide a private space for each program. At ROM-build time and install time, the system will guarantee that each SID is uniquely associated with one executable. SIDs are assigned at compile time and specified in MMP files. If the MMP file does not define a SID, then the tool chain will use UID3 as the SID. If the program does not have a UID3, then the value of KNullUid is assigned. As a consequence, all processes with no SID and a null UID will share the same private directory.

8.4.2.2   *Capabilities and file access*

As well as the SID, there are two capabilities that we created to control access to data-caged directories:

1. TCB – grants write access to executables and shared read-only resources

2. AllFiles – grants read access to the entire file system; grants write access to other processes' private directories.

The access rules are summarized in the following table:

	Capability required to:	
	Read	**Write**
\resource	none	TCB
\sys	AllFiles	TCB
\private\<ownSID>	none	none
\private\<other>	AllFiles	AllFiles
\<other>	none	none

It may sound strange that TCB processes also need the AllFiles capability to be able to read under \sys. This decision was made for the following reasons:

- Capabilities should be fully orthogonal to each other: one should not be a subset of another. This is to eliminate the use of OR in capability checking, which creates ambiguity about what a capability really grants

- We identified a need to provide a capability to grant read access to the entire file system without implying that write access to \sys had to be granted: this reflects the distinction that has been made between TCB and TCE processes.

8.4.2.3 The role of the file server and the loader

All executables are now stored under \sys\bin. The file server enforces the rule that only TCB processes can write into this directory, to ensure that executables cannot be modified. Non-TCB processes cannot inject new code into existing executables and cannot change the capability set. This is a powerful way of ensuring the integrity of executables without requiring that each executable has to be signed and its signature verified every time it is loaded. If executables are installed in directories other than \sys\bin, then this is harmless, as the loader will refuse to load them.

This means that normal processes can no longer scan for executables, as they will not have the permissions to do so. The path of an executable is therefore irrelevant, and only the drive, name and type of file are important. This gives Symbian OS the flexibility to organize the storage of its executables at it sees fit without breaking backwards compatibility. In Symbian OS v9, all executables are stored in \sys\bin; there are no subdirectories. It is even more important than before to choose a "good" name for your executables, for example by prefixing them with your company name. If any clash is identified at install time, the software installer will indicate the conflict to the user and cancel the installation. This may seem harsh, but it is a very effective measure against Trojan horse attacks in which a malicious file tries to be seen as a legitimate one. Another side effect of this decision is that loading is faster, since we have reduced the number of directories to scan and simplified the algorithm used to decide which file to load. See Chapter 10, *The Loader*, if you want to find out more about file loading.

What about installed binaries on removable media – including those that are subst-ed as internal drives? In this case the path <drive>:\sys \bin cannot be deemed to be secure, because the removable medium might have been removed and altered elsewhere. Some tamper evidence is needed to detect whether the contents of a binary file have been changed since they were known to be safe – which was when they were installed. To do this when it first installs an executable onto a removable medium, the Symbian OS installer takes the additional step of computing a secure hash of the binary and storing this in the tamper-proof \sys directory on the internal drive.

Subsequent attempts to load the binary from that medium will fail if a second hash computed at load time does not match the one stored in the internal \sys directory, or if the internal hash does not exist at all.

8.4.2.4   *Sharing files between processes*

Symbian OS has a variety of ways of allowing processes to share data, including publish and subscribe, DBMS (Symbian's relational database) and the central repository (Symbian's service to share persistent settings). These methods, and others, have their uses, but nevertheless we still need a means for one process to share a file with another process under controlled conditions. For example, a messaging application might wish to launch a viewer application on a message attachment, but without revealing all other attachments to that viewer process, or revealing the attachment to all other process. EKA2 gives us the basic building blocks, by providing a way of sharing handles across processes, and the file server supports this feature for file handles.

The process that owns the file opens it in a mode that cannot be changed by the process receiving the file handle without the file server rechecking that file's access policy against the receiving process's credentials.

The receiving process gets access to a shared session and file handles, but it does not get access to the shared file's parent directory or to other files in the same parent directory.

If you want to share files like this, you should be aware that, in the owning process you should open a file server session specifically for file sharing, open any files you wish to share and no others, and then close the session as soon as it is no longer needed (that is, once the receiving process has done what it needs to with the shared files). This is because the session handle is shared, along with the file handle, which means that any other files opened by the owning process in that session may be accessible to the receiving process, which could then increment the file handle numbers and gain access to other files. **Not conforming to this rule is a security hole.**

For more information on shared file handles, please refer to Chapter 9, *The File Server.*

8.5   Summary

In this chapter, I have introduced you to the key concepts in the Symbian OS implementation of platform security. Although I have not fully explored the subject, I hope that I have demonstrated how the kernel, loader and file server have been designed to play their part in making Symbian OS a secure platform. I have shown that this support is provided independently of cryptographic and authentication mechanisms to reduce the impact on the performance of the system and dependency upon those mechanisms:

- Capabilities are used to associate permissions to a program independent of the origin of the program

- Capabilities are used to prevent a program from loading a library that could compromise it.

Finally, I have discussed the file server and its role in data caging. I have shown that data caging provides safe storage for binaries and sensitive data, thus keeping them out of the reach of badly written or malicious code.

In the next chapter, I will explain the operation of the file server.

9

The File Server

by Peter Scobie

RAM disk is not an installation procedure.

Unknown

The file server component, also referred to as F32, manages every file device on a Symbian OS phone; it provides services to access the files, directories and drives on those file devices. This component also contains the loader, which loads executable files (DLLs and EXEs). The loader is covered in Chapter 10, *The Loader*, and in this chapter I will concentrate on the file server.

9.1 Overview

9.1.1 Hardware and terminology

9.1.1.1 Internal drive hardware

We always designate the main ROM drive as "Z:" on a Symbian OS mobile phone. This drive holds system executables and data files and its contents (known as the ROM image) are created by the mobile phone manufacturer when building the device. In fact, the ROM image is normally programmed into Flash memory – Flash is nonvolatile memory that can be programmed and erased electronically. The use of programmable memory for this read-only drive allows the manufacturer to replace or upgrade the ROM image after initial manufacture. In the past, Symbian OS products sometimes used masked ROM to hold the ROM image (or part of it) but this is rarely done now. It takes time to fabricate a masked ROM device with the image and once this has taken place, it is not possible to upgrade the software.

A Symbian OS phone will also have at least one internal drive which provides read/write access, and which the OS uses for the permanent storage of user data. Again, mobile phone manufactures tend to use

Flash memory for this internal drive. Indeed, in certain circumstances, the same memory device can be used for both code and user data storage. Flash memory is made using either NAND or NOR gates – each having significantly different characteristics. Symbian OS supports the storage of code and user data on both NAND and NOR Flash.

Some early Symbian OS products used a RAM disk as the main user data storage device. RAM disks use the same memory as system RAM. Rather than being of fixed size, the system allocates memory to them from the system pool as files are created or extended. Likewise, it frees the memory as data is deleted from the drive. But RAM is volatile storage – data is lost when power is removed. To provide permanent storage, the device has to constantly power the RAM, even when the device is turned off, and it must supply a backup battery to maintain the data, should the main supply fail. Flash memory, on the other hand, retains its contents when power is removed and is also low power and low cost. Because of this, Flash has replaced RAM for permanent user data storage.

Mobile phones do occasionally still make use of a RAM disk, however. If the file server finds that the main user-data drive is corrupt when Symbian OS boots, then it can replace this with a RAM disk, providing a temporary work disk to the OS and allowing the main one to be restored. It can then mount the corrupt disk as a secondary drive, which allows a disk utility to recover data, where possible, and then reformat the drive.

9.1.1.2   Removable media devices

Many Symbian OS phones support removable media devices such as MultiMediaCard (MMC), Secure Digital card (SD card), Memory Stick or Compact Flash (CF). The file server allocates each removable media socket one or more drives, allowing read/write access while a memory card is present. Being removable, these devices have to be formatted in a manner that is compatible with other operating systems. The devices I have mentioned are all solid state rather than rotating media storage devices, but miniature rotating media devices are likely to be used more widely in future, due to their low cost and high capacity. Rotating media devices require more complex power management because of the higher current they consume and their relatively slow disk spinup times.

I will discuss Symbian OS support for MultiMediaCards in Section 13.5.

9.1.1.3   File server terminology

Many types of media device, such as MultiMediaCards and SD cards, require every access to be in multiples of a particular sector size, usually 512 bytes. Thus, the sector is the smallest unit that can be accessed. Other types of media device, such as the ROM, don't have this constraint and allow access in any multiple of a byte.

Throughout this chapter, I will often refer to a media device as a disk. The memory on a disk may be divided into isolated sections, called partitions. Information on the size and location of each partition is generally stored at a known point on the disk – the partition table. For example, most MultiMediaCards keep a partition table in the first sector of the disk. Even when a device has only a single partition, it will still generally have a partition table. Each separate partition that is made available on a Symbian OS mobile phone is enabled as a different drive.

Drives that are allocated to removable media, may, over time, contain different volumes, as the user inserts and removes different removable media devices. So a volume corresponds to a partition on a disk that has been introduced into the system at some time.

9.1.2   F32 system architecture overview

The entire file server system consists of the (shaded) components displayed in Figure 9.1.

The file server, like any other server in Symbian OS, uses the client/server framework. It receives and processes file-related requests from multiple clients. The file server runs in its own process and uses multiple threads to handle the requests from clients efficiently. Clients link to the F32 client-side library (`EFSRV.DLL`), whose API I will describe in Section 9.2. The file server executable, `EFILE.EXE`, contains two servers – the file server itself (which I will describe in detail in Section 9.3) and the loader server, which loads executables and libraries. I will cover this in Chapter 10, *The Loader*.

Because of the differing characteristics of the various types of disk that Symbian OS supports, we need a number of different media formats. For example, removable disks are FAT formatted to be compatible with other operating systems, and the ROM drive uses a format scheme which is efficient for read operation, but which wouldn't be suitable if writes to the drive were required. In general, the file server does not concern itself with the detail of each file system; instead we implement the different media formats as separate file systems, components that are "plugged into" the file server. (The exception to this is the ROM file system, which is built into the file server, for reasons that I will discuss in Section 9.1.2.3.) File system components are polymorphic DLLs that have the file extension ".FSY". These DLLs are dynamically loaded and registered with the file server, normally at system boot time. Figure 9.1 shows a file server configuration with two file systems loaded, `ELOCAL.FSY` and `ELFFS.FSY`. I will describe these and other file systems in Section 9.4.

Before a particular drive can be accessed, it must have a file system associated with it, whereupon it can be said that the drive is mounted. Again, the file server generally carries out this process at system boot time, once the file systems have been loaded. Mounting also involves determining the basic parameters associated with the drive (drive capacity,

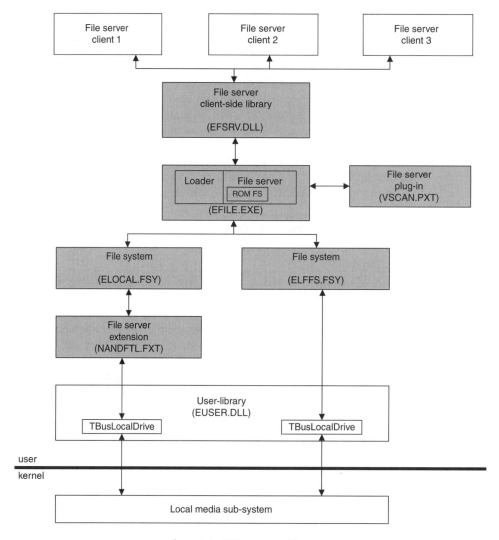

Figure 9.1 F32 system architecture

free space and so on) and initializing the drive specific data held by the file server. A loaded file system may be mounted on more than one drive.

The file systems gain access to the mobile phone's internal and removable disks via a set of device drivers known as the local media sub-system. These drivers are split into a logical device driver layer – the local media LDD (ELOCD.LDD) and a physical device driver layer. The physical device drivers are called media drivers. The user-side interface to the local media sub-system is provided by the class TBusLocalDrive whose methods are exported from the user library (EUSER.DLL). The main functions it provides are those to read, write and format regions of each drive's memory area. I describe the local media sub-system in detail in Section 13.3.

Again, the ROM drive is an exception, as we do not access it through the local media sub-system. Instead, the bootstrap maps this memory area to be user-readable, and the file-server accesses it directly.

For other drives though, the TBusLocalDrive class provides the user-side interface to the physical media. Often, when a file system is mounted on a particular drive, it will interface directly with the TBusLocalDrive instance for that drive. This is the case for the file system ELFFS.FSY shown in the diagram.

However, it is possible to add an extension layer between the file system and the TBusLocalDrive object for a particular drive. These extension layers are known as file server extensions and they are executed user-side. They provide a way to add functionality to a standard file system that is only required for a certain type of drive. They are built as a separate component, and have the file extension .FXT. The file server provides APIs to install an extension and then associate it with a particular drive. For example, as you will see later, a special translation layer is needed to run a FAT file system over a NAND Flash device. Since this layer is not required when using FAT on a RAM disk or a MultiMediaCard, it would not be appropriate to add this functionality to the FAT file system component itself. Instead, we can implement the Flash translation layer (FTL) as a file server extension (NANDFTL.FXT), and use it only on NAND local drives.

The file server also supports file server plug-ins. Built as separate components, with the file extension .PXT, the plug-ins register with the file server and are then able to intercept requests from any file server clients. Plug-ins can be used to support virus scanning, file compression and file encryption software. The plug-in can set a filter for particular types of request (for example file open) and for requests involving a particular path or drive. When a request is intercepted, the plug-in is given the opportunity to issue its own file server requests using the normal F32 client API (so it can scan the file being opened, for example) before deciding on whether to allow the original request to resume. Alternatively, the plug-in can fail the request. The file server allows more than one plug-in to register at the same time. It maintains a strict policy on the order in which it notifies the plug-ins, should their request filters coincide. So, for example, if both a virus scanner and a file-compression plug-in were installed, then the compression software would have to decompress a file before the virus scanner scanned it.

9.1.2.1   *Drive letters*

The file server supports a maximum of 26 drives, each identified (in DOS-like convention) by a different drive letter (A: to Z:). As I said earlier, the main ROM drive is always designated as the last drive, Z:.

Apart from on the emulator, sixteen of the drives (C: to R:) are normally reserved as local drives – that is, they are available for mounting drives on media devices that are located within the phone. Of these, C: is always designated as the main user data drive, and any removable media device is generally designated as D: or E:.

The remaining 9 drives are available as remote drives, or substituted drives.

9.1.2.2   F32 on the Symbian OS emulator

On the Symbian OS emulator, any of the 26 drives can be used for mapping to native drives – that is, mapping directories on the host machine's file system to drives on the Symbian OS file server. We do this by using an emulator-specific Symbian OS file system, which converts the Symbian OS file server calls into calls onto the host operating system's file system. There are two default emulator drives – Z:, which represents the target phone's ROM, and C:, which represents the phone's main user-data storage drive. However, by editing the emulator configuration file (usually EPOC.INI), you can reconfigure these drives to map to alternative locations, and you can map additional native drives.

The emulator is generally configured with only these native drives enabled. However, you can enable additional drives that use emulator builds of the file systems that are used on the actual hardware platforms – for example the Symbian OS FAT file system. You can do this either by editing the emulator configuration file or by configuring ESTART (see Section 13.3.1 and Chapter 16, *Boot Processes*). This can be a useful aid when developing a new file system or debugging an existing one. Apart from the ROM file system, all the standard Symbian OS file systems can be used in this way. The majority of the source code for the emulator builds of these file systems is the same as that used for the hardware platforms. Indeed, the same applies for the logical layer of the local media sub-system. However, these drives use emulator specific media drivers which normally read and write to a binary file on the host machine to emulate the memory area of the disk rather than accessing any media hardware directly.

9.1.2.3   F32 startup

The file server loads and runs early in the Symbian OS boot sequence, immediately after the kernel has been booted. Obviously, we need a special loading mechanism since at this stage neither the loader nor the ROM file system is available. We use a special statement in the ROM image specification (that is, the ROM obey file), to designate the file server as the secondary process in the system. The result is that the main ROM header holds the address of its image in ROM to allow a kernel extension to start it. (Once the file server is running, the loader can start all the other executables in the system.)

Once the file server is loaded, its main thread runs and installs the ROM file system. Again, without the loader and the ROM drive, this can't be done in the same way as a normal file system – this is why we build the ROM file system into the file server executable, rather than having it as a separate library. Next, the file server starts the loader thread, and then an F32 startup thread.

The startup thread, which is a separate thread to allow it to use the file server client API, now runs and continues file server initialization. It initializes the local media sub-system and then executes ESTART.EXE from Z: before exiting.

ESTART completes the file server initialization process, performing operations such as loading and mounting the file systems. Finally it initiates the startup of the rest of Symbian OS. To do this, it usually launches SYSSTART.EXE, the system startup process, but if this is not present, it launches the window server, EWSRV.EXE, instead. Developers who are creating a new phone platform usually customize ESTART to perform platform specific initialization of the file server or other low-level components. In Chapter 16, *Boot Processes*, I will cover system boot in more depth.

9.1.2.4   The text shell

Within the F32 source tree, we have implemented a simple text shell (ESHELL.EXE), which presents the user with a DOS-like command prompt. The shell can be used for running console-mode test programs in a minimal Symbian OS configuration that includes only E32 and F32 components. We also provide a minimal window server (EWSRV.EXE) in the E32 source tree too.

9.2   The file server client API

We have seen that the file server allows clients to access files, directories and drives on the Symbian OS phone. Client programs access the F32 services by linking to EFSRV.DLL, which provides the client API defined in f32file.h.

STDLIB (the Symbian OS implementation of the standard C library) uses this API to add a thin mapping layer to implement *POSIX*-compliant file services. However, in this section I will describe only the file server client API, as this is the most common way for system applications to access file services. In this book, I will provide only an overview of the client API. For more detail, the reader should refer to *Symbian OS C++ for Mobile Phones.*[1]

Not surprisingly, most file services involve communication with the file server. (Only a small number are handled client-side, an example being the services provided by the `TParseBase`-derived file name parsing classes – see Section 9.2.4.)

9.2.1   RFs class – the file server session

All access from client to file server takes place via a file server session. A session is established thus: the client creates an instance of the file server session class, `RFs`, and connects it to the server using the method `RFs::Connect()`. Clients may have more than one session open simultaneously. The kernel assembles the data for session-based requests into a message and passes a message handle to the server. The file server processes the message and passes the result back to the client.

The file server's clients are normally in different processes to the file server – exceptions are the Symbian OS loader, the F32 startup thread (which I described in Section 9.1.2.3), and file server plug-ins. Because of this, most requests on the file server involve the kernel context switching between processes, which can be an expensive operation. However, the file server is a fixed process, which reduces the impact of the context switch considerably (see Section 7.4.1.3).

The file server doesn't use client-side buffering. This is because the way in which its services are used and the types and formats of files it manages are so varied that there aren't any situations in which this could be consistently beneficial. Instead, higher-level Symbian OS components (such as `STORE`) implement techniques to minimize the number of calls they make on the file server.

We associate a current path, including a drive letter, with every file server session. Only one path is supported per session. The file server initializes the path when the client connects the `RFs` object, and changes it only as the client directs.

Many of F32's services are provided by the `RFs` class itself. These include the following groups of services:

- Drive and volume information. Examples include:
  - `DriveList()` to get a list of the available drives
  - `Volume()` to get volume information for a formatted device
- Operations on directories and their entries. Examples include:
  - `Entry()` to get the entry details of a file or directory

---

[1] *Symbian OS C++ for Mobile Phones: Professional Development on Constrained Devices*, by Richard Harrison. Symbian Press.

- – `GetDir()` to get a filtered list of a directory's contents
- – `MkDir()` to create a directory
- Change notification. Examples include:
  - – `NotifyChange()` to request notification of changes to files or directories
  - – `NotifyDiskSpace()` to request notification when the free disk space on a drive crosses a specified threshold value
- File name parsing. Examples include:
  - – `Parse()` to parse a filename specification
- System functions concerning the state of a file system. Examples include:
  - – `CheckDisk()` to check the integrity of the specified drive
  - – `ScanDrive()` to correct errors due to unexpected power down of the phone
- Management of drives and file systems. Examples include:
  - – `SetSubst()` to create a substitute drive – one drive acting as shortcut to a path on another
  - – `AddFileSystem()` to add a file system to the file server
  - – `MountFileSystem()` to mount a file system on a drive.

9.2.2 Sub-session objects

A client may use a session to open and access many different files and directories, and F32 represents each of these by a separate object while it is in use by the client. These objects are known as sub-session objects. There are four sub-session classes:

- The `RFile` class for creating and performing operations on files
- The `RDir` class for reading entries contained in a directory
- The `RFormat` class for formatting a drive
- The `RRawDisk` class, which enables direct drive access.

Creating sub-sessions is much less expensive than opening new sessions. Sub-sessions provide an independent channel of communication within the session. If a client closes a session, the file server automatically closes any associated sub-sessions. This ensures that all fileserver resources are properly freed.

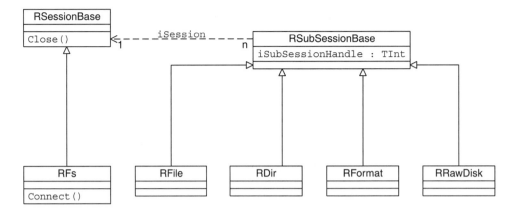

Figure 9.2   F32 client-side classes

Figure 9.2 shows these client-side classes.

`RSessionBase` is the base class for a handle to a session with any Symbian OS server. We derive from this in the file server to provide the `RFs` class. `RSubSessionBase` is the client-side handle to a sub-session. From this, we derive the `RFile`, `RDir`, `RFormat` and `RRawDisk` sub-session classes that I've already introduced.

As I will explain later, each of these client-side session and sub-session objects has a corresponding object on the server-side. Should the client thread terminate unexpectedly before closing the session, then the kernel will send a disconnect message to the file server which will close the session and all its sub-session objects.

It is good practice to close the sub-session objects as soon as they are finished with – to free the corresponding server-side resources involved. Otherwise they will remain allocated until the owning session is closed.

9.2.2.1   RFile class – for creating and performing operations on files

The `RFile` class represents an individual file. It provides methods to create a new file and open an existing file, as well as methods to read from and write to a file, seek to a position within a file, and get or set a file's attributes.

When a client opens a file, it specifies a sharing mode which indicates how (if at all) other programs can access the same file while it is open. If it opens a file with exclusive access, then no other client can access the file until the first client closes it. Read-only sharing means that other clients may access the file – but only for reading. Finally, a client can open a file and allow shared access with other clients for both reading and writing. If a file is already open for sharing, then another program can only open it using the same share mode as that with which it was originally opened. The client can also specify an access mode indicating how the file will be accessed by this particular `RFile` object. This can specify either read-only access or read/write access. The access mode has to be compatible with the sharing mode.

The `RFile` class also provides methods to lock and unlock a range of bytes within a file. A locked region is accessible only through the `RFile` object that claimed the lock. Locking can be used to synchronize updates to a file when more than one program has read/write access to it.

There are a number of variants of the file read and write methods, including synchronous and asynchronous versions. The synchronous version sends the message to the server and waits for the response, suspending the client thread. The asynchronous version returns as soon as the message is sent, allowing the client thread to continue execution while the server processes the request; the client supplies a reference to a `TRequestStatus` object, which the file server signals on completion.

The `RFile` class also provides methods to read or to change the various attributes of a file, such as `RFile::Size()` to return the size of a file in bytes and `RFile::SetSize()` to change the size of a file.

9.2.2.2   RDir class – for reading directory entries

This class is used to read the entries contained in a directory. Like the `RFile` class, it contains both synchronous and asynchronous read methods.

9.2.2.3   RFormat class – for formatting a drive

This class is only used when formatting a drive. This process can take a great deal of time for a large drive, and so the operation is performed in stages, with control returning to the client at the end of each stage. Stages can be performed synchronously or asynchronously. A drive cannot be formatted while any client has files or directories open on it.

9.2.2.4   RRawDisk class – for direct drive access

This class is used for direct disk access – allowing raw read and write operations to the drive. As with formatting, direct access cannot take place while files or directories are open on the drive.

9.2.3   High level file server services

Symbian OS supports a variety of high-level file server services. We implement this higher-level functionality within the client library rather than the server, and each API generally leads to a sequence of calls being made to the file server.

`CFileMan` provides file management services such as moving, copying and deleting one or more files in a path. It allows the client to use wildcards in the specification of the paths and files concerned. CFileMan methods can be configured to operate recursively, which means that they will act on all matching files that they find throughout the source directory's hierarchy. These functions may be performed synchronously or asynchronously. When they operate asynchronously, the operation takes place in a separate thread from the calling client thread. The CFileManObserver class allows user notification during the operation.

The TFindFile class provides methods to search for files in one or more directories either on a single drive or on every available drive in turn. We provide versions of this that accept wildcards in the file specifier.

CDirScan is used to scan through a directory hierarchy, upwards or downwards, returning a filtered list of the entries contained in each directory.

9.2.4   File names

The file server supports long file names. A full file name may contain up to 256 16-bit characters and consists of four components:

- The drive – a single letter and a colon

- The path – a list of directories separated by backslashes which starts and ends with a backslash

- The filename – this consists of every character from that which follows the last backslash to the character preceding the final dot (if an extension is specified)

- The extension – which consists of every character after the final dot (after the final backslash).

For example: `c:\dirA\dirB\dirC\file.ext`.
Symbian provides three classes for parsing filenames, each derived from TParseBase (the base class for filename parsing). All three classes allow you to test whether a particular component is included in a specified filename, and if so, to extract it:

- TParse – this version contains a TFileName object as a buffer to store a copy of the parsed filename. TFileName defines a descriptor long enough to hold the longest file name. Being 256 characters long, it is a relatively large object and should be used with care. For instance, you should avoid allocating or passing a TFileName on the stack

- TParsePtr – this version refers to an external, modifiable buffer

- TParsePtrC – This version refers to an external buffer that cannot be modified.

The last two versions should be used in preference to the first to minimize stack usage.

9.2.5 Data caging and sharing file handles

The EKA2 version of Symbian OS is normally built with platform security enabled. In this secure version, the file server employs the data caging scheme, which I described in Chapter 8, *Platform Security*.

The central theme of data caging is that the file server designates a certain area on the drives that it controls as a restricted system area. This area is only accessible to programs that are part of the Trusted Computing Base (TCB) – that is the kernel, the file server, and the software installer. All executables are located within this system area and the OS will refuse to execute code from anywhere else. In addition, each non-TCB process has its own individual private file area that only it (and a small number of other special components) has access to. We provide a third resource area, which is read-only for non-TCB processes and holds read-only files that are to be shared publicly. All remaining file areas are public and any program can read from them and write to them.

So the data caging mechanism allows processes, and the OS itself, to hide private files from other processes. However, there will be circumstances in which a process will need to share a private file with another chosen process. In other words, a situation in which we want to keep a file safe from most processes, but want the ability to grant access to a chosen process without that process having to have special capabilities. Also we don't want to reveal the full (and private) path of the file in order for the recipient to open it (although we can allow the recipient to know the file's name and extension).

To support this, the EKA2 version of the file server provides new RFile methods that allow a process to pass an open file to another process. Sharing an open file is a two-stage operation. The owner of the RFile object first needs to transfer it to the other process. The RFile class provides three methods for this purpose:

- RFile::TransferToServer() – for passing from client to server

- RFile::TransferToClient() – for passing from server to client

- RFile::TransferToProcess() – for passing from one process to another process.

Let's take a closer look at the last of these, as an example:

```
TInt RFile::TransferToProcess(RProcess& aProcess,
    TInt aFsHandleIndex, TInt aFileHandleIndex) const;
```

This transfers the RFile sub-session object to the process specified by the first argument. In doing this, the file server generates a duplicate handle on this same sub-session object. However, this handle is only useable in the context of the session on which it was created and so the file server must share the session as well as the sub-session object. The duplicate sub-session handle and the session handle are passed to the other process using two of that process's sixteen environment slots. (The slot numbers are specified in the second and third parameters.) The sending process can continue to access the file after it has transferred it. If the sending process closes the file and the session, then the corresponding file server objects are not destroyed – because they have been transferred.

To access the open file that was transferred, the receiving process must adopt the RFile object. Again, three different methods are provided, corresponding to the three file transfer methods:

- RFile::AdoptFromClient() – for a server adopting a file from a client

- RFile::AdoptFromServer() – for a client adopting a file from a server

- RFile::AdoptFromCreator() – for one process adopting a file from another.

Again, let's look at the last of these as an example:

```
TInt RFile::AdoptFromCreator(TInt aFsIndex, TInt aFileHandleIndex);
```

This is used to adopt an open file that was sent using the TransferToProcess() method. The file server retrieves the session and sub-session handles from the environment data slots specified in the two arguments – these must correspond with those specified in the transfer function. The receiving process can then access the file as it would any other open RFile object. The adopted file retains the access attributes that were set when the sending process opened the file.

Although the receiving process shares the session that was used to open and transfer the file, it doesn't have to adopt and manage this shared session directly. Once the receiving process closes the RFile object, both the session and sub-session file server objects are destroyed (assuming the sending process has already done likewise).

Because the session is shared between the two processes involved, it is recommended that the sending process opens a file server session specifically for the transfer. Other files opened in the same session by the sending process could be accessible by the receiving process, which could pose a security risk.

9.3 The file server

As we have seen, the file server handles requests from its clients for all mounted drives. It is a system server, which means that if it panics, the whole OS is restarted. The main file server thread is always one of the highest priority user threads running on the system.

9.3.1 Interfacing with clients

Figure 9.3 shows a diagram of the server-side classes that form the interface with F32 clients.

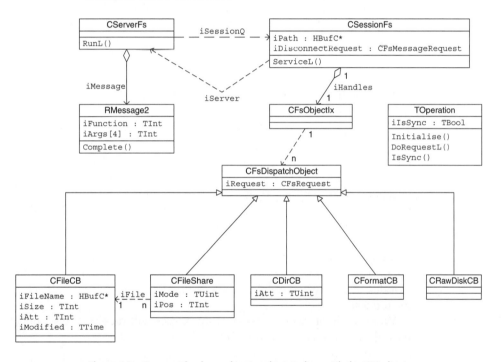

Figure 9.3 Server-side classes forming the interface with the F32 clients

CServerFs is a singleton that is derived from CServer2, the Symbian OS client/server framework's server class. CServerFs is an active object; each time a client request is received, its event-handling method, RunL(), is called to accept that request from the client thread and forward it to the relevant server-side client session.

CServerFs handles the creation of the server-side sessions. A client requests a connection by calling RFs::Connect(), which sends a connect message to the server. If connection is successful, this leads to the creation of an instance of the class CSessionFs, the server-side session object. The session is initialized in the method `CSes-sionFs::CreateL()`. `CServerFs` maintains a queue, `iSessionQ`, of all the sessions open on it.

Each time the server receives a request from an open session, it calls the request servicing method of the relevant session:

```
void CSessionFs::ServiceL(const RMessage2& aMessage)
```

The details of every client request are contained in a message object, `RMessage2`, which is passed as an argument to the service method. `RMessage2` contains a 32-bit operation identifier, which is read by the server using `RMessage2::Function()`. It also holds a copy of the request arguments – up to four 32-bit values. After handling a request, the server conveys a 32-bit result back to the client by calling the message object's base class method:

```
void RMessagePtr2::Complete(TInt aReason) const
```

The class `TOperation` encapsulates a type of operation that the server is able to perform. It contains various data members that categorize the operation, as well as two important methods. The first is `TOperation::Initialise()`, which the server calls prior to request execution. This method parses and preprocesses the data supplied by the client. The second method is `TOperation::DoRequestL()`, which performs the requested operation. The server holds a constant array of `TOperation` objects, containing a separate entry for each operation that it is capable of performing. (This is of the order of 90 different operations.) The session's `ServiceL()` method uses the operation identifier to index this array and obtain the corresponding `TOperation` object for the request.

When a client closes a session, the server will receive a disconnect message and then call this method:

```
void CSessionFs::Disconnect(const RMessage2& aMessage)
```

As we will see shortly, session disconnection can involve more than just deleting the session object.

For each of the client-side sub-session objects that I mentioned in the previous section, there is a corresponding server-side object, and these are all managed by their associated session. The following table lists the server-side sub-session objects and their client/server relationship:

Server-side class	Description	Corresponding client-side class
CFileShare	Abstraction for a client view of an open file.	RFile
CDirCB	Abstraction of an open directory.	RDir
CFormatCB	Abstraction of a format operation.	RFormat
CRawdiskCB	Abstraction for direct drive access.	RRawDisk

Each time the file server creates a server-side sub-session object, for example because a client calls `RFile::Create()`, it adds this object to the object index (`CSessionFs::iHandles`) of the session to which the object belongs. This generates a unique sub-session handle that the server returns to the client-side object, which stores it. After this, the handle is passed as a message argument in each request involving the same sub-session, to identify the appropriate server-side object. If the client closes the session, the file server will first close any sub-session objects still remaining in the object index. Each sub-session class is derived from `CFsDispatchObject`, which deals with the closing of these objects.

The `CFileCB` class represents an open file – the server has to create an instance of this class before access to a particular file is possible. `CFileCB` contains the full file name (including drive and extensions), the file size, the file attributes and the last time the file was modified.

If you look at the previous table, you can see that an `RFile` object is actually a handle on a `CFileShare` rather than a `CFileCB`. This is because many clients may have the same file open, and `CFileShare` corresponds to one client's particular view of the open file. `CFileShare` stores the current file position for its client, together with the mode in which the file was opened. A `CFileCB` object remains instantiated by the server as long as there are one or more `CFileShare` objects open on it. Once the last share is closed, then the file server closes the `CFileCB` object too.

To further illustrate the relationship between the `CFileCB` and `CFileShare` classes, Figure 9.4 shows two clients, each with files open. Client 1 has a single file open. Client 2 has two files open, but one of them is the same as the one opened by Client 1.

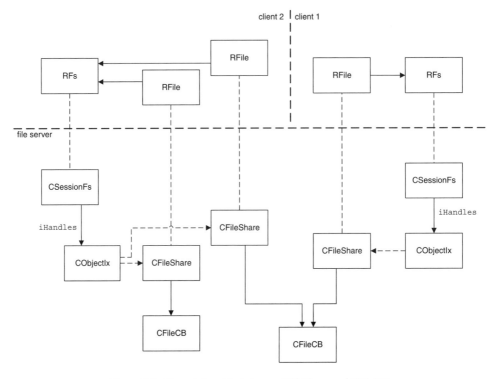

Figure 9.4   The relationship between CFileShare and CFileCB

9.3.2   Processing requests

The EKA1 version of the file server is single-threaded. This single thread processes all requests, for all drives. When the thread blocks, waiting on an I/O operation on a particular drive, it is unable to process requests for any other drive.

We took the opportunity to improve the file server design in EKA2. It is multi-threaded and allows concurrent access to each drive. As well as the main file server thread, there is normally a thread for each logical drive, and a thread for handling session disconnection. So, for example, while the server is processing a request to write a large block of data to a multimedia file on a removable media drive, it is still able to accept and process a read request to an INI file on the main internal user data drive. This design also enables the file server to support file systems for remote drives. These are drives that are connected to the mobile phone via a network connection. Requests to a remote drive could take a very long time to complete. Such requests block the thread associated with the remote drive, but, because it is multi-threaded, the file server can still access the other drives in the system.

A client using asynchronous requests can have requests outstanding concurrently on more than one drive from a single session. With the multi-threaded scheme, these can truly be handled concurrently. On EKA1, although the client may be given the impression that they are handled concurrently, in fact they are processed sequentially.

Figure 9.5 illustrates the running F32 threads in a Symbian OS phone that has a single drive. The main file server thread initially handles all client requests. It goes on to service those requests that don't require any access to the media device itself and those that won't block a thread, before completing them and returning the result to the client. These requests must not block since this will delay the entire file server from processing new requests.

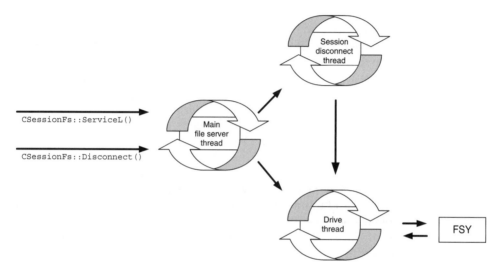

Figure 9.5   The F32 threads

The main thread passes any requests that involve a call down to the file system or that may block to a separate drive thread. We allow requests on drive threads to be "long-running" operations. While these drive threads are busy or blocked handling a request, new requests for the drive are added to a drive-thread queue. In most circumstances, it queues requests in a FIFO order. (There is only one exception to this, which I will talk about later.) All drive threads have the same priority, which is slightly less than that of the main file server thread.

There is a certain overhead in transferring requests to a separate drive thread, and so we avoid this where possible. Some types of drive, such as the ROM drive and the internal RAM drive, never perform "long-running" operations and never block the thread. We designate such drives "synchronous drives", and process all requests for them in the main file server thread – synchronous drives do not have a separate drive thread. However, even with asynchronous drives, we can handle certain requests without access to the media device itself – for example, requests to set or retrieve information held by the file server. We classify these types of operation as "synchronous operations" and the main file server thread always processes these too. (The Boolean member of the `TOp-eration` class – `iIsSync` indicates which operations are synchronous; see Figure 9.3.) I will now list some examples of synchronous operations:

- `RFs::NotifyChange()`

- `RFs::Drive()`

- `RFs::SetSessionPath()`.

As we have seen, when a client closes a session, this can result in the file server having to close down sub-sessions – and this may mean that it has to write to disk. For example, if closing a `CFileShare` object results in the server closing a `CFileCB` object too, the server may need to flush the current size of the file to the disk. If the file is on an asynchronous drive, then this will have to be handled by the drive thread. Also, before the file server destroys a session, it needs to clean up any outstanding requests for that session – and these may be queued or in progress on one or more drive threads. In this case, we may need to wait for a drive thread to unblock before the requests can be unqueued. Again, we can't tie up the main file server thread while these session termination operations take place, and this is why we use a separate thread to manage session disconnection.

Figure 9.6 shows a diagram of the server-side classes that deal with the processing of a request.

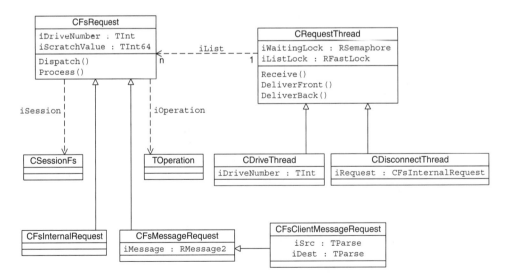

Figure 9.6 The F32 server-side classes which perform request processing

9.3.2.1 Request objects

The abstract class, `CFsRequest`, encapsulates a request within the file server, and we use it to pass these requests from one server thread to another. The initiating thread, which will either be the main file server thread or the session disconnect thread, generates a request object. If the initiating thread cannot handle the request, then this delivers it to the target thread, which will be either a drive thread or the session disconnect thread. The initiating thread may need to store the request in the target thread's request queue until it can be processed. `CFsRequest` has a reference to the corresponding `TOperation` object for the request, `iOperation`. It also has a pointer to the session that originated the request, `iSession`, and a member holding the number of the drive on which the request is to be performed, `iDriveNumber`.

Most requests come from file server clients. However, the server can generate internal requests too:

- `CancelSessionOp`. The session disconnect thread generates this request, and it is delivered to all drive threads, requesting them to cancel any requests they hold for the session being closed

- `DispatchObjectCloseOp`. This is generated when a sub-session object is closed. As I have already mentioned, sub-session closure can result in a write to disk. Because of this, sub-session closure has to be carried out on the correct drive thread for the object. This means that the initiating thread must issue a `DispatchObjectCloseOp` request to the appropriate drive thread.

A separate class derived from `CFsRequest` represents each different type of request. `CFsMessageRequest` encapsulates requests originating from a client, and `CFsInternalRequest` represents an internal file server request. Each of these classes has different `Complete()` methods. Completion of a `CFsMessageRequest` results in the request-handling thread signaling back to the client, by calling `RMessagePtr2::Complete()`. Completion of an internal request means that the handling thread will signal the file server thread that initiated the request.

Some client requests involve one or even two file names as arguments, and so `CFsClientMessageRequest`, derived from `CFsMessageRequest` is provided. This contains two `TParse` members to hold this information. The first such member is `iSrc`, which is used by requests which involve a source path name such as `RFile::Create()` and `RFile::Read()`. Requests that involve both a source and a destination path, such as `RFs::Rename()` and `RFile::Replace()`, also use the second `TParse` member, `iDest`.

Each request processed by the server needs a separate request object, and it is the job of the `RequestAllocator` class to manage the allocation and issuing of new requests. To keep request handling time as short as possible, the request allocator preallocates blocks of empty client request objects. During file server startup, when the first client request is received, it creates the first block of fifteen request objects and adds them to a free list. If ever a request object is required but the allocator's free list is empty, it then allocates a further block of fifteen request objects – up to a maximum of 45. If the allocator ever needs more objects than this, it switches to a new strategy, whereby it allocates and frees individual request objects.

The allocator is responsible for returning the correct type of object for the particular request. When a request object is no longer required, the server informs the allocator, and it returns the object to the free pool.

However, the file server has to be able to handle session and sub-session closure requests without the possibility of failure. This means that for these requests, it must not be necessary for the RequestAllocator to issue new request objects, in case there are none free and there is not enough free memory to allocate a new one. To cope with this, we ensure that the file server always allocates the necessary request objects ahead of receiving a session or sub-session close request. We do this like so:

- Sub-session closure. Each request to open a sub-session results in the request allocator setting aside an internal request object, DispatchObjectCloseOp, to handle sub-session closure

- Session closure. This involves two further types of request in addition to sub-session closure. These are:

  o A request issued from the main thread to the disconnect thread to commence session disconnect. Every CSessionFs object has a "SessionDiconnectOp" message request object as one of its private members (iDisconnectRequest) – see Figure 9.3

  o A request to clean up outstanding requests for the session. The session disconnect thread has a CancelSessionOp internal request object as one of its private members (CDisconnect-Thread::iRequest) – see Figure 9.6.

9.3.2.2 Server threads

As I have already mentioned, as well as the main file server thread, there are two other types of file server threads: the drive threads and the session disconnect thread. Unlike the main thread, which processes each new request as it is received, these other threads may be busy or blocked when a new request arrives, and so they employ a request queue to hold any pending requests. The base class CRequestThread (shown in Figure 9.6) encapsulates a file server thread that accepts requests into a queue and then processes them. Requests can be added to either the start or the end of its doubly linked list, iList. The fast semaphore iListLock prevents access to the list from more than one thread at once. From the CRequestThread entry point, the thread initializes itself and then calls CRequestThread::Receive() in readiness to receive requests. This method waits for a request to arrive from another thread – at which point it calls the request's Process() method. While the request list is empty, CRequestThread waits on the semaphore iWaitingLock. This is signaled by other threads whenever they deliver a new request and the CRequestThread is idle.

The class CDriveThread, which is derived from CRequestThread, handles requests that are carried out on a particular logical drive. The file server creates an instance of this class for each asynchronous drive on the phone, when the drive is mounted. The FsThreadManager class, which contains only static members, manages drive thread allocation and access. When the file server needs to mount a file system on a logical drive, its main thread calls the FsThreadManager to create the corresponding drive thread. However, the mounting of a file system involves an access to the disk itself, and this can only be done from the correct drive thread, so the main thread then sends a mount request to the newly created drive thread. On drive dismount, the drive thread exits, but the file server does not free the drive thread object.

The class CDisconnectThread, also derived from CRequest-Thread, handles session disconnect requests. The file server creates one instance of this class during startup to handle all session disconnect requests. This object is never deleted.

9.3.2.3 Synchronous request handling

Figure 9.7 shows the program flow for the synchronous request: RFs::Drive(). (This request returns drive information to the client.)

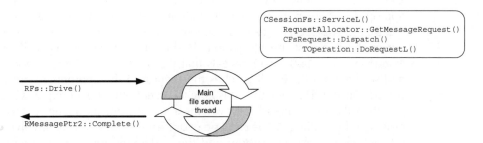

Figure 9.7   Program flow for a synchronous request

On receiving the request, the file server calls CSession-Fs::ServiceL() which executes in the main thread. This acquires a request object, identifies the appropriate TOperation object for this request type and then dispatches the request. CFsRequest::Dis-patch() first calls TOperation::Initialise() to validate the arguments supplied by the client. Next it checks whether or not the operation is synchronous using TOperation::IsSync(). Since the request is synchronous, the main thread processes the request by calling TOperation::DoRequestL(). Finally, the main thread completes the client request by calling RMessagePtr2::Complete().

9.3.2.4   Asynchronous request handling

Figure 9.8 shows the program flow for the asynchronous request RFile::Create() (which creates and opens a file).

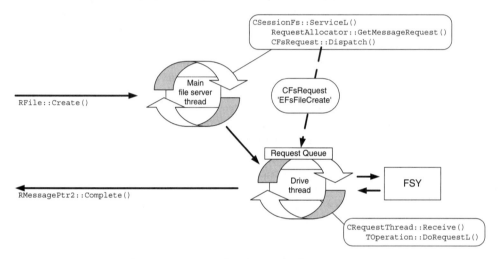

Figure 9.8   Program flow for an asynchronous request

On receiving the request, again the file server calls CSessionFs::ServiceL() to acquire a request object and initialize it with the appropriate TOperation object. Still in the main thread, CFsRequest::Dispatch() calls TOperation::Initialise(), which parses the name of the file supplied. This time, however, the call to TOperation::IsSync() reveals that the operation is asynchronous, and so the main thread dispatches the request to the appropriate drive thread. Once it has done this, it is able to accept other client requests.

When the drive thread retrieves the request from its queue, it processes it by calling TOperation::DoRequestL(). This involves interaction with the file system and the underlying media sub-system. Finally, the drive thread completes the client request by calling RMessagePtr2::Complete().

9.3.2.5   Session disconnection

Figure 9.9 shows the first phase of program flow for session disconnection, RFs::Close(). On receiving the request, the file server's main thread

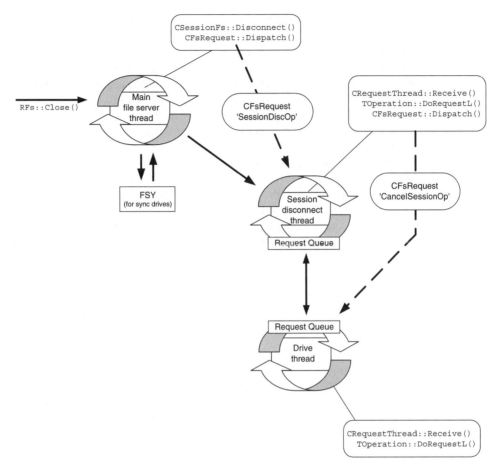

Figure 9.9 Program flow for the first phase of session disconnection

calls `CSessionFs::Disconnect()`. This method first closes any open sub-session objects for synchronous drives. (They can't be closed later, when the disconnect thread issues sub-session close requests to the asynchronous drives, because the main thread is not designed to accept internal requests.)

The next phase is the cleanup of any outstanding requests for the session. However, the main thread passes the responsibility for this and the completion of session disconnection to the disconnect thread by dispatching a "disconnect session" (`SessionDiconnectOp`) request to it. (Remember that for session disconnect, the server can't use the request allocator to acquire this request object, and instead it must use the session's request object: `CSessionFs::iDisconnectRequest`. I discussed this in Section 9.3.2.1.)

When the disconnect thread retrieves the request from its queue, it issues an internal `CancelSessionOp` request to each drive thread in turn, asking each thread to cancel any requests queued for the session in question. (Requests in progress will be allowed to complete, since the drive thread doesn't check its queue again until it has completed its current request). The cancel request is inserted at the front of each drive thread queue, so that it will be the next request fetched by each drive thread. Each drive thread will later signal the completion of its CancelSessionOp request to the disconnect thread.

Figure 9.10 shows the second phase of the program flow for session disconnection, RFs::Close(). Now that the disconnect thread has ensured the cleanup of any outstanding requests for the session, it is able to finish processing the "disconnect session" request it received from the main thread. If any sub-sessions objects remain open – only for asynchronous drives now – then the disconnect thread closes them. Sub-session closure may require the server to write to a disk, so it does this by issuing another internal request, DispatchObjectCloseOp, to each drive concerned.

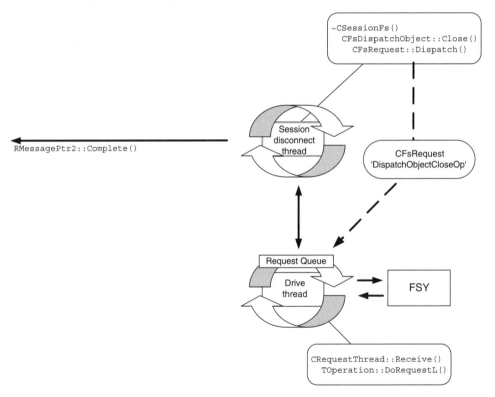

Figure 9.10   Program flow for the second phase of session disconnection

Again each drive thread signals back completion to the disconnect thread. Finally, the session-disconnect thread completes the original client request by calling RMessagePtr2::Complete().

9.3.3   Interfacing with the file system

Figure 9.11 shows a diagram of the server-side classes that form the interface with a file system, with a FAT file system implementation shown as an example. I will now describe these classes.

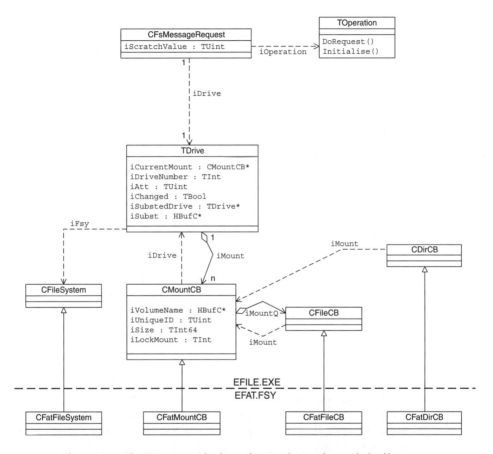

Figure 9.11   The F32 server-side classes forming the interface with the file system

9.3.3.1   TDrive class

We've seen that the file server supports 26 drives (A: to Z:); the TDrive class is the file server's abstraction for a logical drive. It maintains a TDrive instance for each drive, whether or not the drive is currently mounted. As I mentioned in Section 9.1.2, mounting a drive means associating a file system with it. TDrive contains the member iFSys, which is a pointer to a file system factory class, CFileSystem. When iFSys is NULL, the drive is not mounted. (Some drives are available for drive substitution but substitute drives have no associated file system.)

The `TDrive` data member `iAtt` holds a bit-mask of the drive attributes. These attributes are fixed while the drive is mounted with a particular file system. The set of possible drive attributes is as follows:

Attribute	Description
KDriveAttLocal	Drive is local. Uses the local media sub-system (not ROM or remote).
KDriveAttRom	A ROM drive.
KDriveAttSubsted	Drive is a substitute to a path on another drive.
KDriveAttInternal	Drive is internal (as opposed to removable).
KDriveAttRemovable	Drive is removable.
KDriveAttRemote	Drive is remote.
KDriveAttTransaction	Drive employs a file system which is transactional (this is used by STORE).

In fact, in the context of drives, the term "mount" is a little over-used, since we also talk about a volume being "mounted" on a drive. The class `CMountCB` is an abstraction of a volume (or partition). For removable media devices, the file server creates a different `CMountCB` object for each volume introduced into the system. If the user removes a volume from the phone with a sub-session object still open on it (for example, an open file), then the file server cannot destroy the corresponding `CMountCB` object.

`TDrive` maintains an object container, `iMount`, holding all the open mounts on its drive. `TDrive` also keeps a separate `CMountCB` pointer, `iCurrentMount`, corresponding to the volume that is currently present on the phone. For a `CMountCB` object to be destroyed, there must be no sub-session objects open on it and it must not be the current mount.

The Boolean member `TDrive::iChanged` indicates a possible change of volume, and is important for removable media drives. At startup, the file server passes down to the local media sub-system the address of `iChanged` for each local drive that is enabled on the phone. The local media sub-system will then update this variable each time there is a card insertion or removal event for the drive concerned.

Each volume contains a unique identifier – for example, FAT partitions contain a unique ID field in their boot sector. The file server reads this ID when it mounts the volume on the drive and stores it in the corresponding mount object, CMountCB::iUniqueID. If the user changes the media in the drive, then when the file server next accesses that drive, it will find iChanged to be true. The file server then reads the unique ID directly from the new volume to determine if the volume has changed. The server compares the unique ID that it has just read with the ID of each existing mount object stored in the mount queue, to see if it already knows about this volume. If it does, then the corresponding mount object becomes the current mount again. If it does not, then it creates a new mount object.

9.3.3.2 CMountCB class

The volume abstraction, CMountCB, has members holding the size of the volume in bytes, iSize, and the volume name, iVolumeName. It also has a member iMountQ, which is a list of all the files open on the volume.

Its member, iLockMount, is a lock counter, which tracks whether files or directories are opened, and whether a format or raw disk access is active on the volume. The server checks iLockMount prior to processing format and raw disk requests on the drive, as these can't be allowed while files or directories are still open. Similarly it checks this member before opening files or directories on the drive to ensure that a format or raw disk access is not in progress.

9.3.3.3 Request dispatch

Now let us look in a little more detail at what happens when a client request is dispatched to a drive thread.

As I described in Section 9.3.2.4, before it dispatches the request to the drive thread, the server's main thread calls TOperation::Initialise() to preprocess and validate the data supplied by the client. This may involve assembling a full drive, path and filename from a combination of the data supplied and the session's current path. If the request involves a sub-session object (for example, CFileShare) then this process of validation will lead to the identification of the target sub-session object. Rather than discarding this information and recalculating it again in the drive thread when request processing commences, the main thread saves a pointer to the sub-session object in the scratch variable CFsRequest::iScatchValue so that the drive thread can re-use it.

It is also at this initial stage that the main thread translates a request specifying a substituted drive. The data member TDrive::iSubstedDrive provides a pointer to the true drive object (or the next one in the chain), and TDrive::iSubst holds the assigned path on this drive.

The drive thread commences its processing of the request by calling `TOperation::DoRequestL()`. It identifies the appropriate server object to be used to perform the request (often via the scratch variable). Requests translate into server objects as follows:

Client request	Server object
RFs	CMountCB
RFile	CFileCB
RDir	CDirCB
RFormat	CFormatCB
RRawDisk	CRawDiskCB

Request execution continues with the drive thread calling methods on the server object. The first thing it normally does is to check that the target drive is mounted with a volume.

These server object classes form the major part of the API to the file systems. This API is a polymorphic interface – each server object is an abstract class that is implemented in each separate file system DLL. The server manipulates these server objects using the base class's API and this allows it to work with different file systems in different DLLs. In this way, request processing is passed down to the appropriate file system.

9.3.4 Notifiers

As I mentioned in Section 9.2.1, the file server API allows clients to register for notification of various events. These include:

- Standard change notification events:
  - Changes to any file or directory on all drives
  - Disk events such as a drive being mounted, unmounted, formatted, removed and so on
- Extended change notification events. These are changes to a particular file or directory on one or more drives
- Disk space notification events: when free disk space on a drive crosses a specified threshold value.

The client calls to register for notification are asynchronous: they return to the client as soon as the message is sent to the file server. The server doesn't complete the message until the notification event occurs (or the request is canceled). This completion signals the notification back to the client.

The server creates a notification object for each notification request. Figure 9.12 shows a diagram of the classes concerned. CNotifyInfo is the base class for each notification. This contains an RMessagePtr2 member, iMessage, which the server uses to complete the request message when the notification event occurs. It also contains the member iSession, which is a pointer to the session on which the notification was requested. On session closure, the file server uses this to identify any notifiers still pending for the session and cancel them.

CNotifyInfo also stores a pointer to the client's request status object, iStatus, which the client/server framework signals if the notifier is completed. We need this to handle the client's cancellation of a specific notification request. For example, the client can cancel a request for change

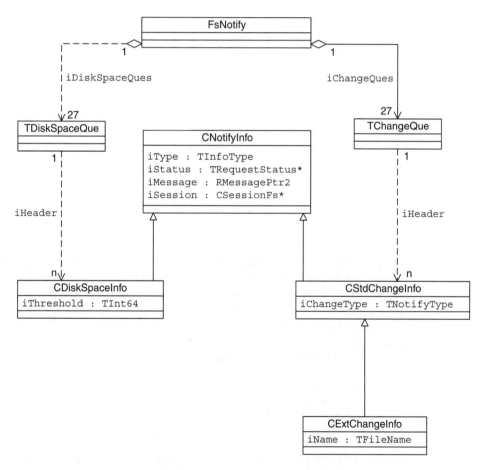

Figure 9.12 The F32 server-side notifier classes

notification using `RFs::NotifyChangeCancel(TRequestStatus& aStat)`, where `aStat` supplies a reference to the request status object of the notifier to cancel. The member `iStatus` is used to identify the specific notifier concerned.

We derive `CStdChangeInfo` from `CNotifyInfo` for standard change notifiers. This in turn is a base class for the extended change notifier class, `CExtChangeInfo`. This class's member `iName` holds the name of the specific file or directory associated with the notifier. We also use the `CDiskSpaceInfo` class, which represents a disk space notifier.

The server uses the static class `FsNotify` to manage the notification objects. `FsNotify` keeps two separate sets of queues, one set for change notifiers and one set for disk space notifiers. Each set has 27 queues within it, one for each supported drive and one more to hold notifiers that apply to all drives.

Users of the F32 notification APIs should be aware of the potential for performance degradation. Each time the server completes any request, it may also have to complete a pending notifier. The server checks the `TOperation` object of the request it is completing, to determine if the request type is one which could potentially trigger either a disk space or a change notifier. If it is, then the server iterates through two queues checking for notifiers in need of completion. (Two queues because one is for the current drive, and one is for notifiers that apply to all drives.) In the case of extended change notifiers, a certain amount of pathname comparison is required, and for disk space notifiers, the amount of free disk space needs recalculating. If there are a large number of notifiers pending, then this can have an impact on file server performance.

9.4   File systems

The file server receives all client requests, but it never accesses the media devices directly. Instead, it passes any requests that require access to the directories and files on the device to a file system. Each file system employs a media format which is appropriate for the characteristics of the devices that use it. Most file systems are implemented as separate file server plug-in DLLs, the exception being the ROM file system, which is built as part of the file server itself. File system DLLs are assigned the file extension: FSY.

Symbian OS supports the following file systems:

- The ROM file system is used for code storage on execute-in-place (XIP) media such as NOR Flash. XIP refers to the capability to execute code directly out of the memory

- The log Flash file system (LFFS) for user-data storage on NOR Flash

- The FAT file system for user-data storage on NAND Flash, internal RAM drives and removable media

- The Read-Only file system (ROFS) for code storage on non-XIP media such as NAND Flash. Code on non-XIP media first has to be copied into RAM for execution.

It is possible for developers to implement their own file system. Normally they would then customize ESTART to load and mount this file system during file server startup. I describe the necessary APIs in Section 9.4.1.6.

9.4.1   File system API

As I mentioned in Section 9.3.3.3, a loadable file system is a polymorphic DLL providing plug-in functionality to the file server by implementing the predefined file system interface classes, which are abstract classes. Each file system implements the API by defining and implementing concrete classes derived from each abstract class.

File systems are dynamically loaded by the file server at runtime – a new one can be added and mounted on a drive without the need to restart the server or interrupt any connected file server sessions. File systems contain a single exported function, which the file server calls when the file system is added to it. This export is a factory function that returns a pointer to a new file system object – an instance of a `CFileSystem`-derived class. The `CFileSystem`-derived class is itself a factory class for creating each of the other file system objects. Having called this export, the server is able to call all other file system functions through the vtable mechanism.

The file system API is defined in `f32fsys.h`. In the following sections, I will discuss the classes of which it is comprised.

9.4.1.1   The CFileSystem class

This is a factory class, which allocates instances of each of the other objects that form the file system API: `CMountCB`, `CFileCB`, `CDirCB` and `CFormatCB`. The file server has only a single `CFileSystem` instance for each loaded file system – even when that file system is mounted on a number of drives.

9.4.1.2   The CMountCB class

This class, which I introduced in Section 9.3.3.2, is the abstraction of a volume. The file server creates an instance of `CMountCB` for each volume introduced into the system.

The functionality that the file system supplies through this class roughly corresponds to that contained within the `RFs` class. So, taking as an example the method `RFs::MkDir()` to make a directory, we find that program flow moves from this client function into `TDrive::MkDir()`

in the file server and then on to `CFatMountCB::MkDirL()` in the FAT file system (`FAT.FSY`). Here is another example:

Client DLL	*File server*	*FAT.FSY*
`RFs::Rename()` →	`TDrive::Rename()` →	`CFatMountCB::RenameL()`

9.4.1.3   The CFileCB class

This class represents an open file. The functionality this class supplies roughly corresponds to the methods contained in the `RFile` class. Again, let's follow the program flow using the `FAT.FSY` as an example:

Client DLL	*File server*	*FAT.FSY*
`RFile::Read()` →	`CFileShare class` →	`CFatFileCB::ReadL()`

The file server has a single object container, which references every `CFileCB` object, across all the drives in the system.

9.4.1.4   The CDirCB class

This class represents the contents of an open directory. This supplies functionality corresponding to the methods contained in the `RDir` class. Again, the file server has a single object container that references every `CDirCB` object across all the drives in the system.

9.4.1.5   The CFormatCB class

This class represents a format operation.

9.4.1.6   Loading and mounting a file system

We add file systems to the file server by calling the client method:

```
TInt RFs::AddFileSystem(const TDesC& aFileName) const
```

The argument `aFileName` specifies the name of the FSY component to be loaded. As I mentioned in Section 9.1.2.3, `ESTART` normally does file-system loading during file server startup.

Once it has been successfully added, a file system can be mounted on a particular drive using the method:

```
TInt RFs::MountFileSystem(const TDesC& aFileSystemName, TInt aDrive) const
```

In this method, `aFileSystemName` is the object name of the file system and `aDrive` is the drive on which it is to be mounted.

The EKA1 version of the file server requires a nominated default file system, which must be called `ELOCAL.FSY`. The EKA2 version of the file server places no such restriction on the naming of file systems, or in requiring a default file system.

If you are developing file systems, there are two methods available which are useful for debugging:

```
TInt RFs::ControlIo(TInt aDrive,TInt,TAny*,TAny*)
```

This is a general-purpose method that provides a mechanism for passing information to and from the file system on a specified drive. The argument `aDrive` specifies the drive number, but the assignment of the last three arguments is file system specific.

Additionally, the following method can be used to request asynchronous notification of a file system specific event:

```
void RFs::DebugNotify(TInt aDrive,TUint aNotifyType,
                      TRequestStatus& aStat)
```

The argument `aDrive` specifies the target drive number, `aNotifyType`, specifies the event, and `aStat` is a reference to a request status object that is signaled when the event occurs.

To trigger the notifier, the file system calls the following method, which is exported by the file server:

```
void DebugNotifySessions(TInt aFunction,TInt aDrive)
```

The argument `aFunction` specifies the event that has occurred and `aDrive` indicates the drive on which this has occurred.

So for example, if when testing, it is required for the test program to issue a particular request when a certain condition occurs in a file system then using `DebugNotifySessions()`, the file system can be configured to complete a pending debug notification request whenever the condition occurs.

All these methods are only available in debug builds.

9.4.2 The log Flash file system (LFFS)

I introduced Flash memory in Section 9.1.1, where I mentioned the different types of Flash that we support in Symbian OS. We designed the log Flash file system to enable user-data storage on NOR Flash devices.

9.4.2.1   NOR Flash characteristics

Flash is nonvolatile memory which can be erased and rewritten. Reading from NOR Flash is just like reading from ROM or RAM. However, unlike RAM, data cannot be altered on Flash just by writing to the location concerned. Flash must be erased before a write operation is possible, and we can only do this erasing in relatively large units (called blocks). To erase, the phone software must issue a command and then wait for the device to signal that the operation is complete. The erase sets each bit within a block to one. Write operations, which are issued in the same way as erases, can then change bits from one to zero – but not from zero to one. The only way to change even a single zero bit back to a one is to erase the entire block again.

Imagine that we need to modify just one byte of data in a block, changing at least one bit from zero to one. (Assume also that we cannot perform the modification by writing to an alternative location in the block that has not yet been written to.) Then, to do this, we have to move all the other valid data in the block to another freshly erased location, together with the updated byte. The new location now replaces the original block – which can then be erased and becomes available for reuse later.

Another characteristic of Flash that we had to consider in our design is that it eventually wears out – there is a limit to the number of times a block can be erased and rewritten.

9.4.2.2   The log

The LFFS is specifically designed to operate with NOR Flash and to protect itself against power loss. To do this, it keeps a log of all its operations (hence the "log" part of the name). It records each modification to the data in the file system by adding an entry at the end of the log describing the operation. So, if a new file is created, this information is added as a log. If the file is subsequently deleted, a log entry indicating that the file is no longer available is added to the log.

Each log entry is of fixed size (32 bytes) and includes a flag that indicates the completion status of the operation. Before each operation is started, the LFFS creates its log entry which it adds to the log with a completion status of "not complete". It then performs the operation, and only when this is fully complete does it modify the status in the log entry to "complete". If an operation is incomplete when power is removed then, when power is restored, the LFFS undoes the operation and any space it had consumed is reclaimed. This system ensures that power loss does not corrupt the file system – although data that is only partially written is lost.

The LFFS uses the key characteristic of NOR Flash to implement this scheme. We've seen that generally we can't change Flash contents without a prior erase cycle. However, we implement an "incomplete" flag status using bits in the one state, and so we can rewrite this flag to zero (the "complete" state) without the need for an erase.

A set of operations are often related to each other, in that the whole set must either be completed, or the set of operations should fail. In other words, all the changes must be committed atomically. As an example of this, consider a large file write involving several data blocks. To handle this requirement, the LFFS uses a transaction mechanism. It marks all log entries that are part of the same transaction with the transaction ID number. It also marks the first entry with a transaction start flag, and the last entry with a transaction end flag. This ensures that partial transactions are never regarded as valid. Either the transaction succeeds and all the associated operations are valid, or the transaction fails and all the operations are invalid. As I mentioned earlier, the LFFS undoes invalid operations, and reclaims the space they consume.

9.4.2.3   *File and directory structure*

Normal file and directory data storage is completely separate from the log. This data is arranged into File Data Blocks (FDBs), which are, by default, 512 bytes in size. However, you could build the LFFS to use larger blocks (up to 4 KB) by changing a constant in one of its configuration header files. Although using a fixed data block size is wasteful of memory for small files, this allows the FDB pointer information to use an FDB index rather than an absolute address, which reduces the data management overhead.

Each FDB has an associated log entry that describes the purpose of the block and provides a pointer to it. However, the log is mainly intended as a record of changes and does not provide a permanent mechanism to track the FDBs that hold a file's data. Instead, the LFFS uses three structures to hold this information.

The first of these structures is an I-node. Each file has a single I-node that holds file-specific data, such as the file type, the file size and a unique I-node number (which is essential in identifying the file).

An I-node also contains fourteen FDB pointers. These are known as the direct pointers, and they hold address information for up to fourteen FDBs that make up the file. With an FDB size of 512 bytes, this structure alone can handle files of up to 7 KB. For larger files, a second structure is involved – the indirect block (IDB). IDBs contain 64 pointers, each addressing either FDBs or further IDBs. The LFFS supports up to four layers of IDBs, giving a maximum file size of approximately 8 GB. An I-node has an indirect pointer for each layer of IDBs.

The organization of a file with a first-level IDB is shown in Figure 9.13. The LFFS gives the FDBs in a file sequential numbers, starting at zero. It gives IDBs the same number as the first FDB that they point to.

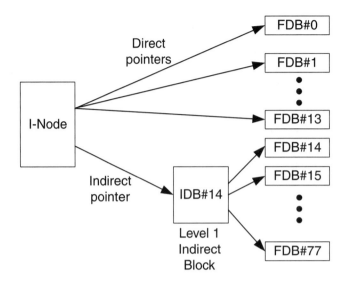

Figure 9.13   The organization of files in the LFFS which uses a first level IDB

The following table lists the fields contained in an I-node:

Field	Size (in bytes)	Description
I-node number	4	The I-node number of the file.
Reference count	2	The number of directory entries referring to this I-node. This is always 1.
File type	2	The type of file referred to by the I-node. The value can be any of the following: 1 = User data file 2 = Directory file 3 = Metadata file.
File length	4	The number of data bytes in the file.
Data block size	4	The size of the FDBs referred to by the I-node and IDBs.
Direct pointers	4 * 14	Pointers to the first 14 FDBs in the file. The first pointer is to FDB#0, the second is to FDB#1, etc.

Field	Size (in bytes)	Description
Indirect pointer L1	4	Pointer to a level 1 IDB. The IDB contains pointers to the FDBs following those found through the direct pointers.
Indirect pointer L2	4	Pointer to a level 2 IDB. The IDB is the root of a 2 level tree with pointers to the FDBs following those found through Indirect pointer L1.
Indirect pointer L3	4	Pointer to a level 3 IDB. The IDB is the root of a 3 level tree with pointers to the FDBs following those found through Indirect pointer L2.
Indirect pointer L4	4	Pointer to a level 4 IDB. The IDB is the root of a 4 level tree with pointers to the FDBs following those found through Indirect pointer L3.

The LFFS uses a third structure to track the I-nodes: the LFFS partition contains a single I-file, which holds an array of pointers to the I-nodes. It adds new I-node references to the I-file at the array entry given by the I-node number. When it deletes a reference to an I-node from the I-file, it sets the array entry to zero. This indicates that the I-node is not in use any more, and a new file can reuse the I-node number.

Collectively, these FDB tracking structures are known as the LFFS metadata. However, the metadata doesn't hold filename or directory information. Instead, we store this information in directory files. These are really just normal data files, except that they are used by the file system, and are not directly visible to clients. A directory file contains an entry for each file in that directory. Directory entries contain the name of the file and the number of the I-node that points to the file's data blocks. A directory entry's size depends on the length of the filename, which can be at most 256 characters.

I-node number 2 always points to the root directory.

9.4.2.4 Segments

To manage the erasing of blocks, the LFFS uses the notion of a segment. A segment is the smallest unit of media space that the file system can erase and consists of one or more consecutive erase blocks. The LFFS views the entire NOR device as a consecutive series of segments. It stores log entries and data entries (file data blocks and metadata) into each segment.

It stores the log starting at the bottom of the segment growing upwards, and the data entries at the top, growing downwards. Figure 9.14 shows the layout of a segment.

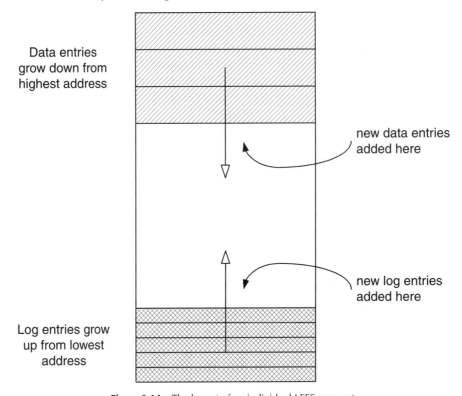

Figure 9.14   The layout of an individual LFFS segment

In this way, the log is split across segments, but log entries always occupy the same segment as their corresponding data entries. The LFFS adds log and data entries to the current segment until that segment eventually becomes full – at which point it moves on to the next erased segment.

Figure 9.15 shows a section of an LFFS partition containing four segments. The segment 2 is the current segment. Segment 1 is full, but segments 3 and 4 are empty.

As it adds and modifies file data, the LFFS moves on from one segment to the next, until it approaches a point where it is running out of media space. However, the total amount of valid data on the device will almost certainly be much less than the capacity of the device.

9.4.2.5   *Reclaiming outdated media space*

When file data is modified, the LFFS has to replace each FDB affected. It adds the replacement FDBs together with their associated log entries to

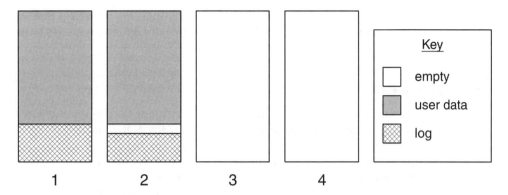

Figure 9.15   The organization of the LFFS across multiple segments

the current segment. At this point, the old FDBs and associated log entries have become out-dated. The LFFS will eventually have to reclaim this space to allow further updates to the drive. However, the LFFS has not yet finished the file update, since it must also change the metadata to point to the new FDBs. This means modifying the file's I-node and IDBs – which will generate yet more out-dated log and data entries. (However, as I will explain in Section 9.4.2.6, this metadata update is deferred until later.) When file data is deleted, this also leaves out-dated log and data entries, which the LFFS needs to reclaim.

Reclaiming out-dated media space is not simple, as this space will normally be spread across many segments, and these segments will also contain valid data. The reclaim process has to identify the segment with the largest amount of dirty data, copy any valid data from that segment, and then erase the segment allowing it to become active again. The LFFS can't allow the device to run out of free space before it attempts a reclaim, because it needs reserve space into which to move the valid data before erasing. It has to reserve at least a segment to ensure this does not happen.

The choice of which segment to reclaim is actually more complex than I have just described. I mentioned earlier that Flash blocks have a limit on the number of erase cycles they can handle. To mitigate this, the LFFS employs a wear-leveling scheme. This scheme aims to keep the erase count of each of the segments roughly equal, to avoid premature failure due to some blocks being used more than others. The LFFS stores the erase count of each segment in a segment header, and the reclaim algorithm takes this into account when identifying the next segment for reclaim. It avoids a segment containing a lot of dirty data but with a high erase count.

Reclaiming a segment can be a slow process. First, the LFFS must copy valid data to another segment, and then it must erase the blocks contained by that segment. If the LFFS did not perform space reclamation until it needed space to service a request, then its performance would be poor. Instead, the LFFS tries to reclaim early by using a reclaim thread. This is a low priority thread that uses what would otherwise be CPU idle time to reclaim data.

9.4.2.6 Roll forward

When the user modifies a file, the LFFS does not update the metadata as part of the same transaction that updates the FDBs. Instead it defers the metadata update until later. It can do this because it can extract the information it needs from the log. We call this update of metadata from the log "roll-forward". To improve performance, the LFFS generally performs roll-forward in batches, using the same low priority background thread that it uses to perform early reclaim. If power is lost after the LFFS has updated the FDBs, but before it updates the metadata, then the write operation is still regarded as successful, because the LFFS can rebuild the metadata from the log when power is restored.

However, the LFFS cannot allow too many metadata updates to accumulate, because this affects reclaiming. This is because it cannot reclaim any segment that contains FDBs whose metadata it has not rolled forward, because this reclaim could destroy information needed to reconstruct the metadata.

9.4.2.7 Caching

The LFFS maintains a cache which holds both read data and pending write data. This cache includes all types of data – not only FDBs, but also metadata and log entries. The cache tracks the pending write data for each file separately, and can therefore act on cached data from only one file. For example, data for a single file can be flushed without having to flush data for any other file. If you are building the LFFS for a new phone platform, you can configure the size of this cache by changing a constant in one of the LFFS configuration header files.

There is also a separate read-ahead cache that reads log entries in groups, for efficiency.

9.4.2.8 Error recovery

If, during a reclaim, the LFFS detects an erase failure on a block, then it marks the entire segment that contains that block as being bad (and no longer available for use). Again, it stores this information in the segment header. The LFFS then identifies another segment for reclaim, leaving the client unaware of the error.

If the LFFS detects a write failure on the current segment, then it reattempts the same write in the next available position on the same segment. It repeats this, moving further through the segment until the write eventually succeeds. This may require the LFFS to move on to the next free segment. Again, the client is unaware of any error. If it has suffered a write error, it is likely that the damaged sector will also suffer an erase error if it is ever reclaimed, which will cause it to be marked as bad at that point. However, assuming the damaged sector is still capable of being read, any valid data it contains will be moved to another segment as part of the normal reclaim process.

By configuring one of the LFFS configuration header files, developers who are creating a new phone platform can build the LFFS so that it keeps segments in reserve to replace bad segments, so that drive capacity isn't reduced in erase failure situations.

9.4.3 The FAT file system

Symbian OS uses the VFAT file system for user-data storage on various media types including removable media, internal RAM and NAND Flash.

On a FAT-formatted volume, the data area is divided into clusters, with a cluster being the smallest unit of data storage that can be allocated to a file. On a given volume, each cluster is the same size and is always a whole number of sectors (see Section 9.1.1.3). Cluster size varies between volumes, and depends on the size of the volume.

A File Allocation Table (FAT) structure is used to track how clusters are allocated to each file. Since the original version of the FAT file system became available, it has been enhanced to support larger volumes. Now there are different FAT file system types, corresponding to differences in the size of the entries used in the FAT data structure. These include FAT12 for 12-bit entries, FAT16 for 16-bit entries and FAT32 for 32-bit entries. Directory information is stored in a directory table, in which each table entry is a 32-byte data structure. The VFAT version of the standard supports long file names, up to 255 characters in length – previous versions supported only "8.3" filenames that can only have eight characters, a period, and a three-character extension. The FAT and VFAT standards are described in many publications and I will not describe them in any more detail here.

To ensure that Symbian OS phones are compatible with other operating systems, it was essential that we used the FAT file system on our removable media. Data on a removable media card that has been formatted and updated on a Symbian OS phone must be fully accessible when removed and introduced into other computer systems, such as a card reader connected to a PC – and vice versa. In some cases, compatibility with other systems can also mandate that internal drives be FAT formatted. This is because some Symbian OS phones support remote access from a host machine (such as a desktop computer) to one or more of their internal drives, by exposing these as USB mass storage devices. For this to work without a special driver on the host machine, these internal drives must be FAT-format.

Symbian OS always formats internal RAM drives using FAT16.

Symbian OS actually provides two builds of the FAT file system – one that supports only FAT12 and FAT16, and a second that supports FAT32 as well. This is because not all Symbian OS licensees require support for FAT32.

9.4.3.1 Rugged FAT version

We build both FAT12/16 and FAT32 in a rugged configuration by default – although developers who are creating a new phone platform can enable the standard version if they wish. The rugged FAT version provides tolerance to situations in which write operations are interrupted due to power failure. This only happens when there is an unexpected loss of battery power, not from the user's normal power down of the phone, because in this case the file server can complete the operation before turning off.

The rugged version alters the way in which the file system updates the FAT tables and directory entries, but this alone can't completely eliminate the possibility of an error due to unexpected power removal. However, it also incorporates a ScanDrive utility, which the file server runs when power is restored to the disk – and this can fix up any such errors. For example, ScanDrive can detect and correct inconsistencies between the FAT table and the directory entries, to reclaim lost clusters. It does this by generating its own version of the FAT table from analyzing the directory entries and then comparing this with the current FAT table. ScanDrive runs at system boot, but only if the phone has been unexpectedly powered down. In normal power down situations, the Symbian OS shutdown server (SHUTDOWNSRVS.EXE) sends notification to the file server of orderly shutdown, using the F32 method RFs::FinaliseDrives(). The file server passes notification down to the FAT file system, and this is then able to update a status flag on the FAT disk. When it starts up, the file system checks the status flag, allowing it to only run ScanDrive when it is needed.

However this power-safe, rugged scheme only applies if the underlying local media sub-system can guarantee atomic sector writes – that is, a sector involved in a write operation is never left in a partially modified state due to power removal, but is either updated completely, or left unmodified. We can provide this guarantee for internal FAT drives that use a translation layer over NAND Flash.

For removable media devices, unexpected power removal may result from the removal of the card from the phone, as well as from the loss of power from the battery. For these devices, we can't usually guarantee atomic sector writes. However, we can minimize the possibility of card corruption due to unexpected power removal, using schemes such as not allowing writes when the battery voltage is low. Another way of minimizing corruption is the use of a card door scheme that provides early warning of the possibility of card removal. Unfortunately these schemes can't catch everything – consider the situation where the phone is accidentally dropped, resulting in the battery being released during a write operation. We could protect against corruption in this scenario with the use of a backup battery that preserves system RAM while the main battery is missing, so that we can retry the original write operation when the main supply is restored. Unfortunately, the use of a backup battery is not popular with phone manufacturers, due to the increase in the bill of materials for the phone.

9.4.3.2 Caching

When we use the FAT file system on either removable media or NAND Flash drives, we always employ two caching schemes to improve performance.

The first of these is a cache for the FAT itself. The file system caches the entire FAT into RAM, for all drives formatted using FAT12 or FAT16, and for any drives formatted using FAT32 whose FAT is smaller than 128 KB. This is a "write-back with dirty bit" type of cache scheme, with the file system flushing all dirty segments at certain critical points throughout each file server operation. This cache is used so that short sequences of updates to the FAT can be accumulated and written in one go. The frequency of cache flushes is higher, for a given operation, if the file system is configured for rugged operation. The segment size within this cache is 512 bytes. This corresponds to the smallest unit of access for the sector-based media that the cache is used for.

However, for larger drives formatted with FAT32, the size of the FAT becomes too large for it to be entirely cached into RAM. Instead, only part of the table is cached. The cache stores up to 256 segments and employs an LRU (Least Recently Used) scheme when it needs to replace a segment. Each segment is still 512 bytes long.

The other type of cache, which we use on NAND Flash and removable media drives, is a metadata cache. This caches the most recently accessed directory entries together with the initial sectors of files. Caching the first part of a file improves the speed of the file server when it is handling client requests to read file UIDs. Each cache segment is again 512 bytes and the file system is built allowing a maximum cache size of 64 segments. Once more, we use an LRU replacement scheme. However, this is a "write through" type cache – it always reflects the contents of the drive.

9.4.3.3 User-data storage on NAND Flash

NAND Flash characteristics

In Section 9.4.2.1, I described the characteristics of NOR Flash. NAND Flash is similar. It is nonvolatile memory that can be erased and rewritten.

Write operations change bits from one to zero, but an entire block must be erased to change a bit from a zero to a one. Again, there is a limit to the number of times a block of NAND Flash can be erased and rewritten.

However, there are a number of differences between the characteristics of NAND and NOR Flash:

- Unlike NOR Flash, NAND Flash devices are not byte-addressable – they can only be read and written in page-sized units. (These pages are 512 bytes or larger, but are always smaller than the erase block size)

- The geometry and timing characteristics of NAND and NOR Flash are different. NAND devices tend to have smaller blocks than NOR devices. Program and erase operations are faster on NAND Flash

- NAND Flash has a low limit on the possible number of partial program cycles to the same page. (After being erased, all bits are in the "one" state. Writing to a page moves some of the bits to a "zero" state. The remaining bits at "one" can still be changed to zero without an erase, using a subsequent write operation to the same page. This is called a partial program cycle.)

As I mentioned at the start of Section 9.4.2, we designed the LFFS specifically to enable user-data storage on NOR Flash. The differences in the NAND Flash characteristics that I have listed mean that LFFS is not a suitable file system for user-data storage on NAND Flash. The most fundamental issue is the low limit on the number of partial page program cycles that are possible on NAND Flash. As we saw, LFFS relies on being able to perform partial programs to update the completion status of each log entry.

The Flash translation layer (FTL)

Instead, Symbian OS uses the FAT file system for user-data storage on NAND Flash. FAT is a file system better suited to the page read/write unit size of NAND.

However, because NAND pages have to be erased prior to a write, and because erase blocks contain multiple pages, we need an additional translation layer for NAND, to provide the sector read/write interface that FAT requires. This is the NAND Flash translation layer (FTL).

The translation layer also handles another characteristic of NAND Flash. When NAND devices are manufactured, they often contain a number of faulty blocks distributed throughout the device. Before the NAND device is shipped, its manufacturer writes information that identifies the bad blocks into a spare region of the NAND device. That is not all – as the FTL writes to good blocks on the device, there is a chance that these will fail to erase or program, and become bad. The likelihood of this occurring increases the more a block is erased. To handle these issues, the translation layer implements a Bad Block Manager (BBM), which interprets the bad block information from the manufacturer and updates it with information about any new bad blocks that it detects. The BBM also controls a reservoir of spare good blocks, and it uses these to replace bad ones encountered within the rest of the device.

The translation layer handles wear leveling, employing a scheme very similar to that used by LFFS. It also provides a system for ensuring the integrity of the data in situations of unexpected power removal, making sure that data already successfully committed to the device is not lost in such a situation – even if power removal occurs part-way through a write or erase operation. Indeed, the FTL is so robust that it can handle the situation in which power removal occurs while it is in the process of recovering from an earlier, unexpected, power removal.

The NAND FTL implementation may be split between a user-side file server extension (see Section 9.1.2) and a media driver. It can also be implemented wholly kernel-side in a media driver. The second scheme tends to result in a smaller number of executive calls between user-side code and the media driver which makes it slightly more efficient.

The first NAND FTL version released by Symbian employed a scheme split between a file server extension and a media driver. We had to split it this way on EKA1, and so we chose the same scheme for EKA2 to provide compatibility between the two versions of the kernel. We later implemented a version of the FTL for EKA2 entirely within a NAND media driver. Whichever scheme is used, the FTL and BBM software is generic to any NAND Flash device. However, the media driver contains a hardware interface layer, which is specific to the particular NAND device in use.

Figure 9.16 shows the components required to support user-data storage on NAND Flash memory.

File delete notification

The FTL operates more efficiently as the amount of free space on the drive increases, since it can make use of the unallocated space in its sector re-mapping process. When a file is truncated or deleted on a FAT device, any clusters previously allocated to the file that become free are marked as available for reuse within the FAT. Normally, the contents of the clusters themselves are left unaltered until they are reallocated to another file. But in this case, the underlying FTL can't benefit from the additional free space – it is not aware that the sectors associated with these clusters are now free. So, when the FAT file system is required to free up clusters – for example, in the call `CFatMountCB::DeleteL()` – it calls down to the next layer using the method:

```
CProxyDrive::DeleteNotify(TInt64 aPos, TInt aLength)
```

This provides notification that the area specified within the arguments is now free. If this layer is a file server extension implementing the FTL, then it can now make use of this information. If no extension is present, then the call can be passed down to the TBusLocalDrive interface, and on to the media driver where again an FTL can make use of the information.

9.4.3.4 Removable media systems

Those Symbian OS phones that support removable media devices must provide a hardware scheme for detecting disk insertion or removal, and it is the local media sub-system that interfaces with this. The file server needs to receive notification of these media change events so that it can handle the possible change of volume, and also so it can pass the information on to any of its clients that have registered for disk event notification.

I have already described (in Section 9.3.3.1) how the file server receives notification of a possible change of volume by registering a data member of the appropriate TDrive class with the local media sub-system.

I also mentioned (in Section 9.3.4) that a client might register for notification of disk events, such as the insertion of a new volume. Instead of using this same TDrive mechanism to handle client notifiers, the file server uses a slightly different scheme. It creates an instance of the CNotifyMediaChange class for each removable media socket. This is an active object that requests notification of media change events, again via the local media sub-system. Each time a request is completed, the active object handles any pending client notifiers and then reissues a request on the local media sub-system for the next media change event.

Media change events are involved in a third notification scheme. For certain critical media access failures, the file server sometimes needs to display a dialogue box on the screen prompting the user to take some action to avoid disk corruption. This dialogue box is launched by an F32 critical notifier. It is used by the FAT file system in situations where a read or write failure has occurred that could result in corruption of the metadata on a volume. These situations include updates to the FAT tables and directory entries, and also running the ScanDrive utility. The dialogue box is only displayed on particular read/write errors. For removable media, these include errors caused by card power-down as a result of a media change event – in this case, the dialogue box prompts the user to replace the disk immediately to avoid disk corruption.

We implement the critical notifier in the class CAsyncNotifier. Each drive can own an instance of this class, and any file system can use it to provide a notifier service. That said, currently only the FAT file system uses it.

CAsyncNotifier uses the RNotifier user library class, which encapsulates a session with the extended notifier server – part of the Symbian OS UI system. When a file system needs to raise a user notification, it creates a session with the notifier server and issues a request on it, specifying the text for the dialogue box. Until the user has responded to the notification, and the request completes back to the file server, the drive thread on which the error occurred is suspended. During this time the file server is unable to process any other requests for that drive. Once the notification has completed, the original operation can be reattempted if needed – for example if the user replaced the disk and selected the "retry" dialogue button.

Since the EKA2 file server has a separate thread per drive, the processing of requests on unaffected drives can continue as normal while a notification is active. It is not so simple to support user notification on the EKA1 version of F32. Here, because it has only a single thread, the file server has to nest its active scheduler so that it can accept a limited set of other requests while the notification is being handled.

File server clients can enable or disable critical notifiers on a per session basis using the method RFs::SetNotifyUser(). The default state is for notifiers to be enabled.

9.4.4 The read-only file system (ROFS)

The read-only file system is part of the scheme used to support the storage of code (that is, ROM components) on non-XIP media such as NAND Flash.

9.4.4.1 The core OS image

As I mentioned in Section 9.4.3.3, NAND Flash devices are not byte-addressable, and they can only be read or written in page-sized units. As a result, they do not support code execute in place (XIP). This means that we need a RAM-shadowing scheme for code stored on NAND devices – the code must be read from the Flash into RAM from where it is then executed. Code on the Flash device must be stored in separate partitions from those used for data storage. Since the code partition is a read-only area, we don't need a FAT format and we can use a simpler linear layout, which is similar to the layout we use for the ROM file system.

One approach we could take is to shadow the entire NAND code area. However, this would use up a lot of RAM! Instead, we normally shadow only a subset of the ROM components permanently, and load the remainder into RAM only when access to them is required.

If you are porting Symbian OS to a new phone platform, you can choose which OS components are permanently shadowed when you specify the contents of the ROM image. At a minimum, this needs to include the kernel, kernel extensions, media drivers, file server, file systems and ESTART. You can include additional components – obviously there is a trade-off between the speed gained by having a component permanently shadowed, against the amount of RAM this consumes. These permanently shadowed components are stored on the Flash device as a separate core OS image. At startup, a core loader program, which is one of the programs used to boot the OS, permanently shadows this entire image in RAM. The core loader does this shadowing before even the standard Symbian OS bootstrap has run.

The phone manufacturer can choose to have the entire core OS image compressed, to reduce the amount of Flash space this consumes. The core loader has to detect whether this is the case and decompress the image where necessary. However, the core OS image is loaded as a single entity and so the core loader does not need the ability to interpret the file system format within it.

9.4.4.2   The ROFS image

The remaining OS components, which are not included in the core OS image, are only loaded into RAM when they are required. The scheme we use loads entire executables and data files into RAM on demand, in much the same way as we load executables from a removable disk. This is not the same as a demand paging scheme, in which components are loaded at a finer granularity (that of a hardware page, usually 4 KB) and in which we would need a more proactive scheme to unload code from RAM that we deem to be no longer in active use.

The ROFS is the entity that reads these OS components from NAND Flash and interprets the linear format of this code area, which is known as the ROFS image.

The standard Symbian OS loader (which I discuss in Chapter 10, *The Loader*) copies entire executables and library files from the ROFS image to RAM, using the file server and the ROFS to read them. The ROFS image also contains data files, such as bitmap files. Clients of the file server issue requests to read sections of these data files, and again the file server uses ROFS to read them from NAND Flash memory. Individual executable files within the ROFS image may be compressed, and it is the job of the standard loader to detect this, and decompress them at load time.

ROFS uses the NAND media driver to read from the NAND device in the same way as the FAT file system does. The NAND region allocated for the ROFS code image may contain bad blocks and again ROFS uses the bad block manager in the media driver to interpret these.

To improve performance, ROFS caches all its metadata (its directory tree and file entries) in RAM. The ROFS file format places file UIDs in the metadata, as well as at the start of the file itself. This means that these UIDs are permanently cached, avoiding the need to make short, inefficient reads from the Flash to retrieve them.

ROFS also employs a small cache for the file data area.

Figure 9.16 shows all the components needed to support code and data storage on NAND Flash memory – including ROFS and the core loader.

9.4.4.3 Booting the OS from NAND Flash

Since it is not possible to execute code directly from NAND Flash memory, a phone using NAND Flash for code storage has to provide hardware assistance so that the processor is able to begin fetching code and can start to boot Symbian OS. Many platforms include a hardware boot loader. This is logic associated with the NAND device that includes a small RAM buffer, and it has the effect of making a small part of the start of the NAND device become XIP.

This XIP area is often very small, typically less than 1 KB, and may be too small to contain the core loader program. Instead a smaller miniboot program is normally the first code to execute, and its function is to locate the core loader program's image, copy it into RAM and then execute it.

Although, as we've seen, the NAND manufacturing process leaves a certain number of faulty blocks distributed throughout the device, usually the manufacturer of the device will guarantee that the first block is good. If the core loader can be contained within this block, then the miniboot program doesn't have to deal with bad blocks at all.

Next the core loader program executes. Its function is to locate the core OS image, copy it entirely into RAM and then find and execute the standard Symbian OS bootstrap. The core loader has to handle existing bad blocks within the core OS image, but not the detection and handling of new bad blocks. It may also have to decompress the core OS image.

The miniboot program and the core loader do not have access to the normal Symbian OS NAND media driver, and so they have to duplicate some of its functionality. If you are creating a new phone platform, you must provide miniboot and core loader programs to suit your particular NAND hardware configuration. Symbian provides reference versions of these, which you can customize.

You must program the following images into the NAND Flash memory for a phone to be able to boot from NAND Flash:

- The miniboot program

- The core loader program

- The core OS image

- The primary ROFS image (and possibly images for secondary ROFS partitions)

- A partition table providing information on the location of all these
  images.

As well as these, phone manufactures will often also program a prefor-
matted user data image into NAND Flash, so that this is available as soon
as the device is first booted.

Phone manufactures must produce tools to program this data into the
phone's NAND Flash memory. Symbian provides a reference tool which
we use on our standard hardware reference platforms, and which you can
refer to. This is the nandloader, NANDLOADER.EXE. When programming
NAND Flash, we include this tool in a normal text shell ROM image,
which we program onto our platform's NOR Flash memory. The platform
boots from this image and runs the nandloader which allows the user to
select and program the various component images into the NAND Flash.
These images can be included in the nandloader ROM image or supplied
separately on a removable media card. Finally the user can restart the
platform, which this time boots from the images now programmed onto
the NAND Flash.

9.4.5   The composite file system

The composite file system is unlike any of the file systems I've described
so far. Although it implements the file system API that I introduced in
Section 9.4.1, it doesn't directly use either the local media sub-system
or a file server extension, as a standard file system would. Instead, it
interfaces with a pair of child file systems. The composite file system is
another part of the scheme we use to support code storage on NAND
Flash.

Once the core loader has loaded the core OS into RAM, the standard
ROM file system (which is embedded into the file server) provides access
to its components in RAM. The ROFS provides access to the rest of the OS
components, which it copies from NAND Flash on demand. Normally,
the file server would mount two different file systems on two separate
drives, but file server clients expect to find all the ROM components on a
single drive – the Z: drive. So we use the composite file system to combine
both file systems. This file system is a thin layer, which simply passes
requests from the file server to either (or both of) the ROM file system or
the ROFS. The composite file system uses the concept of a primary and
secondary file system, where the primary file system is always accessed
first. In this case, ROFS is the primary file system, since the majority of
files are located there.

At system boot, the standard ROM file system is the only file system
that is accessible until ESTART loads and mounts the other file systems.
Before this, on a phone using NAND for code storage, only the core
OS components are available on the Z: drive. ESTART then loads the

composite file system, dismounts the standard ROM file system and mounts the composite file system on the Z: drive in its place. At this point the entire ROM image becomes available on the Z: drive.

Figure 9.16 shows the components required to support code and data storage on NAND Flash, including the composite file system – ECOMP.FSY.

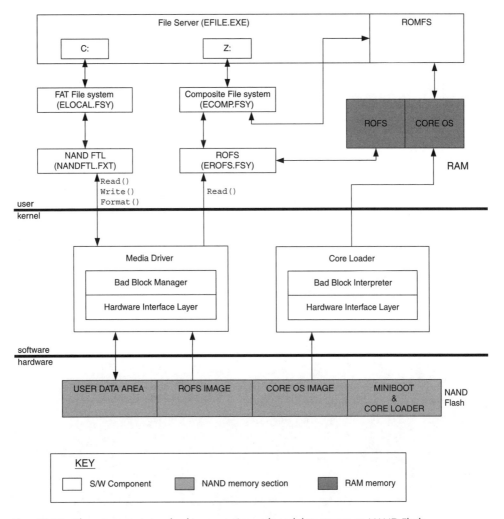

Figure 9.16   The components involved in supporting code and data storage on NAND Flash

9.5   Summary

In this chapter, I have described the F32 system architecture including a brief overview of the client API, followed by a more detailed description of the design of the file server. Next I described the file systems in general terms before looking in detail at the log Flash file system (LFFS), the FAT file system, the read-only file system (ROFS) and the composite file system. In Chapter 10, *The Loader*, I will describe the loader server, which is also part of the F32 component.

10

The Loader

by Dennis May and Peter Scobie

It said, "Insert disk #3" but only two will fit!
Unknown

The file server process contains a second server, the loader server, whose purpose is to load executables (that is, DLLs and EXEs). It runs in a separate thread from the main file server and is implemented using the Symbian OS client-server framework.

In this chapter I describe the process of loading executables and the management of executable code in Symbian OS. In Section 10.3, I show how the loader server operates: how it handles client requests, how it interacts with the file server and I introduce some of the kernel-side code management services. In Section 10.4, I describe kernel-side code management in more detail.

However, before any of this, we should start by examining the format of the executable files that the loader has to handle.

10.1 E32 image file format

This is the Symbian OS executable file format. Symbian provides tools to convert from standard object file formats into the E32 image format: you would use the PETRAN pre-processing tool to convert PE format files (as output by GCC98r2 for example). Similarly, you would use ELFTRAN to convert from the ELF format files produced by ARM's RealView compiler.

You can configure these conversion tools to produce compressed executable files and it is the responsibility of the loader to detect a compressed executable and decompress it on loading.

E32 image files consist of up of nine sections, in the order specified as follows:

1) The image header
The E32ImageHeader. I describe this in Appendix 2, *The E32Image-Header.*

2) Code section – .text
This section contains the executable code.

3) The constant data section – .rdata
This section contains constant (read-only) data. It doesn't exist as a separate entity in an E32 image file. It may exist in the PE or ELF format file from which the E32 image file is derived, but the tools then amalgamate it into the .text section.

4) The import address table (IAT)
This table contains an entry for each function imported by the executable, as follows:

Offset	Description
00	Ordinal of import 1
04	Ordinal of import 2
. . .	
$4(n-1)$	Ordinal of import n
4n	NULL

For each function that the executable imports, the file will contain an import stub function within the code section. When executed, each stub will load the program counter with the value from the corresponding entry of the IAT.

Therefore, when the executable is loaded, the loader has to fix up each entry in the IAT, replacing the ordinal number with the run address of the imported function. It has to calculate the address using the contents of the .idata section of this executable together with the .edata section of the DLL that exports the function requested.

Note that executables originating from ELF format files don't contain an IAT. For these, the tools fix up the import stubs directly – they obtain the location of the stub from the import data section.

The order of the entries in the IAT corresponds precisely with the order that imports are listed in the .idata section.

5) The export directory – .edata
The export directory is a table supplying the address of each function exported from this executable. Each entry holds the start address of the function as an offset relative to the start of the code section:

00	Address of 1st function exported from this executable.
04	Address of 2nd function exported from this executable.
. . .	
4n − 4	Address of last function exported from this executable.

The order of exports in the table corresponds to the order in the DEF file for this executable. The table is not null terminated. Instead, the number of entries in the table is available from the file's image header.

6) Initialized data section – .data

This section contains the initialized data values that are copied to RAM when this executable runs.

7) Import data section – .idata

This section contains data on each function that this executable imports. The loader uses this information to identify each referenced DLL that it also needs to load. Additionally, the loader uses this information to fix up each entry in the import address table (IAT).

The format of this section is as follows:

Field	Description
Size	A word holding the size of this section in bytes (rounded to 4-byte boundary).
Import block for DLL1	
Import block for DLL2	
. . .	. . .
Import block for DLLn	
Name of DDL1	NULL terminated ASCII string.
Name of DLL2	NULL terminated ASCII string.
. . .	. . .
Name of DLLn	NULL terminated ASCII string.

As well as the file name itself, the DLL name string also includes the required third UID. If the file was built with the EKA2 tool set, the name string will also contain the required version number of the DLL (see Section 10.3.1). The loader will have to match all of these when it searches for the imported DLL. The format of the name is as follows, with UID and version in hexadecimal:

```
<filename>{versionNum}[uid3]<extension>
for example, efsrv{00010000}[100039e4].dll
```

The format of each import block depends on whether the executable originated from a PE or an ELF format file. For PE derived files, it has the following format:

Offset	Description
00H	Offset of DLL name from start of .idata section.
04H	Number of imports for this DLL.

For PE-derived executables built with the EKA1 tool set, this import block also contains a list of ordinals for the DLL concerned. However, this information is a duplicate of that contained in the import address table, so import blocks no longer contain this information when built with the EKA2 tool set.

Import blocks for ELF derived files have the following format:

Offset	Description
00H	Offset of DLL name from start of .idata section.
04H	Number of imports for this DLL.
08H	The location of import stub for the 1st function imported from this DLL. (This is an offset within the code segment of the importing executable to the location that will be fixed up with the address of the imported function.)
0CH	The location of import stub for the 2nd function imported from this DLL.
...	...
	The location of import stub for the last function imported from this DLL.

8) Code relocation section
This section contains the relocations to be applied to the code section. The format of the table is shown next:

Offset	Description
00H	The size of the relocation section in bytes (rounded to 4-byte boundary).
04H	Number of relocations.
08H	Relocation information.
0CH	Relocation information.
...	...
Nn	00000H

The format used for the relocation information block differs slightly to the standard Microsoft PE format. It consists of a number of sub-blocks, each referring to a 4 KB page within the section concerned. Each sub-block is always a multiple of 4 bytes in size and has the following format:

Offset	Description
00H	The offset of the start of the 4 KB page relative to the section being relocated.
04H	The size of this sub-block in bytes.
08H	2 byte sub-block entry. The top 4 bits specify the type of relocation: 0 – Not a valid relocation. 1 – Relocate relative to code section. 2 – Relocate relative to data section. 3 – Try to work it out at load time (legacy algorithm). The bottom 12 bits specify the offset within the 4 K page of the item to be relocated.
0AH	2 byte sub-block entry.
...	...

9) Data relocation section
This section contains the relocations to be applied to the data section. The format of the table is the same as that for code relocations.

The nine sections that I have just listed apply to the structure of the executable files as they are stored on disk. However, once an executable has been loaded by the Symbian OS loader, it consists of two separately relocatable regions (or sections). The first is the code section, which includes the code, import stubs, constant data, IAT (if present) and the export directory (.edata). The second is the data section, which includes the un-initialized data (.bss) and initialized data (.data).

10.2   ROM image file format

The format that I described previously applies to executables that are located on drives which are not execute-in-place (XIP) – for example, executables contained within a NAND Flash ROFS image, on the user-data drive (C:) or a removable media disk (D:). On such media, executable code first has to be loaded into RAM (at an address which is not fixed beforehand) before it can be run. However, by definition, for executables stored in XIP memory (such as ROM) there is no need to load the code into RAM for execution.

The ROMBUILD tool assembles the executables and data files destined for the ROM into a ROM image. The base address of the ROM and the address of the data sections are supplied to this tool as part of the ROM specification (that is, the obey file) when it is run. In fact, for certain executables, ROMBUILD itself calculates the address of the data sections. These include fixed processes, variant DLLs, kernel extensions, device drivers and user-side DLLs with writeable static data. With this information, ROMBUILD is able to pre-process the executables, perform the relocations and fix up the import stubs. The result is that on XIP memory, executables have a format that is based on E32 image format but differs in certain ways, which I will now list:

- They have a different file header, TRomImageHeader, which is described in Appendix 3, *The TRomImageHeader*

- They have no IAT; it is removed and each reference to an IAT entry is converted into a reference to the associated export directory entry in the corresponding DLL

- They have no import data (.idata) section; it is discarded

- They have no relocation information; it is discarded

- They include a DLL reference table after the .data section. This is a list of any libraries referenced, directly or indirectly, by the executable that have static data. In other words, libraries with initialized data (.data) or un-initialized data (.bss) sections. The file header contains a pointer to the start of this table. For each such DLL referenced in the table, the table holds a fixed-up pointer to the image header of the DLL concerned. See the following table:

Offset	Description
00H	Flags.
02H	Number of entries in table.
04H	Image header of 1st DLL referenced.
08H	Image header of 2nd DLL referenced.
. . .	. . .
nn	Image header of last DLL referenced.

These differences mean that the size of these files on ROM is smaller than the corresponding E32 image file size.

Another consequence of the pre-processing of the IAT and the removal of the import section for ROM files is that it is not possible to over-ride a statically linked DLL located in ROM by placing a different version of this referenced DLL on a drive checked earlier in the drive search order, such as C:.

10.3   The loader server

The `RLoader` class provides the client interface to the loader and is contained in the user library, `EUSER.DLL`. However, user programs have no need to use this class directly – and indeed they must not use it since it is classified as an internal interface. Instead the `RLoader` class is used privately by various file server and user library methods. These include:

- `RProcess::Create()` – starting a new process
- `RLibrary::Load()` – loading a DLL
- `User::LoadLogicalDevice()` – loading an LDD
- `RFs::AddFileSystem()` – adding a file system.

`RLoader` is derived from `RSessionBase` and is a handle on a session with the loader server. Each request is converted into a message that is sent to the loader server.

Unlike the file server, the loader server supports only a small number of services. These include:

- Starting a process – loading the executable concerned

- Loading a DLL

- Getting information about a particular DLL. (This includes information on the DLL's UID set, security capabilities and module version)

- Loading a device driver

- Loading a locale

- Loading a file system or file server extension.

10.3.1 Version numbering

In EKA1, it is only possible for one version of a particular executable to exist in a Symbian OS phone at any time. This is not the case for EKA2, whose loader and build tools support version numbering – a scheme that associates a version number with each executable. In this scheme, import references state the version number of each dependency. This makes it possible for us to make changes to an executable that are not binary compatible with the previous version, since we can now place both the new and old versions on the device simultaneously. The import section of any preexisting binary that has a dependency on this executable will indicate that it was built against the old version, allowing the loader to link it to that version. At the same time, the loader links new or re-built binaries to the new version. In some cases, rather than have two entire versions of the same DLL, the old version can be re-implemented as a shim DLL, using the functionality in the new DLL, but presenting the original DLL interface.

The EKA2 tools tag each executable with a 32-bit version number, which is stored in the image file header (see Appendix 2, *The E32ImageHeader* and Appendix 3, *The TRomImageHeader*, for details). This number is made up of a 16-bit major and a 16-bit minor number. Regarding linkage, each entry in an executable's import table now specifies the required version number of the DLL concerned (see Section 10.1 for details). Where two or more versions of an executable exist on a device, both will generally reside in the same directory to save the loader searching additional directories. (Indeed, if platform security is enabled, they must reside in the same restricted system directory.) To prevent file name clashes, older versions have the version number appended to the file name (for example, efsrv{00010000}.dll), whereas the latest version has an unadorned name (for example, efsrv.dll). When searching for a candidate executable to load, the loader ignores any version number in the file name – but subsequently checks the version number in the header.

The EKA2 tools tag an executable with a default version number of either 1.0 (for GCC98r2 binaries) or 10.0 (for binaries built with an EABI compliant compiler). The same applies for the default version specified in each element of the import table. This allows inter-working with binaries built with pre-EKA2 versions of the tools, which are assumed to have the version 0.0. (Executables which pre-date versioning can only ever be introduced on non-XIP media. This is because all ROM resident binaries in EKA2-based systems will be built with the new tools.)

We assign a new version number to a DLL each time its published API is changed. If the change is backward compatible (for example, just adding new APIs) and all executables that worked with the original will continue to work with the new version, then we only increment the minor number.

When the new version removes or breaks an existing API, then we increment the major number and reset the minor number to zero. We assign modified APIs a new ordinal number, and remove the original ordinal (leaving a hole). This means that, whether an API is removed or modified, it appears that it has been removed. Of course, it will generally be the case that we break compatibility for just a small number of APIs and the majority of APIs will remain compatible. Executables that don't use removed APIs can then continue to run successfully against the new version. So, whenever APIs are removed, we include information in the image header to indicate which exports are affected (see Appendix 2, *The E32ImageHeader*, for more details).

When it is loading an executable and resolving import dependencies, if the loader finds more than one DLL in the search path that matches the requested name, UID and security capabilities, but has differing version numbers, then it employs the following selection algorithm:

1. If there is a DLL in this set with the requested major version number and a minor version number greater than or equal to the requested minor version number, then it uses that one. If there is more than one of these, then it uses the one with the highest minor version number

2. If no DLL exists satisfying (1), the loader looks for a DLL with a higher major version number than the one requested. If there is more than one of these, then it selects the one with the lowest major version number and the highest minor version number. If the executable does not request any exports that no longer exist in this DLL, then the loader uses it

3. If no DLL exists satisfying (1) or (2), the loader looks for a DLL with the requested major version number. If there is more than one of these, it finds the one with the highest minor version number. If the executable currently being loaded does not request any exports that are not present in this DLL, then the loader uses it

4. If no DLL exists satisfying either (1), (2) or (3) then the load fails.

An implication of the previous algorithm is that as the loader searches for an executable across multiple drives (and multiple paths in non-secure mode), it can't afford to stop at the first match. Instead it has to continue to the end of the search and then evaluate the best match. Fortunately, platform security cuts down the number of paths which have to be searched. The loader cache, which I describe in Section 10.3.3, also reduces the impact of this searching.

10.3.2   Searching for an executable

The EKA2 version of F32 is normally built with platform security enabled – see Chapter 8, *Platform Security*, for more on this. In this secure version, the loader will only load executables from the restricted system area, which is located in the "\sys \bin" directory of a given drive.

In non-secure mode, the loader will load executables from any directory. However, there are a default set of directories where executables are generally located and the loader scans these directories when searching for an executable to load.

10.3.2.1   *Search rules on loading a process*

When a client calls RProcess::Create() to start a new process, it specifies the filename of the executable (and optionally the UID type). If the filename includes the drive and path, then the task of locating the executable is straightforward. When either of these is not supplied, the loader has a fixed set of locations that it searches. This set is much more limited when platform security is enabled. The search rules that it uses are as follows:

1.   If the filename includes a path but no drive letter, then the loader searches only that path, but it does this for all 26 drives

2.   If the filename doesn't contain a path, then instead the loader searches each of the paths that I will now list, in the order given. (Again, for each of these, if a drive letter was supplied then the loader searches these paths only on this specified drive. However, if no drive was supplied either, then it checks all listed paths on all 26 drives)

    ○   sys\bin

    ○   system\bin (non-secure mode only)

    ○   system\programs (non-secure mode only)

    ○   system\libs (non-secure mode only).

When searching all 26 drives, the search order starts with drive Y: and then works backwards through to drive A:, followed finally by the Z: drive. Searching the Z: drive last makes it possible for us to over-ride a particular EXE in the ROM drive by replacing it with an updated version on an alternative drive that is checked earlier in the search order, for example, the C: drive.

When loading a process, the loader follows these rules to select which executable to load:

- Check that the filename and extension match

- Check that the UID type matches (if specified)

- Out of all possible matches, select the one with the highest version number. (Remember, the selection algorithm I described in Section 10.3.1 applies only when resolving import dependencies.)

Once the process executable is loaded, the loader goes on to resolve all its import dependencies. For a non-XIP executable, the name of each DLL that it statically links to is contained in the import data section of the image. The module version and third UID are included in the DLL name (as I discussed in Section 10.1) – but the path and drive are not. Therefore the loader again has to search a fixed set of locations for each dependency:

1. The drive and path that the process executable was loaded from

2. All of the paths listed, in the order given, on all 26 drives in turn:
   - `sys\bin`
   - `system\bin` (non-secure mode only)
   - `system\libs` (non-secure mode only).

When loading DLL dependencies, the properties that the loader checks when searching for a match are more substantial:

- Check that the filename and extension match

- Check that the third UIDs match

- Check that the candidate DLL has sufficient platform security capabilities compared with the importing executable. Refer to Section 8.4.2.1 for precise details of this capability check

- Check that the module versions are compatible. This could potentially include checking the export table bitmap in the image header of a candidate DLL to ensure that an export hasn't been removed.

As I mentioned in Section 10.3.1, when resolving import dependencies, the version numbering selection scheme means that the loader must continue to the end of the search and evaluate the best match.

10.3.2.2   *Search rules when loading a library*

When a client calls `RLibrary::Load()` to dynamically load a library, it may provide a path list as well as the filename of the DLL. Again, if the filename includes the drive and path, the loader loads the DLL from that location. However, if it does not, then the loader searches each of the paths specified in the path list before searching the standard paths for DLL loading, which I listed in the previous paragraph. Again, once the DLL is loaded, the loader goes on to resolve its import dependencies in the same way as I described previously.

10.3.3   The loader cache

From the previous section, you can see that the loading of an executable that has dependencies can involve the loader searching many directories on multiple drives. Furthermore, to determine if a candidate executable fully matches the criteria required by the client or importing executable, then the loader must read header information from those files that match the required filename.

To read directory entries and file headers, the loader server needs to makes requests on the file server and so it permanently has a file server session open. But to optimize the speed at which executables are loaded, and to reduce the number of requests made to the file server, we implemented a loader cache.

For a small number of directories, the loader caches the names of every file that they contain. It stores only the files' "rootnames" in ASCII. The "rootname" is the basic name and extension with any version or UID information removed. We use ASCII since names of executables do not include Unicode characters. (As I showed in Section 10.1, the import section of the image file specifies the names of implicitly linked libraries as 8-bit strings, so an executable with a Unicode name cannot be accommodated within the E32 image format.)

When the loader searches for an executable, if it gets a possible "hit" on a cached root name entry, it further populates the entry (if it hasn't already done so) opening the file and reading the image header to extract the following file data:

- UID triplet

- Module version

- Security information

- Export bitmap – for V-formatted headers (see Appendix 2, *The E32ImageHeader*).

The cache can contain file entries for up to six different directories. It maintains all the file entries for these directories for every mounted drive on the system. It also stores the path to each directory in a linked list.

The class diagram for the loader cache is shown in Figure 10.1. We encapsulate each cached directory by a TDirectoryCacheHeader object. This has an array of pointers, iCache, to all its cached file entries, each of which is represented by an instance of a TFileCacheRecord class, holding the rootname of the file and other cached file data. The pointers are sorted by name, allowing us to perform a binary search for a given rootname.

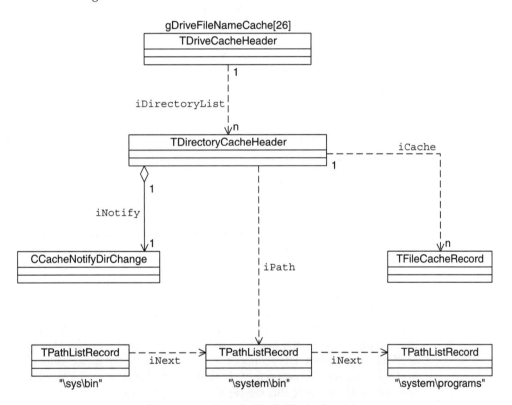

Figure 10.1 Class diagram for the loader cache

We represent each of the 26 drives by a TDriveCacheHeader object; this has a list: iDirectoryList of all the current cached directories on it.

We encapsulate the path name of every cached directory by a TPath-ListRecord object; there is a linked list of up to six of these. In fact, the loader always caches the default directories that it uses. So, in non-secure mode, it always caches these directories: sys\bin, system\bin,

system\programs and system\libs. In secure mode, it always
caches the directory sys\bin. Because of this, the loader only recy-
cles the remainder of the six entries between other directories. Because
the loader tends to search the same paths on each drive, for each directory
path there will generally be a corresponding directory cache on each of
the active drives.

When performing a search, the loader quickly iterates through the
path list, checking whether the directory in question is already cached.
Assuming it is, the loader navigates to the corresponding TDirectoryCacheHeader object via the appropriate drive object, where it can
then scan through each of the file entries.

The cache must accurately reflect the directory filenames for those
directories that it holds. Any changes to these must trigger a refresh before
the next query results are returned. The loader uses file server notifications
for this purpose – one for each drive\path. The CCacheNotifyDir-
Change class handles change notification. Each time a notification is
triggered, the loader destroys that directory cache for the corresponding
drive. This has the effect of forcing a cache reload for that directory when
the drive\path is next queried.

10.3.4 Code and data section management

On Symbian OS, the low level abstraction describing a segment of code
is the DCodeSeg class, a kernel-side object that I will describe in detail
in Section 10.4.1. This class represents the contents of an executable
that has been relocated for particular code and data addresses. Each
DCodeSeg object has an array of pointers to the other code segments to
which it links. In this section I will concentrate on how the loader uses
DCodeSeg objects.

The code segment object for a non-XIP image file owns a region of
RAM, and it is into this that the loader copies the code and data prior
to execution. The kernel allocates space in this RAM region for the code
section, the constant data section, the IAT (if present), the export directory
and the initialized data section, in that order. The loader applies code
and data relocations to this segment.

XIP image files, by definition, can have their code executed directly
from the image file. Likewise, the initialized data section and export
directory can be read directly. Because of this, there is no need for a RAM
region and instead the DCodeSeg object just contains a pointer to the
ROM image header for that file.

The loader needs to create new code segments and manage those that
it has already created. For this purpose, it has a private set of executive
functions, grouped with other loader services into the E32Loader class,
which is contained in the user library. Only threads in the file server

process may use these functions – the kernel panics any other thread trying to use them.

Once it has created a code segment for non-XIP media, the kernel returns the base addresses of the code area and the initialized data area within the segment to the loader. These are known as the code load and data load addresses respectively, and the loader uses them when copying in the various sections from the image file. The kernel also returns the code and data run addresses, and the loader uses this information when applying code and data relocations.

To conserve RAM, the kernel shares code segments whenever possible, and generally only one is required for each executable, even when this is shared between processes – I list the only exceptions later, in Section 10.4.1. So, for example, where a process has been loaded twice, generally the kernel will create only one main code segment for that process. Both processes have their own separate global data chunks, however. When each of these processes is first run, the contents of the initialized data section is copied out of the code segment into this global data chunk.

10.3.5 Loader classes

In Figure 10.2 I show the main classes that the loader server uses. The E32Image class encapsulates a single executable image. When starting a process or dynamically loading a DLL, the loader creates an instance

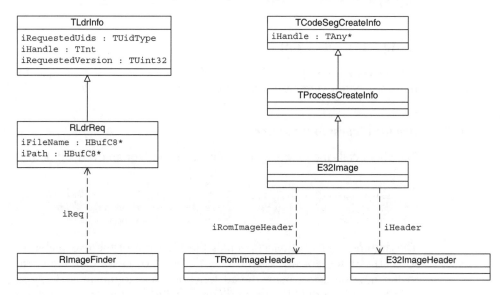

Figure 10.2 Class diagram for the loader server

of this class for the main executable and each statically linked DLL. (For non-XIP media, that includes every implicitly linked DLL, for XIP media, it only includes those which have static data.) The E32Image class has a pointer to a header object appropriate to the type of executable – either a TRomImageHeader object for XIP or an E32ImageHeader object for non-XIP media. The object denoted by iHeader holds a RAM copy of the entire E32ImageHeader, whereas iRomImageHeader points directly to the original header in ROM.

The E32Image class is derived from the class TProcessCreate-Info, which adds information that is only required when creating a new process – such as stack size, heap size and so on. In turn, TProcess-CreateInfo is derived from TCodeSegCreateInfo, which is used to assemble the data required to create a DCodeSeg object. The data member iHandle is a pointer to corresponding kernel-side DCodeSeg object and is used as a handle on it.

The RLdrReq class encapsulates a request on the loader. This is used to store request information copied from the client thread, such as the filename of the executable to load or a path list to search. It is derived from the TLdrInfo class, which is used to pass request arguments from client to server and, if a load request completes successfully, to return a handle on a newly loaded executable back to the client.

The loader uses the RImageFinder class when searching for a particular image file. To perform a search, this uses a reference to an RLdrReq object, iReq, which is the specification for the file being searched for.

10.3.6 Loading a process from ROM

Let us look at the steps involved in loading a process – first looking at the more straightforward case where this is being loaded from ROM.

10.3.6.1 Issuing the request to the server

The client calls the following user library method (or an overload of it):

```
TInt RProcess::Create(const TDesC &aFileName, const TDesC &aCommand,
                      const TUidType &aUidType, TOwnerType aType)
```

The argument aFileName specifies the filename of the executable to load. The descriptor aCommand may be used to pass a data argument to the new process's main thread function. The argument aUidType specifies a triplet of UIDs which the executable must match and aType defines the ownership of the process handle created (current process or current thread).

This method creates an RLoader session object and calls its Con-nect() method, which results in a connect message being sent to the server. Once the connection is established, control returns to the client thread. This then calls RLoader::LoadProcess(), which assembles the arguments passed from the client into a message object and sends this to the server. The kernel then suspends the client thread until the loader completes the request.

On receipt of the message, the server calls the request servicing function belonging to the relevant session, CSessionLoader::ServiceL(). This creates an RLdrReq, a loader request object, and populates it with data such as the filename, command descriptor and so on, reading these from the client thread. Next it allocates an E32Image object for the main process executable and calls the LoadProcess() method on it. Figure 10.3 illustrates this first phase.

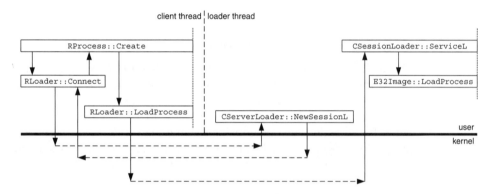

Figure 10.3 Issuing the request to the loader server

10.3.6.2 *Locating the process executable*

The next task to be performed is to search for the main executable file. The loader creates an RImageFinder object and sets its member iReq to the newly created request object, which contains the data specifying the executable. It calls the finder's Search() method – commencing the search scheme as outlined in the first part of Section 10.3.2.1. Assuming the search is successful, the loader now populates the main E32Image object with information on the executable file it has found, by calling the E32Image::Construct() method.

Figure 10.4 shows this second phase. Note that we assume here that the paths searched are not held in the loader cache, and so searching involves making requests on the file server to read the directory entries. The loader also needs to open candidate files to read information from their ROM image header, but this is not shown in the figure. Because the entire ROM image is always mapped into user-readable memory,

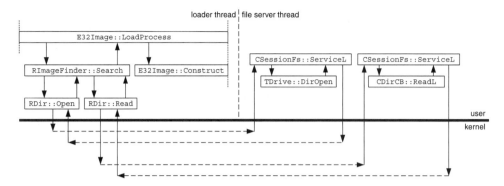

Figure 10.4   Locating the process executable

the loader can access the ROM image headers via a pointer rather than
having to use the file server to read them.

10.3.6.3   Creating the code segment and process

The next stage is to check whether a DCodeSeg object corresponding to this executable already exists (that is, the executable is already
currently loaded). To do this, the loader uses the executive function
E32Loader::CodeSegNext() to request that the kernel search its
entire list of code segments looking for one with a ROM image header
pointer that matches with the one about to be loaded. If a match is found,
the loader sets E32Image::iHandle for this segment, and then opens
it for a second process.

The loader now calls the executive function E32Loader::Process-
Create() to request that the kernel create the process structure, main
thread and global data chunk. This results in a DProcess object being
created for the process. If no DCodeSeg object was found to exist earlier,
this in turn leads to the creation of a DCodeSeg object for this executable.
As I have said, since this is a code segment for a ROM executable, there
is no associated memory area and no need to load any code into the
segment from the executable file or perform any code relocations.

I describe this phase of process loading in more detail at the start of
Section 10.4.3.

10.3.6.4   Processing imports

Next the loader must load any DLLs that the executable depends on and
which contain static data. To do this, it gets the address of the DLL reference table from the ROM image header and starts to process the entries.
Each entry holds a pointer to the image header of the DLL concerned
and, for each, the loader generates a further E32Image object, which
it then populates with information read from the corresponding image

header. The loader must also obtain a `DCodeSeg` object for each entry. This is a procedure that starts in a similar manner to the one performed earlier – searching through the list of existing code segments. However, if it needs a new `DCodeSeg` object, the loader calls the executive function `E32Loader::CodeSegCreate()` to create the object, followed by `E32Loader::CodeSegAddDependency()` to register the dependency in code segments between importer and exporter. If any dependencies themselves link to other DLLs, then they too must be loaded and the loader may call the function that handles loading dependant DLLs, `E32Image::LoadDlls()`, recursively to process these.

Now the loader calls the executive function `E32Loader::CodeSegLoaded()` for each new `DCodeSeg` object created (except that of the `DCodeSeg` belonging to the process executable itself) to mark these as being loaded.

I describe the kernel's involvement in this DLL loading in more detail in Section 10.4.4.

Figure 10.5 shows the program flow as the loader creates the process and handles its import dependencies.

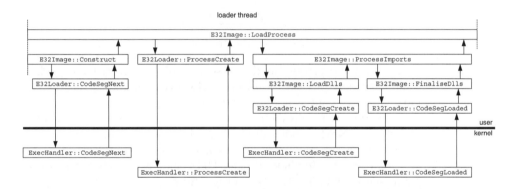

Figure 10.5   Creating the process and handling its import dependencies

10.3.6.5   Completing the request

In the final stage of loading a process, the loader calls the executive function `E32Loader::ProcessLoaded()` to update the state of the new process's thread. (If the `DCodeSeg` object of the process executable is new, and not shared from a preexisting process, this internally marks the `DCodeSeg` object as being loaded.) This function also generates a handle on the new process, relative to the original client thread. The loader then writes the handle back to the client.

Next, the loader deletes all the image objects it has created for the executables involved and closes its own handle on the new process.

Finally it completes the original load process message, and control returns to the client thread. This closes the RLoader session object and the method RProcess::Create() finally returns.

I describe the kernel involvement in this final phase in more detail at the end of Section 10.4.3.

Figure 10.6 shows this last phase.

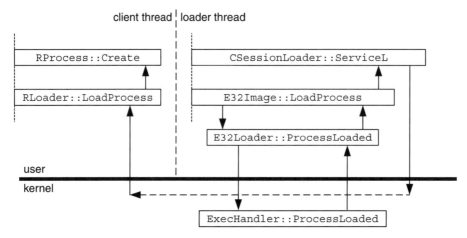

Figure 10.6 Completing the request

Assuming the process load was successful, the client then needs to resume the new process for it to run. However, the loader has done its job by this stage and is not involved in this.

The kernel then calls the process entry point, which creates the main thread heap. Next it copies the initialized data section to its run address and clears the un-initialized data area. Then it calls constructors for the EXE itself and for implicitly linked DLLs. Finally it calls the process's public entry point, the E32Main() function.

There are a number of differences in the way an executable is loaded from ROM on EKA2, compared to EKA1. Firstly, in EKA1 a third server, the kernel server, is involved; this runs in supervisor mode. The loader makes a request on the kernel server, asking it to create the new process. On EKA2, process creation is done in supervisor mode too – but in the context of the loader server. Secondly, in EKA1, the loader copies the initialized data section from ROM to the global data run address as part of the process load operation. However, in EKA2, this data copying is performed kernel-side, and is deferred until the initialization phase of process execution.

10.3.7 Loading a process from non-XIP media

This is similar to the loading of a process from XIP media, but more complex. Since the media is non-XIP, the code must be loaded into RAM for execution. Also, since the import sections and relocations have not been fixed up in advance, these sections need to be processed too.

10.3.7.1 Locating the process executable

The first difference occurs at the point where the loader searches for the process executable. If it needs to load header information from a candidate file (on a loader cache "miss"), then this requires a full file server read request, rather than relying on the ROM image being memory mapped.

10.3.7.2 Creating the code segment and process

The next difference occurs when the loader calls `E32Loader::ProcessCreate()` and the kernel creates a `DCodeSeg` object for the process executable. Since the process is not XIP, the kernel allocates a RAM code segment, associates this with the `DCodeSeg` object and returns the code load address within this segment.

The loader now needs to load the entire code section from the image file into this code segment at the code load address. If it is a compressed

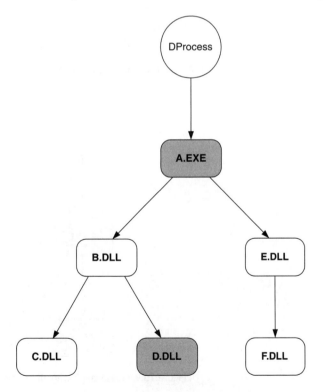

Figure 10.7 Sample non-XIP code graph

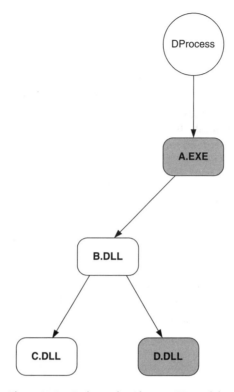

Figure 10.8   Code graph with some XIP modules

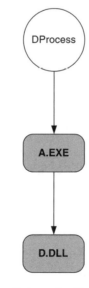

Figure 10.9   Code graph with all XIP modules

executable, the loader also needs to decompress the code section as it loads it. However, unlike on EKA1, the code segment does not have user-write permissions and so the loader can't directly copy data into it. Instead it uses an executive function to perform this in supervisor mode. If decompression is required, the loader reads portions of the code from the file into a buffer, decompresses it, and then makes use of the user library function `UserSvr::ExecuteInSupervisorMode()` to move it from buffer to code segment in supervisor mode. If decompression isn't needed, then no special scheme is required to transfer the code in supervisor mode. The loader simply issues a file server read request, specifying the code load address as the target address. A media driver will perform the transfer and this can use the kernel inter-thread copy function to write to the code segment.

The loader then reads all the rest of the image (after the code section) from the file into a temporary image buffer in one operation, again decompressing if necessary.

Next the loader checks the header information to determine whether the file contains a code relocation section. If so, the loader reads the relocation information from the image buffer and calls a function in supervisor mode to perform each of the relocations on the code section just loaded. (This essentially involves the loader calculating the difference between the code run address provided by the kernel and the base address that the code was linked for. Then it applies this adjustment to a series of 32 bit addresses obtained from the relocation section – see Section 10.1 for more detail.)

If the executable contains an export directory, then the loader fixes up each entry for the run address and writes it into the kernel-side code segment, after the IAT. Again, it uses an executive function to perform this in supervisor mode. (This is only required for PE-derived images. ELF marks export table entries as relocations, so the loader deals with them as part of its code relocation handling.)

If the executable contains an initialized data section, then the loader now copies this from the image buffer into the code segment at the data load address supplied (which is in fact immediately after the code, IAT and export directory).

If the image contains a data relocation section, then the loader applies these relocations in much the same way as it handled code relocations.

10.3.7.3 Processing imports

Next the loader must load all the DLLs referenced by this executable that are not already loaded (rather than just those that contain static data as was the case for XIP images). The procedure is similar to that described for an XIP executable. However, with non-XIP files, the dependency information is contained in the import section rather than a DLL reference table and it specifies the names of the DLLs rather than pointers to their image headers. Hence, for each import block, the loader has to follow the DLL search sequence described in Section 10.3.2.1. It reads each import block from the image buffer and processes it in turn. If a dependency needs to be loaded from non-XIP media, the loader again has to load and relocate its code and data sections, fix up the export tables and so on, in much the same way that it is loading the main executable.

Once this is done, the loader now has to fix up the IAT for the main executable and any dependencies that it has just loaded from non-XIP media. It examines the import sections of each of these executables, which are now loaded in a series of image buffers. It processes the import blocks in turn, identifying the corresponding exporter and loading its export table into a buffer. Then it calls a supervisor function to fix up the entries in the IAT that correspond with this export table.

Once it has processed all the dependencies, the process load request now continues in much the same way as it did for XIP media.

For executables loaded from non-XIP media, the calling of the executive function `E32Loader::CodeSegLoaded()` for the new `DCodeSeg` objects marks the point when the loader has finished loading any data into these segments.

10.3.8   Loading a library file

There are various overloads of the method to load a library but all eventually call:

```
TInt RLibrary::Load(const TDesC& aFileName, const TDesC& aPath,
                const TUidType& aType, TUint32 aModuleVersion)
```

The argument `aFileName` specifies the name of the DLL to be loaded. The descriptor `aPath` contains a list of path names to be searched, each separated by a semicolon. The argument `aType` specifies a triplet of UIDs which the DLL must match and `aModuleVersion` specifies the version that the DLL must match. As versioning was introduced for EKA2, this final argument is not present in the EKA1 version of the method.

This method first creates an `RLoader` session object and establishes a connection with the loader server. Next it calls `RLoader::Load-Library()`, which assembles the request arguments into a message object and sends this to the server.

On receipt of the message, the server handles the request in a similar manner to process load requests. It reads the arguments from the client thread and searches for the specified DLL, following the sequence described in Section 10.3.2.2. Then it creates a `DCodeSeg` object for the DLL and, if loading from non-XIP media, copies the code and initialized data sections into this segment, performing any relocations necessary.

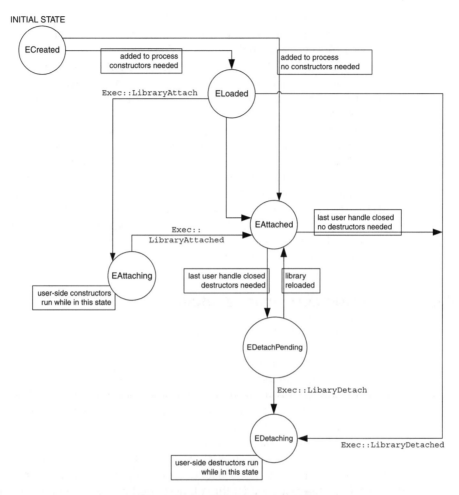

Figure 10.10 DLibrary state machine

Next it processes any dependencies for the DLL and marks every new code segment created as now being fully loaded.

Next it calls the executive function, `E32Loader::Library Create()`, which creates a `DLibrary` object and returns a handle to it. See Section 10.4.4 for more details on this.

Finally, the loader server writes the handle back to the client, deletes the image objects it has created and completes the load library message. Control returns to the client thread which closes the `RLoader` session object.

If the library was loaded successfully, then the method `RLibrary::Init()` is called, still in the context of the client thread. This in turn calls the executive function `E32Loader::LibraryAttach()` to extract the list of entry points for the DLL and all its dependencies. Each entry point is called in turn, passing in the value `KModuleEntryReasonProcess-sAttach` as the entry reason. This runs any C++ constructor functions for static objects associated with these DLLs.

Finally, a call of the executive function `E32Loader::Library-Attached()` signals that the entry points have been completed – marking the library as being attached. The method `RLibrary::Load()` now returns.

Note that, in EKA2, the public DLL entry-point, `E32Dll(TDll-Reason)` is no longer invoked. This function must be present in every EKA1 DLL, to be called when the DLL is attached to or detached from a process or thread. Unfortunately, this entry-point system cannot provide any guarantees that `E32Dll()` will be called with the appropriate parameter at the specified time. Because it is not possible to support this functionality reliably, EKA2 removes support for it. This removal simplifies the kernel-side architecture for managing dynamically loaded code, which improves reliability and robustness.

10.4 Kernel-side code management

The kernel maintains a representation of all the code resident in the system. The representation includes information on which modules link to which other modules (the code graph), which processes each module is used by and whether a given module consists of XIP ROM-resident code or non-XIP RAM-loaded code. The generic concepts involved are implemented in the Symbian OS kernel, but the memory model is responsible for the details of how memory is allocated for RAM-loaded code, and how it is mapped into the address space of each process.

The kernel and memory model only allocate memory for code storage and store information about loaded code; they do not actually load the code. The user-mode loader thread, described in the preceding sections, is responsible for loading images from the file system into RAM, relocating them to the addresses allocated by the kernel and resolving linkages to other modules prior to execution.

10.4.1 Code segments

As we have seen, the main object involved in the management of code is the code segment (`DCodeSeg`). This represents the contents of a single image file (EXE or DLL) relocated for particular code and data addresses. Note that in some memory models, the kernel will create more than one code segment from the same image file if different data section addresses are required. Of course this is expensive in terms of RAM usage, so it only happens if absolutely necessary. The kernel only loads multiple copies where a code segment has writeable static data and is loaded into multiple processes in such a way that the data cannot be at the same address in all those processes. For example, on the moving memory model, a fixed process cannot have its data at the same address as a non-fixed process.

A code segment can be created from an execute-in-place (XIP) image file, in which case it just contains a pointer to the TRomImageHeader for that file. Alternatively it can be created from a non-XIP image file; in this case the code segment owns an amount of RAM into which the loader copies the code. The kernel keeps all code segments on three separate lists. There is a doubly linked list (DCodeSeg::GlobalList) to which it adds code segments in order of creation. There is an array of pointers to DCodeSeg, sorted in lexicographic order of the root name (DCodeSeg::CodeSegsByName). Finally there is an array of pointers to DCodeSeg sorted in order of code run address (DCodeSeg::CodeSegsByAddress). The kernel uses the two sorted lists to allow it to perform a fast binary search for code segments by name, and to allow fast location of the code segment that contains a given run address (to enable C++ exception unwinding to work). The kernel protects these lists, and all other aspects of the global code graph, by the DCodeSeg::CodeSegLock mutex.

Each code segment has an array of pointers to the other code segments to which it implicitly links, thus defining a global code graph (iDepCount specifies how many other code segments this one links to, iDeps points to an array of pointers to the DCodeSegs on which this one depends). This graph is exact for RAM-loaded code segments (that is, all code segments and dependencies are present) but it is reduced for XIP code segments. This reduction takes the form of transitively closing the dependence graph, and then omitting any XIP code segments that have no .data or .bss, or are kernel extensions or variants, and are not the explicit target of a load request. (We avoid creating code segments for these since no actual work is required to load them – the code is always visible, being XIP, and no data initialization is required since there is either no data or it has been initialized by the kernel before the loader even started up. Effectively these DLLs are always loaded.)

A code segment can have various attributes (iAttr), as follows:

- ECodeSegAttKernel – this indicates that the code is intended to execute in supervisor mode. Such code segments will be accessible only in privileged processor modes

- ECodeSegAttGlobal – this indicates that the code should be visible to all user processes regardless of whether they have explicitly loaded it. Used for locales

- ECodeSegAttFixed – this is only used in the moving memory model; it indicates that an EXE code segment is associated with a fixed process and so will be fixed up for a non-standard data address

- ABI attribute – this is a 2-bit field indicating which ABI a code segment conforms to. (ABI stands for Application Binary Interface and covers such things as the calling convention used to pass parameters to functions and receive the return value and the manner in which objects are laid out in memory.) Currently we define two ABIs – GCC98r2 and EABI. We use this attribute to facilitate systems in which multiple ABIs coexist, and multiple versions of the same DLL are present. If we are finding an already-loaded code segment, we must find the one with an ABI matching the importing code segment.

Code segments without either kernel or global attributes are standard user code segments. The kernel needs to attach such code segments to a process before they can execute. It will either perform the attach operation at process load time (for the EXE code segment and its dependencies) or when a running process loads a DLL. Each process maintains a list of all code segments directly attached to it (`DProcess::iExeCodeSeg` points to the main code segment for the process, `DProcess::iDynamicCode` is an array of all explicitly dynamically loaded code segments, each with its corresponding `DLibrary` object). This list only contains directly loaded code segments, not those present solely because they are implicitly linked to by another code segment. Depending on the memory model, non-XIP code segments may either be visible to all user processes or visible only to those user processes to which they have been attached. The multiple memory model uses the latter scheme; the other memory models use the former. Kernel code segments are attached to the kernel process, but they are not mapped and unmapped; the code segment is visible from privileged modes immediately on creation. Global code segments do not need to be attached to any process. They are visible to all processes immediately after creation.

A code segment also has flags (`iMark`), as follows:

- `EMarkListDeps` – temporarily used to mark code segments during traversal of the code graph to add code segments to a dependency list

- `EMarkUnListDeps` – temporarily used to mark code segments during traversal of the code graph to remove code segments from a dependency list

- `EMarkLdr` – indicates that the code segment is in use by a load operation

- `EMarkLoaded` – indicates that the code segment and all its dependencies are fully loaded and fixed up

- `EMarkDataFlagsValid` – indicates that the `DataInit` and `DataPresent` flags are valid (taking into account dependencies)

- `EMarkDataFlagsCheck` – used to mark that a code segment has been visited when calculating the `DataInit` and `DataPresent` flags

- EMarkData – indicates that this code segment has .data/.bss and is not an extension or variant (so may require initialization at load time – extensions and variants are loaded and initialized before the loader comes into existence so don't need to be initialized as a result of any loader operation)

- EMarkDataInit – indicates that either this code segment or one in the sub-graph below it is a DLL with writeable static data, excluding extensions and variants

- EMarkDataPresent – indicates that either this code segment or one in the sub-graph below it has writeable static data, excluding extensions and variants. Note that the difference between EMark-DataPresent and EMarkDataInit is that the former includes EXEs with writeable static data whereas the latter does not

- EMarkDebug – reserved for debuggers.

We need some form of reference count for code segments to cope with the case in which several processes are using a code segment (for example, two instances of the same EXE or two processes loading the same DLL); the kernel can only destroy a code segment when all processes have relinquished their reference on it. A code segment should only be destroyed if no currently running process depends on it, and such dependence may be indirect via implicit linkages from other code segments. We could have done this by reference counting the dependency pointers from each code segment. However, because there may be cycles in the code graph, this scheme makes it difficult to determine when a code segment may actually be removed. The way to do this would be to traverse the graph in the reverse direction – from the exporting code segment to the importing code segment – to see if any process is currently using any of the code segments. This would mean that we would need to maintain two sets of dependence pointers for each code segment, one pointing in each direction in the dependence graph.

In the reference counting scheme we actually use, we do not reference count the dependency pointers. Instead, the reference count of each code segment is equal to the number of processes which currently have the code segment loaded, plus 1 if the (user-side) loader is currently working with the code segment. We indicate the latter case by setting the EMarkLdr flag in the iMark field. When the kernel creates a DCodeSeg object, its access count is 1 and the EMarkLdr flag is set. Following a successful load, each code segment in the new dependency tree will be in this state (unless it was already loaded, in which case the access count will be greater than 1). The kernel then adds the entire dependency tree to the address space of the loader's client process (or the newly created process if an EXE is being loaded), which causes the access count of each code segment to be incremented. Finally, during loader cleanup, the kernel decrements the access counts of all code segments with the EMarkLdr flag set and resets the flag, which leaves all code segments with the correct access count according to the previous rule. The kernel performs the second and third steps (traversing dependence trees or the global code segment list and modifying the access counts of several code segments) with the CodeSegLock mutex held. The access counts of all code segments must be consistent with the previous rule whenever this mutex is free.

To conserve RAM, the kernel shares code segments whenever possible. There will generally only be one code segment for each loaded EXE or DLL with the same code being shared between all processes. There are some exceptions, which all arise from memory model specific restrictions on data addresses:

- On the moving memory model, non-fixed processes share the same data addresses and so they can share all code segments. Fixed processes must have unique data addresses, since we designed them so that a context switch to or from a fixed process should require no change in the virtual to physical memory map. Symbian OS executables and DLLs do not use position independent code or data, so if a DLL needs to have its .data and .bss at a different address in different processes, the kernel must load multiple copies of the DLL and relocate each copy for different code and data addresses. This means that any code segments which either have .data or .bss sections or which implicitly link to other such code segments must be unique to that process

- On the direct memory model and the emulator, all processes must have unique data addresses and so sharing is possible only for code segments which don't have .data/.bss sections and which don't link implicitly (directly or indirectly) to any such code segments.

If such an exceptional case is encountered with a non-XIP image file, the kernel will create a second code segment (that is, a second RAM-loaded copy of the code) from the same image file and relocate it for a different data address. If an exceptional case is encountered with an XIP image file, the kernel can't do this, since XIP files no longer have relocation information present. In this case, the load request is rejected.

To implement sharing of code segments, the loader will search for an already loaded code segment with a root file name (ignoring the drive and path, just including the file name and extension) matching the requested file before attempting to create a new code segment. The kernel provides a "find matching code segment" function for this purpose. It finds the next fully loaded code segment (that is, one that is relocated, and has all imports loaded and fixed up) that matches the provided UIDs and attributes and that can be loaded into the client process. The loader then checks the filename and, if it matches, opens a reference on the matching code segment and on each member of the sub-graph below it, marking each one with EMarkLdr.

To support the exceptional cases where sharing is not allowed, a code segment may have one of two restrictions on its use:

1. If the iExeCodeSeg field is non-null, it indicates that this code segment may only be loaded into a process with that EXE code segment. A code segment which links directly or indirectly to an EXE will have this field pointing to the code segment representing that EXE. This restriction arises in the case where the code segment has an EXE code segment in the sub-graph below it. When this restriction applies, the code segment could potentially be loaded into multiple processes, but these processes must all be instantiations of the same EXE file

2. If the iAttachProcess field is non-null, it indicates that this code segment may only be loaded into that specific process. This restriction arises in the case where the code segment, or one in the sub-graph below it, has .data or .bss and this data must reside at a unique address, for example if the code segment is loaded into a fixed process in the moving memory model. When the iAttachProcess field is non-null, the iExeCodeSeg field points to the EXE code segment of the attach process. The iAttachProcess pointer is reference counted.

Figures 10.7, 10.8 and 10.9 show example code graphs. They depict a process instantiated from an EXE file which links implicitly to five DLLs. Figure 10.7 shows the graph which results where all these modules are non-XIP. Shaded modules signify the presence of writeable static data. Figure 10.8 shows the graph which results from loading the same process if two of the DLLs (E.DLL and F.DLL) are in XIP ROM. Since these DLLs are XIP and they have no writeable static data, they do not appear in the code graph. Figure 10.9 shows the graph resulting from loading the same process where all modules are in XIP ROM. Only the EXE and any DLLs with writeable static data appear in the code graph.

10.4.2 Libraries

The kernel creates a kernel-side library object (DLibrary) for every DLL that is explicitly loaded into a user process (in other words, one that is the target of an RLibrary::Load rather than a DLL that is implicitly linked to by another DLL or EXE). Library objects are specific to, and owned by, the process for which they were created; if two processes both load the same DLL, the kernel creates two separate DLibrary objects. A library has two main uses:

1. It represents a link from a process to the global code graph. Each process has at least one such connection – the `DProcess::iCodeSeg` pointer links each process to its own EXE code segment. The loader creates this link when loading the process. `DLibrary` objects represent additional such links that the kernel creates at run time

2. It provides a state machine to ensure constructors and destructors for objects resident in .data and .bss are called correctly.

Libraries have two reference counts. One is the standard `DObject` reference count (since `DLibrary` derives from `DObject`); a non-zero value for this reference count simply stops the `DLibrary` itself being deleted – it does not stop the underlying code segment being deleted or removed from any process. The second reference count (`iMapCount`) is the number of user references on the library, which is equal to the number of handles on the library opened by the process or by any of its threads. This is always updated with the `CodeSegLock` mutex held. When the last user handle is closed, `iMapCount` will reach zero and this triggers the calling of static destructors and the removal of the library code segment from the process address space. (We need a separate count here because static destructors for a DLL must be called in user mode whenever a library is removed from a process, and those destructors must be called in the context of the process involved. However, the normal reference count may be incremented and decremented kernel-side by threads running in other processes, so it would not be acceptable to call destructors when the normal reference count reached zero.) The loader creates `DLibrary` objects on behalf of a client loading a DLL. A process may only have one `DLibrary` referring to the same code segment. If a process loads the same library twice, a second handle will be opened on the already existing `DLibrary` and its map count will be incremented.

A `DLibrary` object transitions through the following states during its life, as shown in Figure 10.10.

•   `ECreated` – transient state in which object is created. Switches to `ELoaded` or `EAttached` when library and corresponding code segment are added to the target process. The state transitions to `ELoaded` if constructors must be run in user mode and directly to `EAttached` if no such constructors are required; this is the case if neither the DLL itself nor any DLLs that it depends on have writeable static data

•   `ELoaded` – code segment is loaded and attached to the target process but static constructors have not been called

•   `EAttaching` – the target process is currently running the code segment static constructors. Transition to `EAttached` when constructors have completed

- `EAttached` – static constructors have completed and the code segment is fully available for use by the target process

- `EDetachPending` – the last user handle has been closed on the `DLibrary` (that is, the map count has reached zero) but static destructors have not yet been called. Transitions to `EDetaching` just before running static destructors

- `EDetaching` – the target process is currently running the code segment static destructors. Transitions to `ELoaded` when destructors have completed, so that if the library is reloaded by another thread in the same process before being destroyed, the constructors run again.

Problems could be caused by multiple threads in a process loading and unloading DLLs simultaneously – for example, static constructors running in one thread while destructors for the same DLL run in another thread. To prevent this, each process has a mutex (the DLL lock), which protects static constructors and destructors running in that process. The mutex is held for the entire duration of a dynamic library load from connecting to the loader to completion of static constructors for the DLL. It is also held when unloading a library, from the point at which the `iMapCount` reaches zero to the point where the code segment is unmapped from the process following the running of static destructors. The kernel creates the DLL lock mutex, named `DLL$LOCK`, during process creation, but it is held while running user-side code; it is the only mutex with this property.

10.4.3 Loading a process

The kernel's involvement in process loading begins after the loader has completed its search for the requested executable image and decided which of the available files should be used to instantiate the new process. The loader will have created an `E32Image` object on its heap, to represent the new image file it is loading. The loader then queries the kernel to discover if the selected image file is already loaded. The `E32Loader::CodeSegNext()` API, which, like all the `E32Loader` functions, is a kernel executive call, is used for this purpose. If the selected image file is an XIP image, the loader will already have found the address of the `TRomImageHeader` describing it. In this case, the kernel will search for a code segment derived from the same `TRomImageHeader`. If the selected image file is not an XIP image, the loader will know the full path name of the image file and will have read its `E32Image` header. The kernel will search for a code segment with the same root name, same UIDs and same version number. In either case, if the kernel finds that the code segment is already loaded, it returns a "code segment handle" to the loader. This is not a standard Symbian OS handle but is actually just the pointer to the kernel-side `DCodeSeg` object. The loader then calls

`E32Loader::CodeSegInfo()` on the returned handle; this populates the `E32Image` object with information about the code segment being loaded, including full path name, UIDs, attributes, version number, security information, code and data sizes, code and data addresses and export information. The loader then calls `E32Loader::CodeSegOpen()` on the handle. This call checks the `EMarkLdr` flag on the code segment; if this flag is clear, it sets the flag and increments the reference count of the code segment. The `E32Loader::CodeSegOpen()` function then performs the same operation recursively on all code segments in the sub-graph below the original one. At the end of this, the loader has a reference on the code segment and on all the code segments upon which it depends, so these will not be deleted.

If the kernel does not find the selected code segment, the loader populates the `E32Image` object with information read from the `E32Image` header of the selected file.

The loader then calls `E32Loader::ProcessCreate()`, passing in the `E32Image` object; the latter derives from `TProcessCreateInfo`, which contains all the information the kernel needs to create a new process. Figure 10.2 illustrates the relationship of these classes.

The kernel-side handler, `ExecHandler::ProcessCreate()`, verifies that the calling thread belongs to the F32 process and then does some argument marshaling to pass the parameters over to the kernel side. It then calls `Kern::ProcessCreate()` to do the actual work; this function is also used by the startup extension (EXSTART.DLL) to create the F32 process after the kernel has booted.

Actual process creation proceeds as follows:

1. The kernel creates an object of the concrete class derived from `DProcess`. There is only one such class in any given system (`DArmPlatProcess` or `DX86PlatProcess`) and its definition depends on both the processor type and the memory model in use. The generic kernel code calls the function `P::NewProcess()` to instantiate such an object. Once created, this object will contain all the information that the kernel needs to know about the process

2. The kernel stores the command line, UIDs and security information (capabilities, SID and VID) in the new process. It sets the `DObject` name to be the root name of the image file used and calculates the generation number as one greater than the highest generation number of any existing process with the same root name and third UID. If you retrieve the full name of a process, it will be in the form `name.exe [uuuuuuuu] gggg`, where `name.exe` is the root filename, `uuuuuuuu` is the third UID in hexadecimal, and `gggg` is the generation number in base 10

3. The kernel allocates an ID to the process. Process and thread IDs occupy the same number space, beginning at 0 and incrementing

for each new process or thread. If the 32-bit ID reaches $2^{32}-1$, the kernel reboots to ensure uniqueness of IDs over all time. We consider it highly unlikely that this would occur in practice since it would require the system to be active for a very long time without rebooting due to power down

4. The kernel creates the process-relative handles array (DObjectIx) for the new process

5. The kernel creates the process lock and DLL lock mutexes

6. Some platform-dependent initialization of the process object now occurs. Under the moving memory model running on an ARM processor, the kernel just allocates an ARM domain to the process if it is a fixed address process and there is a free domain. Under the multiple memory model, the kernel allocates the process a new OS ASID, a new page directory and a new address allocator (TLinearSection) for the process local address area. Chapter 7 describes OS ASIDs and the address areas used in the multiple memory model. The kernel maps the new page directory at the virtual address corresponding to the allocated OS ASID and initializes it – it copies all global mappings into it if necessary and clears the local mapping area

7. If the process is being created from an already existing code segment, the kernel attaches the existing code segment to the new process. It increments its reference count and creates the process data/bss/stack chunk using the data and bss size information in the code segment. At this point it checks that the run address of the .data section created matches the run address expected by the code segment. If this is not the case (for example, an attempt to create a second instance of a fixed XIP process with .data and/or .bss), the process creation fails

8. If the process is not being created from an existing code segment, the kernel creates a new code segment using the information passed in by the loader. It increments the reference count of the code segment, so that it becomes 2 – one for the loader, one for the new process. I will describe code segment creation in more detail later in the chapter, but essentially, for non-XIP code, the kernel allocates an address and maps RAM to store the code and the initial values of the initialized data. For all code segments, it allocates a data address if necessary. For EXE code segments, the kernel creates the new process's data/bss/stack chunk using the data/bss size information passed from the loader. Finally, the kernel passes run and load addresses for both code and data back to the loader

9. The kernel creates the process's first thread. It sets its DObject name to Main, and sets its stack and heap sizes to the values passed

by the loader; these values were originally read from the `E32Image` header. The kernel marks the thread as "process permanent", which means that if it exits for any reason, the kernel will kill the whole process including any threads that are created after this main one. It also marks the thread as "original", which signifies that it is the first thread. This information is used by the process entry point code – the original thread causes the process static data to be initialized and `E32Main()` to be called, whereas subsequent threads cause the specified thread entry point to be called. The first thread is created with an M-state of `DThread::ECreated`, so it cannot yet be resumed

10. The newly created process is added to the process object container (`DObjectCon`)

11. The kernel creates a handle from the calling thread (the loader) to the new process and passes this handle back to the loader.

After `E32Loader::ProcessCreate()` completes, if a new code segment has been created, the loader needs to load and relocate the code (if not XIP) and load all DLLs to which the new EXE code segment implicitly links – see Section 10.4.4 for more details of this.

Finally, after it has resolved all dependencies, the loader calls `E32Loader::ProcessLoaded()`. This performs the following actions:

1. If a new EXE code segment was created for the process, the kernel calls `DCodeSeg::Loaded()` on it. This performs steps 1 to 3 of the `CodeSegLoaded()` function, described at the end of Section 10.4.4

2. The kernel maps the EXE code segment and all the code segments on which it depends into the process and increments their reference counts

3. The kernel sets the `EMarkLoaded` flag of the EXE code segment to enable it to be reused to launch another instance of the process

4. The kernel changes the first thread's M-state to `DThread::EReady`; it is now ready to be resumed

5. The kernel creates a handle from the loader's client to the new process; the client will eventually use this handle to resume the new process.

After `E32Loader::ProcessLoaded()` has completed, the loader copies the new handle to the process back to the client, and cleans up the `E32Image` object corresponding to the new process. Finally, it completes the client request and control returns to the client.

10.4.4   Loading a library

Similarly to process loading, the kernel's involvement in library loading begins after the loader has completed its search for the requested DLL image and decided which of the available files should be loaded. The loader will have created an `E32Image` object on its heap to represent the new image file being loaded. This procedure is carried out by the loader function `E32Image::LoadCodeSeg()`, which then calls `E32Image::DoLoadCodeSeg()` to perform the actual load; this latter function is also called while resolving implicit linkages to load the implicitly linked DLLs. In a similar way to process loading, the loader then queries the kernel to discover if the selected image file is already loaded. It makes an additional check while searching for a matching code segment – it must be compatible with the process it is destined to be loaded into. An incompatibility can result from any of the following considerations:

- If a code segment links directly or indirectly to an EXE, it may only be loaded into a process instantiated from that EXE. This is because only one EXE file can be loaded into any process; an EXE cannot be loaded as a DLL

- If a code segment has writeable static data or links directly or indirectly to such a code segment, it may only be loaded into a process with which the address of the static data is compatible. This rule affects the moving and direct memory models. A code segment with writeable static data loaded into a fixed process will not be compatible with any other process, and such a code segment loaded into a moving process will be compatible with all moving processes but not with fixed processes.

If the kernel finds that the selected code segment or the file being loaded is an XIP DLL with no .data/.bss and is not the explicit target of the load request, the function `E32Image::DoLoadCodeSeg()` returns at this point. If the DLL is already loaded the function will have populated the `E32Image` object with information about the already-loaded DLL, including its code segment handle. Execution then proceeds in the same way as it would after the creation of a new code segment.

If the kernel does not find the selected code segment, the `E32Image` object is populated with information read from the `E32Image` header of the selected file.

The loader then calls `E32Loader::CodeSegCreate()`, passing in the `E32Image` object; the latter derives from `TCodeSegCreateInfo`, which contains all the information the kernel needs to create a new code segment. Figure 10.2 illustrates the relationship of these classes. The kernel-side handler `ExecHandler::CodeSegCreate()` verifies that the calling thread belongs to the F32 process, and then does some argument marshaling to get all the parameters over to the kernel-side, this time including a handle to the loader's client process, since that is the process into which the new code segment will be loaded. Actual code segment creation then proceeds as follows:

1. The kernel creates a `DMemModelCodeSeg` object; this is the concrete class derived from `DCodeSeg`. There is only one such class in any given system and its definition depends on the memory model in use. The generic kernel code calls the memory model function `M::NewCodeSeg()` to instantiate such an object. Once created, this object will contain all the information that the kernel needs about the code segment

2. The kernel copies the UIDs, attributes, full path name, root name, version number and dependency count (count of number of code segments to which this one implicitly links) into the object. It allocates an array to store the dependency linkages that make up the code graph immediately below this code segment

3. If the code segment is XIP, the kernel stores a pointer to the corresponding `TRomImageHeader` in it

4. If the code segment is a user-side EXE, then the process object with which the code segment was created will have been passed as a parameter. The kernel now creates the data/bss/stack chunk for that process and commits sufficient memory to it to hold the process's .data and .bss sections. On the multiple memory model, this chunk is always at the same virtual address – `0x00400000` on both ARM and IA32. On the moving memory model, the virtual address depends on whether the process is fixed or moving and, if fixed, whether it is XIP. If XIP, the kernel uses `iDataBssLinearBase` from the `TRomImageHeader`. Moving processes have their .data/.bss at `0x00400000`

5. If the code segment is XIP, the kernel copies the `EMarkData`, `EMarkDataPresent` and `EMarkDataInit` flags from the `TRomImageHeader`, and sets the `EMarkDataFlagsValid` flag (since the ROM builder has already looked at all the dependencies). It reads the addresses of code and data, entry point, exception descriptor and export directory from the `TRomImageHeader` and passes them back to the loader. On the moving memory model, an XIP code segment with writeable static data loaded into a fixed process is marked as only available to that process by setting the `iAttachProcess` field of the code segment to point to the process

6. If the code segment is not XIP, the kernel allocates memory to hold size and address information, and copies the size information

from the information passed by the loader. If the code segment has writeable static data, the kernel sets the `EMarkData`, `EMark-DataPresent`, and `EMarkDataFlagsValid` flags, and also sets the `EMarkDataInit` flag if the code segment is not an EXE code segment. If the code segment does not have writeable static data, the kernel cannot determine the status of these flags until it has resolved all dependencies

7. For non-XIP code segments on the moving memory model, the kernel allocates an address and commits memory in either the kernel or user code chunks to hold the actual code. For kernel-side code segments with writeable static data, the kernel allocates space on its heap to store the data. For user-side code segments with writeable static data, the allocation of the data address depends whether the code segment is destined for a fixed or moving process. For moving processes, the kernel allocates an address in the DLL data address range (`0x30000000` to `0x3FFFFFFF`), but does not yet commit the memory. For fixed processes, the kernel creates the process DLL data chunk if necessary and then commits memory to it to hold the static data

8. Non-XIP code segments in the multiple memory model can be user, kernel or global (on the moving model, global is the same as user, since all code is visible to all processes). For kernel code segments, the kernel allocates an address for and commits memory to a special kernel code chunk to hold the code itself, and allocates space for writeable static data on the kernel heap. For global code segments, the kernel allocates an address for and commits memory to a special global code chunk to hold the code itself – writeable static data is not permitted. For user code segments, the kernel allocates an address in the standard user code range and, if necessary, in the user data range too. It allocates sufficient physical RAM pages to hold the code and attaches them to the code segment. At this point, memory is not yet allocated for any static data. The kernel then maps code pages into the current process (F32), at the allocated address

9. The kernel adds the code segment to the three global code segment lists: unordered, ordered by name and ordered by run address

10. The kernel sets the `iAsyncDeleteNext` field (usually zero for a `DBase`-derived object) to point to the code segment itself. This property is used subsequently in kernel executive calls that take a code segment handle to verify that the handle refers to a valid code segment object

11.   The kernel passes the updated code segment information, including the allocated load-time and run-time addresses for the code and data sections, back to the loader.

After the new code segment is created, the loader reads in the code from the file system and relocates it to the address allocated by the kernel. The loader also examines the import section of the loaded DLL and loads all implicitly linked DLLs. This is a recursive process, since each new DLL will have its own implicit linkages, which will require further DLLs to be loaded. When all required DLLs have been loaded, the loader resolves all import references between them. Then the loader calls `E32Loader::CodeSegLoaded()` on each one, finishing with the DLL that was the explicit target of the original load request. In this function, the kernel performs the following actions:

1.   It performs an IMB (Instruction Memory Barrier) operation on the address range of the loaded code. This ensures coherence between the D and I caches on a Harvard cache architecture. (ARM processors with separate instruction and data caches (everything after ARM7) do not maintain coherence between these two caches. So if a memory location is resident in the data cache and is dirty, that is, the value has been modified but not written back to main memory, the new value will not be fetched by an instruction fetch to that location. To ensure that the correct instruction is executed, it is necessary to clean the data cache – to write any modified data in the cache back to main memory – and to invalidate the instruction cache)

2.   On the multiple memory model, if the code segment is a standard user-side code segment, the kernel unmaps it from the loader address space. If the code segment is kernel code, the kernel changes the permissions for the mapping from supervisor read/write to supervisor read-only. If the code segment is global code, it changes the permissions from supervisor read/write to user read-only

3.   The kernel traverses the code graph recursively to ensure that the `EMarkDataPresent` and `EMarkDataInit` flags are set correctly for each code segment

4.   Finally the kernel sets the `EMarkLoaded` flag to indicate that the code segment is fully loaded and ready for use.

At this point, the DLL and all the DLLs on which it depends have been loaded. This is the point at which execution continues after querying the kernel (in the case where the DLL was already loaded). The loader then calls the kernel function `E32Loader::LibraryCreate()`, passing in the code segment handle of the main subject of the load and a handle to the loader's client thread. In this call the kernel first looks at the client process to discover if a DLibrary representing the loaded code segment already exists in that process. If it does, the DLL is already loaded into that process, so the only thing to do is to change the DLibrary state to EAttached if it was originally EDetachPending (since the C++ destructors have not been called there is no need to call the constructors again), and to create a new handle from the client thread or process to the DLibrary, which is then passed back to the loader.

If there is no DLibrary in the client process corresponding to the loaded code segment, the kernel creates a new DLibrary object and attaches it to the process. Then it maps the new code segment and all the code segments in the sub-graph below it into the process address space (and increments their reference counts correspondingly). It creates a new handle from the client thread or process to the new DLibrary and passes it back to the loader. If the main code segment has the EMarkDataInit flag set, the kernel sets the state of the DLibrary to ELoaded, since C++ constructors must be run before it is ready for use; otherwise it sets the DLibrary state to EAttached.

Control then returns to the loader, which writes the new handle back to the client and then completes the load request, at which point control returns to the client thread.

10.5 Summary

In this chapter I have described the process of loading executables and the management of executable code in Symbian OS, from both the file server's perspective, and the kernel's. In the next chapter, I shall go on to look at another key user-mode server, the window server.

11

The Window Server

by Douglas Feather

*"The truth of the matter is that
window management under X
is not yet well understood."*

The Xlib Programming Manual

The window server (or WSERV) works in conjunction with almost every part of Symbian OS, from the kernel to the applications, with the only real exception being the communications sub-systems. Its two main responsibilities are screen management and event management. WSERV receives events from the kernel and passes them to its clients (which are normally applications). It receives commands from clients and updates the screen accordingly. My discussion of these two key responsibilities will make up the backbone of this chapter.

WSERV is started during system boot and runs continually throughout the life of the system. It is a standard system server, being a derived class of CServer2 (or CPolicyServer from Symbian OS v9 onwards) called CWindowServer.

In this chapter I shall also cover animation DLLs (anim DLLs), which are a plug-in to WSERV. I will discuss what an anim DLL is, how to create one and how an anim DLL interacts with events. To illustrate this, I will develop a simple handwriting recognition system.

And of course I will cover windows in great depth – different types of windows, window classes on both the client and server sides, how window objects link together (the window tree), the different regions that windows have, different window effects and how clients can draw to windows. But first I will consider WSERV as the kernel's event handler.

11.1 The kernel's event handler

During system bootup, WSERV calls the function UserSvr::Capture-EventHook(), which tells the kernel that WSERV wants to become the kernel's event handler. To actually receive the events, WSERV then has to call the function `UserSvr::RequestEvent(TRawEvent-Buf& aBuf, TRequestStatus& aStatus)`, passing in the request status of the active object `CRawEventReceiver`, which will then run whenever the kernel has an event waiting. In this way, the kernel passes all its events (for example, digitizer and key events) to WSERV, which then has to perform further processing on these events.

WSERV is not just a simple pipe that passes events on to its clients. It does a lot of processing on the events, discarding some events, acting upon others, creating new events and deciding which client to send the event to. The set of event types that is passed between the kernel and WSERV is not exactly the same as the set of event types that is passed between WSERV and its clients. The kernel is not the only source of events; clients can also generate them, as can anim DLLs and WSERV itself.

As well as passing events to clients, WSERV can pass them to anim DLLs.

11.2   Different types of events

In this section I will list the different types of events that WSERV deals with, and give a brief description of what each type is for. I will describe both the set of events passed from the kernel to WSERV and the set passed from WSERV to the client. Figure 11.1 gives an overview of the paths that events can take within the system. It shows three different threads: the kernel, WSERV and a client of WSERV – the boundaries between these threads are represented by the three dividing lines. The three small boxes represent processing that goes on inside WSERV itself.

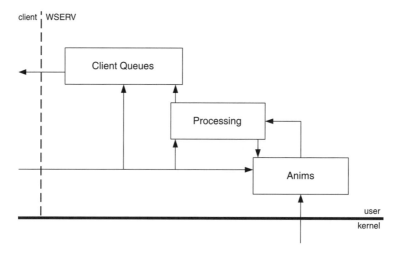

Figure 11.1   WSERV event flow

Although Figure 11.1 does not give the complete picture, it should suffice to give you a feel for how events pass through WSERV.

11.2.1 Events from the kernel to WSERV

The events that are passed from the kernel to WSERV are listed in the class `TRawEvent::TType`. Several of these are to do with pointer events. In the following table, I only list a representative set of the pointer events:

Raw events

Events	Purpose
ENone	A dummy value that is not actually used.
EPointerMove	The pointer or pen has moved position. This could be a move or drag event.
EPointerSwitchOn	The digitizer was pressed and this caused the device to power up.
EKeyDown	A key on the keyboard was pressed.
EKeyUp	A key on the keyboard was released.
ERedraw	The emulator has received a Win32 redraw event.
ESwitchOn	The device has just been powered up.
EActive	The emulator window has gained focus.
EInactive	The emulator window has lost focus.
EUpdateModifiers	The modifier key settings have changed. Sent by the emulator when it regains focus.
EButton1Down	The pen or mouse button 1 has been pressed.
EButton1Up	The pen or mouse button 1 has been released.
ESwitchOff	The device is about to be switched off.
ECaseOpen	The case on a clam-shell device has been opened.
ECaseClose	The case on a clam-shell device has been closed.

I will discuss what happens to key and pointer events later in this chapter. The following table shows how WSERV responds to all the other raw events in the system:

WSERV events

Event	Response
ERedraw	On the emulator, there is a bitmap managed by the screen driver component that contains the complete copy of the display. WSERV calls the function: `CFbsScreen-Device::Update(const TRegion& aRegion)` passing in the full screen area, which updates the screen from the bitmap.
ESwitchOn	Stops the keyboard repeat timer. Puts up the password window if one has been set. Switches on the screen hardware by calling `UserSvr::WsSwitchOn-Screen()`. Sends on events to clients that have requested this notification.
EInactive	Stops keys auto-repeating.
EUpdateModifiers	Resets the state of all the modifier keys.
ESwitchOff	If a client has registered itself for switch-off events, then WSERV sends an event to that client. Otherwise it powers down the device by calling: `UserHal::SwitchOff()`.
EKeyRepeat	Nothing.
ECaseOpen	Same as ESwitchOn except that it does not power up the screen hardware.
ECaseClose	Sends an event to the client that has registered itself to deal with switching off. (Does not power down if such a client does not exist.)

11.2.2 Events from WSERV to its clients

In the next two tables, I show the list of events that WSERV sends to its clients. I will discuss key and pointer events in more detail later in this chapter. The first table contains events that WSERV sends to the relevant client whenever they occur:

Non-client registered events

Event	Meaning
EEventNull	Should be ignored.
EEventKey	A character event.
EEventKeyUp	A key up event.
EEventKeyDown	A key down event.
EEventPointer	An up, down, drag or move pointer event.
EEventPointerEnter	The pointer has moved over a window.
EEventPointerExit	The pointer has moved away from a particular window.
EEventPointerBufferReady	A buffer containing pointer drag or move events is ready for delivery.
EEventDragDrop	A special kind of pointer event. These events can be requested by clients so that they can receive UI widgets by dragging and releasing.
EEventFocusLost	The window has just lost focus.
EEventFocusGained	The window has just gained focus.
EEventPassword	Sent to the owner of the password window when the password window is displayed.
EEventMessageReady	A message has arrived from another application.
EEventMarkInvalid	Internal use only, never sent to clients.
EEventKeyRepeat	Not sent to clients, sent to key click makers.

In the next table I show events that WSERV only sends to clients that register for them – most of these events can be sent to more than one client:

Client-registered events

Event	Meaning
EEventModifiersChanged	One or more modifier keys have changed their state.
EEventSwitchOn	The machine has just been switched on. (This event is not generated on a phone, but is generated on, for example, a Psion Series 5 PDA.)
EEventWindowGroupsChanged	Sent when a group window is destroyed or named.
EEventErrorMessage	Sent when an error, such as out-of-memory, occurs in WSERV. (For more details, see the documentation for TEventCode in the Symbian Developer Library's C++ component reference section.)
EEventSwitchOff	Sent to the client dealing with switch off.
EEventKeySwitchOff	Sent to clients dealing with switch off if the off key is pressed.
EEventScreenDeviceChanged	Sent when the screen size mode changes.
EEventFocusGroupChanged	Sent when the focused group window changes.
EEventCaseOpened	Sent when the clam-shell device is opened.
EEventCaseClosed	Sent to the client dealing with switch off when the clam-shell is closed.
EEventWindowGroupListChanged	Sent when there is a change in group window order.

11.3   How WSERV processes events

WSERV processes events in many stages; some of these are general to all events, in particular the way in which WSERV queues events for the client. Other stages are specific to certain types of events. For example, both pointer events and key events have to undergo special processing.

The first stage WSERV goes through is to process the pointer events – this is so that the main processing of pointer events later on receives pointer events of a standard type. WSERV does various things at this point:

- Filters out Win32 move events for the emulator of a pen-based device

- Where the co-ordinates the kernel has delivered to WSERV are relative to the last position, converts them to absolute co-ordinates for a virtual pointer cursor

- For real devices (that is, not the emulator), WSERV rotates co-ordinates to the current screen rotation. (Screen rotation allows address of the screen in a co-ordinate set rotated by 0, 90, 180 or 270 degrees from the physical co-ordinates of the screen)

- Offsets the co-ordinates to the current screen origin and scaling

- If pointer events are being limited to a sub rectangle of the display, then WSERV restricts the co-ordinates if they are outside of this area.

It is worth noting that rotation does not need to be taken into account in the emulator, because the fascia bitmap rotates, and so the co-ordinates the kernel receives from Win32 are already rotated.

We support the screen origin and scaling functionality from Symbian OS v8.1. By using screen origin and scaling, a user interface designer can allow different applications to address the pixels of the screen with different co-ordinate sets.

Under some circumstances, WSERV turns off its heart beat timer – this normally happens when a client calls RWsSession::PrepareFor-SwitchOff() so that the processor can be powered down to save battery power. In response to each event from the kernel WSERV turns this timer back on (if it's off).

Next WSERV passes the event to any anim DLL that has registered itself as being interested in events. The anim DLL registers by calling the function MAnimGeneralFunctions::GetRawEvents(ETrue). To deliver the event to the anim DLL, WSERV calls the function: MEventHandler::OfferRawEvent(). The anim DLL can consume the event so that WSERV does no further processing; to do this it should return `ETrue` from the `OfferRawEvent` function, otherwise it should return `EFalse`.

From this point onward WSERV treats the different types of events in different ways. This is shown for all events other than key and pointer events, in the "WSERV events" table above.

11.4 Processing key events

There are three kernel events that are directly related to keys: `EKeyDown`, `EKeyUp` and `EUpdateModifiers`. To process these key events, WSERV uses an instance of a `CKeyTranslator`-derived object. This object understands character mappings and modifier keys, and its main purpose is to tell WSERV which characters a particular key press should map to. For example, pressing the "a" key could result in "a" or "A", and it is `CKeyTranslator` that analyzes the state of the shift keys and determines which it should be.

The event `EUpdateModifiers` is passed straight through to the `CKeyTranslator` object. The kernel generates this event in the emulator when the emulator window gains focus from another Windows applications. The data passed with the event tells us the current state of all the modifier keys, and enables the emulator to take into account any changes the user has made to modifier keys while other applications on the emulator host had focus.

11.4.1 Key ups and downs

WSERV processes each up and down event thus:

- It logs the event, if logging is enabled
- It tells the keyboard repeat timer object about the event
- It passes the event to the keyboard translator object
- It checks for any modifier changes
- It queues the key up/down event
- It performs further processing to create the character event (if there is to be one).

The keyboard-repeat-timer object controls auto repeating of key presses. WSERV only receives a single up or down event from the kernel, no matter how long the key is pressed. If a key press maps to a character, WSERV starts a timer, and every time that timer goes off, WSERV generates another instance of the character for the client queue. If the client is responding promptly to the events, then it will get many events for that character, and the timer will have generated all but the first of them.

When a new key down event occurs, WSERV must inform the timer, so that it can cancel the current repeat – this is needed because any key press should change the character the timer generates. Similarly, when a key up event occurs, WSERV informs the timer, so that it can stop the repeat if the key up comes from the currently repeating character.

WSERV calls the keyboard translator object next, using the function:

```
TBool TranslateKey(TUint aScanCode, TBool aKeyUp,
    const CCaptureKeys &aCaptureKeys, TKeyData &aKeyData)
```

As you can see, WSERV passes the scan code of the key event, a Boolean to say whether the key is an up or down event, and the current list of capture keys. The key translator object returns a TBool saying whether the key maps to a character event or if it does, the key translator also returns the following details of the character event in the TKeyData object:

- The code of the character
- The current state of all the modifiers
- Whether the key has been captured.

If the key is captured, the key translator also returns:

- A handle indicating which window captured the object
- Another handle which WSERV uses for its own capture keys.

WSERV capture keys or hotkeys are system wide. There are hotkeys for increasing or decreasing contrast, toggling or turning the backlight on or off and more – you can see the full list in the enum THotKey.

Clients can request events to let them know when certain modifier keys change their state. When this happens, WSERV checks all client requests to see if any are requesting information about the particular change that has occurred. For each such request, WSERV queues an event to the relevant client.

WSERV has to decide which client to send the up or down key event to. Usually it chooses the client that owns the currently focused window – the only exception is if a particular client has requested the capture of up and down events on that particular key. WSERV also sends the event to the key click plug-in in case there is a sound associated with this event.

WSERV now processes those key up or down events that the key translator object decided gave rise to character events. This processing is quite involved and I will describe it in the next section.

11.4.2   Character events

The main steps WSERV performs in processing character events are:

- Calls the key click plug-in
- Deals with capture keys (including WSERV capture keys)
- Determines who should receive the event
- Checks to see if the event has a long capture
- Checks to see if repeat timer should start
- Queues the event.

First, WSERV sends the event to the key click plug-in, if there is one. The key translator object has already returned a flag to say whether the character event should be captured, so WSERV checks this and sets the destination for the event accordingly. If the key has not been captured, then WSERV sends the event to the currently focused window. If the event was captured but WSERV is currently displaying the password window, then WSERV only sends the event if it was captured by the same group window as the password window.

If the character event is one of WSERV's capture keys, then WSERV will have captured it itself. In this case, WSERV will process the event immediately and not send it on to a client.

If the key is either:

- A long capture key, or
- There is currently no repeating key, and the key is allowed to be auto-repeatable

then the repeat timer is started.

Long capturing is a feature that we added in Symbian OS v7.0. It allows a long press of a key to be treated differently from a quick tap. The long-key-press event and the short-key-press event yielded by a single physical key press can differ both in their destination client and the actual character code generated. This feature allows a quick press of a number key on a phone to enter a number into the "dial number" dialogue, while a longer press of the same key could launch the contacts application and jump to first contact starting with a certain letter.

11.5   Processing pointer events

The processing of pointer events is much more complicated than the processing of key events. This is because WSERV calculates which window to send the event to from the exact location of the click. Pointer grabbing and capturing affect it too.

The normal sequence of pointer events starts with a pointer down event, is followed by zero or more pointer drag events, and ends with a pointer up event. It is possible for all of these events to go to the window visible on the screen at the location that they occur. However, there are two features that clients can use to vary this behavior: grabbing and capturing.

If a window receives a down event and it is set to grab pointer events, then WSERV sends all the drag events and the following up event to that window, even if they actually take place over other windows. If a window is capturing, and the down event is on a window behind it, then the window that is capturing will receive the event. If that window is also grabbing, then it will receive the following drag and up events too.

In practice, most windows will grab pointer events and some windows will also capture them too. Capturing allows dialogs to prevent pointer events from being sent to windows behind them.

WSERV takes the following major steps during the processing of pointer events:

- Calculates the actual window the pointer event is on

- Determines if another window's grabbing or capturing means that it should get the pointer event

- Queues enter and exit events if the current window has changed

- Tells the key click plug-in about the pointer event

- For move and drag events, checks the window to see if it doesn't want such events

- If the window has requested it, stores move and drag events in a pointer buffer

- If window has a virtual keyboard and the event occurs on one of the virtual keys, converts the event to a key event

- Checks the event to see if it should be a double-click event, and if a drag-drop event is needed too.

WSERV calculates the actual window that a pointer event occurs in by analyzing the window tree in a recursive way. Starting with top-level client windows, it finds the foremost window at that level that contains the point on which the user clicked. Then it goes on to check each of this window's children, and so it continues, until there are no more children or none of the children contain the point. Then WSERV analyses the windows in the same way again, but this time it checks the capturing flag of each window to see if it should be capturing the event.

When WSERV adds a move or a drag event to the client queue, it checks the event that is currently at the end of the client queue, and if this is an identical event apart from the co-ordinates, then WSERV will just replace the old event with the new one. This means that the client won't get very fine-grained information on pen or mouse moves. This is no problem, indeed it is beneficial, for most applications, but for a drawing application it is not ideal. So, for such applications, WSERV can alternatively store all the events that it gets from the kernel in a buffer, and the client will then get a block of them delivered at once.

11.6   Client queues

WSERV uses client queues to store events while they are waiting to be delivered to the client. There are three different queues for each client; each of these stores a different type of event:

- Redraw events

- Priority key events

- All other events (main queue).

We designed priority key events initially for the OPL programming language and this is the only application to use them to date. While an OPL program was running, the user could press Ctrl+Esc and this would immediately terminate the program. This was because this key was delivered via the priority key queue and so could by-pass all other events.

More generally, we have three queues so that the client can treat different events with different active-object priorities. In general, a client wants to receive pointer and key events before any redraw events that are already queued, so it sets the priority on its active objects for the redraw queue to be lower than those for the main queue.

When WSERV has an event for the client, it places the event in the queue and completes the request status that client has supplied for that queue, so the client knows that there is at least one event waiting. But the system may be busy and WSERV may generate many events before the client has the chance to ask for an event. This means that WSERV has to deal with the problem of the queues overflowing.

11.6.1   Overflow in the priority key queue

We designed this queue to take a single key press instructing the application to close; this means that in this queue we are not interested in multiple occurrences of that key press. So the queue only ever holds the last key press that has the relevant special status – if a new event comes along before the old one is delivered, then the old one is overwritten.

11.6.2 Overflow in the redraw queue

The redraw queue is an array that lists all of the client's windows currently needing a redraw. The array is ordered from front to back so that the window to be redrawn first is the foremost one. If there is enough memory available, the array could expand indefinitely – except that each window can only appear in it once.

If at any time the array cannot be extended, then the redraw queue sets a flag to say that the array is not complete. When the array becomes empty and the flag is set, WSERV scans all the client's windows to find one that needs a redraw. Only when it has scanned all the windows will it clear the flag.

11.6.3 Overflow in the event queue

WSERV uses many tactics to avoid or reduce the effect of overflow in this queue. However, they are not foolproof – it might happen that, in very extreme situations, an event could be lost. However, this has not, to our knowledge, happened in practice, or if it has, it has shown no side effects!

The event queue is a global heap cell – there is only one event queue for the whole system. WSERV grows and shrinks this cell as the number of clients changes. The size of the queue is about 48+2*(number of clients) entries and each entry is 40 bytes, the size of a TWsEvent.

The heap cell is divided into sections and each client is allocated a section. WSERV also has the freedom to change the size of each client section within the cell, growing or shrinking the other clients' sections in response. A particular client's section can have between 2 and 32 entries.

If WSERV needs to queue an event, and there isn't room in the client's section, then obviously it will first try to expand the client's section up to its maximum size of 32 entries. (If the client's section already has 32 entries, then WSERV tries to purge that client's queue – in other words, it tries to find an event that it can delete.) To do this, WSERV first tries to find other clients that have room in their sections and shrink those sections. If this fails, then WSERV makes an attempt to purge an event from one of the other clients' queues. The focused client is the last to be chosen for this operation – WSERV will only purge the focused client's queue if none of the other queues have events that can be purged. If the purge fails then the event will be discarded.

To purge events from a client queue, WSERV will try a variety of tactics, including:

- Deleting an associated pair of up and down pointer events. (If the associated up event hasn't been received yet, it will even delete a down event and later delete the next matching up event)

- Deleting key up or down events from the non-focused client queue
- Deleting matched pairs of key up and down events from the focused client queue. (Most applications ignore these events)
- Merging two modifier change events and deleting one of them
- Deleting matched pairs of focused lost and gained events
- Deleting repeated switch on events
- Deleting these events: key events, pointer enter and exit events, drag drop events, pointer buffer ready events and the following pointer events: drag, move, button repeat and switch on.

11.7   A simple handwriting animation DLL

In this section, I will develop a simple handwriting animation DLL. I won't attempt real character recognition, but I will show all the surrounding framework, including getting the pointer events, drawing the ink on the screen and sending a character event to the application. My intention is to explain the basics of anim DLLs, and especially to show how they can deal with events.

We originally designed anim DLLs for clocks in Symbian OS v5. At this time they provided two main features:

- Accurate timing information. Simple use of a relative CTimer, for example, would provide a clock that would update slower than real time
- The ability for user code to draw to a window while executing inside the same thread as WSERV, thus avoiding delays caused by IPC.

11.7.1   Creating an anim DLL

There are two parts to an anim DLL: the anim DLL itself, which is a plug-in to WSERV, and the client-side code that loads the anim DLL, and controls it.

It is possible to give an anim DLL the standard type "DLL" in the MMP build file, but then you would need to do more work to set it up correctly. It is better to define it with type ANI:

```
TARGETTYPE     ANI
```

The client-side code then calls the following function to load the anim DLL:

```
TInt RAnimDll::Load(const TDesC &aFileName)
```

WSERV then responds by calling ordinal 1 in the anim DLL. This function should return a sub-class of `CAnimDll` to the server:

```
EXPORT_C CAnimDll* CreateCAnimDllL()
  {
  return new(ELeave) CHandWritingAnimDll();
  }
```

This `CAnimDll` sub-class normally has only one function, which creates the anim DLL plug-in object:

```
class CHandWritingAnimDll : public CAnimDll
  {
public: //Pure virtual function from CAnimDLL
  CAnim* CreateInstanceL(TInt aType);
  };
```

Each anim DLL can supply many different sorts of anim DLL objects, and each one can be instantiated many times. But my example handwriting anim DLL will only provide one such object, so the implementation of this function is quite simple:

```
CAnim* CHandWritingAnimDll::CreateInstanceL(TInt )
  {
  return new(ELeave) CHandWritingAnim();
  }
```

`CreateInstanceL()` is called in response to one of the four overloads of the `RAnim::Construct()` client-side functions:

```
TInt Construct(const RWindowBase &aDevice, TInt aType,
                           const TDesC8 &aParams);
TInt Construct(const RWindowBase &aDevice, TInt aType,
      const TDesC8 &aParams, const TIpcArgs& aIpcArgs);
TInt Construct(const RWsSprite &aDevice, TInt aType,
                           const TDesC8 &aParams);
TInt Construct(const RWsSprite &aDevice, TInt aType,
    const TDesC8 &aParams, const TIpcArgs& aIpcArgs);
```

11.7.2   The two types of anim DLL

Originally, anim DLLs only provided the ability to draw to a single window per anim object. This type of anim DLL is now called a "window anim", and to create one you would return an object derived from `CWindowAnim` from `CreateInstanceL()`.

To provide digital ink on-screen, we developed a new type of anim that allowed drawing to a sprite. This is known as a "sprite anim", and to create one you would return an object derived from `CSpriteAnim` from `CreateInstanceL()`. The relationships between these, and other, classes are shown in Figure 11.2.

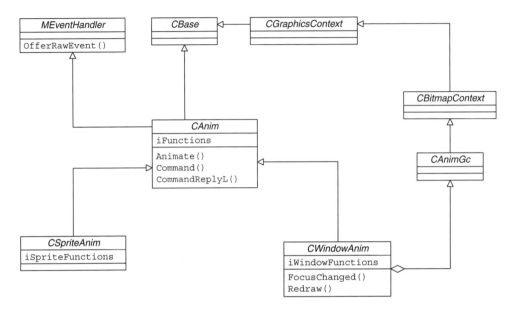

Figure 11.2   Animation class hierarchy

There are two types of functions in the anim interface. Firstly, there are functions in the anim that WSERV calls. These are shown in the diagram as member functions of the four classes: `MEventHandler`, `CAnim`, `CSpriteAnim` and `CWindowAnim`; they are all pure virtual functions and so the anim writer has to provide implementations for the relevant set of these functions, depending on which class she has derived from.

The WSERV functions that an anim can call are provided by means of the member data shown in Figure 11.2. There are four in all, shown with the class they belong to in parentheses:

- `iFunctions` (`MAnimGeneralFunctions`)

- `iSpriteFunctions` (`MAnimSpriteFunctions`)

- `iWindowFunctions` (`MAnimWindowFunctions`)

- `iGc` (`CAnimGc`).

`CAnimGc` provides drawing functions that the window anim uses to draw to its window.

Thus our example `CHandWritingAnim` is a sub-class of `CSprite-Anim`.

11.7.3   Functions a sprite anim must provide

All the derived classes of `CSpriteAnim` must provide all the virtual
functions of that class, `CAnim` and `MEventHandler`, so part of our class
definition will be:

```
class CHandWritingAnim : public CSpriteAnim
  {
public:
  ~CHandWritingAnim();
  //pure virtual functions from CSpriteAnim
  void ConstructL(TAny* aArgs);
  //pure virtual functions from MEventHandler
  TBool OfferRawEvent(const TRawEvent& aRawEvent);
  //pure virtual functions from CAnim
  void Animate(TdateTime* aDateTime);
  void Command(TInt aOpcode,TAny* aArgs);
  TInt CommandReplyL(TInt aOpcode,TAny* aArgs);
private:
  TInt iState;
  CFbsBitmapDevice* iBitmapDevice;
  CFbsBitmapDevice* iMaskBitmapDevice;
  CFbsBitGc* iSpriteGc;
  TBool iIsMask;
  CPointStore* iPointStore;
  };
```

I will talk about the purpose of these functions in the following
sections.

11.7.3.1   Construction

The first anim DLL function that will be called is `CSpriteAnim::`
`ConstructL`. WSERV calls this function when responding to the client's
call to `RAnim::Construct()`. The parameter `aArgs` passed to the
`ConstructL` function is a pointer to a copy of the content of the
descriptor that was originally passed in to the client-side `Construct`
function. It will normally need casting to the correct type.

```
void CHandWritingAnim::ConstructL(TAny* )
  {
  TSpriteMember* spriteMember=iSpriteFunctions->GetSpriteMember(0);
  iIsMask=(spriteMember->iBitmap->Handle()
                           !=spriteMember->iMaskBitmap->Handle());
  iBitmapDevice=CFbsBitmapDevice::NewL(spriteMember->iBitmap);
  if (iIsMask)
    iMaskBitmapDevice=CFbsBitmapDevice::NewL(spriteMember->iMaskBitmap);
  iSpriteGc=CFbsBitGc::NewL();
  iSpriteGc->Reset();
  iState=EHwStateInactive;
```

```
iPointStore=new(ELeave) CPointStore();
iPointStore->ConstructL();
iSpriteFunctions->SizeChangedL();
...
}
```

The call to `GetSpriteMember()` returns details of the sprite that this anim is allowed to draw to. Usually, sprites can animate. To do this, a client needs to give a sprite several members – each member contains one frame of the animation. In this case, the client only needs to create one frame for the ink and thus we specify a value of "0" as the parameter in this function call. This is then checked to see if the client has provided separate bitmaps for the mask and the sprite content. Drawing to any graphics object, such as a bitmap or the screen, requires a device for that object. From a device, we can create a graphics context (or GC) and use this to do the drawing. We now create the following objects – a `CFbsBitmapDevice` for each bitmap and a single `CFbsBitGc` which can be used on both bitmaps.

The state member, `iState`, is initialized to say that no handwriting recognition is currently required. Since the shape drawn on the screen is to be converted to a character, we create a point store so that the detailed shape of the ink can be recorded. The call to `SizeChangedL()` is part of the standard, general initialization of a sprite. It sets up the backup bitmap for the sprite, which needs to be the size of the largest frame. This function will go on to set the parameters for the ink, such as color and line width – this is not shown in the previous code segment.

11.7.3.2 *Receiving events*

Events are received when WSERV calls the function: `MEventHandler::OfferRawEvent()`, see Section 11.3, *How WSERV processes events*. Remember that this function was pure virtual in the base class, and so I have an implementation in my `CHandwritingAnim` class. By default, WSERV will not pass events to anims, so if the anim wants to receive the events, it has to call the function `MAnimGeneralFunctions::GetRawEvents()`, passing in the parameter `ETrue`. Once an event has been passed to the Anim DLL, it has to return a `TBool` to say if it has consumed the event (`ETrue`) or not (`EFalse`):

```
TBool CHandWritingAnim::OfferRawEvent(const TRawEvent &aRawEvent)
  {
  if (iState==EHwStateDeactive)
    return EFalse;
  switch (aRawEvent.Type())
    {
  case TRawEvent::EButton1Down:
```

```
  return HandlePointerDown(aRawEvent.Pos());
case TRawEvent::EPointerMove:
  return HandlePointerMove(aRawEvent.Pos());
case TRawEvent::EButton1Up:
  return HandlePointerUp(aRawEvent.Pos());
default:
  return EFalse;
  }
}
```

The first thing this function does is to check to see if handwriting is turned on. If it is not, it will return `EFalse` to tell WSERV to process the event itself. It also does this if the event is not a pointer event; this is what the `default` part of the switch statement is for. This function then calls three other functions that will process the pointer events. I have not shown an implementation of these functions, but will note that it would be advisable for them to adopt the strategy that if the user clicks and holds for a certain length of time, then this should be treated as a pointer to be sent to applications, rather than for drawing digital ink.

11.7.3.3 Animating

The `Animate()` function is designed for receiving periodic events to update the clock.

```
void Animate(TDateTime* aDateTime);
```

By default, WSERV does not call this virtual function. If an anim does want it to be called, then the anim should call this function:

```
void MAnimGeneralFunctions::SetSync(TAnimSync aSyncMode);
```

The parameter specifies how often to call the `Animate()` function. The options are:

```
enum TAnimSync
  {
  ESyncNone,
  ESyncFlash,
  ESyncSecond,
  ESyncMinute,
  ESyncDay,
  };
```

Clearly `ESyncNone` means that WSERV never animates. The remaining three values tell WSERV to call the animate function after the specified time intervals.

The second value is slightly different. It tells WSERV to animate twice a second. However, these animations are not evenly spaced, every half a second – they happen on the second and after 7/12 of a second. This is so that when the separator character (the ":" in "12:45:37") flashes it will be visible for slightly longer than it is invisible. (WSERV uses the same internal timer to flash the cursor (and sprites), which also are visible for slightly longer than they are invisible.)

To do these animations, WSERV uses a lock timer (possibly the only use of a lock timer in Symbian OS). This timer makes it easy for WSERV to determine if the system is running slowly. Its API is:

```
void CTimer::Lock(TTimerLockSpec aLock);
```

The parameter specifies a particular twelfth of a second. The first time the function is called, the kernel will signal the associated active object when it reaches that point in the second. The second time the function is called, the kernel will only signal the active object if the requested twelfth of the second is within a second of the first requested point. If it is not, the function will return with an error, showing that the system is very busy.

Suppose, for example, that a clock uses this timer to update a display of seconds. Each second, the clock calls the lock timer to ask to be notified when the current second is over. At the next second boundary, the kernel signals the active object. If the active object runs and re-queues itself within that second, everything is fine. If the system is busy and by the time the active object runs and re-queues itself, the second had passed, then the active object will complete with an error telling the clock that it needs to reset itself, rather than just doing an increment.

When WSERV gets an error back from the lock timer, it tells the anim that it should reset itself by passing the current date-time to the animate function. (When things are running normally, it passes NULL to this function.)

Although the handwriting anim does not need to do any animation, it does need a timer. Instead of creating its own timer, it uses the CTimer::Lock() function to receive timer notifications – I will say more on this later.

11.7.3.4 Client communication

The following functions can both receive commands from the client side:

```
TInt CAnim::CommandReplyL(TInt aOpcode, TAny* aArgs)=0;
void CAnim::Command(TInt aOpcode, TAny* aArgs)=0;
```

One difference between them is that the first one can also return a TInt value to the client. It can do this either by returning the value to send back to the client, or by leaving – the leave code will then be sent to the client. Another difference between these two functions is that the first one is sent directly to the window server. This is done because the client needs to know the return value before any more of its code can execute, while the second function will just be stored by WSERV on the client side and sent to the server side later. WSERV calls these functions in response to the client calls to the RAnim functions CommandReply() and Command(), respectively:

```
void CHandWritingAnim::Command(TInt aOpcode,TAny* aArgs)
  {
  THandAnimArgUnion pData;
  pData.any=aArgs;
  switch (aOpcode)
    {
  case EHwOpActivate:
    Activate();
    break;
  case EHwOpDeactivate:
    Deactivate();
    break;
  case EHwOpSetDrawData:
    SetDrawData(pData.DrawData);
    break;
  default:
    iFunctions->Panic();
    }
  }
```

The previous function shows three commands that the client can call on the handwriting anim. These are to turn the handwriting recognition on and off, and to change some display settings, such as line-width and color. The client has to pass a large block of data with this call; this is passed into the function with an untyped pointer. To avoid a cast, we use a union, but of course this provides no more type safety that a cast would – it just makes the code more readable.

```
union THandAnimArgUnion
  {
  const TAny* Any;
  const TBool* Bool;
  const THandwritingDrawData* DrawData;
  };
```

The CommandReplyL() function also provides two functions that the client can call:

```
TInt CHandWritingAnim::CommandReplyL(TInt aOpcode, TAny* aArgs)
  {
  THandAnimArgUnion pData;
```

```
pData.any=aArgs;
switch (aOpcode)
  {
case EHwOpSpriteMask:
  SpriteChangeL(*pData.Bool);
  break;
case EHwOpGetLastChar:
  return iLastGeneratedCharacter;
default:
  iFunctions->Panic();
  }
return KErrNone;
}
```

The first function allows the client to change the bitmaps that are actually used to draw the ink. There is no return value from this function, but it can fail. In this case it will leave and the leave value will be returned to the client. The second function returns the last generated character to the client.

11.7.4 Handling pointer events and updating the sprite

When a pointer down is received, the anim sets a timer. It does this because the pointer event might be a click on a UI feature rather than the start of the drawing of some digital ink. If the user clicks and holds until the timer expires, or clicks and releases without moving the pen, then this indicates a click on a UI feature.

The following routine deals with pointer move events. It only has to deal with them when the handwriting is active and the pen is down, so most states just return EFalse to say that the event has not been consumed:

```
TBool CHandWritingAnim::HandlePointerMove(TPoint aPoint)
  {
  switch (iState)
    {
  case EHwStateWaitingMove:
    {
    cont TInt KMinMovement=5
    TPoint moved=aPoint-iCurrentDrawPoint;
    if (Abs(moved.iX)< KMinMovement && Abs(moved.iY)< KMinMovement)
      return ETrue;
    iSpriteFunctions->Activate(ETrue);
    DrawPoint();
    iState=EHwStateDrawing;
    }
  case EHwStateDrawing:
    break;
  default:
    return EFalse;
    }
  DrawLine(aPoint);
```

```
UpdateSprite();
return ETrue;
}
```

If we are still waiting for the timer to expire (`iState==EHwState-WaitingMove`), and the point is still close to the original down, then the move event is ignored – but it is still consumed. If not, the anim makes the sprite visible by calling the `Activate()` function, then draws a point into the sprite, and updates the state to indicate that drawing is in progress. It then calls the following function to draw a line into the sprite bitmap:

```
void CHandWritingAnim::DrawLine(TPoint aEndPoint)
  {
  iSpriteGc->Activate(iBitmapDevice);
  iSpriteGc->SetPenSize(TSize(iDrawData.iLineWidth,
                            iDrawData.iLineWidth));
  iSpriteGc->SetPenColor(iDrawData.iLineColor);
  iSpriteGc->MoveTo(iCurrentDrawPoint);
  iSpriteGc->DrawLineTo(aEndPoint);
  if (iMaskBitmapDevice)
    {
    iSpriteGc->Activate(iMaskBitmapDevice);
    iSpriteGc->SetPenSize(TSize(iDrawData.iMaskLineWidth,
                              iDrawData.iMaskLineWidth));
    //Mask must be drawn in black
    iSpriteGc->SetPenColor(KRgbBlack);
    iSpriteGc->MoveTo(iCurrentDrawPoint);
    iSpriteGc->DrawLineTo(aEndPoint);
    }
  iCurrentDrawPoint=aEndPoint;
  iPointStore->AddPoint(aEndPoint);
  }
```

The anim uses the same graphics context to draw to the sprite bitmap and to the mask bitmap – it activates that context on the bitmap device of the bitmap in which the drawing is to be done. If there is no mask, then the anim will use the bitmap itself as the mask, and so the ink will have to be drawn in black. If there is a mask, then the line of the digital ink needs to be drawn into the mask and the bitmap. In this case, it should be drawn in black in the mask, but any color can be used for the ink in the bitmap. WSERV stores the end point of the line, so that it can use it as the starting point of the line the next time this function is called. It also stores the point in a buffer so that later on the character recognition algorithm can make an analysis of the ink shape. After the bitmaps are updated, the code calls this function to update the screen (see `CHandWritingAnim::HandlePointerMove` earlier in the chapter):

```
void CHandWritingAnim::UpdateSprite()
  {
  TRect drawTo;
```

```
iSpriteGc->RectDrawnTo(drawTo);
iSpriteFunctions->UpdateMember(0,drawTo,EFalse);
}
```

When any drawing is being done, BITGDI keeps track of which pixels have been drawn to – or at least a bounding rectangle of those pixels. This rectangle is not always pixel perfect, but serves as a good approximation. This rectangle is retrieved by calling `RectDrawnTo()` and this same function also resets the rectangle. Then the function calls the update member function. This is a function provided by WSERV to all sprite anims and its purpose is to correct the screen in the area of this rectangle.

The normal way to update a sprite is to remove it and then draw it again to the screen – but of course if this is done, the screen will flicker. In Symbian OS v5u, we added a way to update a sprite without flicker – this is the function used in the previous code and defined thus:

```
void MAnimSpriteFunctions::UpdateMember(TInt aMember
          ,const TRect& aRect,TBool aFullUpdate);
```

The third parameter to this function tells WSERV whether it should do a full update of the sprite by removing it and redrawing it, or just do an incremental update by redrawing the sprite to the screen. Obviously, when drawing digital ink, the ink only increases, so if we do an incremental update we will get the correct screen content. (It's worth noting that there is one circumstance in which WSERV will do a full update even if an incremental one is requested. If there is no mask bitmap, then the way the bitmap is drawn to the screen is determined by the `iDrawMode` member of the `TSpriteMember` class. If this is not `EDrawModePEN`, then WSERV will always do a full update.)

11.7.5 Sending events

There are two situations in which the anim will need to send (or create) an event. The first is when the ink is converted to a character. The second is when the timer goes off, without the user having moved the pen from the position where it was clicked down. Since the down event itself was consumed, the anim will need to resend it so that the client code can act upon it. This is done in the following code:

```
void CHandWritingAnim::CharacterFinished()
    {
    iState=EHwStateInactive;
    iLastGeneratedCharacter=iPointStore->GetChar();
    TKeyEvent keyEvent;
    keyEvent.iCode=iLastGeneratedCharacter;
    keyEvent.iScanCode=iLastGeneratedCharacter;
```

```
    keyEvent.iModifiers=0;
    keyEvent.iRepeats=0;
    iFunctions->PostKeyEvent(keyEvent);
    iPointStore->ClearPoints();
    iSpriteFunctions->Activate(EFalse);
    ClearSprite();
    }

void CHandWritingAnim::SendEatenDownEvent()
    {
    TRawEvent rawEvent;
    rawEvent.Set(TRawEvent::EButton1Down
            ,iCurrentDrawPoint.iX,iCurrentDrawPoint.iY);
    iFunctions->PostRawEvent(rawEvent);
    iState=EHwStateInactive;
    }
```

There are two functions that allow an anim to send events and they are both illustrated in the previous code and defined in `MAnimGeneral-Functions`. This is one of the classes that allows anims to call functions on WSERV:

```
void PostRawEvent(const TRawEvent& aRawEvent) const;
void PostKeyEvent(const TKeyEvent& aRawEvent) const;
```

`PostRawEvent()` is used by an anim to send the down event. It allows the sending of any raw event (that is, one of the set of events that the kernel sends to WSERV) into WSERV for processing. It's worth noting that the first thing that WSERV will do with the event is to pass it back to any anims that are receiving events – so it would be easy for code to create an infinite loop with bad use of this function! You can send most key events using `PostRawEvent()`, but you would have to send a key up event, a key down event and in some cases up and down events for modifier keys too. This is the reason for the existence of the second function, `PostKeyEvent()`, which allows the sending of an `EEventKey` event.

11.7.6 Client-side code – construction

The client has to create both the anim and the sprite. A class, `CHand-Writing`, is used to own and manage both of these. I have written this class to allow it to be included into any other project that wants to own the handwriting anim:

```
class CHandWriting : public CBase
    {
public:
    CHandWriting(RWsSession& aSession);
    void ConstructL(TSize aScreenSize, RWindowGroup& aGroup,
                            TBool aUseSeparateMask);
```

```
        ~CHandWriting();
        void SetMaskL(TBool aUseSeparateMask);
        void ToggleStatus();
private:
        void CreateSpriteL(TSize aScreenSize, RWindowGroup& aGroup,
                                        TBool aUseSeparateMask);
        void LoadDllL();
        void FillInSpriteMember(TSpriteMember& aMember);
private:
    RWsSession& iSession;
    RAnimDll iAnimDll;
    RHandWritingAnim iAnim;
    RWsSprite iSprite;
    CFbsBitmap *iBitmap;
    CFbsBitmap *iMaskBitmap;
    TBool iActive;
    };
```

The sprite has to be created first as this has to be passed to the function that constructs the anim. We do this using the following two routines:

```
void CHandWriting::CreateSpriteL(TSize aScreenSize,
          RWindowGroup& aGroup,TBool aUseSeparateMask)
    {
    TInt color,gray;  //Unused variables
    TDisplayMode mode=iSession .GetDefModeMaxNumColors(color,gray);
    iBitmap=new(ELeave) CFbsBitmap();
    User::LeaveIfError(iBitmap->Create(aScreenSize,mode));
    TSpriteMember member;
    member.iMaskBitmap=iBitmap;
    if (aUseSeparateMask)
        {
        iMaskBitmap=new(ELeave) CFbsBitmap();
        User::LeaveIfError(iMaskBitmap->Create(aScreenSize,mode));
        member.iMaskBitmap=iMaskBitmap;
        }
    User::LeaveIfError(iSprite.Construct(aGroup,TPoint(),
                 ESpriteNoChildClip|ESpriteNoShadows));
    FillInSpriteMember(member);
    iSprite.AppendMember(member);
    }

void CHandWriting::FillInSpriteMember(TSpriteMember& aMember)
    {
    aMember.iBitmap=iBitmap;
    aMember.iInvertMask=ETrue;        //Must be inverted
    aMember.iDrawMode=CGraphicsContext::EDrawModePEN;
                         //Ignored when using mask
    aMember.iOffset=TPoint();    //Must be 0,0
    aMember.iInterval=0;
    //Not used as only one TSpriteMember in sprite
    }
```

We construct the sprite by calling iSprite.Construct() in the third line from the end of the first routine. All sprites have to be associated with a window, and they will always be clipped to the area of that window. If you specify a group window, as I do in the previous code, then the sprite will be allowed to display over the whole screen. By default, the sprite will also be clipped to the window's visible area. In this case, however, my code specifies the flag ESpriteNoChildClip, which means that this clipping is not done. Thus the hand writing will always be able to appear over the whole screen, even if the group window involved is behind other windows. The other flag, ESpriteNoShadows, means that even if there is a shadow-casting window above the sprite window, WSERV will not shadow the pixels of the sprite. Once the sprite has been created, I add a member or frame to it. This is done in the final two lines of the function.

The other point of note in this function is the color depth with which the sprite's bitmaps are created. When sprites are drawn to the screen, WSFRV uses either BitBlt() or BitBltMasked() from the CFbsBitGc class. These functions execute much faster when the bitmap that they are drawing and the bitmap or screen that they are drawing it to have the same color depth. For a sprite that is normally viewed over a window, it is best to set the sprite's bitmaps to the same color depth as the window. However, for the handwriting anim, where the sprite is effectively viewed over the whole screen, it is best to choose the default color mode of windows, since most applications will be running with this color depth. You can find out what this is by calling the function GetDefModeMaxNumColors().

Having created the sprite, we can create the anim. There are two stages to this – first we ask WSERV to load the anim DLL and then we create the instance of the sprite animation. We do this using the following two functions, the second being called by the first:

```
void CHandWriting::LoadDllL()
  {
  _LIT(DllName,"HandAnim.DLL");
  TInt err=iAnimDll.Load(DllName);
  if (err==KErrNone)
    err=iAnim.Construct(iSprite);
  if (err==KErrNone)
    {
    iAnim.Activate();
    iActive=ETrue;
    }
  User::LeaveIfError(err);
  }

TInt RHandWritingAnim::Construct(const RWsSprite& aDevice)
  {
  TPtrC8 des(NULL,0);
  return RAnim::Construct(aDevice,0,des);
  }
```

To load the anim DLL, you must give WSERV the name of the DLL involved. You do this using an RAnimDll object. Then you need an RAnim-derived class – since the interface of RAnim is protected to force you to derive from it. The interface to the anim constructor has three parameters. These are the sprite of the window, a type and the configuration data packed in to a descriptor. The type allows one anim DLL to have many anim types, this being the way to specify which one to create. In my example, the handwriting anim only has one type, and there is no configuration data used.

11.7.7   Other client-side code

RHandWritingAnim contains several other functions for communicating with the anim. Here are a couple of examples:

```
void RHandWritingAnim::SetDrawData(const THandwritingDrawData& aDrawData)
  {
  TPckgBuf<THandwritingDrawData> param;
  param()=aDrawData;
  Command(EHwOpSetDrawData,param);
  }

TInt RHandWritingAnim::GetLastGeneratedCharacter()
  {
  return CommandReply(EHwOpGetLastChar);
  }
```

The first of these functions tells the handwriting animation to draw the digital ink differently (that is, with different color or line width). This requires the sending of data to the anim – this is packaged into a descriptor using the TPckgBuf class. Since no return value is needed, it can just use the RAnim::Command() function. This will in turn be passed to the function CHandWritingAnim::Command() function.

The second function is passed the code of the last generated character. There is no data to send with this request, so it doesn't need to use a TPckgBuf, but since it does require a reply, it uses RAnim::Command-Reply() and this request gets sent in turn to the function CHand-WritingAnim::CommandReplyL().

11.8   Window objects and classes

Windows are the mechanism that Symbian OS uses to control access to the screen. They are rectangular by default and may overlap each other. They have a front to back order, and this defines which of two overlapping windows is in front. Applications may create and destroy windows. Windows are individually addressable, and an application can draw to only one of its windows at a time. Typically an application will have many windows.

Windows are important since they allow different applications to draw to different parts of the screen at the same time. Furthermore, applications do not need to concern themselves with which part of the screen they are allowed to draw to. An application just draws to its window, and only if that window is visible will it appear on the screen.

In the following sections, I will cover the window tree, the ways in which WSERV navigates this structure, window classes and their structure, the properties of windows, drawing windows and more. I will also cover Direct Screen Access (DSA), which could also be described as drawing without windows.

11.8.1 Diagram of the window tree

Figure 11.3 shows the relationships between different windows. It is presented as an upside down tree. It shows what different window types can appear at which point in the tree.

Figure 11.3 shows four types of windows (although one of them, Group Win, is never displayed and so is not a window as windows are defined above). This diagram is an object diagram in which each row can only contain objects of a certain class type. The different types of windows shown are:

- The root window. WSERV creates this window; it is not directly accessible to any client. It is used as a starting point for the window structure and exists throughout the life of the system. On multiple screen devices there will one of these for each screen

- Group windows. These windows can only be direct children of the root window. WSERV's client creates them, but they do not have any associated screen area. They provide a way for a client to group together some of its windows, so that it can move them together

- Top client window. The third row in the figure consists only of top client windows. These windows are displayable, and so a client will need at least one of these

- Client windows. All the subsequent rows of the diagram consist of client windows. A client can have anything from no client windows to multiple levels of nested client windows.

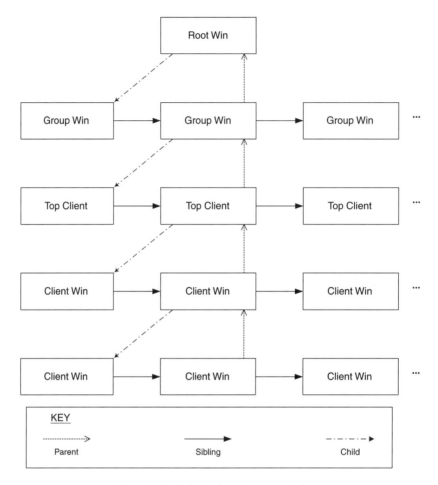

Figure 11.3   Relationships between windows

The following table shows the classes that represent these types of windows, on both the client and server side:

Window type	Client-side class	Server-side class
Root Window	`<none>`	`CWsRootWindow`
Group Window	`RWindowGroup`	`CWsWindowGroup`
Top Client Window	Subclass of `RWindowBase`	`CWsTopClientWindow`
Client Window	Subclass of `RWindowBase`	`CWsClientWindow`

11.8.2 Traversing the window tree

Figure 11.3 contains three different types of arrows. These represent pointers to objects, and give the structure of the window tree thus:

- Parent. These are the arrows that point upward. All windows have a pointer to their parent window on the line above. (Since the root window doesn't have a parent, its pointer will be NULL)

- Child. These are the diagonal arrows down to the left. They show that if a window has any child windows, then it will have a pointer to the first, usually the oldest, such window. (By default the pointer will denote the first window created, but of course the order of the children can be changed, so this is not always the case)

- Sibling. These are the arrows going across to the right. They show that each window knows the next oldest window with the same parent. Siblings form a singly linked list of all windows with the same parent. (As for the child pointer, this oldest to youngest ordering holds at the time the windows are created, but may subsequently be altered.)

These pointers are defined in the server-side class `CWsWindowBase`, which is the base class for all server-side window classes, as I will show later. You can use the pointers to move through the window objects in various ways. For example, to get to the oldest sibling of your parent, you navigate using `iParent->iChild`.

Let's look at a more complex example of the use of these pointers. The following function updates the pointers when a window is removed from the window tree:

```
void CWsWindowBase::Disconnect()
  {
  if (iParent!=NULL)
    {
    CWsWindowBase** prev=&iParent->iChild;
    while ((*prev)!=this)
      prev=&(*prev)->iSibling;
    *prev=iSibling;
    }
  }
```

When a window is removed from the window tree, only one pointer needs to be updated. If the window is the oldest child of its parent, then the parent's child pointer needs to be updated. If it is not, then its next oldest sibling's `iSibling` pointer needs updating. In both cases, the pointers need to be updated to point to the next younger sibling.

11.8.3 Walking the window tree

There are many occasions when the window tree must be traversed in the front to back order, for example:

- When a window is made invisible and the windows that it was covering up need to be exposed

- When a window is made visible and the windows behind it are covered up.

There is a single algorithm for doing the traversal, which is used in many places throughout WSERV, and which I will discuss in this section.

There are two rules that define the front to back order of windows as they are shown on the display:

- A child window is always in front of a parent window

- If two windows are children of the same parent then the older is in front of the younger.

The first rule has the consequence that the root window is always the back-most window. One of the root window's jobs is to clear areas of the display where there are no other windows visible. The color it will use can be set by calling the function `RWsSession::SetBackgroundColor()`.

The walk window tree mechanism is implemented in a single function, `CWindowBase::WalkWindowTree()`, which uses the three pointers that link all windows to traverse the windows in the correct order. `WalkWindowTree()` takes a class with a virtual function as a parameter, and on each new window it finds, it calls the virtual function passing the window as a parameter.

One of the parameters of this function is: `TWalkWindowTreeBase& aWalkClass`. Figure 11.4 shows some of the derived classes and the virtual function on this class – `DoIt()`.

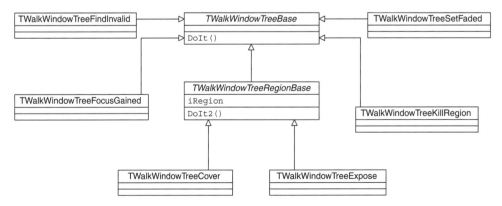

Figure 11.4 Walking the window tree

In all, there are over 20 classes deriving from `TWalkWindowTree-Base` for a variety of different purposes. Some operations only apply to visible windows, hence the need for `TWalkWindowTreeRegionBase`. One of the members of this class is a region, which is initialized to the whole area of the screen. When the operation is applied to each window, the visible area of that window is subtracted from the region and when this region becomes empty no more windows are scanned.

11.8.4 Class structure of windows

Figure 11.5 shows all the classes that we use to represent windows, on both the server and the client sides. You can see that the class structure on the two different sides is not quite the same. The purpose of `RWindowTreeNode` and `CWsWindowBase` is to represent a window that

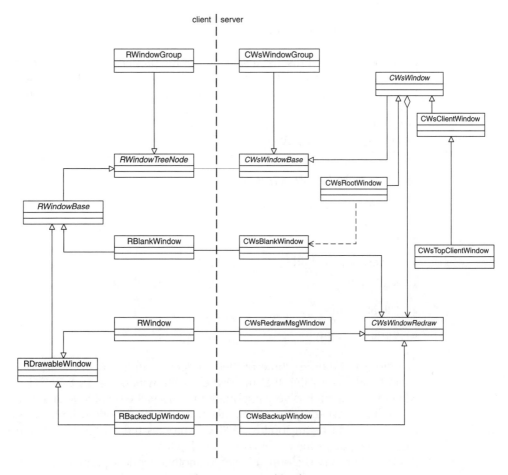

Figure 11.5 Window classes

fits into the window tree at any point. The equivalence of the window-group classes is clear. Yet the other part of the class structure takes a very different shape. On the client side, the class structure is determined by the drawing functionality that each class provides. On the server side, the class structure is more closely related to the window's position in the window tree. The difference in drawing behavior is determined by a plug-in object, which is a class deriving from `CWsWindowRedraw`.

When we consider windows from the drawing point of view, there are three types of windows: blank windows, bitmap backup windows and redraw windows. I will describe the exact differences between these sorts of windows in later sections of this chapter.

The root window, being a derived class of `CWsWindow`, also has a plug-in drawing object. Its type is "blank window" since it is only ever drawn with a solid color; this is shown by a dotted line in the figure.

11.9   Properties of windows

In this section I will discuss a selection of the properties of the different classes of windows. With the exception of the root window, which WSERV creates during bootup, all other windows are created at the request of a WSERV client. Clients are said to own the windows they create. The owner has control of certain properties of the window, while others are assigned by WSERV.

11.9.1   Properties held by all windows

Properties held by all windows include:

- Parent
- Oldest or first child
- Next sibling
- Client handle
- Ordinal priority.

I've discussed the first three of these properties in earlier sections. The client handle is a value that the owner of the window gives to WSERV when it is created. It is very important that this value be unique amongst all windows owned by the client, otherwise the client code will not work as expected. In debug builds, WSERV enforces the uniqueness of the values, and panics the client if they are duplicated.

Ordinal priority is closely related to another window property, known as ordinal position. Ordinal priority is a value set by the owner of a window and it is stored on the server side. Ordinal position concerns a window's position among the other children of its parent. This value isn't stored explicitly, but can be calculated by analyzing the structure of the server-side window classes. The rule is that if two children of the same parent have different ordinal priority then the one that has the highest will always be older and therefore in front of the one with the lowest. If we have a group of children, all with the same priority, then their ordinal position will start at zero and increase through consecutive positive integers. For example, suppose that a window has five children, two of ordinal priority ten and three of ordinal priority zero. Then the two with ordinal priority ten will be the oldest, and in front of the others, and their ordinal positions will be zero and one. Similarly, the three of ordinal priority zero will have ordinal positions zero, one and two.

One use of ordinal priority is to make sure a group window comes in front (or behind) other group windows. For example, the group window associated with the application picker in the UIQ interface has a negative ordinal priority to ensure that it appears behind all the normal applications, which by default have zero for their ordinal priority.

11.9.2 Properties of group windows

Properties of group windows include:

- Name

- Identifier

- Screen device.

The identifier is a number from 1 to 10,000 inclusive that WSERV assigns to each group window. The numbers are unique across all group windows in existence at any one time; they are also allocated cyclically so that when a group window is destroyed, it is unlikely that its identifier will be used again immediately. Identifiers give applications a way of discovering all of the group windows in the system at any time. The APIs in RWsSession use identifiers as a means of referring to group windows:

```
TInt SetWindowGroupOrdinalPosition(TInt aIdentifier, TInt aPosition);
TInt GetWindowGroupClientThreadId(TInt aIdentifier, TThreadId &aThreadId);
TInt GetWindowGroupHandle(TInt aIdentifier);
TInt GetWindowGroupOrdinalPriority(TInt aIdentifier);
TInt SendEventToWindowGroup(TInt aIdentifier, const TWsEvent &aEvent);
TInt FindWindowGroupIdentifier(TInt aPreviousIdentifier,
                const TDesC& aMatch, TInt aOffset=0);
TInt FindWindowGroupIdentifier(TInt aPreviousIdentifier,
                                TThreadId aThreadId);
TInt SendMessageToWindowGroup(TInt aIdentifier,TUid aUid,
                                const TDesC8 &aParams);
```

These functions allow group windows to be listed, interrogated and re-ordered.

There are two API functions for setting and getting a group window's name in the `RWindowGroup` class. In addition, there is one API function in the `RWsSession` class:

```
TInt GetWindowGroupNameFromIdentifier(TInt aIdentifier,
                              TDes &aWindowName);
```

Group window names are used so that the system can get a list of running applications.

It is normal for a WSERV client to create a screen device, `CWsScreenDevice`, which has an associated object of class `DWsScreenDevice` created in the server. The first screen device created by a client becomes the primary screen device for that client. This screen device will be assigned to each group window that that client creates. Group windows created before the primary screen device are never associated with a screen device.

The association of group windows with screen devices is used in systems with more than one screen size mode. (In future, it will also be used in systems with more than one screen.) In this case, each screen device has a screen size mode associated with it. If the current system screen size mode differs from the screen device's screen size mode, then WSERV will make all of the group windows and their children invisible.

11.9.3   Properties of client windows

Client windows have two screen modes and many different areas or regions.

11.9.3.1   Screen modes

The two screen modes (or color depths) are both associated with the screen mode that the client requests. One of these is the drawing mode, which specifies which set of colors can be drawn to the window. The other mode is the hardware mode, which is the minimum mode that the hardware needs to be switched into so that this window can be displayed correctly. A window can request its own drawing mode, but by default WSERV will give it the mode that is specified in the WSINI.INI file using the keyword WINDOWMODE. WSERV calculates the actual drawing mode that a window will get using the requested mode and the modes available on the hardware. In Symbian OS, color modes are specified using the enum `TDisplayMode`. These have a naming convention, depending on whether they are gray scale or color, and the number of colors they contain. So, for example, `EColor64K` is a mode with 65536

Request mode	Drawing mode	Hardware mode
EGray16	EGray16	EColor4K
EColor256	EColor256	EColor4K
EColor64K	EColor64K	EColor64K
EColor16M	EColor64K	EColor64K

non-gray colors. Here are some examples of how the modes get assigned to windows for hardware that supports EColor4K and EColor64K:

The drawing mode is changed to the one requested, unless it requires more colors than the hardware supports.

11.9.3.2 Regions

Windows have many different regions associated with them. I will now discuss some of these. In Symbian OS, we provide a base class, TRegion, which has several derived classes. These classes store a list of disjoint rectangles and can be used to describe a two-dimensional area. There are many manipulation functions for these classes, including functions to add and intersect regions. WSERV makes extensive use of these classes – this is why we recommend that you machine code these classes when porting Symbian OS to new hardware.

Calculating the regions is a time-consuming business. Because of this, WSERV caches the regions after it has first calculated it. Then the next time it needs it, it uses the cached value. This of course means that when an operation takes place that might have changed one of the cached regions, WSERV must discard them all.

Base area

This is the area that the client specifies using the function RWindow-Base::SetShape(). However, the more rectangles that there are in the region describing the area, the greater the processing required when these windows are visible. Thus circular or triangular windows will be particularly inefficient.

By default, windows are rectangular and the same size as their parent. This means that they are full screen if their parent is a group window. Their size can be changed by using the SetSize() function (defined in RWindow or RBlankWindow) or by the SetSizeErr() function (defined in RWindowBase).

Visible area

This is an area that WSERV calculates for each window. It is the area of the window that is not obscured by any other window.

Invalid area

This is the area of a window that is waiting for a redraw. Areas may need redrawing after any of the following:

- They become visible when another window is destroyed or made invisible

- Their window is made visible

- Their window is positioned so it is partly outside the screen and then moved back onto the screen

- Part of their window loses its shadow

- Their window becomes unfaded

- The client calls `Invalidate()` on the window.

Only instantiations of `RWindow` can have invalid areas, since WSERV knows how to draw other window types (see latter section on drawing of windows). The invalid area must be contained in the visible area.

When a window has invalid areas, then WSERV will send it a redraw event. The client can discover the invalid area using the `GetInvalidRegion()` function.

Drawing area

This is the area that WSERV clips drawing to. It is calculated differently, depending on whether the window is being redrawn or not. If it's not being redrawn, then the drawing area is just the visible area less the invalid area. If the window is being redrawn, then the drawing area is the area being redrawn (that is, the area validated by the redraw) less any area that has become invalid since the redraw started.

Shadow area

This is the area of the window that is currently in shadow. When WSERV draws to a window, it actually does the drawing twice. First it draws to the part of the drawing region that is not in shadow, and then it draws to the part that is in shadow. The shadow flag is set for the second drawing.

11.10   Drawing to windows

In this section, I will discuss the different ways to draw to a window and the mechanisms in WSERV to support them.

11.10.1   Drawing of blank windows

WSERV handles the drawing of all blank windows (RBlankWindow) for the client. The client can specify a color for WSERV using the function SetColor(TRgb aColor). When drawing the window, WSERV must take account of the fact that this window could be faded (by calling the RWindowTreeNode::SetFaded() or RWindowBase::Fade-Behind() functions) and that the window could have shadows cast on it. This means that when drawing a blank window, WSERV can use any of four different colors.

11.10.2   Drawing of backup content windows

A client requiring this kind of window must instantiate the class RBackupWindow. These windows could also be called bitmap backup windows, because WSERV keeps the content of the window in a bitmap, so that when the window would otherwise become invalid, WSERV can draw it from the bitmap without needing any co-operation from the owner. WSERV creates a bitmap that is the same size and color depth as the window, and uses this bitmap to mirror the content of the window. Because of the existence of the bitmap, the client must specify the window's color depth when it creates the window. If the client subsequently wants to change the window's size, then the operation may fail if there is not enough memory to change the size of the bitmap.

There are two ways in which the bitmap can be used. When the window is created, the bitmap will store all the parts of the window that are not fully represented on the screen. Situations in which the window's content is not fully represented on the screen include:

- Parts of the window are behind other windows or outside the screen's area

- Parts of the window that have shadow cast upon them

- The window is faded

- There is not enough memory to calculate the area that is fully represented.

However, if the window owner calls the function MaintainBackup() on its window object, then all of the content will also be stored in the bitmap as it changes. The disadvantage of doing this is that most pixels of the window will be drawn twice, to the screen and to the bitmap.

There are two ways in which the two drawings can differ slightly. Firstly, if you are using the DrawBitmap() function, which scales things depending on the twips size of the relevant objects, then the scaling onscreen and in the backup bitmap can be different. This is because the screen and backup bitmap will have slightly different twips to pixel mappings. (This is because the only way to guarantee the same mapping would be to create a backup bitmap the same size as the screen, and of course this would be a waste of memory if the window was small. In any case, the differences are small, being due to rounding errors.) Secondly, the exact color shade can change when copying the content from the screen to the bitmap and back again. If the window is `EColor4K` then the bitmap will also be `EColor4K`. However, the screen may be `EColor64K` because another window that requires this mode is also visible. Even though `EColor64K` has a much richer set of colors, they are not a superset of the colors in `EColor4K`, and sometimes the mappings from one to the other won't be the most ideal.

11.10.3 Drawing to redraw windows

A client requiring this kind of window must instantiate the class `RWindow`. Unlike the windows described in the previous section, WSERV requires co-operation from the client to keep the content of these windows correct. It does this by sending redraw messages to the client telling it that the window content needs redrawing. This happens in the circumstances listed in Section 11.9.3.2, under the title "Invalid area".

A redraw window is either in redraw mode, or not. The mode changes how drawing takes place – the main difference being the drawing area used. This is described in Section 11.9.3.2.

Drawing outside of a redraw is rare in Symbian OS, because of the way that Cone deals with drawing. Cone is a component that makes use of WSERV APIs and provides a framework for the controls used in applications. When a client calls the `DrawNow()` function on a `CCoeControl`, the control invalidates the whole of the control's area and then draws it all again in a redraw.

However, there is nothing to stop a particular application bypassing this mechanism to draw outside of a redraw. This is usually done to update the current content of the window because the application's model has changed – for example, if the user has tapped a key and added another character to a word processor document. This is one of the few situations in which drawing occurs outside of a redraw in Symbian OS. This is because the drawing is done by the component FORM rather than through the normal framework of a control.

Drawing inside a redraw is typically done because an update of the window is needed. That is, part of the window's area has become invalid. WSERV requests a redraw by sending a redraw message to the client to tell it that a specified window needs redrawing. The redraw message also contains a rectangle, to reduce the area of the window that the client needs to draw. The rectangle is the bounding rectangle – that is the smallest rectangle that contains all of the invalid area. The application calls the functions `BeginRedraw()` and `EndRedraw()` on the window object to indicate to WSERV when it wants to do a redraw.

The `BeginRedraw()` function has two variants – one that takes a rectangle and one that doesn't; if the one without a rectangle is used, WSERV will take the rectangle to be the whole of the window. The area that will be drawn by WSERV in response to the draw command is the rectangle that was specified in the `BeginRedraw()` function, intersected with the invalid region. Clearly, if the rectangle specified is greater than the rectangle from the redraw event, then this makes no difference to the redraw. If, it is smaller, then the redraw will only be for part of the invalid region. This will then mean that WSERV must issue another redraw for the remainder of the area that needs drawing. Of course, all this is assuming that no part of the window is invalidated or covered up between WSERV signaling that a redraw is needed and the client acting on the redraw. (If this were to happen, the details become more complicated, but the general principles remain the same.)

Since, in general, a redraw will only draw to part of the window, it is important that the same state of the model (that is, the last drawn content) be reflected in the redraw. To see why, suppose that an application's model changes, but it does not update its window immediately. Then, if it receives a redraw event before it has done the update, it must draw the previous state of the model – because if it drew the current state of the model, part of the window would show the old state while part showed the new. Cone circumvents this requirement, since it always invalidates and redraws the area of the whole control. This means that all the pixels will always be drawn – and so it is safe for the client application to draw the new state of the model.

This section covers redraws from when Symbian OS was first released, until Symbian OS v7.0. In later releases, we have added two new features that complicate things further. These are flicker-free redrawing and redraw command storing, and I will discuss them after I have explained a window property known as "backup behind", which allows redrawing to be avoided in certain circumstances.

11.10.4 Backup behind

Backup behind is a property that you can give to any displayable window as you construct it. It is particularly useful for short-lived windows, such as dialogs.

When such a window first becomes visible, WSERV creates a bitmap and copies into it the part of the screen that will be obscured by this window. Then, when the window is deleted, WSERV doesn't need to issue redraws to the windows that were covered, but can use the backup bitmap to restore them.

This feature is expensive on memory, since it requires a bitmap and a region. Thus we limit its use to one window at a time, and say that if a second window requests this functionality, then the first window will lose it. It is also worth noting that this feature can fail due to lack of memory. However, it works in simple situations and can be very useful in avoiding the IPC required by a redraw.

11.10.5 Flicker-free redrawing

We introduced this feature in Symbian OS v7.0s. For it to work, we need at least one full-screen off-screen bitmap (known as the OSB). There will be one OSB if the keyword "FLICKERFREEREDRAW" is present in the WSINI.INI file, and from Symbian OS v8.0 onwards, there will be two OSBs if the keyword "TRANSPARENCY" appears in this file.

When the OSB exists, WSERV uses it for all redraws. When WSERV receives the begin redraw command, all the graphics contexts are redirected to draw to the OSB. Then, when the end redraw command is received, WSERV copies the content of the off-screen bitmap back to the screen.

The advantage of this is that no pixel will be changed on the screen more than once, removing the chance of flicker during the redraw.

There is one functionality change as a result of drawing in this way. Before we introduced this feature, the content of the window was not changed in the begin redraw step. In particular, if a pixel was not drawn, it would remain unchanged. But now, since the whole area that is being validated by the redraw will be copied from the OSB to the screen in the end redraw, even pixels that are not drawn will be copied from the OSB. Since the content of the OSB is undefined, this is obviously undesirable. So, to avoid this problem, we set the area that is being drawn to the background color of the window (or white if it doesn't have one) in the OSB. However, this has been known to cause problems for some drawing code, which assumed that the previous screen content was still there.

11.10.6 Redraw command storing

In Symbian OS v8.0, we added support for transparent windows. This feature requires that WSERV be able to draw the content of windows upon demand. When the client draws a window, WSERV stores the redraw commands. It does this for all windows, not just windows that might be involved with transparency.

The advantage of this to the client is that, so long as it doesn't change the content of the window, it doesn't have to redraw that window each time part of it becomes invalid – WSERV will just reprocess the commands that it has stored. However, if the content of the window does change, then the client must tell WSERV, so that it can discard the commands it has stored. The client can do this by calling `Invalidate()` on the window object for the area that has changed. It's worth noting that before this feature came along, a client could rely on WSERV issuing a redraw when a window was made visible, and use this as a signal to update its content.

11.11 Direct screen access

This could be described as "drawing without windows", since the drawing commands do not go through WSERV.

Before we introduced this feature, clients could create a screen device object and a graphics context object (defined by the BITGDI component – `CFbsScreenDevice` and `CFbsBitGc`), and then use the latter to draw to any area of the screen. The problem was that this would write over any application that happened to be on the screen at the time! So we designed the direct screen access (DSA) feature to give a well-behaved application a means of drawing directly to the screen using the previously mentioned classes, but restricting it only to the area in which its window is visible. The DSA mechanism allows an application to determine the visible area of its window and also to receive notification when that visible area changes.

To do DSA, a client needs to create an instance of `CDirectScreen-Access`. This class has a very simple interface with only six public functions:

```
static CDirectScreenAccess* NewL(RWsSession& aWs,
  CWsScreenDevice& aScreenDevice, RWindowBase& aWin,
  MDirectScreenAccess& aAbort);
~CDirectScreenAccess();
void StartL();
inline CFbsBitGc* Gc();
inline CFbsScreenDevice*& ScreenDevice();
inline RRegion* DrawingRegion();
```

The first function constructs the object, and the second destroys it. The last three functions provide the objects that you use to do the drawing. The graphics context is already active on the screen, and its clipping region is set to the area that you are allowed to draw to. The last two functions that I list provide a screen device set to the current color depth of the screen and the region that you are allowed to draw to. This is provided in case you ever need to reset the clipping region of the graphics context.

The third function, `StartL`, is the function that you need to call to inform WSERV that you want to start doing DSA. During this function call, the three objects returned by the inline functions will be set up. After you have called this function, you can safely draw to the screen using the provided graphics context.

When WSERV detects that the visible area of the window may be changing, it notifies the client. The client receives this notification through one of the two callback functions that it provided (specified in the class `MDirectScreenAccess`, and passed by the client as the last parameter to the `NewL` of the `CDirectScreenAccess` class). They are:

```
virtual void AbortNow(RDirectScreenAccess::TTerminationReasons aReason)
virtual void Restart(RDirectScreenAccess::TTerminationReasons aReason)
```

The first of these functions is called by the DSA framework to tell the client to abort. When the client has aborted, WSERV must be informed. The framework will do this for you, but only after the client has returned from the `AbortNow()` call. This means that this function should do the minimum amount of work and return as quickly as possible.

When WSERV tells the client that it needs to abort its DSA, it waits to receive the acknowledgment from the client that it has done so. However, it doesn't wait for ever, since the client may have entered some long running calculation or even an infinite loop. So WSERV also waits on a timer. If the timer expires before the client acknowledges, then WSERV continues. If, later on, WSERV gets notification from the client that it has aborted the DSA, then WSERV will invalidate the region in which the DSA was taking place, just in case there had been a conflict between the DSA and another client.

Here are a few other restrictions on what you can do in the `Abort-Now()` function. You can't call WSERV, because then a temporary deadlock will occur. This is because WSERV is waiting to receive the client's acknowledgment that it has aborted, and so will not be able to service the call. Also, since you are not allowed to make calls to WSERV in the `AbortNow()` function, you can't restart the DSA in this function. This is where the other callback is needed, the `Restart()` function. The DSA framework has set up an active object to call this function and it should be called during the next active object run in that thread. The purpose of this function is to give the client the earliest possible opportunity to restart the DSA with the new area.

There is one final restriction on clients performing DSA. This is that, while the DSA is in operation, the client should not make any call to WSERV that will affect the visible area of the window in which the DSA is taking place. Again, if this were to happen, it will cause temporary deadlock – since the client will be waiting for WSERV to make the requested window rearrangement, and WSERV will be waiting for the client to acknowledge that the DSA has aborted.

11.12   Platform security in WSERV

11.12.1   WSERV's command buffer

In Symbian OS, platform security is enforced on client server boundaries (for more on this, see Chapter 8, *Platform Security*). WSERV is no exception to this. However, because of WSERV's command buffer, the implementation differs from that of other servers. Other servers receive a single command sent by the client with a single call to either `RSessionBase::Send()` or the `RSessionBase::SendReceive()`, and the kernel can be instructed which commands (specified with the `aFunction` parameter) need which security capabilities. WSERV has one main command which is called in this function:

```
TInt RWsSession::DoFlush(const TIpcArgs& aIpcArgs)
    {
    return SendReceive(EWservMessCommandBuffer,aIpcArgs);
    }
```

This command tells the server that there is a command buffer waiting for it. WSERV places many individual commands into this command buffer, saying which server object to send the command to, which command or function to execute on that object and any parameters for that command. Each of these commands potentially needs to be policed for the capabilities of the client. Thus we have to do the policing in the server code that executes the commands.

On the server side, each command buffer is unpacked in the function `CWsClient::CommandBufL()`, which passes the commands onto this functions:

```
virtual void CWsObject::CommandL(TInt aOpcode,const TAny *aCmdData)=0;
```

or at least the version of this function in the respective derived class. This means that we must do the policing in the respective `CommandL()` function.

11.12.2   What things does WSERV police?

WSERV checks for three different capabilities – `SwEvent`, `WriteDeviceData` and `PowerMgmt`. The details of which APIs police which capabilities are given in any Symbian OS SDK, so there is no need for me to reiterate here. Instead I will describe the type of API that is policed with each of these capabilities, and the motivation for this policing.

There are various client-side functions that can be used to send an event to a WSERV client. Examples are `RWsSession::SendEventTo-WindowGroup` and `RWsSession::SimulateRawEvent`. These functions are policed by `SwEvent` to spot rogue applications that generate events designed to break other applications.

WSERV has many global settings that can be changed by any client. These include keyboard repeat rate, system pointer cursor list, default fading parameters and current screen size mode. Since these settings affect all clients of WSERV, we must intervene if rogue applications try to set them to bad values. So we police them using `WriteDeviceData`.

WSERV has two APIs that are concerned with switching off the mobile phone. One of these is `RWsSession::RequestOffEvents()`, which an application calls if it wants to receive off events. Only one application can receive these events, as it is then in charge of making sure that the system is ready to be turned off (for example, ensuring all data is saved) and then calling the kernel to power down the device. The other function, `RWsSession::PrepareForSwitchOff()` is called to tell WSERV to stop its timer so that the processor can be switched off – if the timer continued to run it would wake the processor up again. These APIs are both protected by `PowerMgmt`.

11.13 Summary

WSERV has a major role to play in all aspects of the UI of any device. It has rich APIs for dealing with all aspects of event handling, window management and drawing window content, as well as code for managing the different types of event and holding them until clients are ready to receive them. WSERV provides a variety of ways of drawing to the screen, including anim DLLs, redraw windows and direct screen access.

In the next chapter, I shall discuss device drivers and extensions.

12

Device Drivers and Extensions

by Stefan Williams
with Tony Lofthouse

It is pitch dark. You are likely to be eaten by a grue.

Zork I

In the previous chapters of this book, I have concentrated on the fundamental concepts and services that make up the EKA2 kernel, and have
introduced some of the fundamental hardware resources that the kernel
requires, such as the interrupt controller provided in the ASSP class to
provide the access to the millisecond timer interrupt.

The aim of this chapter is to explain how hardware resources are
provided to the system as a whole. For example, the file server requires
access to a variety of media storage devices, while the window server
requires access to the LCD display and touch screen. This chapter will
study the frameworks that exist to allow us to provide support for such
devices.

In particular, I will cover:

- *The device driver architecture* – an overview of device drivers and
  their place in Symbian OS

- *Kernel extensions* – these are key modules required by the kernel at
  boot time, and this section explains how they are created and used
  by Symbian OS

- *The HAL* – this section explains how the hardware abstraction layer
  is used by extensions and device drivers to provide standard device-
  specific interfaces to user-side code

- *Accessing user memory safely* – this section explains how to ensure
  that you are writing safe kernel-side code, fundamental to the stability
  of the system

- *Device drivers* – the user's interface to hardware and peripherals. This section explains the EKA2 device driver model

- *Differences between EKA1 and EKA2* – how the device driver model changed in the EKA2 release of the kernel.

12.1   Device drivers and extensions in Symbian OS

In Chapter 1, *Introducing EKA2*, I introduced the various hardware and software components that make up a typical Symbian OS device, and showed the modular architecture as in Figure 12.1.

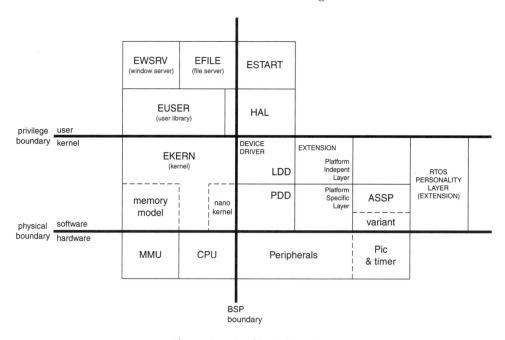

Figure 12.1   Symbian OS overview

12.1.1   What is a device driver?

The role of a device driver is to give a user-side application access to peripheral resources without exposing the operation of the underlying hardware, and in such a manner that new classes of devices may be introduced without modification of that user-side code.

Also, since access to hardware is usually restricted to supervisor-mode code, the device driver (which runs kernel-side) is the means of access to these resources for user-mode client threads.

Device drivers are dynamically loaded kernel DLLs that are loaded into the kernel process after the kernel has booted (either by user request, or by another layer of the OS). They may be execute-in-place (XIP) or RAM loaded, and like other kernel-side code may use writeable static data. (For more details on the differences between XIP and RAM loaded modules, please refer to Chapter 10, *The Loader.*)

Extensions are merely special device drivers that are loaded automatically at kernel boot. I shall say more about them later.

12.1.2 Device driver architecture

The Symbian OS device driver model uses two types of kernel DLL – the logical device driver (LDD) and the physical device driver (PDD). See Figure 12.2. This flexible arrangement provides a level of abstraction that assists in porting between platforms and in adding new implementations of device drivers without impacting or modifying common code and APIs.

12.1.2.1 The logical device driver

The LDD contains functionality that is common to a specific class of devices. User-side code communicates with an LDD via a simple interface class, derived from `RBusLogicalChannel`, which presents a

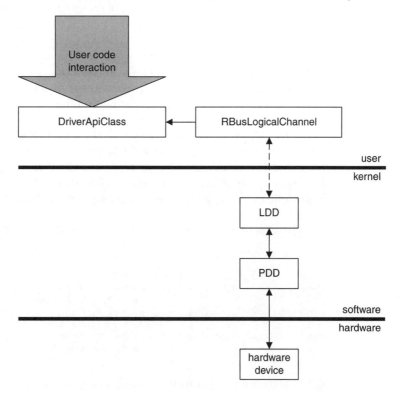

Figure 12.2 Overview of the device driver architecture

well-defined driver-specific API. We use the term "channel" to refer to a single connection between a user-side client and the kernel-side driver.

Since hardware interfaces vary across platforms, an LDD is usually designed to perform generic functionality, using a PDD to implement the device-specific code.

LDDs are dynamically loaded from user-side code but may perform some initialization at boot time if they are configured to do so. I'll explain how this is achieved when I discuss the use of extensions.

Symbian provides standard LDDs for a range of peripheral types (such as media drivers, the USB controller and serial communications devices). However, phone manufacturers will often develop their own interfaces for custom hardware.

12.1.2.2   *The physical device driver*

The physical device driver is an optional component, which contains functionality that is specific to a particular member of the class of devices supported by the LDD. The PDD typically controls a particular peripheral on behalf of its LDD, and obviously it will contain device-specific code. The PDD communicates only with its corresponding LDD, using an API defined by the logical channel, so it may not be accessed directly from a user-side application. The role of the PDD is to communicate with the variant, an extension, or the hardware itself, on behalf of the LDD.

To illustrate this, consider the example of a serial communications device. The generic serial communications LDD (ECOMM.LDD) defines the user-side API and the associated kernel-side PDD interface for all serial devices. It also provides buffering and flow control functions that are common to all types of UART. On a particular hardware platform, this LDD will be accompanied by one or more PDDs that support the different types of UART present in the system. (A single PDD may support more than one device of the same type; separate PDDs are only required for devices with different programming interfaces.) This is demonstrated in the following .oby file, which specifies that the ROM should contain:

1. The generic serial communications LDD (ECOMM.LDD)

2. Two device-specific PDDs (EUART1.PDD, EUART2.PDD).

```
device[VARID] = \Epoc32\Release\Arm4\Urel\16550.PDD
                          \System\Bin\EUART1.PDD
device[VARID] = \Epoc32\Release\Arm4\Urel_SSI.PDD
                          \System\Bin\EUART2.PDD
device[VARID] = \Epoc32\Release\Arm4\Urel\ECOMM.LDD
                          \System\Bin\ECOMM.LDD
```

Both PDDs interface with the generic LDD, which presents a common interface to the hardware to any user of the communications device.

Further examples include:

Driver	LDD	Associated PDD
Sound Driver	ESOUND	ESDRV
Ethernet Driver	ENET	ETHERNET
Local Media Sub-system	ELOCD	MEDNAND
		MEDLFS
		MEDMMC

Similarly to LDDs, PDDs may be configured to perform initialization at boot time.

12.1.3 Kernel extensions

Fundamentally, kernel extensions are just device drivers that are loaded at kernel boot. However, because of this, their use cases are somewhat specialized.

By the time the kernel is ready to start the scheduler, it requires resources that are not strictly defined by the CPU architecture. These are provided by the variant and ASSP extensions, which I have discussed in Chapter 1, *Introducing EKA2*. These extensions are specific to the particular platform that Symbian OS is running on, and permit the phone manufacturer to port the OS without re-compiling the kernel itself.

After initializing the variant and ASSP extensions, the kernel continues to boot until it finally starts the scheduler and enters the supervisor thread, which initializes all remaining kernel extensions. At this point, all kernel services (scheduling, memory management, object creation, timers) and basic peripheral resources (interrupt controller and other ASSP/variant functionality) are available for use.

Extensions loaded at this late stage are not critical to the operation of the kernel itself, but are typically used to perform early initialization of hardware components and to provide permanently available services for devices such as the LCD, DMA, I2C and peripheral bus controllers.

The final kernel extension to be initialized is the EXSTART extension, which is responsible for loading the file server. The file server is responsible for bringing up the rest of the OS. (If you want to find out more about system boot, turn to Chapter 16, *Boot Processes*.)

In Figure 12.1, the extension consists of two components – the platform-independent layer (PIL) and platform-specific layer (PSL). These are analogous to the LDD/PDD layering for device drivers that I discussed earlier. To make porting an extension to a new hardware platform easier, the PIL is generally responsible for providing functionality common to versions of the extension (such as state machines and so on) and defining the exported API, with the PSL taking on the responsibility of communicating directly with the hardware. Therefore, when porting to a new hardware platform only the PSL should require modification.

Note: Some device drivers use the same concept and split the PDD into platform-independent and platform-specific layers. One such example is the local media sub-system – this consists of a generic LDD interface suitable for all media drivers, and a PDD interface which is further divided to handle common device interfaces such as ATA/PCMCIA, NAND or NOR Flash.

12.1.4 Shared library DLLs

The most basic way to offer peripheral resources to other components within the kernel (not to user-mode applications) is to develop a simple kernel DLL (by specifying a `targettype` of `KDLL` in the extension's MMP file). Kernel DLLs can provide a static interface through which other kernel components gain access to the hardware:

```
class MyKextIf
  {
public:
  IMPORT_C static TUint32 GetStatus();
  IMPORT_C static void SetStatus(TUint32 aVal);
  };

EXPORT_C TUint MyKextIf::GetStatus()
  { return *(volatile TUint32 *)(KHwBaseReg); }

EXPORT_C void MyKextIf::SetStatus(TUint aVal)
  { *(volatile TUint32 *)(KHwBaseReg) = aVal; }
```

Of course, a shared library DLL may offer any functionality that may be of use from other components within the kernel (not only access to peripheral resources). However, a kernel DLL is not defined as an extension so is not initialized by the kernel at boot time, so can't make use of writeable static data. Using a kernel extension opens up the opportunity to provide a much richer interface.

12.1.5 Static data initialization

Kernel-side DLLs, such as device drivers and extensions, are only ever loaded and used by a single process, the kernel itself. Hence, they only need one copy of static data (of course, if several threads within the same process require access to this data, the usual care must be taken to avoid synchronization issues).

Writeable static data for ROM-resident kernel-mode DLLs (that is, those declared in the `rombuild.oby` file with the keywords `variant`, `device` or `extension`) is appended to the kernel's static data. Initialization of `variant` and `extension` data occurs at kernel boot time, while initialization of `device` data occurs at device driver load time. Writeable static data for RAM-resident device drivers is placed in an extra kernel data chunk which is mapped with supervisor-only access.

It is important to note that since the kernel itself loads extensions, *they are never unloaded.* Therefore, the destructors for any globally constructed objects will never be called.

12.1.6 Entry points

Each type of kernel DLL has a unique set of characteristics that define how and when the kernel loads them during boot; these are defined by the form of the DLL's entry point. Symbian provides three different entry points, in three different libraries, and you select one by choosing which of these libraries to link against. The tool chain will automatically link in the appropriate library depending on the value of the "`targettype`" field in the DLL's MMP file:

Targettype	Library	DLL type
VAR	EVAR.LIB	Variant kernel extension
KEXT	EEXT.LIB	Kernel extension
PDD	EDEV.LIB	Physical device driver DLL
LDD	EDEV.LIB	Logical device driver DLL

The main entry point for all kernel DLLs is named `_E32Dll`, and its address, represented by `TRomImageHeader::iEntryPoint`, is obtained from the image header. This in turn invokes the DLL specific entry point `_E32Dll_Body`, the behavior of which depends on the type of kernel DLL being loaded.

Note: There is a fourth library, `EKLL.LIB`, which is imported when specifying the `KDLL` keyword for shared library DLLs. Kernel DLLs of this type contain no static data or initialization code, so contain a simple stub entry point.

Before I describe in detail how the kernel controls the initialization of kernel DLLs are during boot, let's take a look at how each library entry point handles construction and destruction of its global C++ objects.

12.1.6.1   *Construction of C++ objects*

Variant extensions – EVAR.LIB

Since the kernel loads the variant extension once, the variant entry point only constructs the DLL's global C++ objects. Destructors are never called:

```
GLDEF_C TInt _E32Dll_Body(TInt aReason)
//
// Call variant and ASIC global constructors
//
  {
  if (aReason==KModuleEntryReasonVariantInit0)
    {
    TUint i=1;
    while (__CTOR_LIST__[i])
      (*__CTOR_LIST__[i++])();

    AsicInitialise();
    return 0;
    }
  return KErrGeneral;
  }
```

Kernel extensions – EEXT.LIB

As with the variant extension, the kernel loads an extension once during boot, so it only constructs the DLLs global C++ objects and never calls their destructors:

```
GLDEF_C TInt _E32Dll_Body(TInt aReason)
//
// Call extension global constructors
//
  {
  if (aReason==KModuleEntryReasonExtensionInit1)
    {
    TUint i=1;
    while (__CTOR_LIST__[i])
      (*__CTOR_LIST__[i++])();
    }
  return KernelModuleEntry(aReason);
  }
```

Device drivers – EDEV.LIB

The kernel loads and unloads device drivers dynamically, so it constructs global C++ objects when loading the DLL, and destroys them when unloading it:

```
GLDEF_C TInt _E32Dll_Body(TInt aReason)
//
// Call global constructors or destructors
//
```

```
{
if (aReason==KModuleEntryReasonProcessDetach)
  {
  TUint i=1;
  while (__DTOR_LIST__[i])
    (*__DTOR_LIST__[i++])();
  return KErrNone;
  }
if (aReason==KModuleEntryReasonExtensionInit1 ||
       aReason==KModuleEntryReasonProcessAttach)
  {
  TUint i=1;
  while (__CTOR_LIST__[i])
    (*__CTOR_LIST__[i++])();
  }
return KernelModuleEntry(aReason);
}
```

12.1.6.2 Calling entry points

As the previous code shows, the kernel invokes _E32Dll with a reason code, which it uses to control how DLLs are loaded. Each reason code is passed during a particular stage in the boot process.

KModuleEntryReasonVariantInit0

Before initializing the variant, the kernel initializes the .data sections for all kernel extensions and passes the reason code KModuleEntryReasonVariantInit0 to all extension entry points. Typically, only the variant extension handles this reason code and, as we have already seen, this is responsible for constructing global C++ objects before invoking AsicInitialise() to initialize the ASSP.

In Chapter 1, *Introducing EKA2*, I pointed out that the base port might be split into an ASSP and a variant. Under this model, the generic ASSP class forms a standard kernel extension that exports its constructor (at the very least). The ASSP class must be initialized at the same time as the variant, so it also exports the function AsicInitialise() to allow its global C++ constructors to be called.

After it has initialized both the variant and the ASSP extensions, the kernel obtains a pointer to the Asic derived variant specific class by calling the variant's first exported function:

```
EXPORT_C Asic* VariantInitialise()
```

This class is described in Chapter 5, *Kernel Services*.

At the end of this process, all of the extensions' .data sections are initialized, and the variant and ASSP extensions are constructed and ready for the kernel to use.

KModuleEntryReasonExtensionInit0

The kernel passes this reason code to all extension entry points that it calls after it has started the scheduler.

This reason code is an inquiry, asking whether the extension has already been initialized. It allows extensions that use the `KModuleEntryReasonVariantInit0` reason code to perform initialization, as I described earlier. If the extension is already loaded, returning any error code (other than `KErrNone`) will prevent the next stage from being performed.

The ASSP DLL returns `KErrGeneral` in response to this reason code to report that it has already been initialized by the variant, as does the crash monitor, which hooks into the variant initialization phase to provide diagnostics of the kernel boot process.

If the extension is not already loaded, the kernel will invoke its DLL entry point with the reason code `KModuleEntryReasonExtensionInit1`.

KModuleEntryReasonExtensionInit1

The kernel passes this reason code to all extension entry points after it has verified that the extension has not already been initialized. This causes the DLL entry point to initialize global constructors before calling `KernelModuleEntry` to initialize the extension itself.

Note that the ASSP kernel extension has already been initialized by this point so will not receive this reason code at this point in the boot process.

KModuleEntryReasonProcessAttach and
KModuleEntryReasonProcessDetach

These reason codes are only handled by `EDEV.LIB`, which is specifically intended to support dynamically loadable DLLs (device drivers). `KModuleEntryReasonProcessAttach` is directly equivalent to `KModuleEntryReasonExtensionInit1` and is used to initialize the driver's constructors. Conversely, `KModuleEntryReasonProcessDetach` calls the driver's destructors. These are called when the relevant code segment is created or destroyed, as described in Chapter 10, *The Loader*.

12.1.7   Accessing user process memory

Kernel drivers and extensions need to ensure that read and write operations involving user process memory are performed safely. There are two scenarios to consider when servicing requests from a user process, depending on whether the request is serviced in the context of the calling thread or a kernel thread.

12.1.7.1 *Servicing requests in calling thread context*

Requests may be fully executed in the context of the calling thread with supervisor-mode privileges. Therefore, if a process passes an invalid address to the handler or device driver, and that address happens to be within the memory of another process or even the kernel itself (either as a result of programming error or deliberate intention), then writing to this address could result in memory corruption and become a potential security risk.

Therefore, you should never attempt to write to user memory directly, either by dereferencing a pointer or by calling a function such as memcpy. Instead, you should use one of the following kernel functions:

```
void kumemget(TAny* aKernAddr, const TAny* aAddr, TInt aLength);
void kumemget32(TAny* aKernAddr, const TAny* aAddr, TInt aLength);
void kumemput(TAny* aAddr, const TAny* aKernAddr, TInt aLength);
void kumemput32(TAny* aAddr, const TAny* aKernAddr, TInt aLength);
void kumemset(TAny* aAddr, const TUint8 aValue, TInt aLength);

void umemget(TAny* aKernAddr, const TAny* aUserAddr, TInt aLength);
void umemget32(TAny* aKernAddr, const TAny* aUserAddr, TInt aLength);
void umemput(TAny* aUserAddr, const TAny* aKernAddr, TInt aLength);
void umemput32(TAny* aUserAddr, const TAny* aKernAddr, TInt aLength);
void umemset(TAny* aUserAddr, const TUint8 aValue, TInt aLength);
```

These provide both word and non-word optimized equivalents to a memcpy function. You should use the kumemxxx versions if your code can be called from both user- and kernel-side code; this ensures that the operation is performed with the same privileges as the current thread. You may use the umemxxx versions if the operation is guaranteed not to be called from kernel-side code. The principles behind these functions are explained in detail in Section 5.2.1.5.

The memget/memput methods described previously are useful when the source and destination pointers and the lengths are provided. However, many APIs make use of descriptors, for which the kernel provides optimized functions. These allow descriptors to be safely copied between the user and kernel process, while maintaining the advantages such as runtime bounds checking that descriptors provide:

```
Kern::KUDesGet(TDes8& aDest, const TDesC8& aSrc);
Kern::KUDesPut(TDes8& aDest, const TDesC8& aSrc);
```

```
Kern::KUDesInfo(const TDesC8& aSrc, TInt& aLength, TInt& aMaxLength);
Kern::KUDesSetLength(TDes8& aDes, TInt aLength);
```

Finally, if you want to copy a descriptor safely in a way that enables
forward and backward compatibility (for example, when communicating
capability packages that may evolve between versions), use the following
methods:

```
Kern::InfoCopy(TDes8& aDest, const TDesC8& aSrc);
Kern::InfoCopy(TDes8& aDest, const TUint8* aPtr, TInt aLength);
```

These provide compatibility by copying only as much data as required
by the target descriptor. If the source is longer than the maximum length
of the target, then the amount of data copied is limited to the maximum
length of the target descriptor. Conversely, if the source is shorter than
the maximum length of the target, then the target descriptor is padded
with zeros.

12.1.7.2 *Servicing requests in kernel thread context*

If a request is made from user-side code to perform a long running
task, control is usually passed back to the user process, while the task
completes in a separate kernel thread. Under these circumstances, you
are no longer in the context of the user thread when you want to transfer
data, so you should use the following methods:

```
Kern::ThreadDesRead(DThread* aThread, const TAny* aSrc,
                TDes8& aDest, TInt aOffset, TInt aMode);
Kern::ThreadRawRead(DThread* aThread, const TAny* aSrc,
                    TAny* aDest, TInt aSize);
Kern::ThreadDesWrite(DThread* aThread, TAny* aDest, const TDesC8& aSrc,
                    TInt aOffset, TInt aMode, DThread* aOrigThread);
Kern::ThreadRawWrite(DThread* aThread, TAny* aDest, const TAny* aSrc,
                    TInt aSize, DThread* aOrigThread=NULL);
Kern::ThreadDesRead(DThread* aThread, const TAny* aSrc,
                    TDes8& aDest, TInt aOffset);
Kern::ThreadDesWrite(DThread* aThread, TAny* aDest, const TDesC8& aSrc,
                    TInt aOffset, DThread* aOrigThread=NULL);
Kern::ThreadGetDesLength(DThread* aThread, const TAny* aDes);
Kern::ThreadGetDesMaxLength(DThread* aThread, const TAny* aDes);
Kern::ThreadGetDesInfo(DThread* aThread, const TAny* aDes,
                    TInt& aLength, TInt& aMaxLength,
                    TUint8*& aPtr, TBool aWriteable);
```

These all take a handle to the client thread as their first argument. You
must obtain this while you are still in user context (such as when the

request is first received, or as we shall see later, when a channel to a device driver is first opened) and store it for use later, when the operation has completed:

```
//request comes in here
iClient=&Kern::CurrentThread();
((DObject*)iClient)->Open();
```

Calling `Open()` on the client thread increments its instance count to ensure that the thread is not destroyed while you are performing the request. When the operation has completed and data has been transferred, you should decrement the threads instance count by calling `Close()`. Then, if the thread is closed while the operation is in progress, thread destruction will be deferred until you have called `Close()` and the thread's usage count has dropped to zero.

12.1.8 Validating the capabilities of the calling thread

As we saw in Chapter 8, *Platform Security*, many APIs must be governed by security capabilities, to avoid an untrusted application gaining access to privileged functionality. You can see this in the LCD HAL handler that I describe in Section 12.3, where the `EDisplayHalSetState` function requires the client to have power management capabilities. Such API policing prevents untrusted applications from being able to deny the user access to the screen.

You use the following kernel API to validate thread capabilities:

```
TBool Kern::CurrentThreadHasCapability(TCapability aCapability,
                                 const char* aContextText)
```

This API simply checks the capabilities of the current thread's process against that specified by `aCapability` and returns `EFalse` if the test fails, at which point you should return an error code of `KErrPermis-sionDenied` to the client and abandon the request. The "C" style string in the second parameter is an optional diagnostic message that is output to the debug port in debug builds (the `__PLATSEC_DIAGNOSTIC_STRING` macro is used to allow the string to be removed in release builds without changing the code).

A request may require more than one capability. If this is the case, you should make several calls to `Kern::CurrentThreadHas-Capability`, since the `TCapability` enumeration is *not* specified as a bitwise field.

12.2   Kernel extensions

Since the ASSP and variant modules are initialized *before* the kernel is initialized, and the kernel loads all extensions before the file server (which itself is loaded by an extension), then there must be some special mechanism in place to load these modules. And indeed there is – extensions are simply execute-in-place DLLs that are specified at ROM build time, allowing the build tools to place the address of the extension in the ROM header. This allows the kernel to initialize extensions without using the loader.

12.2.1   Installing an extension

To install a kernel extension into a Symbian OS ROM image, you need to specify one of the following keywords in the kernel's OBY file:

Variant: The variant extension

Extension: A standard kernel or ASSP extension

The ROMBUILD tool uses these to build the ROM header (represented by the TRomHeader class), which contains two extension lists – iVariantFile contains the list of variants, and iExtensionFile contains the list of all other extensions.

As a consequence of this, extensions are always initialized in the order at which they appear in the kernel's IBY file. This is an extremely desirable feature, as many extensions and device drivers depend on other extensions being present to initialize. The MMC controller is a good example of this, as it depends on the power management extension and possibly the DMA framework too.

Note that although you can specify more than one variant keyword to include several variant extensions in the ROM, the kernel will only initialize one of them. Each variant DLL contains an identifier which specifies which CPU, ASIC and variant it was built for. The build tools place this information in the ROM header, and the bootstrap may later modify it when it copies it to the kernel superpage, thus providing the ability to create multi-platform ROMs. The same principle applies to standard extensions. However, this feature is rarely used in a production device due to ROM budget constraints.

12.2.2   Extension entry point macros

You should define the extension entry point, KernelModuleEntry, when writing a kernel extension, and interpret the supplied reason codes according to the rules I have described. For example, a standard kernel extension entry point would look something like this:

```
TInt KernelModuleEntry(Tint aReason)
  {
  if (aReason==KModuleEntryReasonExtensionInit0)
    return KErrNone;
  if (aReason!=KModuleEntryReasonExtensionInit1)
    return KErrArgument;

  //... do extension specific initialisation here
  }
```

Since all extensions follow the same pattern (and it's easy to make a mistake and difficult to debug what has gone wrong), the kernel provides you with a set of standard macros (defined in kernel.h) that do the hard work for you:

DECLARE_STANDARD_EXTENSION
This is defined by the kernel as follows:

```
#define DECLARE_STANDARD_EXTENSION()
  GLREF_C TInt InitExtension();
  TInt KernelModuleEntry(TInt aReason)
      {
      if (aReason==KModuleEntryReasonExtensionInit0)
        return KErrNone;
      if (aReason!=KModuleEntryReasonExtensionInit1)
        return KErrArgument;
      return InitExtension();
      }
  GLDEF_C TInt InitExtension()
```

Thus reducing the entry point for a standard extension to:

```
DECLARE_STANDARD_EXTENSION()
  {
  // Initialisation code here
  }
```

DECLARE_STANDARD_ASSP
The ASSP extension entry point simply re-invokes the DLL entry point to initialize the extension's constructors:

```
#defineDECLARE_STANDARD_ASSP() \
  extern "C" { GLREF_C TInt _E32Dll(TInt); }
                                            \
  GLDEF_C TInt KernelModuleEntry(TInt aReason)          \
  { return (aReason==KModuleEntryReasonExtensionInit1)\
          ?KErrNone:KErrGeneral; }                    \
```

```
EXPORT_C void AsicInitialise() \
{ E32Dll(KModuleEntryReasonExtensionInit1); }
```

Thus reducing the entry point for the ASSP to:

```
DECLARE_STANDARD_ASSP()
```

You only need to declare this – you don't need to write any extra code.

12.2.2.1 Extensions on the emulator

Since the emulator is based on the Windows DLL model and there is no ROMBUILD stage involved, we are not able to specify the order in which extensions are loaded at build time. To solve this problem, the Symbian OS emulator has its own mechanism for loading extensions, which ensures that the behavior of the emulated platform is identical to that of target hardware.

The kernel loads the emulator's variant extension explicitly by name (`ECUST.DLL`) and invokes the exported `VariantInitialise()` function. This registers the extensions to be loaded by publishing a Publish/Subscribe key named "`Extension`":

```
if (iProperties.Append("Extension",
          "winsgui;elocd.ldd;medint.pdd;medlfs.pdd;
          epbusv.dll;mednand.pdd") == NULL)
  return KErrNoMemory;
```

The emulator-specific parts of the kernel that would be responsible for loading extensions from ROM on target hardware are then able to read this string and explicitly load each DLL in the order it appears in the list.

You should modify this list if you are developing extensions that need to be loaded into the emulator. The code can be found in the `Wins::InitProperties()` function in the source file `\wins \specific\property.cpp`.

12.2.3 Uses of extensions

In this section I will explain some of the most common uses of extensions within Symbian OS. Many extensions such as the power framework, peripheral bus and USB controllers provide asynchronous services for multiple clients – which are usually other extensions and device drivers. The following code demonstrates a common pattern that is used to provide such an interface using an extension.

The interface is usually exported from the extension via a simple static interface class. In this example, the `DoIt()` function will perform some long running peripheral task, followed by a client callback function being invoked to indicate completion:

```
class TClientInterface                  // The Client API
  {
public:
  IMPORT_C static TInt DoIt(TCallback& aCb);
  };

class DMyController : public DBase    // Internal API
  {
public:
  DMyController();
  TInt Create();
private:
  TInt DoIt(TCallback& aCb);
  static void InterruptHandler(TAny* aSelfP);
  static void EventDfcFn(TAny* aSelfP);
private:
  TDfc iEventDfc;
  };

DMyController* TheController = NULL;

EXPORT_C TInt TClientInterface::DoIt(TCallback* aCb)
  {
  return TheController->DoIt(aCb);
  }
```

The client API uses a global instance of the `DMyController` object, which is initialized in the extension entry point:

```
DECLARE_STANDARD_EXTENSION()
  {
  DMyController* TheController = new DMyController();
  if(TheController == NULL)
    return KErrNoMemory;
  return TheController->Create();
  }
```

So all we need to do now is provide the functionality. The simple example that follows simply registers the client callback and talks to the hardware to perform the operation (the detailed mechanism isn't shown here). Upon receiving an interrupt, a DFC is queued within which the client's callback function is invoked:

```
DMyController:: DMyController()
  : iEventDfc(EventDfcFn,this,1)
  {
  iEventDfc.SetDfcQ(Kern::DfcQue0());
  }
```

```
TInt DMyController::Create()
  {
  return RegisterInterruptHandlers();
  }

void DMyController::DoIt(TCallback& aCb)
  {
  RegisterClientCallback(aCb); // Implementation
  EnableInterruptsAndDoIt();   //   not shown
  }

void DMyController::InterruptHandler(TAny* aSelfP)
  {
  DMyController& self = *(DMyController*)aSelfP;
  self.iEventDfc.Add();
  }

void DMyController::EventDfcFn(TAny* aSelfP)
  {
  DMyController& self = *(DMyController*)aSelfP;
  self.NotifyClients();
  }
```

Of course, a real example would do a little more than this, but this is the basic concept behind several extensions found in a real system.

To build this example, you would use the following MMP file:

```
#include        <variant.mmh>
#include        "kernel\kern_ext.mmh"

target          VariantTarget(mykext,dll)
targettype      kext
linkas          mykext.dll

systeminclude   .
source          mykext.cpp

library         ekern.lib

deffile         ~\mykext.def

epocallowdlldata
capability      all
```

The following keywords are of particular importance when building a kernel-side DLL:

VariantTarget – to enable the same source code and MMP files to produce unique binaries for each variant, the VariantTarget macro is used to generate a unique name. Each variant provides its own implementation of this macro in its exported variant.mmh file. Without this macro, each variant would build a binary with the same name and would overwrite the binaries produced for other variants.

The Lubbock variant defines the `VariantTarget` macro as:

```
#define VariantTarget(name,ext) _lubbock_##name##.##ext
```

targettype – by specifying a `targettype` of `kext` in the MMP file, we instruct the build tools to link with EEXT.LIB. This provides the correct version of the `_E32Dll_Body` entry point to initialize kernel extensions.

epocallowdlldata – This informs the build tools that you intend the DLL to contain static data. If you omit this keyword and attempt to build a DLL that requires a. data or. bss section you will encounter one of the following errors:

"Dll '<dllname>' has initialised data."

"Dll '<dllname>' has uninitialised data."

12.2.3.1 Event services

Event services are associated with a single user thread, usually the window server, which calls the `UserSvr::CaptureEventHook()` interface to register itself as the system wide event handler. The thread registers a `TRequestStatus` object by calling `UserSvr::RequestEvent()`; this enables the thread to respond to queued events. Events from hardware such as the keypad, keyboard or digitizer (touch screen) are typically each delivered by their own kernel extension. Taking a keypad as an example, the `DECLARE_STANDARD_EXTENSION()` entry point will initialize the keypad hardware. Key presses will generate interrupts, and their service routine will queue a DFC, which will add key input events to the event service queue using the `Kern::AddEvent()` interface.

The following example shows a key down event for the backspace key being added to the event queue:

```
TRawEvent event;
event.Set(TRawEvent::EKeyDown, EStdKeyBackspace);
Kern::AddEvent(event);
```

See Chapter 11, *Window Server*, for more details on how events are captured and processed.

12.2.3.2 Optional utilities

Symbian OS provides crash debugger and crash logger utility modules. The crash debugger provides post-mortem analysis of fatal errors that may occur during development – usually it is not present in a production ROM. The crash logger, on the other hand, is often placed in production

ROMs so that, for example, the phone manufacturer can diagnose errors that result in a factory return. It is basically a crash debugger that dumps its diagnostic output to a reserved area of persistent storage.

Both modules are implemented as kernel extensions. We want them to be available as early as possible, to provide diagnostics of errors that occur during the early stages of the kernel boot sequence. Because of this, their initialization process is slightly different to other extensions. Rather than using the `DECLARE_STANDARD_EXTENSION()` macro, they implement their own version of the `KernelModuleEntry()` interface, which will register the modules with the kernel during the variant initialization phase, the phase in which all kernel extensions are called with the entry point reason `KModuleEntryReasonVariantInit0`.

See Chapter 14, *Kernel-Side Debug*, for more details on the crash logger and monitor modules.

12.2.3.3 System services

Kernel extensions are also used to provide services to systems outside the kernel, as the following examples demonstrate:

The local media sub-system (ELOCD)
The local media sub-system is a logical device driver that registers as an extension to provide early services to user-side code (in particular, the file server and the loader) during the boot process.

The local media sub-system's kernel extension provides an exported interface class used by media drivers (which are also device drivers and kernel extensions) to register themselves with the system. Because of this, the local media sub-system must be located earlier in the ROM image than the media drivers. `ELOCD` also registers a HAL handler for `EHalGroupMedia` to allow user-side frameworks to query the registered media drivers.

For more details on the local media sub-system and media drivers, please refer to Chapter 13, *Peripheral Support*.

EXSTART
EXSTART is another important extension that must be in the ROM. This extension doesn't export any interfaces – instead its entry point simply queues a DFC to run once, after all kernel-side initialization has completed. This DFC is responsible for locating and starting the file server executable (also known as the secondary process). More information on this process is provided in Chapter 16, *Boot Processes*.

12.3 The hardware abstraction layer

I mentioned earlier that the local media sub-system registers a hardware abstraction layer (HAL) handler to publish information about registered drives to user-side processes. In this section, I'll explain what the HAL does and describe the kinds of services it provides.

Symbian OS defines a set of hardware and information services via the HAL interface. HAL functions are typically simple get/set interfaces, and are used by both kernel and user code.

The OS defines a range of HAL groups, each of which can have a HAL handler function installed. Each HAL group represents a different type of functionality. The following table shows the mapping between each HAL entry (enumerated in THalFunctionGroup) to the associated HAL function (defined in u32hal.h):

EHalGroupKernel	TkernelHalFunction
EHalGroupVariant	TVariantHalFunction
EHalGroupMedia	TMediaHalFunction
EHalGroupPower	TpowerHalFunction
EHalGroupDisplay	TdisplayHalFunction
EHalGroupDigitiser	TdigitiserHalFunction
EHalGroupSound	TSoundHalFunction
EHalGroupMouse	TMouseHalFunction
EHalGroupEmulator	TEmulatorHalFunction
EHalGroupKeyboard	TKeyboardHalFunction

Note: The maximum number of HAL groups is defined by *KMaxHalGroups* (currently set to 32). Because of the limited availability of HAL groups, I recommend that if you do need to add a new group, you should allocate a number from the top end of the available range to avoid conflict with any extension that Symbian may make in the future.

At OS boot, the kernel automatically installs the following handlers:

EHalGroupKernel

The HAL functions in TKernelHalFunction return kernel specific information such as the amount of free RAM, the kernel startup reason and the platform's tick period. The kernel implements these functions itself.

EHalGroupVariant

This HAL group accesses the variant kernel extension. If you are writing a variant extension, then you must provide an implementation of the variant HAL handler within the `Asic::VariantHal()` method of your variant class. This provides a simple low level interface through which the caller can obtain the processor speed and machine ID, select the active debug port, and control the debug LEDs and switches.

EHalGroupDisplay

The LCD extension provides the HAL functions defined by `TDisplay-HalFunction`, which include functions to retrieve the current operating mode of the display, set the contrast, modify the palette and switch the display on or off. This is usually one of the first set of HAL functions that you would implement during a base port.

EHalGroupPower

If a power model is registered with the kernel, it will handle the HAL functions defined by `TPowerHalFunction`. This provides an interface to retrieve information on the state of the power supply, battery capacity and case open/close switches.

Several other HAL groups also have handlers that are implemented and registered by various modules in the OS, depending on the hardware supported by the mobile device.

12.3.1   Registering HAL entries

The `Kern` class exports the following methods to allow modules to register and deregister a HAL group handler:

```
TInt AddHalEntry(TInt aId, THalFunc aFunc, TAny* aPtr);
TInt AddHalEntry(TInt aId, THalFunc aFunc, TAny* aPtr,
                                    TInt aDeviceNumber);
TInt RemoveHalEntry(TInt aId);
TInt RemoveHalEntry(TInt aId, TInt aDeviceNumber);
```

Note: An extension is unlikely to remove a HAL entry as extensions are never unloaded from the system. However, device drivers are dynamically loaded so must remove their handlers as part of their shutdown process.

The arguments to the `AddHalEntry` APIs are the ID of a HAL group, a pointer to the handler function and a pointer to a data structure that will be passed to the handler function. A handler may also take a device number as an argument, so that it can be made device-specific. For example, a second video driver could make itself a handler for display attributes by calling:

```
Kern::AddHalEntry(EHalGroupDisplay, &handler, this, 1).
```

The device number for a HAL function is determined by the top 16 bits of the associated HAL group number passed to the function. If a handler already exists for the HAL group, this handler will not be registered.

The HAL handler function prototype is defined by `THalFunc`.

```
typedef TInt (*THalFunc)(TAny*,TInt,TAny*,TAny*);
```

The arguments to this are the pointer registered with the HAL handler, the HAL function number and two optional arguments, the definition of which are dependent on the HAL function. They are usually used to read or write data passed from the client to the handler.

Let's take a look at how the LCD extension registers its HAL handler with the system. This is done when the extension is initialized:

```
DECLARE_STANDARD_EXTENSION()
    {
    // create LCD power handler
    TInt r = KErrNoMemory;
    DLcdPowerHandler* pH = new DLcdPowerHandler;

    // LCD specific initialisation omitted for clarity

    if(pH != NULL)
        {
        r = Kern::AddHalEntry(EHalGroupDisplay, halFunction, pH);
        }
    return r;
    }
```

This creates the LCD driver and registers a HAL handler (`halFunction`) for the `EHalGroupDisplay` group, passing a pointer to the LCD driver for context when the handler is invoked.

When a client makes a HAL request, `halFunction` is invoked, which is implemented as follows (most HAL functions omitted for clarity):

```
LOCAL_C TInt halFunction(TAny* aPtr, TInt aFunction, TAny* a1, TAny* a2)
    {
    DLcdPowerHandler* pH=(DLcdPowerHandler*)aPtr;
    return pH->HalFunction(aFunction,a1,a2);
    }

TInt DLcdPowerHandler::HalFunction(TInt aFunction, TAny* a1, TAny* a2)
    {
    TInt r=KErrNone;
    switch(aFunction)
        {
        case EDisplayHalScreenInfo:
            {
            TPckgBuf<TScreenInfoV01> vPckg;
            ScreenInfo(vPckg());
            Kern::InfoCopy(*(TDes8*)a1,vPckg);
            break;
            }
```

```
    case EDisplayHalSecure:
       kumemput32(a1, &iSecureDisplay, sizeof(TBool));
       break;

    case EDisplayHalSetState:
    {
    if(!Kern::CurrentThreadHasCapability(ECapabilityPowerMgmt, NULL))
      return KErrPermissionDenied;

    if ((TBool)a1)
      WsSwitchOnScreen();
    else
      WsSwitchOffScreen();
    }

  default:
    r=KErrNotSupported;
    break;
  }
 return r;
 }
```

Note in particular how this example performs API policing and safely accesses user-side memory using the APIs described in Sections 12.1.7 and 12.1.8. These are absolutely essential when implementing HAL handlers, device drivers or any other service that responds to requests from user-side code.

12.4   Device drivers

In this section of the chapter I'll be discussing device drivers in a little more depth. I'll talk about the execution model, and about how to create a device driver. I'll also discuss how user code interacts with a device driver. To make this concrete, I'll be walking through the creation of my own device driver, a simple comms driver. But first, let's look at the device driver counterpart to the extension's entry point macros.

12.4.1   Device driver entry point macros

DECLARE_STANDARD_LDD and DECLARE_STANDARD_PDD
The following macros are provided to support device driver LDDs and PDDs:

```
#define DECLARE_STANDARD_LDD()                                   \
  TInt KernelModuleEntry(TInt)                                   \
    { return KErrNone; }                                         \
  EXPORT_C DLogicalDevice* CreateLogicalDevice()
```

```
#define DECLARE_STANDARD_PDD()                              \
  TInt KernelModuleEntry(TInt)                              \
    { return KErrNone; }                                    \
  EXPORT_C DPhysicalDevice* CreatePhysicalDevice()
```

This would be implemented in an LDD as follows:

```
DECLARE_STANDARD_LDD()
  {
  return new DSimpleSerialLDD;
  }
```

Notice that `KernelModuleEntry` does not provide any initialization hooks. As we shall see later, LDDs and PDDs are polymorphic DLLs which are dynamically loaded after the kernel has booted. Instead, this macro defines the first export to represent the DLL factory function.

DECLARE_EXTENSION_LDD and DECLARE_EXTENSION_PDD

Although device drivers are dynamically loadable DLLs, there may be some instances where a device driver must perform some one-off initialization at boot time. For example, media drivers register themselves with the local media sub-system at boot time to provide information about the number of supported drives, partitions and drive numbers prior to the driver being loaded (this is described in detail in Chapter 13, *Peripheral Support*).

To support this, you should use the `DECLARE_STAND-ARD_EXTENSION` macro previously described, in conjunction with the following macros to export the required factory function:

```
#define DECLARE_EXTENSION_LDD()                          \
      EXPORT_C DLogicalDevice* CreateLogicalDevice()

#define DECLARE_EXTENSION_PDD()                          \
      EXPORT_C DPhysicalDevice* CreatePhysicalDevice()
```

12.4.2 Device driver classes

Throughout this chapter I shall be referring to the various classes that make up the EKA2 device driver framework. Figure 12.3 gives an overview of these classes which you can refer back to while you are reading this chapter.

In Figure 12.3, the white boxes represent classes provided by the EKA2 device driver framework. The shaded boxes indicate classes that must be implemented by the device driver.

Two components make up the logical device driver (LDD) – the LDD factory (derived from `DLogicalDevice`) and the logical channel

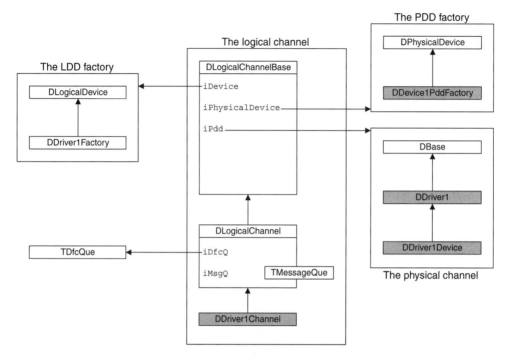

Figure 12.3   The EKA2 device driver classes

(derived from `DLogicalChannelBase`). The LDD factory is responsible for creating an instance of the logical channel, which, as I described in the overview in Section 12.1.2.1, contains functionality that is common to a specific class of devices (such as communications devices). A user-side application communicates with the logical channel via a handle to the logical channel (`RBusLogicalChannel`).

Similarly, two components make up the physical device driver (PDD) – the PDD factory (derived from `DPhysicalDevice`) and the physical channel (derived from `DBase`). As I also described in Section 12.1.2.2, the physical channel is responsible for communicating with the underlying hardware on behalf of the more generic logical channel. The physical channel exists purely to provide functionality to the logical channel, so is not directly accessible from the user side.

Note: In Figure 12.3, two shaded boxes appear in the physical channel (`DDriver1` and `DDriver1Device`). These represent a further abstraction known as the platform-independent and platform-specific layers (PIL/PSL). The PIL (`DDriver1`) contains functionality that, although not generic enough to live in the logical channel, is applicable to all hardware that your driver may be implemented on. The PSL (`DDriver1Device`) contains functionality that is too specific to belong in the LDD or PSL, such as the reading and writing of hardware-specific registers. Such layering is often beneficial when porting your device driver to a new platform, but is optional – so it is up to you when designing your device driver to determine if such layering is appropriate.

12.4.3 The execution model

When a device driver is loaded and a channel is opened to it, it is ready to handle requests. EKA2 provides two device driver models, which are distinguished by the execution context used to process requests from user-side clients. In the first model, requests from user-side clients are executed in the context of these clients, in privileged mode. This functionality is provided by the `DLogicalChannelBase` class, as shown in Figure 12.4.

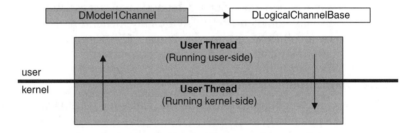

Figure 12.4   Requests handled in user thread context

Alternatively, the `DLogicalChannel` class provides a framework that allows user-side requests to be executed in the context of a kernel thread, as shown in Figure 12.5.

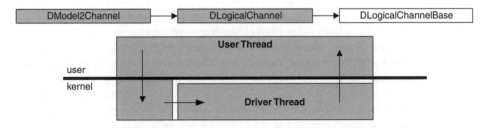

Figure 12.5   Requests handled in kernel thread context

In the latter model, a call to a device driver goes through the following steps:

1. The user-side client uses an executive call to request a service from a driver

2. The kernel blocks the client thread and sends a kernel-side message to the kernel thread handling requests for this driver

3. When the kernel thread is scheduled to run, it processes the request and sends back a result

4. The kernel unblocks the client thread when the result is received.

This model makes device-driver programming easier because the same kernel thread can be used to process requests from many user-side clients and DFCs, thus serializing access to the device driver and eliminating thread-related issues. Several drivers can use the same request/DFC kernel thread to reduce resource usage.

There are two kinds of request: synchronous and asynchronous.

12.4.3.1 Synchronous requests

You would typically use a synchronous request to set or retrieve some state information. Such a request may access the hardware itself, but usually completes relatively quickly. Synchronous requests are initiated by a call to `RBusLogicalChannel::DoControl()`, which does not return until the request has fully completed.

12.4.3.2 Asynchronous requests

An asynchronous request is one which you would typically use to perform a potentially long running operation – for example, one that transmits or receives a block of data from the hardware when it becomes available. The time taken for such a request to complete depends on the operation performed, and during this time the client user-side thread may be able to continue with some other processing. Asynchronous requests are initiated by a call to `RBusLogicalChannel::DoRequest()`, which takes a `TRequestStatus` object as an argument and normally returns control to the user as soon as the request has been issued. Typically, hardware will indicate completion of an operation by generating an interrupt, which is handled by an interrupt service routine (ISR) provided by the driver. This in turn schedules a DFC, which runs at some later time in the context of a kernel-side thread and signals the client user-side thread, marking the asynchronous request as complete.

More than one asynchronous request can be outstanding at the same time, each one associated with its own `TRequestStatus` object, and each identified by a specific request number. The device driver framework puts no explicit limit on the number of concurrent outstanding asynchronous requests; any limit must be enforced by the driver itself. However, the API to cancel a request uses a `TUint32` bit mask to specify the operations to be cancelled, which implicitly prevents you from uniquely identifying more than 32 concurrent request types.

12.4.4 User-side access to device drivers

To put the previous introduction into context, let's take a look at how a user-side application would typically go about initializing and using a simple device driver. The following example shows how a user application might access a serial port. This application simply echoes KBufSize characters from the serial port – of course, a real application would be more complex than this, and would be likely to make use of the active object framework to handle the transmission and reception of data.

```
TInt TestSerialPort()
   {
   // Load the physical device
   TInt err = User::LoadPhysicalDevice(_L("16550.PDD"));
   if (err != KErrNone && err != KErrAlreadyExists)
      return err;

   // Load the logical device
   err = User::LoadLogicalDevice(_L("SERIAL.LDD"));
   if (err != KErrNone && err != KErrAlreadyExists)
      return err;

   // Open a channel to the first serial port (COM0)
   RSimpleSerialChannel serialPort;
   err = serialPort.Open(KUnit0);
   if (err != KErrNone)
      return err;

   // Read the default comms settings
   TCommConfig cBuf;
   TCommConfigV01& c=cBuf();
   serialPort.Config(cBuf);

   c.iRate     = EBps57600;   // 57600 baud
   c.iDataBits = EData8;      // 8 data bits
   c.iParity   = EParityNone; // No parity
   c.iStopBits = EStop1;      // 1 stop bit

   // Write the new comms settings
   err = theSerialPort.SetConfig(cBuf);
   if(err == KErrNone)
      {
      TRequestStatus readStat, writeStat;
      TUint8 dataBuf[KBufSize];
      TPtr8 dataDes(&dataBuf[0],KBufSize,KBufSize);

      // Read some data from the port
      serialPort.Read(readStat, dataDes);
      User::WaitForRequest(readStat);
      if((err = readStat.Int()) == KErrNone)
         {
         // Write the same data back to the port
         serialPort.Write(writeStat, dataDes);
         User::WaitForRequest(writeStat);
         err = writeStat.Int();
         }
      }
   serialPort.Close();
   return(err);
   }
```

This example demonstrates some of the following fundamental device driver concepts:

- Loading of a logical and physical device
  `User::LoadLogicalDevice`
  `User::LoadPhysicalDevice`

- Opening a channel to the device driver
  `RSimpleSerialChannel::Open`

- Performing a synchronous operation
  `RSimpleSerialChannel::Config`
  `RSimpleSerialChannel::SetConfig`

- Performing an asynchronous operation
  `RSimpleSerialChannel::Read`
  `RSimpleSerialChannel::Write`

- Closing the channel to the device driver
  `RSimpleSerialChannel::Close`

In the following sections I'll be discussing the underlying principles behind each of these concepts, both from a user-side perspective and how these operations are translated and implemented by the kernel and device driver.

12.4.4.1   *Loading the driver from user-side code*

As I have previously mentioned, device drivers are kernel DLLs that are initialized by the loader in the same manner as any other DLL; this contrasts with the extensions I mentioned previously, which are XIP modules initialized explicitly by the kernel without the use of the loader. Before a client can use a device driver, its DLLs must be loaded using a combination of the following APIs:

```
TInt User::LoadLogicalDevice(const TDesC &aFileName)
TInt User::LoadPhysicalDevice(const TDesC &aFileName)
```

These functions ask the loader to search the system path for the required LDD or PDD. If you don't supply a filename extension, then the required extension (.LDD or .PDD) will be added to the filename. If the file is found, its UID values are verified to make sure the DLL is a valid LDD or PDD before the image is loaded. Once loaded, the kernel proceeds to call the DLL entry point as described in Section 12.1.6, and this constructs any global objects in the DLL.

After loading the DLL, the loader calls its first export immediately. LDDs and PDDs are polymorphic DLLs, and the first export is defined as the factory function required to create an object of a class derived from either `DLogicalDevice` for an LDD, or `DPhysicalDevice` for a PDD. (I'll describe these classes in detail in the next section.)

As I described in Section 12.2.2, the kernel defines two macros, `DECLARE_STANDARD_LDD` and `DECLARE_STANDARD_PDD`, which are used by the device driver to define both the kernel module entry point and the exported factory function, as shown in the following example:

```
DECLARE_STANDARD_LDD()
    {
    return new DSimpleSerialLDD;
    }
```

If the device driver needs to perform some one-off initialization at system boot time, you should ensure that it is also an extension. In this case, you would use the `DECLARE_STANDARD_EXTENSION` macro discussed in Section 12.2.2 to define the custom kernel module entry point, and use the alternative `DECLARE_EXTENSION_LDD` and `DECLARE_EXTENSION_PDD` macros to export the factory function.

Note: If you are using this feature to allocate resources early in the boot process, consider carefully whether such initialization would be better off being deferred to some later point in the process (such as when the driver is actually loaded or a channel is created). Any resources allocated at boot time will remain allocated until the system is rebooted, which may not be the behavior that you are looking for.

Once the factory object is created, the kernel calls its second phase constructor, `Install()`. You must register an appropriate name for the newly created LDD or PDD factory object with this function (see the following example), as well as performing any other driver-specific initialization as required. If this function is successful, the kernel will add the named object to its kernel object container. The kernel reserves two object containers specifically to maintain the list of currently loaded LDD and PDD factory objects:

Object	Container	Name
`DLogicalDevice`	`ELogicalDevice`	`<ldd>`
`DPhysicalDevice`	`EphysicalDevice`	`<ldd>.<pdd>`

All future references to the name of the device driver should now refer to the object name, rather than the LDD/PDD filename.

The object name is also used to associate a PDD with a specific class of LDD – I'll talk about this more later in the chapter.

Note: Some device drivers deviate from the standard "`<ldd>.<pdd>`" naming convention and define a different prefix for PDD names than the

LDD name. These are usually drivers that don't rely on the kernel's automatic PDD matching framework, and I'll talk about this later.

So, in our simple serial driver, the `Install()` functions would look something like this:

```
// Simple Serial LDD

_LIT(KLddName,"Serial");
TInt DSimpleSerialLDD::Install()
  {
  return(SetName(&KLddName));
  }

// Simple 16550 Uart PDD

_LIT(KPddName,"Serial.16550");
TInt DSimple16550PDD::Install()
  {
  return(SetName(&KPddName));
  }
```

I've already mentioned that the `Install()` function may also be used to perform any initialization that should take place when the driver is first loaded. For example, the driver may create a new kernel thread, allocate shared memory or check for the presence of a required kernel extension or hardware resource.

12.4.4.2 *Verifying that devices are loaded*

Symbian OS provides iterator classes to enable applications to identify which kernel objects are currently present in the system. In particular, `TFindPhysicalDevice` and `TFindLogicalDevice` may be used to identify which device drivers are currently loaded:

```
class TFindPhysicalDevice : public TFindHandleBase
  {
public:
  inline TFindPhysicalDevice();
  inline TFindPhysicalDevice(const TDesC& aMatch);
  IMPORT_C TInt Next(TFullName& aResult);
  };
```

These are derived from `TFindHandleBase`, a base class which performs wildcard name matching on kernel objects contained within object containers, from which a number of classes are derived to find specific types of kernel objects:

```
class TFindHandleBase
  {
public:
```

```
  IMPORT_C TFindHandleBase();
  IMPORT_C TFindHandleBase(const TDesC& aMatch);
  IMPORT_C void Find(const TDesC& aMatch);
  inline TInt Handle() const;
protected:
  TInt NextObject(TFullName& aResult,TInt aObjectType);
protected:
  /**
  The find-handle number.
  */
  TInt iFindHandle;

  /**
  The full name of the last kernel-side object found.
  */
  TFullName iMatch;
  };
```

Each iterator class provides its own implementation of `Next`, which calls the protected `NextObject` method providing the ID of the container to be searched:

```
EXPORT_C TInt TFindPhysicalDevice::Next(TFullName &aResult)
  {
  return NextObject(aResult,EPhysicalDevice);
  }
```

For example, to find all physical devices present in the system, we would use `TFindPhysicalDevice` as follows:

```
TFindPhysicalDevice findHb;
findHb.Find(_L("*"));
TFullName name;
while (findHb.Next(name)==KErrNone)
      RDebug::Print(name);
```

This is precisely the mechanism used by the text window server's PS command, which produces the output shown in Figure 12.6.

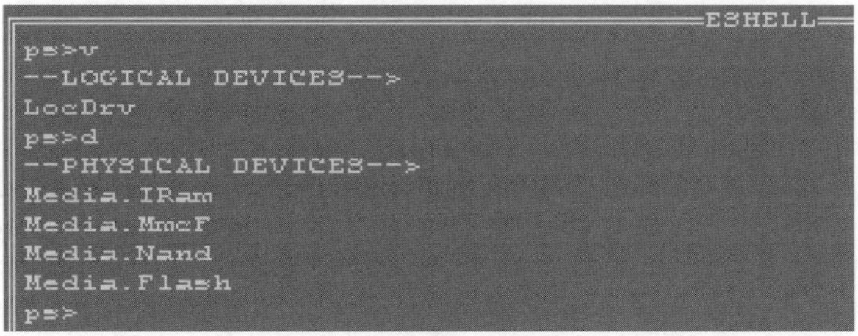

Figure 12.6   Using the text shell's command

12.4.4.3 Unloading the driver

A user-side application can unload an LDD or PDD using one of the following APIs:

```
TInt User::FreeLogicalDevice(const TDesC &aDeviceName)
TInt User::FreePhysicalDevice(const TDesC &aDeviceName)
```

Note that an object name (aDeviceName) is used in this instance, rather than the file name that was used when loading the device. These functions enter the kernel via the executive call:

```
TInt ExecHandler::DeviceFree(const TDesC8& aName, TInt aDeviceType)
```

The aDeviceType parameter identifies the necessary object container (EPhysicalDevice or ELogicalDevice) within which the object is located by name. If the kernel finds the object, it closes it, which will result in deletion of the object and its code segment, if it is not in use by another thread:

```
DLogicalDevice::~DLogicalDevice()
  {
  if (iCodeSeg)
    {
    __DEBUG_EVENT(EEventUnloadLdd, iCodeSeg);
    iCodeSeg->ScheduleKernelCleanup(EFalse);
    }
  }
```

The function call ScheduleKernelCleanup(EFalse) unloads the associated DLL with module reason KModuleEntryReasonProcess-Detach, ensuring that the any static data initialized at DLL load time is destroyed. The EFalse parameter indicates that the code segment is not to be immediately destroyed (since we are still using the code to run the destructor), but is to be added to the garbage list and scheduled for deletion when the null thread next runs.

12.4.5 Opening the device driver

In the previous section, I discussed how device drivers are loaded, creating LDD and PDD factory objects. The next step in using a device driver is to open a channel through which requests can be made. User-side code does this by making a call to RBusLogicalChannel::DoCreate(). (In reality, a client cannot call this method directly, since it is protected. It is called indirectly, via a driver-specific wrapper function, usually named Open(), although this doesn't affect our current discussion.)

```
inline TInt DoCreate(const TDesC& aDevice,
                    const TVersion& aVer, TInt aUnit,
                    const TDesC* aDriver,
                    const TDesC8* anInfo,
                    TOwnerType aType=EOwnerProcess,
                    TBool aProtected=EFalse);
```

The client provides the name of the LDD (again, giving the object name that uniquely identifies the LDD factory), the supported version number, the unit number, an optional PDD name and an optional extra information block. For example:

```
DoCreate(_L("Serial"), version, KUnit0, NULL, NULL);
DoCreate(_L("Serial"), version, KUnit0, _L("16550"), NULL);
```

These examples demonstrate the two different mechanisms that the kernel device driver framework provides for opening channels to device drivers:

1. Automatic search for a suitable physical device (no PDD name is specified)

2. User-specified physical device (a PDD name is provided).

I will discuss both of these methods in the following sections, in which I will show how channels are created using LDD and PDD factory objects.

12.4.5.1   Creating the logical channel – the LDD factory

When you call `RBusLogicalChannel::DoCreate()`, it performs an executive call to create the kernel-side instance of a logical channel (`DLogicalChannelBase`) before initializing the client-side handle:

```
EXPORT_C TInt RBusLogicalChannel::DoCreate(
                        const TDesC& aLogicalDevice,
                        const TVersion& aVer,
                        TInt aUnit,
                        const TDesC* aPhysicalDevice,
                        const TDesC8* anInfo,
                        TInt aType)
    {
    TInt r = User::ValidateName(aLogicalDevice);
    if(KErrNone!=r)
        return r;
    TBuf8<KMaxKernelName> name8;
    name8.Copy(aLogicalDevice);

    TBuf8<KMaxKernelName> physicalDeviceName;
    TChannelCreateInfo8 info;
    info.iVersion=aVer;
    info.iUnit=aUnit;
```

```
    if(aPhysicalDevice)
        {
        physicalDeviceName.Copy(*aPhysicalDevice);
        info.iPhysicalDevice = &physicalDeviceName;
        }
    else
        info.iPhysicalDevice = NULL;
    info.iInfo=anInfo;

    return SetReturnedHandle(Exec::ChannelCreate(name8,
                                  info, aType),*this);
    }
```

The info parameter is of type `TChannelCreateInfo`, which encapsulates the user-supplied version, unit number and optional information block:

```
class TChannelCreateInfo
    {
public:
  TVersion iVersion;
  TInt iUnit;
  const TDesC* iPhysicalDevice;
  const TDesC8* iInfo;
  };
```

The channel creation mechanism in `Exec::ChannelCreate` makes use of the `DLogicalDevice` and `DPhysicalDevice` factory objects that the kernel created when it loaded the device drivers. The logical device is defined in `kernel.h` as follows:

```
class DLogicalDevice : public DObject
    {
public:
  IMPORT_C virtual ~DLogicalDevice();

  IMPORT_C virtual TBool QueryVersionSupported(
                  const TVersion& aVer) const;

  IMPORT_C virtual TBool IsAvailable(TInt aUnit,
                      const TDesC* aDriver,
                      const TDesC8* aInfo) const;

  TInt ChannelCreate(DLogicalChannelBase*& pC,
                  TChannelCreateInfo& aInfo);

  TInt FindPhysicalDevice(DLogicalChannelBase*
          aChannel, TChannelCreateInfo& aInfo);

  virtual TInt Install()=0;
  virtual void GetCaps(TDes8& aDes) const =0;
  virtual TInt Create(DLogicalChannelBase*&aChannel)=0;

public:
  TVersion iVersion;
```

```
TUint iParseMask;
TUint iUnitsMask;
DCodeSeg* iCodeSeg;
TInt iOpenChannels;
};
```

This is an abstract base class – a device driver must provide an implementation of the `GetCaps()`, `Create()` and `Install()` methods, as these are used by the framework when creating the channel.

To create a channel, the kernel-side executive handler, `ExecHandler::ChannelCreate`, first uses the supplied LDD name to search the `ELogicalDevice` container for an associated `DLogicalDevice` factory object. If it finds one, it increments the factory's instance count before validating the supplied unit number against the value of the `KDeviceAllowUnit` flag in `iParseMask`, using the following rules:

1. If the device supports unit numbers, the unit number must be within the range of 0 to `KMaxUnits` (32).

2. If the device does not support unit numbers, the `aUnit` parameter must be `KNullUnit`.

You need to initialize `iVersion` and `iParseMask` in the constructor of your `DlogicalDevice`-derived LDD factory to determine how your device driver is loaded. For example, if my serial driver needs the client to specify a unit number and the relevant PDD to be present in the system, I would code the constructor like this:

```
DSimpleSerialLDD::DSimpleSerialLDD()
  {
  iParseMask = KDeviceAllowPhysicalDevice |
               KDeviceAllowUnit;
  iVersion   = TVersion(KCommsMajorVersionNumber,
                        KCommsMinorVersionNumber,
                        KCommsBuildVersionNumber);
  }
```

The following table summarizes the usage of `iVersion` and `iParseMask`:

`iVersion`	The interface version supported by this LDD. This is used to check that an LDD and PDD are compatible, so you should increment it if the interface changes. The version checking API, `Kern::QueryVersionSupported()`, assumes that clients requesting old versions will work with a newer version, but clients requesting new versions will not accept an older version.

iParseMask   This is a bit mask indicating a combination of:

- KDeviceAllowPhysicalDevice
  The LDD requires an accompanying PDD

- KDeviceAllowUnit
  The LDD accepts a unit number at channel creation
  time

- KDeviceAllowInfo
  The LDD accepts additional device-specific info at
  channel creation time

- KDeviceAllowAll
  A combination of all of these.

iUnitsMask   No longer used by the LDD; present for legacy reasons.

Once the factory object has been identified and its capabilities validated, the kernel calls the driver's channel factory function, DLogicalDevice::Create(). This function is responsible for creating an instance of the logical channel (derived from DLogicalChannelBase) through which all subsequent requests to the driver will be routed:

```
TInt DSimpleSerialLDD::Create(DLogicalChannelBase*& aChannel)
  {
  aChannel = new DSimpleSerialChannel;
  return aChannel ? KErrNone : KErrNoMemory;
  }
```

The kernel returns a pointer to the newly created channel to the framework via a reference parameter, returning an error if it is unable to create the channel. The framework stores a pointer to the DLogicalDevice that created the channel in the channel's iDevice field (so that its reference count may be decremented when the channel is eventually closed), and increments iOpenChannels.

If the logical device specifies that it needs a PDD (indicated by the KDeviceAllowPhysicalDevice flag in iParseMask), then the kernel locates a suitable PDD factory, which is used to create the device-specific physical channel – I will cover this in more detail in the next section. The kernel stores a pointer to the newly created physical channel in the iPdd member of the logical channel.

The kernel framework will now initialize the newly created DlogicalChannelBase-derived object by calling DLogicalChannelBase::DoCreate(), passing in the information contained in the TChannelCreateInfo package supplied by the user. This is the logical channel's opportunity to validate the supplied parameters, allocate additional resources and prepare the hardware for use.

If initialization is successful, the kernel adds the newly created logical channel into the `ELogicalChannel` object container, and creates a handle, which it returns to the user-side client. If it is not, the kernel closes the logical channel and any associated physical device and returns a suitable error.

Note: Being a handle to a kernel object, the client side `RBusLogicalChannel` handle inherits the standard handle functionality described in Chapter 5, *Kernel Services*. By default, the kernel creates an `RBusLogicalChannel` handle with `ELocal` and `EOwnerProcess` attributes, thus restricting usage to the process that opened the channel. Protection may be promoted to `EProtected` by specifying `aProtected = ETrue` in `RBusLogicalChannel::DoCreate`. This will allow the handle to be shared with other processes using the IPC mechanisms available for handle sharing. The handle may never be promoted to an `EGlobal` object.

12.4.5.2 Creating the physical device – the PDD factory

Some LDDs don't require a physical device to be present (two examples being the local media sub-system which takes responsibility for loading its own media drivers and the USB controller which communicates directly with a kernel extension). But the majority of LDDs do need a PDD, since most device drivers rely on hardware with more than one possible variant.

A physical channel is nothing more than a simple `DBase`-derived object, and as such has an interface that is determined only by the LDD with which it is associated. (Contrast this with the logical channel, which must be derived from `DLogicalChannelBase` and conforms to a globally defined interface). It is the responsibility of the `DphysicalDevice`-derived PDD factory to validate and create the physical channel:

```
class DPhysicalDevice : public DObject
  {
public:
  enum TInfoFunction
    {
    EPriority=0,
    };
public:
  IMPORT_C virtual ~DPhysicalDevice();
  IMPORT_C virtual TBool QueryVersionSupported(const TVersion& aVer)
                                                            const;
  IMPORT_C virtual TBool IsAvailable(TInt aUnit, const TDesC8* aInfo)
                                                            const;

  virtual TInt Install() =0;
  virtual void GetCaps(TDes8& aDes) const =0;
  virtual TInt Create(DBase*& aChannel, TInt aUnit, const TDesC8* aInfo,
                                          const TVersion& aVer) =0;
  virtual TInt Validate(TInt aUnit, const TDesC8* aInfo, const TVersion&
                                          aVer) =0;
```

```
  IMPORT_C virtual TInt Info(TInt aFunction, TAny* a1);
public:
  TVersion iVersion;
  TUint iUnitsMask;
  DCodeSeg* iCodeSeg;
  };
```

Notice that this looks very similar to `DLogicalDevice` – not surprising since they perform an almost identical task. However, there are a few differences in the physical device:

- `iParseMask` does not exist

- A `Validate()` method must be provided to support the logical device in searching for suitable PDDs. (I'll show an example implementation of this later)

- An optional `Info()` method may be provided to provide additional device-specific information about the driver. This is currently only used by media drivers (as you can see in Chapter 13, *Peripheral Support*).

Now, let's look at PDD loading in a little more detail.

User-specified PDD

If a PDD name was supplied in the call to `RBusLogicalChannel::DoCreate()`, the kernel first validates the name to ensure that it is a match for the logical channel (that is, it compares the supplied "`<ldd>.<pdd>`" name with the wildcard string "`<ldd>.*`").

If the name is valid, the kernel uses it to locate the corresponding `DPhysicalDevice` object in the `EPhysicalDevice` container.

It then calls the `Validate()` method on this object, passing the unit number, optional extra information block and version number. This is the PDD's opportunity to verify that the version number matches that of the requesting logical channel, and that the requested unit number is supported:

```
TInt DSimpleSerialPDD::Validate(TInt aUnit, const
TDesC8* /*anInfo*/, const TVersion& aVer)
  {
  if(!Kern::QueryVersionSupported(iVersion,aVer)
    return KErrNotSupported;
  if (aUnit<0 || aUnit>=KNum16550Uarts)
    return KErrNotSupported;
  return KErrNone;
  }
```

Automatic search for PDD

Alternatively, if the user-side does not provide a PDD name, but the logical device requires a PDD to be present, then the kernel makes a wildcard search for all DPhysicalDevice objects with the name "<ldd>.*". For each such object, it calls the Validate() function, and the first one which returns KErrNone is taken to be the matching PDD. Note that the order of DPhysicalDevice objects within the container is influenced only by the order in which the PDDs were originally loaded.

Note: This mechanism is useful when there are many PDDs supporting a single LDD, and it is not known in advance which of these PDDs support a given unit number.

Once a suitable physical device has been identified, the kernel opens it (incrementing its reference count) and places the pointer to the DPhysicalDevice in the logical channel's iPhysicalDevice, so that its reference count may be decremented if an error occurs or the channel is closed.

Finally, the kernel calls DPhysicalDevice::Create() on the matching PDD, again passing the unit number, optional extra information block and version number. The device driver must provide this method; it is responsible for creating and initializing the actual DBase derived physical channel:

```
TInt DSimpleSerialPDD::Create(DBase*& aChannel, TInt
aUnit, const TDesC8* anInfo, const TVersion& aVer)
  {
  DComm16550* pD=new DComm16550;
  aChannel=pD;
  TInt r=KErrNoMemory;
  if (pD)
    r=pD->DoCreate(aUnit,anInfo);
  return r;
  }
```

Again, the newly created physical channel is returned by reference, and the kernel places a pointer to it in the logical channel's iPdd field for later use.

12.4.5.3 Advanced LDD/PDD factory concepts

In the previous section, I discussed the basic mechanism by which the LDD and PDD factory classes are used to create a physical channel. Most device drivers follow this simple model, but the framework also provides additional functionality that may be useful for more complex implementations.

Obtaining device capabilities from user-side code

Both DLogicalDevice and DPhysicalDevice define three virtual functions that I haven't yet explained: QueryVersionSupported, IsAvailable and GetCaps. You can implement these in a device driver if you want to provide device capability information to user-side code before it opens a channel. The functions are accessible via the

RDevice class, which is the user-side handle representing the kernel-side LDD factory object. You can obtain this by opening the handle by name, or using the TFindLogicalDevice class described in Section 12.4.4.2:

```
class RDevice : public RHandleBase
    {
public:
    inline TInt Open(const TFindLogicalDevice& aFind,
                    TOwnerType aType=EOwnerProcess);
    IMPORT_C TInt Open(const TDesC& aName,
            TOwnerType aType=EOwnerProcess);
    IMPORT_C void GetCaps(TDes8& aDes) const;
    IMPORT_C TBool QueryVersionSupported(
            const TVersion& aVer) const;
    IMPORT_C TBool IsAvailable(TInt aUnit,
            const TDesC* aPhysicalDevice,
             const TDesC8* anInfo) const;
#ifndef __SECURE_API__
    IMPORT_C TBool IsAvailable(TInt aUnit,
            const TDesC* aPhysicalDevice,
            const TDesC16* anInfo) const;
#endif
    };
```

The implementation of these APIs is driver dependent. For example, our simple serial port may report its version number in the following manner:

```
class TSimpleSerialCaps
    {
public:
    TVersion iVersion;
    };

void DSimpleSerialLDD::GetCaps(TDes8& aDes) const
    {
    TPckgBuf<TSimpleSerialCaps> b;
    b().iVersion=TVersion(KCommsMajorVersionNumber,
                        KCommsMinorVersionNumber,
                        KCommsBuildVersionNumber);
    Kern::InfoCopy(aDes,b);
    }
```

And the user application might obtain this information in this way:

```
RDevice theLDD;
TInt err = theLDD.Open(_L("Serial"));
if(err == KErrNone)
    {
    TPckgBuf<TSimpleSerialCaps> c;
    theLDD.GetCaps(c);
    TVersionName aName = c().version.Name();
    RDebug::Print(_L("Serial Ver = %S\n"), &aName);
    theDevice.Close();
    }
```

Advanced PDD identification

I have described how a logical device may use the KDeviceAllow-PhysicalDevice flag to enable the framework to either find a PDD by name, or by wildcard search. If an LDD does not specify this parameter, it is free to perform its own search for a suitable physical device. In fact, this is precisely the mechanism used by the local media sub-system.

The kernel provides the following kernel-side iterator, which is similar in concept to the user-side TFindPhysicalDevice:

```
struct SPhysicalDeviceEntry
  {
  TInt iPriority;
  DPhysicalDevice* iPhysicalDevice;
  };

class RPhysicalDeviceArray : public
RArray<SPhysicalDeviceEntry>
  {
public:
  IMPORT_C RPhysicalDeviceArray();
  IMPORT_C void Close();
  IMPORT_C TInt GetDriverList(const TDesC& aMatch,
                                     TInt aUnit,
                            const TDesC8* aInfo,
                         const TVersion& aVersion);
  };
```

This class gives the same results as the automatic PDD search provided by the kernel, and it allows a logical channel to identify suitable physical devices according to its own rules. If using this scheme, it is the responsibility of the channel to maintain the list of channels that it has opened, and to define its own identification mechanism. For example, the local media sub-system defines the aUnit parameter to represent the media type of a media driver. For more advanced mechanisms, the aInfo parameter may be used to specify device-specific information when Validate() is called.

12.4.6   Interacting with a device driver

In previous sections, I have explained how device drivers are loaded and channels are opened using the device driver framework. The next stage is to service requests issued from user-side code. There are three main classes involved:

1.   RBusLogicalChannel – the user-side channel handle

2.   DLogicalChannelBase – the kernel-side channel (receives requests in the context of the client thread)

3.   DLogicalChannel – the kernel-side channel (receives requests in the context of a separate kernel thread).

Note: In fact, there are four classes if you include the physical channel, DPhysicalChannel, but since this is a device specific interface, I won't discuss its use until we start looking at our serial driver in more detail.

I have already touched on these classes when discussing how device drivers are loaded and the channel is opened. Now I shall discuss how these are actually used in the context of a real device driver.

12.4.6.1   *RBusLogicalChannel – the user-side channel handle*

The RBusLogicalChannel class is a user-side handle to a kernel-side logical channel (DLogicalChannelBase), and provides the functions required to open a channel to a device driver and to make requests:

```
class RBusLogicalChannel : public RHandleBase
  {
public:
  IMPORT_C TInt Open(RMessagePtr2 aMessage, TInt aParam,
TOwnerType aType=EOwnerProcess);
  IMPORT_C TInt Open(TInt aArgumentIndex, TOwnerType
aType=EOwnerProcess);
protected:
  inline TInt DoCreate(const TDesC& aDevice,
                       const TVersion& aVer,
                       TInt aUnit,
                       const TDesC* aDriver,
                       const TDesC8* anInfo,
                       TOwnerType aType=EOwnerProcess,
                       TBool aProtected=EFalse);

  IMPORT_C void DoCancel(TUint aReqMask);

  IMPORT_C void DoRequest(TInt aReqNo, TRequestStatus& aStatus);
  IMPORT_C void DoRequest(TInt aReqNo, TRequestStatus& aStatus,
TAny* a1);
  IMPORT_C void DoRequest(TInt aReqNo, TRequestStatus& aStatus,
TAny* a1,TAny* a2);

  IMPORT_C TInt DoControl(TInt aFunction);
  IMPORT_C TInt DoControl(TInt aFunction, TAny* a1);
  IMPORT_C TInt DoControl(TInt aFunction, TAny* a1,TAny* a2);
private:
  IMPORT_C TInt DoCreate(const TDesC& aDevice,
                         const TVersion& aVer,
                         TInt aUnit,
                         const TDesC* aDriver,
                         const TDesC8* aInfo,
                         TInt aType);
  };
```

Note: If you have access to the EKA2 source code, you will find that the real class is slightly more complex than the version given here. The extra methods and data are mainly provided to maintain binary compatibility with the EKA1 kernel, since this is the user-side interface to the device driver. See Section 12.5 for more on the differences between the EKA1 and EKA2 device driver framework.

RBusLogicalChannel provides the following functionality:

- Creation of the logical channel (discussed in the previous section)
- DoRequest – performs an asynchronous operation
- DoControl – perform a synchronous operation
- DoCancel – cancel an outstanding asynchronous request.

See Figure 12.7. All but two of the methods provided by RBusLogicalChannel are protected, so the client can do nothing useful with this class directly; it needs a derived interface, specific to the implementation of the device driver. The usual way to do this is to provide a header file to define the class and an inline file to provide the implementation, and include both in the client-side code at build time. As an example, let's look at how I would provide an interface to my example serial driver:

```
class RSimpleSerialChannel : public RBusLogicalChannel
  {
public:
  enum TVer
    {
    EMajorVersionNumber=1,
    EMinorVersionNumber=0,
    EBuildVersionNumber=KE32BuildVersionNumber
    };
  enum TRequest
    {
    ERequestRead=0x0,
    ERequestReadCancel=0x1,
    ERequestWrite=0x1,
    ERequestWriteCancel=0x2,
    };
  enum TControl
    {
    EControlConfig,
    EControlSetConfig
    };
public:
#ifndef __KERNEL_MODE__
  inline TInt Open(TInt aUnit);
  inline TVersion VersionRequired() const;
  inline void Read(TRequestStatus& aStatus, TDes8& aDes);
  inline void ReadCancel();
  inline void Write(TRequestStatus& aStatus, const TDesC8& aDes);
  inline void WriteCancel();
  inline void Config(TDes8& aConfig);
  inline TInt SetConfig(const TDesC8& aConfig);
#endif
  };

#include <simpleserial.inl>
```

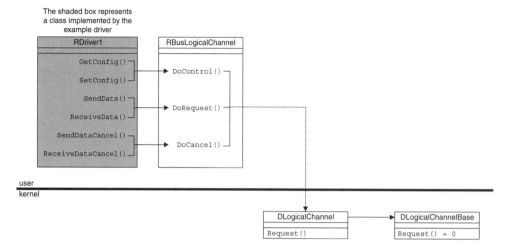

Figure 12.7   Mapping the user-side API to `RBusLogicalChannel`

The implementation is in the corresponding inline file:

```
#ifndef __KERNEL_MODE__
_LIT(KDeviceName,"Serial");

inline TInt RSimpleSerialChannel::Open(TInt aUnit)
  {
  return(DoCreate(KDeviceName,VersionRequired(),
                 aUnit,NULL,NULL));
  }

inline TVersion RSimpleSerialChannel::VersionRequired() const
  {
  return(TVersion(EMajorVersionNumber,
                  EMinorVersionNumber,
                  EBuildVersionNumber));
  }

inline void RSimpleSerialChannel::Read(TRequestStatus&aStatus,
                                                TDes8& aDes)
  {
  TInt len=aDes.MaxLength();
  DoRequest(ERequestRead,aStatus,&aDes,&len);
  }

inline void RSimpleSerialChannel::ReadCancel()
  DoCancel(ERequestReadCancel);

inline void RSimpleSerialChannel::Write(TRequestStatus& aStatus,
                                                const TDesC8& aDes)
```

```
  {
  TInt len=aDes.Length();
  DoRequest(ERequestWrite,aStatus,(TAny *)&aDes,&len);
  }

inline void RSimpleSerialChannel::Config(TDes8& aConfig)
  DoControl(EControlConfig,&aConfig);

inline TInt RSimpleSerialChannel::SetConfig(const TDesC8& aCfg)
  return(DoControl(EControlSetConfig, (TAny *)&aCfg));
#endif
```

Note: These headers are also included in the kernel-side implementation of the device driver, so that it can pick up the version number and request number enumerations. This is why #ifndef __KERNEL_MODE__ is used around the user-side specific methods.

Next I will look at how the kernel handles communication from the user-side application, using the DLogicalChannelBase object.

12.4.6.2   DLogicalChannelBase – the kernel-side channel

DLogicalChannelBase is the kernel-side representation of the user-side RBusLogicalChannel. It is an abstract base class, the implementation of which is provided by the device driver:

```
class DLogicalChannelBase : public DObject
  {
public:
  IMPORT_C virtual ~DLogicalChannelBase();
public:
  virtual TInt Request(TInt aReqNo, TAny* a1, TAny* a2)=0;

  IMPORT_C virtual TInt DoCreate(TInt aUnit,
                     const TDesC8* aInfo,
                     const TVersion& aVer);
public:
  DLogicalDevice* iDevice;
  DPhysicalDevice* iPhysicalDevice;
  DBase* iPdd;
  };
```

I have already discussed the meaning of several members of this class when explaining how a logical channel is created:

- iDevice – a pointer to the LDD factory object that created this logical channel. The framework uses it to close the LDD factory object when the channel is closed

- iPhysicalDevice – a pointer to the PDD factory object that created the physical channel. The framework uses it to close the PDD factory object when the channel is closed

- iPdd – a pointer to the physical channel associated with this logical channel. It is used by the logical channel itself when communicating with the hardware and by the framework to delete the physical channel when the logical channel is closed.

iPhysicalDevice and iPdd are only provided by the framework if the logical device has specified that a physical channel is required by specifying the KDeviceAllowPhysicalDevice flag in DLogicalDevice::ParseMask.

12.4.6.3   Creating the logical channel

The virtual DoCreate() method is the logical channel's opportunity to perform driver-specific initialization at creation time (see Section 12.4.5.1). The device driver framework calls it after creating the logical channel:

```
TInt DoCreate(TInt aUnit, const TDesC8* aInfo, const TVersion& aVer);
```

Typically, a device driver would use this function to perform the following actions:

- Validate that the user-side code has sufficient capabilities to use this device driver

- Validate the version of the driver that the user-side code requires

- Initialize any DFC queues needed by the device driver. (Interrupt handlers would rarely be initialized here – this is usually the responsibility of the physical channel)

- Create and initialize its power handler.

This is how my simple serial driver does it:

```
TInt DSimpleSerialChannel::DoCreate(TInt aUnit, const TDesC8* /*anInfo*/,
                                                 const TVersion &aVer)
    {
if(!Kern::CurrentThreadHasCapability(ECapabilityCommDD,_
      _PLATSEC_DIAGNOSTIC_STRING("Checked by SERIAL.LDD
                            (Simple Serial Driver)")))
      return KErrPermissionDenied;
  if (!Kern::QueryVersionSupported(TVersion(
                  KCommsMajorVersionNumber,
                  KCommsMinorVersionNumber,
                  KCommsBuildVersionNumber),aVer))
      return KErrNotSupported;

  // initialise the TX buffer
  iTxBufSize=KTxBufferSize;
```

```
iTxBuffer=(TUint8*)Kern::Alloc(iTxBufSize);
if (!iTxBuffer)
   return KErrNoMemory;
iTxFillThreshold=iTxBufSize>>1;

// initialise the RX buffer
iRxBufSize=KDefaultRxBufferSize;
iRxCharBuf=(TUint8*)Kern::Alloc(iRxBufSize<<1);
if (!iRxCharBuf)
   {
   Kern::Free(iTxBuffer);
   return KErrNoMemory;
   }
iRxDrainThreshold=iRxBufSize>>1;

return KErrNone;
}
```

Performing the capability check

This should be the very first thing that you do in your `DoCreate()` method. You need to check that the client has sufficient capabilities to use this driver (see Section 12.1.8 and Chapter 8, *Platform Security*, for more information on the EKA2 security model).

Check the version

My `DoCreate()` method also verifies that the version of the device driver is compatible with that expected by the client. As I described in Section 12.4.6.1, both the user and the kernel side share a common header file at build time, and this provides the version number of the API. The kernel provides the `Kern::QueryVersionSupported()` method to enforce a consistent set of rules to all APIs, and this returns `ETrue` if the following conditions are satisfied:

- The major version of the client is less than the major version of the driver

- The major version of the client is equal to the major version of the driver and the minor version of the client is less than or equal to the minor version of the driver.

12.4.6.4 The request gateway function

If you refer back to the `DLogicalChannelBase` class I showed earlier, you may notice that there are no direct equivalents to the `DoControl`, `DoRequest` and `DoCancel` methods that `RBusLogicalChannel` provides. This is because all requests enter the driver via the logical channel's `Request()` gateway method (see Figure 12.8):

```
virtual TInt Request(TInt aReqNo, TAny* a1, TAny* a2)=0;
```

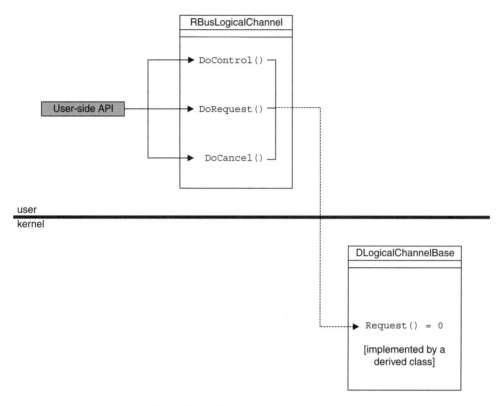

Figure 12.8   The request gateway function

The request gateway function takes a request number and two undefined parameters, which are mapped from the RBusLogicalChannel as follows:

```
RBusLogicalChannel                    DLogicalChannelBase


DoControl(aFunction)                  Request(aFunction, 0, 0)
DoControl(aFunction, a1)              Request(aFunction, a1, 0)
DoControl(aFunction, a1, a2)          Request(aFunction, a1, a2)


DoRequest(aReqNo, aStatus)            Request(~aReqNo, &aStatus, &A[0, 0])
DoRequest(aReqNo, aStatus, a1)        Request(~aReqNo, &aStatus, &A[a1, 0])
DoRequest(aReqNo, aStatus, a1, a2)    Request(~aReqNo, &aStatus, &A[a1, a2])


DoCancel(aReqMask)                    Request(0x7FFFFFFF, aReqMask, 0)
```

The following code shows how the RBusLogicalChannel::Do-
Control() method is implemented:

```
EXPORT_C TInt RBusLogicalChannel::DoControl(TInt aFunction,
                                            TAny *a1,TAny *a2)
    {
    return Exec::ChannelRequest(iHandle,aFunction,a1,a2);
    }
```

And here we show how an RBusLogicalChannel::DoRequest
method is implemented. You can see that the stack is used to pass
parameters a1 and a2. (This stack usage is represented in the previous
table as \&A[a1,a2].)

```
EXPORT_C void RBusLogicalChannel::DoRequest(TInt aReqNo,
                                            TRequestStatus &aStatus,
                                            TAny *a1, TAny *a2)
    {
    TAny *a[2];
    a[0]=a1;
    a[1]=a2;
    aStatus=KRequestPending;
    Exec::ChannelRequest(iHandle,~aReqNo,&aStatus,&a[0]);
    }
```

There is in fact little difference between DoControl() and DoRe-
quest() as far as the kernel is concerned, so DoControl() could
theoretically perform asynchronous operations by passing the address
of a TRequestStatus as one of the user parameters – this is a valid
optimization to make under some circumstances. However, you should
be aware that, although the DLogicalChannelBase framework does
not make any assumptions as to the format of the parameters supplied,
they are crucial to the operation of the DLogicalChannel class – so
any deviation from this pattern should be performed with care.

When understanding the operation of device drivers, it is crucial to
understand the context of requests coming from user-side. These requests
arrive at the gateway function via the following executive call:

```
__EXECDECL__ TInt Exec::ChannelRequest(TInt, TInt, TAny*, TAny*)
    {
    SLOW_EXEC4(EExecChannelRequest);
    }
```

This is a slow executive call which takes four parameters. It runs in
the context of the calling thread, with interrupts enabled and the kernel
unlocked, so it can be preempted at any point of its execution. The
following parameters are defined for this handler:

```
DECLARE_FLAGS_FUNC(0|EF_C|EF_P|(ELogicalChannel+1),
                   ExecHandler::ChannelRequest)
```

Referring back to Chapter 5, *Kernel Services*, this means that the call is
be preprocessed (as indicated by the EF_P[KExecFlagPreProcess]
flag) to obtain the kernel-side object from the supplied user handler using
the ELogicalChannel container, which in turn implies that it must
hold the system lock (as indicated by the EF_C[KExecFlagClaim]
flag). After preprocessing, the kernel invokes this executive handler:

```
TInt ExecHandler::ChannelRequest(DLogicalChannelBase*
        aChannel, TInt aFunction, TAny* a1, TAny* a2)
 {
 DThread& t=*TheCurrentThread;
 if (aChannel->Open()==KErrNone)
   {
   t.iTempObj=aChannel;
   NKern::UnlockSystem();
   TInt r=aChannel->Request(aFunction,a1,a2);
   NKern::ThreadEnterCS();
   t.iTempObj=NULL;
   aChannel->Close(NULL);
   NKern::ThreadLeaveCS();
   return r;
   }
 K::PanicCurrentThread(EBadHandle);
 return 0;
 }
```

The executive handler calls DLogicalChannelBase::Request(),
so this runs in the context of the calling (client) thread. Before calling the
request function, the kernel (a) increments the channel's reference count,
(b) stores the pointer to the channel in the iTempObj member of the
current thread and (c) releases the system lock. Since the request function
may be preempted at any time, these measures ensure that:

- If the current thread exits, the channel is safely closed after servicing
  the request

- Another thread cannot close the channel until the request function
  completes.

12.4.6.5   *Using DLogicalChannelBase::Request*

In the previous section we discussed the context within which DLogicalChannelBase::Request() is called. This has implications for
the design of a device driver using this function. Consider the following
points:

1. A device driver is likely to use hardware interrupts that queue a DFC on a *kernel thread* for further processing. This kernel thread can preempt the `Request()` method at any time

2. Several threads (in the process that opened the channel) may use a single instance of the channel concurrently

3. Several concurrent operations may require access to the same hardware and registers.

So, in all but the simplest device drivers, it is unlikely that the driver will get away with supporting only one asynchronous operation at a time. Depending on the requirements of the driver, it may be acceptable for the client to issue a second request without having to wait for the first to complete – and the same applies to issuing a synchronous request while an asynchronous request is outstanding. Since the completion of an asynchronous operation occurs in a kernel-side DFC thread, and may preempt any processing that the device driver does in user context, you must take great care to avoid synchronization issues – the kernel does not do this for you.

Request synchronization

Most device drivers are either written to perform all processing within the calling thread context, or to perform all processing within the kernel thread. The former is not generally acceptable for long running tasks, as this effectively blocks the client thread from running. A simple way to provide synchronization of requests in the latter case is to provide a single DFC per request (all posted to the same DFC queue). This scheme provides serialization of requests and guarantees that one operation is not preempted by another operation. However, this may not always be a practical solution as it takes time to queue a DFC and time for it to be scheduled to run. If you are performing a simple request (such as a read from a fast hardware register), this delay may be unacceptable.

Device drivers can support a combination of fast synchronous requests (handled in the context of the client thread) and long running asynchronous requests (handled in the context of one or more kernel threads), each of which may require access to the same resources. The kernel provides a set of primitives that should be used when addressing such synchronization issues.

First, the kernel provides a set of primitives to allow you to safely perform operations such as increment, decrement, swap or read/modify/write:

```
TInt NKern::LockedInc(TInt& aCount)
TInt NKern::LockedDec(TInt& aCount)
TInt NKern::LockedAdd(TInt& aDest, TInt aSrc)
TUint32 NKern::LockedSetClear(TUint32& aDest,
                              TUint32 aClearMask,
```

```
                                   TUint32 aSetMask)
TUint8 NKern::LockedSetClear8(TUint8& aDest,
                              TUint8 aClearMask,
                              TUint8 aSetMask)
TInt NKern::SafeInc(TInt& aCount)
TInt NKern::SafeDec(TInt& aCount)
TAny* NKern::SafeSwap(TAny* aNewValue, TAny*& aPtr)
TUint8 NKern::SafeSwap8(TUint8 aNewValue, TUint8& aPtr)
```

And of course, for synchronization, the nanokernel's fast semaphores and mutexes are available:

```
void NKern::FSWait(NFastSemaphore* aSem);
void NKern::FSSignal(NFastSemaphore* aSem);

void NKern::FMWait(NFastMutex* aMutex);
void NKern::FMSignal(NFastMutex* aMutex);
```

However, as the number of request types increases, and we add new DFCs and synchronization objects, the complexity of the driver rises dramatically. What we would like to do is to serialize our requests using a message queue, which is the very scheme employed by the DLogicalChannel framework and which I will explain in the next section.

12.4.7 DLogicalChannel

The DLogicalChannel class is provided to address the synchronization issues I mentioned previously. It supplies a framework within which user-side requests are executed in the context of a single kernel-side thread. It derives from DLogicalChannelBase and makes use of a kernel-side message queue and its associated DFC queue. Additionally, DLogicalChannel overrides the Close() method so that close events are handled safely within the same DFC queue.

Here's how DLogicalChannel is defined in kernel.h:

```
class DLogicalChannel : public DLogicalChannelBase
  {
public:
  enum {EMinRequestId=0xc0000000, ECloseMsg=0x80000000};
public:
  IMPORT_C DLogicalChannel();
  IMPORT_C virtual ~DLogicalChannel();
  IMPORT_C virtual TInt Close(TAny*);
  IMPORT_C virtual TInt Request(TInt aReqNo, TAny* a1, TAny* a2);
  IMPORT_C virtual void HandleMsg(TMessageBase* aMsg)=0;
  IMPORT_C void SetDfcQ(TDfcQue* aDfcQ);
```

```
public:
  static void MsgQFunc(TAny* aPtr);
public:
  TDfcQue* iDfcQ;
  TMessageQue iMsgQ;
  };
```

iDfcQ is a pointer to a DFC queue used to handle client requests.

iMsgQ is a message queue used to handle client requests.

12.4.7.1 *The DFC queue*

A driver based on DLogicalChannel provides a DFC queue to the framework at channel creation time. DLogicalChannel uses this queue to dispatch messages in response to user-side requests received by the Request() function. The driver may use one of the standard kernel queues or provide its own, and to avoid synchronization issues, this queue will usually be the same queue that it uses for DFCs related to hardware interrupts and other asynchronous events. For example, I would initialize my serial driver to use a standard kernel queue like this:

```
TInt DSimpleSerialChannel::DoCreate(TInt aUnit,
          const TDesC8* anInfo, const TVersion &aVer)
  {
  // Security and version control code as shown in the
  // previous example are omitted for clarity.
  SetDfcQ(Kern::DfcQue0());
  iMsgQ.Receive();
  return KErrNone;
  }
```

The pattern I have just shown puts the selection of the DFC queue into the LDD, which is useful if all the physical channels are likely to talk to the same hardware registers or memory, because it ensures that all requests for all channels will be serviced in the same kernel thread.

The kernel provides two standard DFC queues (running on two dedicated kernel threads, DfcThread0 and DfcThread1). These are available for use by device drivers and are obtained using Kern::DfcQue0() and Kern::DfcQue1(). DfcThread0 is a general-purpose low priority thread, which is currently used by serial comms, sound, Ethernet, keyboard and digitizer device drivers, and is suitable for simple device drivers without very stringent real-time requirements. DfcThread1 is a higher priority thread and should be used with care, since inappropriate use of this thread may adversely affect the accuracy of nanokernel timers.

Some device drivers create and use their own thread. This may be specified by the logical channel as I have described previously, or by the physical device itself. The local media sub-system uses the latter method.

The LDD provides a generic interface suitable for all types of media driver, and to allow multiple media drivers to operate concurrently, each media driver is responsible for specifying a DFC queue within which to service requests.

The caution I gave earlier about using DfcThread1 is even more appropriate if your driver creates a thread with higher priority than Dfc-Thread1. In both cases, you must take care not to delay the nanokernel timer DFC by more than 16 ticks.

The following code shows how my logical channel queries the physical device to obtain a device-specific DFC queue:

```
TInt DSimpleSerialChannel::DoCreate(TInt aUnit, const TDesC8* anInfo,
                                              const TVersion &aVer)
    {
    // Security and version control code as shown in the
    // previous example are omitted for clarity.
    SetDfcQ(((DComm*)iPdd)->DfcQ(aUnit));
    iMsgQ.Receive();
    return KErrNone;
    }
```

The physical channel can creates its DFC queue using the following kernel API:

```
TInt r=Kern::DfcQInit(&iDfcQ, iPriority, iName);
```

Alternatively, the physical channel can obtain the DFC queue from some other source, such as a kernel extension. For example, consider the peripheral bus controller which services removable media devices such as PC Card and SDIO devices. Such a controller would typically use a dedicated DFC thread to synchronize its requests, which would be made available for use by device drivers.

DFC queue usage tips

Tip 1: Since several drivers may share the same DFC queue, then the minimum latency of a DFC is the sum of the execution times of all other DFCs executed beforehand. Therefore, DFCs should be kept as short as possible, especially those on shared queues.

Tip 2: Consider your allocation of DFC priorities carefully when designing your device driver. If some events are more critical than others, you can use DFC priorities to ensure that these are serviced before lower priority events. For example, a cable disconnect or media removal notification may be given a higher priority than data transfer events to allow your driver to take emergency action and recover gracefully. However, if you are using a shared DFC queue then choose your priorities carefully to avoid affecting other drivers.

Tip 3: If the DFC queue is obtained from a kernel extension, the queue will be available throughout the life of the system. However, if you create the queue (when the PDD or LDD is opened) then you must destroy it (when the PDD or LDD is unloaded) to avoid resource leaks. There is no kernel API to destroy a DFC queue from outside the DFC queue's own thread, so the standard way to do this is to post a "cleanup" DFC to the queue.

12.4.7.2 The message queue

I described message queues in Chapter 4, *Inter-thread Communication*. In this section, I shall talk about how device drivers make use of message queues.

`DLogicalChannel` uses a message queue (`iMsgQ`) to allow multiple requests from several client-side threads to be queued and handled sequentially by a single kernel-side DFC. This is illustrated in Figure 12.9.

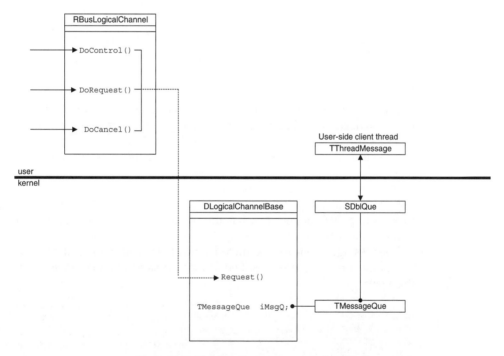

Figure 12.9 The driver's message queue framework

The message queue consists of a DFC and a doubly linked list of received messages (`TThreadMessage` objects). Each user-side thread owns its own `TThreadMessage` object as shown in Figure 12.10.

When issuing a request to a device driver, the driver framework populates the thread's `TThreadMessage` object with the supplied request

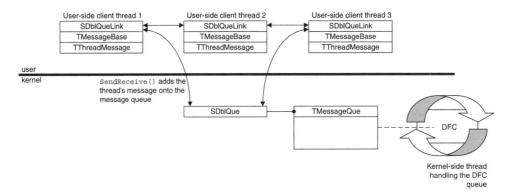

Figure 12.10 The message queue and user threads

parameters before adding the message to the message queue using `SendReceive()`:

```
EXPORT_C TInt TMessageBase::SendReceive(TMessageQue* aQ)
    {
    Send(aQ);
    NKern::FSWait(&iSem);
    return iValue;
    }
```

The calling thread is blocked until the message is delivered and the driver signals that it has received the message by completing it, using `TMessageBase::Complete()`. This does not necessarily mean that the requested operation is done – merely that the message has been received and the driver is ready to accept a new one. If the driver thread is asked to perform a long running task, it will later use a `TRequestStatus` object to signal completion to the client. Since all messages are delivered to the same DFC queue, this has the effect of serializing requests from multiple threads.

The message queue is constructed during the construction of the `DLogicalChannel`, and it is specified as a parameter to that construction in this way:

```
EXPORT_C DLogicalChannel::DLogicalChannel()
    :    iMsgQ(MsgQFunc,this,NULL,1)
    {
    }
```

The `NULL` parameter is the DFC queue, which in this example is initialized in the `DoCreate()` function:

```
SetDfcQ(Kern::DfcQue0());
iMsgQ.Receive();
```

`SetDfcQ` is inherited from `DLogicalChannel`, and is responsible for storing the DFC queue and passing it on to the message queue:

```
EXPORT_C void DLogicalChannel::SetDfcQ(TDfcQue* aDfcQ)
    {
    iDfcQ=aDfcQ;
    iMsgQ.SetDfcQ(aDfcQ);
    }
```

Note that in `DoCreate()`, I called `iMsgQ.Receive()` immediately after setting up the message queue with the appropriate DFC queue. This marks the queue as ready, so that the first message to be received will be accepted immediately. If a message is already available, `iMsgQ.Receive()` immediately queues a DFC to service this message within the context of the device driver's chosen thread. `DLogicalChannel` defines its message queue function like this:

```
void DLogicalChannel::MsgQFunc(TAny* aPtr)
    {
    DLogicalChannel* pC=(DLogicalChannel*)aPtr;
    pC->HandleMsg(pC->iMsgQ.iMessage);
    }
```

`HandleMsg()` is the pure virtual function implemented by the device driver to handle the incoming requests, and I'll explain this in detail shortly. First, I'll explain how messages are added to the queue.

`DLogicalChannel` provides its own implementation of the `Request()` gateway function:

```
EXPORT_C TInt DLogicalChannel::Request(TInt aReqNo, TAny* a1, TAny* a2)
    {
    if (aReqNo<(TInt)EMinRequestId)
      K::PanicKernExec(ERequestNoInvalid);
    TThreadMessage& m=Kern::Message();
    m.iValue=aReqNo;
    m.iArg[0]=a1;
    if (aReqNo<0)
      {
      kumemget32(&m.iArg[1],a2,2*sizeof(TAny*));
      }
    else
      m.iArg[1]=a2;
    return m.SendReceive(&iMsgQ);
    }
```

Remember that this is running in the context of the user-side client thread. This means that `Kern::Message()` obtains the client thread's message object and uses this as a placeholder for the request arguments supplied.

```
EXPORT_C TThreadMessage& Kern::Message()
  {
  return TheCurrentThread->iKernMsg;
  }
```

Now, you may remember that when I discussed the user-side APIs representing the logical channel (Section 12.4.6.4), I described how synchronous requests pass a request number and up to two optional request arguments, while asynchronous requests pass the compliment of the request number, a pointer to a TRequestStatus object and a user-side structure containing two function arguments:

```
RBusLogicalChannel                      DLogicalChannelBase



DoControl(aFunction)                    Request(aFunction, 0, 0)
DoControl(aFunction, a1)                Request(aFunction, a1, 0)
DoControl(aFunction, a1, a2)            Request(aFunction, a1, a2)



DoRequest(aReqNo, aStatus)             Request(~aReqNo, &aStatus, &A[0, 0])
DoRequest(aReqNo, aStatus, a1)         Request(~aReqNo, &aStatus, &A[a1, 0])
DoRequest(aReqNo, aStatus, a1, a2)     Request(~aReqNo, &aStatus, &A[a1, a2])



DoCancel(aReqMask)                      Request(0x7FFFFFFF, aReqMask, 0)
```

A negative request number indicates that an asynchronous DoRequest() operation is being made, so the DLogicalChannel knows to extract the arguments in the appropriate manner (that is, the second argument is allocated on the client stack and represents two arguments which must both be copied and stored before the calling function goes out of scope). A positive number indicates that the operation does not require any special treatment other than a direct copy of the message arguments. Once the arguments have been copied from the user-side thread into the request message, the message is delivered to the appropriate thread using SendReceive(&iMsgQ).

12.4.7.3   Closing the logical channel

DLogicalChannelBase does not provide its own Close() method, but instead relies on the default implementation of the reference counting DObject::Close() method to destroy the channel. In contrast, a DlogicalChannel-based driver makes use of the message queue to destroy the channel. This is necessary because there may be an outstanding DFC or asynchronous request that must be cancelled or completed before we are able to close the channel completely.

A special message, `ECloseMsg`, is reserved for this purpose, and is issued by `DLogicalChannel::Close()` as shown:

```
EXPORT_C TInt DLogicalChannel::Close(TAny*)
  {
  if (Dec()==1)
    {
    NKern::LockSystem();
    NKern::UnlockSystem();
    if (iDfcQ)
      {
      TThreadMessage& m=Kern::Message();
      m.iValue=ECloseMsg;
      m.SendReceive(&iMsgQ);
      }
    DBase::Delete(this);
    return EObjectDeleted;
    }
  return 0;
  }
```

As you can see, this close message is treated exactly the same as any other message, and is delivered to the driver's thread to give it the opportunity to cancel or complete any outstanding DFCs or requests before the channel is finally destroyed. The calls to `NKern::LockSystem()` followed by `NKern::UnlockSystem()` may look odd, but this ensures that nobody else is using the object while the close message is sent and the channel subsequently deleted.

12.4.7.4 Handling messages in the device driver

Messages are handled in a `DLogicalChannel`-derived device driver using the `HandleMsg()` function. Here is my serial driver's implementation:

```
void DSimpleSerialChannel::HandleMsg(TMessageBase* aMsg)
  {
  TThreadMessage& m=*(TThreadMessage*)aMsg;
  TInt id=m.iValue;
  if (id==(TInt)ECloseMsg)
    {
    Shutdown();
    m.Complete(KErrNone, EFalse);
    return;
    }
  else if (id==KMaxTInt)
    {
    // DoCancel
    DoCancel(m.Int0());
```

```
    m.Complete(KErrNone,ETrue);
    return;
    }
if (id<0)
    {
    // DoRequest
    TRequestStatus* pS=(TRequestStatus*)m.Ptr0();
    TInt r=DoRequest(~id,pS,m.Ptr1(),m.Ptr2());
    if (r!=KErrNone)
      Kern::RequestComplete(iClient,pS,r);
    m.Complete(KErrNone,ETrue);
    }
else
    {
    // DoControl
    TInt r=DoControl(id,m.Ptr0(),m.Ptr1());
    m.Complete(r,ETrue);
    }
}
```

Most device drivers follow this pattern, as it draws a clean separation between the different types of request. I use the function ID (obtained from `m.iValue`) to determine if the message is a synchronous or asynchronous request, or a cancel request or a close message. After invoking the necessary handler function, I complete the message, which unblocks the client thread and allows further messages to be processed by the `DLogicalChannel` message-handling framework.

You should also notice also how errors are reported. A synchronous request reports its return value directly to the client, passing the error code via in the call to `m.Complete()`. (`RBusLogicalChannel::DoControl()` returns a `TInt`.) An asynchronous request always completes its message with `KErrNone`, and reports errors back to the client using the client's `TRequestStatus` object. (`RBusLogicalChannel::DoRequest()` has a `void` return type). This ensures that if the client is using the active object framework, then the framework's `CActive::RunError()` method will be invoked if an error occurs when handling an asynchronous request.

12.4.7.5 Handling synchronous requests

Handling a synchronous request is simple – here's my `DoControl` method for the simple serial port channel:

```
TInt DSimpleSerialChannel::DoControl(TInt aFunction, TAny* a1, TAny* a2)
    {
    TCommConfigV01 c;
    TInt r=KErrNone;

    switch (aFunction)
        {
        case RSimpleSerialChannel::EControlConfig:
```

```
    {
    TPtrC8 cfg((const TUint8*)&iConfig, sizeof(iConfig));

    r=Kern::ThreadDesWrite(iClient,a1,cfg,
        0,KTruncateToMaxLength,iClient);
    break;
    }

case RSimpleSerialChannel::EControlSetConfig:
    {
    memclr(&c, sizeof(c));
    TPtr8 cfg((TUint8*)&c,0,sizeof(c));

    r=Kern::ThreadDesRead(iClient,a1,cfg,0,0);
    if(r==KErrNone)
        r=SetConfig(c);
    break;
    }

default:
    r=KErrNotSupported;
    }
return(r);
}
```

The RSimpleSerialChannel::EControlConfig case corresponds to the synchronous user-side API RSimpleSerialChannel::Config() which was defined in Section 12.4.6.1, *RBusLogicalChannel – the user-side channel handle*. To handle this request, a constant pointer descriptor is created to point to the configuration data to be returned to the client, and it is safely written back to user space using the Kern::ThreadDesWrite() API. (Remember, when using DLogicalChannel, all requests are handled within the context of a kernel thread so the appropriate API must be used when writing to user space as described in Section 12.1.7.2.) Note the use of KTruncateToMaxLength – this ensures that the length of data copied back to user space does not exceed the length of the user-side descriptor, and is good practice when passing structures that may change size in future releases of the driver.

RSimpleSerialChannel::EControlSetConfig corresponds to the synchronous user-side API RSimpleSerialChannel::SetConfig(). This is handled in a similar manner to the previous case, this time using the Kern::ThreadDesRead() API to read the configuration data from user space.

12.4.7.6 Handling asynchronous requests

Similarly, asynchronous requests are usually handled by a DoRequest() method which is responsible for setting up the hardware to create an event that will complete the request at some point in the future.

Depending on the nature of the device driver, it may be possible to handle several outstanding asynchronous requests simultaneously. Consider my serial port example for a moment – a duplex link allows simultaneous transmission and reception of data, so I want to allow both a read and a write request to be outstanding simultaneously. However, I want to prevent a client from requesting two simultaneous operations of the same type. The serial port driver handles this by maintaining a copy of the outstanding read/write request status objects (iRxStatus and iTxStatus), and panicking the client if it receives a second request of the same type as an outstanding one. (Panicking is the right thing to do here, as the client's behavior indicates that it has a serious bug.) Other device drivers, such as the local media sub-system, do allow simultaneous requests of the same type to be issued, since a single instance of a media driver may be servicing several file systems which access different partitions on the disk. Such scenarios are handled by forwarding the requests to an internal queue, from which any deferred requests are handled when it is convenient to do so.

Here's how asynchronous requests are handled in my example serial driver:

```
TInt DSimpleSerialChannel::DoRequest(TInt aReqNo,
    TRequestStatus* aStatus, TAny* a1, TAny* a2)
  {
  if(iStatus==EOpen)
    Start();
  else
    return(KErrNotReady)

  TInt r=KErrNone;
  TInt len=0;
  switch (aReqNo)
    {
    case RSimpleSerialChannel::ERequestRead:
      {
      if(iRxStatus)
        {
        Kern::ThreadKill(iClient,EExitPanic,
          ERequestAlreadyPending,KLitKernExec);
        return(KErrNotSupported);
        }

      if(a2)
        r=Kern::ThreadRawRead(iClient,a2, &len,sizeof(len));
      if(r==KErrNone)
        {
        iRxStatus=aStatus;
        InitiateRead(a1,len);
        }
      break;
      }
    case RSimpleSerialChannel::ERequestWrite:
      {
```

```
    if(iTxStatus)
        {
      Kern::ThreadKill(iClient,EExitPanic,
        ERequestAlreadyPending,KLitKernExec);
      return(KErrNotSupported);
        }

    if(!a1)
        a1=(TAny*)1;
      r=Kern::ThreadRawRead(iClient,a2,&len,sizeof(len));
      if(r==KErrNone)
        {
        iTxStatus=aStatus;
        InitiateWrite(a1,len);
        }
      break;
      }
  default:
    return KErrNotSupported;
    }
  return r;
  }
```

Both `ERequestRead` and `ERequestWrite` requests follow the same basic pattern. First, the status of the device is checked to determine if the channel is currently open, and if so the hardware is prepared for data transfer by calling `::Start()`:

```
void DSimpleSerialChannel::Start()
  {
  if (iStatus!=EClosed)
    {
    PddConfigure(iConfig);
    PddStart();
    iStatus=EActive;
    }
  }
```

Since the configuration of a port is specific to the underlying hardware, a call is made to the PDD to set up the required configuration:

```
void DComm16550::Configure(TCommConfigV01 &aConfig)
  {
  // wait for uart to stop transmitting
  Kern::PollingWait(FinishedTransmitting,this,3,100);

  // Select the UART, clear bottom two bits
  iUart->SelectUart();

  TUint lcr=0;
  switch (aConfig.iDataBits)
    {
    case EData8:
```

```
      lcr = T16550UartIfc::K16550LCR_Data8;
      break;
   // ... etc
   }
 switch (aConfig.iStopBits)
   {
   case EStop1: break;
   case EStop2:
      lcr |= T16550UartIfc::K16550LCR_Stop2;
      break;
   }
 switch (aConfig.iParity)
   {
   case EParityEven:
      lcr |=
      T16550UartIfc::K16550LCR_ParityEnable |
         T16550UartIfc::K16550LCR_ParityEven;
      break;
   // ... etc
   }

 iUart->SetLCR(lcr|K16550LCR_DLAB);
 iUart->SetBaudRateDivisor(BaudRateDivisor[(TInt)aConfig.iRate]);
 iUart->SetLCR(lcr);
 iUart->SetFCR(T16550UartIfc::K16550FCR_Enable  |
                T16550UartIfc::K16550FCR_RxReset |
                T16550UartIfc::K16550FCR_TxReset |
                T16550UartIfc::K16550FCR_TxRxRdy |
                T16550UartIfc::K16550FCR_RxTrig8);
 }
```

Notice the use of the `Kern::PollingWait()` API. I don't want to change the port configuration while the UART is transmitting, as this may lead to lost or badly formed data. Since there can be at most 16 bytes of data outstanding (the size of my TX FIFO), then I may simply poll the FIFO until it is fully drained. But rather than waste power and CPU cycles doing this in a code loop, I would prefer that the current thread be put to sleep for a while before checking the status again. The `Kern::PollingWait()` API allows me to do this. It first checks the supplied polling function (`FinishedTransmitting()`) before sleeping the current thread for the specified poll interval (100 mS). This process is repeated until the poll period expires or the polling function returns `ETrue`. Be aware that if you are using this API (or any other method of polling which sleeps the current thread) then *all* the other drivers sharing the DFC thread will also be blocked until the poll is complete. You should take care to ensure that you don't inadvertantly affect the operation of other drivers in the system – particularly if you are running within any of the standard kernel threads.

Similarly, it is the responsibility of the PDD to set up and enable any interrupt-specific configuration:

```
TInt DComm16550::Start()
    {
    // if EnableTransmit() called before Start()
    iTransmitting=EFalse;
    iUart->SetIER(T16550UartIfc::K16550IER_RDAI |
                  T16550UartIfc::K16550IER_RLSI |
                  T16550UartIfc::K16550IER_MSI);
    Interrupt::Enable(iInterruptId);
    return KErrNone;
    }
```

Once the hardware is successfully configured, DSimpleSerialChannel::DoRequest() determines the actual request to be handled (ERequestRead or ERequestWrite) and reads the corresponding request parameters.from user space in exactly the same way as I described when I looked at the handling of synchronous requests in the previous section.

If you refer back to my original definition of the RSimpleSerialChannel API in Section 12.4.6.1, you can see that the message parameters consist of a TRequestStatus object, a 32-bit length (allocated on the user-side stack), and a pointer to a user-side descriptor. These are represented by the aStatus, a1 and a2 parameters respectively. Before starting the request, I must first obtain the length parameter from the user-side stack using the Kern::ThreadRawRead() API, because the stack will go out of scope once the request has been issued (see Section 12.4.6.1 for the implementation of RSimpleSerialChannel::DoRead()). The client-side descriptor (passed in the a2 parameter) is extracted in a similar manner inside the call to InitiateRead() or InitiateWrite(). The implementation of these functions is not shown here, but the same principle applies – the pointer to the user-side data must be safely obtained before the request completes since the user-side stack may go out of scope once the request is issued (the observant reader will notice that in our example user-side function shown in Section 12.4.4 this will not happen because a call to User::WaitForRequest() is made immediately after issuing the request. However, this is a simplified use case – a real application would make use of the active object framework, so you must ensure that your device driver is designed to handle asynchronous requests without making any assumptions as to the behavior of the user-side application).

After the request parameters have been successfully read, the address of the internal request status is stored (in iRxStatus or iTxStatus) so the client can be signaled when the operation is complete. Finally, a call to InitiateRead(a1,len) or InitiateWrite(a1,len) which will start the asynchronous operation requested, eventually signaling the client from a DFC when it has completed.

12.4.7.7 Cancelling asynchronous requests

If the client cancels the asynchronous operation that I described in the previous section, the framework will issue a request with the special value of KMaxTInt(0x7FFFFFFF).

Looking back at Section 12.4.7.4 you can see how the request gateway function intercepted this request:

```
...
else if (id==KMaxTInt)
    {
    // DoCancel
    DoCancel(m.Int0());
    m.Complete(KErrNone,ETrue);
    return;
    }
```

The implementation of my DoCancel method is responsible for:

- Determining which operation is to be cancelled (specified in the first message parameter)

- Tidying up resources specific to the request being cancelled, and cancelling any outstanding DFCs or timers

- Signaling the client that the operation has been cancelled.

```
void DSimpleSerialChannel::DoCancel(TInt aMask)
    {
    TInt irq;
    if(aMask&RSimpleSerialChannel::ERequestReadCancel)
        {
        iRxOutstanding=EFalse;
        iNotifyData=EFalse;
        iRxDesPtr=NULL;
        iRxDesPos=0;
        iRxLength=0;
        iRxError=KErrNone;
        iRxOneOrMore=0;
        iRxCompleteDfc.Cancel();
        iRxDrainDfc.Cancel();
        iTimer.Cancel();
        iTimerDfc.Cancel();
        Complete(ERx,KErrCancel);
        }
    if(aMask&RSimpleSerialChannel::ERequestWriteCancel)
        {
        irq=DisableIrqs();
        iTxPutIndex=0;
        iTxGetIndex=0;
        iTxOutstanding=EFalse;
        iTxDesPtr=NULL;
        iTxDesPos=0;
```

```
    iTxDesLength=0;
    iTxError=KErrNone;
    RestoreIrqs(irq);
    iTxCompleteDfc.Cancel();
    iTxFillDfc.Cancel();
    Complete(ETx,KErrCancel);
    }
}
```

12.4.7.8 Closing the device driver

When the client has finished with the device driver, an `ECloseMsg` will be dispatched to our message handler to allow the driver to tidy free up resources and perform other hardware-specific operations before the channel is finally destroyed (see Section 12.4.7.3):

```
void DSimpleSerialChannel::Shutdown()
    {
    if (iStatus == EActive)
        Stop();

    Complete(EAll, KErrAbort);

    iRxDrainDfc.Cancel();
    iRxCompleteDfc.Cancel();
    iTxFillDfc.Cancel();
    iTxCompleteDfc.Cancel();
    iTimer.Cancel();
    iTimerDfc.Cancel();
    }
```

This is similar to the behavior I described in the previous section, when I talked about the cancellation of an asynchronous request. However, there are some fundamental differences:

- The hardware interface is shut down, using `::Stop()`

- All outstanding requests are completed with `KErrAbort`.

Note also that I do not worry about clearing down any of my member data, since this will be the last message to be received before the channel is finally deleted.

12.4.7.9 Summary

In this section I have discussed the `DLogicalChannel` framework using a simple serial device driver as an example. I'll now conclude by discussing some of the differences between the EKA1 and EKA2 device driver frameworks.

12.5   Differences between EKA1 and EKA2

Before concluding this chapter, I will discuss the fundamental differences between the EKA1 and EKA2 device driver models. I do not intend to explain how to port an existing device driver from EKA1 to EKA2 – please refer to the Device Driver Kit (DDK) documentation, which is available to Symbian Partners, for a detailed explanation of how to do this.

The device driver model in EKA2 has not changed that much from EKA1. EKA1's model was based on the LDD and the PDD and shares such concepts as the LDD factory, the logical channel, the PDD factory and the physical channel with EKA2. The differences are in the detail of how the model is implemented.

The main change is in the way user-side requests are routed and handled kernel side. As you've seen, in EKA2 requests from user-side clients can be executed in the context of a DFC running in a separate kernel-side thread. This means that code running kernel-side can now block – in EKA1 this would have halted the system.

12.5.1   Changes to the user-side API

Both EKA1 and EKA2 use the `RBusLogicalChannel` class to provide the client-side API to a device driver. On EKA1, this is defined as follows:

```
class RBusLogicalChannel : public RHandleBase,
                           public MBusDev
  {
protected:
  IMPORT_C TInt DoCreate(const TDesC& aDevice,const TVersion& aVer,
               const TDesC* aChan,TInt aUnit,const TDesC* aDriver,
            const TDesC8* anInfo,TOwnerType aType=EOwnerProcess);
  IMPORT_C void DoCancel(TUint aReqMask);
  IMPORT_C void DoRequest(TInt aReqNo,TRequestStatus& aStatus);
  IMPORT_C void DoRequest(TInt aReqNo,TRequestStatus& aStatus,TAny* a1);
  IMPORT_C void DoRequest(TInt aReqNo,TRequestStatus& aStatus,TAny*
                                                       a1,TAny* a2);
  IMPORT_C TInt DoControl(TInt aFunction);
  IMPORT_C TInt DoControl(TInt aFunction,TAny* a1);
  IMPORT_C TInt DoControl(TInt aFunction,TAny* a1,TAny* a2);
  IMPORT_C TInt DoSvControl(TInt aFunction);
  IMPORT_C TInt DoSvControl(TInt aFunction,TAny* a1);
  IMPORT_C TInt DoSvControl(TInt aFunction,TAny* a1,TAny* a2);
private:
  TInt CheckBusStatus();
  TInt DoCheckBusStatus(TInt aSocket);
  };
```

This defines four separate types of device driver call:

- `RBusLogicalChannel::DoControl` – perform a synchronous device driver function

- `RBusLogicalChannel::DoSvControl` – perform a synchronous device driver function in the kernel server context

- `RBusLogicalChannel::DoRequest` – initiate an asynchronous device driver operation

- `RBusLogicalChannel::DoCancel` – prematurely terminate an asynchronous device driver operation.

As I described in Section 12.4.6.4, there is little distinction between these operations in EKA2, since all calls are routed to a single gateway function. However, to reduce the effort involved in porting a device driver from EKA1 to EKA2, we have maintained the binary compatibility of this interface (but not the source compatibility). Here's the EKA2 version of the `RBusLogicalChannel` class in full:

```
class RBusLogicalChannel : public RHandleBase
   {
public:
   IMPORT_C TInt Open(RMessagePtr2 aMessage,TInt aParam,TOwnerType
                                        aType=EOwnerProcess);
   IMPORT_C TInt Open(TInt aArgumentIndex, TOwnerType
                             aType=EOwnerProcess);
protected:
   inline TInt DoCreate(const TDesC& aDevice, const TVersion& aVer,
           TInt aUnit, const TDesC* aDriver, const TDesC8* anInfo,
          TOwnerType aType=EOwnerProcess, TBool aProtected=EFalse);
#ifndef __SECURE_API__
   IMPORT_C TInt DoCreate(const TDesC& aDevice,const TVersion& aVer,
                 const TDesC* aChan,TInt aUnit,const TDesC* aDriver,
                const TDesC8* anInfo,TOwnerType aType=EOwnerProcess);
#endif
   IMPORT_C void DoCancel(TUint aReqMask);
   IMPORT_C void DoRequest(TInt aReqNo,TRequestStatus& aStatus);
   IMPORT_C void DoRequest(TInt aReqNo,TRequestStatus& aStatus,TAny* a1);
   IMPORT_C void DoRequest(TInt aReqNo,TRequestStatus& aStatus,TAny*
                                               a1,TAny* a2);
   IMPORT_C TInt DoControl(TInt aFunction);
   IMPORT_C TInt DoControl(TInt aFunction,TAny* a1);
   IMPORT_C TInt DoControl(TInt aFunction,TAny* a1,TAny* a2);
   IMPORT_C TInt DoSvControl(TInt aFunction);
   IMPORT_C TInt DoSvControl(TInt aFunction,TAny* a1);
   IMPORT_C TInt DoSvControl(TInt aFunction,TAny* a1,TAny* a2);
   private:
   IMPORT_C TInt DoCreate(const TDesC& aDevice, const TVersion& aVer,
  TInt aUnit, const TDesC* aDriver, const TDesC8* aInfo, TInt aType);
private:
   // Padding for Binary Compatibility purposes
   TInt iPadding1;
   TInt iPadding2;
   };
```

Note in particular that, on EKA1 any allocation or freeing of memory on the kernel heap must occur within the kernel server, hence the use of the DoSvControl() API. On EKA2, any device driver can now allocate and free memory on the kernel heap providing that either it runs in the context of a kernel-side thread, or, if it runs in the context of a user-side thread it enters a critical section before performing the heap operation by calling NKern::ThreadEnterCS(). However, to make porting a device driver from EKA1 to EKA2 easier we have maintained this API.

The EKA2 version of RBusLogicalChannel contains eight padding bytes to maintain binary compatibility with existing EKA1 clients. These bytes correspond to the member data contained within the now depreciated MBusDevClass from which the EKA1 version of RBusLogicalChannel was derived.

In summary, here's how these operations translate into kernel-side calls on EKA1 and EKA2:

User-side API – RBusLogicalChannel	EKA1 – Kernel-side DLogicalChannel	EKA2 – Kernel-side DLogicalChannelBase
DoControl(aFn)	DoControl(aFn, 0, 0)	Request(aFn, 0, 0)
DoControl(aFn, a1)	DoControl(aFn, a1, 0)	Request(aFn, a1, 0)
DoControl(aFn, a1, a2)	DoControl(aFn, a1, a2)	Request(aFn, a1, a2)
DoSvControl(aFn)	DoControl(aFn, 0, 0)	Request(aFn, 0, 0)
DoSvControl(aFn, a1)	DoControl(aFn, a1, 0)	Request(aFn, a1, 0)
DoSvControl(aFn, a1, a2)	DoControl(aFn, a1, a2)	Request(aFn, a1, a2)
DoRequest(aFn, aStat)	DoRequest(aFn, 0, 0)	Request(~aFn, &aStat, &A[0, 0])
DoRequest(aFn, aStat, a1)	DoRequest(aFn, a1, 0)	Request(~aFn, &aStat,&A[a1, 0])
DoRequest(aFn, aStat, a1, a2)	DoRequest(aFn, a1, a2)	Request(~aFn, &aStat, &A[a1, a2])
DoCancel(aReqMask)	DoCancel(aReqMask)	Request(0x7FFFFFFF, aReqMask, 0)

This highlights a fundamental difference between the EKA1 and EKA2 device driver models – the kernel no longer stores the TRequestStatus pointers (aStat) on your behalf for pending asynchronous operations. There is no limit to the number of outstanding requests that can be handled by a device driver on EKA2, so it is your responsibility as a device driver writer to maintain a list of outstanding requests should you need this functionality.

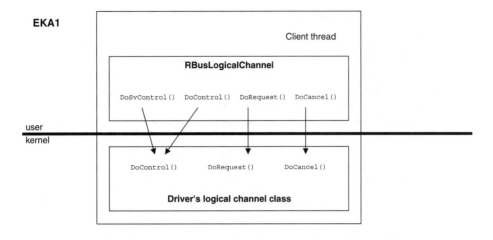

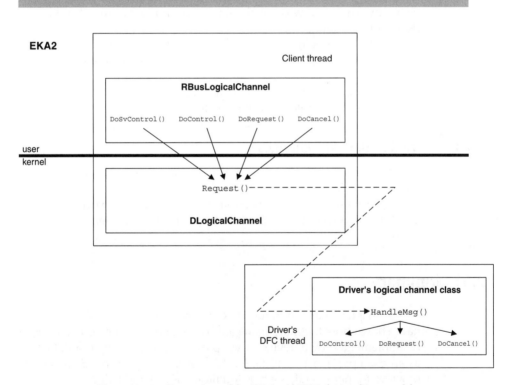

Figure 12.11 Comparison of the EKA1 and EKA2 device driver models

12.5.2 Choice of device driver model

In EKA1, the functions `DoControl()`, `DoRequest()` and `DoCancel()` that you implemented in your logical channel class all ran in the context of the user-side thread. On EKA2, you have the choice of implementing a device driver based on `DLogicalChannelBase` (in which case requests run in the context of the client thread) or `DLogicalChannel` (in which case requests run in a DFC in the context of a kernel-side thread as shown in Figure 12.11).

When porting a device driver from EKA1 to EKA2, you may find it easier to use the functionality provided by the `DLogicalChannel` class, as this helps to avoid synchronization issues by handling all requests in the context of a single thread. If you follow the pattern I described in Section 12.4.7.4, you can simplify migration to the new device driver model by implementing your `HandleMsg()` to determine the type of request, and then call your existing `DoControl()`, `DoCancel()` and `DoRequest()` functions. Of course, you can now rename these, giving them any name you wish, as the names are no longer mandated by the device driver framework.

In EKA1, you could access user memory directly from your kernel-side code. Although this is exceedingly bad practice, it does work. In EKA2, you are unlikely to get away with it as the kernel may (depending on memory model) panic the system with KERN-EXEC 3). You must ensure that you follow the rules set out in Section 12.1.5.

12.5.3 More detailed API changes

In previous sections I have described the fundamental differences between the EKA1 and EKA2 device driver models, but this is in no way a definitive list. For a more detailed discussion of the changes between EKA1 and EKA2 device driver models, please refer to the DDK (available to Symbian Partners).

12.6 Summary

In this chapter I have introduced kernel extensions and device drivers. I have shown how these are managed by the kernel framework and might be implemented by a device driver provider using a simple serial driver as an example. Next I will take a look at the support that Symbian OS provides for peripherals such as MultiMediaCard and USB.

13

Peripheral Support

by Peter Scobie

The nice thing about standards is that there are so many of them to choose from.

Andrew Tannenbaum

In this chapter, I begin by describing more of the services available to device drivers. Then I go on to describe a number of specific device driver implementations – among them media drivers, the MultiMediaCard driver and the USB driver.

The first service, one that device drivers frequently make use of, is direct memory access, or DMA.

13.1 DMA

13.1.1 DMA hardware

DMA hardware allows data to be transferred between a peripheral and system memory without the intervention of the processor. It is used to ease the burden on the processor of servicing peripherals that produce frequent interrupts. This applies equally to transfers involving data received by the phone (data taken from the peripheral and stored in a buffer) or data transmitted by the phone (data taken from a buffer and pushed to the peripheral).

A hardware DMA controller manages a set of DMA channels, each channel providing one direction of communication between the memory and the peripheral (either transmit or receive). Because of this, full duplex communication with a peripheral requires the use of two channels. Many controllers also support DMA transfer directly from one area of system memory to another.

Individual DMA transfer requests can be set up on each channel. These requests can involve a considerable amount of data – an amount that would otherwise involve the processor servicing a series of interrupts. But the use of DMA means that only one processor interrupt is generated, at the end of the transfer. For certain types of peripheral data transfer, such as bulk transfer over full-speed USB, the use of DMA becomes essential to avoid the CPU consuming an excessive proportion of its available bandwidth servicing interrupts.

Symbian OS phones normally provide one or more DMA channels dedicated to the LCD controller, for the transfer of pixel data between a frame buffer and the LCD interface. The LCD controller typically manages these DMA resources itself and they are not available to the main Symbian OS DMA framework, which I am about to describe.

In addition to these LCD channels, most phone platforms provide a limited number of general-purpose DMA channels. Platforms have differing strategies on how these channels are allocated. Some may fix the allocation of each DMA channel to a particular peripheral. Others allow "dynamic" allocation. This second method provides a pool of DMA channels that can be allocated to any peripheral on a first-come first-served basis. This could allow the platform to provide DMA services to more peripherals than there are DMA channels – assuming that device drivers free up DMA channels when they are not in use. With this scheme, however, there is a risk that a device driver might request a DMA channel but find that none are free. So the Symbian OS software framework normally fixes the allocation of DMA channels to particular devices, even when the hardware does not impose this.

Normally, DMA hardware reads and writes directly to physical address space, bypassing the MMU. Let's examine the simplest type of DMA request involving a one-shot transfer to or from a single, physically contiguous memory region. In this case, the DMA channel is supplied with information on the transfer source and destination (each being either a physical memory address or a peripheral identifier), together with the number of bytes to transfer. The request is initiated and the controller interrupts the processor once either the transfer completes successfully, or an error occurs.

DMA controllers often provide support for data to be transferred as a continuous stream as well as a one-shot transfer. This requires more than one set of transfer registers for each channel, allowing a double-buffer scheme to be employed. While the controller is transferring data using one set of registers, the software can simultaneously be programming the second set ready for the next transfer. As soon as the first transfer completes, the controller moves on to process the second one, without interrupting data flow. At the same time the controller signals the end of the first transfer with an interrupt, which signals the software to begin preparing the third – and so on.

Some DMA controllers support scatter-gather mode. This allows a DMA channel to transfer data to and from a number of memory locations that aren't contiguous, all as a single request. The control software has to supply information to the DMA controller, describing the transfer as a linked list of data structures, each specifying part of the transfer. These data structures are known as descriptors. (Not to be confused with the same term widely used in Symbian OS to refer to the family of TDesC derived classes!) The DMA controller acts on each descriptor in turn, and only interrupts the processor at the end of the descriptor chain. Some controllers allow the descriptor chain to be extended while transfer is in progress – another way to facilitate uninterrupted data transfer.

Figure 13.1 shows a setup for scatter-gather DMA transfer from two disjoint blocks of memory into a peripheral.

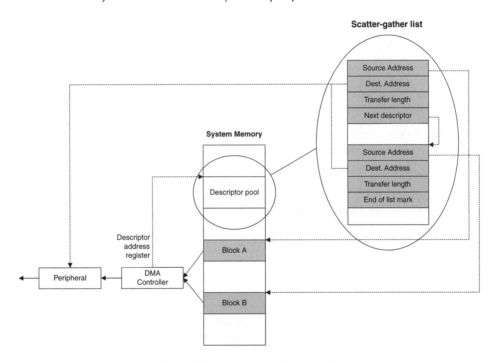

Figure 13.1   Scatter-gather DMA transfer

The scatter-gather list contains two linked descriptors – each providing information on one of the blocks. This list is supplied by the control software, which also loads a descriptor address register in the DMA controller with the address of the first descriptor. The actual descriptor format is generally hardware dependent and often more complex than that shown in the diagram. For example, it may contain information on the addressing mode for the source and destination addresses.

For each channel that involves peripheral-related DMA transfer, the controller normally has to be programmed with information on the burst size and port width of the peripheral. Burst size is the amount of data that has to be transferred to service each individual DMA request from the peripheral device. Many peripherals employ a FIFO buffer and for these, the burst size depends on the size of the FIFO and the threshold level within the FIFO that triggers a DMA request from it (for example, FIFO half-empty or quarter-empty). The port width specifies the granularity of data transfer (for example, byte, half-word and so on).

13.1.2 DMA software framework

Symbian OS provides kernel-side DMA services through its DMA frame-work. We leave the choice of whether or not a particular device will use DMA for data transfer to the developers who are creating a new phone platform – and because of this, the consumers of this service are generally components such as physical device drivers (PDDs) and the platform-specific layers of peripheral bus controllers (see Section 13.4). The framework itself is divided into a platform-independent layer (PIL) and a platform-specific layer (PSL), with both parts being combined into the kernel-side DLL, DMA.DLL. As with most platform-specific components, the PSL interfaces with the controller hardware via func-tions exported from the variant or ASSP DLL. Figure 13.2 shows this arrangement.

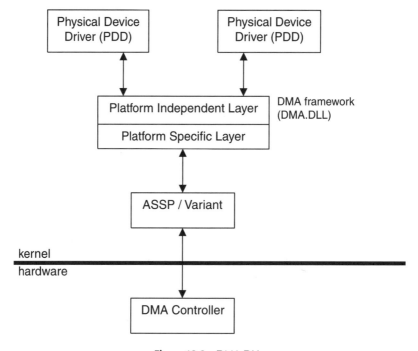

Figure 13.2   DMA.DLL

DMA support may be required by certain peripheral services that are started at system boot time. Because of this, the DMA framework is implemented as a kernel extension and is normally one of the first of these to be initialized by the kernel.

Drivers may request a transfer involving a memory buffer that is specified in terms of its linear address. As I explained in Chapter 7, *Memory Models*, this contiguous linear memory block is often made up of non-contiguous physical areas. Even when a transfer request involves a physically contiguous region of memory, the total length of the transfer may exceed the maximum transfer size that the underlying DMA controller supports. You don't need to worry about this though – the Symbian OS DMA framework performs any fragmentation necessary, due either to requests exceeding the maximum transfer size, or to buffers not being physically contiguous. The framework specifies each fragment with a separate descriptor. If the controller doesn't support scatter-gather then each fragment has to be handled by the framework as a separate DMA transfer – but the framework insulates the device driver from this detail, by only signaling completion back to the driver at the end of the entire transfer.

Figure 13.3 shows a diagram of the classes that make up the DMA framework.

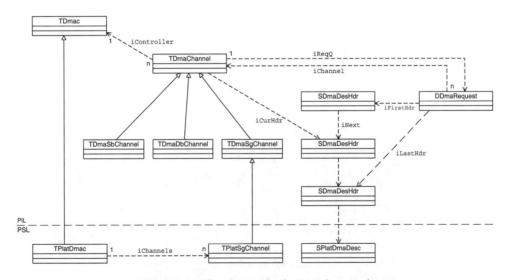

Figure 13.3   Class diagram for the DMA framework

The framework includes the singleton TDmac, which is the abstraction of the DMA controller. This object manages all the DMA channels and defines the main interface between the PIL and PSL. It is an abstract class with each phone platform deriving a controller object from it. This is shown as TPlatDmac on the diagram.

TDmaChannel is the base class for a DMA channel. We derive three different channel classes from this as follows:

- TDmaSbChannel – a single-buffer DMA channel
- TDmaDbChannel – a double-buffer DMA channel
- TDmaSgChannel – a scatter-gather DMA channel.

These in turn are base classes, and the programmers creating a new phone platform will derive a platform-specific channel object from whichever of these is appropriate for the buffering scheme that the controller hardware provides. In the diagram, I've assumed scatter-gather mode and shown it as TPlatSgChannel. When the DMA framework extension is initialized at system boot time, an instance of this derived channel class is created for each general-purpose hardware channel that the controller manages.

The TDmaChannel class is one of the two major elements of the DMA API provided to device drivers. (The other is the DDmaRequest class that I will introduce later.) The main public parts of this class and data members are as follows:

```
class TDmaChannel
    {
public:
  // Information passed by client when opening channel
struct SCreateInfo
    {
    /** ID used by PSL to select channel to open */
    TUint32 iCookie;
    /** Number of descriptors this channel can use. */
    TInt iDesCount;
    /** DFC queue used to service DMA interrupts. */
    TDfcQue* iDfcQ;
    /** DFC priority */
    TUint8 iDfcPriority;
    };

public:
  static TInt Open(const SCreateInfo& aInfo, TDmaChannel*& aChannel);
  void Close();
  void CancelAll();
  inline TBool IsOpened() const;
  inline TBool IsQueueEmpty() const;
protected:
  TDmac* iController;    //DMAC this channel belongs to.
  TDfc iDfc;       //Transfer complete/failure DFC.
  SDmaDesHdr* iCurHdr;    //Fragment being transferred.
  SDblQue iReqQ; //Being/about to be transferred request queue.
  TInt iReqCount; //Number of requests attached to this channel
    };
```

The TDmaChannel class has a pointer to the controller object that manages the channel: iController. It also owns a DFC object iDfc, which is called whenever a request for this channel completes.

Next I will describe the public `TDmaChannel` methods:

```
static TInt Open(const SCreateInfo& aInfo, TDmaChannel*& aChannel);
```

This static method opens the DMA channel identified by the information supplied within the parameter `aInfo`. If the controller is able to open the channel successfully, then it returns a pointer to the appropriate channel object in `aChannel`. A device driver must open each channel that it needs to use – it normally attempts this in its initialization. You can see the format of the structure passed by the driver in the class definition I've just given – it includes a 32-bit channel identifier, which the platform-specific layer uses to identify the corresponding channel object. The rest of the information in the structure specifies the channel configuration. This includes the queue that is to be used for the channel's DFC, and the priority of this DFC relative to others in the same kernel thread.

It is normal for a driver to close any DMA channels used when it has finished with them. It generally does this when the driver itself is being closed using the channel method:

```
void Close();
```

A channel should be idle when it is closed. The following channel method is used to cancel both current and pending requests:

```
void CancelAll();
```

The framework uses descriptor objects to hold transfer request information, whether or not the controller supports scatter-gather. Controllers that do support scatter-gather need the descriptor information to be supplied in a format that is specific to that particular hardware controller. This is shown as the `SPlatDmaDesc` structure on the diagram. If the controller doesn't support scatter-gather, then the framework uses a default descriptor structure, `SDmaPseudoDes` (not shown on the diagram). The pseudo descriptor contains the following information listed. Hardware-specific descriptors generally contain similar information:

1. Transfer source location information. This can be either the address of a memory buffer or a 32-bit value identifying a particular peripheral. For memory addresses, this may hold either the linear or physical address of the buffer

2. Transfer destination location information (same format as 1)

3. The number of bytes to be transferred

4. General information, such as whether the source/destination is a memory address or a peripheral identifier, whether memory addresses contain linear or physical addresses and whether these need to be post-incremented during transfer

5. 32-bits of PSL-specific information provided by the client.

For controllers that do support scatter-gather, because the hardware imposes the structure of the descriptor, it is difficult to include any additional descriptor information required by the framework alone. Therefore, the framework associates a separate descriptor header with each descriptor. This is the SDmaDesHdr structure. The descriptor header is generic and the PIL manipulates descriptors via their associated header. The framework still creates associated descriptor headers even when pseudo descriptors are used.

Each time a driver opens a channel, it has to supply information on the number of descriptors that the framework should reserve for it. This depends on the buffering scheme being used and the maximum number of DMA requests that are likely to be outstanding at any time.

The class DDmaRequest encapsulates a DMA request over a channel. This is the second main element of the DMA device driver API. The main public parts of this class and data members are as follows:

```
class DDmaRequest : public DBase
  {
public:
  // Signature of completion/failure callback function
  typedef void (*TCallback)(TResult, TAny*);

public:
  DDmaRequest(TDmaChannel& aChannel, TCallback aCb=NULL,
      TAny* aCbArg=NULL, TInt aMaxTransferSize=0);
  ~DDmaRequest();
  TInt Fragment(TUint32 aSrc, TUint32 aDest, TInt aCount,
      TUint aFlags, TUint32 aPslInfo);
  void Queue();

public:
  TDmaChannel& iChannel; //Channel this request is bound to
  TCallback iCb;         //Called on completion/failure
  TAny* iCbArg;          //Callback argument
  TInt iDesCount;        //Number of fragments in list
  SDmaDesHdr* iFirstHdr; //The first fragment in the list.
  SDmaDesHdr* iLastHdr;  //The last fragment in the list.
  };
```

Typically a driver will allocate itself one or more request objects for each channel that it has open. The constructor for the DDmaRequest class is as follows:

```
DDmaRequest(TDmaChannel& aChannel, TCallback aCb=NULL, TAny* aCbArg=NULL,
                                              TInt aMaxTransferSize=0);
```

In constructing a request object, the driver must specify the channel with which it is to be used: aChannel. It must also supply a callback function, aCb, which the channel DFC will call when the request completes (either following successful transfer or due to an error). The next parameter, aCbArg, is a driver-specified argument that will be saved by the framework and passed as an argument into the callback function. Often a device driver will pass in a pointer to itself, allowing the callback function to access driver member functions when it is invoked. The final parameter, aMaxTransferSize, is used if the driver needs to specify the maximum fragment size to be applied during the transfer. If the driver does not specify this, then the transfer size defaults to the maximum transfer size that the DMA controller supports, so this parameter is only used when a particular peripheral needs to impose a smaller limit.

Section 13.2.6.1 contains example code showing how a driver might open a DMA channel and construct a request object.

To initiate a DMA transfer, the driver supplies the transfer details and then queues the request object on the channel. Each channel maintains a queue of transfer requests, TDmaChannel::iReqQ. Once a transfer request is complete, the framework de-queues it and invokes the request callback function. The driver is then able to reuse the request object for a subsequent transfer.

A driver is able to queue a series of requests on a channel and, if the channel supports double buffering or scatter-gather, then the framework will manage these so that they are transferred as an uninterrupted stream. However, the framework does continue to invoke each request callback as each request is completed. It's worth noting that the DMA device driver API does not allow a driver to specify a transfer that involves two or more disjoint memory buffers as a single DMA request. But, as I have just explained, if the driver queues separate requests for each memory buffer, the framework can take advantage of a scatter-gather facility to transfer these as an uninterrupted stream.

If a channel is being used to transfer an uninterrupted stream of data, then the channel request queue may contain several requests – the first being the one in progress, and those remaining being pending requests. Information on the total number of requests queued on a channel at any time is held in its data member, TDmaChannel::iReqCount.

Before a request is queued, the driver has to specify the details of the transfer and then allow the framework to analyze these and possibly split

the overall request into a list of smaller transfer fragments. To do this, the
driver calls the following method:

```
TInt Fragment(TUint32 aSrc, TUint32 aDest, TInt aCount, TUint aFlags,
                                          TUint32 aPslInfo);
```

Arguments `aSrc` and `aDest` specify the transfer source and destination
respectively. Each of these can be a linear address, a physical address or
a 32-bit value identifying a particular peripheral. This format is specified
by bit masks in the argument `aFlags`, which also indicates whether
memory addresses need to be post-incremented during transfer. Argument
`aCount` holds the number of bytes to transfer and clients may use
`aPslInfo` to specify 32-bits of PSL-specific information.

Where these request arguments specify a memory buffer in terms of
its linear address, this contiguous linear memory block may consist of
non-contiguous physical areas. In such cases, the fragmentation means
that the framework must split this area into smaller, physically contiguous,
fragments. Later, in Section 13.1.3, I will discuss methods that you can
use to avoid the need for this fragmentation, with the driver allocating
memory buffers that are physically contiguous.

The framework may also have to split large transfers into a series of
smaller fragments – each being smaller than or equal to the maximum
transfer size.

In this way, the framework breaks up the request into a series of
descriptors, each specifying how to transfer one fragment. Each descriptor
has an associated descriptor header, and these headers are formed into
a linked list. The transfer request object contains pointers to the first and
last headers in this list: `iFirstHdr` and `iLastHdr` respectively. When
there is more than one request queued on the channel, then the headers
of all the requests are linked together into a single linked list. During
transfer, the channel maintains a pointer to the header corresponding to
the descriptor currently being transferred, `TDmaChannel::iCurHdr`.
To illustrate this arrangement, Figure 13.4 shows a channel with a three-
fragment request being transferred, and a two-fragment request pending.
The fragment that is currently being transferred is the last one of the first
request.

Once a request has been fragmented, the driver needs to queue it on
its associated channel:

```
void Queue();
```

If this channel is idle, the framework transfers the request immediately;
otherwise it stores it on a queue for transfer later. Once the transfer
completes, either successfully or with an error, the framework executes

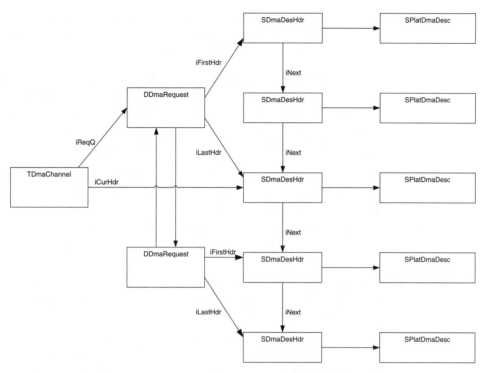

Figure 13.4 Transferring fragmented requests

the callback function associated with the request object. Here the driver should check and handle any transfer errors and queue another DMA transfer if it needs to.

Section 13.2.6.3 contains example code showing how a driver might perform a DMA data transfer.

If you are working with DMA, you need to pay special attention to the way in which you handle data transfers that turn out to be shorter than the requested length, leaving the DMA request outstanding. This is most likely to happen on DMA reads (that is, transfers from peripheral to memory buffer). The normal way in which you would handle this is to timeout the transfer after an appropriate period, at which point the DMA transfer is cancelled. You may then need to initiate the retransmission of the entire data sequence. Alternatively it may be necessary to recover any data that has been transferred to the buffer. If the amount received is not an exact multiple of the burst size, then there may also be data residing in the peripheral FIFO (in other words, trailing bytes).

13.1.3 Memory allocation for DMA transfer

The DMA framework is not responsible for managing the memory buffers used for the DMA transfer. This is left to the users of the framework.

You can't safely perform DMA transfer directly to or from memory that has been allocated to a user process in the normal way – that is, to user chunks. There are a number of reasons for this:

1. While a DMA transfer is in progress to the user chunk, the owning user process might free the memory – or the kernel might do so, if the process dies. This is a problem because the freed memory could be reused for other purposes. Unaware of the reallocation, the DMA controller would continue with the transfer, using the physical addresses supplied, and trash the contents of the newly allocated memory. You can overcome this problem by ensuring that the driver opens the chunk representing the user memory for the duration of the transfer – but this can be inefficient

2. A process context switch may change the location of the memory. To be suitable for DMA, the memory needs to be available to the kernel at a fixed location

3. The peripheral may mandate DMA to a specific physical memory region and the allocation of user-mode memory doesn't allow this attribute to be specified

4. Since the DMA controller interfaces directly with the physical address space, it bypasses the MMU, cache and write buffer. Hence, it is important to ensure that DMA memory buffer and cache are coherent. One way to achieve this is to disable caching in the buffers used for DMA transfer. Again, the allocation of user-mode memory doesn't allow these caching and buffering options to be specified.

You can avoid all these problems by allocating the DMA buffers kernel-side, and so it is usual for device drivers that support DMA to do the allocation of memory that is to be used for DMA transfers themselves.

The example code that follows shows how a driver would use a hardware chunk to allocate a buffer that is non-cacheable and non-bufferable to avoid cache incoherency issues. This creates a global memory buffer – accessible kernel-side only. By using RAM pages that are physically contiguous, this also avoids the issue of memory fragmentation.

```
TUint32 physAddr=0;
TUint32 size=Kern::RoundToPageSize(aBuffersize);

// Get contiguous pages of RAM from the system's free pool
if (Epoc::AllocPhysicalRam(size,physAddr) != KErrNone)
  return(NULL);

// EMapAttrSupRw - supervisor read/write, user no access
// EMapAttrFullyBlocking - uncached, unbuffered

DPlatChunkHw* chunk;
```

```
if(DPlatChunkHw::New(chunk,physAddr,
   size,EMapAttrSupRw|EMapAttrFullyBlocking) != KErrNone)
   {
   Epoc::FreePhysicalRam(physAddr,size);
   return(NULL);
   }

TUint8* buf;
buf=reinterpret_cast<TUint8*>(chunk->LinearAddress());
```

On the other hand, you may have reasons that make it preferable to allocate DMA buffers that are cached – for instance if you want to perform significant data processing on data in the buffer. You can do this using the same example code – but with the cache attribute `EMapAttrFullyBlocking` replaced with `EMapAttrCachedMax`. However, to maintain cache coherency, you must then flush the cache for each DMA transfer.

For a DMA transfer from cacheable memory to peripheral (that is, a DMA write), the memory cache must to be flushed before transfer. The kernel provides the following method for this:

```
void Cache::SyncMemoryBeforeDmaWrite(TLinAddr aBase, TUint aSize,
                                               TUint32 aMapAttr);
```

For DMA transfer from peripheral to cacheable memory (that is, a DMA read), the cache may have to be flushed both before and after transfer. Again, methods are provided for this:

```
void Cache::SyncMemoryBeforeDmaRead(TLinAddr aBase, TUint aSize,
                                               TUint32 aMapAttr);
void Cache::SyncMemoryAfterDmaRead(TLinAddr aBase, TUint aSize);
```

It's worth pointing out that only kernel-side code can access the types of hardware chunk I've described so far. So, if the ultimate source or destination of a data transfer request is in normal user memory, you must perform a two-stage transfer between peripheral and user-side client:

1. DMA transfer between peripheral and device driver DMA buffer

2. Memory copy between driver DMA buffer and user memory.

Obviously a two-stage transfer process wastes time. How can it be avoided? In the previous example buffer-allocation code, if you set the access permission attribute to `EMapAttrUserRw` rather than `EMapAttrSupRw`, the driver creates a user-accessible global memory buffer. The driver must then provide a function to report the address of this buffer as part of its user-side API. Note that you can't make these chunks accessible to just a limited set of user processes and so they are not suitable for use when the chunk's contents must remain private or secure.

A much more robust scheme for avoiding the second transfer stage is for client and driver to use a shared chunk as the source or destination of data transfer requests between peripheral and user accessible memory. I will discuss this in the next section.

13.2   Shared chunks

As described in Section 7.3.1, chunks are the means by which memory is allocated and made available to code outside of the memory model. In Symbian OS, we represent chunks by DChunk objects, and we support various types of these. I mentioned user chunks and hardware chunks in the previous section, and discussed the problems with DMA transfer involving these chunk types.

In this section I describe a third type of chunk – the shared chunk. These provide a mechanism for device drivers to safely share memory buffers with user-mode code. Shared chunks are only available on EKA2. They should not be confused with global chunks, (created for example using RChunk::CreateGlobal()) which are also accessible by multiple user processes. However global chunks, being a type of user chunk, have all the problems that I listed in the previous section when accessed by device drivers.

Another type of chunk is the shared I/O buffer. These are supported in EKA1, but deprecated in EKA2, and also allow memory to be safely shared between kernel and user code. However, unlike shared chunks, these buffers have the drawback that only one user-side process at a time can open them. Another difference is that, for a user-side application to access a shared chunk, it must create a handle for that chunk and assign it to an RChunk object. For shared I/O buffers, there is no user-mode representation. Instead the user process is generally just supplied with an address and size for the buffer by the driver that performs the user process mapping.

We represent a shared chunk with a DChunk object. This class is internal to the kernel – it has no published methods – but instead the Kern class publishes a set of methods for performing operations on shared chunks. The following sections describe these methods and provide an example of their use.

13.2.1   Creating a shared chunk

Only kernel-side code can create shared chunks, by using the following function:

```
TInt Kern::ChunkCreate(const TChunkCreateInfo& aInfo,
    DChunk*& aChunk, TLinAddr& aKernAddr, TUint32& aMapAttr);
```

The argument aInfo is used to supply details of the attributes of the chunk required. If chunk creation is successful, the function returns with aChunk containing a pointer to the new chunk object. This object owns a region of linear address space, but it is empty – the kernel has not committed any physical RAM to it. You have to map either RAM or I/O devices to the chunk before it can be used. The argument aKernAddr returns the base address of this linear address space in the kernel process – only kernel code can used this address. The argument aMapAttr returns the mapping attributes that apply for the chunk created. The caller will often save this value and pass it as an argument into the DMA cache flushing functions described in Section 13.1.3. I will talk more about these mapping attributes later in this section.

The structure TChunkCreateInfo is used to specify the attributes of the required chunk. This is defined as follows:

```
class TChunkCreateInfo
    {
public:
    enum TType
        {
        ESharedKernelSingle = 9,
        ESharedKernelMultiple = 10,
        };
public:
    inline TChunkCreateInfo();
public:
    TType iType;
    TInt iMaxSize;
    TUint32 iMapAttr;
    TUint8 iOwnsMemory;
    TInt8 iSpare8[3];
    TDfc* iDestroyedDfc;
    TInt32 iSpare32[2];
    };
```

The member iType specifies the type of shared chunk, which can be one of the following values:

Type	Description
EsharedKernelSingle	A chunk that may only be opened by one user-side process at a time.
EsharedKernelMultiple	A chunk that may be opened by any number of user-side processes.

The member `iMaxsize` specifies the size of the linear address space to reserve for the chunk.

The member `iMapAttr` specifies the caching attributes for the chunk's memory. This should be constructed from the cache/buffer values for the `TMappingAttributes` enumeration defined in the file `\e32\include\memmodel\epoc\platform.h`. Frequently used values are:

1. `EMapAttrFullyBlocking` for no caching

2. `EMapAttrCachedMax` for full caching.

However, it is possible that the MMU may not support the requested caching attribute. In this case, a lesser attribute will be used, with this being reported back to the caller of `Kern::ChunkCreate()` via the parameter `aMapAttr`.

You should set the member `iOwnsMemory` to true if the chunk is to own the memory committed to it. This applies where that memory is RAM pages from the system's free pool. If I/O devices will be committed to the chunk or RAM set aside at system boot time, then `iOwnsMemory` should be set to false.

You can supply a pointer to a DFC, `iDestroyedDfc`. This DFC is then called when the chunk is destroyed.

The members `iSpare8[3]` and `iSpare32[2]` are reserved for future expansion.

13.2.2 Destroying a shared chunk

Chunks are reference-counted kernel objects. When the kernel creates them, it sets the reference count to one, and each subsequent open operation increases this count by one. Closing a chunk decrements the access count by one. When the count reaches zero, the chunk is destroyed. Shared chunks are closed using the following function:

```
TBool Kern::ChunkClose(DChunk* aChunk);
```

The parameter `aChunk` is a pointer to the chunk that is to be closed. If this results in the chunk object being destroyed then the function returns true, otherwise it returns false.

The kernel may destroy chunks asynchronously, and so they may still exist after the close function returns. If you need to know when a chunk is actually destroyed, then you should supply a DFC when you create the chunk, using the member `iDestroyedDfc` of the `TChunkCreateInfo` argument. The kernel then queues the DFC when it finally destroys the chunk, which is after the point when the kernel guarantees that the memory mapped by the chunk will no longer be accessed by any program.

13.2.3   Committing memory to a shared chunk

Once a shared chunk has been created, you need to commit either RAM or I/O devices to it before it can be used. We provide four functions for this.

The first function that I show is used to commit a set of RAM pages with physically contiguous addresses from the system's free pool of memory:

```
TInt Kern::ChunkCommitContiguous(DChunk* aChunk, TInt aOffset, TInt aSize,
                                 TUint32& aPhysicalAddress);
```

The argument `aChunk` is a pointer to the chunk into which the memory should be committed.

The argument `aSize` holds the size of the region to commit, and `aOffset` holds an offset within the chunk's linear address space that should become the start of the committed memory region. The units for both these arguments are bytes and both must be a multiple of the MMU page size. (Use the function `Kern::RoundToPageSize(TUint32 aSize)` to round up to the size of an MMU page).

On return, the final argument, `aPhysicalAddress`, is set to the physical address of the first page of memory that has been committed. This is useful for DMA transfer. By using `aPhysicalAddress` as a base, you can specify memory locations within the committed area in terms of physical address, saving the DMA framework from the overhead of converting from a linear address.

This function can create a buffer within the shared chunk, which is equivalent to the physically contiguous buffer created in the example code in Section 13.1.3.

We provide a similar function, which commits an arbitrary set of RAM pages from the system's free pool. In this case these aren't necessarily physically contiguous:

```
TInt Kern::ChunkCommit(DChunk* aChunk, TInt aOffset, TInt aSize);
```

You can use a third function to commit a specified physical region to a shared chunk. For example, a region that represents memory mapped I/O or RAM that was set aside for special use at boot time:

```
TInt Kern::ChunkCommitPhysical(DChunk* aChunk, TInt aOffset, TInt aSize,
                               TUint32 aPhysicalAddress);
```

The first three arguments are identical to those described for the first version of the function. The fourth argument, `aPhysicalAddress`, is the physical address of the memory to be committed to the chunk (which again must be a multiple of the MMU page size).

The fourth function is similar, except that this time the physical region is specified as a list of physical addresses. The list must contain one address for each page of memory to be committed, with the length of the list corresponding to size of the region to be committed:

```
TInt Kern::ChunkCommitPhysical(DChunk* aChunk, TInt aOffset, TInt aSize,
                             const TUint32* aPhysicalAddressList);
```

13.2.4 Providing access to a shared chunk from user-side code

As I have already mentioned, before a user-side application can have access to the memory in a shared chunk, the kernel must create a handle to the chunk for it. The following function is used to create such a handle. If successful, the function also maps the chunk's memory into the address space of the process to which the specified thread belongs. It also increases the access count on the object:

```
TInt Kern::MakeHandleAndOpen(DThread* aThread, DObject* aObject)
```

The argument `aThread` specifies the thread which is to own the handle and `aObject` specifies the shared chunk to which the handle will refer. The function returns the handle (that is, a value greater than zero) if it is successfully created. Otherwise, a standard error value (less than zero) is returned.

The handle is normally passed back to the user thread, where it is assigned to an `RChunk` object, using one of the methods derived from `RHandleBase` – either `SetHandle()` or `SetReturnedHandle()`. Once this has happened, it normally becomes the responsibility of that application to close the handle once it no longer needs access to the shared chunk.

13.2.5 Providing access to a shared chunk from kernel-side code

A user application that has obtained access to a shared chunk from one device driver may wish to allow a second driver access to that shared chunk. In this case, the second device driver needs a method to obtain a reference to the chunk object and the addresses used by the memory it represents. Before code in the second device driver can safely access the memory in the shared chunk, it must first open that chunk. Once this is done, the reference counted nature of chunk objects means that the shared chunk and its memory will remain accessible until it closes the chunk again.

A user application can pass a shared chunk handle to a device driver, which can then use the following function to open it:

```
DChunk* Kern::OpenSharedChunk(DThread* aThread, TInt aChunkHandle,
                                               TBool aWrite);
```

The argument `aChunkHandle` supplies the handle value, and `aThread` is the thread in which this is valid. You use the Boolean `aWrite` to indicate whether you intend to write to the chunk memory or not. To give an example of how you might use this argument, imagine that the user application intends to write to a chunk that contains read-only memory – in this case, the error that is returned can be handled gracefully when the chunk is opened rather waiting until a fault occurs much later on.

The function returns a pointer to the chunk if the chunk handle is valid for the thread concerned, is of the correct shared chunk type and opens successfully. If the function is successful in opening the chunk, the access count on the chunk will of course be incremented.

In some cases, a user application and a driver would have been able to transfer data using a shared chunk, except that the driver only supports a descriptor-based API, rather than an API designed specifically for shared chunks. A similar scenario is where driver and user application can transfer data via a shared chunk, but the user application obtained the data source or destination information from another application, and so this was presented to it as a normal descriptor rather than a chunk handle. In both cases, the driver will receive information on the data, via a descriptor, in the form of an address and a size.

If the driver wishes to optimize the case in which the data address resides in a shared chunk, it won't be able to use the open function I described previously, since it doesn't have a chunk handle. Instead it can make use of the following method below to speculatively attempt to open a shared chunk:

```
DChunk* Kern::OpenSharedChunk(DThread* aThread, const TAny* aAddress,
                                        TBool aWrite, TInt& aOffset);
```

If the address `aAddress` supplied is within a shared chunk that is mapped to the process associated with thread `aThread`, then the function returns a pointer to the chunk. If not, then it returns zero. When a chunk pointer is returned, the chunk access count is incremented and the argument `aOffset` returns the offset within the chunk corresponding to the address passed.

Let's make this clearer with an example. Suppose we have a media driver that is designed to optimize data transfer to data addresses that are within a shared chunk. For example, a request might come via the file server from a multimedia application to save data to a file from a buffer in a shared chunk. The file server and media driver only support descriptor-based APIs, but if the driver uses the `Kern::OpenSharedChunk()` function, then we can still optimize the transfer using the shared chunk.

Once the driver has opened the chunk, it next needs to obtain the address of the data within it. Remember that shared chunks may contain uncommitted regions (gaps) and the driver needs to detect these to avoid making an access attempt to a bad address, which would cause an exception. There are two functions provided for this – the first obtains just the linear address, the second also obtains the physical address. Taking the first of these:

```
TInt Kern::ChunkAddress(DChunk* aChunk, TInt aOffset, TInt aSize,
                                     TLinAddr& aKernelAddress)
```

If chunk `aChunk` is a shared chunk, and if the region starting at offset `aOffset` from the start of the chunk and of size `aSize` (both in bytes) contains committed memory, then the function succeeds. In this case, the argument `aKernelAddress` returns the linear address in the kernel process corresponding to the start of the specified region. However, if the region isn't within the chunk, or the whole region doesn't contain committed memory, then an error is returned. Now the second function:

```
TInt Kern::ChunkPhysicalAddress(DChunk* Chunk, TInt aOffset, TInt aSize,
 TLinAddr& aKernelAddress, TUint32& aMapAttr, TUint32& aPhysicalAddress,
                                     TUint32* aPageList)
```

The first four arguments are identical to those described for the previous function. If the function is successful, the argument `aMapAttr` will contain the mapping attributes that apply for the chunk, and the argument `aPhysicalAddress` will contain the physical address of the first byte in the specified region. The argument `aPageList` returns the addresses of each of the physical pages that contain the specified region.

13.2.6 An example driver using a shared chunk for DMA transfer

To illustrate how shared chunks can be used, let us consider as an example a minimal device driver for an unspecified peripheral. Our driver supports only one type of request – the asynchronous transmission of data out of the phone from a memory buffer residing within a shared chunk. The user-side interface to the driver is as follows:

```
const TInt KMyDeviceBufSize=0x2000;     // 8KB

class RMyDevice : public RBusLogicalChannel
  {
public:
  enum TRequest
    { EWriteBuf=0x0,EWriteBufCancel=0x1,};
  enum TControl
    { EGetChunkHandle,EGetBufInfo,};
#ifndef __KERNEL_MODE__
public:
  inline TInt Open();
  inline TInt GetChunkHandle(RChunk& aChunk);
  inline TInt GetBufInfo(TInt aBufNum,TInt& aBufOffset);
  inline void WriteBuffer(TRequestStatus& aStatus,
          TInt aBufNum,TUint aBufOffset,TInt aLen);
#endif
  };
```

The driver creates a shared chunk when it is opened. At the same time, it commits memory to two separate buffers within the chunk, each of size KMyDeviceBufSize, and each containing physically contiguous RAM pages.

To gain access to these buffers, the user application must first create a handle on the chunk, using the method GetChunkHandle(). This maps the chunk's memory into the address space of the process. The application obtains a pointer to the base of this region using the method RChunk::Base(). The application must then determine the offsets of the two buffers relative to this base address using the method GetBufInfo() – the argument aBufNum specifying the buffer and aBufOffset returning its offset.

Now the application can fill a buffer with the transmission data – taking care not to access beyond the perimeter of the buffer, as this would normally cause it to panic. Finally, the application issues a request to transmit the contents of the buffer using the method WriteBuffer(). The argument aBufNum identifies which buffer should be used for the transfer and the argument aBufOffset provides the offset within this to start the transfer from. Argument aLen provides the number of bytes to transfer.

When exchanging information on data locations within a shared chunk between driver and user code, you must always take care to specify this information as an offset rather than an address, since the chunk appears at different addresses in the address spaces of the different processes. Of course, the same applies when exchanging this information between user processes.

Again, since this user-side interface header is also included in the kernel-side implementation of the driver, I use `#ifndef__KERNEL_MODE__` around the user-side specific methods to prevent compiler errors when building the kernel-side driver – see Section 12.4.6.1 for more details.

Here is the driver class definition:

```
// Driver object making use of shared chunks
class DMyDevice : public DBase
  {
  ...
private:
  TInt CreateChunk(TInt aChunkSize);
  void CloseChunk();
  TInt MakeChunkHandle(DThread* aThread);
  TInt InitDma();
  static void WrDmaService(DDmaRequest::TResult aResult, TAny* aArg);
  TInt InitiateWrite(TInt aBufNo,TUint aBufOffset,
    TInt aLen,TRequestStatus* aStatus);
private:
  DThread* iClient;
  TRequestStatus* iWrStatus;
  DChunk* iChunk;
  TLinAddr iChunkKernAddr;
  TUint32 iBuf1PhysAddr;
  TUint32 iBuf2PhysAddr;
  TDmaChannel* iDmaChannel;
  DDmaRequest* iDmaRequest;
  };
```

The member `iChunk` is a pointer to the shared chunk created and `iChunkKernAddr` is the base address of this in the kernel process. The member `iClient` is the user thread that opened the channel. This will be used when creating a handle on the shared chunk for that thread. The members `iBuf1PhysAddr` and `iBuf2PhysAddr` save the physical addresses of the two buffers. This information will allow us to specify physical rather than linear addresses for DMA data transfers from these buffers, which is more efficient.

13.2.6.1   Operations on opening and closing the driver

The following code shows how the driver creates the shared chunk and commits memory to the pair of buffers. It commits physically contiguous RAM pages and disables caching. Each buffer is the shared chunk equivalent of that created in the example code, shown in Section 13.1.3. In this case, we leave an uncommitted page either side of each buffer; these act as guard pages. If the user application writes beyond the buffer region when it is filling one of the buffers with the transmission data, this will panic the application rather than corrupting adjacent memory regions in the chunk:

```
TInt DMyDevice::CreateChunk(TInt aChunkSize)
  {
// Round the chunk size supplied upto a multiple of the
// MMU page size. Check size specified is large enough.
aChunkSize=Kern::RoundToPageSize(aChunkSize);
__ASSERT_DEBUG(aChunkSize>=((3*KGuardPageSize)+
  (KMyDeviceBufSize<<1)),Panic(KMyDevPanicChunkCreate));

// Thread must be in critical section to create a chunk
NKern::ThreadEnterCS();

// Create the shared chunk.
TChunkCreateInfo info;
info.iType = TChunkCreateInfo::ESharedKernelMultiple;
info.iMaxSize = aChunkSize;
info.iMapAttr = EMapAttrFullyBlocking; // No caching
info.iOwnsMemory = ETrue;    // Using RAM pages
info.iDestroyedDfc = NULL;   // No chunk destroy DFC
DChunk* chunk;
TUint32 mapAttr;
TInt r = Kern::ChunkCreate(info,chunk,iChunkKernAddr, mapAttr);
if (r!=KErrNone)
    {
    NKern::ThreadLeaveCS();
    return(r);
    }

// Map two buffers into the chunk - each containing
// physically contiguous RAM pages. Both buffers
// surrounded by 4K guard pages.
TInt bufOffset=KGuardPageSize;
r=Kern::ChunkCommitContiguous(chunk,bufOffset,
                      KMyDeviceBufSize,iBuf1PhysAddr);
if (r==KErrNone)
  {
  bufOffset+=(KMyDeviceBufSize+KGuardPageSize);
  r=Kern::ChunkCommitContiguous(chunk,bufOffset,
                      KMyDeviceBufSize,iBuf2PhysAddr);
  }
if (r!=KErrNone)
    Kern::ChunkClose(chunk); // Commit failed - tidy-up.
else
    iChunk=chunk;

NKern::ThreadLeaveCS();
return(r);
  }
```

The following code shows how the driver closes the chunk again:

```
void DMyDevice::CloseChunk()
  {
// Thread must be in critical section to close a chunk
NKern::ThreadEnterCS();

// Close chunk
if (iChunk)
    Kern::ChunkClose(iChunk);
```

```
// Can leave critical section now
NKern::ThreadLeaveCS();
}
```

Next we see how the driver initializes the DMA objects required for data transfer. First it opens a DMA channel for data transfer. In this simple example, it only asks the framework to reserve one descriptor, since we assume a controller supporting a single buffer scheme and we allow only one DMA request to be outstanding at any time.

KPlatDevice1TxChan is the platform-specific channel identifier, which in this example selects data transmission over the peripheral device concerned. The driver elects to use DFC thread 0 to queue the DMA channel's DFC. Next it constructs a single request object, specifying the callback function as DMyDevice::WrDmaService() and passing a pointer to itself as the callback argument:

```
TInt DMyDevice::InitDma()
  {
  // Open and configure the channel for data
  // transmission
  TDmaChannel::SCreateInfo info;
  info.iCookie = KPlatDevice1TxChan;
  info.iDesCount = 1;
  info.iDfcPriority = 4;
  info.iDfcQ = Kern::DfcQue0();

  TInt r = TDmaChannel::Open(info,iDmaChannel);
  if (r!=KErrNone)
    return(r);

  // We're only ever going to have one
  // outstanding transfer
  iDmaRequest = new DDmaRequest(*iDmaChannel, DMyDevice::WrDmaService,
                                                               this);
  if (iDmaRequest == NULL)
    return(KErrNoMemory);
  return(KErrNone);
  }
```

13.2.6.2 Getting a handle on the shared chunk

Next we see the how the driver creates the chunk handle for the user-thread concerned:

The inline code that follows shows how the user application assigns the handle created for it by the driver to the RChunk object passed into the "get handle" method:

```
inline TInt RMyDevice::GetChunkHandle(RChunk& aChunk)
  {
  return aChunk.SetReturnedHandle (DoControl(EGetChunkHandle));
  }
```

```
TInt DMyDevice::MakeChunkHandle(DThread* aThread)
  {

  TInt r;
  // Thread must be in critical section to make a handle
  NKern::ThreadEnterCS();
  if (iChunk)
  r=Kern::MakeHandleAndOpen(aThread,iChunk);
  else
  r=KErrNotFound;
  NKern::ThreadLeaveCS();
  return(r);
  }
```

13.2.6.3 DMA data transfer using the shared chunk

The user application initiates data transfer using the following method:

```
TInt RMyDevice::WriteBuffer(TRequestStatus& aStatus, TInt aBufNum,
                            TUint aBufOffset,TInt aLen);
```

Next we see how the driver initiates transfer over the DMA channel in response to this. To calculate the source memory address, it combines the buffer offset passed by the client with the physical address of the start of the buffer that it saved earlier. KPlatDevice1TxId is the transfer destination information – an identifier for the peripheral concerned:

```
TInt DMyDevice::InitiateWrite(TInt aBufNo, TUint aBufOffset,
                              TInt aLen,TRequestStatus* aStatus)
  {
  // Validate buffer no, buffer offset
  // and length supplied
  iWrStatus=aStatus;

  // Platform specific code to enable TX on device
  TUint32 src=(aBufNo==1)?iBuf2PhysAddr:iBuf1PhysAddr;
  TUint32 dest=KPlatDevice1TxId;
  TInt r=iDmaRequest->Fragment((src+aBufOffset),
    dest,aLen,(KDmaMemSrc|KDmaIncSrc|KDmaPhysAddrSrc),0);
  if (r != KErrNone)
    return(r);
  iDmaRequest->Queue();
  return(KErrNone);
  }
```

Finally we see the driver's DFC callback function handing the end of the DMA transfer. In this example, it simply checks whether the transfer was successful or not and completes the request back to the user application. In a more complex implementation it might check if there is more data to be transferred:

```
void DMyDevice::WrDmaService(DDmaRequest::TResult aResult, TAny* aArg)
  {
  DMyDevice &driver = *((DMyDevice*)aArg);

  // Platform specific code to disable TX on device
  TInt r = (aResult==DDmaRequest::EOk) ? KErrNone : KErrGeneral;
  Kern::RequestComplete(driver.iClient, driver.iWrStatus,r);
  }
```

13.3 Media drivers and the local media sub-system

13.3.1 Local media sub-system overview

Media drivers are a form of PDD (physical device driver) that are used almost exclusively by the file server to access local media devices. Phones contain both fixed media devices that are internal to the phone such as NAND/NOR flash disks, and removable media devices such as MultiMediaCards and SD cards. The set of media drivers installed on a device, together with a local media LDD (logical device driver) and a user-side interface class, are referred to as the local media sub-system. Figure 13.5 shows an overview of the architecture. In this example, I show a Symbian OS phone containing three local drives:

1. A NAND user data drive (C:)

2. A MultiMediaCard drive (D:)

3. Code stored in NAND (Z:).

As we saw in Section 9.3.3.1, the file server supports at most 26 drives, each identified by a different drive letter (A: to Z:). For the file server, the TDrive class is the abstraction of a logical drive, and when a drive is mounted, this class provides the interface with the associated file system. Of the 26 drives supported, 16 are allocated as local drives – that is, they are available for mounting drives on media devices that are located within the phone. This is more than on EKA1, which only supports nine local drives.

The interface to the local media sub-system is provided by the TBus-LocalDrive class. Each instance of this user-side class represents a channel of communication with a local drive and to establish a channel, a client must connect a TBusLocalDrive object to a specified drive. A single instance of the TBusLocalDrive class can be switched between different drives.

The file server always contains 16 separate TBusLocalDrive instances – one for each local drive. Those drive objects that correspond

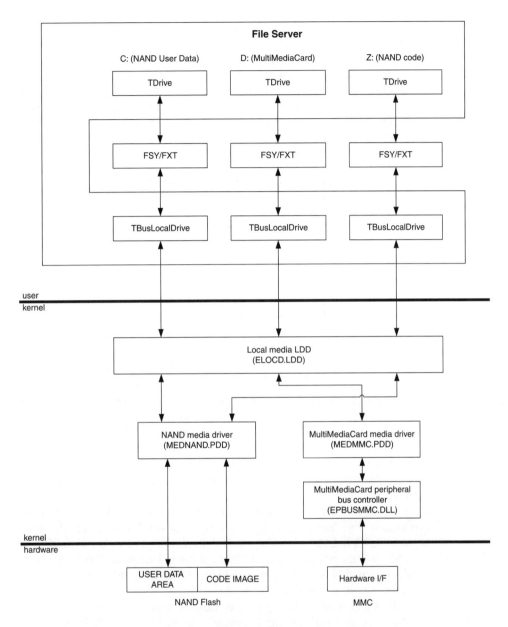

Figure 13.5 Local media sub-system overview

to the drives that are supported on a particular platform are kept permanently connected. Each of the file systems and the file server extensions access their respective drive hardware using the corresponding file server local drive object. Programs other than the file server may also instantiate their own TBusLocalDrive object to access a local drive – for example, a low-level disk utility might do this. So you can see that two or more channels can be open on the same drive simultaneously.

Local drives are distinguished by their drive number (0–15). ESTART is an executable started during system boot, which completes the initialization of the file server and is responsible for handling the mapping between drive letter and the local drive number. This can be configured for each platform. However, apart from the emulator, most platforms adopt the default local drive-mapping scheme, which is:

Local drive number	Drive letter
0	C:
1	D:
2	E:
. . .	. . .
14	Q:
15	R:

Figure 13.5 shows drive Z: mapped to a local drive, which seems to deviate from the mapping scheme I've just described. In fact, this mapping to Z: happens because the composite file system combines the ROFS and ROM drives into a single drive designated as Z: – see Section 9.4.5. Without the composite file system, the ROFS local drive would be mapped to a drive letter in the range shown in the previous table.

The rest of the local media sub-system consists of kernel-side components. This includes a logical device driver layer called the local media LDD (ELOCD.LDD) together with a set of installed media drivers, which are essentially physical device drivers. However, the local media sub-system differs in a number of ways from a standard device driver configuration, as I will now describe.

The local media LDD abstracts various aspects of an interface with a local media device: for example, the handling of disks that have been divided into more than one partition. This LDD is involved in any connection to a local drive – which means that any functionality specific to a particular family of media device (NAND, MultiMediaCard and so on) is implemented in the media driver rather than the LDD. The result is that rather than each media driver abstracting just the platform specifics, it generally also includes a portion that is generic across those platforms that support the same family of media. Indeed, certain media drivers don't directly control the hardware interface at all – instead they use the services provided by a peripheral bus controller (see Section 13.4) that handles hardware interfacing. Such media drivers then become completely platform-independent and are built as part of the set of generic E32 components. An example of this is the MultiMediaCard driver, which uses the generic services of the MultiMediaCard peripheral bus controller.

Other media drivers do control the hardware interface themselves, and so contain both platform-specific and generic elements. These drivers are built as part of the platform variant, but they do include generic source files from E32 as well as variant-related source. The NAND flash media driver is an example of this type of driver. As with most platform-specific components, this type of media driver interfaces with the media hardware via functions exported from the variant or ASSP DLLs.

The EKA2 local media sub-system architecture differs from that provided on EKA1, where there is no local media LDD. The EKA1 architecture is less modular as in this case the kernel contains the equivalent functionality.

Figure 13.5 shows the file server mounting the two NAND device partitions as two separate drives. When both are connected, two open channels exist on the NAND device. However, rather than this resulting in two separate PDD objects, requests for both channels are fed into a single media driver PDD object. This is another aspect that differs from a standard driver configuration.

Before it is possible to connect to a local drive, a media driver or kernel extension must have registered for that drive. Registering involves specifying a local media ID that identifies the media device family. After this is done, only media drivers that support that particular family will open on that drive. On a particular platform, there may be multiple media drivers present for a certain media ID. A media driver may support only a small sub-set of the media devices within that family: for example, the sub-set might be constrained to devices from a particular manufacturer, or to devices with a particular part number. So a ROM image might include two versions of a NAND media driver to support two different NAND parts that the phone could be built to contain. However, other media drivers will include support for a wider sub-set and some drivers, for example the MultiMediaCard media driver, aim to support the whole family of devices.

The set of media IDs that are supported and the list of local drives that are allocated to each ID are highly dependent on the target hardware platform. Each variant includes the header file, variantmediadef.h, where this information is specified.

Removable media drives normally involve a Symbian OS peripheral bus controller as well as a media driver to manage the removable media bus. Here, the platform-specific code lies in the controller extension rather than the media driver, and so it is normally the controller that registers for such drives. In this situation, there could be multiple media drivers associated with that controller, each supporting a different type of removable memory card. For example, a platform including the SD card controller may contain drivers for both the user and protected area SD card sections.

The following table lists the possible media IDs. The association between ID and media device family can vary between platforms. What is essential is that each media family supported on the platform has a unique ID. However, the most common media types supported on Symbian OS have acquired default IDs which are shown in the table:

Local media ID	Default media device family
EFixedMedia0	Internal RAM
EFixedMedia1	NOR flash
EFixedMedia2	NAND flash
EFixedMedia3	–
EFixedMedia4	–
EFixedMedia5	–
EFixedMedia6	–
EFixedMedia7	–
ERemovableMedia0	MultiMediaCard/SD
ERemovableMedia1	PC card
ERemovableMedia2	Code Storage Area (SDIO)
ERemovableMedia3	–

Note that the definition of media IDs for removable media devices has altered between EKA1 and EKA2. On EKA1, the ID indicates the slot (or socket) number rather than the media device family.

Media drivers and the local media LDD are generally built as combined device driver and kernel extension components. Being extensions means that the kernel will call their DLL entry points early in its boot process (before the file server is started), and it is at this stage that each media driver registers itself for one or more of the local drives.

Later on, during the initialization of the file server, a separate F32 startup thread runs, and this continues local media sub-system initialization. It loads the local media LDD and then attempts to load all media drivers it finds, by searching for "MED*.PDD" in the system directory (\Sys\Bin\) on the ROM file system (Z:). Like any other drivers, media drivers and the local media LDD export a function at ordinal 1 to create a driver factory object – and the kernel calls this export for each driver as they are loaded. Once the relevant factory objects have been created, it becomes possible to connect to the corresponding local drives.

ESTART completes the initialization of the file server. As well as being responsible for configuring the mapping between drive letter and the local drive number, it is also responsible for assigning an appropriate file system, and possibly a file server extension to each active drive. However, this has to be co-ordinated with the media ID assigned for each of these drives – that is, with the contents of variantmediadef.h for the platform concerned.

ESTART may use one of two methods for determining this local drive file system configuration. The first is to use a platform-specific local drive mapping file – an ASCII text file which specifies precisely which file system/extension to associate with which local drive. (This can also be used to customize the mapping between drive letter and the local drive number.) The second method is to allow ESTART to automatically detect which file system to mount on which local drive, by allowing it to interrogate the capabilities of each local drive and then use this information to decide an appropriate FSY. This second scheme is not as efficient as the first and therefore tends only to be used for development reference platforms, where the flexibility of drive mapping is more important than the time taken to boot the system. The local drive file system configuration performed by ESTART is discussed further in Chapter 16, *Boot Processes*.

During ESTART, the file server connects to all the active drives on the platform and reads their drive capabilities. So before file server initialization is complete, media drivers will normally be open on all these drives.

13.3.2 User-side interface class

Figure 13.6 shows the derivation of the TBusLocalDrive class. Normally, the user-side interface to a device driver consists solely of an RBusLogicalChannel-derived class containing only inline methods. In this case, RLocalDrive provides this thin class. However, here we further derive TBusLocalDrive from RLocalDrive to provide the local media user interface and this contains functions exported from the

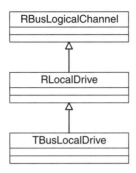

Figure 13.6   Derivation of TBusLocalDrive

user library (EUSER.DLL). TBusLocalDrive adds code to handle the user-side processing of drive format and password protection operations. However, the main reason for the derivation of TBusLocalDrive from RLocalDrive is to preserve compatibility with EKA1. It is needed there so that it can perform the far greater amount of user-side processing, which is necessary to cope with the issues associated with handling asynchronous I/O in device drivers.

These are the major elements of the public interface to the TBusLocalDrive class:

```
class TBusLocalDrive : public RLocalDrive
    {
public:
  TBusLocalDrive();
  TInt Connect(TInt aDriveNumber, TBool& aChangedFlag);
  void Disconnect();
  TInt Caps(TDes8& anInfo);
  TInt Read(TInt64 aPos,TInt aLength,const TAny* aTrg,
     TInt aMessageHandle,TInt aOffset);
  TInt Write(TInt64 aPos,TInt aLength,const TAny* aSrc,
     TInt aMessageHandle,TInt aOffset);
  Format(TFormatInfo& anInfo);
  Format(TInt64 aPos,TInt aLength);
  TInt Enlarge(TInt aLength);
  TInt ReduceSize(TInt aPos, TInt aLength);
  TInt ForceRemount(TUint aFlags=0);
  SetMountInfo(const TDesC8* aMountInfo, TInt aMessageHandle)
    };
```

The method Connect() is used to open a channel to the specified local drive, aDriveNumber. The second parameter, aChangedFlag, is used to provide notification that a drive remount is required. Once the drive is connected, this flag is set true on each media change. When connecting to each local drive, the file server passes in a reference to the data member iChanged belonging to the corresponding TDrive object, and this is how it receives notification of a possible change of volume – see

Section 9.3.3.1. The method `Disconnect()` dissociates the object from any drive.

Next I will list the standard local media operations. The `Caps()` method returns information on the capabilities of a connected drive. Three forms of both the read and write methods are provided (although I've only listed one of each for brevity). The read version shown is the one used for inter-thread communication. It fully specifies the target memory location:

```
TInt Read(TInt64 aPos,TInt aLength,const TAny* aTrg, TInt aMessageHandle,
                                                      TInt aOffset);
```

This method reads `aLength` bytes from offset `aPos` on the drive. Parameter `aTrg` is a pointer to a target descriptor in memory and `aOffset` specifies the offset within this to start storing the data. Parameter `aMessageHandle` is a handle to the message object associated with the F32 client request and this allows the local media LDD to identify the target thread. The corresponding inter-thread write method is also shown.

Two versions of the `Format()` method are provided. The first is used when formatting the entire connected drive – that is, setting each memory element of the drive to a default state and detecting any hardware faults across the drive. The second method is used to format (or erase) just a specified region within the drive.

The methods `Enlarge()` and `ReduceSize()` are used to control the size of a variable sized disk – typically only used for internal RAM drives.

The method `ForceRemount()` is used to close the media driver currently associated with the drive and force the local media sub-system to reopen the most appropriate driver. This is useful in situations where a new media driver has recently been installed on the system. `ForceRemount()` is then used to replace the existing driver with the new version. Also, some media drivers may need to be supplied with security information to open. This is achieved using the `SetMountInfo()` function. `ForceRemount()` is then used to retry the opening the driver once the appropriate mount information has been supplied.

A second media change notification scheme, in addition to that provided via the `TBusLocalDrive::Connect()` method, is available from the base class `RLocalDrive`. This is the method:

```
RLocalDrive::NotifyChange(TRequestStatus* aStatus);
```

The file server also uses this second scheme. The active object `CNotifyMediaChange` makes use of it when requesting notification of media change events to pass on to F32 clients – see Section 9.4.3.4.

13.3.3   Local media LDD

Figure 13.7 shows the main classes that comprise the local media LDD. The diagram also includes the `TBusLocalDrive` class and the main NAND media driver class to show the relationships between the local media LDD and these other components.

I will now describe these classes.

13.3.3.1   *The DLocalDrive class*

The class `DLocalDrive` is the local drive logical channel abstraction. An instance of this class is created each time a `TBusLocalDrive` object is connected to a local drive, and destroyed each time it is disconnected. If two channels are connected to the same drive, then two instances of this class will exist. `DLocalDrive` is derived from the abstract base class for a logical channel, `DLogicalChannelBase`. In this case, however,

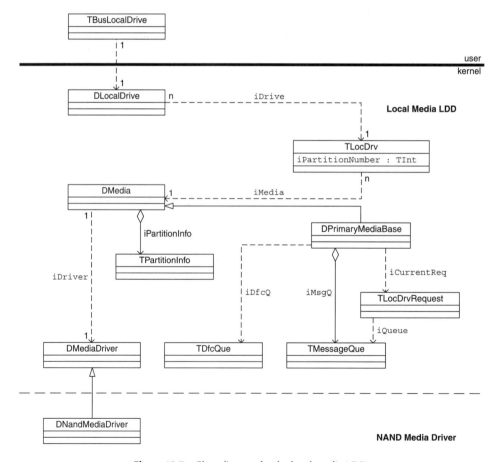

Figure 13.7   Class diagram for the local media LDD

the fact that it derives from this rather than `DLogicalChannel` does not imply that requests on the channel are always executed in the context of the client thread. Media drivers can also be configured to perform requests in a kernel thread – as we will see shortly.

The `DLocalDrive` class contains the member `iDrive`, a pointer to an associated `TLocDrv` object.

13.3.3.2   The TLocDrv class

`TLocDrv` encapsulates the local drive itself and, unlike the `DLocalDrive` class, there is always just a single instance of this class per local drive. When a driver or extension registers for a set of local drives (normally during kernel boot), a `TLocDrv` instance is created for each. Since it is not possible to de-register drives, these objects are never destroyed. Each `TLocDrv` instance represents an individual partition on a media device, so if a media device contains multiple partitions, then a separate `TLocDrv` object is required for each one.

The `TLocDrv` class contains the member `iMedia`, a pointer to its associated `DMedia` object.

13.3.3.3   The DMedia class

The `DMedia` class is the abstraction for a media device. It owns a single media driver, `iDriver`, which it uses to perform any access to the media hardware. It also owns a `TPartitionInfo` object, `iPartitionInfo`, which holds information on each of the partitions contained on the media. Here is the class definition:

```
class TPartitionEntry
  {
public:
  // Start address of partition, described as the relative
  //offset in bytes, from the start of the media.
  Int64 iPartitionBaseAddr;

  // The length of the partition, in bytes.
  Int64 iPartitionLen;

  // Boot Indicator record, currently unused.
  TUint16 iBootIndicator;

  // Describes the type of partition.
  TUint16 iPartitionType;
  };

const TInt KMaxPartitionEntries=0x4;
class TPartitionInfo
  {
public:
  TPartitionInfo();
```

```
public:
  Int64 iMediaSizeInBytes; //Total size of media in bytes.
  TInt iPartitionCount;     //No of partitions on media.
  TPartitionEntry iEntry[KMaxPartitionEntries];
  };
```

The `TLocDrv` class contains a partition number, `iPartitionNumber`. This indicates the element of the partition array in the associated `DMedia` object, `TPartitionInfo::iEntry[]`, which holds the data for that partition. Local drive requests are specified in terms of an offset relative to the start of the partition. By retrieving partition information from the appropriate `DMedia` object, the request is converted into an absolute address on the media device and then passed on to the media driver.

When a driver or extension registers for a set of local drives, it must also specify the number of associated `DMedia` objects required. Hence, drive registration is also the point at which the `DMedia` objects are allocated and again, they are never destroyed. A peripheral bus controller must specify at least one separate media object for each card slot that it controls. Some peripheral bus controllers may need to register for more than one media object per card slot if they are required to support dual media cards. For example, a single SD card, containing both a user and a protected area, requires separate media drivers for both areas, and so needs at least two `DMedia` objects available. As far as Symbian OS is concerned, this is effectively a dual function, or dual media card.

Where removable media are concerned, the relationship between `TLocDrv` and `DMedia` objects can change as the user of the phone removes one memory card and inserts another. The SD card configuration that I've just described requires two `DMedia` objects, with each having a single associated `TLocDrv` object. If this card were removed and replaced by a MultiMediaCard containing two partitions, then this would require only one `DMedia` object, with two associated `TLocDrv` objects.

Figure 13.8 shows various `TLocDrv` and `DMedia` combinations that could result from different cards being inserted into a single card slot.

13.3.3.4   The DPrimaryMediaBase class

In the previous section I described how each media driver or extension (for the remainder of this section I shall refer to these merely as drivers) that registers for a set of local drives also has to register for a set of `DMedia` objects at the same time. This media set must contain just one primary media object. This object is responsible for controlling the overall state of the media (for example, whether power is applied, whether the partition information has been determined and so on). The `DPrimaryMediaBase` class, which is derived from `DMedia`, provides this functionality. The driver that performs drive registration is responsible for creating the primary media object itself, which it then passes over to

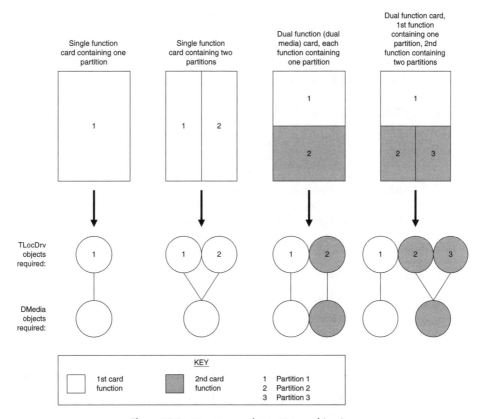

Figure 13.8 TLocDrv and DMedia combinations

the local media sub-system for ownership. If further media objects are specified in the set, then the local media sub-system itself creates DMedia instances for these on behalf of the driver.

The DPrimaryMediaBase class contains the member iDfcQ, a pointer to a DFC queue. As we have seen earlier in the book, a DFC queue is associated with a kernel thread. If the driver that creates the DPrimaryMediaBase object assigns a DFC queue to this member, then this configures the media set so that its requests are implemented in the context of the kernel thread associated with that DFC queue. The driver may use a standard kernel queue or create its own. If iDfcQ is left null, then this configures the media set so that its requests are executed in the context of the client thread.

Each local drive request is encapsulated as a TLocDrvRequest – a class derived from TThreadMessage, the kernel message class. A request ID is defined for every request type. TLocDrvRequest contains information pertaining to the request, including the ID and any associated parameters such as the drive position, length and source/destination location.

Requests for an entire set of DMedia objects are all delivered to the primary media object. This takes place in the context of the calling client thread (normally a file server drive thread). The DPrimaryMediaBase class owns a kernel message queue, iMsgQ. If the media is configured to use a kernel thread, then each request is sent to the queue and the client thread then blocks waiting for the message to complete. Meanwhile, in the context of the kernel thread, the request is retrieved from the queue and dispatched to the appropriate media driver for processing (which normally takes place within driver interrupt service routines and subsequent DFCs). If the media is configured to use the client thread, then requests are not queued, but instead dispatched straight to the media driver to be processed in the context of the client thread.

I discussed the differences between implementing driver requests in the context of the client thread or a kernel thread in Chapter 12, *Drivers and Extensions*.

13.3.3.5   *Local drive power management*

However, before a connected local drive is ready to process its first request, it must first be mounted. For certain media this can be a relatively long and complex task that is often handled asynchronously, while the client thread is blocked. It consists of the following phases:

1. Apply power and reset the media device, then wait for it to stabilize

2. Attempt to open each media driver loaded (installed). Each one that opens successfully is assigned to one of the media objects in the media set

3. Acquire the partition information for each media object for which a driver has opened successfully, and from this determine the relationship between DMedia and associated TLocDrv objects. This typically involves reading data from the media device itself.

For media configured to use the client thread for execution (typically these are fixed media devices), drive mounting commences as soon as any local drive is connected to the media device. For media configured to use a kernel thread, drive mounting is deferred until the first request on the drive takes place – this generally being a request from the file server to read the drive capabilities.

The point at which drive dismounting occurs – that is, when all media drivers are closed for the media set and when power is removed – again depends on the type of media. For removable media devices, this is performed on each of the following occasions:

1. When a media removal event occurs, that is, the media door has been opened or the device has been removed

2.   When the phone is being turned off or switched into standby mode

3.   When a power-off request from a peripheral bus controller is received – it might do this after a period of bus inactivity to save power.

Cases 2 and 3 are collectively known as normal power down events.

In case 1, subsequent drive re-mounting does not occur until the first access to the drive after the door has been closed again. In case 2, it only occurs after the phone has been brought out of standby – on the first subsequent access to the drive. In case 3, it occurs on the next access to the drive. For removable media devices, closing and re-opening the media drivers is necessary in each of these power-down situations because the user could exchange the media device while power is removed. This is particularly likely, of course, in the case of a media removal event. An exchange could involve the introduction of a completely different type of media device into the phone. If so, then on a subsequent re-mounting of the drive, a different media driver will be opened (assuming that the new device is supported).

Irrespective of whether they are configured to use the client thread or a kernel thread for execution, it is likely that the drives for fixed media devices will remain mounted as long as there are `TBusLocalDrive` objects connected. In this situation, it is left to the media driver to implement its own power management policy, as it deems appropriate for the media – for example, power saving during periods of inactivity.

Before power is removed from a removable media device in response to a normal power down event, the local media LDD first notifies each of the affected media drivers of the impending power down. This is not the case on a media removal event.

13.3.3.6   Media change handling

The local media LDD is also responsible for providing user-side notification of media change events. When the peripheral bus controller notifies the local media LDD of either a media removal event or the presence of a card, following a door close event, then the local media LDD passes on this notification. Each event can potentially trigger both of the user notification schemes described in Section 13.3.2.

In the EKA1 version of the local media sub-system, the local media sub-system must also signal normal power down events to the user-side, as far as the `TBusLocalDrive` class, so that any subsequent drive-mounting may be performed asynchronously. This is no longer necessary with EKA2 since drive mounting can be handled asynchronously kernel-side.

13.3.4 Media drivers

A media driver is a special form of a physical device driver. The class DMediaDriver is the abstract base class from which all media drivers must be derived. Here are the major elements of the public interface to this class:

```
class DMediaDriver : public DBase
  {
public:
  DMediaDriver(TInt aMediaId);
  virtual ~DMediaDriver();
  virtual void Close();
  virtual TInt Request(TLocDrvRequest& aRequest)=0;
  virtual TInt PartitionInfo(TPartitionInfo &anInfo)=0;
  virtual void NotifyPowerDown()=0;
  void Complete(TLocDrvRequest& aRequest, TInt aResult);
  void PartitionInfoComplete(TInt anError);
  };
```

The method Request() is the main request handling method, which is called by the associated primary media object to deal with a request received for that drive. A reference to the corresponding request object is passed as a parameter.

Not all requests require access to the media hardware. Even when such access is required, requests can be processed very quickly for fast media memory such as internal RAM. However, any request that involves accessing the media hardware has the potential to be a long-running operation. Even just to read a few bytes, we may need to bring the device out of power saving mode, spin up a rotating disk and so on. To cope with this, the driver may complete requests either synchronously or asynchronously. The return value to the Request() method indicates the mode adopted, as follows:

Return value	Meaning
KErrCompletion	Request has been completed synchronously and the outcome was successful.
KErrNone	Request has been initiated successfully but is still in progress and will be completed asynchronously.
KMediaDriverDeferRequest	Request is not yet initiated since another is in progress – defer the request until later.
Other system-wide error code	Request has failed (during the synchronous phase of processing).

When a request is to be performed asynchronously, then its completion is signaled back to the LDD using the method `Complete()`.

The local media LDD calls the method `PartitionInfo()` during drive mounting to get partition information for the media device. Again, this operation may be performed either synchronously or asynchronously as indicated by the method's return value. If performed asynchronously then the method `PartitionInfoComplete()` is used to signal back completion to the LDD.

In response to a normal power down event, the local media LDD calls the method `NotifyPowerDown()` to allow the driver to terminate any outstanding requests and power down the device. However, for removable media devices, the peripheral bus controller takes care of powering down the bus.

13.4 Peripheral bus controllers

Symbian OS supports a number of peripheral bus standards for removable memory and I/O cards:

- MultiMediaCard
- SD card
- PC card
- Memory stick.

Symbian OS implements a software controller for each, and these controllers provide a set of generic kernel-side services that is available to device drivers and media drivers alike. There are many similarities between each of these peripheral bus systems: to share functionality common to each and to unify the interface to these components as far as possible, we have encapsulated these common characteristics into a set of abstract base classes for peripheral bus controllers which I will briefly describe in this section.

The features common to removable peripheral cards and their associated bus interface hardware include:

- Detection and handling of card insertion and removal events
- Support for the hot removal of cards – that is, removing a card when the bus is in operation
- Control of the bus power supply in relation to insertion and removal events and bus activity
- Adjustment of hardware interface characteristics according to the capabilities reported by the cards

- Rejection of cards that aren't compatible with the hardware interface – for example, low voltage cards, cards which consume too
  much current when active and so on

- Support for dual and multi-function cards.

Figure 13.9 shows part of the class diagram for a peripheral bus controller – the MultiMediaCard controller. It shows each of the peripheral
bus controller base classes, and the classes derived from these for the
particular MultiMediaCard controller case. It also shows some of the
local media sub-system classes that I've already described, to show their
relationships with the peripheral bus controller.

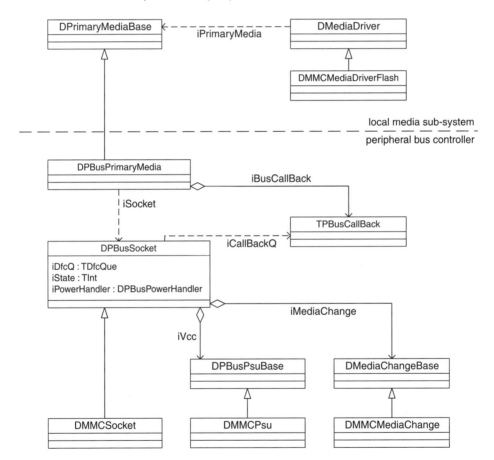

Figure 13.9 Class diagram for a peripheral bus controller (using the MultiMediaCard controller as an
example)

I discussed the DPrimaryMediaBase class in Section 13.3.3. Part of
the local media sub-system, this is the object responsible for controlling

the overall state of a media device or set of related media devices. For fixed media, this class is instantiated directly. However, for media involving a peripheral bus controller, a derived version is provided, DPBusPrimaryMedia. This class abstracts the interface between the local media sub-system and a peripheral bus controller – passing on requests from the sub-system to apply power to removable media devices and providing notification back of media change and power down events. The media driver base class, DMediaDriver, contains a pointer to its associated primary media object, iPrimaryMedia. For peripheral bus related media drivers (such as the MultiMediaCard media driver, DMMCMediaDriverFlash shown), this pointer is used to gain access to other peripheral bus objects via the DPBusPrimaryMedia object.

Associated with each DPBusPrimaryMedia object, there is a peripheral bus socket object, iSocket. This is a major element of every peripheral bus controller that essentially encapsulates a bus controller thread. Often, this also corresponds to a physical card slot for an individual removable media card – but not always. For example, if a platform contains two physical slots, each with separate hardware control, such that cards in both slots can be enabled and can actively be transferring data simultaneously, then each slot needs to be allocated a separate socket object. However, if the two slots are connected with a common set of control signals such that only one slot can be actively transferring data at any given time (as is the case with a MultiMediaCard stack), then the pair should be allocated a single socket object.

DPBusSocket is the abstract base class for a socket, with each type of controller providing a derived version – in this case a DMMCSocket class. The DPBusSocket class owns a DFC queue, iDfcQ and at system boot time each socket allocates itself a separate kernel thread to process DFCs added to this queue. I mentioned in Section 13.3.1 that peripheral bus controllers register for their associated removable media local drives, rather than leaving this to the relevant media drivers. Registering also involves setting a DFC queue for the primary media object, which is then used for handling all requests for these local drives. A peripheral bus controller always assigns this to the DFC queue of the relevant DPBusSocket object and so the socket's kernel thread is used for handling these local drive requests.

The DPBusSocket derived object oversees the power supply and media change functionality associated with the socket – owning an associated PSU object, iVcc and media change object, iMediaChange.

DPBusPsuBase is the abstract base class for the main bus power supply for the socket. Again, each type of controller provides a derived version – DMMCPsu in this case. The power supply can be set to one of three desired states:

PSU state	Definition
EPsuOff	PSU is turned off.
EPsuOnCurLimit	PSU is turned on in a current limited mode: some supplies can be turned on in a mode that supplies a limited amount of current to the card. If a card draws excessive current then this causes PSU output voltage droop, which can be detected. Normally the PSU is only placed in this mode for a brief period, before being turned fully on. For PSUs that don't support current limit mode, this state is treated in the same way as EPsuOnFull.
EPsuOnFull	PSU is turned fully on.

While the supply is in either of its ON states, it can be configured to monitor the PSU output voltage level every second. The method used to perform voltage checking varies between platforms. If the voltage level goes out of range, then the PSU is immediately turned off. This PSU object also implements a bus inactivity timer (using the same 1 second tick). The controller resets the timer on each transfer over the bus. The PSU object can be configured so that if the timer is allowed to expire, this causes the associated socket to be powered down. The programmers creating a new phone platform set the duration of the inactivity period.

Similarly, each type of controller provides a derived version of the class DMediaChangeBase, which handles the insertion and removal of media on the socket. The derived class interfaces with the media change hardware – providing notification of media change events.

DPBusSocket also owns a power handler object, iPowerHandler. It registers this with the kernel-side power manager to receive notification of phone transitions into the standby or off state, and transitions out of standby, back into the active state.

The socket object combines status information from its power supply, media change and power handler objects into an overall power state, iState. The following six different socket states are defined:

Power state	Definition
EPBusCardAbsent	Either no card is present or the media door is open.
EPBusOff	The media door is closed and a card is present, but it is not powered up.

Power state	Definition
EPBusPoweringUp	A request has been received from the local media sub-system or an I/O driver to power up the card and this is now in progress. This normally involves applying power, waiting for the PSU to stabilize, applying a hardware reset to the card and, finally, interrogating the capabilites of the card.
EPBusPowerUpPending	A request has been received to power up the card just as the phone is being placed in standby mode. Power up is deferred until the phone comes out of standby.
EPBusOn	The card has successfully been powered up and initialized.
EPBusPsuFault	In the process of powering up the card, it has been discovered that the power supply range for the card is not compatible with that of the host phone, or a hardware problem with the card has resulted in it drawing excessive current. The card is now powered off and no more power up requests will be accepted on this socket until a new card is inserted (that is, a media change event occurs).

I've assumed one physical card slot per socket object to simplify these descriptions.

Figure 13.10 shows the power state transition diagram. Referring still to Figure 13.9, clients of a controller, such as media drivers, use the TPBusCallBack class to implement peripheral bus event service routines. These objects must be configured with details of the bus event concerned, and then queued on the appropriate socket object. The event of interest can be either a peripheral bus interrupt or a change in the status of the socket power state. Each TPBusCallBack object has an associated callback function supplied by the client, and, once queued, this is called on each occurrence of the event until the object is de-queued again. In the case of power state changes, information is passed to the callback indicating the new power state.

Each DPBusPrimaryMedia object owns a callback object, iBus-CallBack, which it queues with the corresponding socket object for notification of power state changes. Of primary interest are card insertion/removal events, which it passes on to the local media LDD to trigger user-side media change notification. Power-down events are also

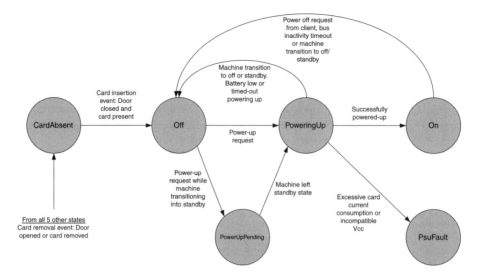

Figure 13.10   Socket power state transition diagram

signaled to the local media sub-system and lead to the relevant media drivers being closed, as do card removal events – see Section 13.3.3.5.

13.5   MultiMediaCard support

13.5.1   MultiMediaCard overview

MultiMediaCards are miniature solid-state removable media cards about the size of a postage stamp. There are two main types:

1.   Read-only memory (ROM) cards

2.   Read/write cards – which generally use Flash memory.

Both types support a common command interface. In the case of Flash cards, this allows the host to write to any data block on the device without requiring a prior erase to be issued. This means that there is no need for the phone to implement a flash translation layer.

The standard MultiMediaCard provides a 7-pin serial bus for communication with the host computer. Cards may support two different communication protocols. The first is MultiMediaCard mode, and support for this is mandatory. The second, based on the Serial Peripheral Interface (SPI) standard, is optional and not supported on Symbian OS. MultiMediaCard mode involves six of the card signals: three as communication signals and three which supply power to the card. The communication signals are:

Signal	Description
CLK	One bit of data is transferred on the CMD and DAT lines with each cycle of this clock.
CMD	Bidirectional command channel – used to send commands to the card and to receive back responses from it.
DAT	Bidirectional data channel – for data transfer between host and card.

This arrangement allows commands and responses to be exchanged over the CMD line at the same time that data is transferred over the DAT line. The maximum data transfer rate for standard cards is 20 Mbits/sec. However, high-speed 13-pin MultiMediaCards are available that can employ eight data signals, and here the maximum transfer rate is 416 Mbits/sec.

The MultiMediaCard architecture allows more than one card to be attached to a MultiMediaCard bus, with each card being connected to the same signals, and no card having an individual connection. A MultiMediaCard controller on the host machine – the bus master – controls this group of cards, known as a card stack. Communication over the bus begins with the controller issuing a command over the CMD line. There are two types of these: broadcast commands are intended for all cards, while, fairly obviously, addressed commands are intended for the addressed card only. Of course, many commands produce a response from the card. In the case of data transfer commands, such as the reading or writing of data blocks, data transfer commences over the DAT line after the command is issued. For normal multiple block transfers, this data flow is only terminated when the controller issues a stop command. Single block transfers end without the need for a stop command.

A minimal card stack that consists of only one card has a point-to-point connection linking that card and the controller, but you should be aware that this doesn't alter the communication protocol required.

13.5.2 Software MultiMediaCard controller

In the two previous sections, I introduced the software MultiMediaCard controller in Symbian OS, which provides a generic kernel-side API to media drivers. Figure 13.5 showed its position in relation to the local media sub-system. Here I will describe it in more detail.

Symbian OS also supports SD/SDIO cards, and we derive the software controller for these from the same MultiMediaCard classes. The MultiMediaCard specification also includes an I/O card class. For both of these reasons, we designed the MultiMediaCard controller to support I/O cards too. The clients for these I/O services are device drivers.

The MultiMediaCard controller is implemented as a peripheral bus controller, which means that we derive it from the peripheral bus controller base classes described in Section 13.4. Like the DMA framework, the MultiMediaCard controller is divided into a platform-independent layer (PIL) and a platform-specific layer (PSL). In this case, the two are built as separate kernel extensions, as shown in Figure 13.11. In this case too, the PSL normally interfaces with the controller hardware via functions exported from the variant or ASSP DLL.

The basic architecture of the MultiMediaCard controller, and its relationship with a media driver is shown in Figure 13.12.

Figure 13.12 omits the peripheral bus controller base classes, which I showed in Figure 13.9.

On most phones, the MultiMediaCard controller manages only a single card stack – although it can be configured to control as many as

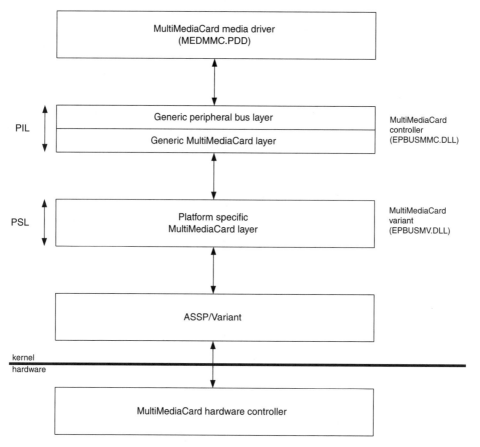

Figure 13.11   The components of the MultiMediaCard controller

MultiMediaCard controller　　　　　　**MultiMediaCard media driver**

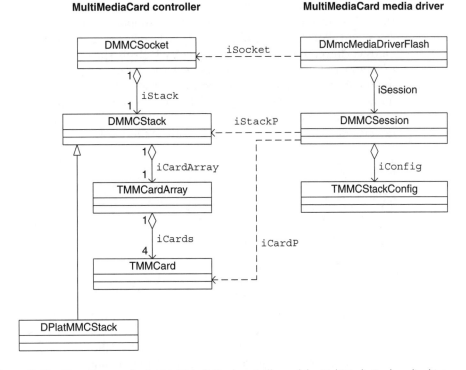

Figure 13.12 Class diagrams for the MultiMediaCard controller and the MultiMediaCard media driver

four stacks. Each stack is implemented as a peripheral bus socket, which means that it has an associated kernel thread. We create an instance of the class DMmcSocket (derived from the peripheral bus socket base class DPBusSocket) for each stack. We make a distinction between this socket object – which oversees the bus power supply and media change functionality – and the object that controls access to the card stack, DMMCStack.

The DMMCStack class is responsible for issuing commands over the bus, receiving responses back from the cards, transferring card data, and the control of the bus clock speed. All of this involves the management of the MultiMediaCard hardware interface. The MultiMediaCard specification defines a set of predefined command sequences (called macro commands) for complex bus operations, such as identifying the cards present in the stack, reading more than one block from a card and so on. The DMMCStack class has been designed to implement these macro commands. It is an abstract class, which defines the main interface between the PIL and PSL. Each phone platform provides a derived stack object – shown as DPlatMMCStack on the diagram – which normally deals with such issues as hardware interface control, DMA transfer and the servicing of card interrupts.

The class `TMMCard` is the abstraction of a MultiMediaCard within the stack. The Symbian OS software controller supports up to four cards per stack, and allocates a card object for each. Clients can gain access to these cards via the corresponding stack object, which also provides information on number of cards supported on this particular phone platform (that is, the number of card slots allocated to the stack). The stack owns a card array object, `TMMCardArray`, which manages the cards. The `TMMCard` class is one of the main elements of the MultiMediaCard API provided to drivers. Here are some of the public parts of this class:

```
class TMMCard
  {
public:
  TMMCard();
  inline TBool IsPresent() const;
  TBool IsReady() const;
  inline TMMCMediaTypeEnum MediaType() const;
  inline TUint DeviceSize() const;
  virtual TUint MaxTranSpeedInKilohertz() const;
  };
```

MultiMediaCards can be inserted or removed at any time and the method `IsPresent()` indicates whether there is currently a card present in the slot concerned. `IsReady()` indicates whether the card is powered, initialized and ready to accept a data transfer command.

The method `MediaType()` returns one of the following values to indicate the type of card present:

EMultiMediaROM	Read-only MultiMediaCard
EMultiMediaFlash	Writeable MultiMediaCard
EMultiMediaIO	I/O MultiMediaCard

`DeviceSize()` returns the total capacity of the card in bytes. However, this doesn't take account of how this memory has been partitioned. (Partition information for the card is normally stored in a partition table in the card's first data block – which has to be read using a block read command by the media driver.)

`MaxTranSpeedInKilohertz()` returns the maximum supported clock rate for the card.

The `DMMCSession` class provides the other main part of the client interface to the MultiMediaCard controller. A `DMMCSession` represents a unit of work for the stack, and is used to issue commands – either to the entire stack using a broadcast command, or to an individual card in the stack. Each client creates its own instance of this class, and associates it with the stack object, iStackP, concerned. The client must also associate it with a card object, iCardP, if the session is to be used to send addressed commands. To issue a request, the client configures the session object with the relevant information for the request and submits it to the stack. The DMMCSession class contains methods for initiating macro commands, as well as lower level methods allowing a client to control the stack in a more explicit manner. Here are some of the public parts of this class:

```
class DMMCSession : public DBase
  {
public:
  virtual ~DMMCSession();
  DMMCSession(const TMMCCallBack& aCallBack);
  void SetupCIMReadBlock(TMMCArgument aDevAddr,
      TUint32 aLength, TUint8* aMemoryP);
  void SetupCIMWriteBlock(TMMCArgument aDevAddr,
      TUint32 aLength, TUint8* aMemoryP);
  void SetupCIMReadMBlock(TMMCArgument aDevAddr,
      TUint32 aLength, TUint8* aMemoryP, TUint32 aBlkLen);
  void SetupCIMWriteMBlock(TMMCArgument aDevAddr,
      TUint32 aLength, TUint8* aMemoryP, TUint32 aBlkLen);
  TInt Engage();
  inline TUint8* ResponseP();
  };
```

When creating a DMMCSession object, the client supplies a callback function as part of the class constructor. Once a client has engaged a session on the stack, the controller will inform it of the completion of the request by calling this callback function.

Next, you can see four methods used to configure the session for data transfer macro commands. The first pair of methods involves single block transfer. Looking at the first of these in detail:

```
void SetupCIMReadBlock(TMMCArgument aDevAddr, TUint32 aLength,
                                    TUint8* aMemoryP);
```

This configures the session for a single block read from the card. When submitted, the stack starts by issuing a command to define the block length as aLength bytes for the subsequent block read command. Then it issues a read single block command – reading from offset aDevAddr on the card into system memory beginning at address aMemoryP. No stop command is required in this case.

The second pair of methods involves multi-block transfer. This time, I will look at the write version in more detail:

```
void SetupCIMWriteMBlock(TMMCArgument aDevAddr, TUint32 aLength,
                                    TUint8* aMemoryP, TUint32 aBlkLen);
```

When submitted, the stack issues a command to define the block length as
aBlkLen bytes for the subsequent block write command. It then issues a
write multiple block command to continually transfer blocks from the host
to the card, starting at address aMemoryP in system memory, and offset
aDevAddr on the card. Once aLength bytes have been transferred, the
stack issues a stop command to terminate the transfer. Engage() is used
to enque the session for execution on the DMMCStack object once it has
been configured.

ResponseP() returns a pointer to a buffer containing the last command response received by the session.

The controller is designed to accept more than one client request on
a stack at any given time. This could happen on multi-card stacks, or on
single card stacks containing multi-function cards where multiple drivers
have session engaged simultaneously. The controller attempts to manage
the sessions as efficiently as it can, by internally scheduling them onto
the bus. When the current session becomes blocked waiting on an event,
the controller will attempt to reschedule another session in its place.

13.5.3   Bus configuration and error recovery

Referring still to Figure 13.12, the class TMmcStackConfig is used to
hold bus configuration settings for a stack. These settings are such things
as the bus clock rate, whether to try re-issuing commands on error,
how long to wait for a response from the card and so on. The stack
owns an instance of this class (not shown on the diagram) containing
the default settings that are normally applied. Each session also owns an
instance of this class, the member iConfig, which normally contains
a copy of the defaults. However, if it chooses, the client may over-ride
the configuration settings for any bus operation it submits by altering the
contents of iConfig. These changes only remain in effect for the period
that the session remains current.

The controller is normally configured to automatically retry failed
operations when any of the following errors are detected:

- Timeout waiting for a command response from a card

- A CRC error is detected in a response

- A timeout waiting for data transfer to commence during a data read
  or write command

- A CRC error detected in a data block during data transfer.

For certain other errors, such as if the card state is found to be inconsistent
with the command being issued, the controller will attempt to recover by
re-initializing the entire stack before retrying the failed operation.

13.5.4   Card power handling

When the controller detects a door-open event, it tries to remove power from the card as soon as possible. It does not remove power immediately if a bus operation is in progress, because it wouldn't be a good idea to remove power from a card in the middle of writing a block, as this could corrupt the block. In this case, power-down is deferred until the end of the MultiMediaCard session. Attempts to engage a new session while the door is open will fail immediately though.

So, to avoid the situation in which a card is physically unplugged while a command is still completing, driver requests have to be kept short enough to ensure that they can always be completed in the time between the door open event and the time the card is physically removed. This means that long multi-block write commands have to be avoided, despite the improved rate of data transfer they provide over shorter block transfers. It is very important that the phone provides a door mechanism and circuitry that gives early warning of potential card removal.

The controller is normally configured to implement a bus inactivity power-down scheme to save power. If the inactivity period elapses, then the controller automatically removes power from the cards. The length of this inactivity timeout period is set by the particular mobile phone.

As I said in Section 13.3.3.5, the local media sub-system does not initialize removable media devices as soon as they are inserted, but instead waits until the first request on the drive. Nevertheless, this request generally arrives almost immediately after card insertion, because applications receive notification of the disk insertion event from the file server and then interrogate the new card.

For MultiMediaCards, initialization involves applying bus power and then performing the card identification process. This entails issuing a series of broadcast and addressed commands over the bus, and is handled asynchronously by the controller. (All requests on the stack that involve bus activity are inherently long running operations that have to be handled asynchronously.) Initialization proceeds as follows.

First, the cards in the stack are reset, and then their operating voltage range is ascertained to ensure this is compatible with that of the host phone. The host reads the 128-bit unique ID that identifies each card. It then allocates each card a shorter Relative Card Address (RCA), which is used thereafter to address that card. Finally, the host reads back data from the card concerning its operating characteristics, to check that these are compatible with the host. Now the card is available for data transfer. This entire process is carried out in the first phase of drive mounting – before any media drivers are opened.

I/O drivers don't use the local media sub-system, and so they need to ensure that the bus is powered and the stack is initialized when they open. However, once an I/O driver has opened successfully, it doesn't need to bother about the card subsequently becoming powered down again. If the controller receives a data transfer request for a card that has been powered down due to a normal power down event it automatically applies power and initializes the stack first.

13.6 USB device support

13.6.1 USB overview

Universal Serial Bus (USB) is a bus standard for connecting peripheral and memory devices to a host computer. It supports hot insertion and removal of devices from the bus – devices may be attached or removed at any time. The bus consists of four signals: two carrying differential data and two carrying power to the USB device. The USB specification revision 2.0 defines three data rates:

Data rate	Data transfer rate
USB High Speed	Up to 480 Mbits/sec
USB Full Speed	12 Mbits/sec
Limited capability low speed	1.5 Mbits/sec

The USB system consists of a single host controller connected to a number of USB devices. The host includes an embedded root hub that provides one or more attachment points. The host is the bus master and initiates all data transfers over the bus. Each USB device passively responds to requests addressed to it by the host.

The host is often a desktop computer, but a supplement to the USB specification introduces a dual-role USB device. As well as being a normal USB device, this kind of device is also able to take on the role of a limited USB host, without the burden of having to support full USB host functionality. This is the On-The-Go (OTG) supplement aimed at portable devices.

Many USB devices implement just a single function – USB keyboards and data storage devices are examples of these – but multi-function devices are also possible. These are called composite devices, an example being a USB headset that combines a USB headphone and microphone. Likewise, although the functionality of most devices remains static, some devices can alter the USB function or functions they implement. A mobile phone is an example of this – it may use various different USB functions to exchange data with a host computer. Related USB devices that provide similar functionality are grouped into USB device classes, and standard protocols are defined to communicate with them. This means that a generic device class driver on the host machine can control any compliant device. Many classes are further subdivided into subclasses. The USB Implementers' Forum assigns unique codes to each class and subclass, and USB devices report these codes for each function they support. Examples of USB classes include the USB Mass Storage class for devices such as MultiMediaCard readers, and the Communications Device class for modem devices.

A USB device is made up of a collection of independent endpoints. An endpoint is the terminus of a communication flow between host and device that supports data flow in one direction. Each endpoint has its own particular transfer characteristics that dictate how it can be accessed. Four transfer types are defined:

Transfer type	Description
Bulk	Used for transferring large volumes of data that has no periodic or transfer rate requirements (for example, a printer device).
Control	Used to transfer specific requests to a USB device to configure it or to control aspects of its operation.
Isochronous	Used where a constant delivery rate is required (for example, an audio device). Given guaranteed access to USB bandwidth.
Interrupt	Used to poll devices that send or receive data infrequently, to determine if they are ready for the next data transfer.

Every USB device contains at least one input and one output control endpoint – both with endpoint number zero (ep0). The host uses this pair to initialize and control the device. Full speed devices can have a maximum of 15 input and 15 output endpoints, in addition to ep0. Each USB function on a device has an associated set of endpoints, and this set is known as an interface.

Before a device can be used, it must first be configured. This is the responsibility of the host, and is normally done when the device is first connected. In a process known as bus enumeration, the host requests information on the capabilities and requirements of the device. The data returned specifies the power requirements of the device. It also describes each interface, in terms of its class type, the endpoints it contains and the characteristics of each endpoint. This is the device configuration. Certain devices offer alternative configurations. This information is contained in a set of device descriptors – once more, these are not to be confused with Symbian OS descriptors! The host checks whether it can support the power and bandwidth requirements, and that it has a compatible class driver. It may also have to select the configuration of choice. The host is said to have configured the device by selecting and accepting a configuration.

An interface within a configuration may also have alternative settings that redefine the number of associated endpoints or the characteristics of these endpoints. In this case the host is also responsible for selecting the appropriate alternate setting.

A Symbian OS phone is unlikely to be configured as a standard USB host because such devices have to be able to supply a high current to power devices attached to the bus. Until now, most Symbian OS phones have been configured as USB devices and connected to a USB host computer. Classes supported by Symbian OS include the Abstract Control Model (ACM) modem interface – this is a subclass of the Communications Device Class (CDC) and provides serial communications over USB. It is used for backup, restore and data synchronization with a desktop computer. Another class Symbian OS supports is the Mass Storage class, which allows direct access to certain drives on the phone from the host computer.

We expect that Symbian OS OTG devices will be produced in the near future. These will be able to be used as host computers, interfacing with USB devices such as printers, video cameras and mass storage devices.

13.6.2   USB software architecture

The standard Symbian OS USB software architecture provides support for USB device (or client) functionality. Our implementation is designed to work with a hardware USB Device Controller (UDC). UDCs provide a set of endpoints of varying transfer type (bulk, control and so on), of varying direction (IN, OUT or bidirectional) and varying packet size. UDCs normally allow these endpoints to be grouped together into various different USB interfaces and configurations. This means that a single Symbian OS phone can be configured for different USB device functions so long as it contains the appropriate (device) class driver. This also means that as long as the UDC provides enough endpoints, the phone can be configured as a multi-function device.

Figure 13.13 shows an overview of the Symbian OS USB software architecture.

As an example, Figure 13.13 shows the setup for a phone configured as a combined Abstract Control Model (ACM) and mass-storage USB device. (However, when the host configures a device containing multiple functions, it enables each of these and requires a class driver for each. In practice, it can be difficult to obtain the corresponding composite host-side driver setup for this type of combined functionality.)

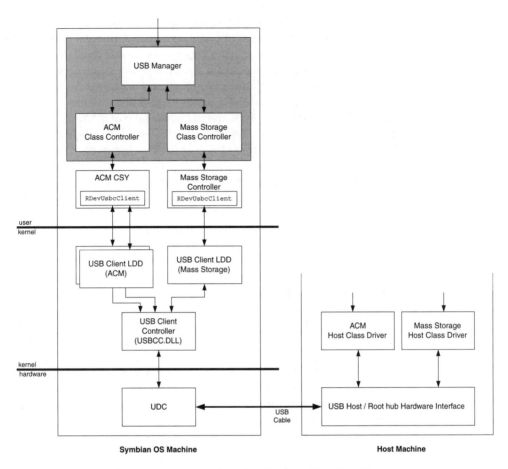

Figure 13.13 An overview of the Symbian OS USB architecture

The USB manager ensures the orderly startup and shutdown of all the USB classes on the Symbian phone, as well as allowing its clients to determine the status of these classes and to be informed of changes in the overall USB state. To this end, the USB Manager implements a class controller for each supported class on the device. A class controller provides the interface between the USB manager and the class implementation – but does not implement any class functionality itself.

USB class implementations normally exist in a separate thread from the USB manager. To gain access to the USB hardware (UDC), the USB class implementation must open a channel on the USB client device driver. The class `RDevUsbcClient` provides the user-side interface to this driver. Each channel supports only a single main USB interface (although it may support multiple alternate interfaces). This means that class implementations that use two or more main interfaces must open multiple channels.

Once a channel has been opened, the class implementation is able to read the USB capabilities of the phone to determine the total number of endpoints, their type, direction, maximum packet size, availability and so on. If the phone provides the required USB resources, and they are not already in use, the class implementation then sets up each USB interface by setting a class type and claiming its endpoints. All the channels automatically have access to ep0, and of course each of them can make a request on it. The other endpoints may only be used by a single channel, and can't be shared. Each channel may claim up to five endpoints as well as ep0.

The ACM class is implemented as a comms server (C32) plug-in, or CSY. Clients that wish to use this CSY do so via the C32 API. The ACM comprises two interfaces. The first is a communications interface consisting of an interrupt endpoint and a control endpoint (ep0) for transferring management information between host and device. The second is a data interface consisting of a pair of bulk endpoints (one IN, one OUT) – this acts like a legacy serial interface. This means that this class opens two channels on the USB client driver – one for each interface.

The mass storage controller provides the mass storage class implementation, which is built as a file system component (MSFS.FSY). It is implemented using the Bulk-Only Transport protocol (a protocol specific to USB) which provides a transport for the communication of standard SCSI Primary Commands (SPC) between host and device. This requires a single USB interface consisting of a pair of bulk endpoints (one IN, and one OUT) over which the majority of the communication takes places, and a control endpoint (ep0) to issue class-specific requests and clear stall conditions.

Each USB client LDD manages client requests over each endpoint and passes these on to the USB client controller. It also creates and manages the data buffers involved in transferring data to and from the UDC.

The USB client controller is a kernel extension that manages requests from each of the channels and controls the hardware UDC. It is divided into a platform-independent layer (PIL) and a platform-specific layer (PSL).

This architecture allows the current USB function (or functions) of the phone to be changed without the need to physically remove the USB cable or restart the phone. The USB manager allows classes to be started or stopped, and doing so will result in new USB interfaces being setup or existing ones released. The USB driver API also supports the simulated removal and insertion of the cable (so long as the hardware interface does too). However, the host assumes that once a device has been enumerated, the functions described will be available until disconnection. The host is also unable to discover new classes that are started after enumeration. This means that the host sees such changes in USB function as the removal of one device and the attachment of a different one, which causes it to re-enumerate. This terminates any active USB communication.

The software architecture I have described supports only Full Speed USB 2.0 device functionality – not USB Host or OTG. Neither does it support USB High Speed.

The kernel-side components and the UDC handle the USB device protocol layer, whereas the various class implementers handle the USB device side of the class layers. The next section concentrates on the device protocol layer implementation.

13.6.3   USB client controller and LDD

Figure 13.14 shows part of the class diagram for the USB client controller and LDD.

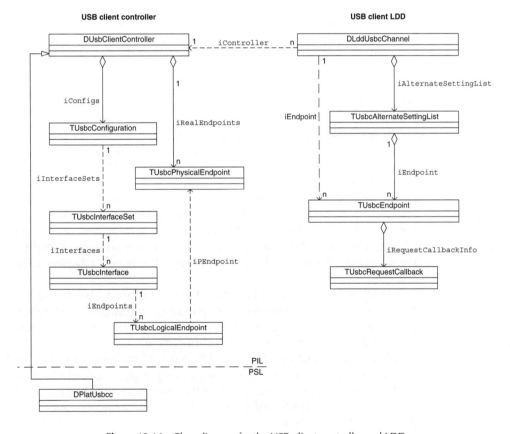

Figure 13.14   Class diagram for the USB client controller and LDD

13.6.3.1   The USB controller

DUsbClientController is a singleton that embodies the USB device
controller; it is an abstract class that defines the interface between the PIL
and the PSL. Each platform provides a derived controller object, shown as
DPlatUsbcc on the diagram, which handles USB functionality specific
to the platform UDC – such as the management of data transfer over an
endpoint. Use of DMA is recommended for USB transfers, and the PSL
handles all aspects of DMA data transfer.

The main role of the controller is the handling of packets on ep0,
and the relaying of LDD read and write transfer requests from the other
endpoints. The PIL part of the controller processes and responds to all
standard USB device requests, (as described in chapter 9 of the *Universal
Serial Bus Specification Revision 2.0*[1]) – if they are not already handled
by the UDC hardware itself.

The controller also creates and manages the USB descriptor pool (or
database). Descriptors contain information about the properties of specific
parts of the USB device in a well-defined format, and they are propagated
to the host – normally during enumeration. The USB client API allows
class implementers to specify and alter many of the elements of each
different type of descriptor as well as to add class-specific descriptors.
However to preserve the USB device's integrity, the controller creates
other parts of the descriptors itself and clients of the controller cannot
alter these.

The class TUsbcPhysicalEndpoint is the abstraction for a physical
endpoint present on the device. At system boot time, the controller creates
an instance of this class for each endpoint that the UDC supports – and
these are never destroyed. The controller class owns these objects and
holds them in the array iRealEndpoints. An endpoint capabilities
class is associated with the TUsbcPhysicalEndpoint class (this is
not shown on the diagram). This class stores information on the set
of endpoint types, directions and maximum packet sizes supported by
the endpoint. Physical endpoints are used at the interface between PIL
and PSL.

The TUsbcConfiguration object encapsulates a USB configuration. The Symbian OS USB client API only supports a single configuration
per device and so the controller owns just one instance of this class,
iConfigs, which it creates at system boot time.

As I mentioned earlier, Symbian OS supports multiple interfaces (or
USB functions) within this single configuration. It also supports alternate
USB interfaces – so an interface within the configuration may have alternative settings, each potentially having differing numbers of endpoints or
differing endpoint characteristics.

---

[1] *Universal Serial Bus Specification Revision 2.0*, www.usb.org

To accommodate multiple interfaces, the configuration object manages an array of TUsbcInterfaceSet objects, iInterfaceSets. Each set object corresponds to an individual main interface within the configuration. It is called an interface set because, for interfaces with alternative settings, this object represents the set of alternative interfaces supported. A configuration consisting of a single main interface has just a single interface set object. Each set object is created when the associated LDD client requests a first interface on the channel (which might be the first of a number of alternative settings) and destroyed when the last setting is released. Remember that there can only be one main interface (and therefore one interface set) per channel.

The interface set manages an array of TUsbcInterface objects: iInterfaces. Each interface object encapsulates one of the alternate interface settings. For interfaces without alternative settings, only a single instance of this class is created. For interfaces that do have alternative settings, the associated set object keeps track of the current alternative setting. A TUsbcInterface object is created each time an LDD client is successful in requesting an interface and destroyed when that setting is released again.

Associated with each TUsbcInterface object is a group of endpoint objects that make up (or belong to) that interface setting. However, these are logical endpoint objects – TUsbcLogicalEndpoint. An interface may claim up to a maximum of five endpoints in addition to ep0. Each is locally numbered between one and five and the LDD client uses this number to identify an endpoint when it issues requests. This number need not correspond to the actual endpoint number of the UDC. (LDD clients can discover the physical endpoint address of a logical endpoint by requesting the endpoint descriptor for the endpoint). When an interface is being created, the controller is supplied with the details of each of the endpoints required by the client. It scans through the list of physical endpoints, searching for ones that are available and that have matching capabilities. Obviously, interface setting can only succeed if the search is successful for all endpoints specified within the interface. If successful, a TUsbcLogicalEndpoint instance is created for each – and this has the same lifetime as the associated interface object. TUsbcLogicalEndpoint holds information on endpoint transfer type, direction and maximum packet size together with a pointer to its corresponding physical endpoint object, iPEndpoint.

13.6.3.2   *The USB client LDD*

The class DLddUsbcChannel is the USB client LDD channel object – an instance being created for each main interface that is set on the UDC. It is derived from logical channel base class DLogicalChannel – which means that channel requests are executed in the context of a kernel thread. A DFC queue is associated with the controller object, and this determines which kernel thread is used to process these requests. It is set on a per-platform basis, with the default being DFC thread 0. The channel owns an instance of the `TUsbcAlternateSettingList` class for each alternative setting that exists for the interface, `iAlternateSettingList`. In turn, each alternative setting object owns an instance of the `TUsbcEndpoint` class for each endpoint that it contains, apart from ep0. Instead, the channel owns the `TUsbcEndpoint` instance for ep0 and also maintains a pointer to each of the endpoint objects for the current alternate interface via `DLddUsbcChannel::iEndpoint`. An important function of the `TUsbcEndpoint` class is to manage the buffers used for data transfer. However, the channel object owns these buffers since they are shared with other endpoints in the interface.

Up to three hardware memory chunks, each containing physically contiguous RAM pages, are allocated to every channel object, and these chunks are each divided into separate buffers for use during data transfers. All IN endpoints (that is, ones which transfer data back to the host) share one chunk, OUT endpoints share the second, and the third is used for ep0. These chunks are created when an interface is first set on the channel. The size of chunk for ep0 is fixed, containing four 1024-byte buffers. However, fairly obviously, the size of the IN and OUT chunks depends on the number of IN and OUT endpoints that are included in the interface. The number of buffers created for each of these endpoints is fixed, but the size of the buffers is configurable by the LDD client, using bandwidth priority arguments specified when setting an interface. A single buffer is created for each IN endpoint and four buffers are created for each OUT endpoint. The default buffer size for Bulk IN is 4 KB, and for Bulk OUT it is 4 KB too. We have selectable OUT endpoint buffer sizes for performance reasons – large buffer sizes are recommended for high bandwidth data transfers. Since different alternate interfaces may specify different groups of endpoints and different buffer sizes, the chunks often have to be reallocated each time the LDD client sets a different alternative interface. (The chunk size finally used is the maximum of each alternate setting's requirements.)

The `TUsbcRequestCallback` class encapsulates an LDD transfer request. It holds data specifying the request, together with a DFC that the controller uses to call back the LDD when transfer completes. The `TUsbcEndpoint` class owns a request object, `iRequestCallbackInfo`, which it uses to issue requests to the controller. A channel can have asynchronous requests outstanding on all of its endpoints at once, and this includes ep0. Since ep0 is shared with other channels, the client controller has to manage multiple requests on the same endpoint.

13.6.4 The mass storage file system

This is quite different from any other file system. It contains null implementations of the file system API described in Section 9.4.1, and, when it is mounted on a drive, that drive is inaccessible from the Symbian OS device. Instead, the desktop host computer is allowed exclusive block level access to the drive. The mass storage file system implements the mass storage controller function that I introduced in Section 13.6.2, which involves the handling of SCSI commands received from the host via a USB client device driver channel. The file server is not involved in the processing of the commands. Instead they are processed entirely by the mass storage controller. Being a file system component, it has access to the media device concerned via the local drive interface class, TBusLocalDrive. You should note that if the drive has a file server extension mounted on it (for example a NAND drive with the flash translation layer implemented in a file server extension), then all media accesses are routed through the extension. This allows Symbian OS to support a mass storage connection to a NAND flash drive, as well as to a normal FAT drive. Only FAT-formatted drives may be connected as mass storage drives. Drives C: or Z: cannot be connected, because these must always be accessible to the rest of the OS.

The mass storage file system is not normally loaded automatically during file server startup. Instead, a USB mass storage application (a component provided by the phone manufacturer) loads it later, and also mounts the file system on a particular drive. However, before it does this, the application has to dismount the FAT file system from that drive. This can only happen if there are no file or directory resources open on the drive. This may mean that the application has to request that the user shuts down certain applications that have these resources open.

Once the mass storage connection is terminated, the same application is responsible for dismounting the mass storage file system and re-mounting the FAT file system again.

Figure 13.15 shows the two configurations of a NAND drive configured for mass storage connection. The first configuration shows it mounted and accessible from a Symbian OS device. The second shows it disconnected from the Symbian OS device, with a host computer accessing the drive.

Granting direct access to a drive on the Symbian OS phone from a host machine poses a security threat. To counter this, all drives available for mass storage connection are subject to the same restrictions as removable drives. For instance, installed binaries on the mass storage drive could be altered while the desktop computer is remotely accessing the drive. So we need tamper evidence to detect if the contents of these binary files have been altered since they were known to be safe, at install time. Section 8.5.2.3 covers this in a little more detail.

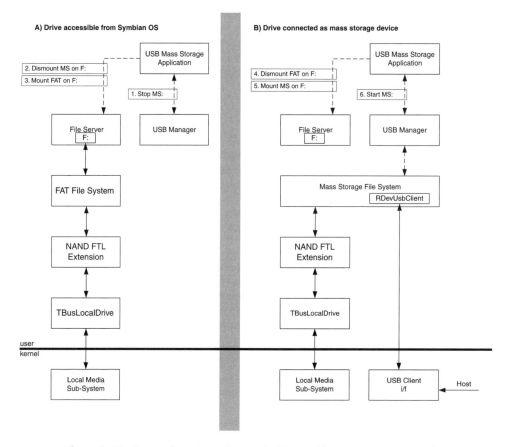

Figure 13.15   Two configurations of a NAND drive used for mass storage connection

13.7   Summary

In this chapter, I began by describing two more of the services available to
device drivers and peripheral bus controllers: DMA and shared chunks.
I went on to describe media drivers and the local media sub-system.
Then I examined peripheral bus controllers – looking specifically at the
MultiMediaCard controller as an example. Finally, I introduced the kernel-
side components of the USB software architecture and the USB mass
storage file system. In the next chapter, I will describe debugging in the
Symbian OS environment.

14

Kernel-Side Debug

by Morgan Henry

A computer lets you make more mistakes faster than any invention in human history-with the possible exceptions of handguns and tequila.

Mitch Ratcliffe

This chapter describes how the Symbian kernel architecture supports a range of debuggers and other useful development tools. It describes the types of tools available for development of kernel and application level software, and how the kernel implements and interacts with them.

The reader should be familiar with EKA2's device driver model, memory model and scheduler.

14.1 Overview

The emulator provides the primary development environment for Symbian OS (see Figure 14.1). For most application and middleware development, the behavior of the emulator is sufficiently close to the behavior of Symbian OS on retail handsets to allow us to develop the majority of our software inside this environment.

As I described in Chapter 1, *Introducing EKA2*, we have made several improvements to the design of the emulator in EKA2. It now shares a significant amount of code with the kernel, nanokernel and scheduler. As a result, the emulator is a much more faithful representation of the behavior of the kernel on a target phone. This has made the EKA2 emulator suitable for the development of some types of kernel-side software, even including the development of device drivers that are not sensitive to the underlying hardware.

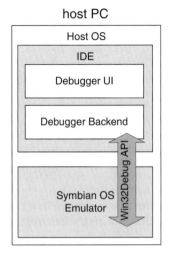

Figure 14.1   Emulator debug architecture

However, even with these improvements, there are occasions when application and kernel developers will need to move out of the emulated environment, and into a hardware environment. This is necessary for:

- Development of hardware-specific device drivers

- Diagnosis of defects that stubbornly appear only on a target mobile phone

- Software that is timing sensitive

- Software with dependencies on exotic peripherals only found on mobile phones.

Where the emulator can no longer assist you with your debugging tasks, EKA2 provides features to support debug on target hardware.

EKA2 is architected to support remote debuggers. The design aims were to provide direct kernel support for as much of the embedded tools market as possible, whilst remaining vendor independent. The new interface builds on experience with EKA1 phones, hopefully easing the integration task faced by those providing new tools.

The APIs described in this chapter provide operating system support for a number of debug tools:

- Emulator debugger for hardware agnostic application and middleware development

- Run-mode, target resident debuggers primarily focused on debugging applications, middleware, real-time and hardware-sensitive software.

- Hardware assisted stop-mode debuggers, primarily focused on debugging the kernel, device drivers and other kernel-mode software

- Post-mortem debuggers

- Trace output

- Profilers.

But first, let's look at how EKA2's architecture supports debugging.

14.2 Architecture

Debuggers need much more information, and much more control over the kernel than any other piece of software. This section describes how the Symbian OS kernel and each of the tools that I just listed interact with each other.

14.2.1 Emulator debuggers

In the emulator world, both the debugger IDE and Symbian OS are citizens of the host PC operating system. As I described in Chapter 1, *Introducing EKA2*, each Symbian OS thread maps onto a native Win32 thread – this allows the IDE to treat Symbian OS just like any other Win32 application. To observe and control Symbian OS threads, the debugger attaches to them by using the native Win32 debug APIs. While attached, the debugger will be notified of any events that affect the thread, such as breakpoints or termination. Both Symbian OS kernel and application threads can be debugged in this way. While it is attached, the emulator debugger has complete control over the execution of Symbian OS threads.

This method of debugging is extremely powerful, since existing state-of-the-art Windows development tools can be used to debug Symbian OS. This makes it an attractive development environment for much hardware-agnostic software.

14.2.2 Run-mode debuggers

The type of target debugger most familiar to application and middleware developers is the remote "run-mode" debugger (Figure 14.2). The debugger UI runs on a host PC, and controls threads running on a target operating system through a proxy running remotely on the target mobile

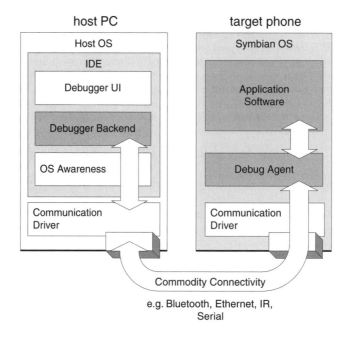

Figure 14.2   Run-mode debug architecture

phone. Debuggers with this "remote debug" capability are common in the embedded technology industry.

In the Symbian environment, the host PC runs a debugger, which connects to the target phone running Symbian OS. The connection is over any common communications channel supported by Symbian OS, such as serial, Bluetooth, IR, USB or Ethernet.

The host debugger talks to a remote debug agent, running on Symbian OS, which performs actions on its behalf. It is the debug agent that directly observes and manipulates the application threads being debugged by the host. The debug agent will also report any information it believes is relevant for the debugging session back to the host. To reduce the number of information and event messages sent over the communications link, the host debugger will typically elect to observe and control only a few threads. The debug agent will report only those events and data that affect these attached threads.

The debugger remains mostly transparent to the rest of the system. This has the benefit that protocol stacks, timing-dependent software, and any software interacting with the real world environment will continue to function as normal during a debug session. This makes this type of debugger attractive to third-party application and middleware developers. However, these debuggers are not generally suitable for kernel or device driver development. In this architecture, the debug agent and the communication channel are directly, and indirectly, clients of the Symbian

OS kernel. Any attempt by the debugger to suspend parts of the kernel would result in a hung system, making the agent and communication channel inoperable.

The remainder of this section examines the components of the run-mode debug architecture in more detail. Figure 14.3 shows how the debugger communicates with its remote debug agent, and how the agent interacts with Symbian OS.

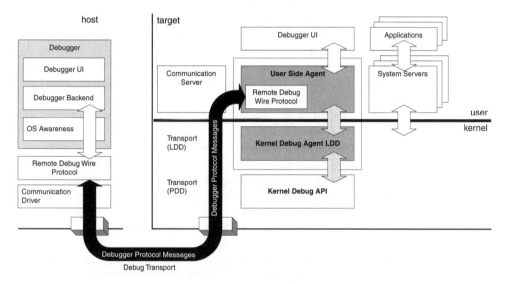

Figure 14.3   Host debugger and debug agent on target platform

14.2.2.1   *Remote debug wire protocol*

The backbone of this debugger environment is the remote debug wire protocol. This carries debug messages between the host debugger and the target, over the physical connection. The flow of these high-level protocol messages is shown in black on the diagram. The debugger communicates with the target to acquire information about threads and processes running on the target. It typically asks the target to perform thread- or process-relative memory reads and writes, control the execution flow of threads, and set/remove breakpoints. The target will also notify the debugger of interesting events occurring on the mobile phone.

14.2.2.2   *Debug agent*

An essential component of this communication is the debug agent running on the target. This component translates the debugger's messages in the wire protocol into actions and requests for the Symbian OS kernel. (These are shown with cross-hatching.) The agent is a privileged client of the operating system, and encapsulates a significant amount of the "OS awareness" on behalf of the host debugger.

The debug agent comes in two parts. The kernel-side agent is tightly bound into the kernel via the kernel debugger API to give it the level of control and information it requires. The API (covered in Section 14.3) allows the agent to capture system events, suspend and resume threads, get and set thread context, shadow ROM, read and write to non-current processes, and discover information about code segments, libraries, and other kernel objects. The user-side agent implements the wire protocol and is responsible for setting up the communication channel. It can do this by talking to the comms server or by opening a channel to the communications driver directly. It is also a client of the file server for the upload and download of files into the file system. On phones that enforce platform security, it will also need to negotiate with the software install components to install uploaded executables. The debug agent may also use other APIs and servers.

The two parts communicate over the standard (RBusLogicalChannel) device driver interface – see Chapter 12, *Device Drivers and Extensions*, for more on this. Symbian does *not* define a common API here, because the functionality provided by the agent is largely dependent on the tool or wire protocol in use. (EKA1 does provide a debugger interface (RDebug), however, this proved not to be widely adopted, and is only really suitable for the GDB monitor, "GDBSTUB".)

There are a number of debugger wire protocols available. At the time of writing, the following implementations exist for Symbian OS:

- GDBSTUB implements the open GNU remote debug wire protocol on EKA1

- MetroTrk implements the Metrowerks proprietary protocol on EKA1

- MetroTrk implements the Metrowerks proprietary protocol on EKA2.

14.2.2.3   *OS awareness*

On the host side, the debugger's OS awareness module interprets any operating system specific information for the rest of the debugger. This module is the host-side partner of the debug agent for Symbian OS – it encapsulates any methods and implementations that the debugger needs to communicate effectively with the target platform and that are not part of the core debugger. This could include items such as:

- Establishing a connection to the target

- Discovering which processor core is being debugged

- Discovering which version of the OS is available

- Defining which OS specific objects should be displayed as part of the OS object visualization.

The OS awareness module is an intrinsic part of the debugger-OS integration package and is usually supplied with the IDE.

14.2.2.4 Responsibilities

In this architecture the agent has the following responsibilities:

- Implementation of high-level wire protocol. It must provide an implementation of the protocol that matches the host debugger in use. For example, GDB uses the GNU remote debug wire protocol

- Configuring the debug connection. The agent must open and configure the communication channel to enable the connection to the host. For example, it should configure the serial port, or open a TCP/IP connection. For convenience, it may also provide a UI

- Uploading files and executables onto the target. Executables are built on the host PC and must be uploaded to the mobile phone for execution. Supplementary data files also need to be transferred. On a secure build of Symbian OS, the debug agent must use software install components to install the executable. The debugger may choose to use commercial PC connectivity software

- Implementation of CPU instruction stepping, and instruction decode. This is a fundamental capability of any debugger. The agent can implement instruction stepping of a suspended thread in a couple of ways: firstly, through software simulation of the instruction at the program counter, or secondly, by placing a temporary breakpoint at the next program-counter target address and resuming the thread. The agent must identify potential branches, which requires an instruction decode

- Capturing user-thread panics, and exceptions. Knowing that an application has died is essential for a developer. The debug agent registers with the kernel to receive notification when a thread panics, causes an exception, or otherwise terminates. When notified, the debugger can open the thread for diagnosis and relay the information to the developer

- Implementation of JIT debug triggers. ''Just In Time'' debugging catches a thread just *before* it executes a panic or exception routine. Capturing a thread early, before it is terminated, allows the developer to more closely inspect what went wrong, before the kernel removes the thread. In some cases, the developer can modify context, program counter, and variables to recover the thread

- Implementation of software breakpoint handler. Software breakpoints are implemented as undefined instructions. The agent must register to capture undefined exception events, and then handle any that are actually breakpoints. If the breakpoint is intended to be thread-specific, the handler must check the ID of a triggered thread against the breakpoint's intended target – if it does not match, then the thread should be resumed. If the breakpoint is placed in shared code, then there are further complications – the agent must implement an algorithm for efficiently handling multiple false triggers from untargeted threads. The agent must also be able to resume a thread that was incorrectly triggered without missing further valid triggers – that is, it must be able to execute the instruction under the breakpoint for the current thread without removing the breakpoint

- Breakpoint housekeeping. Add and remove breakpoints as libraries and processes are loaded and unloaded. For the developer's convenience, the debugger often makes it possible to set breakpoints in code that is not yet loaded. The debug agent defers the application of the breakpoint until the OS loads the target code. The agent can do this by registering to be notified of library and process load events. The agent is also responsible for shadowing ROM code to allow breakpoint instructions to be written

- Communicating addresses of code and process data to host. For executable to source-code association to work effectively, the host must relocate the executable's symbolic debug information to match the memory address of the corresponding code and data on the target. The debug agent must discover where the kernel has loaded each executable section and relay this to the debugger.

14.2.3   Hardware-assisted debuggers

Many debuggers in the embedded world provide support for ASICs equipped with JTAG ICE hardware.

The Joint Test Action Group defined and established the IEEE 1149.1 standard for boundary-scan hardware test and diagnostics. This standard is commonly referred to as JTAG. The interface has since been adopted as a popular access port for CPU control to support software debugging activities using the embedded In-Circuit Emulator (ICE) common on ARM hardware.

The ICE allows the target processor to be halted and subsequently controlled by the host at the instruction level. This provides features such as instruction level step, hardware breakpoint support, remote memory reads and writes, and CPU register manipulation. The JTAG port can also provide an additional real-time data channel for a debugger protocol (Figure 14.4).

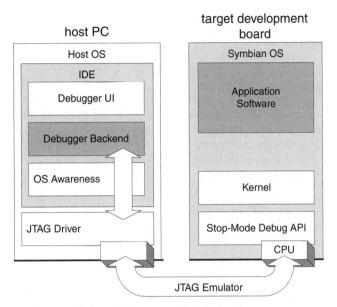

Figure 14.4 Stop-mode debug architecture

The host side runs a debugger with the ability to drive a connection to a JTAG emulator, such as ARM's RealView ICE, Lauterbach's ICD, and so on.

A hardware-assisted debugger will work adequately with Symbian OS with almost no additional support, just as it would with many other OSes. The debugger can immediately provide raw CPU/instruction level debugging and an unvarnished view of the current memory map.

This low-level view of the target can be improved when the debugger implements "OS aware" features. The host provides the necessary Symbian OS intelligence to interpret the simple memory and register read/write semantics of JTAG as high-level operating-system events, messages and objects. To assist the host in this task, the stop-mode debug API on the target provides metadata describing the layout of key kernel objects. Using this metadata, the host debugger can navigate the kernel's data structures to determine the current state of the kernel and all running applications.

The host then interprets this information and presents it to the developer in a meaningful manner to provide the following high-level debug functionality:

- Thread-relative memory read and writes
- Thread-relative breakpoints
- Multi-process and memory model awareness
- Kernel object display.

Using this approach, some tools vendors can support integrated stop-mode kernel and stop-mode application debugging.

The ability to halt the processor makes a hardware-assisted debugger an essential tool for debugging kernels, device drivers, and any other kernel-mode software that requires a significant amount of hardware "bit-twiddling". However, while the debugger holds the CPU, it has limited usefulness for debugging real-time software and live communication stacks. Once the CPU has been halted, the real-time protocols that interact with the outside world will invariably fall over.

Figure 14.5 shows the interactions between the host debugger, the stop-mode debug API, and the kernel in more detail.

While the host debugger has control of the target CPU, the target is not running any kernel or application code; the CPU is frozen. Because of this, and in contrast to run-mode debuggers, there is little opportunity for a target-side debug agent to run, and no high-level wire protocol. The interface between the host debugger and target has only "simple" or "flat" register and memory read/write semantics (shown in black). Compared to the run-mode architecture, the host side debugger must encapsulate a far greater amount of knowledge about how to interact with Symbian OS. The host must understand:

- Scheduling and kernel locking strategy

- Per-process memory mapping

- How the kernel lays out its data structures.

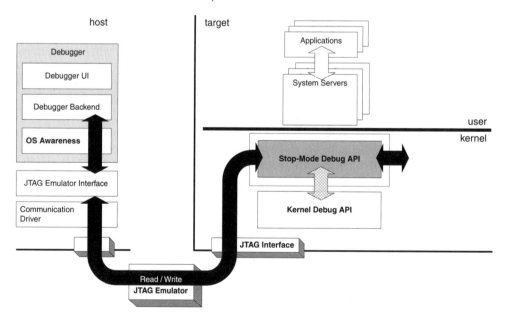

Figure 14.5 Stop-mode debugger architecture

Most modern stop-mode development tools have a generic OS abstraction and can support this host-side requirement.

The stop-mode debug API is responsible for ensuring all the information the debugger requires is available and valid. It presents metadata encapsulating the layout of the kernel's objects (such as processes, threads and memory chunks). The kernel continually updates the content while the target is running (shown with cross-hatching). This ensures that the metadata is consistent and valid whenever the data is required.

Hardware-assisted debuggers make effective post-mortem analysis tools. Even after a full system crash, much of the kernel data is intact, and can be inspected through the stop-mode debug API.

Section 14.5 shows in detail how the Symbian OS debugger architecture supports hardware-assisted debuggers.

14.2.4   Post-mortem analysis tools

Under Symbian OS, we use post-mortem tools to analyze the cause of crashes and hangs after software has failed. The analysis can apply to specific executables, or to whole-system crashes. The tool is dormant on the target, waiting for a trigger from the operating system indicating abnormal termination. In response to this trigger, the tool will gather information from the kernel and system servers about the crash to present to the debugger. Some tools (for example, `D_EXC` and the crash logger) save a human-readable context dump to a file that can be analyzed off the phone. Others (for example, the crash debugger) are interactive, and allow the developer to interrogate the host over a communications link.

The debug API provides triggers and hooks for various system events, on which to hang the post-mortem analysis tools. Code can be installed and run on events such as: hardware exceptions, thread death, kernel death and trace output.

For more details, see the documentation for `TEventCode` in the Symbian Developer Library's C++ component reference section.

Usage information for the previously mentioned crash debugger post-mortem tool can be found in the Symbian Developer Library Device Driver Guide for EKA2 versions of Symbian OS.

Figure 14.6 shows the details of the post-mortem tool on the target. You can see that this architecture is similar to the run-mode architecture, with the host PC side omitted. In fact, the set of kernel interfaces used by both tool-types are largely the same. In the post-mortem case, the kernel-side agent uses the kernel debug API to register with kernel events associated with thread termination. The user-side agent is responsible for outputting the information over a communications channel or to disk.

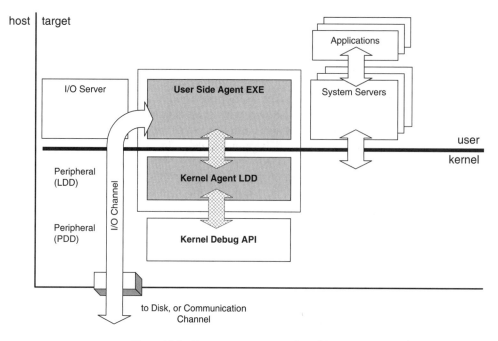

Figure 14.6   Target post-mortem tools architecture

A good example of this architecture is the D_EXC tool. This implements a minimal kernel debug agent (MINKDA) and a user-side agent (D_EXC). Source code for these tools is available at these locations:

```
\base\e32utils\d_exc\d_exc.cpp
\base\e32utils\d_exc\minkda.cpp
```

14.2.4.1   *Analyzing post-mortem dump*

To save ROM, the Symbian OS build tools strip symbolic debug information from all executables before they reach the mobile phone. This means that the post-mortem tools on the target have very little contextual information to annotate the crash dump. This can be a particular problem when attempting to read stack traces. To solve this, Symbian provides tools for the host that match up addresses found in the post-mortem dump and the symbolic debug information on the host.

MAKSYM is a command-line tool that cross-references the log file generated when building a ROM image with the verbose linker output that contains the executable symbols. The output is a text file that lists the address of every global and exported function in the ROM. This file can be used to interpret addresses found in post-mortem dumps. MAKSYM symbolic output is essential for diagnosing problems when using the crash logger or crash debugger. Similarly, two other tools – PRINTSYM and PRINTSTK – use the MAKSYM symbolic output to interpret D_EXC output. More information on using these tools can be found in the Symbian Developer Library.

14.3 The kernel debug interface

Debug tools will use many of the general purpose APIs provided by the kernel. In addition, we provide the kernel debug interface to specifically support the remaining requirements of all these tools. In this section, I will describe the features of the kernel debug interface, namely:

- Kernel event notification

- Thread context API

- Code and data section information

- Shadowing ROM pages.

Other features typically used by debug tools are:

- Kernel resource tracking (kernel object API)

- Thread-relative memory read and write.

Kernel objects and the kernel object containers are covered in Section 5.1, and I describe thread-relative memory access for the moving and multiple memory models in Chapter 7, *Memory Models.*

The kernel debug functionality is optional, since you will not always want to allow intrusive debug tools onto production mobile phones. The__DEBUGGER_SUPPORT__ macro enables the kernel features required specifically for a debugger implementation. You'll find this defined (or not) in the variant MMH file. (The project definition files for the variant are typically named \base\<variant>\variant.mmh. See \base\lubbock\variant.mmh for an example.) You can check at run-time if your build of the kernel includes these features by calling.

```
TBool DKernelEventHandler::DebugSupportEnabled();
```

By default, software and ROM images supplied on the Symbian OS DevK-its are built with debug support enabled. However, phone manufacturers may choose to switch it off.

14.3.1 Kernel event notification

The kernel exposes an API to allow a debug agent to track kernel activity, and if necessary respond to it. We chose the events exposed through this API to allow the most important features of a debug agent to be implemented. Of course, other kernel-side software can use them too.

The following events can be captured:

- User-side software exceptions, occurring when the user thread calls `User::Panic` or `RThread::RaiseException()`. Typically on ARM processors, the latter will be caused by an integer divide by zero exception. Debuggers will report the exception or panic details to the developer for diagnosis. Post-mortem tools can also trigger on these events to save context for later analysis

- Hardware exceptions: for example, code aborts, data aborts, invalid instruction, memory access violation and floating-point co-processor divide by zero. These are obviously very important in aiding the developer with her diagnosis. It is also often possible for the developer to use the debugger to alter thread context and variables to re-try the instruction. Importantly, software breakpoints are commonly implemented as undefined instructions – the debug agent uses the hardware exception event to implement the breakpoint handler

- Thread scheduled for the first time. The run-mode debug agent uses this event to apply any uncommitted thread-specific breakpoints that apply. Deferring the breakpoint commit is especially useful if the breakpoint is in shared code where false triggers may cause noticeable performance degradation

- Kernel object updates. When a process, thread or library is created or destroyed, or a process's attributes are updated, an event is generated. (Process attribute changes can be caused by a name change, or a chunk being added or removed from the process.) Debuggers, more than most other software, care about what code is running on the mobile phone. The debug agent often uses these notifications for housekeeping tasks: process and library creation events are indications that new code has been loaded to the phone, which the debug tool may like to annotate or commit breakpoints to

- Thread object updates. These happen when a thread terminates, or thread attributes are updated (always a thread name change). These events are usually reported to the developer for information

- Chunk object updates. These happen when a chunk is created or destroyed, or memory is committed or de-committed from a chunk, or a chunk's size is adjusted: for example, creating a thread or a heap, or calling `RChunk::Create()`. A stop-mode debugger closely monitors the memory mappings created by the kernel. To avoid crashing the target while it is halted, it must be certain that addresses it is attempting to access are actually mapped in. Other debug tools may also present this information to the developer

- Code objects. These events happen when a user-side library (DLL) is loaded, closed or unloaded, or code segments are loaded or unloaded: for example, using `RLibrary::Load()`, `RProcess::Create()` or `RLibrary::Close()`. As I mentioned earlier, library events are indications that new code has been loaded or unloaded to the phone. The debug tool may like to take this opportunity to annotate or commit breakpoints in the new code

- Device drivers are loaded or unloaded, using APIs such as `User::LoadLogicalDevice()`

- User-side trace output – this indicates that `RDebug::Print()` has been called. Debuggers and tracing tools may want to capture calls to the trace port to allow the string to be redirected to an alternative output channel. (See Section 14.6 for more on this.)

14.3.1.1   Kernel events reference documentation

A detailed description of each event can be found in the Symbian Developer Library's C++ component reference section, and in the source for `TKernelEvent` in `kernel\kernel.h`. A summary is provided here:

TKernelEvent	Meaning
EEventSwExc	The current user-side thread has taken a software exception, (`User::RaiseException()`). The exception type is provided as the first argument to the handler. `NKern::UnlockSystem()` has been called by the kernel. The current thread can be discovered from `Kern::CurrentThread()`. (See Chapter 6, *Interrupts and Exceptions*, for more on exceptions.)
EEventHwExc	The current thread has taken a hardware exception. A pointer to the structure on the stack containing the thread context is the passed as the first argument. This structure is CPU specific. For the ARM processor the structure is `TArmExcInfo`. This pointer has the same value as returned by `DThread::Context()`. (Again, see Chapter 6, *Interrupts and Exceptions*, for more on exceptions.)
EEventAddProcess	Event delivered when a process is created (that is, during a call to `RProcess::Create` or `Kern::ProcessCreate`).

`TKernelEvent`	**Meaning**
	Argument 1 points to the process being created. Argument 2 points to the creator thread (which may not be the current thread). In some cases, the creator thread cannot be reliably determined and this will be set to NULL. The process being created is partly constructed (and has no threads and no chunks). The event is triggered just after creation.
`EEventUpdateProcess`	Event delivered after a process attribute change. Currently this applies only to process renaming and a change to the address space through chunk addition/removal, though we may extend it in the future. Argument 1 points to the process being modified. The process lock may be held. The event is triggered just after the name change, just after a chunk is added, or just before a chunk removal.
`EEventRemoveProcess`	Event delivered when a process terminates. The first argument points to the process (`DProcess`) being terminated. The current thread is the kernel server thread. The process is partly destructed, so its resources should be accessed only after checking they still exist.
`EEventLoadedProcess`	Event delivered immediately after a process is created (that is, during a call to `RProcess::Create` or `Kern::ProcessCreate`). Argument 1 points to the process. The process being created is fully constructed.
`EEventUnloadingProcess`	Event delivered when a process is being released, but before its code segment, stack chunk and so on are unmapped. Argument 1 points to the process. The process being released is fully constructed.
`EEventAddThread`	Event delivered when a user or kernel thread is created (that is, during a call to `RProcess::Create`, `RThread::Create` or `Kern::ThreadCreate`). The thread being created is fully constructed but has not executed any code yet.

`TKernelEvent`	Meaning
	Argument 1 points to the thread being created. Argument 2 points to the creator thread (which may not be the current thread).
`EEventStartThread`	Event delivered when a user or kernel thread is scheduled for the first time. The thread has not executed any code yet. The current thread is the thread being scheduled. Argument 1 points to the thread being scheduled.
`EEventUpdateThread`	Event delivered after a thread attribute change. Currently this applies only to thread renaming but we may extend it in the future. Argument 1 points to the thread being modified.
`EEventKillThread`	Event delivered when a user or kernel thread terminates. The current thread and argument 1 is the thread being terminated. This is in the `ECSExitInProgress` state, and so cannot be suspended. The thread's address space can be inspected.
`EEventRemoveThread`	Event delivered when a user or kernel thread is about to be closed. The current thread is the kernel thread. Argument 1 points to the thread being terminated. The thread is partly destructed so its resources should be accessed only after checking if they still exist.
`EEventNewChunk`	Event delivered when a chunk is created. Argument 1 points to the chunk being created.
`EEventUpdateChunk`	Event delivered when physical memory is committed to or released from a chunk. Argument 1 points to the chunk being modified.
`EEventDeleteChunk`	Event delivered when a chunk is deleted. Pointer to the chunk is provided as an argument.
`EEventAddLibrary`	Event delivered when a user-side DLL is explicitly loaded.

`TKernelEvent`	Meaning
	Argument 1 points to the `DLibrary` instance being loaded. Argument 2 points to the creator thread. `DLibrary::iMapCount` is equal to 1 if the DLL is loaded for the first time into the creator thread's address space. If the DLL is being loaded for the first time, any global constructors haven't been called yet. The DLL and all its dependencies have been mapped. The system-wide mutex `DCodeSeg::CodeSegLock` is held.
`EEventRemoveLibrary`	Event delivered when a previously explicitly loaded user-side DLL is closed or unloaded (that is, a call to `RLibrary::Close`). Argument 1 points to the `DLibrary` instance being unloaded. `DLibrary::iMapCount` is equal to 0 if the DLL is about to be unloaded. If the DLL is about to be unloaded, its global destructors have been called but it is still mapped (and so are its dependencies). The system-wide mutex `DCodeSeg::CodeSeg-Lock` is held when this event is triggered.
`EEventAddCodeSeg`	Event delivered when a code segment is mapped into a process. Argument 1 points to the code segment, and argument 2 points to the owning process. The system-wide mutex `DCodeSeg::CodeSegLock` is held.
`EEventRemoveCodeSeg`	Event delivered when a code segment is unmapped from a process. Argument 1 points to the code segment. Argument 2 points to the owning process. The system-wide mutex `DCodeSeg::CodeSegLock` is held.
`EEventLoadLdd`	Event delivered when an LDD is loaded. Argument 1 points to the LDD's code segment (which is an instance of `DCodeSeg`). The current thread will always be the loader thread. The event is triggered *before* the LDD factory function is called.

`TKernelEvent`	Meaning
`EEventUnloadLdd`	A LDD is being unloaded. The current thread is always the loader thread. The LDD's code segment (`DCodeSeg` instance) is passed as argument 1.
`EEventLoadPdd`	A PDD has been loaded. The current thread is always the loader thread. The first argument is the PDD's code segment (`DCodeSeg` instance). The PDD factory function has not been called yet.
`EEventUnloadPdd`	Event delivered when a PDD is unloaded. The current thread is always the loader thread. The first argument points to the PDD's code segment (`DCodeSeg` instance).
`EEventUserTrace`	Event delivered when `RDebug::Print` has been called in user-side code. The current thread is the user-side caller. Argument 1 points to the user-side buffer containing the Unicode string for printing. The characters cannot be accessed directly, because they are in user-space, so they string must copied using `kumemget()`. The event is delivered in a thread-critical section, so the call to `kumemget()` must be protected with `XTRAP`. Argument 2 holds the length of the string in characters. The size of the buffer is twice the length. On exit from the event handler use `DKernelEventHandler::ETraceHandled` to prevent further processing of the trace request by the kernel.

14.3.1.2   *Kernel event dispatch*

To issue an event, the kernel calls `DKernelEventHandler::Dispatch()` at the appropriate place in the code. Some wrapper macros are provided for this function, to conditionally compile the event dispatch, including it only when debugger support is enabled (that is, when `__DEBUGGER_SUPPORT__` is defined, and `DKernelEventHandler::DebugSupportEnabled()` is true).

```
// Dispatch kernel event aEvent
#define __DEBUG_EVENT(aEvent, a1)
#define __DEBUG_EVENT2(aEvent, a1, a2)

// Dispatch kernel event aEvent if condition aCond is true
#define __COND_DEBUG_EVENT(aCond, aEvent, a1)
```

The previous table shows the guarantees that are made for each event about the current state of the kernel and the object passed in.

14.3.1.3   Kernel event capture

When implementing a debug agent, you will need to provide event handlers for the events you wish to capture. In this section, I will discuss how this is done.

To capture events, you simply create an instance of DKernelEventHandler and add this to the kernel's event handler queue. During construction, you provide a pointer to your event handler function, and some private data. The next time any event is issued, each event handler in the queue will be called in order.

```
// Derive an event handler class

class DMyEventHandler : public DKernelEventHandler
  {
public:
  DMyEventHandler();
private:
  static TUint EventHandler(TKernelEvent aEvent,
            TAny* a1, TAny* a2, TAny* aThis);
  };

DMyEventHandler::DMyEventHandler()
  : DKernelEventHandler(EventHandler, this)
  {}
```

The kernel will maintain an access count on the handler so, when the time comes, it can correctly ascertain when it is safe to destruct the object. The kernel won't destroy the object if there are any threads currently executing the handler. When cleaning up, you should use the Close() method to remove the object rather than deleting it.

You can now implement the event handler function. The first parameter of the hander indicates the type of the event. The event type determines the semantics of the next two (void *) parameters. The function is always called in the thread-critical section.

The following simple code snippet shows a handler that counts the total number of processes started by the kernel since the handler was installed:

```
TUint gAllProcessesCount = 0;

TUint DMyEventHandler::EventHandler(TKernelEvent aEvent,
                         TAny* a1, TAny* a2, TAny* aThis)
  {

  switch (aType)
    {
  case EEventAddProcess:
    // increment the process counter
    gAllProcessesCount++;
    default:
    break;
    }
  return DKernelEventHandler::ERunNext;
  }
```

Inside the hander you can use the following functionality:

- Reading/writing of thread memory

- Getting/setting of the thread's context information. If the context is changed, the remaining handlers will not have access to the original context

- Signaling threads, mutexes and other synchronization objects

- Waiting on mutexes and other synchronization objects

- Suspending the thread.

Your handler's return value, a bit-field, determines what happens next:

- If bit ERunNext is not set, the kernel will not run any more handlers for this event

- If the event is a user trace, setting bit ETraceHandled will stop any further processing of the trace command by the kernel. This is useful if you want to intercept the trace for processing yourself, and prevent the kernel outputting it to the usual debug channel

- If EExcHandled is set, the kernel will *not* perform the usual cleanup code for the thread that generated the exception. (The kernel won't generate a "KERN-EXEC 3" and won't make an attempt to destroy the thread object.)

It is worth noting that we may choose to extend the set of events that the kernel generates in the future. The handler should take care to respond to any unknown TKernelEvent values by returning ERunNext.

Example code for testing the capturing of hardware exceptions and panic events can be found here:

```
\base\e32utils\d_exc\d_exc.mmp
```

14.3.1.4   *Context switch event*

To complete the set of notifications available to a debug agent, the kernel provides a context switch event. This event is triggered on every change to the currently scheduled thread. This notification is particularly useful for the implementation of software profilers – for example, to record the length of time spent in each thread.

In this API, we wanted to allow a device driver or extension to provide a callback function that would be called by the scheduler after every context switch. During the implementation, we were conscious that this was impacting a critical part of the scheduler and we were not prepared to compromise its performance.

The cost for a typical implementation of the callback mechanism on an ARM processor would be three instructions:

1. Load the function pointer for the callback

2. Compare it to NULL

3. Execute the callback if non-NULL.

This three-instruction cost is paid at every call to the scheduler, even if the callback function is not provided.

To work around this performance impact, we devised an alternative mechanism for installing the callback function: the kernel provides two implementations of the scheduler code segment affected by the callback. The kernel also provides functions to replace the fast version (with no callback) with the slower version that supports the callback hook.

The kernel publishes the following functions:

```
NKern::SchedulerHooks(TLinAddr &start, TLinAddr &end)
```

This returns the address in the scheduler where the callback trampoline should be placed. (This is located towards the end of the scheduler, after it has selected the new thread to run.)

```
NKern::InsertSchedulerHooks()
```

This is the function for patching-in the callback trampoline. It constructs a branch-and-link instruction to the callback trampoline and inserts it at the address returned by `NKern::SchedulerHooks`. It performs a write to an instruction in the scheduler code, which is usually in ROM – so you must shadow the ROM first.

In the general case in which no software is using the event, this implementation has zero speed overhead. Because of this, the API is a little more awkward to use, but this is clearly a compromise worth making for an API that has only a few specialized clients, and affects such a performance critical area of the nanokernel.

Tools that wish to use the context switch event are responsible for shadowing the appropriate area of scheduler code, and calling the function to patch the scheduler. Let's look at some example code.

First we install the scheduler hooks by shadowing the appropriate area of ROM, and then we call the `NKern::InsertSchedulerHooks()` function to patch the scheduler:

```
TInt InsertSchedulerHooks()
    {
    // Get range of memory used by hooks
    TLinAddr start,end;
    NKern::SchedulerHooks(start,end);

    // Create shadow pages for hooks
    TUint32 pageSize=Kern::RoundToPageSize(1);
    for(TLinAddr a=start; a<end; a+=pageSize)
        {
        NKern::ThreadEnterCS();
        TInt r=Epoc::AllocShadowPage(a);
        NKern::ThreadLeaveCS();
        if(r!=KErrNone && r!=KErrAlreadyExists)
            {
            RemoveSchedulerHooks();
            return r;
            }
        }
    // Put hooks in
    NKern::InsertSchedulerHooks();

    // Make I and D caches consistent for hook region
    Cache::IMB_Range(start,end-start);
    return KErrNone;
    }
```

Now the hooks are installed, we can ask to be called back on every context switch:

```
// Ask for callback
NKern::SetRescheduleCallback(MyRescheduleCallback);
```

The callback function that you provide must have the following prototype:

```
void MyRescheduleCallback(NThread* aNThread);
```

You can temporarily disable context switch callbacks by passing a NULL function pointer to NKern::SetRescheduleCallback(). To completely remove the rescheduling hooks, we do the following:

```
void RemoveSchedulerHooks()
    {
    // Prevent rescheduling whilst we
    // disable the callback
    NKern::Lock();

    // Disable Callback
    NKern::SetRescheduleCallback(NULL);

    // Invalidate CurrentThread
    CurrentThread() = NULL;

    // Callback now disabled...
    NKern::Unlock();

    // Get range of memory used by hooks
    TLinAddr start,end;
    NKern::SchedulerHooks(start,end);

    // Free shadow pages which cover hooks
    TUint32 pageSize=Kern::RoundToPageSize(1);
    NKern::ThreadEnterCS();
    for(TLinAddr a=start; a<end; a+=pageSize)
            Epoc::FreeShadowPage(a);
    NKern::ThreadLeaveCS();
    }
```

Your callback function will be called with the kernel preemption lock held, during a reschedule. (For more information on rescheduling see Section 3.6.) As I've said, this area of code is performance sensitive, and your callback function should therefore use as few processor cycles as possible.

The callback function you provide should be of the type TReschedu-leCallback (see INCLUDE\NKERN\NKERN.H). The kernel passes a pointer to the newly scheduled NThread as a parameter to your function. In some cases you will need to find the Symbian OS thread that corresponds to this nanokernel thread. You can construct it as follows:

```
DThread* pT = _LOFF(aNThread, DThread, iNThread);
```

Before doing this, you should first check that the thread really is a Symbian OS thread, and not a thread belonging to the personality layer, as shown in Section 3.3.3.1.

Example code for testing the scheduling hooks and event capture can be found here:

```
\base\e32\kernel\kdebug.cpp
\base\e32test\debug\d_schedhook.cpp
\base\e32test\debug\d_eventtracker.cpp
```

14.3.2 Thread context API

The kernel exposes an API that allows debug agents to get and set user-side thread context. The API allows the thread context to be retrieved and altered for any non-current, user-side thread. This allows the debugger to display register state for any thread in the system, access any thread's stack to display a stack trace and modify program flow.

The nanokernel does not systematically save all registers in the supervisor stack on entry into privileged mode, and the exact subset that is saved depends on why the switch to privileged mode occurred. So, in general, only a subset of the register set is available, and the volatile registers may be corrupted.

Function	Description
`e32\include\kernel\kernel.h` `DThread::Context(TDes8 &)`	Retrieve the user thread context to the descriptor provided. This is a virtual method, implemented by the memory model, (`DArmPlatThread::Context()` in `e32\KERNEL\ARM\CKERNEL.CPP`).
`INCLUDE\NKERN\NKERN.H` `NKern::ThreadGetUserContext`	Get (subset of) user context of specified thread. See `nkern\arm\ncthrd.cpp` for more information.
`INCLUDE\NKERN\NKERN.H` `NKern::ThreadSetUserContext`	Set (subset of) user context of specified thread. See `nkern\arm\ncthrd.cpp` for more information.

The current thread context can also be read from user-side code by using the method `RThread::Context()`.

Example test code that exercises thread context can be found in:

```
base\e32test\debug\d_context.h
base\e32test\debug\d_context.cpp
base\e32test\debug\t_context.cpp
```

14.3.2.1   *Context type*

We've seen that, on entry to privileged mode, the nanokernel does not systematically save all registers in the supervisor stack. To improve performance, it only pushes registers when it needs to.

To retrieve and modify the user context for any non-current threads, we need to discover exactly where on its stack the thread's context has been pushed. To do this, we must work out what caused the thread to be switched from user mode. The set of possibilities is enumerated in the type `NThread::TUserContextType` (include\nkern\arm\nk_plat.h)

```
// Value indicating what event caused thread to enter
// privileged mode.

enum TUserContextType
  {
  EContextNone=0, // Thread has no user context
  EContextException=1, // Hardware exception
  EContextUndefined,
  EContextUserInterrupt, // Preempted by interrupt
  // Killed while preempted by int taken in user mode
  EContextUserInterruptDied,
  // Preempted by int taken in executive call handler
  EContextSvsrInterrupt1,
  // Killed preempted by int taken in exec call hdler
  EContextSvsrInterrupt1Died,
  // Preempted by int taken in executive call handler
  EContextSvsrInterrupt2,
  // Killed preempted by int taken in exec call handler
  EContextSvsrInterrupt2Died,
  EContextWFAR, // Blocked on User::WaitForAnyRequest()
  // Killed while blocked on User::WaitForAnyRequest()
  EContextWFARDied,
  EContextExec, // Slow executive call
  // Kernel-side context (for kernel threads)
  EContextKernel,
  };
```

The kernel does not keep a record of this type, since it is not usually required. The value is calculated only on demand, by calling:

```
IMPORT_C TUserContextType NThread::UserContextType();
```

Apart from the previous context functions, the stop-mode debug API is the primary client for this API (see Section 14.5.2).

14.3.3   Code and data section information

When an executable is loaded from disk, the loader dynamically allocates code and data chunks for it, as I discussed in Chapter 10, *The Loader*.

The linear address of these chunks is unlikely to match the link address in the executable's symbolic debug information, so the debugger has to determine the address allocated by the loader, which allows it to relocate the symbolic debug information to match the run address.

The kernel exposes APIs to get the base addresses of code, data and BSS sections for any library or process:

```
\generic\base\e32\include\e32cmn.h

class TModuleMemoryInfo;
```

```
\generic\base\e32\include\e32std.h

TInt RProcess::GetMemoryInfo(TModuleMemoryInfo& aInfo);
TInt RLibrary::GetRamSizes(TInt& aCodeSize, TInt& aConstDataSize)
TInt RProcess::GetRamSizes(TInt& aCodeSize, TInt& aConstDataSize,
        TInt& anInitialisedDataSize, TInt& anUninitialisedDataSize)
```

```
generic\base\e32\include\kernel\kern_priv.h

TInt DCodeSeg::GetMemoryInfo(TModuleMemoryInfo& aInfo, DProcess*
                                                        aProcess);
```

`TModuleMemoryInfo` returns

- The base address of the code section (.text)
- The size of the code section
- The base address of the constant data section (.rdata)
- The size of the constant data section
- The base address of the initialized data section (.data)
- The base address of the uninitialized data section (.bss)
- The size of the initialized data section.

The D_EXC logger shows these APIs in use:

```
\base\e32utils\d_exc\minkda.cpp
```

14.3.4 ROM shadow API

The kernel publishes APIs that allow debug agents to shadow pages of ROM in RAM. This allows the debugger to set and clear breakpoints in the ROM address range.

Function defined in `memmodel\epoc\platform.h`	Description
`Epoc::AllocShadowPage`	Allocates a shadow page for the given address. Returns `KErrAlreadyExists` if the ROM page has already been shadowed.
`Epoc::FreeShadowPage`	Frees a shadow page for the given address.
`Epoc::FreezeShadowPage`	Freezes a shadow page for the given address, that is, the page is made read-only.

The thread must be in its critical section when these calls are made. The thread can enter its critical section with `NKern::ThreadEnterCS()`, and exit with `NKern::ThreadLeaveCS()`.

The implementations of these functions can be found in `memmodel\epoc\mmubase\mmubase.cpp`. They are memory model-dependent.

Example code demonstrating the ROM shadow API can be found here:

```
\generic\base\e32test\mmu\d_shadow.h
\generic\base\e32test\mmu\d_shadow.cpp
\generic\base\e32test\mmu\t_shadow.cpp
```

14.4   Target debugger agents

The kernel debug interface provides the foundation for building and integrating tools into the Symbian OS platform. In this and subsequent sections of this chapter, I will describe how the different types of tools are implemented on top of this API.

14.4.1   Debug agent

A debug agent for a run-mode debugger must translate the debug protocol requests received from its host debugger into actions for the kernel and other Symbian OS servers.

The responsibilities for the debug agent were outlined in Section 14.3.2. However, the division of responsibilities between the agent and host is flexible: for example, it is possible to implement CPU instruction step on the host or the target, but it is almost always the case that the host performs the relocation of symbolic debug information for source association.

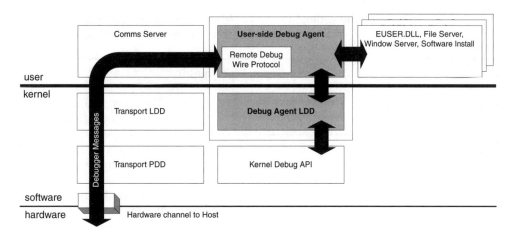

Figure 14.7 User-side and kernel-side debug agent for a run-mode debugger

Figure 14.7 shows the architecture of the debug agent. You can see from the diagram that the debug agent has dependencies on other components in the system, such as the user library, file server and software install. Because of this, it is not possible to place breakpoints in any of those components. These components are essential to the correct operation of the debug agent – suspending any threads serving the debug agent will make the agent inoperable. For example, if the debugger has configured the serial port as the debug channel, you cannot place a breakpoint in the communication server's serial protocol module.

In EKA1, it was not possible to place breakpoints anywhere in the user library because the kernel was linked to this library too. This is no longer a problem in EKA2, since kernel-side software now has its own utility library.

Similarly, if the user-side agent depends on functionality in any other server, then it will not be able to debug that server.

The debugger implementation should seek to minimize these restrictions. This usually involves providing a duplicate implementation for the private use of the debug agent.

14.4.2 JIT debugging

Symbian OS supports JIT debugging directly for the emulator only. However, the debug agent can implement JIT on target hardware, by placing JIT debug traps (implemented as breakpoints) on the common termination points for user-side threads. The address of these functions in EUSER.DLL can be discovered by using the `RLibrary::Lookup()`

method on the ordinal for each. When a JIT breakpoint is triggered, the "reason" information can be discovered from the thread's context.

Function	Ordinal (gcc build)	
`RThread::Panic()`	812	The category is in r1, the panic number is in r2.
`RProcess::Panic()`	813	The category is in r0, the panic number is in r1.
`RThread::RaiseException()`	868	R0 holds the exception number.
`User::RaiseException()`	1910	R1 holds the exception number.

14.4.3 Breakpoints

The handling of hardware exceptions is critical for the functioning of a run-mode debugger on ARM platforms. Software breakpoints are implemented by replacing code at the break location with an "undefined instruction", or the "BKPT" opcode on ARM v5 processors. When the thread executes the undefined instruction, the CPU will generate an exception.

You can write software breakpoints to RAM-loaded code by modifying the code chunk's permissions. You can write them to code in ROM by first shadowing the target page of ROM in RAM (as I discussed in Section 14.3.4). When writing breakpoints into a code area, you should make certain that the cache is coherent with the modified code in RAM. This will ensure that the breakpoint instruction is committed to main RAM before the code is executed. The cache operations required to maintain coherence are dependent on the mobile phone's memory architecture, but a call to the instruction memory barrier function (`Cache::IMB_Range`) specifying the modified address range will perform the necessary operations. (I discussed caches and memory architectures in more detail in Chapter 2, *Hardware for Symbian OS.*)

Once a breakpoint is set, the kernel debug agent can capture its breakpoint exceptions by installing an event handler for `EHwEvent`.

When the exception handler is run, the debug agent can determine what to do next. If the exception was not due to a breakpoint set by the debugger, then the agent can pass the exception onto the next handler (and ultimately the kernel). If the exception was a breakpoint intended for the current thread, then the agent can suspend the thread with `DThread::Suspend()`, then replace the instruction removed by the breakpoint and notify the host debugger via the user-side agent.

14.5 Stop-mode debug API

The vast majority of hardware platforms supported by Symbian OS are ICE-enabled. Kernel developers and those porting the operating system to new hardware often have access to development boards exposing the JTAG interface, and allowing the use of CPU-level debuggers.

The main problem with OS support in a stop-mode debugger is that there is little or no opportunity for the operating system to run code on behalf of the debugger to enable it to perform the tasks it needs. There is no debug agent, and no high-level wire protocol between host and target; communication is through remote memory reads and writes initiated over JTAG. While the CPU is halted, the debugger must do all the data discovery and object manipulation for itself by rummaging around inside the kernel – the "OS awareness" is pushed onto the host.

However, Symbian OS publishes an API to make this a little easier. It is a table-driven interface onto the data and kernel objects: a virtual "map" of the kernel. We implement the map as a memory structure that can be easily navigated with memory reads initiated over the JTAG interface.

Thread and process awareness is common in the run-mode debuggers used for application development, but far less common in JTAG stop-mode debuggers. Using the API provided, it is possible to integrate the following features into a stop-mode debugger:

- Thread and process awareness
- Thread-specific breakpoints
- Memory management awareness
- Code segment management.

The EKA2 stop-mode debug API is similar in principle to the API provided in EKA1. However, EKA2 has one significant design change. We made this change with the intention of improving performance and reducing interference in timing characteristics of the target when a debugger is attached.

The EKA1 solution copied key information from the kernel into a "debug log" for convenient access by the debugger. EKA2 does not copy information – instead, the debugger must locate the information in-place. This design improves the performance of Symbian OS while the debugger

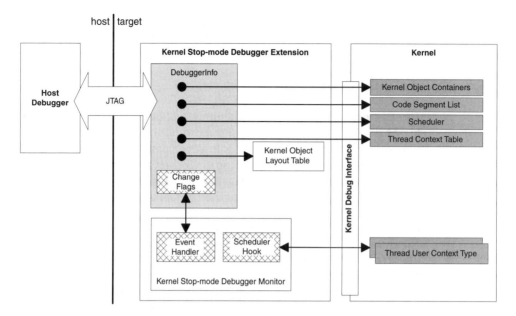

Figure 14.8   Stop-mode debugger interface

is attached, at the cost of a slightly more complex client interface (see Figure 14.8).

The stop-mode debugger API is built on top of the kernel's core debug APIs. It is implemented as a kernel extension (KDEBUG.DLL), which is enabled simply by including it in a ROM. For most variants, you can do this simply by defining the STOP_MODE_DEBUGGING macro. Alternatively, you can add the following line to <variant>rom\kernel.iby:

```
extension[VARID]=
\Epoc32\Release\<assp>\urel\KDEBUG.DLL \System\Bin\kdebug.dll
```

The DDebuggerInfo interface implemented by the KDEBUG extension is the debugger's gateway into the kernel. The host initially locates the gateway from a pointer stored at a constant address in the superpage:

```
DDebuggerInfo* TSuperPage::iDebuggerInfo
```

(The superpage is used for communication between the bootstrap and the kernel, and is described in Section 16.2.2.1.)

The gateway contains:

- The object layout table, which provides a virtual "map" of the kernel's data types, to allow them to be navigated. The table also isolates the debugger from minor changes in layout of kernel objects

- Pointers to the kernel's object containers for threads, processes, libraries, memory chunks, semaphores, and so on

- Access to the scheduler for information about the current thread, and current address space

- Access to the kernel's locks that indicate the validity and state of various kernel objects

- A mechanism for retrieving the context of any non-current thread.

The KDEBUG extension installs an event handler, which it uses to update "change flags". These flags can be read by the host debugger to determine if any new kernel objects have been removed (for example, thread death) or created (for example, library loaded).

The extension has a minimal impact on performance when installed. Furthermore, there is no overhead on the phone software since the interface can be entirely removed on phones that don't expose JTAG hardware, without re-compiling the kernel.

The implementation can be found here:

```
e32\include\kernel\kdebug.h
e32\kernel\kdebug.cpp
```

14.5.1 Kernel object layout table

The kernel object layout table provides the host debugger with a virtual map of the kernel's data structures. The table is an array of offsets of member data from the start of the owning object.

Given a pointer to a kernel object, the address of any object of a known type, and any of its members can be found by looking up the offset in the table and adding it to the object pointer.

Using this method, and starting from the DDebuggerInfo object, the host debugger can walk the kernel's data structures by issuing the appropriate memory reads over JTAG.

The table layout (host interface) is defined in this header file:

```
e32\include\kernel\debug.h
```

Here is a small section of this file so that you can see what it looks like:

```
e32\include\kernel\debug.henum TOffsetTableEntry
  {
  // thread info
  EThread_Name,
  EThread_Id,
```

```
EThread_OwningProcess,
EThread_NThread,
EThread_SupervisorStack,

// scheduler info
EScheduler_KernCSLocked,
EScheduler_LockWaiting,
EScheduler_CurrentThread,
EScheduler_AddressSpace,

// and so on ...
}
```

The constants published in this file correspond to indices in the object table defined by the stop-mode debug API.

```
const TInt Debugger::ObjectOffsetTable[]=
  {
  // thread info
_FOFF(DThread, iName),
_FOFF(DThread, iId),
_FOFF(DThread, iOwningProcess),
_FOFF(DThread, iNThread),
_FOFF(DThread, iSupervisorStack),

  // scheduler info
_FOFF(TScheduler, iKernCSLocked),
_FOFF(TScheduler, iLock.iWaiting),
_FOFF(TScheduler, iCurrentThread),
_FOFF(TScheduler, iAddressSpace),

  // and so on ...
  }
```

Symbian builds and delivered this table with every release of the kernel. Indirection through the table provides a level of binary compatibility for the host debugger – the indices will not change between releases of the OS, even if the actual layout of kernel objects does change.

14.5.2   Thread context

Acquiring the thread context of any non-current thread presents a challenge for a stop-mode debugger. It is worth examining the solution in a little more detail.

The context for the current thread is always available directly from the processor. The context for any non-current thread is stored in its supervisor stack. However, as I mentioned in Section 14.3.2, it is not always straightforward to determine where the registers are placed in the stack frame – or, indeed, which register subset has been saved, and in which order the registers were pushed. This will depend on the reason the switch to privileged mode occurred: the thread's user context type. (I list the TUserContext types in Section 14.3.2.1.)

In a multi-session debugger, where non-current threads may be visible, the host debugger needs to be able to identify the context of any thread *at any time* – it must always be able to determine the user context type for a thread.

The kernel does not routinely store this information, so the stop-mode debug API installs a scheduler callback to update the thread's context type on every reschedule. The result is stored in the NThread object:

```
inline TInt NThread::SetUserContextType()
```

The context type value can be used as an index into the user context tables. This will yield a structure that describes the layout of the thread's stack, as shown in Figure 14.8.

```
static const TArmContextElement* const*
NThread::UserContextTables();
```

```
const TArmContextElement* const ThreadUserContextTables[] =
  {
  ContextTableUndefined, // EContextNone
  ContextTableException,
  ContextTableUndefined,
  ContextTableUserInterrupt,
  ContextTableUserInterruptDied,
  ContextTableSvsrInterrupt1,
  ContextTableSvsrInterrupt1Died,
  ContextTableSvsrInterrupt2,
  ContextTableSvsrInterrupt2Died,
  ContextTableWFAR,
  ContextTableWFARDied,
  ContextTableExec,
  ContextTableKernel,
  0 // Null terminated
  };
```

This structure holds 18 pointers to tables (one for each thread context type). Each item is an array of TArmContextElement objects, one per ARM CPU register, in the order defined in TArmRegisters:

```
// Structure storing where a given
// register is saved on the supervisor stack.
class TArmContextElement
  {
public:
  enum TType
    {
    // register is not available
```

```
        EUndefined,
        // iValue is offset from stack pointer
        EOffsetFromSp,
        // iValue is offset from stack top
        EOffsetFromStackTop,
        // value = SP + offset
        ESpPlusOffset,
    };
public:
  TUint8 iType;
  TUint8 iValue;
    };

enum TArmRegisters
    {
    EArmR0   = 0,
    EArmR1   = 1,
    EArmR2   = 2,
    EArmR3   = 3,
    EArmR4   = 4,
    EArmR5   = 5,
    EArmR6   = 6,
    EArmR7   = 7,
    EArmR8   = 8,
    EArmR9   = 9,
    EArmR10  = 10,
    EArmR11  = 11,
    EArmR12  = 12,
    EArmSp   = 13,
    EArmLr   = 14,
    EArmPc   = 15,
    EArmFlags = 16,
    EArmDacr  = 17,
    };
```

The `TArmContextElement::iType` determines how the register location should be calculated. Figure 14.9 shows an example of a *thread context table* and its associated *thread context state*.

The algorithm for obtaining a thread context is intended to be run on the host by a stop-mode debugger. Here it is:

```
reg_value GetSavedThreadRegister(<thread>,<reg-id>)
    {
    type = READ(thread, EThread_UserContextType)
    IF ( KernelLock != 0 )
      RETURN "Kernel Locked"
    IF (thread == CurrentThread)
      RETURN "Register not saved - current thread"

    // Select the appropriate context table
    ContextTable = READ(DDebuggerInfo::iThreadContextTable)
    ContextTable = READ(ContextTable[Type])

    // Get stack pointer and stack top
    SP = READ(<thread>,EThread_SavedSP)
    StackTop = READ(<thread>, EThread_SupervisorStack)
        + READ(<thread>,EThread_SupervisorStackSize)
```

```
// Get the iType and iValue fields for this
// register from the thread context table
iType  = READ( &ContextTable[<reg-id>].iType )
iValue = READ( &ContextTable[<reg-id>].iValue )

// Now handle the cases and calculate the
IF ( iType == OFFSET_FROM_SP )
  RETURN READ( SP[iValue] );
ELSE
  IF( iType == OFFSET_FROM_STACK_TOP)
    RETURN READ( StackTop[-iValue] );
  ELSE
    IF( iType == SP_PLUS_OFFSET)
      RETURN SP[iValue];
    ELSE
      // Other case currently not used by OS
      RETURN "Register Not Valid"
}

// Read field <offset-tag> from <object>
val READ(<object>, <offset-tag>)
  {
  offset = OffsetTable[<offset-tag>]
  pointer = <object>
  RETURN READ( pointer[offset] )
  }
```

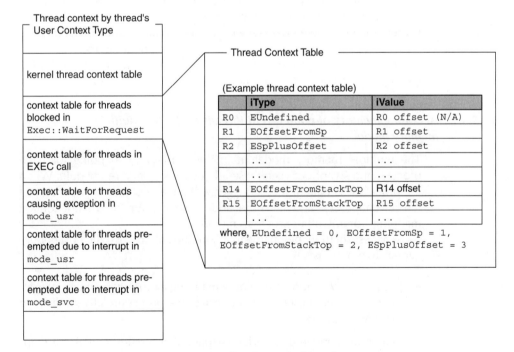

Figure 14.9 Thread context table and state

Note that in some states, the Symbian OS kernel exploits the conventions in the ARM-Thumb procedure call standard and thus not all registers in the thread's context will be saved. Typically, the argument registers (that is, R0–R3) are not saved because the caller throws those registers away – so reading the thread context for these registers will return garbage values. This is harmless for user code, and it should be harmless for the debugger too. The debugger, if it has the capability, may choose not to show these registers at all.

14.5.3 Memory of non-current threads

Reading and writing to the current process's memory is straightforward – the process's data will be mapped into its run address, and the host can follow all pointers relative to the current process directly.

However, if the host wants to read and write to an address in a process that is not currently scheduled, it must take into account that the memory may not be available in the current address space, or may appear at a different logical address. The debugger must move to an address space in which the memory is available, and translate the process-relative pointer from its run address into an equivalent pointer in the new address space.

The implementation is memory-model specific. It is an equivalent operation to the DThread::RawRead() and DThread::RawWrite() methods that the kernel uses when transferring data between processes.

To perform this operation, the debugger must understand how the kernel's memory model works. I will give a short description of the method for each memory model, and you can find more detail in the stop-mode debugger integration guide. I describe the kernel's memory maps for the moving and multiple memory models in Chapter 7, *Memory Models*.

14.5.3.1 *Accessing memory of non-current threads under the multiple memory model*

The multiple memory model maintains a memory mapping for each process, and swaps between these address spaces at a reschedule. When the processor is halted, the debugger will have access to the memory of the current process and the kernel address space, but this will not contain mappings for any other process's memory.

To access memory belonging to a non-current process, the host debugger has two options:

- Create a new temporary memory mapping exposing the memory from the non-current process, then translate the process-relative pointer to the new mapping

- Temporarily move to an address-space that already contains a mapping for the target memory.

The former is the method used by the `DThread::RawRead()` and `DThread::RawWrite()` methods. For the host debugger, it is likely to be more practical to simply re-use the address space for the target process that is provided by the kernel.

The host can change the address space by modifying the appropriate MMU registers. (For ARMv6 processors the debugger programs the ASID and TTBR with the values provided in the target `DProcess` object.) Once in the appropriate address space, the process-relative pointer can be used to access the memory.

14.5.3.2   *Accessing memory of non-current threads under the moving memory model*

The moving memory model maps the current process's memory into the run section. All non-current processes are mapped into the kernel's home section, and are only visible to the kernel. When the processor is halted, the debugger can grant itself access to the kernel's memory by modifying the MMU access control register, DACR.

To use a process-relative pointer to access memory belonging to a non-current process, the host debugger must obviously take into account where in the home section the kernel has mapped the process's memory chunks. It is most efficient to use the same calculation that is implemented by the kernel's `DThread::RawRead()` and `DThread::RawWrite()` methods, which I will now briefly describe.

To perform the pointer translation, the debugger iterates through the process's list of chunks (`DMemModelProcess::iChunks`) until it finds the chunk with an address range that covers the target address. The home address can now be calculated as:

```
home_address = chunk.iChunk.iHomeBase +
               target_address - chunk.iDataSectionBase
```

14.5.3.3   *Accessing memory of non-current threads under the direct memory model*

The direct memory model maintains only a single memory mapping that is valid for current and non-current processes. It is sufficient for the debugger to ensure that it has read/write access permissions before using a process-relative pointer.

14.5.4   Kernel state

The host debugger may halt the target processor at any time. This means that the debugger might find kernel data structures in an indeterminate state – for example if the kernel was interrupted in the middle of updating them. Before walking the kernel data structures, the debugger must ensure that the kernel is self-consistent.

The debugger can determine this by examining the kernel and system locks that are exposed through the debug API. The kernel and system locks show when it is safe to access kernel objects, see Section 3.6. If any of the locks are non-zero, the debugger cannot assume that either the thread list or the MMU mappings are in a consistent state. This means that it is unsafe to walk the kernel's data structures. Most debuggers relay this information to their user via the IDE's UI, by graying out the OS visualizations. The debugger could also repeatedly step the processor, until the locks are cleared.

14.6   Kernel trace channel

The kernel provides tracing support as the lowest common denominator debugging tool. The trace port is available for all software, from the bootstrap and device drivers, right up to C++ applications. Software can output trace strings through the trace port to assist with development and diagnosis.

By default, most hardware platforms will configure a serial port as a debug channel to allow the ASCII strings to be picked up by a host PC with a standard terminal program.

The trace support is extended on some base ports to allow the debug strings to be redirected to another port. Usually this would be another serial port, but it can also be a dedicated hardware debug channel. For example, the kernel implements debug trace over the JTAG data channel for ARM CPUs.

Being able to redirect the kernel trace is invaluable during system integration, where conflicts may arise between high-level software and the trace port.

Figure 14.10 shows the program flow from the two clients (in light gray) to the output to hardware (in dark gray).

14.6.1   Redirect user trace

Any application-trace strings that are passed into the kernel through the RDebug::Print() functions can be captured and redirected by a device driver. The capture facility is part of the kernel event notifier described in Section 14.3.1. The driver can handle the trace string and terminate the trace, or it can pass it back to the kernel for processing as usual.

This method can be used to capture trace strings for redirection to an alternative output channel, or for analysis. For example:

- Capture the trace strings and package them for sending over a wire protocol to a host debugger. The host debugger can then display the string in a console or output window

- Redirection to a file, on target, for later download and analysis

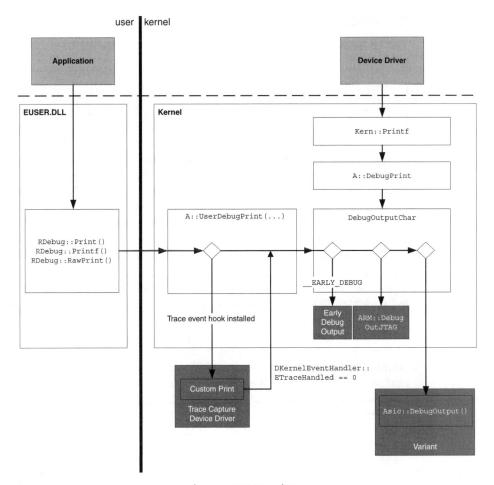

Figure 14.10 Kernel trace

- Redirection to RAM, for performance
- Redirection to dedicated trace hardware
- Redirection to an analysis tool.

Symbian provides example code that demonstrates the use of this API to capture user-side trace and display it in a console window on the mobile phone:

```
\base\e32test\debug\t_traceredirect.cpp
\base\e32test\debug\d_traceredirect.cpp
\base\e32test\debug\d_traceredirect.h
```

14.6.2 Debug output

The channel used to output the trace is determined by the `DebugOut-`
`putChar()` function:

```
void DebugOutputChar(TUint aChar)
// Transmit one character to the trace port
// (for debugging only)
```

The default implementation for ARM platforms is defined in `\base\`
`e32\kernel\arm\cutils.cpp`. If the `__EARLY_DEBUG` macro is
defined, then this function can be replaced by linking-in a custom
implementation. Custom "early debug" implementations are provided
as a convenience to developers porting Symbian OS to new hardware,
for use during the early stages of porting, when other communications
channels are unreliable or not available. If the debug port, `TheSu-`
`perPage().iDebugPort`, is set to `Arm::EDebugPortJTAG` then the
kernel outputs the string to the JTAG co-processor data channel (CP14).
If the variant DLL is available (that is, `Arm::TheAsic` is defined), then
the string is handed to the variant for output.

The kernel doesn't make any attempt to arbitrate access to the destination port. You will find that if the kernel trace and some other
communications protocol, such as PPP, are being directed to the same
port, then the two serial streams will be interleaved. In such cases, the
communications protocol is likely to fail.

Kernel-side software can use the trace channel by calling

```
Kern::Printf();
```

User-side software uses a slow exec call, `Exec::DebugPrint`,
which is available through the following function wrappers provided
in `EUSER.DLL`:

```
RDebug::Print();
RDebug::Printf();
RDebug::RawPrint();
```

The trace will appear on the port specified in

```
TheSuperPage().iDebugPort
```

This value can be set in a number of ways:

- Call `Hal::Set(EDebugPort, <port>)`

- The `DEBUGPORT <port>` ESHELL command

- The `DEBUGPORT <port>` ROMBUILD keyword.

The kernel defines the following values for `port`:

Constant	Port number	Header file	Meaning
`Arm::EDebugPortJTAG`	42	`kernel\arm\arm.h`	Send trace strings to ARM co-processor 14.
`TRomHeader:: KDefaultDebugPort`	−1	`e32rom.h`	Send trace strings to the default port.
`KNullDebugPort`	−2	`e32const.h`	Don't output trace strings.
	other	`variant header`	Send the trace to the variant.

The semantics of other port values are defined by the ASIC. Some ASICs implement these as port numbers (for example, 0, 1, 2, 3, and so on) and others use hardware port addresses.

For example, on the Lubbock platform, when the port is set to 3, the trace appears on the serial port labeled "BTUART". Any other value means the trace appears on the port labeled "FFUART".

On the "H2" reference platform, when port is set to 2, trace output goes to COM3, and when it is set to 0, the trace goes to COM0.

14.6.3 Caveats

There are some problems with this style of tracing which are worth noting. Tracing alters timing. For most user-side software, this will not be a problem. However, with time-critical software such as kernel code, peripheral code and communication stacks, the addition of trace output may cause it to fail. Also, if the defect you are diagnosing is timing-dependent, such as a race condition, then adding trace output can make the problem move somewhere else, making it harder to track down.

Timing problems are compounded if a slow output channel, such as a serial UART is used. You can mitigate the problem by outputting less trace information, or by switching to a faster trace channel. The throughput of the JTAG data channel is typically greater than a serial UART. For some tasks, you may need to use an even faster channel, such as dedicated trace hardware or logging to RAM. You can implement the latter by using the user trace capture API provided by the kernel, see Section 14.3.1 for more details.

Another side effect of compiling trace strings into your code is that its "shape" changes – functions and data move address and also move relative to each other. As a consequence the code may change too (for example, the size of relative branches). Again, this can occasionally affect the reproducibility of your defect.

The kernel also has some tracing blind spots – if you are tracing during power down, you will find that you tend to lose whatever was in the FIFO when the ASIC was moved to a low-power mode. This makes the quality of the trace unpredictable.

14.6.4   Kernel trace in practice

To aid development, we have liberally placed debug trace strings throughout the kernel code, so the activities of the system can be observed.

The kernel trace strings are wrapped in a macro (__KTRACE_OPT) that is expanded only in debug builds. The strings are categorized into 30 functional areas (e32\include\nkern\nk_trace.h), so you can choose to get trace output from only the areas you are interested in. F32 follows a similar model.

Macro	Bit number	Trace strings relating to
KHARDWARE	0	Hardware abstraction layer
KSERVER	2	DServer
KMMU	3	Memory model
KSEMAPHORE	4	Semaphores
KSCHED	5	Scheduler
KPROC	6	DProcess
KDUBUGGER	8	Kernel-side debug agents
KTHREAD	9	DThread
KDLL	10	DLLs
KIPC	11	IPC v1 and v2
KPBUS1	12	Peripheral bus controller

Macro	Bit number	Trace strings relating to
KPBUS2	13	Peripheral bus controller
KPBUSDRV	14	Peripheral bus driver
KPOWER	15	Power management
KTIMING	16	DTimer
KEVENT	17	Kernel events
KOBJECT	18	DObject
KDFC	19	DFCs
KEXTENSION	20	Kernel extensions
KSCHED2	21	Scheduler
KLOCDRV	22	TLocalDrive
KTHREAD2	24	DThread
KDEVICE	25	Logical and physical device drivers
KMEMTRACE	26	Memory allocations
KDMA	27	DMA framework
KMMU2	28	Memory model
KNKERN	29	Nanokernel

Tracing can be enabled using any of these methods:

- ROMBUILD `kerneltrace` keyword
- `User::DebugMask()`
- ESHELL `trace` command.

We changed the syntax of the trace command between v9.0 and v9.1 of Symbian OS to allow more trace bits to be allocated. More information is available from the Symbian Developer Library in the Base Porting Guide for EKA2 versions of Symbian OS and the C++ component reference section.

14.7   Summary

Symbian's primary development environment for applications and middleware is the EKA2 emulator. Symbian also supports development tools for target hardware, for the development of kernel-side and hardware dependent software.

The core building block of the debug architecture is the kernel debug interface. This interface is designed to support many of the development tools that are common to the embedded technology tools industry – that is, remote software on-target debuggers, hardware assisted on-target debuggers, post-mortem analysis tools, system trace and profilers.

The kernel debug architecture delivers the high level of information and execution control required to build powerful debugging and analysis tools.

Stop-mode kernel debugging and stop-mode application debugging is supported on mobile phones with JTAG ICE hardware. The stop-mode debug interface provides a method for the hardware assisted debugger to fully explore the operating system and extract information about kernel objects even while the target CPU is halted. The debugger implements Symbian OS awareness and kernel object visualizations using this interface. This improves the model of the operating system available to developer through the debugger.

The architecture supports software run-mode debuggers that are suitable for application and middleware development on mobile phones. These debuggers running on the PC talk to a proxy debug agent on the target, which is a privileged client of the kernel. This style of debugger allows system services to continue running during a debug session. However, they are not generally suitable for development of kernel-side software. EKA2 provides the necessary primitives required to implement the debug agent. The functionality provided includes the kernel event notification API to notify the debug agent of significant events, an interface to control thread execution and retrieve context, information about executable code and data sections for the relocation of symbolic debug information, and functionality to support setting breakpoints in ROM.

The architecture supports both interactive and non-interactive post-mortem analysis tools for the examination of kernel and application state at the point of thread or system death. In addition, the kernel provides primitive kernel tracing for defect diagnosis during development of kernel-side software.

In the next chapter, I will look at how Symbian OS manages a phone's power resources.

15

Power Management

by Carlos Freitas

All power corrupts, but we need the electricity.

Anon

Mobile phones are battery-powered devices. In the majority of cases, the battery is the only available source of energy – the exception being the times when the mobile phone is being recharged. Even with today's most advanced developments, rechargeable batteries are still characterized by:

- The limited amount of power they can supply at any given time

- The limited period for which they can supply electrical energy before exhaustion – the depletion of the active materials inside a cell must be replenished by recharging

- The hysteresis of the depletion–recharge cycle, which shortens the life-span of a battery.

So it is fair to say that the supply of power on a mobile device is quite constrained.

The problem is compounded by the need to keep the size and weight of battery components as small as possible. At the same time, new features are being added that use more power, or users are operating phones in power-consuming states (such as gaming or audio/video playback) for longer periods of time.

Because of this, mobile phone hardware has gained new energy-saving features, which require software monitoring and control. It is the primary goal of the operating system's power management architecture to define and implement strategies to use energy efficiently, to extend the useful life-time of the batteries, to increase the period of time for which the device can be used between recharges and at the same time, to allow the use of services required by the user of the device at any given time and at an acceptable level.

From the point of view of the phone's hardware components, there are a number of factors that the power management policy and implementation need to address, such as:

- Each hardware component's requirement on power resources at a given time

- The component's state with respect to power consumption and availability

- The component's transition time to a "more available" state (for executing both externally initiated tasks and background tasks), including the restoration of the status prior to the transition to the "less available" state

- The component's current workload and how this maps to the range of possible states

- The component's response time to an input that requires processing (such as the input from an interface port) whilst in each state and its ability to keep up with a sudden inflow of data.

Power management also deals with the operational state of the mobile phone as perceived by its user. That perception is primarily based on the availability of the user interface. The device is seen to be operational when the user can interact with the UI. On the other hand, the device is perceived to be unavailable when the UI seems to be unavailable, for example when the display is off or is displaying a screen saving image. The user expects the transition from unavailable to available to be fast and invariable.

The user also has the perception of an "off" state from which it takes a considerably longer time to return back to an "on" state.

The user perception of the operational state of the device may differ from the actual state of the hardware or the interpretation the operating system has of that state. For example, the user may perceive the device to be "off" when the screen is off, but background tasks or data transactions may well be going on. In this case, the device may be able to readily return to a perceived operational state with no loss of data and state. Equally, the phone can present itself to its user as fully operational, because the UI is active and available, while in fact significant portions of the hardware may be powered off, or only a fraction of the total processing bandwidth may be available for utilization.

In summary, the power management implementation is responsible for, on behalf of the operating system:

- Controlling the state and the power requirements of the hardware components

- Extending the useful life of the battery component and the period the device can be used in between recharges

- Managing the user's perception of the phone operational state.

From this, it is clear that power management must be implemented at all levels of the operating system. Let me give a couple of examples:

1. There may be a UI-specific policy that decides to switch the display backlight or the display itself off after a period of user inactivity

2. A client of the services provided by an input port may decide to allow the controlling device driver to move the input port hardware to a low power state after a period of inactivity (no transactions through that port).

Symbian OS favors a distributed approach to power management, with components at different layers of the OS responsible both for managing their requirements on system power, and the impact of their actions on the availability of the phone. They achieve this in co-operation with other interdependent components, which can be at any level of the OS.

This chapter is mostly concerned with the implementation of power management at the kernel level of Symbian OS, and its interface to user-side components, but I will refer to other parts of the framework whenever necessary.

15.1 Power states

The kernel-level implementation of power management is responsible for managing the power state of hardware components such as the CPU and peripherals. The factors that are used to identify the state the component is in include:

- Its ability to retain data while in that state

- Its requirement on the level of system power resources, such as voltage, clock, current, and so on

- The response time to internal or external events while in that state

- Its transition time to the next "more available" state

- Its internal processing load at the time of transition to that state, and what parts of the component are involved.

The kernel-side framework sees a hardware component's power state as one of:

1. Off – moving a hardware component to this state is a result of removing the power supply to the component. Data and state are lost, the component's power consumption becomes negligible and it has no requirement on any power resource. The component will have no ability to respond to external events, and will have the longest transition time to any other state

2. Standby – in this power state, the hardware component may not have the ability to preserve data and state, but the power framework software can restore them when it transitions the component to a "more available" state, so long as it saved the previous state's status elsewhere before the transition to standby. The requirements on power resources can be significantly lowered, for one of two reasons – either no status preservation is required, or the component has a fully static operation and no internal processing takes place. The component may preserve some ability to detect and service external events, but the response time is generally long and will impact the component's performance

3. Retention – in this state the requirements on power resources are reduced to only those necessary to preserve the component's data, internal state and the ability to detect external or generate internal events. The component is not performing any active tasks, it is not involved in any data transactions and no internal processing is taking place. The response times to external or internal events, as well as the transition time to a state where the events can be processed, may be long enough to impact the system's performance

4. Idle – this is usually a transitory state, or a mode. The hardware component has finished processing a task and no request for further service has been placed on it. No connected component is acting on any inputs, nor are new internal events being generated. The component has the capability to respond to new events and process them. Its state and data are preserved. Its power consumption may be reduced, but that does not lead to lowering the requirements it has on system power resources. Depending on a number of circumstances which I will explain later in this chapter, the power management framework may move the component to a lower power state or keep it in this state until a request for processing data or events is placed upon it (by the OS or by a connected component)

5. Active – a hardware component in this state is processing tasks, data or events generated internally and received from its inputs. Its requirement on power resources is as high as necessary to guarantee that this processing takes place at the level of availability required. It may have pending tasks or requests for processing.

Not all hardware components support all these power states, and some components are capable of intermediate states, usually different variations of the retention state.

Transitions between power states may be triggered by user actions, requests from the clients of the services provided by these components, the need to save power, changes to the state of power resources used by the component, and so on. These states apply to the CPU and peripherals independently, so it is possible that, at a given time, different hardware components of a phone will be in different power states.

For example, it is possible that the CPU might enter the idle state if it has no scheduled tasks and there are no anticipated events requiring its attention, while a peripheral has an outstanding request for servicing incoming data. The OS power management must be able to make a decision to either move the CPU to a lower power mode or to leave it in its present state. The decision depends on, for example, the response time to transition the CPU back to the active state and service any requests issued by the peripheral, and is also based on the permissible degradation of service provided by the peripheral for the request it is servicing.

Transitioning the CPU to and from some of these states has an impact on the rest of the system. For instance, transitioning the CPU to the off or standby state will result in open applications being terminated with loss of state and data (unless it is saved elsewhere). On returning from standby to the active state, the same applications must be restored to their previous context.

Given their wider impact, in Symbian OS we consider off, standby and active to be system-wide states, and the transitions between those states, system-wide transitions.

Peripheral transitions to low power states that are not the result of a system-wide transition may need to be agreed with their clients at other levels of the OS, given the possible degradation of the quality of service they provide to those clients.

15.2 Power framework

The kernel power framework is responsible for:

- Managing the transitions of processor core and peripherals between power states

- Making use of the energy-saving features of the hardware, detecting and responding to events which may trigger power state transitions

- Managing the hardware components' requirements on system power resources.

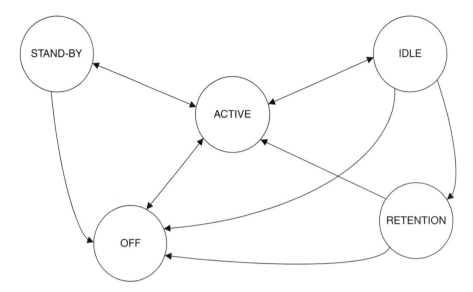

Figure 15.1 Typical CPU state transition diagram

The implementation of the framework straddles several software components, including the kernel, device and media drivers, extensions and peripheral controllers, the base port, the hardware adaptation layer (HAL).

The framework is made up of a built-in basic framework and mandatory and optional portions that must be implemented as part of the port of Symbian OS to a new hardware platform (Figure 15.1).

15.2.1 Basic framework

The basic power management framework is primarily concerned with system-wide power transitions – in other words, transitioning the processor core and peripherals as a group between the off, standby and active power states.

15.2.1.1 Power manager

The power manager is at the core of the framework and provides the API between the user and kernel levels of the framework. It co-ordinates the transition of the CPU, peripherals and hardware platform between the various system-wide power states, provides the interface to other parts of the kernel, and coordinates the interactions of the other components of the framework.

15.2.1.2 Power controller

The framework uses the variant-specific power controller to control the power behavior of CPU and other parts of the hardware platform.

The power controller may also provide a way of controlling the power resources of the platform.

15.2.1.3 Power handlers

The framework uses power handlers to control the power behavior of peripherals. This means that power handlers are associated with peripheral drivers. The implementation of power handlers may be customized at the driver level and/or at the variant level.

15.2.1.4 Wakeup events

The basic power management framework provides support for wakeup events. These are hardware events specific to each low power state, which, if they occur during a system-wide power transition, may result in the transition being cancelled or even reverted. If they occur during standby, they may trigger a return to the active state. Wakeup events for the standby or off states usually relate to user interactions or timed sources. The framework provides support for tracking these events (at peripheral driver or platform-specific levels) and notifying the user-side software component responsible for initiating the system-wide power transition of their occurrence.

15.2.1.5 CPU idle

The basic framework provides support for transitioning the CPU in and out of idle mode. The transition to this mode is triggered when there are no threads ready to run, and the kernel schedules the null (also known as the idle) thread as a result. In specific circumstances, some CPUs can be moved to a more power-saving retention state, and that would be handled by the platform-specific implementation of the idle mode handling.

15.2.1.6 Power HAL

There is a power-related group of functions that can be executed kernel-side in response to a call to the `HAL` class's `Get(...)` or `Set(...)` APIs (or for certain functions, through calling `UserHal` or `UserSvr` class APIs). This group is identified by the enumerated value `EHal-GroupPower`. The framework should also provide an object to handle this group of functions. This group of functions allow user-side components to gain access to the kernel power framework to obtain certain information or set the power behavior of selected hardware components.

15.2.2 Basic power model overview

The basic power framework only gives external visibility to the system-wide power states, which I will now enumerate:

```
enum TPowerState
  {
  EPwActive,
  EPwStandby,
  EPwOff,
  EPwLimit,
  };
```

The model relies on a user-side component to initiate the transitions to standby and off states. There should only be one such component in the system and it must have power management capabilities (for more on capabilities, see Chapter 8, *Platform Security*). This component is currently the shutdown server but that may change in the future to be the domain manager – see Chapter 16, *Boot Processes*, for more on this.

The kernel power framework was developed with the interface exported by the domain manager in mind (Figure 15.2), so I will assume throughout this chapter that the domain manager is the user-side

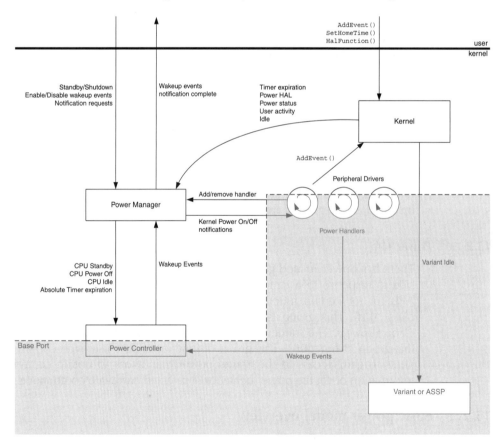

Figure 15.2   Basic framework block diagram

component responsible for initiating system-wide transitions. In the majority of cases, the behavior of the kernel framework will be the same if the shutdown server is used instead – I will describe any exceptions where relevant.

Transitions to standby or off are not instantaneous – from the moment the user requests the shutting down of the phone, until the framework is requested to perform the transition at kernel level there is typically a lengthy preparation phase in which UI state and application data are saved, and applications are shut down. We therefore want wakeup events that are detected kernel-side to be communicated to the initiator of the transition during the preparation phase. This component may on receiving a wakeup event, cancel or reverse the preparations for the system-wide transition – restoring the previous state of UI and applications.

Wakeup events are hardware-specific, and the kernel-level part of the framework maps a set of events to each target low power state. The shutdown server or domain manager must be able to set a target low power state for a system-wide transition and enable the wakeup events for that state. It must also be able to request notification of their occurrence, and in time, request the kernel framework to transition to that state.

When deciding to stop or reverse the preparations to a system-wide transition to a low power state, the initiator of the system-wide transition must be able to request the disabling of wakeup events for the previous target low power state, and set the target state to active. It must also be able to cancel the request for notification of wakeup events.

Once the kernel-side power framework has initiated a transition, the user-side initiator cannot stop that transition – although a wakeup event may still prevent it taking place.

The power manager manages the kernel-side transitions.

All of the user-side requests that I've mentioned are routed to the power manager. This receives a request to power off or go to standby state, and dispatches notifications to other components that manage the transition of CPU and peripherals to those states.

Peripheral drivers for peripherals that need to be powered down as a result of a system-wide transition to standby or off must own a power handler. When these peripheral drivers are started, they need to register with the power manager for notifications of system-wide power transitions – the power manager keeps a list of registered power handlers. When the peripheral driver object is destroyed, it should de-register its power handler with the power manager.

The power manager notifies every registered peripheral driver of an imminent power down through its power handler. Upon receiving these notifications, peripheral drivers should change the power state of the peripheral they control so as not to compromise the eventual system-wide power transition that is taking place.

As peripheral power down may take some time, each power handler owns a fast semaphore, which the power manager waits on, after requesting it to power down the peripheral. This semaphore is signaled upon completion of the peripheral power down.

After all peripherals have powered down, the power manager should request the CPU to power down. To do this, it calls down to the power controller.

If the target state of the system-wide power transition is off, instruction execution terminates soon after the call to the power controller is issued. If the target state is standby, the CPU is eventually brought back to the active state when a wakeup event occurs. Instruction execution is resumed inside the power controller call, and then control is returned to the power manager, which then powers up all peripheral drivers owning a registered power handler, and waits for them to power up, in a sequence that is the reverse of the power down that I explained previously.

Wakeup events may also occur during the user-side transition, and if they are enabled, should be propagated up to the component that initiated that transition.

Wakeup events are monitored at the variant-specific level, so every request to enable or disable them should be propagated down to the power controller.

Each system-wide low power state (standby and off) may have a different set of wakeup events. So, if the domain manager requests the enabling of wakeup events when the target state is already a low power state the power manager will disable the set corresponding to the previous low power state, before enabling the set corresponding to the new low power state. If the domain manager requests the disabling of wakeup events, the power manager assumes that it decided to stop or reverse the transition, so it is sets the target state to active.

The power controller may monitor wakeup events directly, or delegate this to a peripheral driver. In the latter case, the peripheral driver must notify the power controller of the occurrence of a wakeup event, and the power controller then propagates the notification to the power manager, which completes any pending user-side request for notification.

If the target low power state of a system-wide transition is standby, and a wakeup event happens after the kernel framework is requested to transition, but before the CPU is moved to that state, then the implementation should not complete the transition. If no event occurs, it will return when a detected wakeup event finally occurs.

Another important function of the kernel power framework is to detect the moment when the CPU idles. This can be used to move the CPU and platform to a power-saving state. Such decisions must be taken at variant-specific level, and therefore must involve the power controller.

The kernel notifies the power manager every time the null thread is scheduled to run. A power manager implementation calls down to the power controller's platform-specific implementation, which may decide to move the CPU to a low power retention state, possibly in cooperation with other components such as peripheral drivers.

There is an alternative mechanism to allow user-side components to communicate with the kernel-side framework – the HAL. This component provides APIs that any user-side component with power management capabilities may call to obtain information on power supplies and control the power behavior of certain peripherals (display, pointing devices, external case or flip, and so on).

Finally, the framework may include a battery-monitoring component, which is implemented at variant level. I will discuss this in greater detail later in the chapter.

15.2.2.1 Initialization

Early on during kernel boot (see Chapter 16, *Boot Processes),* when the microkernel is initialized, the global power manager object is created. As a power manager must own a pointer to a power controller, a dummy power controller is also created. The power manager will later replace this pointer with a pointer to a real power controller.

The power controller is typically implemented in a kernel extension; when this extension is started the power controller is created and registers with the power manager. Registering results in the power manager replacing the dummy pointer with a pointer to the real power controller. It also sets up a global pointer in the kernel, `K::PowerModel`, to point to the power manager, in this way providing the kernel with the means to access the power framework.

The base porter may not want to have a power-controller-specific kernel extension, but instead have the `Variant` object, part of the variant DLL, create and own one.

The power controller extension entry point will usually create a platform-specific handling object for the `EHalGroupPower` group of functions and register it with the power manager.

Typically, it will also create a battery monitor component at this stage, if one is to be implemented.

Finally, as the kernel starts each peripheral driver, it will register its power handler with the power manager.

15.2.2.2 API description

Let's now look at each component and its public exported interface in detail.

The user-side interface
The basic power management framework can be accessed from user-side via the `Power` class. This class provides static methods for enabling

and disabling wakeup events, requesting or canceling notification of occurrence of wakeup events and moving the kernel-side components to one of the low power states, standby or off.

```
class Power
  {
public:
  IMPORT_C static TInt EnableWakeupEvents(TPowerState);
  IMPORT_C static void DisableWakeupEvents();
  IMPORT_C static void RequestWakeupEventNotification(TRequestStatus&);
  IMPORT_C static void CancelWakeupEventNotification();
  IMPORT_C static TInt PowerDown();
  };
```

All of these functions are exported by EUSER, and gain access to the kernel-side power framework in the usual way, via executive calls. Here is a description of the public API:

- EnableWakeupEvents(). This function is used to set the target low power state for a system-wide transition and to enable wakeup events for that state. If the target state is neither EPwStandby nor EPwOff, it returns KErrArgument

- DisableWakeupEvents(). This function is used to disable wakeup events for the current target low power state for the system-wide transition in progress. If the current target power state is neither EPwstandby nor EPwoff, the call returns immediately

- RequestWakeupEventNotification(). This is the only asynchronous function; it is used to request notification of any wakeup events that happen during the preparation to transition the system to a low power state, or after the system has entered standby. Only one pending request is allowed at a time – if another request is already pending, the function returns KErrInUse

- CancelWakeupEventNotification(). This call is used to cancel a pending wakeup event notification request. If, at the time this function is called, the notification request is still pending, then it returns KErrCancel

- PowerDown(). This function requests the kernel framework to move the CPU and peripherals to a low power state. If the target low power state is standby, this function returns when a wakeup event occurs. If the target low power state is off, this call never returns.

The power manager
The power manager has no public exported APIs.

The kernel-level power management framework offers an abstract class (DPowerModel) as a template for the implementation of a power manager:

```
class DPowerModel : public DBase
  {
public:
  virtual void AbsoluteTimerExpired() = 0;
  virtual void RegisterUserActivity(const TRawEvent& anEvent) = 0;
  virtual void CpuIdle() = 0;
  virtual void SystemTimeChanged(TInt anOldTime, TInt aNewTime) = 0;
  virtual TSupplyStatus MachinePowerStatus() = 0;
  virtual TInt PowerHalFunction(TInt aFunction, TAny* a1, TAny* a2) = 0;
  };
```

This class defines the interface between the power framework and the rest of the kernel. It mandates a number of functions that should be implemented by a power manager. The kernel uses the global pointer I mentioned earlier, K::PowerModel, to call these functions. Here is a description of the DPowerModel API:

- CpuIdle(). The kernel calls this function every time the null thread is scheduled to run

- RegisterUserActivity(). The kernel calls this function every time an event is added to the event queue. Peripheral drivers that monitor user interaction (such as pressing a key, tapping the touch screen, opening or closing the phone) may add events kernel-side. A user-side component may also add events using the userSvr API AddEvent(), which is exported from EUSER.DLL. The function takes a reference to the raw event as a parameter, so a power manager implementation may choose to respond differently to different events

- PowerHalFunction(). The kernel's HAL function that handles EHalGroupPower calls this function, passing an identifier to the function to be executed. The power manager implementation should call a platform-specific handling function

- AbsoluteTimerExpired(). The kernel calls this function every time an absolute timer completes. (An absolute timer is one that expires at a specific date and time.) A power manager implementation should call a power controller's platform-specific implementation, which may regard it as a wakeup event for an impending system-wide transition

- SystemTimeChanged(). The kernel calls this function every time the software RTC (and eventually the hardware RTC, if one exists) is updated in response to a call to user::SetHomeTime()

- `MachinePowerStatus()`. The kernel calls this function whenever the framework's exported API `Kern::MachinePowerStatus()` is called. `MachinePowerStatus()` should query the battery monitoring component if one is implemented kernel-side.

The current implementation of the power manager in Symbian OS also offers:

- A kernel-side implementation of the corresponding user-side `Power` class APIs

- Management of and interface to power handlers

- Management of and interface to the power controller.

Here's the make up of the current Symbian OS power manager:

```
class DPowerManager : public DPowerModel
  {
public:
  void CpuIdle();
  void RegisterUserActivity(const TRawEvent& anEvent);
  TInt PowerHalFunction(TInt aFunction, TAny* a1, TAny* a2);
  void AbsoluteTimerExpired();
  void SystemTimeChanged(TInt anOldTime, TInt aNewTime);
  TSupplyStatus MachinePowerStatus();

public:
  static DPowerManager* New();
  TInt EnableWakeupEvents(TPowerState);
  void DisableWakeupEvents();
  void RequestWakeupEventNotification(TRequestStatus*);
  void CancelWakeupEventNotification();
  TInt PowerDown();
  void AppendHandler(DPowerHandler*);
  void RemoveHandler(DPowerHandler*);
  void WakeupEvent();
  ...
  };
```

Kernel-side implementation of user-side API

The following methods are called in response to corresponding `Power` class calls:

- `DPowerManager::EnableWakeupEvents()` enables tracking of wakeup events for a valid target low power state (standby or off)

- `DPowerManager::DisableWakeupEvents()` disables tracking of wakeup events for the target low power state

- `DPowerManager::RequestWakeupEventNotification()` enables the delivery of wakeup event notifications to the client that requested it, whenever one occurs

- `DPowerManager::CancelWakeupEventNotification()` stops the power manager from delivering wakeup event notifications to the client that requested them

- `DPowerManager::PowerDown()` initiates the kernel-side transition of CPU and peripherals to the target low power state. If the target state is standby, when a wakeup event arrives, it delivers a notification to the client if a request is pending.

These functions need access to the platform-specific powercontroller, which is protected against concurrent access and re-entrance with a mutex. Therefore, the corresponding `Power` class functions execute inside a critical section to prevent the calling thread that holds the mutex from being suspended or killed.

Management and interface to power handlers

The `DPowerManager::AppendHandler` API adds the power handler to the list of controlled objects, and the `DPowerManager::Remove-Handler` API removes it.

Management and interface to power controller

`DPowerManager::WakeupEvent()` checks if the power state is valid and completes any pending client's request for wakeup event notification.

The power handler

The `DPowerHandler` class is intended for derivation. The software component that owns the power handler must implement the pure virtual functions and may include other APIs (for example, to allow the handler to request power related resources):

```
class DPowerHandler : public DBase
    {
public:
  // to be implemented by kernel-side power framework
  IMPORT_C ~DPowerHandler();
  IMPORT_C DPowerHandler(const TDesC& aName);
  IMPORT_C void Add();
  IMPORT_C void Remove();
  IMPORT_C void PowerUpDone();
  IMPORT_C void PowerDownDone();
  IMPORT_C void SetCurrentConsumption(TInt aCurrent);
  IMPORT_C void DeltaCurrentConsumption(TInt aCurrent);
public: // to be implemented at component-specific level
  virtual void PowerDown(TPowerState) = 0;
  virtual void PowerUp() = 0;
  ...
    };
```

The APIs (exported from EKERN.EXE) with a default implementation are:

- A constructor to allow the creation of power handler objects owned by peripheral drivers. The constructor simply sets the name for this power handler from the argument passed in. (The name is only used for debug purposes.) Typically the peripheral driver-specific derived constructor will set up other relevant parameters

- Add(). Called by the component that owns the power handler to add it to the list of power handlers that receive notifications of power state changes. Calls DPowerManager::AppendHandler()

- Remove(). Called by the component that owns the power handler to remove it from the list of power handlers that receive notifications of power state changes. Calls DPowerManager::RemoveHandler(). Like the Add(), this function acquires a mutex that is also held by the implementation of PowerUp() and PowerDown(). Hence, the device driver writer must guarantee these calls are issued from inside a critical section to prevent the calling thread from being suspended or killed when owning a mutex

- PowerDownDone(). This is called by the component that owns the power handler, after it has performed all the required internal actions to guarantee that the system-wide power transition that is taking place can be accomplished

- PowerUpDone(). This is called by the component that owns the power handler, after it has performed all the required internal actions to guarantee that the system-wide transition that is taking place can be accomplished

- SetCurrentConsumption() and DeltaCurrentConsumption(). These APIs have been deprecated and should not be used

- A destructor to allow destruction from peripheral driver code.

Ownership of power handlers

Next I will discuss the ownership of power handlers. The following kernel-side software components may own power handlers:

- Kernel extensions that control simple peripherals (for example display, digitizer and keyboard) and which can be accessed from user-side through the HAL or through unique kernel interfaces, and peripherals which provide services to other peripherals (for example, an internal inter-component bus) usually enforce a policy of having a single client at a time and therefore may own, or in the majority of cases derive from, DPowerHandler

- Device drivers may control more than one unit of the same type of peripheral and so they allow multiple simultaneous clients or channels (one per unit). In this case the channel usually owns the power handler. If you are implementing an LDD/PDD split, then the logical (or physical) channel object will create and own a pointer to the power handler

- Some device drivers may enforce a single channel policy. In this case, the logical device may own the power handler

- Peripheral bus controllers are used to extend access to the system bus (or any bus internal to the device) to external peripherals. They may be able to support multiple physical interfaces, in which case each interface implementation should own a power handler. Examples of these are the PCMCIA and MMC/SD/SDIO bus controllers

- In other instances, controllers only support one physical interface but multiple logical instances. In this case the controller itself will own the power handler – this is the case of the USB controller.

The power controller

The power controller object must derive from the DPowerController class. This class provides APIs for initiating CPU-specific preparations for going to low power states, enabling/disabling tracking of wakeup events at platform-specific level and allowing peripheral drivers to notify the occurrence of wakeup events that they track:

```
class DPowerController : public DBase
  {
public: // Framework
  IMPORT_C DPowerController();
  IMPORT_C void Register();
  IMPORT_C void WakeupEvent();
  ...
public: // Platform-specific power component
  virtual void Cpuidle() = 0;
  virtual void EnableWakeupEvents() = 0;
  virtual void DisableWakeupEvents() = 0;
  virtual void AbsoluteTimerExpired() = 0;
  virtual void PowerDown(TTimeK aWakeupTime) = 0;
  ...
  };
```

The APIs (exported from EKERN.EXE) with default implementation are:

- A constructor to allow a platform-specific component (such as the variant DLL or the power controller kernel extension) to create a power controller. The default implementation sets the power controller power state to active. The platform-specific constructor will usually register the power controller with the power manager

- `Register()`. This API registers a power controller with the power manager. The implementation of `Register()` replaces the power controller object pointer with a pointer to this one

- `WakeupEvent()`. Calls the power manager to notify it of a wakeup event.

The power HAL handler

This is the prototype of a platform-specific handling object for the power HAL group of functions:

```
class DPowerHal : public DBase
  {
public:
  IMPORT_C DPowerHal();
  IMPORT_C void Register();
public:
  virtual TInt PowerHalFunction(TInt aFunction, TAny* a1, TAny* a2) = 0;
  };
```

The APIs (exported from `EKERN.EXE`) with default implementation are:

- An exported constructor to allow a platform-specific component to create a handling object

- `Register()`. This registers the power handling function with the power manager.

15.2.3   Walkthrough of user-initiated shutdown

Now that I have explained the role of each component of the framework and their APIs, let's look at how they are used on a user-initiated transition to standby or off.

The shutting down of the phone is typically triggered by the user pressing a power button. In other cases, defined by a UI policy, it may be triggered by a user inactivity timer. These events are detected at kernel level and propagated to the user-side component that manages the system shutdown, currently the shutdown server.

The shutdown server starts the transition by notifying active applications that a transition is imminent, allowing them to save status and shut down.

It is only after all this is done that the shutdown server requests the kernel framework to transition the CPU, peripherals and the hardware platform to the target state.

The reverse applies to the transition from standby to active, with the CPU and peripherals transitioning first, and then a notification generated at the kernel framework level being propagated upwards to the shutdown server which is responsible for transitioning the rest of the system.

I will describe the processes of shutting down and restarting and the user-level components involved in more detail in the next chapter, *Boot Processes*.

Let us now look at the sequence of events in the kernel level framework during a transition to standby or off.

The way in which the user-side shutdown initiator hooks into the kernel framework varies, with the shutdown server calling `User-Hal::SwitchOff()` (see Section 15.2.3.6) which then calls the `Power` class APIs, and the domain manager calling those APIs directly. In either case, the calls are always made in the sequence I will now describe.

The sequence starts with a call to `Power::EnableWakeup-Events()`, passing the target low power state as an argument (`EPw-standby` or `EPwoff`). This goes through an executive call to the kernel in a critical section, and ends up in the power manager. The power manager sets the target state, and then calls the derived `DPowerController` object's platform-specific implementation of `EnableWakeupEvents()`. As I have said before, this will either enable wakeup events directly in hardware, or call to relevant drivers.

The next function to be called in the sequence is `Power::Request-WakeupEventNotification()`. This goes through an executive call, inside a critical section, to the power manager. The power manager simply saves the pointers to the `TRequestStatus` object and the requester client thread.

If the power manager receives a notification that a wakeup event has occurred at any point during the transition to a low power state, or after the transition to standby, it uses the pointers to the request status object and the client thread to complete the request (with `KErrNone`).

The final function in the sequence is `Power::PowerDown()` which initiates the kernel-side shutdown. Again this goes through an executive call, inside a critical section, to the power manager. The power manager performs the following sequence:

1. Notifies every registered power handler of power down, by calling the driver-specific implementation of `DPowerHandler::Power-Down()` and passing the target power state. The driver-specific implementation may shut down the peripheral removing its power source (if the target state is off) or move it to a low power state, relinquishing its use on power resources, and possibly leaving some of its subsystems operational for detection of wakeup events (if the target state is standby)

2. Waits for all the power handlers to complete powering down. Completion is signaled by the peripheral driver calling `DPower-Handler::PowerDownDone()`

3. Acquires the tick queue mutex to stop tick timers being updated

4. Calls `DPowerController::PowerDown()`, passing the time for the next absolute timer expiration (in system ticks)

5. The platform-specific power controller function prepares the CPU for, and transitions it to, the low power state. If the target state is off, instruction execution terminates. If the target state is standby, execution is halted until a wakeup event occurs or an absolute timer expires, when execution resumes, the power controller restores the state of the CPU and core peripherals and control returns back to the power manager

6. Back in the power manager, it is safe to set the power state to active. The power manager wakes up the second queue (a different queue, used for second-based timers and driven by the tick queue), which will resynchronize the system time with the hardware RTC. If waking up on an absolute timer, this will queue a DFC to call back any timers which have expired and restart second queue. The power manager releases the timer mutex

7. At this point the power manager notifies all registered power handlers of the transition to the active state by calling the driver-specific implementation of `DPowerHandler::PowerUp()`. This may restore the peripheral state and power it up

8. As before, the power manager waits for all power handlers to finish powering up, which is signaled by the peripheral driver calling `DPowerHandler::PowerUpDone()`

9. Finally, the power manager simply completes the request for notification of wakeup events if one is pending.

15.2.3.1   *Remapping standby state to off state*

As I mentioned before, the shutdown server is currently the user-side component responsible for initiating a shutdown. It does that by calling `UserHal::SwitchOff()` which requests the kernel framework to transition to standby. It is likely that the device creator will want the shutdown sequence to end in the power supply to the CPU and peripherals being removed to prolong the life of the device's battery – unless the device includes a backup battery which could be used to power the self-refreshing SDRAM in standby state. In this case, the base porter may remap the standby state to off.

15.2.4   Customizing the basic framework

The framework includes several abstract classes that are intended as prototypes for platform-specific (or driver-specific) components. Those porting Symbian OS to new hardware would implement these framework components as part of the base port, or in the case of power handlers, as peripheral drivers.

This customization of the framework implements mandatory functions that deal with:

1. Peripheral transitions when a system-wide transition occurs, to or from the standby state, or to the off state

2. CPU transitions when a system-wide transition occurs, to or from the standby state, or to the off state

3. CPU transitions to and from the idle mode

4. Tracking of standby wakeup events

5. Handling of power-related HAL functions.

15.2.4.1 *Peripheral power down and power up*

A `DPowerHandler` class derived object requires the following functions to be implemented:

- `PowerDown()`. This requests peripheral power down. The power manager calls this function during a transition to the standby or off state

- `PowerUp()`. This notifies the peripheral of a system power up. The power manager calls the power handler's `PowerUp()` when returning from standby back to the active state.

After receiving a request to power down, a peripheral driver should execute the necessary actions to power down the peripheral and ancillary hardware (unless it is required for detection of wakeup events and the target state is standby). This may include requesting the removal of the power supply, and also releasing the requirements on other power resources such as clocks and power supplies.

After this is done, the driver should signal to the power manager that the peripheral has powered down by calling the power handler's `PowerDownDone()` method.

After it receives notification of system power up, a peripheral driver may decide to power up the peripheral and ancillary hardware. The decision depends on the internal operational state of the peripheral driver before the transition to standby. The peripheral driver should also signal to the power manager that the call has completed by calling the power handler's `PowerUpDone()` method.

`PowerDown()` and `PowerUp()` are called in the context of the user-side component that requested the system-wide transition. `Power-DownDone()` and `PowerUpDone()` can be called from that same thread, or from the peripheral driver's thread (before or after the corresponding `PowerDown()` or `PowerUp()` functions return).

Note that `PowerUp()` and `PowerDown()` are only used on transitions to and from the standby or active states or transitions to off state. The peripheral hardware is typically powered up on opening a peripheral driver and down on closing it, and its power state changes when the driver uses or releases it – and all of this should be fully managed by the driver software.

15.2.4.2   *CPU power down and power up*

A `DPowerController` class derived object requires an implementation of `PowerDown()` which deals with the CPU transition between the standby, active and off states. The power manager calls the power controller's `PowerDown()` function to move the CPU to a low power state. `PowerDown()` runs in the context of the shutdown server (or domain manager). If one or more wakeup events occur during execution of the call, but before the power state is entered, the `PowerDown()` call should return immediately.

`PowerDown()` takes an argument (`aWakeupTime`), which is a system time value; if it is not null and the target state is standby, it specifies the time when the system should wakeup. This is the time when the next absolute timer will expire. Typically the implementation starts by checking that this time is in the future, and then programs the RTC (real time clock) module to generate an event at the specified time, which will cause a return to the active state. For this to happen, the call should enable RTC event detection during standby. The implementation of `PowerDown()` must make sure that setting the RTC to wakeup in the future will not cause it to wrap around, as the maintenance of the system time depends on the knowledge of when this happens. In this case, the RTC should wakeup the CPU just before it is about to wrap.

If `aWakeupTime` is null, the system will only wake up from standby when a wakeup event occurs. When this happens, the CPU wakes up and the `PowerDown()` function resumes and restores the status that was saved before entering standby. At that point, there is no need to call `WakeupEvent()` – upon returning from this function the power manager will notify any client which requested notification of wakeup events.

If the target state is off, then `PowerDown()` will never return. Usually the power controller turns off the CPU power supply.

Preparation to go to standby state
In the standby state, the CPU's and core peripherals' clocks and even their power supplies, may be suppressed. This means that their internal state

is not preserved. In this case, PowerDown() should save this internal state, so that it can be restored when the system wakes up. This is done as follows:

- CPU state. Saves all registers (on ARM – the current mode, banked registers for each mode, and stack pointer for both the current mode and user mode)

- MMU state. On ARM saves the control register, translation table base address, domain access control (if supported)

- Flushes the data cache and drains the write buffer

- Core peripherals. Saves the state of interrupt controller, I/O pin function controller, external (memory) bus state controller, clock controller, and so on.

When this data is saved to SDRAM, PowerDown() should place the device in self-refresh mode. If the SDRAM device allows partial bank refresh, and support has been implemented to query bank usage, PowerDown() can set the used banks to self-refresh, and power down unused banks of memory. Obviously this uses less power.

Usually PowerDown() would leave peripheral subsystems that are involved in the detection of wakeup events powered and capable of detection.

PowerDown() should also disable tick timer events and save the current count of this and any other system timers; it should enable any relevant wakeup events, and disable any others.

On entering the standby state, instruction execution halts. PowerDown() can do this simply by stopping the CPU clock, if this has used a fully static architecture. A wakeup event will restart the CPU clock, and execution resumes.

On returning from standby state, when PowerDown() resumes execution, it should restore the CPU and core peripherals' state that it saved prior to going to standby.

15.2.4.3   CPU idle

A DPowerController class derived object requires an implementation of CpuIdle(), which deals with CPU transition to idle state.

The idle state is a transitional state, often the gateway to a power-saving retention mode. In Section 15.2.2.1, I will look at how the CPU can be moved to these retention states.

Variant-specific idle
As I mentioned previously, the scheduling of the null thread is what signals the CPU idle condition.

The null thread is the first thread to start on a device at boot time, and it runs before the power manager has been registered with the kernel. Therefore, an alternative to the power manager's own `CpuIdle()` function must be provided, as a pure virtual method of the `Asic` class:

```
class Asic
  {
public:
  ...
  // power management
  virtual void Idle()=0;
  ...
  };
```

This function is typically a dummy implementation, provided by the `Asic` class derived `Variant` class. Once the power manager has been registered, the kernel will call its `CpuIdle()` function instead.

15.2.4.4   Enabling access to power controller from other kernel-side components

It is common that other kernel-side components such as the variant, or peripheral drivers, need access to the power controller. This has no built-in accessible interfaces, other than to the power manager. When porting Symbian OS, the base porter may therefore wish to implement a derived power controller exported method to return a pointer to itself and an interface class, in this way:

```
class TXXXPowerControllerInterface
  {
public:
  ...
  // to allow Drivers access to power controller
  IMPORT_C static PowerController* PowerController();
  inline static void RegisterPowerController(
              DXXXPowerController* aPowerController)
              {iPowerController=aPowerController;}
public:
  ...
  static DXXXPowerController* iPowerController;
  };

EXPORT_C DXXXPowerController*
   TXXXPowerControllerInterface::PowerController()
  {
  return &iPowerController;
  }
```

The power controller derived object's constructor should register the power controller with the interface, which is best done at construction time:

```
DXXXPowerController::DXXXPowerController()
  {
  Register(); //register power ctrllr with power manager

  // register power controller with interface
  TXXXPowerController::RegisterPowerController(this);
  }
```

15.2.4.5 Handling of wakeup events

When the CPU and peripherals move to the standby state, their responsiveness and availability are greatly reduced. This is accepted by the user who has chosen to switch the phone off and the framework uses that acceptance to save power.

However, at the OS level, we need to enable a minimum capability to respond to user interactions, so that the framework can transition the phone back to a more available state when the user switches the phone back on. Also, some internal events, such as expiry of absolute timers, must be able to bring the phone back to a more available state.

A DPowerController-derived object should implement the following pure virtual functions to handle wakeup events:

- EnableWakeupEvents()

- DisableWakeupEvents()

- AbsoluteTimerExpired().

EnableWakeupEvents()

Typically, the domain manager (or shutdown server) will start a transition to standby by requesting the kernel power framework to start monitoring wakeup events and notify it of their occurrence.

As a result, the power manager calls the power controller's Enable-WakeupEvents() to enable detection at platform-specific level.

Monitoring wakeup events

The power controller may monitor some wakeup events directly. If that is the case, the implementation of EnableWakeupEvents() programs the hardware components involved in their detection, and hooks a handling function to service the event. This is commonly achieved with the use of an interrupt – the ISR should schedule a DFC to notify the power manager of the event.

More commonly, peripheral drivers monitor wakeup events. In this case, the implementation of EnableWakeupEvents() should store whether the event is enabled, like so:

```
class DXXXPowerController : public DPowerController
```

```
     {
public: // from DPowerController
  ...
  void EnableWakeupEvents();
  void AbsoluteTimerExpired();
  void DisableWakeupEvents();
  ...
public:
  DXXXPowerController();
  ...
private:
  TInt iWakeupEventMask;
  ...
  };

void DXXXPowerController::EnableWakeupEvents()
  {
  ...

// Set iWakeUpMask to a bit mask with one bit set for
// each relevant wakeup event for the standby state
  if(iTargetState==EPwstandby)
     iWakeupEventMask=myMask;
  }
```

There are two possible schemes:

1. Upon the occurrence of the event, the driver checks with the power controller to see if the event is enabled, and if it is, notifies the power manager by calling the power controller's `WakeupEvent()` method. (It checks by calling an API such as the next example `IsWakeupEventEnable(...)`, and passing a bit mask containing the wakeup event that it is interested in.)

```
public:
inline TBool IsWakeupEventEnabled(Tint aWakeupEvent)
  {
  (iWakeupEventMask & aWakeupEvent) ?
             return ETrue : return EFalse;
  }
```

2. The driver notifies the power controller whenever a wakeup event it monitors occurs, using an API such as the next example `NotifyWakeupEvent()`, and passing a bit mask containing the wakeup event that it monitors; the API checks to see if the wakeup event is enabled, and if it is, notifies the power manager by calling the `WakeupEvent()` method.

```
public:
inline void NotifyWakeupEvent (Tint aWakeupEvent)
```

```
{
if(iWakeupEventMask & aWakeupEvent) WakeupEvent();
}
```

Obviously, for either of these schemes to work, the peripheral driver must have access to the power controller as I described previously.

DisableWakeupEvents()

`DisableWakeupEvents()` either disables the detection of wakeup events directly in hardware, if the power controller monitors them, or it signals to the peripheral driver that monitors them to stop notifying the power controller of their occurrence.

AbsoluteTimerExpired()

Absolute timer expiration is typically a monitored wakeup event; the servicing of `AbsoluteTimerExpired()` should simply notify the power manager of a wakeup event:

```
void DXXXPowerController::AbsoluteTimerExpired()
  {
  if (iTargetState == EPwstandby) WakeupEvent();
  }
```

15.2.4.6   *Handling of power HAL group of functions*

A `DPowerHal`-derived object requires an implementation of `Power-HalFunction()`, which provides the platform-specific handling of a group of HAL functions.

The HAL component provides user-side access to certain platform-specific functions. It uses the following public exported APIs:

```
class HAL : public HALData
  {
public:
  IMPORT_C static TInt Get(TAttribute aAttribute, TInt& aValue);
  IMPORT_C static TInt Set(TAttribute aAttribute, TInt aValue);
  ...
  IMPORT_C static TInt Get(TInt aDeviceNumber,
               TAttribute aAttribute, TInt& aValue);
  IMPORT_C static TInt Set(TInt aDeviceNumber,
               TAttribute aAttribute, TInt aValue);
  };
```

These can be called with an attribute specifying what function is to be executed at platform-specific level.

The set of HAL attributes that may need to be handled by the `Power-HalFunction()` function are:

- `EPowerBatteryStatus` – used with `HAL::Get(...)` only, see Section 15.3.1.3

- `EPowerGood` – used with `HAL::Get(...)` only, see Section 15.3.1.3

- `EPowerBackupStatus` – used with `HAL::Get(...)` only, see Section 15.3.1.3

- `EPowerExternal` – used with `HAL::Get(...)` only, see Section 15.3.1.3

- `EPowerBackup` – used with `HAL::Get(...)` only, see Section 15.3.1.3

- `EAccessoryPower` – used with `HAL::Get(...)` only, see Section 15.3.1.3

- `EPenDisplayOn` – used with `HAL::Set(...)` to enable switching the display on when tapping the touch panel, or `HAL::Get(...)` to query if tapping the touch panel will switch the display on

- `ECaseSwitchDisplayOn` – used with `HAL::Set(...)` to enable switching the display on when opening the phone lid, or `HAL::Get(...)` to query if opening the phone lid will switch the display on

- `ECaseSwitchDisplayOff` – used with `HAL::Set(...)` to enable switching the display off when closing the phone lid, or `HAL::Get(...)` to query if closing the phone lid will switch the display off.

The `DPowerHal` derived object's `PowerHalFunction(...)` will be called in response to HAL calls with any of the previous attributes and is passed one of the following parameters (in place of the `aFunction` argument) to indicate what function to perform at this level:

- `EPowerHalSupplyInfo` – called in response to `HAL::Get(...)` with `EPowerBatteryStatus`, `EPowerGood`, `EPowerBackupStatus` or `EPowerExternal`. Returns a device-specific information structure that is usually kept by the battery-monitoring component (if one exists at this level – see Section 15.3.1.3)

- `EPowerHalBackupPresent` – called in response to `HAL::Get(...)` with `EPowerBackup`, used to query for the presence of a backup battery (see Section 15.3.1.3)

- `EPowerHalAcessoryPowerPresent` – called in response to `HAL::Get(...)` with `EAccessoryPower`, used to query for the presence of accessory power (see Section 15.3.1.3)

- `EPowerHalSetPointerSwitchesOn` – called in response to `HAL::Set(...)` with `EPenDisplayOn`, may be used to enable switching the display back when tapping the touch sensitive panel. On periods of user inactivity, the window server may request the switching off of the display and backlight to conserve power. This is part of a system-wide power policy, which is not the object of this chapter

- `EPowerHalPointerSwitchesOn` – called in response to `HAL::Get(...)` with `EPenDisplayOn`, used to query if tapping the screen will switch the display back on

- `EPowerHalSetCaseOpenSwitchesOn` – called in response to `HAL::Set(...)` with `ECaseSwitchDisplayOn`, may be used to enable switching the display back on when opening any external encasement (lid on a clam shell device, the sliding panel, and so on)

- `EPowerHalCaseOpenSwitchesOn` – called in response to `HAL::Get(...)` with `ECaseSwitchDisplayOn`, used to query if opening the case will switch the display back on

- `EPowerHalSetCaseCloseSwitchesOff` – called in response to `HAL::Set(...)` with `ECaseSwitchDisplayoff`, may be used to enable the switching off of the display when closing the case. Again, this may be part of a system-wide power policy taken care by a component not covered by this chapter

- `EPowerHalCaseCloseSwitchesOff` – called in response to `HAL::Get(...)` with `ECaseSwitchDisplayoff`, used to query if closing the case will switch the display off.

As I mentioned previously, `PowerHalFunction` may be invoked in response to a user-side component call to a `UserSvr` class exported API, `HalFunction(...)` – an export from EUSER.DLL:

```
class UserSvr
  {
public: ...
  IMPORT_C static TInt HalFunction(TInt aGroup,
                 TInt aFunction, TAny* a1, TAny* a2);
  IMPORT_C static TInt HalFunction(TInt aGroup,
                 TInt aFunction, TAny* a1,
                 TAny* a2, TInt aDeviceNumber);
  ...
  };
```

There are a number of other argument values that `PowerHalFunction` function may be invoked with if using `UserSvr::HalFunction(...)`, such as:

- `EPowerHalOnoffInfo` – used to read a `TOnoffInfoV1` structure. This structure is used to record the display switch on/switch off behavior

- `EPowerHalSwitchoff` – this may be used to request a system-wide transition to standby and is provided for binary compatibility with previous versions of the OS. When this is serviced, an `ESwitchoff TRawEvent` will be added to the event queue, from where the window server will pick it up and call `UserHal::Switchoff()`, which will request a transition to standby (see Section 15.2.2). This behavior is customizable at the UI level, and the UI integrator may change it to merely switch UI peripherals such as the display, keypad and touch screen off, leaving the rest of the phone operational

- `EPowerHalTestBootSequence` – this may be used to indicate if the machine is being booted in device-specific test mode.

The following argument values have been deprecated and do not require handling:

- `EPowerHalSetAutoSwitchoffBehavior`

- `EPowerHalAutoSwitchoffBehavior`

- `EPowerHalSetAutoSwitchoffTime`

- `EPowerHalAutoSwitchoffTime`

- `EPowerHalResetAutoSwitchoffTimer`

- `EPowerHalSetBatteryType`

- `EPowerHalBatteryType`

- `EPowerHalSetBatteryCapacity`

- `EPowerHalBatteryCapacity`

- `EPowerHalAutoSwitchoffType.`

15.3 Typical power management

15.3.1 Extending the basic framework

We can identify a number of areas where extending the existing basic framework will result in power savings or increased ability to control and monitor power consumption. These extensions can mostly be done at the base port level. The extensions I will propose next utilize the existing framework functionality.

15.3.1.1   *Resource management*

Recent mobile phone designs define a number of power resources, such as clock frequencies, voltages and switchable power rails. Software can control these resources independently for each hardware component (CPU and peripherals).

Power resources vary in complexity, from simple binary resources that can be switched on or off almost instantaneously to resources that can be set at different voltage levels or that take a while to change state. There are even resources that may only be changed in conjunction with other resources.

And, of course, some resources are shared between hardware components, and controlling them should be based on tracking their usage.

The base port controls power resources. The base porter needs to provide interfaces for the use of:

1. Peripheral drivers, to be able to change the resources used by the peripherals they control

2. The software component responsible for setting the operating point of the CPU when processing a task (see Section 15.5.1)

3. The derived `DPowerController CpuIdle()` function. This routine maps resource state to retention state, and may need to change the state of other resources to achieve the CPU retention state desired (see Section 15.3.1.2).

Controllable power resources may be spread across several functional areas of the ASIC and external components. However, in most cases, it is possible to concentrate the control of power resources on a single software component, the resource manager (Figure 15.3), which offers a conceptual representation and interfaces for all resources. The base porter may also decide to include resource management as part of the power controller kernel extension.

Let's now look at a suggested template for the resource manager. This will be based on an `XXXResourceManager` class:

```
class XXXResourceManager
  {
public:
  enum TResource // a list of controllable resources
                 (e.g clocks, voltages, power lines)
    {
    SynchBinResourceUsedByZOnly,
```

```
    AsynchBinResourceUsedByZOnly,
    // ... other non-shared binary resources, synchronous
                                        or asynchronous
    BinResourceSharedByZAndY,
    // ... other shared binary resources, synchronous
                                        or asynchronous
    SynchMlResourceUsedByXOnly,
    AsynchMlResourceUsedByXOnly,
    // ... other non-shared multilevel resources, synchronous
                                            or asynchronous
    MlResourceSharedByXAndW,
    // ... other shared multilevel resources, synchronous
                                        or asynchronous
  };

void InitResources(); // initialises power Resources
                        not initialised by Bootstrap

// interface for non-shared resources

inline void Modify(TResource aResource, TBool aOnoff);
// for non-shared binary resources
inline void ModifyToLevel(TResource aResource, Tint
    aLevel);  // for non-shared multilevel resources
// the following functions may be used by
            Drivers/Extensions or the idle routine to
            determine what resources are On or off
            or their levels
inline TBool GetResourceState(TResource aResource);
                    // for non-shared binary resources
inline TUint GetResourceLevel(TResource aResource);
                // for non-shared multilevel resources
public:
// interface for shared resources

SharedBinaryResourceX iSharedBResource;
inline SharedBinaryResourceX* SharedBResourceX()
            {return & iSharedBResource;}
//   ...    other shared Binary resources,
                    synchronous or asynchronous
SharedMultilevelResourceY iSharedMlResource;
inline SharedMultilevelResourceY* SharedMlResourceY()
            {return & iSharedMlResource;}
//   ...    other shared Multilevel resources
};
```

If the resource manager needs to be available to the Variant component, or used early in the boot sequence, I recommend that the entry point of the kernel extension be written as follows:

```
static XXXResourceManager TheResourceManager;
static DXXXPowerHal* XXXPowerHal;

GLDEF_C TInt KernelModuleEntry(TInt aReason)
  {
  if(aReason==KModuleEntryReasonVariantInit0)
```

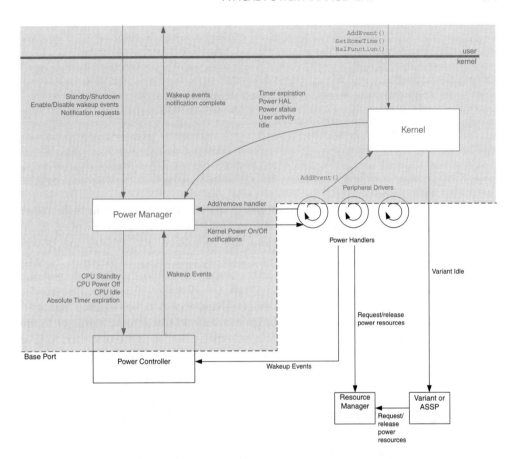

Figure 15.3 Framework block diagram with resource manager

```
  {
  // Start the Resource Manager earlier so that
        Variant and other extension could make use of
                                  Power Resources
  __KTRACE_OPT(KPOWER, Kern::Printf("Starting
                    Resource controller"));
  new(&TheResourceManager) XXXResourceManager;
  TheResourceManager.InitResources();
  return KErrNone;
  }
else if(aReason==KModuleEntryReasonExtensionInit0)
  {
  // Returning KErrNone here ensures we are called
later with aReason==KModuleEntryReasonExtensionInit1.
  return KErrNone;
  }
else if(aReason==KModuleEntryReasonExtensionInit1)
  {
```

```
    __KTRACE_OPT(KPOWER, Kern::Printf("Starting power
                                      controller"));
  XXXPowerHal = new DXXXPowerHal();
  if (!XXXPowerHal)
    return KErrNoMemory;
  DXXXPowerController* c = new DXXXPowerController();
  if(!c)
    return KErrNoMemory;
  return KErrNone;
  }
  return KErrArgument;
}
```

This allows the kernel startup sequence to create the resource manager
at `Variant` component creation time. The entry point is invoked again
when other kernel extensions are initialized and creates the power
controller.

Alternatively, the `Variant` component could create, and own the
resource manager.

To give the variant and device drivers access to the resource manager,
the power controller could export a method that returns a pointer to the
resource manager object. This scheme is similar to the one used to give
access to the power controller object as I explained in Section 15.2.3.5:

```
class TXXXPowerControllerInterface
  {
public:
  ...
  // to allow Variant/Drivers/other Extensions access to Resource Manager
  IMPORT_C static XXXResourceManager* ResourceManager();
  ...
  };

EXPORT_C XXXResourceManager*
        TXXXPowerControllerInterface::ResourceManager()
  {
  return &TheResourceManager;
  }
```

Resources may be shared by several hardware components; the existing
framework already has a template to model the interface required by a
binary-shared resource:

```
class MPowerInput
  {
public:
  virtual void Use() = 0;
  virtual void Release() = 0;
  };
```

A shared binary resource deriving from this class needs to implement the pure virtual functions:

- `Use()`. Signals that the power resource is in use. A driver calls this function when it needs the resource to be turned on. A typical implementation associates a counter, initially zero, with the object. `Use()` increments the counter and, if the counter's value changes from 0 to 1, turns the resource on

- `Release()`. Signals that the power resource is not in use. A driver calls this function when it no longer needs the source to be on. `Release()` would decrement the counter I mentioned previously. If the counter's value changes from 1 to 0, `Release()` turns the resource off.

The implementation may add other functions to get the current usage count or resource state. Usage count is especially important as some resources have a maximum acceptable load. When the cumulative load (usage count) on a resource equals its maximum, any attempt to increase its usage count should fail.

Multi-level resources may also be shared. The control model I mentioned previously is not appropriate for such resources – users will want to increase or decrease the level of the resource, rather than switch it on or off. The implementation needs to keep track of the current level of the resource and the requirement of each of the resource users. If a user asks to increase the level, then this is done (up to the maximum acceptable level). But if the user requests a lowering of the present level, then the level is reduced to the maximum requirement from all users. If the requestor does not have the highest level, then there will be no change.

The considerations made previously regarding the maximum cumulative load still apply; however in the case of multi-level resources, the maximum acceptable load may be different for different levels.

A generic shared multi-level API template could look like this:

```
class SharedMultilevelResource // Multilevel Shared Input
    {
public:
    virtual void IncreaseToLevel(TUint aLevel, TInt aRequester) = 0;
    virtual void ReduceToLevel(TUint aLevel, TInt aRequester) = 0;
    virtual TUint GetResourceLevel() = 0;
    };
```

The `aRequester` parameter on the APIs identifies the user that is requesting a level change.

Finally, there are power resources that cannot be instantaneously varied, requiring, for example, a stabilization period after being changed.

These need to be addressed differently. The software component that requested the resource change needs to wait for the resource to be stable before proceeding. Busy-waiting inside kernel-side components is strongly discouraged in EKA2, especially as the stabilization times may be long. A better alternative is to put the thread to sleep for a period of time, after which the thread can poll the resource again. The base porter can use `Kern::PollingWait()` for this purpose.

You should note that most device drivers use the same kernel thread and so when this thread sleeps, waiting for a resource to stabilize, other device drivers will be also be held up. If the resource stabilization time is long enough to impact the performance of other drivers on the same thread, the device driver which controls the resource may need to create its own kernel thread and change the resource from there. This thread can sleep without affecting the performance of other drivers, and then can call back to the main driver thread when the resource change finally takes place.

Given the multi-threaded nature of EKA2, we advise the base porter to write code that accesses resources with the kernel locked to guarantee their consistency. This is mandatory for shared resources, when accesses can be performed from different threads. If an interrupt service routine can read or change resources, interrupts should also be disabled around any access points.

15.3.1.2 Moving the CPU to retention from idle

Certain CPUs support a number of low power states distinguished by their ability to retain status, their different power requirements and their wakeup time.

Moving to one of these low power retention states is a non-system-wide power transition that can be wholly managed by the base port part of the kernel framework. In fact, transitions in and out of these low power retention states should be transparent to the rest of the system. If it is likely that a transition to a retention state may have an impact on other parts of the system at a given time then the base port code should not move the CPU to that state at that time, even if the opportunity presents itself.

Let's consider the actions needed to move the CPU to a low power retention state. I've said that the transition will happen in the power controller's platform-specific `CpuIdle()` function.

To guarantee the maximum uninterrupted idle time, some events need to be disabled during that period. The best example of such an event is the system tick – the periodic timed interrupt that is the basis for all timing in EKA2, and is provided by a hardware timer. This is commonly known as idle tick suppression.

The idle time can be predicted as the time until the next timer in the system is due to expire. The CpuIdle() implementation can examine the nanokernel timer queue (NTimerQ) which provides this information. The power framework already has an API to return the number of system ticks before the next NTimer expiration, the function IdleTime(), which is a member of the NTimerQ class. The CpuIdle() implementation can now suppress the system tick for that period, and program the hardware timer to skip the required number of ticks.

When the hardware timer finally wakes the CPU, CpuIdle() can simply adjust the system tick count and reset the hardware timer to produce the regular ticks again. To adjust the system tick count, CpuIdle() may use the function Advance(), which is a member of the NTimerQ class, passing it the number of suppressed ticks.

The CPU may wake up as a result of an event rather than the expiration of the hardware timer. In this case, the implementation of CpuIdle() needs to read the hardware timer, work out the number of integral system ticks suppressed and adjust the system tick count. It must also reprogram the hardware timer to generate the next (and subsequent) system ticks.

Sometimes waking up from a retention state can take longer than several system ticks. In that case, CpuIdle() should program the hardware timer to wake the CPU up at a time given by the next NTimer expiration minus the number of ticks it takes to wake up from that state.

This waking up from a retention state happens inside the null thread – this means that the post amble needed to restore the status should be kept as short as possible. Both preamble and post-amble routines should be executed with interrupts disabled, to stop them from being preempted.

It often happens that while the CPU is in the retention state, it is not able to perform the periodic refreshing that SDRAM needs. In this case, the SDRAM must be placed in self-refresh mode before going into the retention state, with the CPU reassuming control of refreshing it after waking up.

The choice of low power retention state is connected with the current status of the phone's power resources. The idle transition routine must have the ability to inspect the state of relevant resources, by interrogating the resource manager. This interface also allows the state of resources to be modified as needed.

The CPU is moved to a low power retention state by a wait-for-interrupt type instruction, which will suspend instruction execution until an enabled hardware event occurs.

Naturally, events other than the hardware timer interrupt may have the ability to wake the CPU up from the retention state; these are wakeup events for that state. Wakeup events for the retention state include not only hardware events that result from user interaction (screen tapping, key press, and so on) and timed alarms as for the standby state, but also the events that result from other peripherals' operation (such as receiving a unit of data from an input peripheral, a media change resulting from inserting or removing a removable media device) device timeouts, and more. These events should be left enabled or explicitly enabled prior to moving the CPU to retention state.

If a wakeup event other than the timer's expiration brings the CPU back from idle state, the CpuIdle() implementation must determine how many ticks were effectively skipped, and adjust the system tick count accordingly, before resetting the hardware timer to produce regular ticks. CpuIdle() can do this simply by examining the hardware timer's current count. However the adjustment needs to take in consideration that the effective elapsed time may not be an integral number of system ticks.

Finally, the base porter may decide, on longer periods of CPU idle, to transition the CPU to a state that is not capable of state retention, such as the standby state I described previously. To transition to this state, the CpuIdle() routine needs to save the status of the CPU and possibly that of some peripherals, as I described previously. Although this results in greater power savings, extreme care must be taken, as the transition into and out of such a state may severely impact the performance and real-time guarantees of the system.

15.3.1.3 *Battery monitoring and management*

The majority of Symbian OS mobile phones that were in the market as this book was written were based on a two-chip solution, with one processor dedicated to the telephony application and associated signaling stacks, and the other for Symbian OS. In this case, the telephony processor usually performs battery monitoring and management. Symbian OS gets the battery information through the communication channel between the two devices.

However, in the future we may see single-chip and even single-core solutions becoming more common. For single-core solutions, Symbian OS will provide battery monitoring and management. The base port will do the actual monitoring of battery levels. The framework must offer an interface to read the levels from the battery hardware-controlling component. It also needs to register and propagate any battery related events.

The management of the information provided by the battery monitoring involves notifying applications and other user-side components of level changes or critical conditions. For example, when the battery level drops below a certain level, the system-wide power policy might be that the window server must ask the screen driver to switch the display driver to a different mode, lowering the resolution and refresh rate to conserve power. The OS power policy must include provisions to keep the user of the phone informed of the battery level and warn him/her when the level drops below the safety threshold or when a charger has been connected.

The policy may even force a transition to a low power state, if the battery level drops below a critical threshold.

A user-side battery manager component should communicate with the battery monitoring part of the framework (a kernel-side component).

Certain device drivers may also have an interest in battery levels or notification of battery events.

The kernel framework has a template for a battery monitor as provided by DBatteryMonitor class:

```
class DBatteryMonitor
  {
public:
  IMPORT_C DBatteryMonitor();
  IMPORT_C void Register();
public:
  virtual TSupplyStatus MachinePowerStatus() = 0;
  virtual void systemTimeChanged(TInt anOldTime, TInt aNewTime) = 0;
  };
```

This class includes an exported constructor to allow the platform-specific power kernel extension to create the monitor, and a Register() function, which the entry point of this extension should invoke after the monitor object is created, to register the battery monitor with the power manager. These two public APIs are exported by EKERN.EXE.

The battery monitor object may derive from this class, and be owned by the power controller kernel extension.

In version 9.1 and below, Symbian OS allows the mapping of charge levels to four possible values: "zero", "very low", "low" and "good" as given in the TSupplyStatus enumeration:

```
enum TSupplyStatus
  {
  EZero,
  EVeryLow,
  ELow,
  EGood
  };
```

This is likely to change to a system that uses a percentage of charge level, as this would give finer graduations.

There is one pure virtual function that must be implemented by the battery monitor, and that forms its mandatory interface to the kernel (the other function, `SystemTimeChanged()` has been deprecated):

- `MachinePowerStatus()`. This function should read and return the state of the battery with respect to charge level (as one of the `TSupplyStatus` enumerated values). If external power is connected, the function should return `EGood`. Device drivers call this function before starting operations whose successful conclusion depends on the battery charge level – for example, operations that lead to substantial increases in power consumption, or take a long time to complete. They access the function through another framework API, `Kern::MachinePowerStatus()`.

There is no built-in feature to notify device drivers of asynchronous battery events, such as a drop in charge beyond a critical level. The device creator could implement this at base port level: the battery monitor could provide an exported method to allow drivers to register an interest in being notified of battery events. The battery monitor would maintain a list of pointers to driver objects. Obviously, when a driver was closed, it should deregister with the battery monitor:

```
class DXXXBatteryMonitor : public DBatteryMonitor
  {
public:
  ...
  inline void RegisterForBatteryNotifications(
                           DPowerHandler* aPowerHandler)
    {
    NKern::Lock();
    aPowerHandler->iNextBt=iHead;
    iHead=aPowerHandler;
    NKern::Unlock();
    }
  inline void DeRegisterForBatteryNotifications(
                           DPowerHandler* aPowerHandler)
    {
    NKern::Lock();
    DPowerHandler** prev = &iHead;
    while (*prev != aPowerHandler)
    prev = &(*prev)->iNextBt;
    *prev = aPowerHandler->iNextBt;
    NKern::Unlock();
    }
public:
  ...
  DPowerHandler*      iHead;
  };
```

Peripheral drivers could register with the battery monitor using a power controller exported API (implemented by the base port) which returns a pointer to the battery monitor:

```
class TXXXPowerControllerInterface
  {
public:
  ...
  // to allow Variant/Drivers/other Extensions access
                                     to battery monitor
  IMPORT_C static DXXXBatteryMonitor* BatteryMonitor();
  inline static void RegisterBatteryMonitor(
                  DXXXBatteryMonitor* aBatteryMonitor)
    {iBatteryMonitor=aBatteryMonitor;}
public:
  ...
  static DXXXBatteryMonitor* iBatteryMonitor;
  };

EXPORT_C DXXXBatteryMonitor*
        TXXXPowerControllerInterface::BatteryMonitor()
  {
  return &iBatteryMonitor;
  }

// battery monitor constructor
DXXXBatteryMonitor::DXXXBatteryMonitor()
  {
  Register(); // register battery monitor with power manager
  TXXXPowerController::RegisterBatteryMonitor(this);
        // register battery monitor with the interface
  }
```

The driver's power handler-derived object could have a method that the battery monitor would call when an event occurs that the driver is interested in. This method could either execute the driver-specific handling of the event in the context of the battery monitor, or schedule a DFC to execute in the driver's thread. For example:

```
class DXXXPowerHandler : public DPowerHandler
  {
public:
  ...
  inline void NotifyBattEvent(TInt aEvent)
    {
    NKern::Lock();
    iBattEvent=aEvent;
    iBattEventDfc.Enque();
    NKern::Unlock();
    }
public:
  ...
  DPowerHandler* iNextBt;
```

```
    TInt NotificationMask;
    };
```

Here `aEvent` is a bit mask indicating what battery event has occurred.

When an event occurs, the battery monitor could simply notify all drivers that are interested in that event by calling the previous API for their power handlers. This should be done from a thread context (for example a DFC):

```
// to be called after reading the event off the hardware
                                      battery component
DXXXBatteryMonitor::NotifyBattEvent(TInt aEvent)
  {
  DPowerHandler* ph = iHead;
  while (ph)
    {
    if(ph->NotificationMask&aEvent)
      ph->NotifyBattEvent(aEvent);
    ph = ph->iNextBt;
    }
  }
```

The scheme I have just described could be improved to have a priority associated with each driver, which will be reflected in the order the monitor notifies drivers.

The battery monitor should be responsible for maintaining a power supply information structure as summarized by the framework's existing `TSupplyInfoV1`:

```
class TSupplyInfoV1
  {
public:
  SInt64 iMainBatteryInsertionTime;
  TSupplyStatus iMainBatteryStatus;
  SInt64 iMainBatteryInUseMicroSeconds;
  TInt iCurrentConsumptionMilliAmps;
  TInt iMainBatteryConsumedMilliAmpSeconds;
  TInt iMainBatteryMilliVolts;
  TInt iMainBatteryMaxMilliVolts;
  TSupplyStatus iBackupBatteryStatus;
  TInt iBackupBatteryMilliVolts;
  TInt iBackupBatteryMaxMilliVolts;
  TBool iExternalPowerPresent;
  SInt64 iExternalPowerInUseMicroSeconds;
  TUint iFlags;
  };
```

This information is base-port specific and the monitoring component may decide to use these fields as it sees fit.

The power framework and the HAL provide the user-side software battery-management component with an embryonic interface to the battery monitor.

The following set of HAL attributes can be used:

- `EPowerBatteryStatus` – this is used to query the value of `iMain-BatteryStatus` from the previous structure. This is the charge level of the battery (normalized to one of the `TSupplyStatus` enumerated values)

- `EPowerGood` – this returns `ETrue` either if external power is connected or if the current battery charge level is above "low"

- `EPowerBackupStatus` – this is used to query the value of `iBackupBatteryStatus` which is the charge level of a backup battery, if present

- `EPowerExternal` – this is used to query the value of `iExternalPowerPresent` which is `ETrue` if external power, such as the charger, is connected

- `EPowerBackup` – this can be used to query for the presence of a backup battery

- `EAccessoryPower` – this can be used to query for presence of accessory power, such as for example, drawing power from a USB cable.

The implementation of `PowerHAL::PowerHalFunction(...)` should therefore call the battery monitor when it is passed one of the previous arguments.

It may be that this interface is not enough for the needs of a battery manager component. If that is the case, we suggest the use of a device driver for the purpose of communicating with the battery monitor. The battery monitor would then have a set of exported functions, which would be called by an LDD loaded by the battery manager, which offers a channel for interfacing to the battery manager (Figure 15.4).

15.3.1.4 Monitoring environmental inputs

Certain environmental factors such as temperature may have an impact on the power state of CPU and peripherals, and so need to be monitored. For example if the CPU temperature rises above a certain level, the power framework may need to reduce its clock speed to prevent damage. As a further example, certain mobile SDRAM devices have a temperature compensated self-refresh rate, for which software that monitors the case temperature needs to input the current temperature range.

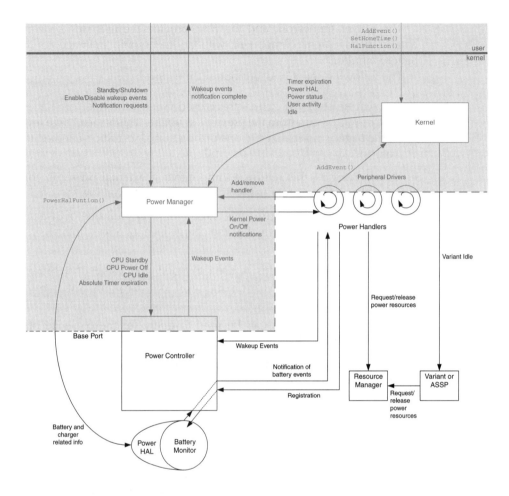

Figure 15.4   Framework block diagram with battery monitor

The base port may need to provide software routines to monitor the environmental inputs using hardware sensors and communicate the state of these to other parts of the kernel power framework.

Peripheral low power retention state support

Peripheral devices, even those which are integrated as part of the main ASIC, may be capable of operation at low power, and may be transitioned to that mode of operation under software control. These low power states map to the retention state that I described in Section 15.1.

Device driver software usually powers up the peripheral device it controls at channel creation time. If a peripheral is controlled by a kernel extension, it is usually powered up at kernel boot time. However, this does not mean that the peripheral device will be used immediately or that power resources used by that peripheral need to be turned on at the level corresponding to peripheral device activity.

We recommend that if a peripheral device is idling, it should be moved to a low power state, if supported. The peripheral driver-specific part of the power framework should do this.

The definition of peripheral idle may vary from peripheral to peripheral but may be generally defined as not servicing any requests from its clients and not performing any internal tasks not directly related to service of a client request.

Any power-saving measures undertaken by the peripheral driver must be transparent to the users of the peripheral. If the time it takes a peripheral to return to a more available state and service a request has no impact on the performance of peripheral driver or their clients, then it is safe to move the peripheral to a low power state when it reaches an idle condition (Figure 15.5).

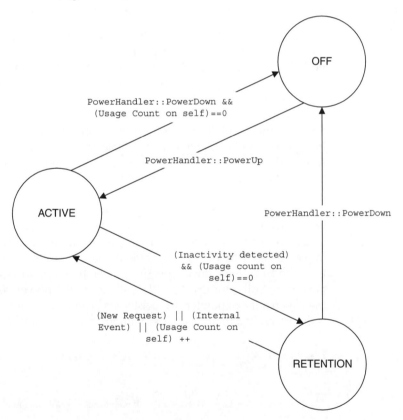

Figure 15.5 Typical peripheral state transition diagram

The SDIO bus controller implementation is a good example of peripheral inactivity monitoring:

1. When the bus power supply is turned on, a periodic inactivity timer with a period of one second is started

2. On timer expiration, the ensuing callback function checks if a device using the bus has locked the controller. If this is not the case, and the required number of seconds (iNotLockedTimeout) has expired since turning the power supply on, the bus is powered down. The inactivity timer is stopped

3. If the bus controller is locked (it is in use by a device on the bus) but a longer timeout period (given by iInactivityTimeout) expires, then the device that has locked the bus is notified every second from then on and may decide to deregister itself, which unlocks the controller, thus allowing it to power down on the next second tick, and move to a device-specific sleep mode.

15.3.1.5 *Notifying peripheral drivers of imminent CPU transition to retention state*

The base porter may want peripheral drivers to be notified that the CPU has entered the idle state. Depending on their current functional state, peripheral drivers may decide to either transition the peripheral to a retention state or stop the CPU transition to that state. In other cases, certain peripherals will have to be placed in a different mode of operation to track any events which will bring the CPU back from the retention state.

The kernel's null thread issues notifications that the CPU is idling. The base port should implement the notification mechanism. This mechanism should do nothing that results in scheduling another thread; it cannot block. At best it may initiate a power resource change, but may not wait for its completion.

Base porters could give their peripheral drivers a callback function, which would execute synchronously and would be called from the CpuIdle() routine. Next I will give an example of how this could be implemented. The platform-specific power controller object could have a method to allow driver-specific power handlers to register with the power controller for CpuIdle() callbacks. The power controller could then keep a list of pointers to registered drivers. When the power handler is destroyed, it should deregister with the power controller:

```
class DXXXPowerController : public DPowerController
  {
  ...
public:
  inline void RegisterWithCpuidle(DPowerHandler* aPowerHandler)
    {
    NKern::Lock();
    aPowerHandler->iNextCi=iHead;
    iHead=aPowerHandler;
```

```
  NKern::Unlock();
  }
inline void DeRegisterWithCpuidle(DPowerHandler* aPowerHandler)
  {
  NKern::Lock();
  DPowerHandler** prev = &iHead;
  while (*prev != aPowerHandler)prev = &(*prev)->iNextCi;
  *prev = aPowerHandler->iNextCi;
  NKern::Unlock();
  } public:
...
DPowerHandler*      iHead;
  };
```

The driver's power handler should keep pointers to the static synchronous, non-blocking, non-waiting callbacks that can be called from the power controller. There are two callbacks: one that is called when entering the CPU idle state, and the other that is called when leaving this routine, for example:

```
typedef void (*TCpuIdleInCallBack)(TAny* aPtr);
typedef void (*TCpuIdleOutCallBack)(TAny* aPtr);

inline static void EnterIdle(TAny* aPtr);
inline static void LeaveIdle(TAny* aPtr);

class DXXXPowerHandler : public DPowerHandler
  {
public:
  ...
public:
  ...
  TCpuIdleInCallBack iEnterIdleCallback;
  TCpuIdleOutCallBack iLeaveIdleCallback;
  };
```

At construction time, `iEnterIdleCallback` is set to point to `EnterIdle()` and `iLeaveIdleCallback` to `LeaveIdle()`.

When entering the `CpuIdle()` function, the power controller calls the registered drivers, using the power handler callback pointer mentioned previously. The callback functions execute in the null thread context.

```
...
DPowerHandler* ph = iHandlers;
  while (ph)
    {
    ph->iEnterIdle(ph);
    ph = ph->iNext;
    }
...
```

When the CPU wakes up, and just before leaving the `CpuIdle()` function, the power controller calls the registered drivers:

```
...
DPowerHandler* ph = iHandlers;
  while (ph)
    {
    ph->iLeaveIdle(ph);
    ph = ph->iNext;
    }
...
```

15.3.1.6 *Power management for peripherals that provide services to other peripherals*

Some peripherals provide services that are used by other peripherals in the same system – these peripherals may require a separate driver to control them. Examples are intelligent internal buses such as I²C and SPI, DMA controllers, embedded PCI controllers and so on. The power state of these peripherals at any given time must be related to the power states of the peripherals they provide services to. It is important that their control model takes this into consideration.

If a peripheral provides services to another peripheral, it must not power down until the client peripheral has powered down – and of course it must power up before the dependent peripheral has any need for its services.

One way in which the base porter can guarantee this is to have the requests from its client drivers powering the slave peripheral up, and only powering down when the client driver powers down. If the slave peripheral driver's power handler's `PowerDown()` is called, it should wait until the all its client drivers power down before powering down the hardware it controls. Requests from the client peripheral's drivers will have to yield and wait for the slave peripheral to power up.

Peripherals that provide services to other peripherals may be capable of moving into a retention state. The principles of control discussed for general peripherals still apply: peripherals will be allowed to go to retention state if no request is being serviced or background task performed and if the latency of the retention state does not impact the performance of the client drivers.

Peripherals may provide services to more than one other peripheral, such as is usually the case with DMA controllers or inter-component buses (Figure 15.6). These peripherals can be seen as shared power resources, especially if they allow multiple simultaneous clients. They should implement a usage counting mechanism that will allow their drivers to know if the peripheral is in use, and decide when to power up or down, and if it is safe to go to retention state.

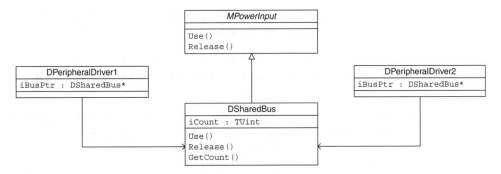

Figure 15.6 Example shared peripheral

In the previous example, the shared peripheral driver object derives from `MPowerInput` exposing a `Use()/Release()` interface to the client drivers.

If the shared peripheral's retention state latency does not have an impact on the performance of the client drivers, then the client drivers may call `Use()` whenever they issue a request for service to the shared driver, and `Release()` when the request is complete. If the impact of the latency cannot be dismissed, the client drivers will need to keep the shared peripheral in operation for longer periods, possibly for the entire duration of their own operational cycle.

15.3.2 Writing a power-aware device driver

Now let's look at how to implement power management for a "real life" device driver. I will use a simplified serial comms driver and will apply some of the concepts I have just described.

I make the following assumptions:

1. The peripheral hardware supports all five power states: off, standby, retention, idle and active. This is not a common situation: in most cases there is no distinction between standby and off states and in some others, there is no support for retention state. I also assume that I can move the peripheral to a particular power state by setting requirements on certain power resources (clock, voltage and power supply), and by a hardware register programming sequence

2. The peripheral hardware uses a clock input that can only be on (when the peripheral is in active, idle or retention states) or off (when the peripheral is moved to standby or off states). This clock input is shared with another peripheral. The peripheral hardware operates at different voltages depending on the power state: 100% of maximum voltage for the active state, 50% of maximum voltage for the retention

state, and 20% of maximum voltage for the standby state. And, finally, the power supply to the peripheral can be cut off or restored

3. The peripheral retention state is of negligible latency, that is, it can come back from retention to the active state quickly enough to service a request

4. In my example, the LDD software moves the peripheral to a different power state, for simplicity, while in a "real-life" device driver the LDD should call the PDD to perform the transition

5. The driver thread can change the power resources used by this peripheral instantaneously, which means that it can wait, with no impact on either its own performance, or that of its clients or the system.

The peripheral driver software routines implement a state machine:

1. When a channel is opened the peripheral is moved to the idle state

2. If the peripheral is in the idle state when a request is made, it moves to the active state

3. After the request is completed, the peripheral moves back to idle

4. When in the idle state, the peripheral waits for a period of time (the inactivity timeout) and if no request is made, it moves to the retention state

5. If the peripheral is in the retention state when a request is made, it moves to the active state

6. When the null (or idle) thread runs, it calls a driver function which checks if the peripheral is idling, in which case the driver callback initiates the peripheral's move to retention state and cancels the inactivity timer. It also delays any device timeouts until the CPU wakes up

7. If the peripheral is in one of the active, idle or retention states, the power manager may request a power down to either the standby or the off state

8. The peripheral can only leave standby if the power manager requests a power up, in which case the driver software moves it to idle and starts the inactivity timer

9. When the channel is closed, the driver software shuts down the peripheral (moving it to the off state).

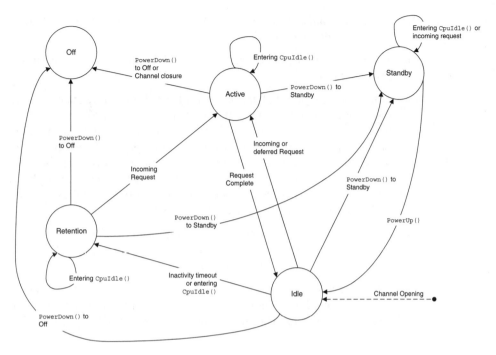

Figure 15.7 Example serial comms driver state machine

The state diagram shown in Figure 15.7 applies.

15.3.2.1 *Thread and synchronization issues*

The driver power management functions execute in different contexts:

1. The power manager's `PowerUp()` and `PowerDown()` are called from the thread of the user-side component responsible for the system transition

2. Requests from a client (including closing the channel) are issued from the client's thread but their servicing and their completion execute in the driver's thread. Channel opening executes in the client's context

3. The inactivity timer's expiration generates an interrupt

4. The callbacks that are called when entering or leaving `CpuIdle()` execute in the null thread.

Thus, we must take some care to guarantee that execution is performed in the right sequence:

- We must protect both the peripheral's and the power resource's state changes against the preemption of the executing thread

- The power manager's `PowerUp()` and `PowerDown()` must schedule DFCs to execute in the driver's thread

- The inactivity timer interrupt must schedule a DFC to execute in the driver's thread

- Transitions to the off state, or to and from the standby state, involve the calling of other power handlers and take some time: it might happen that a request comes in, or the null thread gets to run, after our driver's power handler moves to its low power state, and before the CPU reaches that state. This might also happen after the CPU wakes up but before our driver's power handler moves the peripheral back to the active state. Service requests and the `CpuIdle()` entry callback must check the current power state

- We must cancel the inactivity timer and the ensuing DFC on every state change, apart from when moving from the idle state to the retention state (since this is caused by its own expiration)

- The `CpuIdle()` entry and exit callbacks run with interrupts disabled (as I mentioned in Section 15.2.2.1). They cannot be preempted, and always run in sequence, even if the CPU never reaches the retention state

- The CPU idle (null) thread may run while a request is being serviced (for example, if the driver blocks waiting on a hardware event), or at any time during the power down or power up sequence. The driver's `CpuIdle()` entry callback needs to check if the peripheral state is idle

- When the client closes the channel to the driver, the kernel sends a request as a kernel-side message to the driver that needs to be completed before the driver object is destructed. The completion of a kernel-side message may block, so the power-down or power-up DFCs, or the null thread, may run between the driver shutting down and the driver object (and the associated power handler) being destructed. We must check for this and skip any operations that result in attempting to operate on a peripheral that has already powered off.

15.3.2.2 Class definitions

```
// COMM.H
#include <xxxpower.h> // platform specific power definitions
                           including power controller, Resource
                                                        Manager
#include <kpower.h>    // framework power definition including
                           power handlers
```

```
/// ... other include files
typedef void (*TCpuidleInCallBack)(TAny* aPtr);
typedef void (*TCpuidleOutCallBack)(TAny* aPtr);

class DSerialDriverPowerHandler : public DPowerHandler
  {
  enum TPowerState
    {
    EActive,
    EIdle,
    ERetention,
    EEtandby,
    EOff
    };
public: // from DPowerHandler
  void PowerUp();
  void PowerDown(TPowerState);
public:
  DSerialDriverPowerHandler(DChannelSerialDriver* aChannel);
public:
  void RegisterCpuIdleCallback(TBool aRegister);
public:
  DChannelSerialDriver* iChannel;
  XXXResourceManager* iResourceManager;
  DXXXPowerController* iPowerController;
  DPowerHandler*      iNextCi;
  TCpuIdleInCallBack iEnteridleCallback;
  TCpuIdleOutCallBack iLeaveidleCallback;
  TPowerState iPowerState;
  TBool iStandby;
  };

class DChannelSerialDriver : public DLogicalChannel
  {
public:
  enum TState {EOpen,Eactive,EClosed};
public:
  DChannelSerialDriver();
  ~DChannelSerialDriver();
  // ... other Serial Driver public methods
protected:
  virtual TInt DoCreate(TInt aUnit, const TDesC8* anInfo,
                        const TVersion& aVer);
  virtual void HandleMsg(TMessageBase* aMsg); // entry point
                                  for all requests
  void Complete(TInt aMask, TInt aReason);  // exit point
                                  for all requests
  void Shutdown(TBool astandby); // if ETrue, going to standby
  void MoveToActive();
  void MoveToRetention();
  void DoPowerUp();

  // ... other Serial Driver protected methods
private:
  static void PowerUpDfc(TAny* aPtr);
  static void PowerDownDfc(TAny* aPtr);
  static void TimerCallBack(TAny* aPtr);
  static void TimerDfcFn(TAny* aPtr);
```

```
  void InactivityDfc(TAny* aPtr);

  // ... other Serial Driver private methods
public:
  DCommPowerHandler* iPowerHandler;
  TDfc iPowerUpDfc;
  TDfc iPowerDownDfc;
  TState iStatus;     // interaction between standby and driver's Close
  TBool iMsgHeld;     // ETrue means a message has been held up waiting
                         the end
                         of from standby transition
  NTimer iTimer;      // inactivity timer
  TDfc iTimerDfc;     // inactivity timer DFC
  TBool iCancelled;   // ETrue if device timeouts were cancelled
                         when Enteridle() was called
  // ... other Serial Driver public data members
  };
```

The device driver class (DChannelSerialDriver) has a pointer to the power handler (DSerialDriverPowerHandler). It owns an NTimer that is used to track inactivity. It offers methods to power the peripheral hardware up and down, and move it to the retention and the active states.

The power handler has pointers to the power controller and resource manager. It has pointers to the two callbacks that will be called on entering and leaving the power controller's CpuIdle() function.

15.3.2.3   Driver object construction

```
DChannelSerialDriver::DChannelSerialDriver()
//
// Constructor
//
   :
  iPowerUpDfc(DChannelSerialDriver::PowerUpDfc,this,3),
  iPowerDownDfc(DChannelSerialDriver::PowerDownDfc,this,3),
  iTimerDfc(DChannelSerialDriver::TimerDfcFn,this,3),
  iTimer(DChannelSerialDriver::TimerCallBack,this)
  ...
   {
   ...
  iStatus=EOpen;
   }
```

When the driver DLL is loaded the kernel calls its entry point, which then creates the driver object.

The device driver object's constructor sets up the DFCs that will be issued when the power manager asks to power the peripheral up or down, and the DFC that is called when the inactivity timer expires. It also sets up the callback that the timer interrupt will call.

15.3.2.4 Channel opening

```
TInt DChannelSerialDriver::DoCreate(TInt aUnit, const
          TDesC8* /*anInfo*/, const TVersion &aVer)
//
// Create the channel from the passed info.
//
  {
  ...
  // set up the correct DFC queue
  SetDfcQ(((DComm*)iPdd)->DfcQ(aUnit)); // Sets the DFC
      queue (iDfcQ) to be used by this logical channel
  iPowerUpDfc.SetDfcQ(iDfcQ);
  iPowerDownDfc.SetDfcQ(iDfcQ);
  iTimerDfc.SetDfcQ(iDfcQ);
  ...
  iMsgQ.Receive();
  // create the power handler
  iPowerHandler=new DSerialDriverPowerHandler(this);
  if (!iPowerHandler)
    return KErrNoMemory;
  iPowerHandler->Add(); // add to power manager's list
                                     of power handlers
  iPowerHandler->RegisterCpuIdleCallback(ETrue);
                             // register with CpuIdle
  DoPowerUp();

  return KErrNone;
  }
```

When the client creates a channel to access this driver the `DoCreate()` function above is called. This:

1. Sets the DFC queue to be used by the driver. The power up, power down and inactivity timer DFCs all execute in the context of that DFC queue, in this way avoiding any preemption problems

2. Activates the message delivery queue for this driver's requests

3. Creates the driver's power handler object and registers it with the power manager. Note that the device driver framework calls `DoCreate()` inside a critical section, making it possible to call the power handler `Add()` function from within it.

```
DSerialDriverPowerHandler::DSerialDriverPowerHandler(
                      DChannelSerialDriver* aChannel)
    :   DPowerHandler(KLddName),
        iChannel(aChannel),
        iPowerState(EIdle),
        iEnterIdleCallback(EnterIdle)
        iLeaveIdleCallback(LeaveIdle)
```

```
{
iResourceManager=
    TXXXPowerControllerInterface::ResourceManager();
                    // get pointer to Resource Manager
}
```

The power handler constructor sets up the pointer to the device driver object, and also sets up the pointers to the two callback functions. It obtains a pointer to the resource manager to allow it to access the power resources controlled by it

4. The `DoCreate()` function calls a method provided by the power handler to register with the power controller. This allows the calling of the callback from `CpuIdle()`

```
void DSerialDriverPowerHandler::RegisterCpuIdleCallback(
                                        TBool aRegister)
  {
  if(aRegister)              // register
    {
    iPowerController=
        TXXXPowerControllerInterface::PowerController();
    iPowerController->RegisterWithCpuIdle(this);
    }
  else                       // deregister
    {
    iPowerController->DeRegisterWithCpuIdle(this);
    iPowerController=NULL;
    }
  }
```

5. Finally the `DoCreate()` function calls `DoPowerUp()` to power up the peripheral hardware, setting the driver's power state to idle. It starts the inactivity-monitoring timer:

```
void DChannelSerialDriver::DoPowerUp()
  {
  iTimer.Cancel();
  iTimerDfc.Cancel();

  NKern::Lock();
  iPowerHandler->iPowerState=DSerialDriverPowerHandler::EIdle;
  iResourceManager->ModifyToLevel(XXXResourceManager::VoltageSerial,
                                                          100);
                        // request 100% voltage level
  iResourceManager->SharedClock()->Use();  // assert
                                request on shared clock
  iResourceManager->Modify(XXXResourceManager::PowerSupplySerial,
                                                          ETrue);
                        // turn power supply on (if off)
  // ...write to peripheral registers to set peripheral in
                                          active state
  NKern::Unlock();
```

```
    Complete(EAll, KErrAbort);

    iTimer.OneShot(KTimeout, ETrue);  // restart inactivity timeout
    }
```

15.3.2.5 Incoming requests

Client requests are delivered as kernel-side messages, which will be executed in the driver's thread context (`iDfcQ`). So, when the function `HandleMsg()` is executed, it marks the start of the execution of a client's request by this driver:

```
void DChannelSerialDriver::HandleMsg(TMessageBase* aMsg)
  {
  TInt state=iPowerHandler->iPowerState;

  if(state==(TInt)DSerialDriverPowerHandler::Eoff) return;

  if(state==(TInt)DSerialDriverPowerHandler::Estandby)
    {
    // postpone message handling to transition from standby
    iMsgHeld=ETrue;
    return;
    }

  TThreadMessage& m=*(TThreadMessage*)aMsg;
  TInt id=m.iValue;
  if (id==(TInt)ECloseMsg)
    {
    Shutdown(EFalse); // off
    iStatus = EClosed;
    m.Complete(KErrNone, EFalse);
    return;
    }
  else
    {
    if(iPowerHandler->iPowerState!=
                    DSerialDriverPowerHandler::EActive)
                            // if already active, skip
    MoveToActive(); // a request has been made, move
                                      to active
    if (id==KMaxTInt)
      {
      // DoCancel
      DoCancel(m.Int0());
      m.Complete(KErrNone,ETrue);
      return;
      }
    if (id<0)
      {
      // DoRequest
      TRequestStatus* pS=(TRequestStatus*)m.Ptr0();
      TInt r=DoRequest(~id,pS,m.Ptr1(),m.Ptr2());
      if (r!=KErrNone)
```

```
       Kern::RequestComplete(iClient,pS,r);
     m.Complete(KErrNone,ETrue);
     }
   else
     {
     // DoControl
     TInt r=DoControl(id,m.Ptr0(),m.Ptr1());
     m.Complete(r,ETrue);
     }
   }
 }
```

As I explained earlier, a request may arrive while the driver is being powered down or powered up. The function checks to see if the peripheral is powering down: if it is then the request will not be serviced. If the peripheral is being transitioned to standby, or just returning from it, the function defers the servicing of the request until the peripheral has powered on.

If the client is not requesting the closure of the driver, the peripheral hardware must be moved to the active state in anticipation of performing request-related actions. We do this by calling the MoveToActive() function:

```
void DChannelSerialDriver::MoveToActive()
  {
  iTimer.Cancel();
  iTimerDfc.Cancel();

  NKern::Lock();
  iPowerHandler->iPowerState=DSerialDriverPowerHandler::EActive;
  iResourceManager->ModifyToLevel(XXXResourceManager::VoltageSerial,
                                                             100);
                            // request 100% voltage level
  iResourceManager->SharedClock()->Use();
                            // assert request on shared clock
  // ...write to peripheral registers to set peripheral in active state
  NKern::Unlock();
  }
```

This function requests power resources that are compatible with the active state, sets the driver's power state to active and writes to the peripheral register to move it to active state.

15.3.2.6 *Inactivity detection*

When a request is completed, the driver calls the Complete() function. This function is also called when shutting down. It checks the power state, and if this is active, sets it to idle and restarts the inactivity-monitoring timer.

```
void DChannelSerialDriver::Complete(TInt aMask, TInt aReason)
  {
  if (aMask & ERx)
    Kern::RequestComplete(iClient, iRxStatus, aReason);
  if (aMask & ETx)
    Kern::RequestComplete(iClient, iTxStatus, aReason);
  if (aMask & ESigChg)
    Kern::RequestComplete(iClient, iSigNotifyStatus, aReason);

  TInt state=iPowerHandler->iPowerState;
  if(state==(TInt)DSerialDriverPowerHandler::EActive)
    {
    iPowerHandler->iPowerState=DSerialDriverPowerHandler::EIdle;
    iTimer.OneShot(KTimeout, ETrue);
    }
  }
```

The timer callback is called in the context of the system tick interrupt. The callback simply schedules a DFC to execute in the driver's thread context:

```
void DChannelSerialDriver::TimerCallBack(TAny* aPtr)
  {
  // called from ISR when timer completes
  DChannelSerialDriver *pC=(DChannelSerialDriver*)aPtr;
  pC->iTimerDfc.Add();
  }

void DChannelSerialDriver::TimerDfcFn(TAny* aPtr)
  {
  DChannelSerialDriver *pC=(DChannelSerialDriver*)aPtr;
  pC->InactivityDfc();
  }
```

A state change might occur between the timer being started and the DFC executing, so this function needs to check if the power state is still idle. If it is, then the peripheral hardware is moved to the retention state:

```
void DChannelSerialDriver::InactivityDfc(TAny* aPtr)
  {
  DChannelSerialDriver *pC=(DChannelSerialDriver*)aPtr;
  if(pc->iPowerHandler->iPowerState==
                      DSerialDriverPowerHandler::Eidle)
  pC->MoveToRetention();
  }
```

We move to retention state like this:

```
void DChannelSerialDriver::MoveToRetention()
  {
  // may be called from Null thread: must not block or
                              schedule another thread
  NKern::Lock();
  iPowerHandler->iPowerState=
                 DSerialDriverPowerHandler::ERetention;
  iResourceManager->ModifyToLevel(XXXResourceManager::VoltageSerial, 50);
                        // request 50% voltage level
  iResourceManager->SharedClock()->Use();
                        // assert request on shared clock
  // ...write to peripheral registers to set peripheral
                              in retention state
  NKern::Unlock();
  }
```

15.3.2.7   Entering and leaving CPU idle

Because we registered for `CpuIdle()` callbacks, when the power controller's `CpuIdle()` is entered, the power controller calls the driver using the `iEnterIdleCallback` pointer. I discussed this in Section 15.2.2.1.

```
inline static void EnterIdle(TAny* aPtr)
  {
  // called with interrupts disabled
  DSerialDriverPowerHandler* d = (DSerialDriverPowerHandler*)aPtr;
  if (d->iChannel->iStatus != EClosed)  // not closing
    {
    if(d->iPowerState==DSerialDriverPowerHandler::EIdle)
      {
      d->iChannel->iTimer.Cancel();
      d->iChannel->iTimerDfc.Cancel();

      // ...Cancel device timeouts
      d->iChannel->iCancelled=ETrue;
      d->iChannel->MoveToRetention();
      // this must be synchronous, non-blocking, non waiting
      }
    }
  else
    // race condition: driver was already closed (ECloseMsg)
            but the PowerHandler has not deregistered yet
    {}
  }
```

This function checks to see if the peripheral is in the idle state, and moves it to the retention state. It stops the inactivity-monitoring timer.

The null thread may run between the request to close the channel being serviced and the driver object being destroyed – at that time the power handler has not yet deregistered itself with the power controller. We need to check for that condition.

Just before leaving the CpuIdle() function, the power controller calls the driver using the iLeaveIdleCallback pointer:

```
inline static void LeaveIdle(TAny* aPtr)
  {
  // called with interrupts disabled
  DSerialDriverPowerHandler* d =
                    (DSerialDriverPowerHandler*)aPtr;
  if (d->iChannel->iStatus != EClosed) // not closing
    {
    if(d->iChannel->iCancelled)
      {
      // ...Restarts device timeouts
      }
    }
  else
    // race condition: driver was already closed (ECloseMsg)
             but the PowerHandler has not deregistered yet
    {}
  }
```

If device timeouts were cancelled, the driver restarts them.

15.3.2.8 Power manager initiated power down and power up

The power manager calls the power handler's PowerDown() and PowerUp() functions in the power manager's client context. Their implementation may require lengthy operations or may even block. So it is best if they both schedule DFCs to execute in the driver's context, in this way also guaranteeing that they will not preempt each other.

```
void DSerialDriverPowerHandler::PowerUp()
  {
  iChannel->iPowerUpDfc.Enque();
  }

void DSerialDriverPowerHandler::PowerDown(TPowerState aState)
  {
  (aState==EPwStandby)? iStandby=ETrue:iStandby=EFalse;
  iChannel->iPowerDownDfc.Enque();
  }
```

The power-down DFC moves the peripheral hardware to either the standby or the off state, depending on the target power state, and then acknowledges the transition:

```
void DChannelSerialDriver::PowerDownDfc(TAny* aPtr)
  {
  DChannelSerialDriver* d=(DChannelSerialDriver*)aPtr;
  if (d->iStatus != EClosed)
      d->Shutdown(iStandby);
  else
            // race condition: driver was already closed (ECloseMsg)
                      but the PowerHandler has not deregistered yet
    {}
  d->iPowerHandler->PowerDownDone();
  }
```

When shutting down, we abort all pending requests, cancel timers and
DFCs, and stop the peripheral hardware function. The requirements on
power resources are reduced to a level compatible to the standby state. If
going to the off state, we turn off the power supply.

```
TInt DChannelSerialDriver::Shutdown(TBool astandby)
  {
  ...
  Complete(EAll, KErrAbort); // complete any pending requests

  iTimer.Cancel();
  iTimerDfc.Cancel();
  iPowerUpDfc.Cancel();
  iPowerDownDfc.Cancel();

  NKern::Lock();
  if(astandby)
    iPowerHandler->iPowerState=
                  DSerialDriverPowerHandler::EStandby;
  else
    iPowerHandler->iPowerState=
                      DSerialDriverPowerHandler::EOff;

  iResourceManager->ModifyToLevel(
              XXXResourceManager::VoltageSerial, 20);
                      // request 20% voltage level
  iResourceManager->SharedClock()->Release();
              // relinquish requirement on shared clock
  if(aStandby)
    {
    // ...write to peripheral registers to set peripheral in
                                          standby state
    NKern::Unlock();
    return;
    }
  iResourceManager->Modify(
      XXXResourceManager::PowerSupplySerial, EFalse);
    // turn power supply off
  NKern::Unlock();
  }
```

The power-up DFC moves the peripheral hardware to the idle state by calling the `DoPowerUp()` function that I described previously.

A power manager-initiated move to standby is not instantaneous; a request may arrive after the peripheral has moved to standby or before it has powered back up. The `HandleMsg()` function will defer the request to be serviced until the power handler is powered back up.

```
void DChannelSerialDriver::PowerUpDfc(TAny* aPtr)
    {
    DChannelSerialDriver* d=(DChannelSerialDriver*)aPtr;
    if (d->iStatus != EClosed) // if not closing by client's request
        d->DoPowerUp();
    else
        // race condition: driver was already closed
                (ECloseMsg) but the PowerHandler has not
                                        deregistered yet
        {}
    d->iPowerHandler->PowerUpDone();
    if (d->iMsgHeld)
      {
        __PM_ASSERT(d->iStatus != EClosed);
        d->iMsgHeld = EFalse;
        d->HandleMsg(d->iMsgQ.iMessage);
      }
    }
```

Again, we check the window of opportunity between closing the channel and deregistering the power handler for any power manager initiated transitions, and if any, skip those transitions.

15.3.2.9   *Channel closure and destruction*

The closing of the channel results in the sending of an `ECloseMsg` message to the driver. This is serviced by the `HandleMsg()` and results in the shutting down of the driver and the powering off of the peripheral.

We also delete the driver object:

```
DChannelSerialDriver::~DChannelSerialDriver()
//
// Destructor
//
    {
    if (iPowerHandler)
      {
        iPowerHandler->RegisterCpuIdleCallback(EFalse);
                        // deregister with CPU idle
        iPowerHandler->Remove(); // deregister with power manager
        delete iPowerHandler;
      }
    ...
    }
```

The destructor deregisters the power handler with both the power manager and the power controller and calls the power handler's destructor.

15.3.3   Emergency shutdown (power loss)

Emergency shutdown is a situation that results from sudden loss of power supply, such as when the mobile phone battery is removed.

There are two possible approaches for handling an emergency shutdown situation:

1. If there is a short-term alternative power source, such as that provided by a SuperCap (high capacitance capacitor), which is capable of supplying power for a few milliseconds, and there is a mechanism for notifying drivers and user-side software components, then the emergency situation can be handled before power failure

2. If there is no alternative power source, and hence no time left to handle the emergency situation before power failure, then the power failure event should be dealt with after the device is rebooted. We must provide a mechanism to mark a shutdown as an "orderly" or "emergency".

If we have a short-term alternative power source, then the notification of an emergency shutdown should be distributed to a chosen subset of the peripheral drivers:

*   Drivers for peripherals that draw a significant amount of power should shut down first and as speedily as possible after the notification. These might include the display and backlight, hard disk drives, and so on

*   Drivers for peripherals that may be affected by a sudden loss of power, such as media drivers for external storage media that are susceptible of media corruption in the event of power loss, can then finish their current operation. For example, they can complete their current sector write, and shut down gracefully.

If there is no short-term alternative power source, peripherals will just power down on power loss without any finalization. Upon rebooting, the system checks each of the critical peripherals for possible corruption, and attempts to fix it. The file server scans every internal persistent media drives that are marked as "not finalized", and fixes up any errors. Removable media may also be corrupted by sudden power loss, so they will be scanned on notification of insertion.

In a system where there is a backup power source capable of guaranteeing the preservation of the contents of volatile system memory, it is possible to complete any aborted writes to persistent memory, as the data will still be in SDRAM when rebooting.

The kernel framework does not currently have a built-in mechanism for the distribution of emergency shutdown notifications. However, if battery monitoring is implemented at the framework level, you can implement such a mechanism, along the lines of the one I described in Section 15.3.1.3. The sudden power loss event should be serviced as speedily as possible, which is done best if it is capable of interrupting instruction execution – this means that the battery monitor component should hook a hardware interrupt (on ARM, an FIQ) to the event.

The driver code that services the notification should also handle it as speedily as possible – for example, it should complete the minimum of work to guarantee that the media will be restored when rebooting, and then power down. No time should be wasted completing requests or waiting for freed resources to reach their final state.

15.4 Managing idle time

15.4.1 CPU idle time

The typical utilization profile of a hardware component, CPU or peripheral, is usually characterized by brief periods of intense activity with high requirements on processing bandwidth, followed by longer periods of idleness (Figure 15.8). This matches the usage model of most mobile phones: the device is left constantly on, even when it is in someone's pocket or left downstairs for the night.

Bursts of CPU activity may be triggered by user interaction, or interrupts from a peripheral or a timer working in the background. This activity is

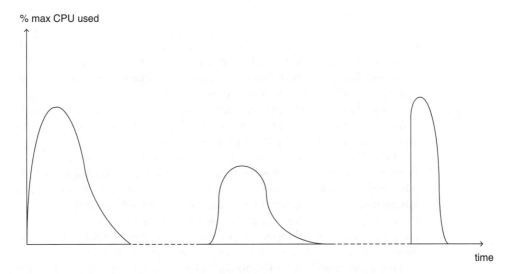

Figure 15.8 Typical CPU usage

linked to higher power consumption whilst the periods of idleness are linked with the entering of a power-saving mode, provided by most modern CPUs. These can be entered automatically, or under software control, to save power during periods of low activity.

I have previously provided a definition for these power-saving modes – or retention states – and I have examined the support that exists, or needs to be implemented in the framework, to move the CPU to them. I will now discuss the utilization of idle time.

15.4.1.1 *Choosing a CPU retention state*

As we have seen, the kernel notifies the power framework of when the CPU enters a period of inactivity by calling the power manager's CpuIdle() function. This function must decide whether to reduce the availability of the CPU by moving it to a low power retention state and reduce power consumption, or keep it in a more available state, with less or no power savings. There are also usually several gradations of retention that we can select.

The first factor in the determination of the retention state is the estimated uninterrupted length of idle time. We have already described how this idle time can be obtained from the kernel. Moving in (and out) of a retention state requires preparation, and usually, the more complex the preparations, the more the power savings that will result. A more power-efficient retention state usually requires a longer wakeup time too. Therefore, the longer the estimated idle time, the more power-efficient the selected retention state can be.

Another factor is the power resource utilization at the time when the decision is made; due to the interdependency between resources, it may only be possible to move the CPU to a low power retention state if certain resources are already off or being used only at a low level. The higher the power savings on a retention state, the lower should be the overall resource utilization profile. Also, on moving the CPU to retention state, more peripherals can be turned off or have their power requirement levels lowered, resulting in even greater power savings.

When choosing the CPU retention state, we need to take into consideration the state of certain peripherals – mainly the ones used for data input or the detection of unlatched external events.

Often the user will enable certain peripheral functions and leave them inactive but in an operational state for long periods of time: this often happens when infrared or Bluetooth are enabled, or when an I/O function card is connected to an externally accessible peripheral bus. If these peripherals are servicing a request when the null thread is entered, then they must be left operational, and this in itself could prevent the moving of the CPU to a more power-efficient retention state.

These peripherals have the ability to interrupt the CPU idle mode and request CPU processing time. Investigating the power resource state may give a view of what peripherals are in the active state and which have already powered down, thus helping us to choose the retention state.

Waking up from a retention state usually takes a fairly long time. We must choose a CPU retention state whose wakeup time will permit the correct operation of all peripherals that were left operational, and lead to the servicing of their requests for CPU attention on time – that is, with no data loss, correct and with the timely servicing of events.

The analysis of past CPU workload may be relevant for the choice of retention state, as it can give an indication of the future requirements. For example, if an episode requiring high CPU bandwidth is suddenly followed by a period of inactivity then it is probable that the task yielded, waiting for some hardware event to occur. Once the hardware event happens, the task can be expected to resume as soon as possible. In this case a retention state with a lower latency should be chosen.

The current battery charge level may also be important in the choice of a retention state. If the level is low, this does not necessarily lead to the choice of a less power hungry retention state. In fact, as the charge level approaches a critical threshold when applications and drivers should be notified, the decision to move the CPU to retention must be carefully weighed against the need to wake up on time to service the sending of the notifications.

15.4.1.2 *SDRAM power management*

When in a retention state, the CPU is usually unable to refresh SDRAM – and without cell refreshing, in which the cell charge level is periodically restored, the contents of memory will be lost. We can place SDRAM devices in a self-refresh mode, where their internal controller takes over the duty of refreshing the memory cell charge without the external CPU intervention. All we need is to maintain a power supply to the device and to supply a clock source to it – then we send a command to the SDRAM controller. Once this is done, the CPU can be moved to retention mode.

If we are using mobile SDRAM, we can reduce power consumption during the periods when the CPU is sleeping, by enabling self-refresh only for the memory banks that are actually in use.

To do this, we need to ensure that pages containing valid data are arranged to occupy as few memory banks as possible. This means that periodic re-organization of the memory pages, or defragmentation, needs to take place. Mobile SDRAM defragmentation typically happens during periods when the CPU has no other tasks to perform – that is, in the null thread. When the CPU is defragmenting memory, it cannot be moved to a retention state.

The power savings that result from a partial refresh of the memory device need to be carefully weighed against the increased overall power consumption stemming from the reduction of CPU idle time. You might achieve a balance by using only part of the idle time available for memory defragmentation, and using the rest as a power-saving retention state time.

15.4.1.3   *Interaction between CPU retention and peripheral operation*

If, when the CPU enters an idle period, the software investigates the state of peripherals and acts on them, it may further reduce power consumption:

- If the peripheral driver is not servicing any request, or if it is waiting on a signal from its client, it may be possible to move the peripheral to a retention mode. Its client will not request its services again until the CPU wakes up. Moving as many peripherals as possible to the retention state usually leads to freeing power resources

- Peripherals that are responsible for detecting wakeup events may power down to a high latency state and only leave the systems responsible for detecting those events powered up and operational. Given the wider time constraints associated with user input, the latency has no impact on the ability to service the input

- Even if the peripheral cannot be transitioned to a low power state, we may be able to take other actions that result in increasing the idle time, such as skipping periodic device timeouts or increasing their period

- We can turn off the LCD backlight, and lower the LCD refresh rate

- We can notify external devices on a peripheral bus such as MMC or USB, so that they may enter a low power mode.

Obviously, some of these actions need to be reversed when the CPU leaves the retention state.

15.4.1.4   *Event reduction*

Certain applications use periodic timers to poll the state of particular software resources. These timers will wake up the CPU from its retention mode, only for the application to realize that no change to the resource has been made. The effect of this is to shorten the period that the CPU can be in a retention state, making the choice of more complex and power-efficient states impossible. At the worst, if these timer ticks are too frequent, they may prevent transitions to the power-saving retention states altogether.

Because of this, an effort has to be made to reduce the use of such timers and move to an event-driven architecture whenever possible.

Some peripheral drivers use interrupt driven I/O for data exchanges with the peripherals they control; this also has a negative impact on CPU idle time, as events are generated at a high rate, to signal transfers of small units of data. A better alternative is to use DMA, which enables transfers of larger amounts of data with a much lower signaling rate. This is especially relevant as some CPUs may go into a retention state while the DMA controllers are operational.

Display drivers for refreshed displays whose frame buffers are placed in system memory can be optimized for event reduction. During periods of CPU idle, no new display content is being generated, and no updates to the frame buffers occur. It is also unlikely that the user is interacting with the mobile phone. Therefore we recommend two different policies for LCD refresh rates: one that refreshes the LCD at the "normal" rate when the CPU is active, and another, for when the CPU is idling, that lowers the refresh rate and relies on the persistence of the display for longer periods of time in between refreshes. Obviously, lowering the LCD refresh rate increases the intervals between the CPU having to wake up and service DMA requests to refresh the display.

With the introduction of "Smart LCD" panels with their own controller and memory, the control model can be simplified; these displays can be placed in a mode in which they refresh from their internal frame buffer. This buffer keeps the last frame sent to the controller. The display can therefore be disconnected from the CPU bus during periods while this is in retention mode.

15.4.2   Peripheral idle time

Peripheral devices may spend considerable time idling. Even when a peripheral driver is controlled by a device driver that has an open channel, it might happen that no requests for service will be issued for considerable periods of time.

Earlier, I mentioned that if a peripheral is idling then it could be moved to a low power retention state. Peripheral drivers cannot estimate when their clients will issue requests for their services. Thus, the decision to move the peripheral to a retention state depends on that peripheral's ability to wakeup when a request is issued, and to service it on time without compromising the performance of the client.

15.5   Advanced power management

A number of improvements to the kernel power framework are being considered in line with the current developments.

15.5.1   CPU workload prediction and voltage and frequency scaling

Power consumption of an electronic component, such as a transistor or a gate, is directly proportional to the operating frequency and to the square of the operating voltage:

$$P = K \times f \times V^2$$

Hardware manufacturers have been taking advantage of this with improvements in the utilization of the physics of the silicon which allow electronic components to work at lower voltages and higher frequencies, without increasing the overall power consumption, as the previous formula clearly shows.

This static model has its limitations: as the transistor's operating threshold voltage is lowered, so the leakage current increases, resulting in the increase of static power and increased dissipation (which causes additional problems in removing the additional heat).

More recently, another approach based on dynamically varying the factors that contribute to power consumption has been favored:

- Hardware manufacturers design devices (CPU, peripherals) for which voltage and frequency can be dynamically adjusted without disruption of operation

- The operating system uses this feature to always require the lowest power consumption from the CPU without reducing the perceived performance of the system.

Another look at the physics of the silicon tells us that when reducing the supply voltage of a switching gate, the propagation delay across that gate increases. In other words, a reduction in operating voltage of a hardware component such as the CPU must be accompanied by a reduction of operating frequency.

The reverse of this principle may be used in favor of lowering the power consumption; if the frequency is reduced, the operating voltage can be reduced accordingly. Let us see how this could be beneficial.

Analyzing the operational cycle of the CPU reveals a "bursty" profile (Figure 15.9): tasks or episodes are executed at nominal clock frequency followed by "gaps" corresponding to periods of idle time.

If the clock frequency of the CPU was adjusted to allow each episode to complete before the next one, no degradation of system performance would occur (Figure 15.10).

It must be noted that if the total energy per task (the area inside each of the boxes) remained the same, no overall gain in power savings would occur. In fact the power performance would be poorer, as with

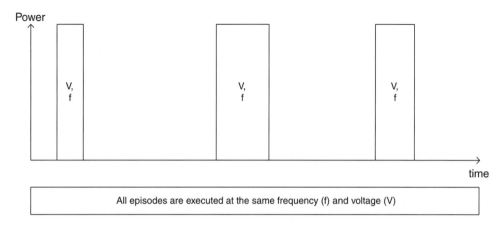

Figure 15.9 Typical CPU episode profile (assuming low power idle time)

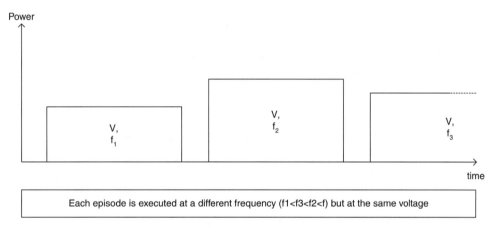

Figure 15.10 Episode profile with frequency adjusted per episode

the reduction of idle time no power savings could be made from moving the CPU to a retention state.

However, if we lower the clock frequency per task, we can lower the voltage supply to the CPU accordingly, resulting in a significant reduction in power consumption (Figure 15.11).

If, at the moment the CPU enters an idle period, it is possible to predict when the next episode is going to require CPU attention, then it is possible to continuously adjust the frequency (and voltage) and still allow each episode to complete before the next one is due to start.

Algorithms which perform an analysis of idle time and predict CPU workload in real time have recently been developed. These algorithms require the kernel, which is responsible for scheduling the tasks and tracking the idle condition, to be instrumented to collect the relevant information.

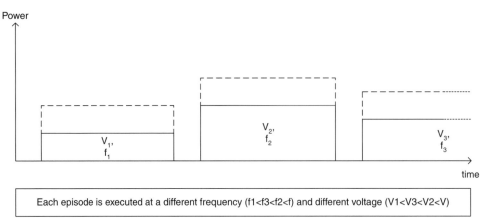

Each episode is executed at a different frequency (f1<f3<f2<f) and different voltage (V1<V3<V2<V)

Figure 15.11   Task profile with frequency and voltage adjusted per episode

Usually the software component that contains the algorithms that perform the prediction and ultimately decide upon an operating point is a higher level component. It may be able to receive input from certain critical applications, which "hint" at a required performance level, and may support different switchable policies corresponding to different modes of device operation – such as "gaming", "media playback", "call-only mode" and so on.

The system has requirements on the kernel framework:

- APIs to allow collecting the workload information from the kernel

- An interface to the resource manager to allow the modification of the operating parameters (voltage, clock frequency)

- May have an interface to certain critical device drivers to allow those to request a performance level. Device drivers may have a knowledge of the probability of unpredictable future events that require CPU attention (data input, interrupts), and this information is not available to the workload prediction component.

A possible optimization to the "just-in-time" strategy I have just described might involve searching for periods in the CPU operational cycle when performance is independent of clock frequency. Examples of these include activities related to periods of intensive memory or I/O port access, when the CPU has to wait for these to return the data, or polling of an I/O port. These tend to be fairly common for wireless peripherals and disk I/O.

Identifying such periods will make it possible to lower the CPU clock frequency (and voltage) to match that of the peripheral it is accessing, resulting in energy saving without impacting the performance of the task.

Finally, it is possible that for certain CPU loads the strategy of lowering the clock frequency and operating voltage to a level that still allows deadlines to be met may result in less power savings than would be possible by running the episodes at a higher frequency and then saving power by transitioning the CPU to a low power mode when it is idling – even during the short periods in between tasks. It must be noted that neither transitioning the CPU to and from a low power mode nor changing the speed and operating voltage is cost free; energy is spent on both preparing the transition and in the transition itself and there are latencies associated with both. The software component responsible for setting the operational point for the CPU operation needs to be able to make the decision about what strategy results in greater economies of power but still meets the service requirements.

15.5.2   Peripheral low power states and quality of service

As I mentioned earlier in this chapter, some peripherals may be retention state capable. The retention states that they can be transitioned to are characterized not only by lower power consumption, but in some cases also by a higher latency, that is, a diminished ability to respond to external events within the time constraints required for the correct operation of the peripheral.

The peripheral driver should make the decision to move the peripheral to a low power state and choose a state based upon:

1. Which point of the operational cycle the driver is in: is the peripheral idling; are there any pending requests for service?

2. Is the peripheral able to detect incoming data or external events whilst in that state?

3. Is the response time of the peripheral to incoming data or events whilst in that state within the service constraints associated with a pending request for service?

4. For events that repeat, for example a stream of data, the transition time to the active state is important: even if the initial event is detected and transition to active started, will the peripheral be able to detect/service the next event?

It may be possible that a peripheral reaches an idle condition even when the peripheral driver has a pending request for services. It may be still possible to transition the peripheral to a low power state if that state's latency does not have an impact on the peripheral's ability to service the request. As an example of this, consider keyboard or touch screen drivers, where the associated peripheral still has the ability to detect a key press or touch sensitive panel tap and generate an interrupt, even when the peripheral is in a low power state. Given that the clients of these peripherals have very tolerant constraints for servicing those events and their repeat rate is usually of the order of tens of milliseconds (after debouncing filters have been applied), it is quite natural that these peripherals be moved to a low power state every time they finish processing an event (even though their operation implies they need to be ready for the next incoming event).

However it may also be that the client of the services provided by the peripheral can, in certain stages of its operational cycle, be more tolerant to the peripheral lowering its response time to input data or events, even though in other stages it has a much more stringent requirement on the peripheral. In other words, the quality of service required from the peripheral may not always be constant.

This situation is particularly common with peripherals used for tracking and servicing input data streams. As an example consider an IR peripheral: the constraints on response time during the discovery phase of the operation, when devices search for the presence of another device with which to initiate a transaction, are considerably lower than when the devices are already engaged in a transaction. The protocol even makes allowance for loss of data during that phase.

Another common situation relates to peripherals that even in their operational state may be able to work with different levels of power resources such as clocks or voltages on power lines. Their responsiveness to their client's requests varies according to their requirement on those power resources.

Therefore it is possible to envisage a system where clients of services provided by peripherals negotiate the quality of service provided by these peripherals with their drivers. To achieve this, special APIs need to be put in place. We will call them peripheral quality of service (QoS) APIs.

Peripheral QoS APIs allow peripheral drivers to know, at any time, the quality of service required by their clients. There are two ways in which peripheral quality of service specifications may be implemented:

1. The peripheral enters an idle period but has a pending request for service. The peripheral driver notifies its client. Then it's up to the client to allow or disallow the relaxing of the quality of service. When given permission to relax quality of service, the driver will adjust this according to its own needs

2. The client specifies the quality of service required for each request of service from the peripheral when placing the request. This may be expressed as, for example, a percentage of the maximum degradation allowed for the request, or as a range of discrete values, and it takes into consideration the requirements of the client, not the driver.

Peripheral QoS APIs allow the device driver to ensure the lowest requirement on platform power resources at all times and initiate the peripheral transition to a low power state whenever the quality of service required by its clients permits it. This can happen even with a pending request, not only when the peripheral is idling. This results in further lowering power consumption of the entire system.

Depending on which of the methodologies for setting the quality of service provided by peripherals is implemented, the strategy for transitioning peripherals to a low power state and the impact on system power and performance is different:

1. In the case where the peripheral driver notifies the client of an idle condition and receives permission to relax quality of service, it will transition the peripheral to a low power state, releasing the requirements on power resources (turn voltages or clocks off or lower their values). If the peripheral is in that state and the CPU enters its idle mode, the routine responsible for investigating the state of power resources sees the resources used by that peripheral as unused and assumes the CPU can safely be transitioned to a retention state without affecting the performance of the peripheral's driver or its client. Therefore the client of the services offered by the peripheral needs to make the decision to allow the relaxing of the quality of those services based not only on peripheral wakeup time but also upon CPU wakeup time, possibly from the retention state with the longer wakeup time

2. In the case where the client sets the quality of service required for each request, the peripheral driver will know if it can transition the peripheral to a low power state when the peripheral reaches an idle period whilst servicing the request. The choice of a peripheral low power state is determined by the requirement on service quality. This strategy allows a finer granularity of control, and supports multiple peripheral low power states. The drawback is that when the CPU reaches the idle mode the framework will need to investigate the quality of service required for the request the peripheral is servicing with each relevant peripheral driver before deciding on the CPU retention state to move to.

It is possible that for some peripherals one of these methods is preferable to the other; for others a combination of these two methods may be preferable, with the client setting the QoS for each request, allowing the driver to map to the lowest possible requirement on power resources, and then notify its client of periods of inactivity and receive from them confirmation that it is valid to transition the peripheral to a low power state.

15.5.3   Matching of energy sources and loads

The operational curve of a battery – relating the power it supplies to the current that is demanded of it – is only linear for a small region of that curve. Other factors such as temperature and age also affect its ability to release energy. Therefore the energy it releases for a given level of charge is not constant.

The duty cycle of a phone – the cycle of run/idle – creates a variable peak-to-average energy consumption which speeds up the discharge of the battery and reduces its useful life (Figure 15.12).

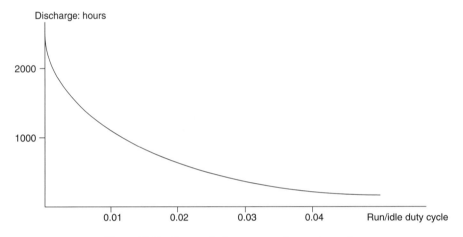

Figure 15.12   Battery discharge versus duty cycle graph

Mobile phone manufacturers may decide to incorporate multiple energy sources in their designs, to be used in conjunction with the main battery or as an alternative power source. Those energy sources may include SuperCaps, rechargeable buffer batteries, and so on.

These energy sources may be switched in and out of the energy supply to supplement or replace the main battery, matching corresponding load changes or providing backup for the main power supply. This should be done under software control.

Software will monitor the load and use a framework to switch the sources in or out.

15.5.4   SDRAM partial refresh

Mobile phone designs may include mobile SDRAM components capable of partial array self-refresh. This feature allows for the power consumed during self-refresh to be directly proportional to the amount of memory refreshed. The memory device is organized as a number of power banks and software can set the number of banks that can be self-refreshed, starting from one end (Figure 15.13).

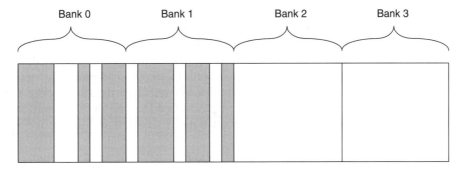

Figure 15.13 Banks of SDRAM on a mobile phone

SDRAM can be placed in self-refresh mode during the periods when the CPU is not accessing it, for example, CPU standby and retention states.

To make use of the features provided by this type of memory and reduce system power consumption, the framework must be able to:

1. Identify the geometry of the memory device – the number of power partitions and how they map to physical addresses

2. Track the utilization of pages on each power partition

3. Guarantee an optimal utilization of physical RAM, with the page frames in use arranged to reside on as few power banks as possible, and all at one end of the power partition list

4. Provide the functionality to enable partial self-refresh when necessary.

The geometry of the device is determined by the bootstrap and passed to the kernel via the super page. During the early phases of nanokernel initialization, the RAM allocator object that deals with the mapping of memory used by the OS to physical RAM is created and can map the number of power banks and the number of pages per power bank, thus creating a power partition address map.

Whenever physical memory is allocated or freed, the RAM allocator marks the pages as used or free. When memory is allocated, the algorithm that maps it to physical RAM should attempt to find the required number of pages at the lower end of the power partition address map. This may not always be guaranteed. Also, when physical RAM is freed, gaps will be left in the RAM address map which may or may not be fully re-used when an allocation of a number of contiguous pages less than or equal to the number of pages freed takes place.

Therefore the OS may need to implement a more aggressive strategy for rearranging physical RAM, such as ensuring that used pages are all at contiguous physical addresses at the low end of the power partition address. This defragmentation of physical RAM may be a time-consuming operation, and this must be taken in consideration when deciding when it needs to run. One option is to launch the operation when the CPU has no other threads in the ready list, that is, when the null thread is scheduled to run. In Section 15.3, I mentioned the risk of the defragmentation routine encroaching itself into CPU low power retention time – therefore there has to be some mechanism in place to allow the coordination of the triggering of the defragmentation task, its duration and the `CpuIdle()` routine.

A possible defragmentation algorithm investigates if the number of used pages at the higher address end of the power partition map is less than the number of free pages at the lower address end, and, if it is, starts copying those pages. The algorithm must also be able to determine if it is be able to copy all the pages within the allocated time. If it is interrupted before it completes the copy, it should abandon copying and relinquish control of the CPU to any other thread that needs to run as a result of the interruption. When it finally resumes, it needs to be able to determine which pages were copied and which were abandoned, as well as whether it should retry copying the pages that were abandoned, or if those have been invalidated as a result of the interruption.

Finally, the routines which prepare the CPU and platform to enter the standby or retention states must be able to obtain a list of what power banks are used and their locations, mark only these to be refreshed, and power down all others.

15.6 Summary

In this chapter, I have described the power management framework of Symbian OS in some detail. Next I shall look at how Symbian OS boots up.

16

Boot Processes

by Andrew Thoelke and Carlos Freitas
with Jon Coppeard

There is only one satisfying way to boot a computer.

J.H. Goldfuss

A description of how Symbian OS operates, manages hardware resources and provides services for application software is incomplete without an explanation of how it takes the hardware from an uninitialized, powered-off state to one in which the system is fully ready for action.

In this chapter I will walk through the boot process for mobile phones that run the operating system from execute-in-place (XIP) Flash memory, such as NOR Flash, and then describe the differences needed to support non-XIP media, such as NAND Flash.

The opposite process, shutdown, also deserves some attention. I will go on to explain how Symbian OS responds to a request to switch off, describing the design of the current *Shutdown Server* and the forthcoming *Domain Manager* architectures.

16.1 Operating system startup

The process of *bootstrapping* an operating system is a carefully managed operation. The different stages of initialization must be correctly sequenced to avoid services being initialized before the services they depend on are ready.

Figure 16.1 illustrates the main stages of OS initialization for an XIP Flash memory device. However, before I explain why the memory technology makes a difference to the boot process, we should start at the very beginning, or perhaps even a little earlier.

To successfully initialize the hardware and OS, it is important to know what state the hardware will be in immediately after it has been switched

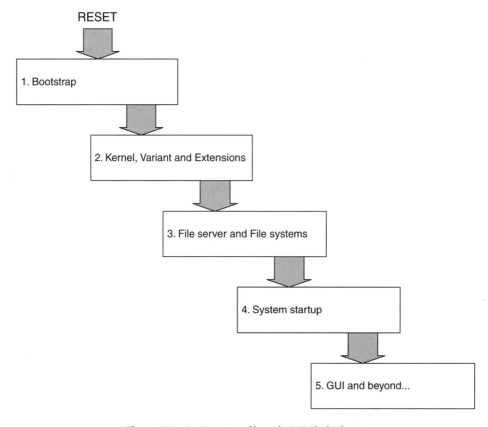

Figure 16.1   Main stages of boot for XIP Flash phone

on or reset. For the most part, the OS has to assume that hardware is in an
"unknown" state because the boot process may arise from several causes.

For example, after a mobile phone is switched on, the CPU, MMU
and memory controller are in the most primitive state: clocks are set to
low frequencies, the MMU is disabled, only memory essential for reset
is visible and RAM will contain garbage. On the other hand, following
a software reset these components are typically already initialized. The
initialization carried out during the boot process must be robust enough
to handle any reason for reset.

Switching on the phone triggers the CPU and MMU to reset. This
disables the MMU and causes the CPU to jump to a well-known location
to execute the reset code. On ARM CPUs, this is address 0x00000000,
which is usually referred to as the *reset vector*. Obviously there must be
some code at physical address zero for this to work and hence some
hardware – usually this will be some masked ROM or XIP Flash.

Mobile phones typically use some form of Flash memory to store
the OS image and built-in software. Although this is significantly more

expensive (and slower) than masked ROM, there are two substantial advantages:

- Mobile phones are complex products and often require an update during their lifetime. Flash memory enables the OS to be over-written or upgraded ("reflashed")

- Masked ROM takes time to manufacture. This introduces a delay of several weeks between the software being ready and the production of the phone. "Several weeks" is a lot of phone sales.

Some types of non-volatile memory, such as NOR Flash, can be treated by the memory controller as directly accessed, read-only memory. This allows program code to execute directly from Flash memory, which makes initial system startup much simpler. It is interesting to compare this to desktop systems where the operating system resides on hard disk and must be loaded into RAM before it is possible to start executing any of the code. There are some Flash technologies, such as NAND Flash, that cannot support execute-in-place and thus require a boot process that more closely resembles that of a desktop OS. In Section 16.2.1 I will look at how Symbian OS supports booting from NAND Flash, and discuss why you might choose to boot from NAND, given this inefficiency.

But now, let's return to the boot process.

16.1.1 High level process

As the OS starts up, the boot process runs through, broadly speaking, five stages. I say "broadly" because the later stages can be broken into more discrete steps. However, this book is primarily about the operation of the kernel and file server, so as the later boot stages are related to general OS services and user interface initialization I will not cover them in depth.

Figure 16.1 illustrates these main stages. The beginning of each stage is marked by the execution path entering a specific new process within the operating system, and each stage ends when the services provided by that process are ready for use by the OS.

Before examining each stage in more detail, I will provide an overview of each stage and what it achieves before it hands over to the next process in the chain.

1. Switching the phone on triggers a hardware reset. The first software that is executed after this is known as the bootstrap. On entry to the bootstrap, the execution environment is very primitive, and the bootstrap is tasked with providing a basic execution environment for the kernel process

2. On entry to the kernel, the CPU is now running at full speed and an execution stack allows typical C++ code to be run. However, there

is still only a primitive memory environment and only one execution path. Static data is now initialized and interrupts are masked. Once kernel and base support package (BSP) initialization is complete, there is full management of CPU, memory, power and peripherals and the second OS process is started

3. At this stage in the boot there is a fully functional micro-kernel that supports multiple multi-threaded, protected user-mode processes. However, the OS has not yet provided the means to instantiate new processes, to extract file-based data from the Flash or to persist data in read/write Flash memory. The process of establishing all of these services falls to EFILE.EXE and its supporting process, ESTART.EXE

4. All of the kernel, user library and file server services are now fully initialized ready for the rest of the OS to begin its boot process – a job that is given to the *system starter* process. The system starter manages the initialization of the rest of the OS system services in an ordered manner, and can also provide monitoring and restart for those which terminate unexpectedly. The precise order in which the persistence, communications, multimedia, security and other services are started is controlled by a script and is phone-specific

5. Once enough of the system services are running, the primary GUI service, the *window server*, can be started. This now allows initialization of the other UI services and the applications that make up the aspect of the OS that is most evident to the user.

This is a standard sequence for booting the phone. According to this process, the OS services for displaying images or animations, or playing audio become available quite late in the boot. This does not reconcile with the typical experience of using a Symbian OS phone – in practice phones often use lower level graphics services to display images during boot without demanding that the full screen-sharing capabilities of the window server are available.

It is worth looking in more detail at some of the work done in the earlier stages of boot to understand how the OS brings the services online in a carefully orchestrated manner. Many of the interesting events or activities can be seen in Figure 16.2, which provides a graphical "history" of booting EKA2 on development hardware.

The horizontal lanes each show a particular related area of the OS or hardware that requires initialization during startup – for example, activities that are to do with initializing memory and memory services are in the central lane.

The four main vertical divisions show when execution passes from one executable to another during boot. The first two each represent one of the stages referred to earlier, while the last two together make up stage three of the startup. The total elapsed time for these stages of boot is less than one second.

Boot Timeline

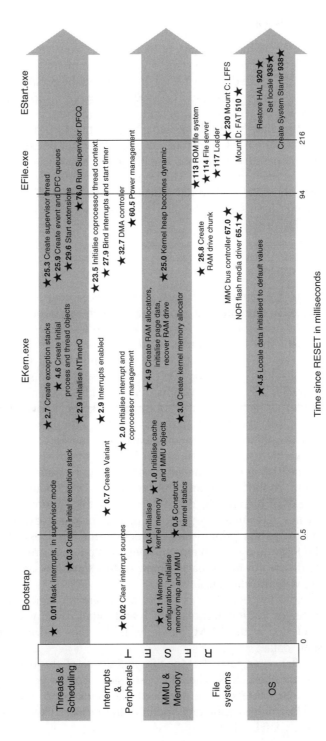

Figure 16.2 Key events during the first few stages of booting Symbian OS

16.1.2   The bootstrap

On entry to the bootstrap, `bootrom.bin`, very little is certain about the processor or hardware state. The CPU and memory will be set to run at safe, slow speeds, the MMU is disabled and the only CPU general register that is known to be good is the PC in supervisor mode (`R15_SVC`) – and that will be zero at the very start of the bootstrap.

Immediately, the bootstrap modifies the CPU mode to run in SVR mode with all interrupts masked. Any interrupt or exception at this stage would cause a fault, because the CPU registers for these states have not yet been initialized. The bootstrap then initializes hardware, starting with the CPU and MMU, and clears interrupts. The bootstrap creates an execution stack and points the supervisor stack pointer, `R13_SVC`, to this memory.

16.1.2.1   The superpage

From here, the bootstrap starts populating a structure called the superpage. This is a structure that is shared between the bootstrap and the kernel and is used for passing information determined by the bootstrap to the kernel. This is information such as addresses of key ROM locations (such as the root directory), location and size of memory banks, and various other values that are calculated by the bootstrap. The superpage is always allocated at a known virtual address, specific to each memory model – which is how the bootstrap and kernel know where to put it and find it. All other bootstrap data is lost after completion.

The bootstrap determines the available memory, both RAM and ROM. It does this using a combination of explicit information in a table provided by the BSP, and dynamic probing to determine memory address, size and width. At the end of this, the superpage will contain a record of all the blocks of memory in the system. With this information, the bootstrap creates and initializes the RAM page allocator. Next it allocates, clears and maps the primary page directory and first page table, then maps the ROM and other memory model-related data structures. It also maps hardware I/O in the page tables. At this stage, the MMU is switched to use virtual addressing.

Now the bootstrap is ready to prepare the kernel for execution. It allocates the initial thread stack and initializes it according to the size requested in the ROM. Similarly, it allocates and initializes the kernel static data.

After some final BSP-specific initialization, the bootstrap is ready to execute the kernel. The supervisor stack pointer is changed to point to the initial thread stack (the bootstrap stack is no longer used) and the CPU branches to the entry point of the *primary* executable in the ROM, usually EKERN.EXE.

16.1.3   The kernel

On entry to the kernel, the CPU is now running at full speed, the execution stack allows typical C++ code to be run, the memory hardware sub-system is tuned and the MMU provides virtual addressing. However, the memory environment is still primitive – the static data is initialized but there is no free pool allocator and there is only one execution path. Interrupts are still disabled.

The kernel starts by initializing all the CPU execution modes, although they will all share a common stack for now. This enables exceptions to be detected and diagnostics produced rather than generating errors that are difficult to debug. Next the kernel runs C++ constructors for static kernel objects, and we are ready to enter the C++ entry point for EKERN.EXE: `KernelMain()`.

The kernel performs its initialization by running a number of initialization routines, init-0 to init-3. At each stage, core kernel initialization is performed and equivalent initialization routines are run in the BSP to allow the initialization of phone-specific hardware.

16.1.3.1   Init-0

From `KernelMain()` the initial thread first invokes `P::CreateVariant()`, which does phase zero of the initialization. That is, it initializes and constructs the static data objects for all BSP extensions, and then does the same for the variant. The variant must be initialized after the extensions, as the initialization of the variant may depend on one or more extensions having been through this phase already. Finally, the variant's exported `Initialise()` function is called to do early initialization and provide the kernel with a pointer to the singleton `Asic` object.

16.1.3.2   Init-1

Now that the BSP static objects are initialized and ready, the second action the initial thread takes is to call `K::InitialiseMicrokernel()`. This prepares various kernel and BSP objects in sequence:

- The `Mmu` and `Cache` management objects
- Coprocessor management
- Interrupt dispatchers
- Some ISRs
- Exception mode stacks for IRQ, FIQ, ABT and UND modes.

At this point, some three milliseconds into the boot, the kernel can unmask interrupts safely, although there are no interrupts enabled yet. The nanokernel timer period is now set from the variant information.

The kernel creates an initial free store allocator over the memory reserved by the bootstrap, but this heap is not yet able to grow dynamically or support multiple threads. However, the kernel can now support dynamic object creation:

- The kernel initializes locale data to default values
- The kernel creates a `DProcess` object to represent the EKERN process
- The kernel creates a `DThread` object to represent the currently running initial thread, which will become the "null" (or idle) thread.

The kernel now unlocks the scheduler and is ready to start scheduling threads. The kernel creates the supervisor DFC queue but does not yet create the thread to service the DFCs, This allows `TDfc` objects to be created, bound and even added to this DFC queue during early initialization – once the kernel creates the thread, it will process the queue and execute these DFCs.

16.1.3.3   Init-2

We now have a viable heap allocator and scheduler. The next step is to complete initialization of the memory manager. This creates all the virtual address region allocators and the RAM allocator mutex used to protect the manager. It also recovers any contents of the RAM drive that survived a warm reset.

The final coprocessor initialization creates the default thread context for saved coprocessor state.

Now the rest of the kernel resource management machinery can be brought into existence:

1. The object containers are created with their mutexes, and the initial process and thread are added to these

2. A chunk representing the already existing kernel heap is created and set up, and the heap's mutex is created. A second chunk to contain supervisor mode stacks is created. The kernel heap is now "mutated" into a dynamic heap – the kernel now has full memory allocation capabilities

3. The debugger interface is initialized

4. Publish and subscribe is initialized

5. The power model is initialized

6. The code management system is initialized.

The final act of the initial thread during boot is to create and resume the kernel supervisor thread – startup now continues in the context of that thread.

Eventually the null thread will run again, and will then enter a loop in `KernelMain()`, repeatedly running a low priority garbage collection process, and after that requesting the `Asic` object to take the processor into some form of idle state.

16.1.3.4 Init-3

The supervisor thread now initializes several more kernel services:

- The kernel side of the HAL system
- The event queue
- The default DFC queues
- The RAM drive chunk
- The tick- and second-timer system.

The supervisor then invokes the variant's init-3, which will at last enable the kernel timer services – and, now that the kernel is fully functional, initialize various other interrupt handlers and sources.

Finally, the supervisor now runs the export entry point for each extension in turn, in this way initializing the phone's BSP piece by piece. There are many more extensions than are shown in the timeline in Figure 16.2. I have only included a few of the key ones that provide services used elsewhere in this chapter.

The last such extension is always `ExStart` – this is dedicated to constructing the second process "by hand", and so initializing EFILE.EXE and resuming this as the first user-mode process.

16.1.4 The file server

At this stage in the boot, we have a fully functional micro-kernel that supports multiple multi-threaded, protected user-mode processes. However, the OS has not yet provided the means to instantiate new processes, to extract file-based data from the Flash or to persist data in read/write Flash memory. The establishment of all of these services falls to EFILE.EXE, the designated *secondary* executable, and its supporting process ESTART.EXE.

EFILE starts by creating the infrastructure for the file server:

- The secondary thread for processing disconnect requests
- The object container classes for shared resources
- The `TDrive` objects providing the logical media interface to the file systems.

The file server mounts the first file system (the XIP ROM file system on drive "Z:") manually, and this allows the file server service to be created.

The file server now creates the loader thread, which provides the executable loader service for the rest of the OS, and waits for it to signal that it is ready. The loader initializes itself by creating the server objects and initializing its filename cache.

The file server now completes initialization of the local drive collection and prepares its notification service before creating a final slave thread to continue startup. Finally it begins to service file server requests.

The OS can now service load requests against executable files found in the XIP ROM (as this is the only file system that is mounted!). The slave thread picks up the trail and now makes requests to the loader to install the local media sub-system drivers and physical media drivers, preparing the file server for mounting the full set of file systems. The last action of the slave thread is to create the second user process: ESTART.EXE.

ESTART does phone-specific initialization, which is why it is separated from the generic EFILE.EXE. ESTART initializes the local file systems one by one, installing and mounting the required file systems over each medium – for example LFFS on a NOR Flash memory. ESTART can also be configured to use error detection and repair tools (such as scandisk) on file systems that were not shutdown in an orderly way – or to format disks when the phone is booted for the first time.

Once the read/write file systems are available, ESTART locates the persistent HAL settings on the internal drive and restores them to the HAL. This is also where the current language and locale settings are identified and restored from disk.

When we reach this point, all of the kernel, user library and file server services are now fully initialized and ready for the rest of the OS to begin its startup process. ESTART has done its job, and it now creates the next process in the chain, the system starter.

16.1.5 The system starter

The system starter provides a framework for the mobile phone to start and maintain all of the services necessary for normal operation. This framework is driven by a configuration file that the phone manufacturer constructs. The system starter also allows for multiple startup scenarios (some of which are described in Section 16.2.2) by supporting the selection of different configuration files.

Just as with the kernel and file server, the order in which the system services are initialized is important. This is to respect dependencies between services and to ensure that vital services are started first. In particular, on a mobile phone one would like the telephone functionality to be ready as soon as possible.

During normal system boot, we would expect that this component would first start the various low level communications, audio and graphics services. One vital server to initialize before the user interface can appear is the window server (discussed in Chapter 11, *The Window Server*), which provides shared access to the UI hardware on the phone, such as the display, keypad and touch screen.

Once the window server is running then the rest of the application and UI framework can initialize, and finally the telephone application is run.

16.2 Alternative startup scenarios

16.2.1 Booting from NAND Flash memory

In Section 16.1, I briefly described NAND Flash memory, and particularly noted its inability to be used for XIP software. In Chapter 9, *The File Server*, I discussed this type of Flash and its use for both user data storage and for storing built-in software. That alone is not enough to enable the system to boot from such memory, because the ROFS (read-only file system) relies on the kernel, file server and loader to copy the executable code into memory and prepare it for execution. So how do we get these fundamental services running to support loading the main OS from a ROFS image?

Figure 16.3 shows the modified startup stages for booting from NAND Flash. There are now two extra stages before the bootstrap is run:

1a.   NAND Flash provides a very basic XIP service to allow a system to boot – the first 512-byte sector of the memory can be shadowed into some internal RAM and executed from there. This first sector must contain enough code to carry out the first step in loading the entire OS. The miniboot does this, by providing the essential CPU and memory setup, before loading the rest of the first Flash block (typically 16 KB) into RAM and continuing execution from there

1b.   The program in this larger block is the *coreloader*. This understands the partitioning of the NAND Flash and the bad block algorithm, which I discussed in Chapter 9, *The File Server*. This allows it to locate and load the core image into RAM. The core image is an XIP image, which must at least contain all of the code required to initialize the kernel and file server and install the ROFS file system. The core image may be compressed, as this saves space in the Flash. Once the core image is loaded, the core loader executes the entry point in the XIP image (the bootstrap) and boot continues as for the XIP sequence for a while.

The XIP boot sequence is then modified once more – during file system initialization. The file system configuration for NAND Flash typically will combine both the XIP ROM file system and the ROFS file system under a single drive identifier, as I described in Chapter 9, *The File Server*. This

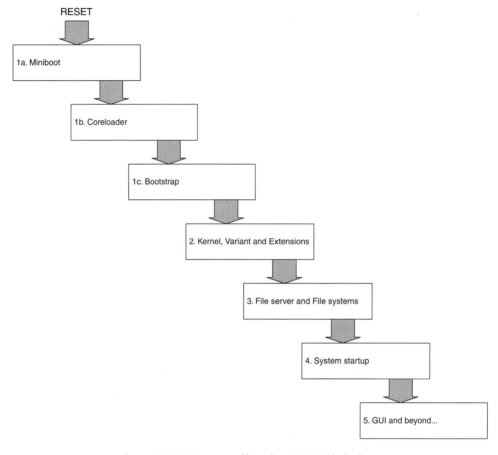

Figure 16.3   Main stages of boot for a NAND Flash phone

allows built-in software that expects to be "in ROM" to be in the usual place – drive "Z:".

Given all this extra effort and delay during startup it is worth asking, what is the value of using NAND Flash for non-volatile storage in mobile phones? The answer is the same issue that prompted the question: performance. NAND Flash provides similar performance to NOR Flash for reading, but can write data three or four times faster. This will become very important for mobile phones that have multi-megapixel cameras or allow download of music tracks from a PC – NOR Flash is too slow for these use cases.

16.2.2   Other reasons for startup

The boot process usually starts because the user switched on the mobile phone, in which case the standard startup process is likely to be followed.

However, there are circumstances in which we follow alternative boot sequences, for example:

- A phone that is powered off displays its charging status when plugged into an electrical supply

- In the factory, when it is first switched on, the phone runs a series of diagnostic "self tests" to verify that the hardware and software are all functioning correctly

- While the phone's firmware (in other words, the Flash memory on which Symbian OS resides) is being updated, Symbian OS cannot safely be running. Depending on how the update software is implemented, this startup sequence may diverge inside the bootstrap before the kernel runs.

In the majority of Symbian phones, it is not the Symbian kernel that is initially aware of the reason for boot. The bootstrap provides a little information to the kernel through the superpage in the form of iBootReason, but this usually indicates only the difference between a cold boot (hardware power on) and a warm boot (software reset and reboot). Most often, the baseband software determines the reason for booting and provides this information to Symbian OS early on – for example in ESTART. The system starter uses this information to select the configuration file that corresponds to this startup scenario.

16.2.3   Booting in the emulator

The introduction of process emulation makes it possible for the emulator to "boot" in a way that is much closer to the real thing. The most significant differences are:

1.   The object that replaces the bootstrap

2.   Running different "types" of emulator.

16.2.3.1   Bootstrap

EPOC.EXE is the standard bootstrap program. It is a Win32 executable and its sole reason for existence is to call BootEpoc() in EUSER from its Win32 entry point. BootEpoc() takes a single Boolean parameter, ultimately used to determine if the emulator should automatically run a program after boot is completed.

BootEpoc() loads the kernel DLL dynamically and looks up the Symbian OS entry point, _E32Startup, by name. If it is successful, this entry point is then invoked, passing in BootEpoc()'s parameter. The kernel's _E32Startup() function first runs the kernel's static data constructors, then saves the parameter for later and calls the kernel's

`BootEpoc()` function. This function does emulator specific initialization before calling the common kernel startup code in `KernelMain()`.

16.2.3.2 Variant and extensions

With no ROM, the kernel cannot immediately find the variant and extensions to load.

The variant is always called ECUST.DLL and `P::CreateVariant()` dynamically loads it – the DLL entrypoint is located as for other emulator DLLs, and called as normal for the variant. `A::CreateVariant()` then invokes the first ordinal in the variant, passing in the previously saved parameter that was originally passed to `BootEpoc()` by EPOC.EXE. Variant initialization then proceeds as usual.

The list of extensions to load is retrieved from the variant as the "extensions" property. These are dynamically loaded, in order, and their Symbian OS DLL entry points are called as normal for extensions. The last of these should be EXSTART, which creates a process based on the EFILE.EXE image – the file server.

16.2.3.3 E32START

File server initialization proceeds as normal, the last action being to create a new process from the E32STRT.EXE image. This is the emulator equivalent of the ESTART.EXE that I describe in Chapter 16. It carries out the same initialization tasks, but provides some additional features for the emulator.

E32STRT determines which UI to run based on its configuration properties: it can run the graphical window server, the text shell or run without any UI at all.

E32STRT then checks to see how the emulator was bootstrapped. If it was started by EPOC.EXE, it exits leaving the UI to run and the emulator boot has completed. If not, it retrieves the program and command line to auto-execute from the "AutoRun" and "CommandLine" properties, creates that process, waits for it to exit and after that terminates the emulator. This latter course of action gives the same behavior that you see in the EKA1 emulator when you run an EXE from the Windows command line.

16.3 Operating system shutdown

Now that I have covered startup, I will move on to describe its opposite: shutdown. From the user's point of view, startup and shutdown are symmetrical activities. From the software perspective, there is little in common:

- Startup is a baton-passing exercise, which takes the mobile phone from a primordial state to one where all services are running, in a carefully sequenced procession. This sequence is a consequence of the system design and our main interest lies in how it is achieved

- Conversely, shutdown is an activity which must be orchestrated, bringing the running system to a state in which it is safe to "pull the plug" and remove power. I will discuss some design details here to help explain the way in which shutdown is managed.

Shutdown – which involves shutting down the phone, closing all open applications and saving data that has changed in the current session – is normally initiated by a user action, such as pressing a power button or a power-off key. Shutdown also occurs in response to other user or network based activities:

- Restoring data from a backup can invalidate much of the OS state: it is easier to restart the entire system than to synchronize all system services with the new configuration data

- Firmware over the air (FOTA) update. In-place update of the Symbian OS firmware requires that Symbian OS is not executing at the time. Once the update is downloaded to the phone, the phone will need to restart in "update" mode.

In all of these scenarios, the shutdown can be managed in an orderly way to ensure that persistent data is saved correctly.

Sometimes, however, the cause of shutdown is less controlled. For example, some software faults in critical system services are unrecoverable and result in an immediate software reset. Or, a loss of power results in a very rapid shutdown of the system, even though a little residual power is available to complete critical disk activities. In such cases the startup process must make its best effort to recover the state of the data on the mobile phone, and repair any problems that it discovers. Some of this work is done in ESTART as it mounts the file systems – if the system did not shutdown cleanly, it can check for errors in the file system and may even reformat the file system if it cannot be repaired.

System shutdown may result in critical hardware components such as the CPU and most peripherals having their power removed (transition to the off state) – or it may leave these components in a standby state, from which it is possible to return to an operational (active) state without rebooting.

There are currently two architectures available that can be used to manage shutdown of the entire OS. The shutdown server is used in phones today, whereas the domain manager is a new component that will eventually replace the shutdown server in this role. I will look at the design of both these architectures.

16.3.1   The shutdown server

The shutdown server is the current architecture that is used to manage controlled shutdown in Symbian OS.

Shutdown is typically initiated by a dedicated kernel-level component such as a device driver or kernel extension, or by the variant detecting a power button press, a power hotkey tap, the closing of the phone's cover, or some other mechanism.

A user-side component may also initiate a shutdown sequence, by calling the UserSvr class exported API HalFunction(TInt aGroup, TInt aFunction, TAny* a1, TAny* a2) with EHalGroupPower as the identifier for the HAL group of functions and EPowerHalSwitchOff as the identifier for the function to execute. This could be used, for example, when the detection of the power key press is not done by a software component executing on the main application processor: instead the user-side component that is used as a communication channel to the baseband software will call the HalFunction API. The servicing of the UserSvr call is done by the platform-specific part of the kernel power framework, as I explained in Chapter 15, *Power Management*.

As a result of detecting the hardware event corresponding to the physical action, or servicing the UserSvr call as I have just described, a TRawEvent having one of the following types is added to the event queue:

- ESwitchOff – added by the servicing of the UserSvr call

- EKeyOff – added by the driver that detects the key presses

- ECaseClose – added by the platform-specific component that monitors the state of the phone's lid.

The window server receives the event, and translates it into a TEventCode type:

- EEventSwitchOff in place of ESwitchOff

- EEventKeySwitchOff in place of EKeyOff

- EEventCaseClosed in place of ECaseClose.

The window server will then either send the event to a registered component that requested it or, if no component is registered to receive off events, request the kernel to power down by calling UserHal::SwitchOff().

All current Symbian OS mobile phone have a UI component – the Look And Feel, or LAF, shutdown manager – that would previously have registered with the window server to receive such events. Implementing this policy in the UI allows the shutdown behavior of the phone to be customized according to the UI model it employs.

The shutdown manager object should derive from `CLafShutdown-ManagerBase` and implement a policy on when to shutdown the mobile phone.

```
class CLafShutdownManagerBase : public CBase
  {
protected:
  inline CLafShutdownManagerBase(MShutdownEventObserver& aObserver);
protected:
  MShutdownEventObserver& iObserver;
  };
```

The policy can involve listening for events such as the ones I have just listed, monitoring user inactivity using inactivity timers, and more.

A typical implementation has the LAF shutdown manager opening a session with the window server at creation time and queuing a request for the notification of "off" events. When it does receive such an "off" event, the LAF shutdown manager decides if it should result in a power down or just the sending of state and data save notifications to applications.

The shutdown server is at the center of the shutdown architecture. It derives from `MShutdownEventObserver`, as follows:

```
class MShutdownEventObserver
  {
public:
  virtual void HandleShutdownEventL(MSaveObserver::TSaveType aAction,
                                                   TBool aPowerOff)=0;
  virtual CArrayFix<TThreadId>* ClientArrayLC()=0;
  virtual TBool IsClientHung(TThreadId aId) const=0;
  virtual void GetShutdownState(TBool& aPowerOff,
          TBool& aAllSessionsHavePendingRequest)
const=0;
  };
```

The implementation of the mandatory API by a shutdown server enables the LAF shutdown manager to:

- Request the sending of save notifications to registered components, possibly followed by a shutdown

- Return a list of registered clients

- Enquire if a registered client is still processing the save notification

- Obtain the shutdown status after a shutdown request has been issued.

When the UI creates the shutdown server, the shutdown manager is also created and its `iObserver` member is set to reference the shutdown server.

Software components that need to be notified of an imminent shutdown create sessions with the shutdown server to receive save notifications. An example of such a component is a UI-specific save observer, which acts as a gateway for save/shutdown notifications on behalf of UI applications. Upon receiving a save notification, a save observer propagates the request to all running applications which will then save their data/status, close dialogs, exit, and so on.

The notification mechanism is based on an asynchronous request, which is placed on the shutdown server when a client creates a session with it. Clients of the shutdown server typically own a CSaveNotifier object that provides them with an interface to the shutdown server:

```
class CSaveNotifier : public CActive
  {
public:
  IMPORT_C static CSaveNotifier* NewL(MSaveObserver& aObserver);
  IMPORT_C ~CSaveNotifier();
  IMPORT_C void DelayRequeue();
  IMPORT_C void Queue();
  IMPORT_C void HandleError(TInt aError);
  ...
  };
```

The API allows for:

- Creating a session with the shutdown server that will queue an asynchronous request for shutdown notification

- Closing the session and canceling a pending request

- Delaying or stopping a shutdown sequence after the client received the notification, and resuming the sequence

- Notifying the shutdown server of an error in its internal save/shutdown sequence.

Clients of the shutdown server must also implement an MSaveObserver interface:

```
class MSaveObserver
  {
public:
  enum TSaveType
    {
    ESaveNone,
    ESaveData,
    ESaveAll,
    ESaveQuick,
    EReleaseRAM,
```

```
    EReleaseDisk,
    };
public:
  virtual void SaveL(TSaveType aSaveType)=0;
  };
```

Thus, when notified of an "off" event, the LAF shutdown manager calls the shutdown server's `HandleShutdownEventL()` API, specifying if a power down is required and specifying what save action is required from its clients (as a `TSaveType`). The LAF shutdown manager may also do this as a result of detecting a period of user inactivity.

The shutdown server manages the shutdown sequence. The servicing of `HandleShutdownEventL()` saves the locale and HAL settings that may have changed during the current session and, if a saving action of any type is required, notifies all registered clients that have pending save notification requests, by completing those requests. If a registered client does not yet have a pending request, then it will be notified immediately after it issues the request for notification.

After receiving a save notification, clients of the shutdown server call the `SaveL()` method (from `MSaveObserver`) which will perform client-specific status saving actions corresponding to the `TSaveType` argument passed.

Clients must then re-queue a request with the shutdown server. If a power down is required, the shutdown server will ask the kernel to shutdown only after all its clients have re-queued requests with it.

The shutdown server requests kernel shutdown by invoking the `User-Hal::SwitchOff()` API (an export from EUSER.DLL):

```
EXPORT_C TInt UserHal::SwitchOff()
  {
  TInt r = Power::EnableWakeupEvents(EPwStandby);
  if(r!=KErrNone)
  return r;
  TRequestStatus s;
  Power::RequestWakeupEventNotification(s);
  Power::PowerDown();
  User::WaitForRequest(s);
  return s.Int();
  }
```

This entire sequence is illustrated in Figure 16.4.

I have already discussed the `Power` class APIs invoked by this function in Chapter 15, *Power Management*. Be sure to note that:

- The target power state selected by `UserHal::SwitchOff()` is standby, as was the case with the EKA1 power management. However, as the implementation of `Power::PowerDown()` will call down to platform-specific code, phone manufacturers can interpret this

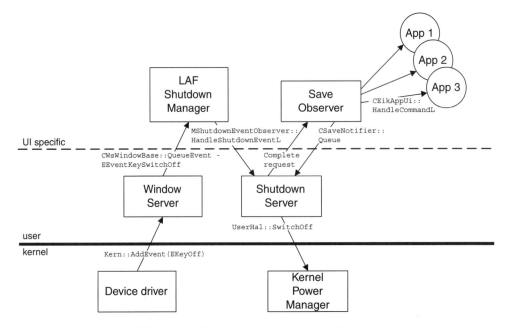

Figure 16.4 Flow of activity after a power off event

request by powering down the hardware (CPU, peripherals) instead of transitioning them to a standby state

- The new shutdown architecture using the domain manager (discussed in the following section) leaves the choice of target power state to the LAF domain controller

- Wakeup events are enabled but, if they occur they have no impact on the transition once initiated.

16.3.2 The domain manager

As I mentioned earlier, in the future an architecture based upon domain management will be used as a replacement to the current scheme based around the shutdown server.

16.3.2.1 Overview

This alternative scheme is based on the concept of power domains, which may be populated with applications, and which are organized as dependency trees that represent the domain hierarchy (see Figure 16.5). Each node on the dependency tree represents a domain and is identified by a domain ID – an identifier number. Applications at the top of the tree, residing in parent domains, will usually provide services to those in child domains, or will manage the resources that they need to use. In this way

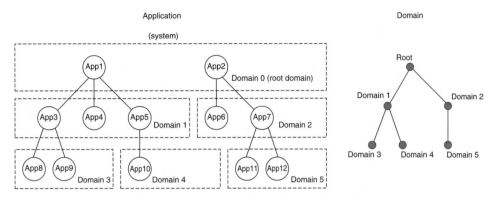

Figure 16.5 Application dependencies and the domain hierarchy

the applications on one node of the domain tree have a dependency on the node above, and so on. This dependency is taken into consideration when a domain is activated, put into standby or shutdown.

Domains can be in one of three possible power states: active, standby or off. Domains can be independently requested to transition between these different power states.

If a transition is applied to the root domain (the top of the tree) then the transition is a *system transition*. A system transition is one that is also applied to the kernel via the `Power` API, once the root domain has completed its transition. The system can transition from the active to the standby or off states – this is, of course, shutdown. The transition to active state is only allowed from the standby state and cannot be initiated by a call to the domain manager. This transition starts when the kernel wakes up from its standby state and reports the wakeup event to the domain manager, which then recovers from standby state by transitioning the domain tree back to active.

The transition of a domain to standby or off always starts with the transition of all the domain's child domains, followed by the transition of the target domain itself. A domain transition to the active state always starts with the transition of that domain, followed by the transition of its entire list of child domains.

Domain trees are static and are specified at system build time in the domain policy DLL. At system startup time, when the domain tree is loaded from this DLL, domains in the tree have no member applications. Applications will join the relevant domain as they startup.

We permit a maximum of 256 domains.

Applications are allowed to join domains, or disconnect from them, at any time. Once an application has joined a domain, it will remain a member of that domain until it explicitly relinquishes membership.

Membership of a domain gives an application the ability to request notification of the domain's power state changes. The application can decide on what action it should take on receiving this notification. Usually, on receiving a notification for a transition to a low power state, an application will save data related to its current state.

Domain state change notification is implemented using the publish and subscribe mechanism that I discussed in Chapter 4, *Inter-thread Communication*. State changes are published as property value changes. A state property identifier – a UID – has been reserved for this purpose, as have 256 sub-keys for the maximum possible number of domains. Applications that want to receive domain state notification simply subscribe to the state property.

Applications can join more than one domain and be notified of power state changes affecting all the different domains that they belong to. Applications may act upon the notification differently for each of the different domains they belong to, or for each type of state change they are notified about. For example, an application may save its data and state to persistent storage on domain shutdown, or save it to RAM on domain standby.

16.3.2.2 Design and APIs

The domain managed architecture is shown in Figure 16.6. The domain manager is a user-side system server, which manages application membership to domains as well as system-wide and domain-specific power state transitions. It owns the domain tree.

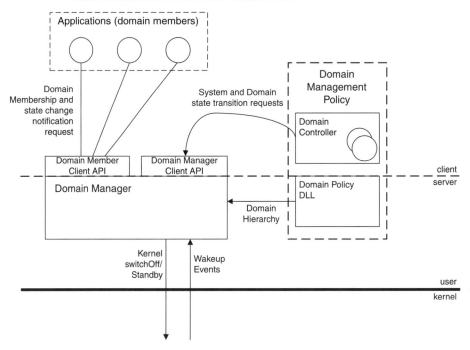

Figure 16.6 Domain management architecture

The domain manager gets the description of the domain tree from the domain policy DLL at system boot time when the domain manager is created; the domain policy DLL contains a "recipe" – or specification – to allow it to build the domain tree. Once loaded, the domain tree can never be modified.

The domain management policy is also responsible for triggering system-wide and domain-specific power state transitions. A component in the UI will provide a domain controller to implement these aspects of the policy, in a similar way to that in which the LAF shutdown server provides UI specific policy in the shutdown server architecture.

A domain controller has to connect to the domain manager, using the domain manager client API. The domain controller is required to have the `PowerMgmt` capability to request transitions, protecting the phone from malicious software. Once a connection is created, the controller can request a system or domain transition. After the transition has completed – which is signaled asynchronously – the controller should disconnect. Only one connection is allowed at any given time.

The domain manager client API is provided by the `RDmDomainManager` class:

```
class RDmDomainManager
  {
public:
  IMPORT_C static TInt WaitForInitialization();
public:
  IMPORT_C TInt Connect();
  IMPORT_C void Close();
  IMPORT_C void RequestSystemTransition(TPowerState,
                         TRequestStatus& aStatus);
  IMPORT_C void RequestDomainTransition(TDmDomainId, TPowerState,
                                  TRequestStatus& aStatus);
  IMPORT_C void CancelTransition();
  IMPORT_C void SystemShutdown();
  };
```

This class offers methods to allow a domain controller to:

- Synchronize with the domain manager initialization before creating a session with it

- Create a controlling session with the domain manager

- Request system-wide transitions – to "standby" or "off"

- Request domain-specific transitions

- Cancel a system-wide or domain specific transition

- Disconnect from the domain manager.

Applications use the domain member client to interface to the domain manager. This client is a user-side DLL that encapsulates the domain membership and the state transition protocols. No platform security capabilities are required to use this interface to the domain manager.

The domain member client API is provided by the RDmDomain class:

```
class RDmDomain
  {
public:
  IMPORT_C TInt Connect(TDmDomainId aId);
  IMPORT_C void RequestTransitionNotification(TRequestStatus&
                                              aStatus);
  IMPORT_C void CancelTransitionNotification();
  IMPORT_C TPowerState GetPowerState();
  IMPORT_C void AcknowledgeLastState();
  IMPORT_C void Close();
  };
```

It offers methods to allow applications to:

- Request membership of a domain

- Request notification of domain state changes

- Cancel a request for notification of domain state changes

- Enquire the current state of a domain

- Acknowledge a state change notification

- Disconnect from a domain.

16.3.2.3 Shutdown sequence

When the domain controller requests a system-wide transition by calling the domain manager client exported API RequestSystemTransition() specifying standby or off as the power state, or by calling SystemShutdown() (which is a convenient wrapper for a PowerOff transition request), the domain manager will perform the following sequence of actions:

1. Enable wakeup events for the target state (by calling Power::EnableWakeupEvents(...) and passing the target power state)

2. Request notification of the occurrence of any wakeup events by calling Power::RequestWakeupEventNotification()

3. Notify all applications in the domain tree of the imminent transition, and wait for them to complete their transition. Notifications are

issued taking into consideration the dependency between these components: applications that depend on resources offered by others are notified before those they depend on, and are shutdown first. In this way, resources are not released prematurely and are always available for applications that need them during the shutdown sequence. This orderly issuing of notifications also guarantees the speediest shutdown

4. If no wakeup event has been notified, the domain manager creates a session with the file server and calls the RFs class's API FinaliseDrives(). This iterates over every local or internal drive (that has a file system already mounted and has a media mounted that is not write protected) calling a file system-specific mount control block method (FinaliseMountL()). This may simply mark the drive as having been successfully finalized and not needing to be scanned the next time the phone is rebooted. This signals the completion of the user-side preparations to shutdown: at this point all user-side components that needed to save data or state must have already done so. The method can therefore mark the mount as read-only to prevent any spurious writes

5. At this point, if no wakeup event has been notified, the domain manager asks the kernel framework to power down the CPU and peripherals: Power::PowerDown().

You might have noticed that steps 4 and 5 are just special cases of the domain transitions – and that one could view the file server and kernel as being nodes above the root domain in the hierarchy. Although it is possible to implement the file server shutdown as a domain transition, it is simpler at present to implement this transition as a special case. This is true in particular due to the need to support both shutdown architectures at present.

It may happen that halfway through the system shutdown, the domain controller decides to interrupt the transition (for example, if part of the system cannot be transitioned at this time). It may do so by calling the domain manager client exported API CancelTransition(), which results in the following sequence of actions being performed:

1. Wakeup events for the current transition are disabled and the power framework's target state is reset to active by calling Power::DisableWakeupEvents()

2. Wakeup event notification is canceled by calling Power::CancelWakeupEventNotification()

3. The shutdown notification is canceled for registered applications.

16.3.2.4 *Migration from the current architecture*

The domain manager and its domain member client interface can replace the shutdown server and the save notification mechanism by implementing save observers as nodes in the domain tree (that is, as power domains) and using the LAF shutdown manager in the role of domain controller.

Domain management offers some advantages over the current shutdown server architecture:

1. Shutdown is "orderly": it takes into consideration the dependencies between components

2. Shutdown of the file server is controlled

3. Wakeup events are monitored during shutdown (see Section 16.4).

16.4 Operating system sleep and wakeup events

Within the current shutdown framework, some events may not lead to fully shutting down the phone via the `UserHal::SwitchOff()` API. Instead, moving it to a silent running mode, characterized by switching off the user interface, may be a more appropriate action, leaving the phone able to respond to incoming calls and quickly return to a running state. A clamshell phone may switch to silent running mode while the lid is closed and awake again when it is opened.

Such an operational mode may also be used at the beginning of a full shutdown operation, to provide feedback to the user that the mobile phone is switching off.

In this case, the UI observer of the `EEventCaseClosed` can simply disable appropriate hardware through the HAL or other device drivers:

```
HAL::Set(HAL::EDisplayState, 0);
HAL::Set(HAL::EKeyboardState, 0);
HAL::Set(HAL::EPenState, 0);
```

Recovering from such a state usually happens because of a wake up event, generated by events such as the user pressing the on key, the phone being opened or an alarm going off.

I have already introduced the concept of wakeup events in Chapter 15, *Power Management*. In that chapter, I defined wakeup events as hardware events that, occurring while the platform is in low power state, may be capable of initiating a transition to an operational state. The kernel can also track them while the OS is preparing the platform transition to a low power state. If they are reported during that stage, they will lead to the canceling or even the reversing of the transition. Wakeup events can therefore play an important role during system shutdown.

Suppose the system has transitioned to a low power state such as the standby state, which does not require a full system reboot and leaves some systems operational (namely those involved in the detection of wakeup events). If a wakeup event then occurs, it is initially handled by the kernel power framework, which will restore the hardware platform to the state prior to the transition.

The current shutdown framework, based upon the shutdown server and LAF shutdown manager, relies on the kernel power framework sending an `ESwitchOn` event (or an `ECaseOpen` event if waking up was triggered by opening the phone lid) when waking up from the low power state. This may be done by the BSP part of the kernel framework.

The window server captures the events, translates them into `EEvent-SwitchOn` or `EEventCaseOpened` and sends them to a component that registered for "on" events (typically the LAF shutdown manager). The LAF shutdown manager will then perform whatever actions are required to restore the UI and applications to a state corresponding to the phone operational mode. Typically:

```
HAL::Set(HAL::EDisplayState, 1);
HAL::Set(HAL::EKeyboardState, 1);
HAL::Set(HAL::EPenState, 1);
```

In a shutdown architecture based upon the domain manager, the domain controller requests a system transition to standby by calling the domain manager client asynchronous API `RequestSystemTransition()` and passing a `TRequestStatus`. The domain manager asks the kernel framework for notification of wakeup events before the transition to standby.

After waking up the platform, the kernel power framework completes the domain manager notification, which will then complete the domain controller's request, thus notifying it of a system wakeup.

On a domain-manager-controlled shutdown, the domain manager also monitors wakeup events during the OS shutdown sequence. At any point in that sequence before the kernel is requested to transition, a wakeup event may occur. For example, the user of the phone may change her mind and press the power button again. Or an alarm from a user-side software component may go off.

The kernel power framework completes the domain manager wakeup notification request, thus notifying it of the occurrence of the wakeup event. Upon receiving the notification, the domain manager performs the following actions:

1. Disables wakeup events and resets the kernel power framework target state to active by calling `Power::DisableWakeupEvents()`

2. Cancels the shutdown notification for applications that have not yet shutdown

3. Sends notifications to applications to transition back to the active state.

16.5   Summary

In this chapter I have demonstrated what happens during the first and the last few seconds of execution of Symbian OS – how the operating system bootstraps itself into existence and how it safely shuts itself down again.

In the next chapter, I will consider performance, and discuss how you can get the most out of EKA2.

17

Real Time

by Dennis May

*If I could explain it to the average person, I wouldn't have been worth
the Nobel Prize.*

Richard Feynman

In this chapter, I will discuss real time systems, the support that operating
systems must provide to enable them and how we designed EKA2 to
support them.

17.1   What is real time?

The term "real time" is often misunderstood. The canonical definition
of a "real time system" is the following, taken from the Usenet group
comp.realtime[1] and credited to Donald Gillies:

> A real-time system is one in which the correctness of the computations
> not only depends upon the logical correctness of the computation but also
> upon the time at which the result is produced. If the timing constraints of
> the system are not met, system failure is said to have occurred.

Essentially, a real time system has a set of tasks which it must perform,
and at least one of those tasks has a deadline by which it must complete
otherwise the system will fail to operate correctly. A system may perform
both real time and non-real time tasks; the former are the ones with strict
deadlines.

Some examples are useful at this point:

1.   An engine management system has several tasks that need to be done
     on each revolution of the engine, such as operating the fuel injectors

---

[1] See FAQ posting on comp.realtime

and triggering the ignition spark. If these tasks do not occur at the correct times, the engine will either perform badly or not function at all. To get an idea of how much accuracy is required, a typical engine has a maximum working angular velocity of 6000 rpm, or 100 revolutions per second. For optimum performance, the timing needs to be adjusted to within 1% of a revolution, so this equates to a timing margin of less than 100 μs

2. Most communication protocols include timeouts to guard against the possibility of data being lost in transit through an unreliable network or transmission medium. If a computer system running one of these protocols does not respond in time, the peer will assume the data has been lost and will retransmit it unnecessarily or possibly even terminate the connection. Typical values of the timeouts range from a few milliseconds to several minutes depending on the protocol concerned.

A common misapprehension about the term real time is that it implies that the system must operate very quickly. This is not necessarily the case – a deadline may be known about well in advance but still be critical. A well-known example here is the problem of ensuring that servers were year 2000 compliant before that date. Another example is the second one I just gave, in which the deadline may be of the order of seconds or even minutes, which is for ever for a computer!

17.1.1 Hard and soft real time

In Section 17.1 I give a black and white definition of real time. In reality a lot of systems have varying degrees of tolerance to missed deadlines. This leads to the following definitions:

A **hard** real time system or task is one in which a missed deadline causes complete system failure, as described in Section 17.1.

A **soft** real time system or task is one in which a missed deadline causes a reduction in system performance. Typically, the greater the margin by which the deadline is missed, the greater is the reduction in performance, and for some value of the margin the system has failed.

Examples of soft real time systems include:

1. A user interface responding to input from the user. The objective here is to provide apparently instant response. Research indicates that the user will perceive a response within 100 ms as instantaneous, and so the "deadline" is 100 ms from the user's input. However if the response takes 200 ms, no one is likely to mind. If it takes a second, the system could appear sluggish and if it takes more than a minute with no response at all, the user will probably think the device is broken

2. In most cases the communication protocol example in Section 17.1 is actually a soft real time task. If the deadline is missed, the peer entity will retransmit, which will waste bandwidth and reduce throughput but will not cause catastrophic failure.

17.2 Real time operating systems

We have given definitions of real time systems and tasks. An operating system cannot be real time in the sense that I have just discussed. Instead the term "real time operating system" (usually abbreviated to RTOS) refers to an operating system that is capable of running real time applications. In this section I will discuss some of the properties that an RTOS should have.

17.2.1 Tasks and scheduling

A real time system will generally consist of several logically separate but interacting tasks each with their own deadline. It may also contain non-real time (or soft real time) tasks. The most important task for any RTOS is to schedule the tasks for execution on the processor in such a way that the deadlines of the real time tasks are always met. In analyzing whether this is possible, the following simplified model of task execution is often used. Consider that the system has a set of n tasks, denoted $\tau_1, \ldots, \tau_n$. Each task is assumed to run periodically. Task τ_i is triggered every T_i seconds, runs for a maximum time C_i and is expected to finish within time D_i of being triggered. In reality tasks will have a variable execution time, but to ensure that deadlines can be met the worst case execution time (WCET) is assumed. Similarly, aperiodic tasks can be incorporated by treating them as periodic with period equal to the minimum possible time between invocations of the task. We define the response time (R_i) of a task τ_i to be the time from the task being triggered to the task completing. Figure 17.1 illustrates these task-timing parameters.

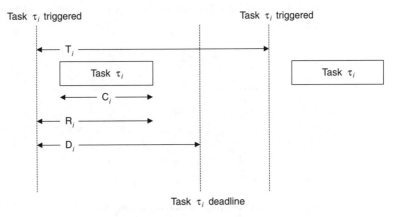

Figure 17.1   Task timing parameters

17.2.1.1　*Cyclic scheduling*

The simplest means of ensuring that tasks all run when necessary is cyclic scheduling. It does not require interrupts and is the only method available on systems without interrupts. This method is often used in simple deeply embedded systems such as engine management, and would look something like this:

```
void main()
  {
  wait_for_next_tick();
  do_task1();
  do_task2();
  do_task3();
  }
```

This shows three tasks, all with the same period. To handle tasks with periods which are multiples of the same lowest period, the scheduler loop or task functions can be modified so that they only execute the task every *m* ticks for some value of *m*. Alternatively, for more flexibility, a major/minor cycle scheme may be employed where the system period is the least common multiple of the periods of all tasks and within each period each task executes several times. In both schemes, problems will be encountered fitting tasks into the schedule. Consider the following two tasks:

- Task 1 runs for 1 ms every 2 ms, deadline 2 ms
- Task 2 runs for 1.5 ms every 4 ms, deadline 4 ms.

It is not possible to execute task 2 continuously for 1.5 ms since then task 1 would miss its deadline. Instead, task 2 must be divided into two pieces, each of which has an execution time <1 ms. These pieces can then be fitted into the "gaps" between invocations of task 1. So you end up with:

```
void main()
  {
  wait_for_next_tick();
  ++tick_count;
  do_task1();
  if (tick_count & 1)
    do_task2_second_half();
  else
    do_task2_first_half();
  }
```

Figure 17.2 illustrates task execution under this scheduling scheme.

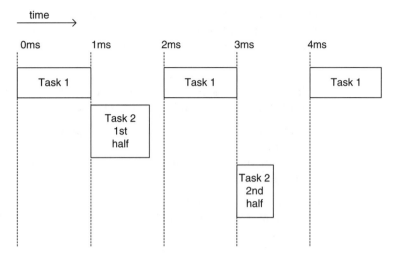

Figure 17.2

The partitioning of task 2 must be done by hand and the code must be modified to preserve any necessary state in global data, so that it can be communicated from the first to the second half.

Cyclic scheduling has some advantages – it can be implemented on very small systems without interrupts, there is no preemption to worry about, and it is guaranteed to meet all deadlines provided the schedule has been correctly calculated. However it also has major disadvantages:

- It has problems dealing with periods that are not multiples of the smallest period in the system. Tasks with periods that are not simple multiples of one another will give rise to very complicated schedules. To work round this limitation, tasks often end up being run more frequently than required, which wastes processor time

- Adding a new task to the system is difficult. The new task will probably need to be manually partitioned into several pieces with lots of state communicated between the pieces using global data

- Maintenance is difficult. An increase in the execution time of any of the task pieces may require a complete rethink of the cyclic schedule, even if that increase does not actually overload the processor

- Sporadic events are handled badly. They must be polled for, and time must be budgeted for them in every cycle even though in most cases that time is not required. This leads to poor processor utilization.

17.2.1.2 *Preemptive scheduling*

Cyclic scheduling is a completely co-operative scheduling method – there is no preemption. Once a task begins execution, it must complete before any other task can gain control of the processor – and this is the root of the major problems with cyclic scheduling. To overcome these problems, preemptive scheduling is used. A preemptive system has the following characteristics:

- Interrupts are used to signal external events. An interrupt will have some way, direct or indirect, of triggering a task

- The tasks in the system are ordered in some way; for real time systems, they are generally ordered by how urgent they are. This ordering may be constant or it may change with time depending on circumstances

- When a task is triggered, its urgency is compared with that of the currently executing task. If the new task is more urgent, the current task is suspended and the new task begins execution immediately. If the new task is less urgent, it is simply placed on a list of pending tasks – the ready list

- When a task completes execution or waits for an external event to occur, it is suspended and control is passed to the most urgent task on the ready list.

Note that when control is passed from one task to another, the operating system automatically saves the state of the old task so that it can resume it later. Thus the operating system effectively does the partitioning of tasks into smaller pieces for you and so tasks can simply be written as a single unit. Adding a new task is simple; all that you have to do is to assign it a priority and check that the system can still be scheduled correctly with the new task included (in the sense that each task completes within its deadline). Similarly, an increase in the execution time of any task doesn't require any extra work rearranging the schedule, just a check that the system can still be scheduled correctly. Task periods don't have to be integer multiples of each other – each task simply runs when it needs to. Similarly, sporadic tasks are not a problem – they only use processor time when they actually run. Preemptive scheduling also deals with non-real time tasks; these are simply placed at the bottom of the ordering and so they run whenever no time critical tasks need the processor.

Preemptive scheduling solves the major problems of cyclic scheduling. However it brings some problems of its own:

- Resource sharing. Since tasks are started and stopped automatically by the OS it is possible that they will contend for use of a shared resource

- It is more difficult to check that a set of tasks can be scheduled correctly.

17.2.1.3 *Static priority based scheduling*

This is the most common form of preemptive scheduling, at least among real time operating systems. Each task is assigned a fixed priority when it is created, and these priorities determine which tasks preempt which other tasks. The actual priority values used are derived using a very simple rule from the deadlines of the various tasks. The tasks are placed in increasing deadline order – that is, the task with the shortest deadline has the highest priority and so on. This is known as *deadline monotonic scheduling*.

This result was proved in the well-known paper by Liu and Layland[2] for the case where $D_i = T_i$ and the more general result for $D_i < T_i$ was proved by Leung and Whitehead.[3] For the case where $D_i = T_i$ the resulting priority assignment is called *rate monotonic scheduling*. For this case the Liu and Layland paper also derives a simple sufficient condition for a task set to be scheduled correctly by the rate monotonic algorithm; this is possible provided that

$$u \le n(2^{1/n} - 1)$$

where u is the total CPU utilization given by

$$u = C_1/T_1 + C_2/T_2 + \cdots + C_n/T_n$$

That is, u is the proportion of the CPU time used. For large n, the limit is

$$u = \ln 2 = 0.6931 \ldots$$

So a task set satisfying the assumptions can be scheduled correctly using a rate monotonic fixed priority assignment provided that the CPU utilization does not exceed 69%. The condition is sufficient but not necessary and is usually pessimistic. In reality, task periods tend to be multiples of each other and this increases maximum possible utilization. If every task period is a multiple of the next shorter period, 100% utilization is theoretically possible.

Static priority based scheduling is by far the most common scheduling method used in real time systems. Even though it is not theoretically optimal, it is good enough for a large number of real world systems. It is also very simple to implement, which makes it suitable even for small, memory-limited systems. It can be implemented with fast, constant time algorithms, improving utilization and predictability when OS overheads

[2] Liu, C.L. and J.W. Layland, "Scheduling algorithms for multi-programming in a hard real-time environment", *Journal of the Association of Computer Machinery (ACM)* **20**(1), Jan. 1973, pp. 46–61.
[3] Leung, J.Y.T. and J. Whitehead, "On the complexity of fixed-priority scheduling of periodic, real-time tasks", *Performance Evaluation (Netherlands)* **2**(4), Dec. 1982, pp. 237–250.

are taken into account. Finally, its behavior under overload is predictable. As the system becomes more overloaded, the lowest priority tasks are delayed first. This makes it suitable for systems containing both real time and non-real time tasks.

17.2.1.4 *Deadline driven scheduling*

In the static priority scheme that I have just described, the scheduler never actually examines the deadlines of any tasks. It simply uses a fixed ordering specifying which tasks are generally more urgent than which others. However this is suboptimal, as illustrated by the following example:

- Task 1 runs for 50 ms every 100 ms, deadline 100 ms
- Task 2 runs for 60 ms every 140 ms, deadline 140 ms.

This cannot be scheduled by any static priority scheme. To see this, consider what happens when both tasks are triggered at the same time. If task 1 has higher priority, the response time for task 2 is 160 ms, since task 1 runs twice before task 2 completes. If task 2 has higher priority, the response time for task 1 is 110 ms. This task set is illustrated in Figure 17.3.

This task set can be scheduled by a dynamic priority scheme. In fact the Liu and Layland paper also proves that *earliest deadline first (EDF) scheduling* is optimal. In this algorithm, whenever a scheduling decision is required the task with the deadline closest to expiry is selected. Note

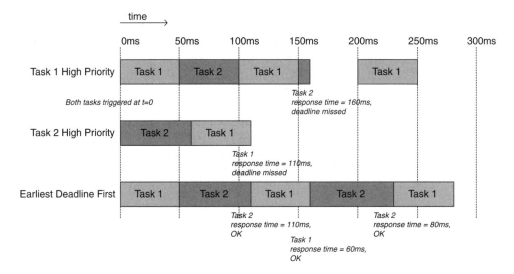

Figure 17.3 Suboptimality of static priority scheduling

that for a given set of tasks eligible for execution this policy will not always choose the same task to run – the decision made depends on how close each task's deadline is, which depends on the past history of the system – how the system got to the present state. The EDF algorithm is optimal in the sense that, provided the total CPU utilization of the tasks does not exceed 100%, then the task set can be scheduled by EDF.

There are two main problems with EDF scheduling. The first is that it is relatively complex to implement, and so introduces higher OS overheads than simple priority scheduling. The other problem is that it is unstable under overload. It is unpredictable which task will miss its deadline if the system is overloaded. This makes pure EDF scheduling unsuitable for systems containing both real time and non-real time tasks.

17.2.2 Predictability

The results on scheduling algorithms that I referred to previously make certain assumptions about how the system operates. Chief among these are the assumptions that task switching takes zero time and that a higher priority task is never prevented from running by a lower priority task. If the latter situation does occur, it is termed *priority inversion*. There is also the implicit assumption that the execution time of each task is known, or at least that it is bounded.

17.2.2.1 OS services

The time taken for task switching can be accounted for by assuming that a task switch takes place at the beginning and end of each task, so adding twice[4] the context switch time to each task's execution time gives an estimate (actually pessimistic) for the effect of context switching time.

To obtain predictable task execution times, the execution time of any operating system services used by that task must be predictable. The time taken by the operating system to switch tasks must also be predictable. Thus we arrive at our first requirement for an RTOS – task switching and OS services must have predictable, or at least well bounded, execution times. Obviously to maximize the proportion of processor time spent doing useful work these overheads should be as small as possible. However in a choice between an algorithm with a constant execution time and one with an execution time which is usually small but may

---

[4] To see why two context switch times are added, consider tasks A and B. Suppose A is part way through running when B becomes ready and preempts A. There is a context switch from A to B and then another from B to A when B completes. So the total delay to task A is the execution time of task B plus twice the context switch time – in other words, as if task B had twice the context switch time added to its execution time. On the other hand, when the end of one task and the beginning of another coincide then there is only one context switch to be added. This is why the estimate obtained is pessimistic.

occasionally be very large, the former should be chosen even though it may be slower on average.

17.2.2.2 *Interrupts*

Consider now the effect of hardware interrupts on the system. These may be considered as tasks with a very high priority – higher than any software-defined tasks. The tasks with the very shortest deadlines will be implemented as interrupt service routines. However, not all interrupts are equally urgent. An interrupt from a keyboard controller can probably wait 100 ms or so without any problem, whereas a receive interrupt from a 16550 UART must be serviced within 700 μs or data may be lost. In particular, some interrupts may have longer deadlines than some software defined tasks. According to the deadline monotonic scheduling rule, these interrupts should have lower priority than the tasks. However, the hardware will automatically preempt any task whenever an interrupt is signaled. There are three possible ways around this problem:

- Use a periodic task to poll for the long deadline interrupt at an appropriate priority. This has the disadvantage that the task uses processor time and consumes energy even when the interrupt is inactive

- Modify the interrupt masks of all peripherals in the system on every task switch so that certain tasks can mask certain interrupts. This approach is probably the best in principle but is complicated to implement unless the hardware is specifically designed to support it. Some processors support prioritized interrupts – typically 7 or 15 levels. It would be simple to allow the processor interrupt mask level to be modified by the scheduler on a task switch and then to assign the interrupts with long deadlines a low hardware priority. However other hardware does not have such a prioritization scheme and so would require many peripheral registers to be modified on each task switch, which would severely impact the efficiency of task switching

- Make the service routine for the long deadline interrupt as short as possible to minimize its impact on the rest of the system. In fact all it needs to do is to clear the peripheral's interrupt condition and then trigger a software task to do the real processing at an appropriate priority.

EKA2 employs the third option to solve this problem.

17.2.3 Mutual exclusion

In any preemptive system, there must be a means for a task to gain exclusive access to system resources for a time. Without such a mechanism, two or more tasks accessing the same resource will interact in an unpredictable manner. For example, consider two tasks both incrementing the same variable. On the ARM processor this involves executing the following sequence of instructions:

```
LDR     R1, [R0]     ; load register R1 with variable
ADD     R1, R1, #1   ; add 1 to register R1
STR     R1, [R0]     ; update variable with new value.
```

If two tasks both execute this sequence and the first task executes the first instruction of the sequence before the second task gains control, the sequence of instructions executed is:

(task 1) load variable into R1

(task 2) load variable into R1

(task 2) add 1 to R1

(task 2) store R1 into variable

(task 1) add 1 to R1

(task 1) store R1 into variable.

It can be seen that the effect of this sequence is to increment the variable only once instead of twice.

The measures commonly employed to prevent such contention take various forms, listed next. They all amount to ways to specify a group of code fragments and to ensure that at any time at most one thread of execution is present in the group. This property is called *mutual exclusion*. Ways of achieving mutual exclusion include:

- Use a single atomic instruction. This is the most efficient where possible but is limited in that only certain operations are possible. On ARM architecture 4 and 5 processors, the only atomic instruction is to swap the contents of memory with a register

- Disabling hardware interrupts. On a single processor system this ensures that no other task can gain control of the processor. On a multiple processor system spin locks must be used in conjunction with disabling local interrupts to prevent a task running on another processor from entering an excluded code section. Virtually every OS disables interrupts in some places since, other than atomic instructions, it is the only way of protecting resources accessed by both interrupts and software tasks. In particular, managing the interaction of interrupts with software tasks generally requires disabling interrupts

- Disabling preemption. Similar to disabling interrupts, but only protects against other software tasks, not against hardware interrupts.

Both disabling interrupts and disabling preemption are fairly drastic measures since they delay all other tasks, not just those that might contend for a particular resource

- Use an OS-provided synchronization object, such as a semaphore or mutex. These have no effect on scheduling of tasks unless the tasks contend for the protected resource.

Any method of mutual exclusion is a source of priority inversion since a high priority task may be held up waiting for a resource, which is currently locked by a lower priority task. The schedulability analysis referred to in Section 17.2.1 can be extended to account for mutual exclusion provided that the time for which priority inversion occurs is bounded. Thus we must ensure that:

- The time for which interrupts are disabled is bounded. In fact, to produce an OS of the greatest utility, this time must be minimized, since the maximum time for which interrupts are disabled gives a lower bound on the guaranteed response time for an external event

- The time for which preemption is disabled is minimized. This time, along with the time taken by all ISRs in the system, determines the fastest possible response time by a software task

- Mutual exclusion locks are held for a bounded time

- The OS provides a mutual exclusion primitive that minimizes priority inversion.

The last point here requires some explanation. Consider a standard counting semaphore used to protect a resource and consider two tasks τ_1 and τ_2 which both require access to the resource. Suppose τ_1 has a higher priority than τ_2 and that τ_2 holds the semaphore. Task τ_1 is then triggered, attempts to acquire the semaphore, and is blocked, leaving τ_2 running. So far all is well, but now consider what happens if a third task τ_3 with priority intermediate between that of τ_1 and τ_2 begins running. Now τ_2 cannot run and so it cannot exit the locked section and release the semaphore at least until τ_3 finishes, and τ_1 cannot resume until τ_2 releases the semaphore. So effectively the higher priority task τ_1 cannot run until the lower priority task τ_3 finishes, even though there is no contention for resources between them. You can see that τ_1 could be delayed for a very long time through this mechanism. On a system with non-real time tasks as well as real time tasks, it could be delayed indefinitely. This scenario is the classic unbounded priority inversion scenario that caused problems with the 1997 Mars Pathfinder mission.

There are two main ways to avoid this problem. Both involve the operating system providing a special object, superficially similar to a semaphore, but designed specifically for mutual exclusion applications. Such an object is usually called a *mutex*.

The Mars Pathfinder lander touched down on Mars on the 4th of July 1997, and initially performed well. But a few days after landing, it started experiencing total system resets, each of which lost some of the gathered data. Pathfinder contained a shared memory area used to pass information between different components of the system. A high priority bus management task ran frequently to move data in and out of the shared area. Access to the shared area was protected by mutexes, and these did not employ priority inheritance.

A low priority task ran infrequently to gather meteorological data, and used the shared area to publish that data. This task would acquire a mutex, write to the shared area and then release the mutex. If it were preempted by the bus management task, the latter could be blocked waiting for the meteorological data task to complete.

There was also a communications task, which ran with priority between those of the tasks already mentioned. This was a relatively long running task. Occasionally it would preempt the meteorological data task just at the time when it held the mutex and the bus management task was blocked on the mutex. In that case the bus management task could not run until the communications task completed. When the bus management task was delayed too long a watchdog timer triggered a system reset.

The problem was fixed by changing the mutex so that it employed priority inheritance, which I will describe next.

17.2.3.1 *Priority inheritance*

Under the priority inheritance scheme, whenever a task τ_2 holds a mutex M and another task τ_1 of higher priority is blocked on M then the priority of τ_2 is raised to that of τ_1. When the task eventually releases M, its priority is returned to normal.

If the counting semaphore in the classic unbounded priority inversion scenario is replaced by a priority inheritance mutex, you can see that the problem no longer occurs. Instead, when task τ_1 attempts to acquire the mutex, it is blocked and τ_2 resumes, but now running with the priority of τ_1. Now when task τ_3 is triggered, it does not preempt τ_2, and τ_2 continues running until it reaches the end of the protected code fragment and releases the mutex. It then returns to its normal priority and task τ_1 immediately resumes and claims the mutex. So, in this case, the delay to any task wanting to claim the mutex is limited to the maximum time for which the mutex is held by any lower priority task.

17.2.3.2 *Priority ceiling protocol*

Under the priority ceiling protocol, each mutex has a *ceiling priority*, which is the maximum priority of any task that can acquire the mutex.

The algorithm is very simple. A task acquires a mutex by saving its current priority and then raising its priority to the mutex ceiling priority. It releases the mutex by restoring its priority to the value saved while acquiring the mutex. Note that we don't need to test whether the mutex is held when acquiring it – it can't be held since, if it were, the holding task would have raised its priority to at least as high as the current task and so the current task would not be running.

This scheme is very simple and efficient and also provides the most predictable blocking times. A high priority task can be delayed by at most one low priority task holding a mutex, and that delay comes all in one block before the task actually starts running. The maximum blocking time for a task τ_i is just the maximum time that any mutex with a ceiling priority higher than that of τ_i is held by any task with priority lower than that of τ_i. Once task τ_i starts running it never waits for a mutex.

The priority ceiling protocol is very good for deeply embedded, closed, hard real time systems. To use it, the following conditions must be satisfied:

- Static priority based scheduling must be used, with no time slicing for tasks at the same priority

- The set of tasks which may use a particular mutex must be known at system build time

- Tasks must not block waiting for an event while holding a mutex. This would invalidate the rule that a task never needs to wait for a mutex.

You can see that none of these conditions can be guaranteed to hold for an operating system capable of loading and executing arbitrary code at run time.

17.3   EKA2 and real time

Now that I have explored some of the problems faced by real time operating systems and looked at some of the solutions they employ, I will look at how we have attempted to solve these problems in EKA2. EKA2 was designed with several requirements that are relevant to our problem:

- It must be an open operating system; that is it must be capable of loading and executing arbitrary code at run time. This is really a corollary of the next point but is so significant that it warrants an explicit statement

- It was to be a replacement for EKA1. Hence it should have the same functionality and should be compatible with existing application level code written for EKA1

- It was to have sufficient real time capabilities to run the frame-level and multiframe-level activities of a GSM signaling stack. This includes layers 2 and 3, and part of layer 1, depending on how the hardware is arranged.

The first point eliminates many of the schemes discussed in Section 17.2: it eliminates cyclic scheduling and pure EDF scheduling, for reasons that I've mentioned previously. So, the scheduling algorithm that we selected was static priority based scheduling, with time slicing between threads at the same priority. We chose this because it is the simplest algorithm, which gives acceptable performance for both real time and non-real time applications, and because the APIs inherited from EKA1 assumed it! We set the number of priority levels at 64, because EKA1 allowed up to 26 different priorities to be explicitly set by applications, and signaling stacks require as many as 30 priorities.

17.3.1 The nanokernel

Once the scheduling algorithm is decided, the other requirements for a real time OS are minimizing priority inversion times and ensuring predictability of execution times for OS services. Minimizing priority inversion times entails minimizing the time for which interrupts and pre-emption are disabled. This is the role of the nanokernel. The nanokernel provides the most basic services of an operating system: threads, scheduling, mutual exclusion and synchronization of threads, and managing the interaction of interrupts with threads. The nanokernel is small (around 7% of the total code volume of the kernel) but it encapsulates most of the places where interrupts or preemption are disabled. This allows us to maintain tight control over these sections.

I have discussed the nanokernel in more detail in previous chapters of this book, so I will not repeat myself here. Instead I will just describe some of the design decisions that we made for the sake of real time performance.

17.3.1.1 The ready list

To ensure that we have predictable execution times for OS services, we need to be able to perform operations on the thread ready list in predictable times. The operations we need are:

- Adding a thread to the ready list
- Removing a thread from the ready list
- Finding the highest priority ready thread.

We achieve this by using 64 separate linked lists, one for each priority level. We also have a 64-bit mask, in which bit n is set if and only if the list for priority n is non-empty. This scheme eliminates the need to scan the list for the correct insertion point when adding a thread. To find the highest priority ready thread, we do a binary search on the bit mask and the result is used to index the array of 64 lists.

This same structure, referred to as a *priority list* in the EKA2 documentation, is used in other parts of the kernel whenever a priority ordered list is required.

See Section 3.6 for more on this subject.

17.3.1.2 *Nanokernel timers*

We encountered a similar problem with timers; we wanted to allow timers to be started from interrupt service routines for efficiency reasons. We couldn't use a simple delta list, because adding a timer to such a list would involve a linear time search through the list to find the insertion point. Instead we chose to use a two-level system. If the timer is due to expire in the next 32 ticks, we place it directly on one of the 32 final queues; the system tick interrupt then inspects one of these on each tick (in a round-robin fashion) and completes any timers on it. But if the timer is due to expire after 32 ticks, then we first add it to a pending queue. A thread then sorts the timers on the pending queue into an ordered queue. When a timer at the head of the ordered queue gets within 32 ticks of its expiry time, the same thread will transfer it to the relevant final queue. In this way, the starting and stopping of timers become constant time operations.

17.3.1.3 *Fast mutexes*

One of the main purposes of the nanokernel is to localize all the non-preemptible sections of code in the system. For this to be practical, the nanokernel has to provide a very fast mutual exclusion primitive that still allows preemption of the critical section by unrelated threads. To be useful for real time applications, this mechanism also needs to provide a means of limiting priority inversion times. Because EKA2 must support an open system, the priority ceiling protocol cannot be used, and so some form of priority inheritance is needed.

We designed fast mutexes to provide the solution to this problem. A fast mutex consists of two fields – a pointer to the nanokernel thread, which currently holds the mutex (or null if the mutex is free), and a flag (the waiting flag), which indicates that some action has been deferred because the mutex was locked. To lock a fast mutex, a thread first inspects the holding thread pointer. If this is null, the thread simply claims the mutex by writing its own address into the holding thread pointer and then proceeds. This makes fast mutexes very fast in the case where there is no contention. If the mutex is held by another thread, the nanokernel sets the waiting flag and then performs an immediate context switch directly to the holding thread (which must be of lower priority than the blocked thread). The blocked thread remains on the ready list – this is not the case when blocking on other wait objects. So, this is how we get priority inheritance – because the blocked thread is still on the ready list, a reschedule will only be triggered if a thread with a higher priority than the blocked thread is made ready. Otherwise the holding thread will continue running until it releases the mutex. At that point it checks the waiting flag and, if it is set, triggers a reschedule. This will then switch to the blocked thread.

There are two restrictions on the use of fast mutexes that we impose to guarantee predictable real time behavior:

1. Fast mutexes cannot be nested

2. A thread may not block on another wait object while holding a fast mutex.

We impose these restrictions so that the scheduler can always find the next thread to run in a bounded time, even when the preferred thread (that is, the highest priority ready thread) is currently blocked on a fast mutex. We have placed assertions in the debug build of the kernel to flag violations of these rules to those porting Symbian OS and writing device drivers.

17.3.1.4 *Context switching*

Under the moving memory model (used on ARM architecture 4 and 5 processors), a context switch between threads belonging to different user-side processes can be a time consuming procedure. It may involve, in the worst case:

- Moving all the chunks attached to the current data section process to the home section

- Protecting all chunks attached to the last user process to run

- Moving all chunks attached to the new process from the home section to the data section

- Flushing the processor data cache.

On processors with large data caches and slow memory interfaces, this could take more than 500 μs – this is a measured value from one such system. If all this work were done directly by the scheduler, with preemption disabled, this would add 500 μs or more to the worst case thread latency. We didn't consider this to be acceptable performance – not all context switches require the full list of actions listed. Switches to kernel threads and threads in certain user processes can occur much faster and so should have lower guaranteed latency. To achieve this goal, we perform the modification of page directory entries and the flushing of the data cache with preemption enabled. Essentially, the kernel restores the registers for the new thread, so that the system is using the new thread's supervisor stack, then re-enables preemption before restoring the correct MMU configuration. The new thread then establishes its own MMU configuration. Clearly we need some protection to prevent multiple threads modifying the page tables simultaneously, and so we ensure that code holds the system lock fast mutex while performing these operations.

17.3.2 The Symbian OS kernel

17.3.2.1 *Bounded and unbounded services*

The services provided by the Symbian OS kernel are partitioned into two classes – bounded and unbounded. The bounded services obviously have bounded execution times, and are therefore suitable for real time applications. The unbounded services have no guaranteed upper limit on their execution times. The list of unbounded services includes:

- Object creation and destruction, including thread and process creation, IPC session creation and destruction
- Opening handles on existing objects
- Finding objects by name or by ID
- Symbian OS timer services (`RTimer::After()` and `RTimer::At()`).

In most cases, the unbounded services involve the allocation or freeing of memory on the kernel heap or in the global free page pool. This is because the algorithms used to manage the free page pool and the kernel heap do not have bounded execution times.

The bounded services include:

- Mutexes (`DMutex` and `RMutex` classes)
- Semaphores (`DSemaphore` and `RSemaphore` classes)
- Asynchronous request processing
- Device driver access
- Message queues (`RMsgQueue` and `DMsgQueue` classes)
- Client/server IPC message send and receive
- Thread control (suspend, resume, change priority, kill)
- Finding objects from a user handle.

We achieve mutual exclusion in bounded services by using fast mutexes, usually the system lock. To ensure maximum predictability for these services, the time for which the system lock is held continuously must be bounded and the bound minimized. We employ various measures to minimize this time, generally involving breaking down operations into sections between which the system lock is released.

For example, under the moving memory model, which I discussed in Section 17.3.1.4, the MMU related part of context switching could take a long time. Rather than holding the system lock for the whole duration, we make periodic checks to see if there is any contention for the system lock. We make this check every 512 bytes or every 1 KB (depending on type of cache) during the cache flush, and after moving or changing permissions of each chunk. If a higher priority thread is waiting on the system lock, we abort the context switch, release the system lock and allow the higher priority thread to run.

Similarly, during an inter-process data copy, we must hold the system lock to prevent the remote process' chunks from being moved while they are being accessed. Again, we make a check for contention after every 512 bytes are copied. If no contention is detected, the copy can continue immediately, but if contention is detected, we must release the system lock and reacquire it. In this case, we have to recheck the remote address, because the chunk involved may have been moved (or even deleted) while the system lock was released. This algorithm is illustrated in flowchart form in Figure 17.4.

17.3.2.2 Symbian OS mutexes

We designed Symbian OS mutexes for cases where mutual exclusion is needed but the restrictions on the use of fast mutexes cannot be observed. This situation arises in two main ways – either from a requirement for nested mutexes, or from a requirement for mutual exclusion in user-side code. We don't allow user-side code to hold fast mutexes since it cannot be trusted to conform to the restrictions on their use.

Symbian OS mutexes differ from fast mutexes in the following ways:

- They can only be used by Symbian OS threads (DThread) rather than by raw nanokernel threads. This has significance for personality layers, which I will describe later in this chapter

- They can be nested. A thread may hold a single mutex several times, provided that thread releases it the same number of times. A thread may hold a mutex while already holding a different mutex

- Threads can block while holding a Symbian OS mutex.

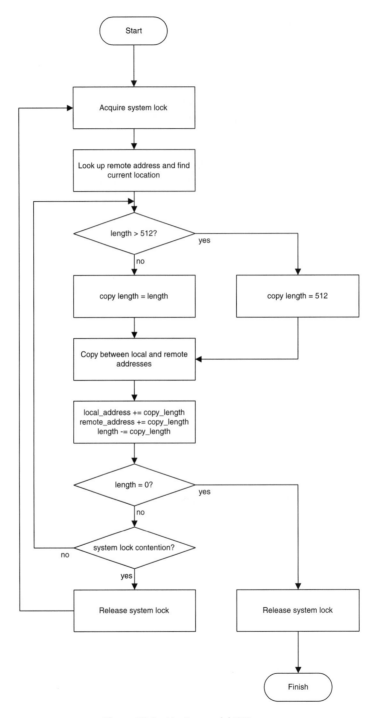

Figure 17.4 Moving model IPC copy

In Chapter 3, *Processes and Threads*, I covered the operation of Symbian OS mutexes in some detail. Here I will just speak from a real time perspective and say that we designed these mutexes to ensure that:

1. So far as is possible, the highest priority thread that requests a mutex holds it

2. The length of time for which point 1 is not true is minimized.

We use priority inheritance to meet this goal. In this case, priority inheritance does not come for free but has to be explicitly managed by the kernel. We use priority lists (which I described in Section 17.3.1.1) to hold the list of threads waiting to acquire a mutex and the list of mutexes held by any thread. We prioritize the latter according to the highest priority thread waiting on them, and use this to work out the required scheduling priority of the holding thread to comply with the rules of priority inheritance.

17.3.3 Latencies and performance

In this section I will define some key performance measurements that we use to verify the real time capabilities of EKA2. I will go on to give actual measured values for certain hardware platforms.

Figure 17.5 illustrates these measurements. The scenario depicted in this figure is as follows: at time t_0, a hardware interrupt occurs. It happens that interrupts are disabled at time t_0 and so thread X0 continues executing for a while. When X0 re-enables interrupts, the processor's response to the interrupt begins. The interrupt preamble and dispatcher run and, at time t_1, the first instruction of the service routine for the particular interrupt is executed. The elapsed time between t_0 and t_1 is known as the *interrupt latency*, denoted l_{isr} in the diagram.

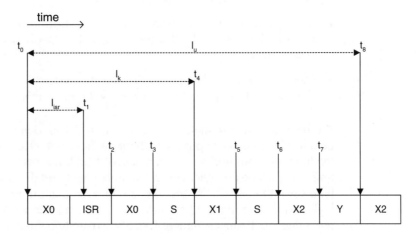

Figure 17.5 Latencies

The interrupt service routine finishes at time t_2, having woken up a high priority kernel thread X1 (by way of an IDFC or DFC, not shown). However, the interrupted thread X0 has disabled preemption, so at time t_2 thread X0 resumes execution until it re-enables preemption at time t_3. The scheduler S runs at this point, and thread X1 starts running at time t_4. The elapsed time between t_0 and t_4 is known as the *kernel thread latency*, denoted ℓ_k in the diagram.

Thread X1 finishes execution at time t_5, having woken up a high priority user-side thread X2. The scheduler S runs again and schedules X2. X2 immediately tries to acquire the system lock fast mutex and is blocked by thread Y. Thread Y runs long enough to release the system lock and then thread X2 runs again, with the system lock held, at time t_8. The elapsed time between t_0 and t_8 is known as the *user thread latency*, denoted ℓ_u in the diagram.

Worst-case interrupt latency is equal to the maximum time interrupts are disabled plus the execution time of the preamble and dispatcher. Interrupts can be disabled either by the kernel or by the base port and device drivers. When measuring the performance of the kernel only the former is of interest.

Worst-case kernel thread latency includes the maximum time for which preemption is disabled and the time taken to switch from an arbitrary thread to a kernel thread.

Worst-case user thread latency includes, in addition, the maximum time for which the system lock is held. The reason for including this is that most user threads will require the system lock to be held at some point before they can run and do useful work. This is a consequence of the following observations:

- On the moving memory model, the system lock must be held before context switching to the user thread

- If a Symbian OS asynchronous request (TRequestStatus) must be completed to make the thread run, that involves acquiring the system lock

- Most executive calls need to acquire the system lock; for example communication with a device driver will require this.

We measure the parameters ℓ_{isr}, ℓ_k and ℓ_u in the following way. We set up a hardware timer to produce a periodic interrupt. (This can simply be the timer used to produce the nanokernel tick, but it could be a separate timer.) It must be possible to read the timer count and deduce the elapsed time since the last tick. If possible, the measurement timer is set up as a high priority interrupt (FIQ on ARM), so that other peripheral interrupts do not influence the measurement. We also create two threads – one kernel thread running a DFC queue and one user thread. The priorities of these two threads are set at 63 and 62 respectively so that they preempt all the other threads in the system. Under the moving memory model, we usually ensure that the user thread belongs to a fixed process. Each periodic tick interrupt triggers a DFC on the kernel thread, and that thread then wakes up the user thread by signaling its request semaphore. We record the elapsed time from the last tick at the beginning of the ISR, the DFC, and just after the user thread wakes up. We also record maximum values for each of these times. We run stress test programs in the background to ensure that sections of kernel code that disable interrupts and preemption and that hold the system lock are exercised.

Measured performance parameters for some specific hardware platforms are given in the following table:

Parameter	Assabet	Series 5mx
Worst case interrupt latency	9 μs	25 μs
Typical interrupt latency	3 μs	
Worst case kernel thread latency	34 μs	120 μs
Typical kernel thread latency	13 μs	
Worst case user thread latency	63 μs	250 μs
Typical user thread latency	26 μs	
Thread switch time	2 μs	12 μs

The Assabet platform uses a 206 MHz SA1110 processor with code and data both stored in 32-bit wide SDRAM clocked at 103 MHz.

The Series 5mx platform uses a 36.864 MHz ARM710T processor with code and data both stored in 32-bit wide EDO DRAM.

In general, worst-case latencies are dominated by memory access speed rather than by processor clock frequency. This is because on typical hardware used for Symbian OS, a memory access requires several processor clock cycles – for example the random access time of SDRAM (60 ns) equates to 12 processor clock cycles on Assabet. A large difference between typical and worst case execution times can also be expected on this hardware. The best case execution time occurs when all code and data involved are present in the processor caches, so no slow external memory accesses are needed. Obviously, the worst-case execution time occurs when none of the code or data is present in the caches, so a large number of slow memory accesses are required – we ensure this is the case in our tests by running the stress test programs previously mentioned.

17.4   Real time application – GSM

This section gives a brief explanation of the GSM cellular system and an outline of how it might be implemented, with particular emphasis on the real time aspects.

17.4.1   Introduction to GSM

Data is transmitted over the radio channel at a bit rate of 270.833 kHz (=13 MHz/48, period 3.69 μs). The spectrum used for GSM is divided into channels spaced 200 kHz apart. These channels are time-division multiplexed into eight timeslots, numbered 0 to 7. Each timeslot lasts for 156.25 bit periods (577 μs) and eight consecutive timeslots (one of each number) make up one frame (4.615 ms). In the original GSM system (prior to GPRS and high speed circuit switched data services) each mobile receives only one timeslot per frame. If the mobile is transmitting, the transmission occurs three timeslots after the receive. Of the 156.25 bit periods in a burst, 148 actual data bits are transmitted (except for random-access bursts, which transmit only 88 bits). The other 8.25 bit times are used to allow the mobile to ramp its power up and down in such a way to avoid excessive spurious emissions.

The 4.615 ms TDMA frames are numbered modulo 2715648 ($= 26 * 51 * 2048$). The frame number is used to divide a single physical radio channel into a number of logical channels, which use frames on a periodic basis. The frame number is also used as a parameter by the frequency hopping and encryption algorithms. The logical channels are:

Channel name	Description
Frequency correction channel (FCCH)	Base-station to mobile only. Consists of a pure sine wave burst with a frequency 67.7 kHz above the carrier frequency, equivalent to all data bits = 1. Used to allow the mobile to find the synchronization channel and to correct its internal frequency reference sufficiently to be able to receive it. Transmitted in timeslot 0 of frames numbered 0, 10, 20, 30, 40 modulo 51.
Synchronization channel (SCH)	Base-station to mobile only. Used to enable the mobile to establish precise time and frequency synchronization, including the frame number. The current frame number between 0 and 2715647 is transmitted in the SCH burst. Transmitted in timeslot 0 of frames numbered 1, 11, 21, 31, 41 modulo 51.

Channel name	Description
Broadcast control channel (BCCH)	Base-station to mobile only. Carries information about the cell configuration (number of frequencies, number of paging slots, etc.) of a particular base station. Transmitted in timeslot 0 of four consecutive frames starting with a frame numbered 2, 12, 22, 32, 42 modulo 51.
Paging channel (PCH)	Base-station to mobile only. Used to send paging messages to mobiles; a paging message is a request for the mobile to access the network (for example, for an incoming call).
Access grant channel (AGCH)	Base-station to mobile only. Used to assign the mobile a dedicated channel in response to a mobile accessing the base station. Once a dedicated channel has been set up, a dialogue can occur between the mobile and base station.
Cell broadcast channel (CBCH)	Base-station to mobile only. Used to transmit miscellaneous information, usually of a network-specific nature, such as dialing codes to which cheaper call rates apply.
Random access channel (RACH)	Mobile to base station only. Used by the mobile to request access to the network, for example, to originate a call or in response to a paging message.
Stand-alone dedicated control channel (SDCCH)	Both directions. This is a low-rate (just under 800 bps) channel that is used for the initial phase of call setup (authentication, ciphering, call setup message, etc.), SMS transmission and for network accesses that are not user-initiated (for example, location updating).
Traffic channel (TCH)	Both directions. This is a high-rate (13 kbps) channel that is used for the duration of a call to transfer encoded speech or user data.
Slow associated control channel (SACCH)	Both directions. This is a low-rate (~400 bps) channel that is used mainly for the transmission of surrounding cell information while the mobile is using a TCH or SDCCH. It is also used to allow the mobile to send or receive SMS while a call is in progress. In the latter case, every other SACCH message is SMS-related and

Channel name	Description
	every other one surrounding cell-related. This channel is always associated with a TCH or SDCCH, and its bursts are time-division multiplexed with those of the TCH or SDCCH (different frame numbers).
Fast associated control channel (FACCH)	Both directions. This is a high-rate (9200 bps) channel used to send signaling messages while a call is in progress. This is mainly used to send handover messages. This channel is always associated with a TCH and its bursts replace some of the TCH bursts.

There are four different types of burst used:

Burst type	Used on	Description
Frequency	FCCH	This consists of a pure sine wave with a frequency 67.7 kHz (one quarter the bit rate) above the carrier frequency. This is equivalent to a burst where all data bits are 1.
Sync	SCH	This consists of 148 transmitted bits, and can be decoded on its own. The first and last 3 bits are 0 (called tail bits). The middle 64 bits are the midamble, which I describe next. The remaining 78 bits are encoded data bits, derived from 25 bits of user data.
Random Access	RACH	This consists of 88 transmitted bits and can be decoded on its own. The first 52 bits are the preamble, which serves the same function as the midamble for the other bursts. The remaining 36 bits are encoded data bits, derived from 8 bits of user data.
Normal	All others	This consists of 148 transmitted bits. The first and last three bits are tail bits (0). The middle 26 bits are the midamble. The two bits on either side of the midamble are called stealing flags – they differentiate between signaling and traffic channels. The remaining 114 bits are encoded data bits.

The midamble (preamble for RACH) is used to enable the receiver to get the precise timing of the burst, and to compensate for the effects of multipath distortion. By correlating the received midamble bits with the known value of the midamble, the receiver can get the timing of the burst and also estimate the multipath distortion on the radio channel. It can then compensate for the multipath distortion and make an estimate of the received data bits. This process is performed by the equalizer in the receive chain.

The stealing flags are always set to 1 except on traffic channels, where they are used to differentiate between TCH and FACCH bursts (0 = TCH, 1 = FACCH).

In general (apart from FCCH, SCH and RACH), more than one burst is required to make a meaningful data block. The data to be transmitted is first passed through a forward error correction encoder (either one or two stages) then the bits are interleaved (reordered) and divided between a number of bursts (4, 8 or 19). The encoding used is:

Channel	Encoding
SCH	Start with 25 bits of user data. Append 10-bit CRC check code. Pass through half-rate convolutional encoder. This gives $(25 + 10 + 4) * 2 = 78$ bits. The extra 4 bits are needed to flush out the convolutional encoder.
RACH	Start with 8 bits of user data. Append 6-bit CRC check code. Pass through half-rate convolutional encoder. This gives $(8 + 6 + 4) * 2 = 36$ bits.
BCCH, PCH, AGCH, CBCH, SDCCH	Start with 23 bytes = 184 bits of user data. Pass through a FIRE block encoder that appends 40 parity check bits. Then pass through a half-rate convolutional encoder. This gives a total of $(184 + 40 + 4) * 2 = 456$ bits. These bits are divided between the transmitted bursts in four consecutive frames.
TCH speech	Start with 260 bits of compressed speech data. Split these into 50 class Ia, 132 class Ib and 78 class II bits. Calculate and append a 3-bit CRC check code to the class Ia bits. Pass the class Ia and class Ib bits through a half-rate convolutional encoder. Append the class II bits, unencoded. This gives a total of $(50 + 3 + 132 + 4) * 2 + 78 = 456$ bits. Divide these into eight sets of 57 bits and spread them over eight half-bursts, in combination with the previous and successive speech blocks.
TCH data	For 9600 bits per second data, start with 240 bits of user data. Pass through a half-rate convolutional encoder to give $(240 + 4) * 2 = 488$ bits. Puncture the code by omitting 32 specified bits to give 456 bits of encoded data. Divide these into 19 sets of 24 bits and spread them over 19 consecutive traffic bursts, in combination with other data blocks.

Channel	Encoding
FACCH	Channel encoding as for BCCH, but divide resulting 456 bits into eight sets of 57 and spread over eight half-bursts as for full-rate speech TCH.
SACCH	Channel encoding as for BCCH, but the four bursts are transmitted with a 26-frame gap between them instead of in consecutive frames, thus giving a throughput of 23 bytes per 104 frames.

On the receive side, the process is reversed, with bits from various equalized bursts being stored until there are enough bursts to make a decodable block. The bits are then de-interleaved (reordered into an order which the error correction decoder can make sense of) and passed through a Viterbi convolutional decoder. If necessary, the output of the Viterbi decoder is then passed through a FIRE decoder or a CRC check.

Encryption is performed on SDCCH, TCH, FACCH and SACCH. A special algorithm is used (A5.1 or A5.2) which takes the frame number and the encryption key as parameters and produces two 114-bit blocks of encryption data, one for receive and one for transmit. The receive block is exclusive-ORed with the output of the equalizer prior to de-interleaving. The transmit block is exclusive-ORed with the output of the interleaver prior to addition of the midamble and stealing flags. The key used for encryption is generated by the SIM as part of the authentication process. Whenever a mobile tries to connect to the network, the base station will perform a challenge/response authentication procedure. The base station sends a random number to the mobile and this is passed to the SIM where it is used as input to the A3 algorithm in conjunction with a secret key (K_i) which never leaves the SIM, but which is also known to the network. The A3 algorithm produces two outputs – SRES and K_c. The SRES is sent back to the base station in response to the authentication request, and the K_c is used as the encryption key for subsequent traffic.

17.4.2   Idle mode

When a mobile phone is not actively being used it spends most of its time in idle mode. In this mode the phone performs receive operations only. The following operations are performed by a phone in idle mode:

1. Periodically receive the BCCH for the cell on which the mobile phone is camped. This tells the mobile when it should listen for paging requests and which frequencies it should monitor for neighbor cells

2. Periodically receive the paging channel as indicated by the BCCH message. Paging messages are transmitted in four consecutive frames

and any particular mobile must listen every 102*N frames, where N is between 2 and 9 inclusive, so approximately every 1 to 4.5 seconds

3. Monitor the signal strength of neighbor cells as indicated in the BCCH message. If a neighbor cell is received consistently better than the current cell for a period of time the mobile will move to the neighbor cell

4. Send location update messages to the network both periodically (around every 30 minutes) and following a change of cell where the old and new cells are in different location areas. Base stations are grouped into location areas and an incoming call to a mobile will result in paging messages being transmitted by all base stations in the last reported location area. Of course to send a message to the network the mobile must briefly leave idle mode.

17.4.3   Traffic mode

When a call is in progress, the mobile phone is in traffic mode. The phone receives a burst in 25 out of every 26 frames and transmits in around 60% of frames. The GSM traffic channel operates on a period of 26 frames, used as follows:

Frame mod 26	Description
0 to 11	Encoded speech bursts or FACCH bursts
12	SACCH burst or idle slot
13 to 24	Encoded speech bursts or FACCH bursts
25	Idle slot or SACCH burst

A single 20 ms speech frame is spread between eight consecutive frames, overlapped with the preceding and following speech frame. Four SACCH bursts are required to make up a meaningful data block, so one block is received and transmitted every 104 frames. This is too slow for seamless handover between cells so when necessary some bursts normally used for speech are "stolen" for signaling messages. The SACCH bursts are staggered between timeslots – the first of a group of four occurs when frame number modulo 104 equals 13*TN, where TN is the timeslot number between 0 and 7. This was done so that base stations (which must obviously process all timeslots) only need to perform one SACCH encode and decode every 13 frames rather than eight all at once.

While a call is in progress the mobile phone performs the following operations:

1. Receive traffic bursts, pass them through the GSM speech decoder and out to the speaker

2. Accept audio from the microphone and pass it through the GSM speech encoder. If someone is actually speaking, transmit the encoded speech in traffic bursts. During periods of silence no transmission occurs to save battery power

3. Receive SACCH bursts and decode them. They contain instructions as to precise transmission timing (to compensate for the propagation times of the signals between the mobile phone and base station), the transmit power that the phone should use and the neighboring cells that the phone should monitor

4. Monitor the indicated neighboring cells. The signal level from each one should be measured and additionally FCCH and SCH bursts are received from each one to get the precise frequency and timing in case a handover is required. All this activity occurs in the "idle" slot. The 26 frame period of the traffic channel is deliberately chosen to be coprime to the 51 frame period of the control channels so that the FCCH and SCH bursts of the neighbor cell will eventually occur during the idle slot

5. Transmit the measured signal levels on the neighboring cells back to the base station in the SACCH bursts

6. Receive and act on handover commands transmitted on the FACCH.

17.4.4   GSM hardware

A typical GSM mobile implementation consists of the following functional blocks:

- RF stages
- Baseband converters
- Timing controller
- Encryption unit
- DSP
- Microcontroller
- SIM interface
- Miscellaneous (LCD, keyboard, earpiece, microphone, battery charging circuitry).

The original GSM frequency band has 124 channels, spaced 200 kHz apart. The mobile receive frequency is $935+0.2n$ MHz, the mobile transmit frequency is $890+0.2n$ MHz where n is the channel number between 1 and 124. On the receive side, the signal is amplified and downconverted using a frequency synthesizer for channel selection. A quadrature mixer is used, producing two baseband signal outputs I and Q (in-phase and quadrature components – the result of mixing the received signal with two different carriers 90° out-of-phase). On the transmit side, the I and Q signals from the modulator are mixed up using another quadrature mixer to produce the final RF frequency for feeding to the PA (power amplifier). The PA output level is adjustable by a separate DAC output.

The baseband receive ADC samples both the I and Q receive channels. It may also contain some of the channel filtering (in which case it oversamples the I and Q signals and filters them digitally). The output of the baseband receive ADC is one I and one Q sample, of ~10 bits each, every GSM bit period (3.69 μs). Each receive burst will produce around 160 sample pairs (must receive more samples than there are bits to account for timing errors).

The transmit modulator converts the bits to be transmitted into varying I and Q voltages according to the specification in the GSM standard (GMSK modulation). Essentially, a 1 bit causes the phase of the carrier to advance by 90° and a 0 bit causes the phase to be retarded by 90°; however some low-pass filtering is applied so that the phase changes smoothly, with the previous 3 bits making a significant contribution to the carrier phase at any time. This is done to reduce the bandwidth of the transmitted signal. The modulation is done digitally and the output converted to I and Q signals by the baseband transmit DAC.

At least three other baseband converters are required. A DAC is required to control the output power level while transmitting. A FIFO store is required to feed this DAC so that the power can be ramped up and down at the beginning and end of the transmit burst (one output sample per half bit-period). An ADC and DAC are required for the microphone and earpiece. These both work at a sampling rate of 8 kHz and resolution of 13 bits.

A versatile timing controller is required, which can be programmed to a resolution of one-quarter bit period. This is used to switch various parts of the hardware on and off at the correct time, and to initiate receive and transmit operations at the correct time. The timing controller is synchronized with the received signal from the base station after FCCH and SCH receive.

The DSP usually performs the following functions:

- Reading received data from the baseband receive ADC
- Frequency burst detection
- Sync and normal burst equalization

- Channel encoding

- Channel decoding

- Speech encoding

- Speech decoding

- Assembly of bursts for transmission

- Buffering of audio samples

- Generation of sidetone and miscellaneous GSM-specified tones.

The DSP may also perform a certain amount of the low-level control and scheduling functions. The split of these between the DSP and microcontroller varies between implementations. It is implementation dependent whether the timing controller is configured by the DSP or the microcontroller.

The microcontroller performs the following tasks:

- Some of the layer 1 control functions (implementation-dependent split with DSP)

- Layers 2 and 3 of the GSM protocol stack

- Control of screen and keyboard, battery monitoring, and possibly charging

- User interface functions

- Control of the SIM interface

- Extra processing for data traffic channels.

The SIM interface connects the SIM (subscriber identity module – smart card) to the microcontroller. It is essentially a UART, but operates in a half-duplex mode. The SIM has only one data line and it is used for both reading and writing to the SIM. There is a specified protocol for this interface, which is usually implemented in hardware.

17.4.5   A GSM stack on EKA2

As an illustration of a real time application running on EKA2, I will consider the implementation of a GSM protocol stack. Obviously, only an outline will be given and not all scenarios will be considered – a real stack requires many man-years of development! I will assume that all processing is done on the main ARM processor and there is no DSP – while, in principle, this could be achieved on high end ARM devices such as ARM1136, in practice no-one would actually do so, because it would be inefficient in terms of power consumption, cost and the number of cycles available for application processing.

I will assume the following hardware configuration:

• Timing controller has free running counter at four times the GSM bit rate which wraps to zero at 5000 quarter bits, that is, one GSM frame period

• There are several match registers that can trigger an event. This event can be an interrupt to the processor, switching on or off some piece of hardware such as the frequency synthesizer, the receive chain or the transmit chain, the start of a receive or the start of a transmission

• Once a receive starts, the processor is interrupted whenever 16 sample pairs are available and these must be read before the next interrupt occurs

• Before a transmission starts the data to be transmitted must be loaded into a TX buffer and the power ramp up and ramp down masks must be loaded into a power control buffer

• Frequency synthesizer needs 500 μs to lock before beginning RX or TX

• Equalizing a received burst, channel encoding or decoding and speech encoding or decoding takes 250 μs maximum

• Scanning for a FCCH burst takes 10 μs maximum per 16 sample pairs.

A processor interrupt is triggered once every frame in the same place so that a frame count can be maintained.

17.4.5.1 *Frequency burst receive*

The main activities related to FCCH burst reception are shown in Figure 17.6.

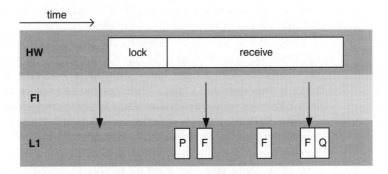

Figure 17.6 Frequency burst search

In Figure 17.6, the HW line shows what the hardware is doing, the FI line indicates the time of the once-per-frame interrupt and the "L1 Task" line shows which software tasks are in progress.

The tasks involved are:

(i) Programming the hardware with the frequency to receive and the time at which to start the receive. This is shown as task P. This task is triggered by the main layer 1 state machine when a frequency burst search is required

(ii) Reading blocks of 16 sample pairs from HW buffer to main memory buffer. This task is not shown since it is too frequent. It is triggered by the baseband receive ADC interrupt

(iii) Processing the received samples to search for a frequency burst. This is shown as task F, although it occurs more frequently than is shown. It is triggered by task (ii)

(iv) On either finding a frequency burst or timing out, shut down the hardware and start the next operation if any. This is shown as task Q. It may be necessary to search for up to 11.25 frame times – the worst case occurs when you start the receive just after the beginning of the FCCH burst and the next burst starts in 11 frames. This task is triggered by the per-frame interrupt following either the detection of a frequency burst or a timeout.

Task (ii) has the shortest deadline (16 bit periods or 59 μs), so I will implement this as an ISR. In fact with a hard deadline as short as this, it would be best to use the ARM processor's FIQ interrupt. The other tasks must run in a thread context. It would be inefficient to schedule a thread at this frequency – it would use around 10% of the processor time context switching. It is also unnecessary. Instead, task (iii) will be triggered every 10 receive interrupts. The deadline for task (iii) depends on how much buffering is used. If there is enough buffering for 480 sample pairs (around 2 K) the deadline would be $320*3.69 \, \mu s = 1180 \, \mu s$, since the task is triggered when there are 160 sample pairs available and must complete before the buffer fills.

Tasks (i) and (iv) are triggered by the per-frame interrupt and need to complete quickly enough to set up hardware for the following frame. A convenient time for the per-frame interrupt is two timeslots into the frame, since it then does not clash with either the receive or transmit windows and allows six timeslots for any setup to complete before the next frame. This is 3.460 ms. However, 500 μs is required for the synthesizer to lock before the next receive and so the deadline for tasks P and Q is 2.9 ms. So task P and Q should have lower priority than task F. In fact in this case the same thread could be used for all three tasks since these tasks never execute simultaneously anyway.

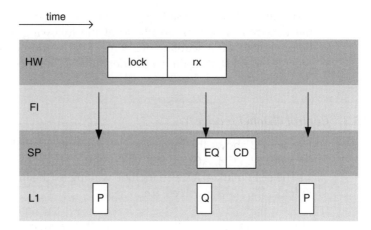

Figure 17.7 Sync burst receive

17.4.5.2 *Sync burst receive*

The activities involved in receiving an SCH burst are shown in Figure 17.7. The tasks involved are:

(i) Programming the hardware with the frequency to receive and the time at which to start the receive. This is shown as task P. This task is triggered by the main layer 1 state machine when an SCH burst receive is required

(ii) Reading blocks of 16 sample pairs from HW buffer to main memory buffer. This task is not shown since it is too frequent. After 11 blocks have been received, task (iii) is triggered. 176 sample pairs are used instead of the usual 160 since there is generally more uncertainty about the precise timing of a sync burst, since the only timing information may have come from the previous FCCH receive. Non-FCCH bursts contain a known sequence of bits (the midamble) which can be used to estimate the burst timing accurately

(iii) Pass the 176 received sample pairs through the sync burst equalizer (EQ). This calculates the precise timing of the burst and demodulates it

(iv) Pass the demodulated burst through the channel decoder (CD). This corrects any errors in the received burst. This task is triggered by the end of the EQ task

(v) Reprogram the hardware to stop the receive occurring again. This is shown as task Q. It is triggered by the per-frame interrupt following the receive period.

As before, task (ii) has the shortest deadline, at 59 μs, and I implement it directly in the FIQ. The EQ and CD tasks together have to meet a deadline of ten timeslots −176 bit periods, or 5.1 ms, in order for the decoded data to be available at the following frame interrupt. As before task (i) has a deadline of 2.9 ms. Task (v) must complete before the receive would start again, so the deadline is six timeslots minus 500 μs, or 2.9 ms.

17.4.5.3   *Control channel receive*

Figure 17.8 shows the reception of a control channel block. This could be a BCCH, PCH, AGCH, SDCCH or SACCH accompanying SDCCH.

The tasks marked RX also include waiting for the frequency synthesizer to lock. The tasks involved are:

(i)   Programming the hardware with the frequency to receive and the time at which to start the receive. This is shown as task P. The main layer 1 state machine triggers it when an SCH burst receive is required

(ii) Reading blocks of 16 sample pairs from HW buffer to main memory buffer. After 10 blocks have been received, task (iii) is triggered. 160 sample pairs give sufficient leeway to cope with small errors in the burst timing. There is no need to reprogram the hardware after a burst receive since the next receive will automatically be initiated when the timer wraps round

(iii) Pass the 160 received sample pairs through the normal burst equalizer (EQ). This calculates the precise timing of the burst and demodulates it

(iv) Pass the four demodulated bursts through the de-interleaver and channel decoder (CD). This corrects any errors in the received data. This task is triggered by the end of the fourth EQ task

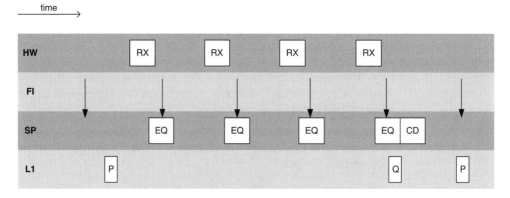

Figure 17.8   Control channel receive

(v)   Reprogram the hardware after the final burst receive so that another receive does not occur. This is shown as task Q. It is triggered by the frame interrupt following the final burst receive.

Task deadlines are the same as for the sync burst receive, apart from the EQ task on its own. The deadline for this is that it should finish before the next receive starts, which is a time lapse of seven timeslots, or 3.9 ms.

17.4.5.4   *Control channel transmit*

Figure 17.9 shows the transmission of a control channel block. This could be either an SDCCH or SACCH accompanying SDCCH.
Tasks marked TX include waiting for the frequency synthesizer to lock. The tasks involved are:

(i)   Passing the data block to be transmitted through the channel encoder and interleaver and adding the midambles, stealing flags and tail bits to produce four 148-bit bursts for transmission. This is shown as task CE in the figure. The main layer 1 state machine triggers it when an SDCCH or accompanying SACCH transmission is required

(ii) Programming the hardware with the frequency to transmit and time at which to start transmission. This is shown as task P and is triggered by the end of the CE task or by an interrupt at the end of the previous transmit burst if there is one

(iii) Transferring each burst to the transmit data buffer. This is shown as task T on the diagram. Task T is triggered by the end of task P or by the end of a transmit burst

(iv) Reprogram the hardware after the final burst transmission so that another transmission does not occur. This is shown as task Q. It is triggered by the end of the final transmit burst.

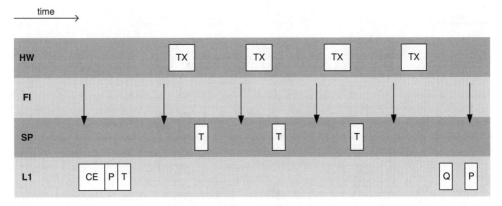

Figure 17.9   Control channel transmit

The deadline for task CE, P and the first task T is 500 μs before transmission is due to start, so approximately 1 frame period, since transmission starts three timeslots into the next frame. If a previous transmit operation is in progress the deadline for CE is unchanged, but the deadline for P and T is reduced to six timeslots or 3.4 ms. The subsequent task T invocations are triggered by the end of the transmission and must complete before the start of the next transmission. Hence the deadline there is seven timeslots (3.9 ms).

17.4.5.5 *Control channel simultaneous receive and transmit*

Figure 17.10 shows the simultaneous transmission and reception of a control channel block. This only occurs with an SDCCH in one direction and an SACCH accompanying SDCCH in the other.

The tasks involved are:

(i)   Pass the transmit data block through the channel encoder and interleaver (CE). Add midambles, stealing flags and tail bits to produce bursts for transmission. This task is triggered by the main layer 1 state machine when a simultaneous SDCCH receive and transmit is required

(ii) Programming the hardware with the frequency to receive/transmit and the time at which to start the receive and transmission. This is shown as task P. It is triggered by the end of the CE task or the end of the previous transmit burst if there is one

(iii) Reading blocks of 16 sample pairs from HW buffer to main memory buffer. This task is triggered by an interrupt from the receive ADC when 16 sample pairs are available. After 10 blocks have been received, task (ii) is triggered

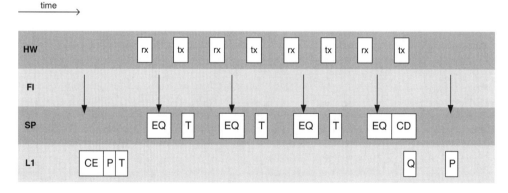

Figure 17.10   Control channel TX + RX

(iv) Pass the 160 received sample pairs through the normal burst equalizer (EQ). This calculates the precise timing of the burst and demodulates it. This task is triggered by the receive ISR when 160 sample pairs have been received

(v) Pass four demodulated bursts through the de-interleaver and channel decoder (CD). This corrects any errors in the received data. This task is triggered by the end of the last EQ task

(vi) Transfer each traffic burst to the transmit data buffer. This is shown as task T on the diagram. This task is triggered either by the end of the P task or by the end of the previous transmit burst

(vii) Reprogram the hardware after the final burst transmission so that another receive/transmit does not occur. This is shown as the task Q. It is triggered by the end of the final transmit burst.

Task deadlines are as for the separate receive and transmit operations already described.

17.4.5.6 *Traffic channel*

Figure 17.11 shows the operation of a full rate traffic channel (TCH). The line marked FN shows the frame number modulo 26. Frames 21 to 1 are shown since they illustrate both the normal reception and transmission of traffic bursts and activity in the idle slot.

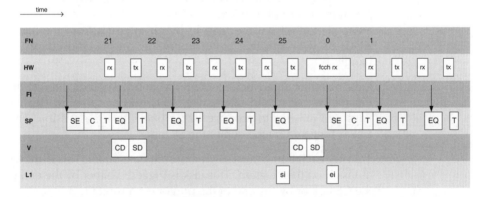

Figure 17.11   Traffic channel

The tasks involved are:

(i) Reading blocks of 16 sample pairs from HW buffer to main memory buffer. This task is triggered by an interrupt from the receive ADC when 16 sample pairs are available. After 10 blocks have been received, task (ii) is triggered. In most cases there is no need to reprogram the hardware after a burst receive since the next receive will automatically be initiated when the timer wraps round. The exception is the case shown where a different activity may be performed in the idle slot

(ii) Pass the 160 received sample pairs through the normal burst equalizer (EQ). This calculates the precise timing of the burst and demodulates it. This task is triggered by the receive ISR when 160 sample pairs have been received

(iii) Pass eight half-bursts from the previous 8 frames through the de-interleaver and channel decoder (CD). This corrects any errors in the received data. This task is triggered by the end of the EQ task in frames 3, 7, 11, 16, 20, 24 modulo 26

(iv) Pass the decoded data through the speech decoder (SD) and output the resulting audio to the speaker. This task is triggered by an interrupt from the audio DAC. Note that owing to slight errors in the locally generated audio sampling frequency relative to the base station's frame timing (generated from a precise frequency source) the task needs to handle buffer underflows and overflows. Underflow would normally be handled by repeating the previous sample and overflow by discarding a sample

(v)   Read audio data from the microphone and, when 20 ms worth of samples are available, pass them through the speech encoder (SE) to produce a traffic data block. This task is triggered by the per-frame interrupt in frames 3, 7, 12, 16, 20, 25 modulo 26. The audio data itself will be read in by an interrupt from the audio ADC. As with task (iv), buffer underflow and overflow must be handled

(vi) Pass the traffic data blocks containing encoded speech through the channel encoder and interleaver (CE). Add midambles, stealing flags and tail bits to produce traffic bursts for transmission. This task is triggered by the end of the SE task

(vii) Transfer each traffic burst to the transmit data buffer. This is shown as task T on the diagram. This task is triggered either by the end of the CE task or by the end of the previous transmit burst

(viii) Decode an SACCH data block after every 4 SACCH bursts. This task is not shown on the diagram. It is triggered by the end of the EQ task for frames $13*TN+78$ modulo 104

(ix) Encode an SACCH data block prior to the beginning of each group of four SACCH bursts. Triggered by a layer 2 SACCH block becoming available in frames between $13*TN-12$ and $13*TN-1$ modulo 104

(x) Reprogram the hardware to perform the required activity in the idle slot (task marked si on the diagram). This could either be a neighbor cell power measurement, which requires a 160 bit receive, a neighbor cell FCCH burst search, which requires a 1408-bit receive, or a neighbor cell SCH burst receive, which a requires a 176-bit receive starting at an arbitrary offset within a frame. This task is triggered either by the frame interrupt for the frame before the idle slot or by an extra interrupt at timer wraparound if the idle slot activity commences more than two timeslots into the idle frame

(xi) Reprogram the hardware for normal TCH activity following the idle slot (task marked ei on the diagram). Triggered either by the start of an idle slot power measurement or SCH receive, or by the frame interrupt during an idle slot FCCH receive

(xii) Process the samples received during the idle slot. This consists of either a simple power measurement, a frequency burst search or an SCH equalization and channel decode. This task is triggered by the end of the idle slot activity

As ever the deadline for task (i) is 59 μs, and this task runs directly in the ISR. Task (ii) should complete before the next burst receive, so the deadline is seven timeslots, or 3.9 ms. Tasks (v), (vi) and the first (vii) of each four form a group and their deadline is nine timeslots (5.1 ms) since the transmitted data must be available before the next transmit slot. Tasks (iii) and (iv) form a pair and their deadline is governed by the maximum allowed round trip delay time for GSM of 100 ms. After taking account of the fact that it takes eight frames to receive a speech block and eight frames to transmit one, we find that a deadline of four frame periods (18 ms) is permissible for tasks (iii) and (iv).

Tasks (viii) and (ix) only occur once every 104 frames. Their deadlines, in combination with the layer 2 and layer 3 processing of SACCH messages, are determined by the fact that a received SACCH message should have been processed in time for the next idle slot, and that an SACCH message for transmission must be assembled in the time between the previous idle slot and the first SACCH transmit frame. Thus a deadline of 12 frames (55 ms) is acceptable for each direction of SACCH processing.

The worst case for task (x) is an SCH receive starting immediately after the TX burst finishes (RX starts timeslot 5), which is two timeslots after the frame interrupt. Thus the deadline for task (x) is 1.1 ms. The worst case for task (xi) is an SCH receive starting just before timeslot 5 in the idle slot. The task must have completed by the start of timeslot 7 to set up for the next normal receive. Hence again the deadline is two timeslots, or 1.1 ms.

The result of task (xii) will not be needed before the next SACCH transmission, so this shares the deadline of 55 ms with other SACCH processing.

17.4.5.7 Layer 1 threads

From my earlier discussion, you can see that the real time deadlines involved in GSM layer 1 fall into five clusters. I list these in the following table:

Deadline	Context	Tasks
59 µs	FIQ	Reading 16 sample pairs from baseband receive ADC into main memory.
1 ms	L1 Thread	Main layer 1 state machine, idle slot setup and teardown during traffic mode, control channel encode.
3–5 ms	SP Thread	Receive equalization, control channel decode, traffic channel encode, speech encode.
18 ms	V Thread	Speech decode, traffic channel decode.
55 ms	SA Thread	Idle slot data processing, SACCH channel encode and decode.

Each of the tasks that I've mentioned in the preceding sections (apart from the baseband receive ISR) would be implemented as a DFC running on one of the four threads in the table. The priorities of these threads would be set in the order L1, SP, V, SA (highest to lowest).

17.4.5.8 Layers 2 and 3

Messages received on BCCH and PCH during idle mode are passed to layer 3 of the GSM protocol stack. Signaling messages received or transmitted on either SDCCH, SACCH or FACCH go through a small layer 2 as well, which discriminates between messages meant for the different parts of layer 3.

Layer 3 of GSM is split into three main pieces:

- **RR (Radio Resources).** This is responsible for allocation and management of radio frequencies and timeslots. Allocation of a channel (SDCCH or TCH) to a mobile, change of channel or handover between base stations are handled by RR, as is the reporting of measurements on neighboring cells, which is used to determine when to hand over a call

- **MM (Mobility Management).** This is responsible for keeping the network informed of each mobile's approximate position via location update messages

- **CC (Call Control).** This is responsible for setting up and closing down voice calls and data calls and for sending and receiving SMS messages.

Deadlines for processing messages in these layers range from four frames (18 ms) to seconds. Typically MM runs in a single thread and CC runs in two threads – one for calls and one for SMS. SMS can be sent and received while a call is in progress; every other SACCH message is used for SMS in this case. RR typically uses several threads (up to 10).

If you were writing a GSM stack for EKA2 from scratch, I would recommend putting layer 3 in a user-side process. This is because there would be no problem achieving latencies of 18 ms there, and running user side makes debugging easier.

17.5 Personality layers

17.5.1 Introduction

Every Symbian OS product will need to incorporate some type of mobile telephony stack, and usually also a Bluetooth stack too. These two items have the following features in common:

- They are large complex pieces of software in which the phone manufacturer has made a considerable investment

- They have significant real time requirements

- They generally run over some type of RTOS, either a proprietary one or a standard commercial RTOS such as Nucleus Plus, VRTX or OSE.

In the rest of this chapter, I will refer to any such software block as a legacy real time application (LRTA).

One way in which you could incorporate an LRTA into a mobile phone is by running it on its own CPU, separate from the one that runs Symbian OS. There are some advantages to this solution – the LRTA need not be modified and it is completely isolated from the Symbian OS software, reducing the integration burden. However, there are also disadvantages – mainly the cost of the extra processor and the accompanying memory. So, let us assume that the separate processor solution is too expensive, and that the LRTA must run on the same CPU as Symbian OS. There are essentially three ways of achieving this:

1. Modify the source code (and possibly design) of the LRTA to run directly over Symbian OS – either as a purely kernel-mode device driver, or as a combination of kernel and user mode components

2. Implement a system in which both Symbian OS and the LRTA RTOS run concurrently. You could do this either by placing hooks into the Symbian OS kernel at strategic places (interrupt and possibly other exception vectors) to allow the RTOS to run, or by implementing some kind of "hypervisor" that performs context switches between the two operating systems. This would require modifications to both operating systems to make calls to the hypervisor to indicate thread switches, priority changes and so on

3. Implement a personality layer over the EKA2 kernel, which provides the same API as the RTOS, or at least as much of it as is required by the LRTA. The RTOS itself can then be dispensed with and the LRTA can run using EKA2 as the underlying real time kernel.

I alluded to the first of these options in Section 17.4.5. Nevertheless, this option is unlikely to be viable because of the time it would take to modify the LRTA, the risk involved in doing so and the problem of creating a second distinct version of the LRTA that then increases the phone manufacturer's maintenance burden.

The second option suffers from the following problems:

- Performance is degraded because of the hooks that are called on every interrupt and every executive call, even if they are not related to the LRTA. The hypervisor system will degrade performance even more due to the presence of more hooks and a whole extra layer of processing on interrupts

- The hooks add additional complication and risk of defects to particularly sensitive areas of code

- Inserting hooks into the Symbian OS kernel to allow the RTOS to run whenever it wants to destroys the real time performance of EKA2 since a low priority thread in the LRTA will take precedence over a high priority thread in Symbian OS. The hypervisor system would not necessarily suffer from this problem but would be considerably more complicated and incur a larger performance penalty

- The hooks become extremely complicated and hard to manage if more than one RTOS needs to run, for example if both a GSM signaling stack and a Bluetooth stack are required and each uses a different RTOS.

For these reasons, Symbian prefers option 3 as a solution to this problem. In the rest of this section I will describe how such a personality layer may be implemented.

17.5.2 The RTOS environment

Even the most minimal RTOS provides the following features:

- Threads, usually scheduled by static priority-based scheduling with a fixed number of priorities. Round robin scheduling of equal priority threads may be available but is usually not used in real time applications. Dynamic creation and destruction of threads may or may not be possible

- At least one mechanism for thread synchronization and communication. Typical examples would be semaphores, message queues and event flags. There is wide variation between systems as to which primitives are provided and what features they support. Again, dynamic creation and destruction of such synchronization and communication objects may or may not be supported. Mutual exclusion is often achieved by simply disabling interrupts, or occasionally by disabling rescheduling

- A way for hardware interrupts to cause a thread to be scheduled. This is usually achieved by allowing ISRs to make system calls which perform operations such as signaling a semaphore, posting a message to a queue or setting event flags, which would cause a thread waiting on the semaphore, message queue or event flag to run. Some systems don't allow ISRs to perform these operations directly, but require them to queue some kind of deferred function call. This is a function that runs at a lower priority than hardware interrupts (that is, with interrupts enabled) but at a higher priority than any thread – for example a Nucleus Plus HISR (High-level Interrupt Service Routine). The deferred function call then performs the operation that causes thread rescheduling.

Most RTOSes also provide a timer management function, allowing several software timers to be driven from a single hardware timer. On expiry, a software timer may call a supplied timer handler, post a message to a queue or set an event flag.

RTOSes may provide other features, such as memory management. This is usually in the form of fixed size block management, since that allows real time allocation and freeing. Some RTOSes may also support full variable size block management. However most RTOSes do not support the use of a hardware MMU. Even if the RTOS does supports it (OSE does), then the real time applications generally do not make use of such support, since they are written to be portable to hardware without an MMU.

17.5.3   Mapping RTOS to EKA2

I will now assume that the real time application expects a flat address space with no protection, as would be the case on hardware with no MMU. To get this behavior under EKA2, the application must run in supervisor mode in the kernel address space. The obvious way to do this is to make the real time application plus personality layer a kernel extension; this will also ensure that it is started automatically, early on in the boot process.

In general, a real time application will have its own memory management strategy and will not wish to use the standard Symbian OS memory management system. To this end, at boot time the personality layer will allocate a certain fixed amount of RAM for use by the real time application. For a telephony stack this will be around 128 KB–256 KB. The personality layer can do this either by including the memory in the kernel extension's. bss section or by making a one-time allocation on the kernel heap at boot time. Depending on the LRTA's requirements, the personality layer may manage this area of RAM (if the RTOS being emulated provides memory management primitives) or the LRTA may manage it.

The personality layer will use a nanokernel thread for each RTOS thread. It will need a priority-mapping scheme to map RTOS priorities, of which there are typically 64 to 256 distinct values, to the 64 nanokernel priorities. As long as the real time application does not have more than 35 threads running simultaneously (which is usually the case) it should be possible to produce a mapping scheme that allows each thread to have a distinct priority. If you do need to exceed this limit, you will have to fold some priorities together.

The nanokernel does not support most of the synchronization and communication primitives provided by standard RTOSes. You will have to implement any such primitives required by the LRTA in the personality layer. This basically means that the personality layer has to define new types of object on which threads may wait. This in turn means that new N-states (discussed in Chapter 3, *Processes and Threads*) must be defined to signify that a thread is waiting on an object of a new type; generally each new type of wait-object will require an accompanying new N-state. To make a thread actually block on a new type of wait object, you would use the following nanokernel function:

```
void NKern::NanoBlock(TUint32 aTimeout, TUint aState, TAny* aWaitObj);
```

You should call this function with preemption disabled since it removes the current thread from the scheduler ready list. The parameters are as follows:

- aTimeout is the maximum time for which the thread should block, in nanokernel timer ticks; a zero value means wait for ever. If the thread is still blocked when the timeout expires the state handler (which I discuss next) will be called

- aState is the new N-state corresponding to the wait object. This value will be written into the NThreadBase::iNState field

- aWaitObj is a pointer to the new wait object. This value will be written into the NThreadBase::iWaitObj field.

You can use the TPriListLink base class of NThreadBase to attach the thread to a list of threads waiting on the object; note that you must do this after calling the NanoBlock() function. Since preemption is disabled at this point, a reschedule will not occur immediately but will be deferred to the next point at which preemption is re-enabled.

Every thread that wants to use a new type of wait object must have a nanokernel state handler installed to handle operations on that thread when it is waiting on the new type of object. A nanokernel state handler is a function with the following signature:

```
void StateHandler(NThread* aThread, TInt aOp, TInt aParam);
```

The parameters are as follows:

- aThread is a pointer to the thread involved

- aOp indicates which operation is being performed on the thread (a value from enum NThreadBase::NThreadOperation)

- aParam is a parameter that depends on aOp.

The state handler is always called with preemption disabled. The possible values of aOp are described in the following table:

aOp	Description
ESuspend	Called if the thread is suspended while not in a critical section and not holding a fast mutex. Called in whichever context NThreadBase::Suspend() was called from. Requested suspension count is passed as aParam.
EResume	Called if the thread is resumed while actually suspended and the last suspension has been removed. Called in whichever context NThreadBase::Resume() was called. No parameter.

aOp	Description
EForceResume	Called if the thread has all suspensions cancelled while actually suspended. Called in whichever context `NThreadBase::ForceResume()` was called. No parameter.
ERelease	Called if the thread is released from its wait. This call should make the thread ready if necessary. Called in whichever context `NThreadBase::Release()` was called. `aParam` is the value passed into `NThreadBase::Release()` to be used as a return code. If `aParam` is nonnegative this indicates normal termination of the wait condition. If it is negative it indicates early or abnormal termination of the wait; in this case the wait object should be rolled back as if the wait had never occurred. For example a semaphore's count needs to be incremented if `aParam` is negative since in that case the waiting thread never acquired the semaphore.
EChangePriority	Called if the thread's priority is changed. Called in whichever context `NThreadBase::SetPriority()` is called. This function should set the `iPriority` field of the thread, after doing any necessary priority queue manipulations. The new priority is passed as `aParam`.
ELeaveCS	Called in the context of the thread concerned if the thread executes `NKern::ThreadLeaveCS()` with an unknown `iCsFunction`, that is negative but not equal to `ECsExitPending`. The value of `iCsFunction` is passed as `aParam`.
ETimeout	Called if the thread's wait timeout expires and no timeout handler is defined for that thread. Called in the context of the nanokernel timer thread (DfcThread1). No parameter. This should cancel the wait and arrange for an appropriate error code to be returned. The handler for this condition will usually do the same thing as the handler for `ERelease` with a parameter of `KErrTimedOut`.

When a thread's wait condition is resolved, you should call the following nanokernel method:

```
void NThreadBase::Release(TInt aReturnCode);
```

The parameter is usually KErrNone if the wait condition is resolved normally (for example the semaphore on which it is waiting is signaled). A negative parameter value is used for an abnormal termination – in this case the wait object may need to be rolled back. You should call the Release method with preemption disabled. It performs the following actions:

- Calls the state handler with ERelease and the return code. If the return code is negative this should remove the thread from any wait queues and roll back the state of the wait object. In any case it should call NThreadBase::CheckSuspendThenReady() to make the thread ready again if necessary

- Sets the NThreadBase::iWaitObj field to NULL and cancels the wait timer if it is still running

- Stores the supplied return code in NThreadBase::iReturnCode.

The final piece of the puzzle for simple personality layers is the mechanism by which ISRs cause threads to be scheduled. Most RTOSes allow ISRs to directly perform operations such as semaphore signal, queue post and set event flag – usually using the same API as would be used in a thread context. The EKA2 nanokernel does not allow this – ISRs may only queue an IDFC or DFC. The way to get round this limitation is to incorporate an IDFC into each personality layer wait object. The personality layer API involved then needs to check whether it is being invoked from an ISR or a thread, and in the first case it will queue the IDFC. The API also might need to save some other information for use by the IDFC; for example it may need to maintain a list of messages queued from ISRs, a count of semaphore signals from ISRs or a bit mask of event flags set by ISRs. Checking for invocation from an ISR can be done using the NKern::CurrentContext() API.

```
class NKern
  {
  enum TContext
    {
    EThread=0,         // execution in thread context
    EIDFC=1,           // execution in IDFC context
    EInterrupt=2,      // execution in ISR context
    EEscaped=KMaxTInt  // emulator only
    };

// Return a value indicating the current execution
// context. One of the NKern::TContext enumeration
// values is returned.

  IMPORT_C static TInt CurrentContext();
  };
```

Hardware interrupts serviced by the LRTA need to conform to the same pattern as those serviced by Symbian OS extensions or device drivers. This means that the standard preamble must run before the actual service routine, and the nanokernel interrupt postamble must run after the service routine to enable reschedules to occur if necessary. You can do this by calling the standard `Interrupt::Bind()` provided by the base port during LRTA initialization (possibly via a personality layer call if it must be called from C code).

I will illustrate these points with an example. Consider the implementation of a simple counting semaphore, with the following properties:

1. Semaphores are created at system startup, with an initial count of zero

2. Any personality layer thread may wait on any semaphore. The wait operation causes the count to be decremented; if it becomes negative the thread blocks

3. Any personality layer thread may signal any semaphore. The signal operation causes the count to be incremented; if it was originally negative the highest priority waiting thread is released

4. Semaphores may be signaled directly by ISRs.

Since we have a new wait object, we need a new N-state and a state handler to deal with threads in the new state. We make the following declaration for personality layer threads:

```
class PThread : public NThread
  {
public:
  enum PThreadState
    {
    EWaitSemaphore = NThreadBase::ENumNStates,
    };

public:
  static void StateHandler(NThread* aThread, TInt aOp, TInt aParam);
  void HandleSuspend();
  void HandleResume();
  void HandleRelease(TInt aReturnCode);
  void HandlePriorityChange(TInt aNewPriority);
  void HandleTimeout();
  };
```

The semaphore object itself must have a count and a list of waiting threads. This list must be priority ordered since threads are woken up in priority order. Also, threads that are suspended while waiting must be kept on a separate list since they are no longer eligible for execution when the semaphore is signaled. We make the following definition for our semaphore class:

```
class PSemaphore
  {
public:
  static void CreateAll();
  PSemaphore();
  void WaitCancel(PThread* aThread);
  void SuspendWaitingThread(PThread* aThread);
  void ResumeWaitingThread(PThread* aThread);
  void ChangeWaitingThreadPriority(PThread* aThread,
                                   TInt aNewPriority);
  void Signal();
  void ISRSignal();
  static void IDfcFn(TAny*);

public:
  TInt iCount; // semaphore count
  TInt iISRCount; // number of pending ISR signals
  TDfc iIDfc; // IDFC to signal semaphore from ISR
  SDblQue iSuspendedQ; // suspended waiting threads
  // list of waiting threads
  TPriList<PThread, KNumPriorities> iWaitQ;
  static TInt NumSemaphores;
  static PSemaphore* SemaphoreTable;
  };
```

I will first examine semaphore creation:

```
void PSemaphore::CreateAll()
  {
  NumSemaphores = semaphore_count;
  SemaphoreTable = new PSemaphore[semaphore_count];
  __NK_ASSERT_ALWAYS(SemaphoreTable != NULL);
  }

PSemaphore::PSemaphore()
  : iCount(0),
    iISRCount(0),
    iIDfc(iDfcFn, this)
  {
  }
```

The PSemaphore::CreateAll() method is called when the personality layer initializes. It allocates and initializes an array of sema-phore_count (this is a configuration parameter) semaphore objects on the kernel heap. Since personality layer initialization takes place in an extension entry point, it occurs in the context of the supervisor thread (see Chapter 16, *Boot Processes*) and so it can make use of the kernel heap.

The second method, the semaphore's constructor, initializes the count and ISR count to zero, the wait queues to empty and sets up the callback function for the IDFC.

Now let's consider a thread waiting on a semaphore:

```
extern "C" int semaphore_wait(int sem_id, int time_ticks)
  {
  if (time_ticks < WAIT_FOREVER)
    return BAD_TIME_INTERVAL;
  if (TUint(sem_id) >= TUint(PSemaphore::NumSemaphores))
    return BAD_SEM_ID;
  PSemaphore* s = PSemaphore::SemaphoreTable + sem_id;
  PThread* t = (PThread*)NKern::CurrentThread();
  TInt r = OK;
  NKern::Lock();
  if (time_ticks == NO_WAIT)
    {
    if (s->iCount <= 0)
      r = TIMED_OUT;
    else
      --s->iCount;
    NKern::Unlock();
    return r;
    }
  if (--s->iCount < 0)
    {
    TInt waitp;
    waitp = (time_ticks == WAIT_FOREVER) ? 0 : time_ticks;
    NKern::NanoBlock(waitp, PThread::EWaitSemaphore, s);
    s->iWaitQ.Add(t);
    NKern::PreemptionPoint();
    if (t->iReturnValue == KErrTimedOut)
      r = TIMED_OUT;
    }
  NKern::Unlock();
  return r;
  }
```

We have declared the public API provided by the personality layer with C linkage since most LRTA code is written in C. The function first validates the semaphore ID and timeout parameters, and then looks up the semaphore control block from the ID (just a simple array index in this case). If a non-blocking call is required (NO_WAIT) the semaphore count is checked; if positive the count is decremented and OK returned, otherwise the count is left alone and TIMED_OUT returned. If blocking is permitted the count is decremented. If it becomes negative the current thread is blocked for a maximum of time_ticks nanokernel ticks (for ever if WAIT_FOREVER). The blocked thread is placed in the new N-state PThread::EWaitSemaphore. When the thread eventually wakes up the wake up reason (iReturnValue) is checked. If this is KErrTimed-Out, the wait was timed out so TIMED_OUT is returned to the caller, otherwise the wait ended normally with the semaphore being signaled, so OK is returned.

The code to signal a semaphore is complicated by the fact that the API must work whether it was called from a thread or an ISR:

```
extern "C" int semaphore_signal(int sem_id)
  {
  if (TUint(sem_id) >= TUint(PSemaphore::NumSemaphores))
    return BAD_SEM_ID;
  PSemaphore* s = PSemaphore::SemaphoreTable + sem_id;
  TInt c = NKern::CurrentContext();
  if (c == NKern::EInterrupt)
    {
    s->ISRSignal();
    return OK;
    }
  NKern::Lock();
  s->Signal();
  NKern::Unlock();
  return OK;
  }

void PSemaphore::Signal()
  {
  if (++iCount <= 0)
    {
    // must wake up next thread
    PThread* t = iWaitQ.First();
    iWaitQ.Remove(t);
    t->Release(KErrNone);
    }
  }

void PSemaphore::ISRSignal()
  {
  if (NKern::LockedInc(iISRCount)==0)
    iIDfc.Add();
  }

void PSemaphore::IDfcFn(TAny* aPtr)
  {
  PSemaphore* s = (PSemaphore*)aPtr;
  TInt count;
  count = (TInt)NKern::SafeSwap(0, (TAny*&)s->iISRCount);
  while (count--)
    s->Signal();
  }
```

Again we declare the public API with C linkage. The function begins by validating the semaphore ID argument and looking up the PSemaphore object from the ID. Then it checks the current execution context. If it was called from within an ISR, it calls ISRSignal(), otherwise it calls Signal() with preemption disabled.

Signal() increments the semaphore's count; if the count was originally negative, it takes the first thread off the wait queue (which is priority ordered, so it gets the highest priority waiting thread) and releases it.

Note that the wait queue cannot be empty since a semaphore count of−N implies that there are N threads on the wait queue.

If the semaphore is signaled from an ISR, we can't wake up the first waiting thread immediately, since neither the semaphore wait queue nor the thread ready list is guaranteed to be consistent during ISRs. Instead, we atomically increment the `iISRCount` field. If `iISRCount` was initially zero the semaphore's IDFC is queued. The IDFC atomically reads `iISRCount` and zeros it again, then signals the semaphore the required number of times.

Finally, let's examine the state handler used for personality layer threads, and its associated methods.

```
void PThread::StateHandler(NThread* aThread, TInt aOp, TInt aParam)
    {
    PThread* t = (PThread*)aThread;
    switch (aOp)
        {
        case NThreadBase::ESuspend:
            t->HandleSuspend();
            break;
        case NThreadBase::EResume:
        case NThreadBase::EForceResume:
            t->HandleResume();
            break;
        case NThreadBase::ERelease:
            t->HandleRelease(aParam);
            break;
        case NThreadBase::EChangePriority:
            t->HandlePriorityChange(aParam);
            break;
        case NThreadBase::ETimeout:
            t->HandleTimeout();
            break;
        case NThreadBase::ELeaveCS:
        default:
            __NK_ASSERT_ALWAYS(0);
        }
    }

void PThread::HandleSuspend()
    {
    switch(iNState)
        {
        case EWaitSemaphore:
            ((PSemaphore*)iWaitObj)->SuspendWaitingThread(this);
            break;
        default:
            __NK_ASSERT_ALWAYS(0);
        }
    }

void PThread::HandleResume()
    {
    switch(iNState)
```

```
      {
      case EWaitSemaphore:
        ((PSemaphore*)iWaitObj)->ResumeWaitingThread(this);
        break;
      default:
        __NK_ASSERT_ALWAYS(0);
      }
    }

void PThread::HandleRelease(TInt aReturnCode)
  {
  switch(iNState)
    {
    case EWaitSemaphore:
      if (aReturnCode<0)
        ((PSemaphore*)iWaitObj)->WaitCancel(this);
      else
        CheckSuspendThenReady();
      break;
    default:
      __NK_ASSERT_ALWAYS(0);
    }
  }

void PThread::HandlePriorityChange(TInt aNewPriority)
  {
  switch(iNState)
    {
    case EWaitSemaphore:
      ((PSemaphore*)iWaitObj)->ChangeWaitingThreadPriority(this,
                                      aNewPriority);
      break;
    default:
      __NK_ASSERT_ALWAYS(0);
    }
  }

void PThread::HandleTimeout()
  {
  switch(iNState)
    {
    case EWaitSemaphore:
      ((PSemaphore*)iWaitObj)->WaitCancel(this);
      break;
    default:
      __NK_ASSERT_ALWAYS(0);
    }
  }

void PSemaphore::WaitCancel(PThread* aThread)
  {
  if (aThread->iSuspendCount == 0)
    {
    iWaitQ.Remove(aThread);
    ++iCount;
    }
  else
    aThread->Deque();
```

```
  aThread->CheckSuspendThenReady();
  }

void PSemaphore::SuspendWaitingThread(PThread* aThread)
  {
  // do nothing if already suspended
  if (aThread->iSuspendCount == 0)
    {
    iWaitQ.Remove(aThread);
    ++iCount;
    iSuspendedQ.Add(aThread);
    }
  }

void PSemaphore::ResumeWaitingThread(PThread* aThread)
  {
  aThread->Deque();
  if (--iCount<0)
    iWaitQ.Add(aThread);
  else
    {
    aThread->iWaitObj=NULL;
    aThread->Ready();
    }
  }

void PSemaphore::ChangeWaitingThreadPriority(PThread* aThread,
                                             TInt aNewPriority)
  {
  if (aThread->iSuspendCount == 0)
        iWaitQ.ChangePriority(aThread, aNewPriority);
  else
        aThread->iPriority = (TUint8)aNewPriority;
  }
```

The state handler calls different PThread methods according to which operation is being performed on the thread. Each of these PThread methods then performs the appropriate operation on the object on which the thread is waiting, depending on the N-state.

If a thread is suspended while waiting on a semaphore, the code first checks the thread's suspend count. The suspend count is zero if the thread is not suspended and $-N$ if it has been suspended N times. If the thread was already suspended, no action is required. Otherwise we move the thread from the semaphore's wait queue to its suspended queue. We then increment the semaphore count to preserve the invariant that (if negative) it equals minus the number of threads on the wait queue.

If a thread is resumed while waiting on a semaphore, we remove it from the semaphore's suspended queue, where it was placed when it was first suspended. Then we decrement the semaphore's count, balancing the increment when the thread was suspended. If the count becomes negative, we add the thread to the semaphore's wait queue and it remains in the PThread::EWaitSemaphore state. If the count is non-negative, we make the thread ready. Note that the state handler is only called when a thread is resumed if all suspensions have been cancelled, so there is no need for us to check the thread's suspend count.

If a thread is released while waiting on a semaphore, we check the reason code for the release. If this reason is KErrNone, this is a normal release event – in other words the semaphore has been signaled and the thread's wait condition has been resolved normally. In this case we call CheckSuspendThenReady() on the thread, which makes it ready, provided that it is not also explicitly suspended. If the reason code is not KErrNone, the wait has been cancelled – for example because the thread was terminated. In this case, we detach the thread from the semaphore – either from the wait queue or suspended queue depending on whether the thread is also suspended. If we detached it from the wait queue, we increment the count, balancing the decrement when the thread waited on the semaphore. Finally, we call CheckSuspendThenReady() on the thread. The effect is to reverse the actions taken when the thread waited on the semaphore.

If a timeout occurs on a thread waiting on a semaphore, we take the same action as a release with reason code KErrTimedOut, so the semaphore wait is cancelled. If a thread's priority is changed while it is waiting on a semaphore, the thread's position on the semaphore wait queue needs to be adjusted. If the thread is also suspended, its position on the suspended queue needn't be changed, but we do need to modify the thread's iPriority field.

17.5.4 Symbian–LRTA communication

If the functionality of the LRTA is to be available to Symbian OS applications, we need a mechanism by which Symbian OS code and the LRTA may communicate with each other. In practice this means:

1. It must be possible for a Symbian OS thread to cause an RTOS thread to be scheduled and vice-versa

2. It must be possible for data to be transferred between Symbian OS and RTOS threads in both directions.

It is usually possible for a Symbian OS thread to make standard personality layer calls (the same calls that RTOS threads would make) to cause an RTOS thread to be scheduled. This is because the nanokernel underlies both types of thread and most "signal" type operations (that is, those that make threads ready rather than blocking them) can be implemented using operations which make no reference to the calling thread, and which are therefore not sensitive to the type of thread they are called from. The semaphore-signal operation in the previous example code falls into this category – a Symbian OS thread could use this to signal a personality layer semaphore.

In the other direction, it is not possible for a personality layer thread to signal a personality layer wait object and have a Symbian OS thread wait on that object. The most straightforward way for RTOS threads to trigger the scheduling of a Symbian OS thread is to enque a DFC on a queue operated by a Symbian OS thread. Another possibility is for the Symbian OS thread to wait on a fast semaphore, which could then be signaled by the RTOS thread; however the DFC method has a better fit with the way device drivers are generally written. A device driver is needed to mediate communication between Symbian OS user mode processes and the LRTA, since the latter runs kernel side.

Data transfer between the two environments must either occur kernel-side or via shared chunks. It is not possible for any RTOS thread to access user-side memory via the IPC copy APIs, since these access parts of the Symbian OS DThread structure representing the calling thread (for example to perform exception trapping). If you want to use shared chunks, they must be created by a Symbian OS thread, not by a personality layer thread. This is because creating Symbian OS objects such as chunks requires waiting on DMutex objects, which only Symbian OS threads may do. The chunks would either be created at personality layer initialization or by the device driver used to interface Symbian OS with the LRTA. Shared chunks can be useful as a way to reduce copying overhead if bulk data transfer is necessary between the two domains.

Some possibilities for the data transfer mechanism are:

- A fairly common architecture for real time applications involves a fixed block size memory manager and message queues for inter-thread communication. The memory manager supports allocation and freeing of memory in constant time. The sending thread allocates a memory block, places data in it and posts it to the receiving thread's message queue. The receiving thread then processes the data and frees the memory block, or possibly passes the block to yet another thread. It would be a simple proposition to produce such a system in which the memory manager could be used by any thread. In that case, a Symbian OS thread could pass messages to RTOS threads in the same way as other RTOS threads do. Passing data back would involve a special type of message queue implemented in the personality layer. When the personality layer wanted to send a message to a Symbian OS thread, it would enque a DFC. That DFC would then process the message data and free the memory block as usual. This scheme combines the data transfer and scheduling aspects of communication

- You could use any standard buffering arrangement, for example circular buffers, between the LRTA and the device driver. You could prevent contention between threads by the use of nanokernel fast mutexes, on which any thread can wait, or by the simpler means of disabling preemption or interrupts.

17.6 Summary

In this chapter I have explored real time systems and the challenges they present to an operating system. I have looked at several solutions to these challenges and examined their pluses and minuses. Then I presented the solutions that we chose for EKA2, looked at the measurements typically made on real time OSes and gave the results for EKA2. After that, I discussed the hardware and software issues that need to be considered when building real time applications for EKA2. In the second half of the chapter, I gave a quick overview of the GSM system, while considering how it might be implemented under EKA2. Finally, I showed how personality layers enable existing real time software to be ported to EKA2 with minimum effort, and I gave an example of how you might implement such a personality layer. In the next chapter, I will look at how you can ensure the best performance when using EKA2.

18

Ensuring Performance

by Jasmine Strong with Dennis May

The best way to accelerate a PC is at 9.8 m s^{-2}.

Jane Sales after Marcus Dolengo

In a real-time environment, ensuring acceptable performance is not as simple as one might expect. A real-time system has been defined as one in which the validity of the results depends not only on the logical correctness of the results, but also on the timeliness of their delivery. EKA2 provides a number of constructs and techniques for ensuring that code executes not only at a sufficient rate but also within an acceptable time frame.

We can, therefore, aim to improve code performance in two areas: in its flat-out speed, and in its ability to respond to real-world events that require software intervention. The provision of real-time behavior within the EKA2 operating system requires not only that code runs quickly, but also that drivers and, to a lesser extent, application software be careful to act as a good neighbor. Sometimes the fastest algorithm can compromise the real-time behavior of the rest of the system, and so best throughput must be sacrificed in order to provide better real-time performance. For example, inter-process communication in EKA2 is not quite as fast as it was under EKA1 because the kernel now pauses every 512 bytes to check if there is contention for the system lock. This allows anything that might be waiting on the system lock with higher priority than the current thread to run in good time, rather than having to be suspended for the duration of the whole operation, which could be many milliseconds. On the user-side, this problem is already solved for you. As long as an application cannot set its priority too high, the design of EKA2 prevents it from adversely affecting the real-time behavior of other software in the system.

The analysis of code performance on an interrupt-heavy system is a complex topic and quite controversial in parts. This analysis is complicated further because the typical architectures that run EKA2 have more advanced and complex memory systems than earlier platforms. Care must be taken in the board support package, device drivers, kernel extensions, and in the use of file systems to ensure that these complex issues are sensitively handled. It is all too easy to compromise system performance with a single bit error in the configuration of a memory controller, or to allow an unforeseen interaction in a device driver to substantially increase latency.

To deliver a product with high performance requires that you understand the factors that contribute to system performance – both software factors such as context switch time and contention for exclusive locks and hardware factors such as memory access times, I/O throughput and cache architecture – and that you design the software around these. The real-time behavior of the OS is more fully described in Chapter 17, *Real Time*. In this chapter I concentrate on performance and I do not duplicate the material found there.

Before you start to modify any of the code in your system you must first profile and measure the existing performance. Only by careful testing and analysis can you truly understand how and where the performance is being consumed. Guessing at what to optimize will not solve your problems.

18.1   Writing efficient code

Writing highly efficient code for ARM processors is not as straightforward as it might at first seem. With the advent of the Thumb instruction set (see Chapter 2, *Hardware for Symbian OS*, for details), the performance gap between the most space-efficient code and the most time-efficient code has widened considerably. To write rapid code you need not write large portions of the application in assembly language. You can get 90% of the benefit in 10% of the time with care in the design phase. Of course you can use all the usual optimization strategies such as using binary searches rather than linear searches, using ASCII instead of Unicode if possible and using the most efficient available algorithm. But ARM processors have some quirks that make their performance levels vary in a way that is different from some other processors. Here are some techniques that can help.

18.1.1   Avoid tight loops

Tight loops (by "tight loop" I mean one that has only a very brief operation inside it) are very inefficient in ARM9 and earlier CPUs because these processors do not have branch prediction hardware. The lack of this hardware entails that the branch at the end of the loop incurs a time penalty while the pipeline is flushed and reloaded from the start of the loop. If the operation inside the loop requires only a few cycles, the branch penalty cycles can take more time than the actual operation.

XScale, ARM11 and all future cores have branch prediction hardware and do not suffer from the above looping problem. Their hardware predicts branch instructions that will be taken based on past history of the code and heuristic rules. If a branch is correctly predicted the CPU will continue execution without a penalty, unpredicted branches will incur a pipeline flush penalty. ARM11 goes one step further with branch folding. Predicted branch instructions are removed from the pipeline and the branch target instruction is executed immediately thus saving one more cycle.

Sometimes, of course, you can't avoid writing code that does this sort of thing, and in these cases you may decide to "unroll the loop" by performing more than a single operation in each iteration. You must weigh the increased code size produced by unrolling the loop against the improved execution time it gives. For example, take this memory checksum function:

```
TInt trivial_checksum(TInt8* aBlock, TInt aLen)
  {
  TInt i=0;
  TInt8* j;

  for (j=aBlock; j<aBlock+aLen; j++)
    i+=*j;

  return i;
  }
```

Compare this to an unrolled version:

```
TInt trivial_checksum_unrolled(TInt8* aBlock, TInt aLen)
  {
  TInt i=0;
  TInt8* j;
  TInt8* endptr;

  endptr=aBlock+aLen;

  for (j=aBlock; j<endptr; )      // we unroll this to degree 5
    {
    if (j<endptr) i+=*j++;
    else
      break;

    if (j<endptr) i+=*j++;
    else
      break;

    if (j<endptr) i+=*j++;
    else
      break;

    if (j<endptr) i+=*j++;
    else
      break;
```

```
  if (j<endptr) i+=*j++;
  else
    break;
  }
return i;
}
```

While the unrolled version is clearly much larger and more difficult to read, because it branches much less frequently it will execute much more rapidly than the non-unrolled version. If you use this technique to unroll loops, be sure to check the assembled output from the compiler to ensure that it does what you want.

The easiest way to ensure that you're using a fast, unrolled operation is to use one provided by Symbian OS. The library-provided memory and string operations are very thoroughly unrolled, so will execute quickly without bloating your application. For example, the provided implementation of Mem::Copy() is very fast indeed.

18.1.2   Optimize the general case

Code often has a "general case" that executes very often and a "special case" that only executes much more infrequently. If you can determine which case happens most often and make this general case faster, even at the expense of a little performance in the special case, you can improve the overall performance of your program markedly.

18.1.3   Don't repeatedly make small requests

If you have a list of items to get when you go shopping, do you get in your car, drive to the supermarket, take a trolley around, buy the first thing on the list, come home, look at the second thing, get in the car, drive to the supermarket, take a trolley around, buy it, come home, look at the third thing on the list, and so on? That would be crazy, and would waste a lot of time, effort and fuel.

Nevertheless, many people release code that does things exactly like this! It's even worse in code, because it defeats many of the performance-improving features of processors: the cache, which depends upon spatial and temporal locality to do its job, and burst transfer modes, which depend upon the high probability of handling more than one datum at a time.

If your program needs to open a file or any other kind of server connection, be aware that there are significant overheads in setting up a connection. If you repeatedly open a connection, perform a small operation and then close it again, you will waste huge amounts of processor time, memory bandwidth and battery power.

Similar provisos apply to image handling methods: while most of the image handling APIs provide methods for querying the values of single pixels, it is very inefficient indeed to perform single pixel operations on a large number of pixels. There is a significant overhead in every method invocation and an even bigger overhead in every IPC. It is important to make every one count.

File input and output is the same. These classes provide block methods for a reason: making a fileserver request takes a significant amount of time over and above the time required to actually fulfill the request. Use the block read and write methods if you need to read or write more than one character. In some cases, this can be literally thousands of times faster.

Memory allocation can also be slow, so you may wish to avoid repeatedly invoking memory allocation functions. I describe some approaches to improving the performance of memory allocation later in Section 18.2.9.

18.1.4 Performance differences between ARM platforms

Different ARM processors, even at the same clock frequencies, have different performance characteristics. With ARMv6 processors now becoming available, these differences have become very significant. If you're an application developer, you will want your code to work well on all ARM-compatible processors to maximize your audience. To achieve this, it's important to understand some of the differences between ARM platforms. Symbian OS has historically supported three-and-a-half ARM architectures. I'll ignore the ARMv3 and ARMv4 architectures because they are no longer supported by Symbian OS, and turn instead to the two that are actively supported today.

- **ARMv5:** Most mobile application processors in production at the time of writing are ARMv5 processors. Typical ARMv5 processor cores include the ARM926EJ at the heart of the Texas Instruments OMAP1610 and 1710 chips and many manufacturer-specific ASICs. ARMv5 retained substantial compatibility with ARMv4, needing only fairly minor changes to operating systems and almost no changes to application code. Most ARMv5 processors run at frequencies between 100 and 200 MHz, though XScale is currently available at speeds up to 700 MHz. ARMv5 processors usually reach speeds of 180MIPS, while some high performance variants occasionally exceed 250MIPS. XScale can reach speeds of 500MIPS, though it is usually restrained to a more sedate pace by mobile memory systems.

- **ARMv6:** This new architecture promises to improve performance with a number of new features, including dynamic branch prediction similar to that introduced in XScale, a new and very much improved physically-tagged cache architecture, support for symmetric multiprocessing, branch folding and other substantial improvements.

ARMv6 is much more than an incremental improvement over ARMv5. ARM1136JF-S, as used in the Texas Instruments OMAP2420, Freescale MXC and other mobile ASICs, was the first ARMv6 processor to become available. Because of ARMv6's Prefetch Unit and branch folding capabilities, ARMv6 processors may execute more than one instruction per clock cycle. ARMv6 processors are very fast and routinely exceed 400MIPS. Some ARM1136JF-S based ASICs are expected to reach clock frequencies of nearly 700 MHz. These processors will return figures of around 750MIPS. As they also have a vector floating point unit and SIMD instruction set, the performance available from these processors is considerably in excess of that available on the more common and cheaper ARMv5 solutions.

18.1.4.1 Applying optimizations

Many factors will influence the selection of optimizations that you choose to perform. If your device is short of memory, you might decide to forego time performance in order to use Thumb code, which is typically about 70% of the size of ARM code. Conversely, if your device is short of processing power, you might decide that the 20% faster execution of ARM code is a better compromise for your application. Depending on what your code does, ARM might be much faster than Thumb, particularly if you need multiword arithmetic or other things that are improved by instructions that are only available in ARM state. Your choice of optimizations will also depend on which processor you expect your code to run on. For example, there's little need to unroll loops if your code will only run on processors with branch prediction such as ARM1136JF-S and XScale.

In general, you have to target your code at the slowest processor it will run on. If you are aiming for the installed base of EKA2-based Symbian OS devices, these will all be ARMv5 or higher, which means that they have Harvard architecture caches,[1] at least 5-stage pipelines and they support the Thumb instruction set. If your performance is limited by the amount of code that can fit in the instruction cache, you may find that your performance is actually improved by compiling to a Thumb target. However, this is rare, especially on ARMv5 platforms where every process switch potentially eliminates useful content from the data cache. Performance on these devices is generally limited by the high rate of data cache misses due to these flushes.

The memory systems on mobile phone platforms are usually quite slow, and so, to alleviate the performance problems this creates, ARM processors have caches. The cache is a special area of memory that is used to keep a local copy of words that are also used in main memory.

---

[1] The Harvard architecture separates the instruction stream from the data stream, which potentially allows any instruction to access memory without penalty.

Cache memory is very expensive, so most processors do not include very much of it. In ARM systems, the processor cache is always incorporated into the processor chip.

- **ARMv5:** All ARMv5 application processors to date have a Harvard memory architecture. Most ARMv5 processors have at least 16 KB of instruction cache, with ARM926 often implemented with asymmetrical instruction and data caches. 16 KB of instruction and 8 KB of data is a common split. XScale usually has 32 KB each of instruction and data cache.

- **ARMv6:** ARMv6 defined a new cache architecture. While all ARM architectures place the memory management unit outside the processor core, architectures before ARMv6 also dictated that the caches may use only virtual addresses. This meant that when Symbian OS switched processes and those processes occupied the same virtual addresses, then we needed to clean and flush the caches (partially, at least). This is time consuming and generally to be avoided. The avoidance of cache flushing was the primary motivation behind the design of Symbian OS features such as the "moving" memory model and fixed processes. ARMv6 alleviates this problem by incorporating a cache with knowledge of the physical addresses that underlie the virtually addressed contents of the cache (that is, it's a virtually indexed, physically tagged cache). This means that it doesn't have to be flushed nearly so often, which makes process switching much faster and more power efficient. At the time of writing, the only ARMv6 processors available are the ARM1136JF-S and the ARM1176JZ-S. ARM1136 cores often have 32 KB each of instruction and data cache, though they may have much more.

18.1.4.2 The influence of caches

Caches are the main source of unexpected interactions that affect program execution speed. For example, a benchmark that repeatedly performs a simple operation may show a two microsecond context switch, but this is only possible because the cache is filled early in the test and remains filled throughout. On a real system where the threads being switched do actual work, the contents of the cache are displaced, which makes context switching much slower. Also, because caches contain scattered pieces of information from throughout main memory and have to be able to find that information very quickly, they use something called "tag RAM". Tag RAM is even more expensive than the rest of the cache, so to reduce the amount needed, spatial locality is exploited by organizing the cache into "lines", typically of eight 32-bit words each. Each line has a single tag, and will be filled in from main memory in a single operation: an eight-word burst. It is much faster to do this than to fetch eight single words from memory: it may even be more than eight times faster, because many memory systems require a delay between requests.

When a processor with a cache is running code and data that fits entirely within the cache, it is said to be "running from cache". Running from cache has a number of benefits: primarily, it is considerably faster than running from DRAM or, even slower, flash memory. It also generates fewer memory bus cycles, which in turn saves power. If the DRAM is not used for some time, some DRAM controllers will even close pages and place them in retention mode, reducing power consumption even further.

When the code and data in the current active set does not quite fit inside the cache, lines will have to be evicted from the cache to make room for each successive new datum or instruction that the program flow encounters. It is not uncommon for items of data to be repeatedly evicted and reloaded. This unwelcome state of affairs is known as "thrashing". The choice of algorithm used to select lines to evict from the cache determines the processor's behavior when thrashing. Many of the processors described in this chapter support two algorithms, round robin (RR) and random replacement. RR replacement evicts lines in turn, whereas random replacement selects them at random. When an RR cache is thrashing, the performance of the processor drops off extremely quickly: it falls off a "performance cliff". On the other hand, when a randomly replaced cache starts to thrash, its performance degrades more gracefully. For this reason, random replacement is to be preferred to round robin. On processors where the replacement algorithm is a run-time option, this is configured using a CP15 configuration register setting in the base port; it is very important to ensure that this is configured appropriately.

18.1.5 Alignment

Since ARM processors generally only handle word-aligned memory operations, accessing non-single-byte quantities that are not aligned to a word boundary is not as fast as accessing ones that are. The `Mem::Copy()` method is very heavily optimized, using a special "twister" algorithm to copy unaligned data using aligned memory access cycles. This makes it about three times faster than a conventional implementation of `memcpy()` for both unaligned copies and for copies in which the source is not aligned with the destination. Similarly, particularly on ARM926EJ platforms, the memory interface does not generate burst accesses for cache missing `STM` or `LDM` instructions that are not aligned to a 16 byte boundary. The `Mem::` methods include code to alleviate these problems, and their performance is very close to the theoretical maximum.

In some situations you may choose to modify your code to place important members of structures in aligned locations. Packing structs can help to save memory but may significantly reduce the available memory bandwidth on these processors. ARM926EJ is a very popular core at the time of writing and can be found in many mobile phones. ARM926EJ cache lines are eight words long, so to be aligned, an address must be divisible by 32.

18.1.6 Pragmatism, not idealism

Unfortunately, there is only a finite amount of work that any processor can do in one second, and that amount depends on the nature of the work. While the processors available to mobile phone applications now would have been astonishingly powerful as recently as ten years ago, they aren't that powerful compared to workstation processors. Mobile phone manufacturers have to choose processors based on their benchmark scores. That is, they use figures published by manufacturers, measured using programs designed to advertise how fast their processors are. The problem with this is that the performance of a processor is entirely dependent on what it's being asked to process. The application binary environment, compiler and even the instruction set may have been tweaked to improve benchmark performance! That's all very well as long as your application does the same sort of thing as the benchmark, and *only* the same sort of thing – rather than a mixture of different operations. To make a safer estimate, it's important to have a set of representative, mixed operation benchmarks, timing how long it takes to perform actual user operations, using real applications. The user interface can be as important as the application engine itself in these tests.

It's not a simple operation to take a set of benchmark results, perform an examination of a very different problem, and say with certainty that problem x can be solved with processor y in time t. It is, therefore, very important to define the scope of your application with this in mind. The manufacturer's benchmarks, such as Dhrystone, running on the "bare metal" of the machine, may demonstrate performance far in excess of that actually available in a real-time, multithreaded, interrupt-rich environment. Treat these benchmarks as you do all other forms of advertising!

18.1.7 Memory throughput

ARM systems have fairly fast memory systems. They consist of a large DRAM, accessed by the processor through a cache, prefetch buffer and a write buffer. The cache usually consists of around 16 KB of very fast memory, which is usually run at the same speed as the processor core itself. This is necessary in the ARM architecture because almost every cycle will issue an instruction.

All ARMv5 and later processors have a write buffer, which is a simple FIFO queue that accepts data to be written to memory. It serves to decouple the processor pipeline from the core's data port so that if the cache misses on the data to be written, the processor pipeline does not stall. The size of the FIFO is usually eight words, and the words are usually not required to be ordered in any way.

ARM systems today use a wide variety of different interconnects and memory types, but most current systems use synchronous DRAM, similar to SDRAM or DDR RAM, attached to essentially transparent interconnects. These clock at around half the processor core speed, though with the trend towards increased core speeds this is likely to change in the near future. Power consumption and processor package pin count constrain mobile memory systems more than component cost, which means that most mobile platforms use 16-bit wide memory interfaces. This essentially limits the maximum sustained bandwidth of their memory interfaces to one word every four core cycles. This variable remains remarkably consistent across new and old processors.

However, in practice this limit can never be achieved. SDRAM is line-oriented, that is, it is designed in such a way that a "row address" is applied, taking between two and seven cycles depending on the type of RAM, then a "column address" is applied, returning data usually between two and three cycles later. Subsequent words from the same row can then be fetched in subsequent cycles without delay. This "burst mode" is very useful in cached architectures like ARM, where whole lines of eight words are generally fetched at any time, and can make memory access several times faster.

The exact management of RAM parameters is beyond the scope of this book, but is critical to the performance of the system as a whole. It is very important to ensure that systems have their RAM configured correctly.

18.2 Maintaining real-time performance

18.2.1 Techniques and limitations

This section explores some techniques for writing code with real-time performance requirements and also for writing code that does not compromise the real-time requirements of other code. It also explains some of the limitations of EKA2 for real-time systems.

18.2.1.1 Task partitioning

The first thing you should consider when writing any real-time software is how to partition the desired functionality into separate tasks, according to the deadlines involved. Some of these tasks may run as interrupt service routines, others will run in threads with varying priority levels. You should only do the minimum amount of work needed to meet a deadline at any given priority level. Work that is less urgent should be postponed to lower priority tasks, where it will not hold up more urgent activities. This is especially important for tasks which run as ISRs, since these run in preference to threads. Interrupts should always be kept as short as possible.

The following table gives a rough guide to the thread priority ranges that would be used for tasks with certain deadlines:

Priority	Deadline range	Comments
0	–	Null (idle) thread.
1–15	–	Normal application priorities.
16	–	Kernel cleanup activities.
16–24	–	System servers (file server, window server and so on).
25–26	>100 ms	Media drivers.
27	>20 ms	General device drivers. The "default" DFC thread (DfcThread()) runs at this priority.
28–31	2–20 ms	"Real-time" priority Symbian OS user processes.
28–47	2–20 ms	High priority kernel-side threads and personality layer threads. Priorities above 31 are not directly accessible user-side and must be set using a device driver.
48	2–20 ms	Nanokernel timer thread.
49–63	100 µs–10 ms	Personality layer threads.
IDFC	100 µs–1 ms	Personality layer routines to enable ISRs to wakeup threads.
ISR	10 µs–1 ms	

Threads that run in normal Symbian OS user processes, with priorities of EPriorityForeground or lower, have absolute priorities between 1 and 15. Various Symbian OS servers with high legacy code content, which were not written with real-time performance in mind, inhabit priorities 16–24 and so it is not possible to give any meaningful real-time guarantees for code running at these priorities. At the high end of the spectrum, the deadlines possible at each priority depend on the speed of the hardware and how the base port is written. On very fast hardware it should be possible to service deadlines of 100 µs with a priority 63 kernel thread, provided the base port does not have long ISRs. On slower hardware, tasks with deadlines of 1 ms will need to be ISRs.

18.2.1.2 *Avoid priority inversion*

When choosing a mutual exclusion method for use in software that must meet real-time deadlines, you should take care to minimize the time for which priority inversion exists. The following methods are available:

1. Lock-free algorithms

Lock-free algorithms for updating data structures make use of atomic memory access instructions such as SWP on ARMv5, LDREX/STREX on ARMv6 and locked instructions on IA32.

The ARM SWP instruction atomically interchanges the contents of a register with the contents of a memory location. The instruction is atomic with respect to other code running on the same processor (simply by virtue of being a single instruction, so not interruptible between the read and write) and also with respect to accesses by other bus masters. No other bus master in the system can access the memory location referred to in between the read and write part of the SWP.

The ARM LDREX and STREX instructions make use of an *exclusive access monitor*, which on systems with only a single processor is just a single bit hardware flag. The flag is usually clear, or, in ARM's terminology, in the *Open Access* state. Executing an LDREX instruction loads the contents of a memory location into a register and sets the flag (puts it into the *Exclusive Access* state). Executing a STREX instruction checks the state of the flag. If it is in the *Exclusive Access* state, the contents of the register is written into a memory location and a value of 0 is written into the result register. If the flag is in the *Open Access* state, no memory write occurs and the result register is set to 1. In either case, the flag is reset to the *Open Access* state by a STREX instruction. The usage of these instructions is illustrated here:

Use of LDREX and STREX

```
; Atomically increment the memory location at [R1]
; Return the original memory contents in R0

1 LockedInc:
2       LDREX   R0, [R1]
3       ADD     R2, R0, #1
4       STREX   R3, R2, [R1]
5       CMP     R3, #0
6       BNE     LockedInc
```

Line 2 reads the original value of the memory counter and places the monitor into the *Exclusive Access* state. Line 3 increments the value.

Line 4 writes the new value to memory, provided the monitor is still in the *Exclusive Access* state. Lines 5 and 6 retry the entire operation if the store at line 4 found the monitor in the *Open Access* state.

To ensure the correct functioning of such routines, the operating system must perform an STREX as part of the interrupt preamble. This will cause the monitor to be reset to the *Open Access* state if any interrupt occurs between the load and store, which in turn will cause the load-increment-store to be retried.

For more details on the operation of the LDREX and STREX instructions, refer to the *ARM Architecture Reference Manual*.[2]

The IA32 architecture supports many instructions that both read and write a memory location. Since interrupts cannot occur within a single instruction these instructions are automatically atomic with respect to code executing on the same processor. If atomicity with respect to other bus masters is required – for example on a system with more than one CPU sharing memory – you can apply the LOCK prefix to the instruction. This causes the CPU to output a lock signal which prevents any other bus master getting in between the read and write parts of the instruction.

Lock-free algorithms are recommended where possible for both kernel- and user-side use, since they are usually very fast, but can only be used for certain tasks. The tasks for which they can be used depend on the set of atomic instructions available on the processor in question.

As an example of a lock-free algorithm, consider adding elements to the end of a singly linked list. The following example shows some code to do this.

Lock-free singly linked list add

```
; Add the element pointed to by R0 to a singly linked
; list pointed to by R1. The first word of
; each element is the link pointer, which points
; to the next element in the list or is zero if this
; is the last element.
; The list itself consists of two pointers - the first
; points to the last element on the list (zero if the
; list is empty), and the second points to the first
; element in the list (again zero if the list is
; empty).

1       MOV     R2, #0
2       STR     R2, [R0]
3       SWP     R2, R0, [R1]
4       STR     R0, [R2]
5       CMP     R2, #0
6       STREQ   R0, [R1, #4]
```

Lines 1 and 2 set the link pointer of the element being added to zero, since it is the last element. Line 3 atomically gets the address of the

---

[2] *ARM Architecture Reference Manual*, by Dave Seal. Addison-Wesley Professional.

current last element and sets the element being added as the last element. Line 4 sets the link pointer of the previous last element to the one just added. Lines 5 and 6 set the element just added as the first element if the list was initially empty. It can be seen that this algorithm works even if the function is called simultaneously in multiple threads.

2. Disabling interrupts
This method is only available kernel side, and it must be used if any of the contending tasks runs in an ISR, unless a lock-free algorithm can be used. The duration for which interrupts are disabled should not exceed the maximum time for which the kernel disables interrupts. A good rule of thumb is that it should not exceed 10 μs.

3. Disabling preemption
This method is only available kernel side and it must be used if any of the contending tasks runs in an IDFC, unless a lock-free algorithm can be used. The duration for which preemption is disabled should not exceed the maximum time for which it is disabled by the kernel. A good rule of thumb is that it should not exceed 30 μs.

4. Fast mutexes
Use of a fast mutex is the recommended method for mutual exclusion between kernel-side threads. Both Symbian OS threads and nanothreads can use it. If the system lock is used, it should not be held for longer than the kernel holds it. A reasonable rule of thumb for this is that it should not be held for more than 100 μs.

5. Symbian OS mutexes
Symbian OS mutexes are available to both kernel- and user-side code. They are slower than methods 2–4, and so we only recommend them for critical sections that are entered relatively infrequently (periods in the millisecond range) and for critical sections that contain other nested critical sections protected by fast mutexes – because fast mutexes cannot nest. Obviously these mutexes are only available to Symbian OS threads.

6. Threads
Our final method is the use of a single thread to run multiple tasks, one at a time. This can be the simplest method and should work well provided that the tasks have similar deadlines and execution times. The nanokernel's DFC queues make this method particularly simple to use, and the different DFC priorities within the same queue can be used to cope with whatever differences there are in task deadlines. This method is the slowest since it involves two context switches, instead of a mutex wait and signal.

For user-side code, only methods 1, 5 and 6 are available. The RFastLock primitive available to user code is faster than RMutex but it does not implement any form of priority inheritance so will generally be unsuitable for applications requiring real-time guarantees.

18.2.1.3 Algorithm selection

For an application with real-time constraints, the algorithm that you would choose for a particular function is often different from the one that you would choose in the absence of those constraints. This is because you need an algorithm with predictable execution time. This may not be the fastest algorithm in the average case, and it may be less memory efficient than other algorithms.

For example, when you are managing a list of N elements, you should use constant time or logarithmic time algorithms rather than algorithms that are linear or higher order, unless the value of N is well bounded. So, you would generally use doubly linked lists rather than singly linked lists if you need to insert and/or remove items from the middle of the list. If the list must be ordered according to some key, then you can use a priority list structure (as in Section 17.3.1.1) if the number of possible key values is small, or you can use a tree-based structure.

To sort a list of N elements, where N is known, you should prefer heap sort to quick sort, even though quick sort has lower average execution time. This is because quick sort has a pathological worst-case execution time proportional to N^2.

Lists come in intrusive and non-intrusive varieties. Intrusive lists require that the objects on the list include reserved space used for management of the list, so that the object must "know" what lists it will potentially be added to. Non-intrusive lists do not make such demands; instead any memory required for management of the list is allocated dynamically when the object is added to the list and freed when the object is removed from the list. For real-time applications you should clearly prefer intrusive lists, since non-intrusive lists require memory allocation and freeing when adding and removing elements, which spoils, or at least makes it more difficult to achieve, real-time behavior.

18.2.1.4 Hardware issues

The design of the hardware places fundamental limits on how well real-time applications will run on that hardware. I have already mentioned that memory bandwidth has a large effect on achievable interrupt and thread latencies.

There can also be other more subtle problems, one example being the effect of DMA on memory bandwidth. Generally DMA controllers have higher bus arbitration priority than the CPU, so the CPU is stalled while DMA accesses occur. This problem is most apparent with high-resolution, high-color displays which use main memory for the frame buffer.

Certain peripheral designs can also seriously damage real-time performance. Peripherals that generate very frequent interrupts to the processor, generally as a result of inadequate internal buffering or lack of DMA capability, can be a particular problem. The archetypal example of this is a USB controller with no buffering or DMA. Running flat out at 12 Mbit/sec this will generate an interrupt every 40 μs (one per 64-byte USB packet). Such a high interrupt rate will use a large proportion of the processor bandwidth. Even trying to shorten the ISRs by deferring work to a thread will cause problems, unless the processor is very fast, because the two thread switches (to and from the thread handling USB) every 40 μs will use an unacceptable percentage of processor time and will result in degradation of the USB data transfer rate. Ideally a peripheral delivering data at this rate would either buffer the data internally or (more likely) use DMA to transfer data to or from memory without needing processor intervention. In either case the rate of interrupts would be greatly reduced.

18.2.1.5 *Software limitations*

The most obvious limitation on real-time software under Symbian OS is that, with the exception of the bounded kernel services, most Symbian APIs do not have bounded execution times. Non-kernel APIs such as file system access and other system servers generally do not provide any real-time guarantees. One (but not the only) reason for this is that most of them rely on unbounded kernel services, most notably memory allocation and freeing.

When you are writing real-time software to run under EKA2, the first thing to bear in mind is that the standard dynamic memory allocation primitives do not provide any real-time guarantees. There are two main reasons for this:

Firstly, the default algorithm used to manage an application's heap memory (the RHeap class) is address-ordered first fit, using a simple linked list of free cells. It may need to search many free cells to find one that is capable of satisfying an allocation request, or to find the correct place in which to insert a cell that is being freed.

Secondly, if there is no free cell large enough to satisfy a request, the algorithm requests more memory from the global free page pool. Even though a request for a single page can be completed in a known time, the pool is protected by a mutex which could be held for a long period if another thread is also performing memory allocation or freeing. This means that accesses to the global pool cannot be performed in a known time.

There are two main techniques for avoiding this problem. The first is to avoid dynamic memory management altogether in time-critical sections of code. Instead you should allocate all memory blocks at initialization time and free them when the application or operation terminates.

The second technique is to replace the standard RHeap allocator with a custom allocator designed to offer predictable execution times – for example an allocator based on a small number of fixed block sizes. The allocator will need to be seeded with a fixed amount of memory from the global pool when the real-time application initializes. Why didn't Symbian provide such an allocator? The address-ordered first-fit algorithm used by the standard Symbian OS RHeap class is a good general-purpose algorithm that provides low memory overhead and acceptable performance for most applications without making any assumptions about the size and pattern of allocations made by the application. Custom allocators can take advantage of their knowledge of the particular application involved, especially of the sizes of allocations made, and can give real-time guarantees without compromising on space efficiency. Alternatively, they may trade space efficiency for bounded execution time. The custom allocator approach has the advantage that any standard library functions used in the same thread or process also use the predictable algorithms. Of course this doesn't help with allocations occurring in the kernel or in server processes; these must simply be avoided in time critical code.

Another fundamental limitation of Symbian OS for real-time software is that it is an open OS. Subject to the restrictions of platform security, any code, even that which is written long after the mobile phone was designed and built, may be loaded onto the phone and executed. There is no way for programs to declare real-time deadlines to the OS, and no way for the OS to make use of such information. The user could run many applications, all requiring real-time guarantees, and there is no way for the OS to indicate that it cannot provide the required guarantees to all the applications. In the strictest sense, real-time guarantees can only be given to code supplied with the mobile phone by the manufacturer, and even then only if aftermarket applications are restricted to the lower levels of the thread priority spectrum.

As well as ensuring that your code runs quickly enough to deliver acceptable results without consuming too much power, it's also essential to ensure that it doesn't damage system response times. There are several places where latency can be measured, and at all of these it can prove a problem. These locations are in interrupt service routines (ISRs), delayed function calls (DFCs and IDFCs) and user threads, in order of increasing response time (illustrated in Figure 18.1). The vast bulk of code in the system runs in one of these three environments, so it's very important not to slow down any of them unduly. The basic problem is how to enforce and maintain scheduling priority over short timescales? This is the "priority inversion" problem and hinges on one question: how long can an urgent process, triggered by some event that is not directly associated with program execution, be delayed because the system is busy with a less urgent task?

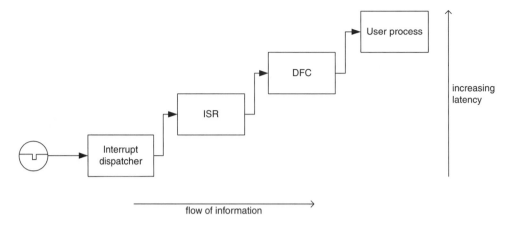

Figure 18.1 Order of events

Various locks, mutexes and processes in the system contribute to these delays. The "worst-case latency" is determined by several variables:

- The length of time for which preemption is disabled

- The length of time for which interrupts are disabled

- The length of time for which each mutex in the system is held

- The length of time it takes to change to the higher-priority process.

For a detailed explanation of latencies please refer to Chapter 17, *Real Time*.

18.2.2   Reducing ISR latency

The interrupt service routine is the second piece of code to run after a hardware interrupt has been asserted. The first is the interrupt vector handler, which has one job – to call the appropriate ISR as quickly as possible. During the ISR, you can do a little work, or you can queue a DFC to perform a larger job later when the kernel is less busy, or you can do both. ISRs must execute quickly because, in systems not supporting nested interrupts, no interrupt can occur during their execution; the longer they run, the higher the system's overall latency. If you need to do a lot of work in response to an interrupt, you should use a DFC if at all possible. Since ISRs are the first code that executes in response to a hardware event, ISR latency is critical to the system's real-time performance. It must be kept as low as possible. To ensure that interrupt latency is kept low, you must not mask interrupts for more than a very few instructions if you can possibly avoid doing so. Code that was acceptable in a non-real-time EKA1 environment often masked interrupts for long periods of time while servicing peripherals. This is no longer acceptable; you must find a better method.

Some systems support "nested interrupts". Nested interrupts allow interrupts to occur during the execution of an ISR, by switching out of IRQ mode while the ISR runs. This can help to reduce latency at the ISR level. However, since non-ISR code cannot execute until the last ISR completes, using nested interrupts will not help to improve DFC or user thread latency. I discuss nested interrupts in more detail in Chapter 6, *Interrupts and Exceptions*.

If your system needs interrupt latency to be even lower than the IRQ mechanism can provide, you may be able to use an FIQ (Fast Interrupt reQuest) instead, to provide extremely rapid service for a very few events. FIQs take advantage of a processor-supported very fast context switch mechanism to provide very low assertion-to-ISR latency. EKA2 disables both FIQ and IRQ interrupts in some places, however, so the shortest possible worst-case latency dictated by the hardware can never be realized. You can only use FIQs if your hardware supports them. FIQ interrupts take priority over IRQ interrupts, and can execute their service routines during ISR execution. FIQs should only be used in cases of dire necessity and their service routines must complete as quickly as possible, as they cannot be interrupted by anything else. The FIQ dispatcher is part of the ASSP, and should always be written in assembly language. Because FIQs are supported by a large number of banked registers, FIQ service routines have a lower overhead than IRQ service routines. They do not need to use the stack as much as an IRQ service routine, which means they may execute more quickly and pollute the data cache less. The FIQ banked registers are useful as work registers, but they can't be used for FIQ-to-FIQ persistence unless FIQs never queue IDFCs or DFCs directly, only doing it via an IRQ. The FIQ postamble uses the banked registers as work registers.

I discuss interrupts in general, nested interrupts and FIQs more fully in Chapter 6, *Interrupts and Exceptions*.

18.2.3 Reducing DFC latency

DFCs are the basic tool for doing anything in response to an interrupt. In a real-time environment, there is no time for the interrupt preamble to prepare the system to offer a full and flexible execution environment for the interrupt service routine to run in. Because at the time of an interrupt the kernel could be in almost any state, it's not possible to access kernel data structures freely during an ISR. Instead, EKA2 offers DFCs and IDFCs. These provide a method for your interrupt handler to get work done after the system exits interrupt mode. In addition to allowing interrupt handlers to actually get work done, DFCs also encourage you to keep interrupt routines short, which is a very good thing indeed to do.

Since so much work has to be done in DFCs, their latency is as important as interrupt latency. While the similarity in names between

IDFCs and DFCs might lead you to expect that they are different varieties of the same thing, they are actually completely different. They are usually treated as quite separate entities, because they behave in very different ways. Because IDFCs are invoked with the kernel lock equal to 1, there are some restrictions on which kernel functions they may interact with. IDFCs are queued by ISRs and will run immediately after the kernel finishes interrupt dispatch. If you need to do some work to finish servicing an interrupt, then an IDFC is an obvious place to do it. However, you should be warned that time spent in an IDFC will increase DFC and user thread latency. For this reason, you should use IDFCs sparingly and with care. in fact, we only recommend the use of IDFCs for the implementation of personality layers and when an ISR needs to make a thread other than a DFC thread ready. IDFCs run in the order in which they were queued, so there can be a delay if other IDFCs are pending. Of course, ISRs take priority over IDFCs and will run before them.

So, if we don't recommend IDFCs, how about DFCs? Although they do run later, a high-priority DFC will run almost as soon as the last IDFC finishes. The only difference between a priority 63 DFC and an IDFC is the time taken for the scheduler to run and switch to the DFC thread, which should be of the order of two microseconds. No MMU manipulation or cache reload penalty is involved, since DFCs run in a kernel thread.

18.2.4   DMA and its impact on latency

DMA has both advantages and disadvantages over programmed I/O. A DMA controller is an essential part of most phone platforms, as nearly all of them include DMA-driven display controllers. These display controllers perform a regular burst of memory accesses every few microseconds in order to feed a line buffer in the LCD panel driver. Because the display hardware's need for pixel data is constrained by the physics of the LCD panel, the DMA that fills it must have a very high priority if the display is not to be disrupted by other system activity. Because the display DMA will have higher priority than the microprocessor core, it is likely that on occasion the processor will be effectively stalled while the display DMA completes.

While there is nothing that can be done to alleviate this particular problem, it's important to bear it in mind when designing systems that use DMA while relying upon the low latency of the rest of the system. If your DMA controller supports multiple priority levels, you should select the lowest priority level that allows your driver to work appropriately. If your DMA needs to be of a very high priority, or your DMA controller does not support multiple priority levels, make sure the transfers are short or, at least, that the latency they will introduce is acceptable to your system.

On the other hand, DMA controllers can transfer data very quickly without polluting the CPU cache. By leaving the CPU cache populated, latency to the ISRs and exception vectors can be significantly improved compared with a software copy – improvements of the order of hundreds of cycles are not uncommon.

18.2.5   Priority inversion

Another source of DFC and user thread latency is priority inversion caused by disabling preemption. Anything that disables interrupts or holds certain locks (for example, the preemption lock) too long will prevent the scheduler from running when it ought to, causing a priority inversion (that is, a thread that should have been suspended will continue to run while the higher priority thread that should run in its place will remain suspended). IDFCs and DFCs will not run until the scheduler is able to run. From the point of view of any thread that needs the processor, this appears as if the scheduler was slow in returning control. If you can possibly avoid it, do not claim any system locks. If you must claim them, use them as briefly as possible to reduce priority inversion time. The preemption lock (also known as the kernel lock) and the system lock are particularly important in this respect, as they stop important scheduler processes from proceeding. Other kernel locks are sometimes held for long periods in other places, but they should still be used judiciously.

Unless you are implementing a personality layer, there are no points where the board support package will be entered with the kernel locked. The personality layer N-state extension hooks are the only place where the kernel calls out to the BSP while it is locked. If you are implementing such functions, be sure they run quickly.

As I explained earlier, IDFCs also run with the kernel locked.

18.2.6   DFCs and DFC threads

As I explained in Chapter 6, *Interrupts and Exceptions*, DFCs have one of eight priorities (between 0 and 7) and belong to a DFC thread. Higher priority threads obviously run their DFCs before lower priority threads, and within one thread, the kernel runs higher priority DFCs before lower priority ones. This means that you need to choose your DFC thread and priority carefully to ensure that your DFC does not prevent more important DFCs from running when they need to. Since many services will use DFCs, there is the potential for wide-ranging performance impact. If you have created your own DFC thread, it may be acceptable for your DFCs to block, run indefinitely or otherwise not terminate for some time. But be aware that while a DFC is running, no other DFCs in the same thread will receive a share of the processor. It is completely unacceptable to place blocking or slow DFCs in system DFC threads as this will severely damage performance. If you have multiple drivers provided as a unit, for example in a base port, it may be desirable to create a DFC thread and share it between all the drivers. Be aware that if any of your DFCs block, there could be interactions between otherwise separate drivers that may not be predictable and will probably not be desirable.

18.2.7 Reducing user thread latency

Neither DFCs nor user threads can be scheduled while the preemption (kernel) lock is held. The system lock prevents user-side memory from being remapped, so must be claimed before memory copies between user-side processes, or between kernel-side and user-side memory take place; otherwise an interrupt or a reschedule could occur during the copy and cause problems by removing memory that was allocated and available at the start of the copy. For this reason, it's essential to avoid large memory copy operations. In fact, IPC copies are paused every 512 bytes to allow the system lock to be checked for contention. If contention is detected, the system lock is released and relocked, allowing the contending thread to claim the system lock and run in the intervening period. If you need to copy large areas of user-side memory around from kernel-side routines, it is important to bear the duration of the system lock in mind. It might even be worth thinking about redesigning your architecture to use a shared chunk instead of copying.

18.2.8 Mutual exclusion techniques

When code runs in an environment in which it may be interrupted, some sections of that code may need to be "protected" from being executed out of order, from being re-entered, or from their data structures being modified "behind their backs". The most common way of doing this is with a mutex. Obviously, since mutexes revolve around preventing code from running until it is convenient for it to do so, this can have some impact on latency, and so care is needed to avoid adverse consequences.

Disabling interrupts: Since multitasking in the system is based on interrupts, a very lightweight way to achieve exclusion from re-entry for a very short sequence of code is to disable interrupts before it, and re-enable them afterwards. This is almost never an appropriate thing to do for long pieces of code, and may break in multiprocessor environments (for example, environments like OMAP where the DSP may be running concurrently to the ARM processor) or in cases where a call during that code causes a reschedule. Obviously, since no interrupts can be serviced while interrupts are disabled, this strategy has the potential to significantly increase worst-case interrupt latency. You should only ever disable interrupts for a very few instructions, and you should consider 30 μs with interrupts disabled the absolute maximum. For example, the kernel queue handling functions disable interrupts only for the innermost critical portion of their execution. Some kernel functions require interrupts to be enabled on entry, so this strategy is not suitable for driver operations that may interact with them.

Writing your code so that it doesn't need to be locked (a lockless implementation) is another possibility: Lockless implementation isn't really a mutual exclusion method, but I've included it here because it falls into the same general category of techniques for ensuring consistency in concurrent code.

Disabling preemption: If your code does not need protecting from the effects of interrupt service routines themselves, it may not be necessary to disable all interrupts. Merely holding the kernel lock is enough to prevent rescheduling from taking place. This is enough to prevent another thread from interfering with your protected code, and has the advantage that it does not increase interrupt service latency at all. However, DFCs will not run until the kernel lock is released, and, as we noted earlier, holding the kernel lock constitutes a potential priority inversion, so you must not hold it for long: 30 μs should be considered a maximum.

Using a fast mutex: The nanokernel provides a very fast special case of mutex. The interface to fast mutexes is the class NFastMutex, this class is exposed via NKern:: methods. Fast mutexes have a few limitations on their use. For example, waiting on a fast mutex constitutes blocking, so you cannot do this in an IDFC or ISR. You also must release fast mutexes before your thread attempts to terminate or block. Fast mutexes can't be nested, either. These limitations are more fully explored in Chapter 3, *Threads, Processes and Libraries.* The nanokernel will ensure that threads are not suspended while they hold a fast mutex. It will treat threads that hold a fast mutex as if they are in a critical section and will not suspend them while they hold the mutex.

Using a conventional mutex: The Symbian OS layer provides various sophisticated synchronization objects, including a fully featured mutex, a condition variable object and a counting semaphore. Symbian OS semaphores support multiple waiting threads (unlike nanokernel fast semaphores) and release waiting threads in priority order. As I discussed in Chapter 3, *Threads, Processes and Libraries,* Symbian OS mutexes are fully nestable and they support priority inheritance. Symbian OS mutexes are covered in Chapter 3, *Threads, Processes and Libraries.*

The kernel and memory model use Symbian OS mutexes extensively to protect long-running critical code sections. However, these wait objects are comparatively heavyweight and the overhead of using them may not be worth the convenience. What's more, since they are implemented by the Symbian OS layer, they can't be used in code that runs at nanokernel level. If you need to block or wait while holding a mutex, or you may have more than one waiting thread, you must use a Symbian OS mutex. If you will hold the mutex for longer than 20 ms, you should consider using a Symbian OS mutex in any case, as the overall overhead will be small when the frequency with which the mutex code will run is considered.

Using a DFC queue thread: Because the DFCs in a DFC queue thread will be called in priority order, they can provide a useful measure of mutual exclusion. The DFCs in a single queue will never execute concurrently. This means that the queuing mechanism guarantees that any one DFC can never interrupt another in the same thread. This can provide all the protection you need to manage some forms of buffer.

18.2.9 Memory allocation

Nanokernel threads, IDFCs and interrupt service routines cannot use the standard Symbian OS memory allocation APIs, since they obviously contain internal state, and this may be inconsistent when the relevant mutex is not held. ISRs and IDFCs cannot block, as described in Chapter 6, and therefore they cannot wait on a mutex. Since this means that they cannot claim the mutex, they can't guarantee allocator consistency and therefore cannot claim memory. As we've seen, the nanokernel does not contain any code relating to memory allocation and depends on the Symbian OS layer to allocate memory for it.

The `RHeap` allocator conducts a linear search through the array describing the cells in the arena it allocates from, looking for free cells; when it finds a free cell it then has to check if the cell is large enough to contain the request. This process is memory-efficient but not particularly fast and may not complete in a reasonable length of time. Also, if interrupts could allocate memory, the allocator would have to be re-entrant. The design of a re-entrant allocator is extremely difficult and would significantly complicate the memory system's overall design. Therefore these methods are not available to any real-time process.

If you're trying to write code to run quickly, you may choose to avoid allocating memory during sections that must run quickly. There are several approaches to this problem.

Avoid allocating memory at all: Running entirely from stack is fairly efficient, and is an option available everywhere in the system. Even interrupt routines have stack, but stack space under Symbian OS is very limited, and of course stack-based ("automatic") variables are local, so they may not be useful as structures to be passed around by reference. Different contexts have different stacks. Be aware that the stack limit under Windows (that is, the emulator) is not the same as it is in a real device. Windows has a larger stack limit than the real devices do, so code may fail to run on real devices even if it works on the emulator.

Allocate statically: If you allocate a single block of heap memory when your program starts, you can sub-allocate parts of it by defining a data structure containing all the necessary objects. This approach is extremely efficient and has almost no overhead, as no allocation process happens at run time. Many video applications use this approach, and it works well, but it is very inflexible. While it can easily become unmanageable, it has the advantage that it makes it easy to integrate C++ with assembly language routines, since all the offsets from the start of the allocated block are known at compile time and can be included statically in the source.

Write your own allocator: This is an approach similar to static allocation, but more flexible. You allocate a large block of memory at startup time and then use a simple allocator routine to distribute it. There are many high-performance memory allocation routines discussed in the literature; some work by using a hash table, thereby reducing the general case time needed for an allocation, and others use fixed-length cells, simplifying the search. Some high-performance network protocol implementations use both fixed-length cells and hash tables. These methods are extremely effective in reducing time taken to allocate memory. In Symbian OS you may even choose to replace RHeap's allocator for your application, so that all allocations will benefit from your faster algorithm. This is discussed in Section 3.3.1.3.

18.2.10   Performance in the emulator

The EKA2 emulator provides a few ways to help application developers simulate the performance of a real mobile phone. Only one of these, the emulation LFFS media driver, is of production quality, but the others are there to try if you think that they might help.

18.2.10.1   Media performance

We provide a way to change the general performance of the file system. You can inject small, not-too-noticeable delays into the file system code, by setting the "DiskRead" and "DiskWrite" values in the emulator initialization file, epoc.ini. These values specify the read and write speed to emulate in units of microseconds/KB, and we act on them by injecting delays into file system calls using the millisecond timer. This is still at the experimental stage, and so is rather approximate.

You can change the performance of the LFFS media driver in a more robust way. The [emulation] LFFS media driver, which uses a memory mapped file for the flash image, can be parameterized by settings in epoc.ini to have performance similar to most NOR flash hardware. Coupled with the LFFS file system, this gives quite realistic performance for this file system on a PC.

18.2.10.2   CPU performance

The HalData::ECpuSpeed HAL item is read/write on the emulator, which means that by writing a low value to it, you can slow down the speed of the emulated CPU. We act on this item by making the emulator timer system consume some fraction of the CPU time when the emulator is busy.

18.3   Summary

In this chapter I have discussed techniques that will help you to improve the performance of your software. However, all the tweaks and tricks in the world are no substitute for a good, efficient design. In a deeply object-oriented environment it is easy to lose sight of what is really happening to your processor and memory. I hope that this chapter will have made the underlying processes a little more familiar to you.

Techniques such as unrolling and flattening recursive routines into iterative ones can improve the performance of an algorithm, but if that algorithm is inherently suboptimal, it's better to avoid it. A little care during the design phase of your project can save a lot of scraping for cycles later on.

Symbian OS mobile phones are getting faster and faster every year, and there is no end to this scaling in sight. The software stacks that run on them are getting larger and more powerful, and users are expecting more and more from their phones. EKA2 was designed to provide capabilities for the next generation of devices, smaller, faster and cheaper than ever. In the rich, real-time environment it provides, performance is more important than ever. Every cycle consumes a few nanojoules, and every nanojoule has to come out of a battery that is more compact than the one fitted to the last model. Cycles are an endangered species; treat them like the precious commodity they are.

Appendix 1

Glossary

The following glossary explains the meanings of some of the less common and Symbian OS-specific acronyms used within this book.

ABI	Application Binary Interface
ACM	Abstract Control Model
AGCH	Access Grant CHannel
AP	Application Processor
ASIC	Application-Specific Integrated Circuit
ASID	Application Space IDentifier
ASSP	Application-Specific Standard Part
BBM	Bad Block Manager
BCCH	Broadcast Control CHannel
BP	Baseband Processor
BPP	Bits Per Pixel
BSP	Board Support Package
BPK	Base Porting Kit
CBCH	Cell Broadcast CHannel
CDC	Connected Device Configuration
CISC	Complex Instruction Set Computer
CLZ	Count Leading Zeros
CPL	Current Privilege Level
CPSR	Current Program Status Register
CS	Code Segment
DACR	Domain Access Control Register
DDK	Device Driver Kit
DFC	Deferred Function Call
DMA	Direct Memory Access
DSA	Direct Screen Access
DSP	Digital Signal Processor

ECC	Error Correction Code
EDF	Earliest Deadline First
EIP	Extended Instruction Pointer
ELF	Extended Linker Format
EKA1	EPOC Kernel Architecture 1
EKA2	EPOC Kernel Architecture 2
ESP	Extended Stack Pointer
FAT	File Allocation Table
FACCH	Fast Associated Control CHannel
FDB	File Data Block
FIFO	First In, First Out
FCCH	Frequency Correction CHannel
FIQ	Fast Interrupt reQuest
FOTA	Firmware Over-The-Air
FTL	Flash Translation Layer
GC	Graphics Context
GDT	Global Descriptor Table
HAL	Hardware Abstraction Layer
IAT	Import Address Table
ICE	In-Circuit Emulator
IDB	Indirect Data Block
IDE	Integrated Development Environment (if related to debugging)
	Integrated Drive Electronics (if related to disk drives)
IDFC	Immediate Deferred Function Call
IDT	Interrupt Descriptor Table
IMB	Instruction Memory Barrier
IPC	Inter-Process Communication
ISR	Interrupt Service Routine
ITC	Inter-Thread Communication
LDD	Logical Device Driver
LFFS	Log Flash File System
LRTA	Legacy Real-Time Application
LRU	Least Recently Used
MDF	Multimedia Device Framework
MMC	Multi Media Card
MMF	Multi Media Framework
MMU	Memory Management Unit
OOM	Out-Of-Memory

OPL	Open Programming Language, the
OSB	Off-Screen Bitmap
OTG	On-The-Go
PASR	Partial Array Self Refresh
PCH	Paging CHannel
PCM	Pulse Code Modulation
PDD	Physical Device Driver
PIC	Programmable Interrupt Controller
PIL	Platform-Independent Layer
PIM	Personal Information Management
PM	Power Management
PSL	Platform-Specific Layer
QoS	Quality of Service
RACH	Random Access CHannel
RCA	Relative Card Address
ROFS	Read Only File System
RPL	Requestor Privilege Level
RTC	Real-Time Clock
RTOS	Real-Time Operating System
SACCH	Slow Associated Control CHannel
SCH	Synchronization CHannel
SDCCH	Stand-alone Dedicated Control CHannel
SDK	Software Development Kit
SID	Secure IDentifier
SOC	System-On-Chip
SPC	SCSI Primary Commands
SWI	SoftWare Interrupt
TCB	Trusted Computing Base
TCE	Trusted Computing Environment
TCH	Traffic Channel
TCSR	Temperature Compensated Self Refresh
TLB	Translation Look-aside Buffer
TR	Task Register
TSS	Task State Segment
TTBR	Translation Table Base Register
TWIP	TWentIeth of a Point
UART	Universal Asynchronous Receiver/Transmitter
UDC	USB Device Controller
UID	Unique IDentifier

VFP	Vector Floating Point
VIC	Vectored Interrupt Controller
VID	Vendor IDentifier
VT	Video Telephony
XIP	eXecute In Place

Appendix 2

The E32ImageHeader

This section describes the image header for Symbian OS executable files, as defined in the file F32IMAGE.H. There are three formats for the E32ImageHeader:

- Basic format – header contains no compression, security or version number information

- J-format – header may contain compression information. In addition to the basic format fields, if the compression type (at offset 1C) is nonzero, the header includes an extra field holding the uncompressed size of the file

- V-format – the executable contains versioning and security information. In addition to the basic and J-format fields, the header includes extra security and versioning related fields.

Basic format fields:

Offset (hex)	Description of field
00	UID 1
04	UID 2
08	UID 3
0C	Checksum of UIDs.
10	Signature ("EPOC" = 0x434F5045).
14	CRC-32 of entire header for V-format, CPU identifier for original and J-formats.

18	Version number of this executable – a 16-bit major and a 16-bit minor version number. This is used in link resolution (V-format only). In original format, this contained a checksum of the code, but this was never used.
1C	Type of compression used (UID or 0 for none).
20	Version of PETRAN/ELFTRAN which generated this file.
24	Time at which file was generated, in standard EPOC encoding (microseconds since 00:00:00 01-01-00AD).
2C	Flags field – see later in this appendix for more details.
30	Code size (includes constant data, IAT and export directory).
34	Initialized data size.
38	Heap minimum size (only used for EXEs).
3C	Heap maximum size (only used for EXEs).
40	Stack size (only used for EXEs).
44	BSS (zero-filled data) size.
48	Offset in code of entry point.
4C	Code base address (where code is linked for).
50	Data base address (where data is linked for).
54	Number of DLLs referenced.
58	Offset into the file of the export address table.
5C	Number of entries in export address table.
60	Size of text section (offset of IAT within code section).
64	Offset in file to code section.
68	Offset in file to data section.
6C	Offset in file to import section.
70	Offset in file to code relocations.

74	Offset in file to data relocations.
78	Priority of this process (only used for EXEs).
7A	CPU (0x1000 = X86, 0x2000 = ARM).

For J-formatted headers, if the "Type of compression" field is nonzero, then the following field will be present. For V-formatted headers, it is always present:

7C	Uncompressed size of the file.

For V-formatted headers, the following fields will be present:

80	Security information (capabilities, secure ID, vendor ID).
90	Offset from start of code section to exception descriptor (for C++ exception unwinding) + 1. Bit 0 is set if this is valid, bit 0 is clear if there is no exception descriptor.
94	Spare.
98	Size of bitmap description holes in the export table.
9A	Format of bitmap describing holes in the export table (described later in this appendix).
9B	Bitmap describing any holes in the export table. This is a variable length field.

The flags field at offset 2C in the header is a bitmapped field, defined as follows:

Bits	Size in bits	Description
0	1	Executable type: 0 – EXE 1 – DLL

1	1	Whether to call entry point (not used in EKA2): 0 – call entry point 1 – don't call entry point
2	1	Whether this is a fixed address EXE: 0 – not fixed address 1 – fixed address
4–3	2	ABI: 0 – GCC98r2 1 – EABI
7–5	3	Entry point type: 0 – EKA1 1 – EKA2
23–8	16	Reserved
27–24	4	Header format: 0 – Basic 1 – J-format 2 – V-format
31–28	4	Import format: 0 – Standard PE format 1 – ELF format 2 – PE format without redundant copy of import ordinals. Standard PE format is only used with original and J-format headers. V-format headers are either ELF or PE without redundant import ordinals.

For V-formatted headers, the field describing the format of the export table bitmap may have one of the following values:

Value	Description
00H	No holes, all exports are present.
01H	A full bitmap is present, that is, there is one bit for each export directory slot – a 1 indicates export present, a 0 indicates export absent.
02H	A sparse bitmap is present (granularity 8). This consists of two sections. The first section contains one bit for each group of eight

	consecutive export directory slots. A 0 bit indicates that all these slots contain valid exports and no further description of them is necessary. A 1 bit indicates that at least one of the eight exports is absent, and there is a bit mask byte in the second section describing which of the eight is present. The bytes in the second section occur in the same order as the bits in the first section.
FFH	XIP file.

Appendix 3

The TRomImageHeader

This section describes the image header for Symbian OS executable files in ROM. This is defined in the file E32ROM.H:

Offset (hex)	Description of field
00	UID 1
04	UID 2
08	UID 3
0C	Checksum of UIDs.
10	Entry point of this executable (absolute address).
14	This executable's code address.
18	This executable's data address.
1C	Code size (includes constant data).
20	Text size (code size – size of constant data).
24	Data size.
28	BSS (zero-filled data) size.
2C	Heap minimum size (only needed for EXEs).
30	Heap maximum size (only needed for EXEs).
34	Stack size (only needed for EXEs).

38	Address of DLL reference table. (This is a list of the DLLs referenced by this executable which have static data.)
3C	Number of functions exported by this executable.
40	Export directory address.
44	Security information (capabilities, secure ID, vendor ID).
54	Version number of the tools used to generate this image file.
58	Flags field (see below).
5C	Priority of this process (only needed for EXEs).
60	Data and BSS linear base address – where this image file expects its data to be when it runs.
64	Next extension. Address of ROM entry header of subsequent extension files. This field is only used if there is more than one extension. The first extension is found using the `TRomHeader`.
68	A number denoting the hardware variant – used to determine if this executable can run on any particular system.
6C	The total data size (including space reserved for DLLs – for fixed address EXEs in moving memory model).
70	Version number of this executable – a 16-bit major and a 16-bit minor version number. This is used in link resolution.
74	Address of exception descriptor for this image (used in C++ exception unwinding). Zero if no exception descriptor present.

The flags field contains the following flags:

Bit number	Description
31	`KRomImageFlagPrimary` – set if the file is a primary, that is, a kernel image.
30	`KRomImageFlagVariant` – set if the file is a variant DLL image.
29	`KRomImageFlagExtension` – set if the file is a kernel extension.

28	`KRomImageFlagDevice` – set if the file is a device driver.
27	`KRomImageFlagSecondary` – set if the file is a secondary, that is, the file server.
26	`KRomImageFlagData` – set if the file has .data/.bss and is not an extension or variant.
25	`KRomImageFlagDataInit` – set if the file or any of its dependencies have .data or .bss. Linkages to EXEs are not counted in this assessment.
24	`KRomImageFlagDataPresent` – set if the file or any of its dependencies have .data or .bss. Linkages to EXEs are counted.
23	`KRomImageFlagExeInTree` – set if this file links directly or indirectly to an EXE. If this is the case the EXE is listed first in this file's DLL reference table.
5, 6, 7	3-bit field indicating the entry point type – values the same as in `E32ImageHeader`.
3, 4	2-bit field indicating the ABI – values the same as in `E32ImageHeader`.
2	Set if this image is a fixed address EXE.
0	Set if this image is a DLL, clear if it is an EXE.

Appendix 4

Bibliography

ARM System-on-Chip Architecture (2nd Edition), by Steve Furber.
Addison-Wesley Professional.
ISBN: 0201675196

Symbian OS Explained: Effective C++ Programming for Smartphones, by
Jo Stichbury.
Symbian Press.
ISBN: 0470021306

ARM Architecture Reference Manual, by Dave Seal.
Addison-Wesley Professional.
ISBN: 0201737191

Symbian OS C++ for Mobile Phones, Volume 1: Professional Development on Constrained Devices, by Richard Harrison.
Symbian Press.
ISBN: 0470856114

Universal Serial Bus Specification Revision 2.0
www.usb.org

Liu, C.L. and J.W. Layland, "Scheduling algorithms for multi-programming in a hard real-time environment," *Journal of the Association of Computer Machinery (ACM)*, **20**(1), Jan. 1973, pp. 46–61.

Leung, J.Y.T. and J. Whitehead, "On the complexity of fixed-priority scheduling of periodic, real-time tasks", *Performance Evaluation (Netherlands)* **2**(4), Dec. 1982, pp. 237–250.

For up-to-date information on EKA2 and phones developed on it, please consult the Symbian website ***www.symbian.com***

Information on current and forthcoming books can be found on the Symbian Press webpage ***www.symbian.com/books***

Index